Praise for *Redeeming Economics*

"The scope of Mueller's intellectual ambition in this book is truly astonishing, as is the scope of the research involved. . . . People should invest the time needed to read, absorb, and promote this important book."
— JENNIFER ROBACK MORSE, Ph.D., in *The Family in America: A Journal of Public Policy*

"For years I've watched John Mueller combine markets with morality to help fix what's broken. Both Washington and Wall Street sorely need *Redeeming Economics*."
— LARRY KUDLOW, host of CNBC's *Kudlow and Company*

"John Mueller is that rarest of thinkers and writers: one who can make the 'dismal science' thoroughly engaging at a very human level—a man who knows his economics but never loses sight of people amidst a forest of data. *Redeeming Economics* is sure to provoke cries of 'I protest!' from various sorts of economists, and just as sure to demand some needed rethinking on everyone's part."
— GEORGE WEIGEL, Distinguished Senior Fellow at the Ethics and Public Policy Center

"At the very least, John Mueller has written a bold, interesting, and thought-provoking book. But he may have done much more. He may have written a book that could fundamentally reground the discipline of economics and reorient the study of political economy. Serious students and thoughtful practitioners of both politics and economics need to read and reflect upon this work."
— WILLIAM KRISTOL, editor of the *Weekly Standard*

"By restoring two millennia of lost economic theory and tracing its links with sound economic policy, John Mueller's *Redeeming Economics* should revolutionize the teaching and practice of political economy—not only in the United States but in every national community dedicated to the authentic common good."
— LEWIS E. LEHRMAN, cofounder of the Gilder-Lehrman Institute of American History, author of *Lincoln at Peoria*

"*Redeeming Economics* provides an original perspective on economics, one that is soundly based in the work of three giants in the intellectual history of Western civilization: Aristotle, Augustine, and Aquinas. Anyone with either a practical or scholarly interest in economics would do well to take a close look at this book."
— ANDREW V. ABELA, chairman of the Department of Business and Economics at the Catholic University of America

"*Redeeming Economics* achieves a double miracle: resurrecting the economic insights of ancient and medieval thinkers, and making a mathematically rigorous case that these deserve a central place in the policy debates of the present. It's hard to imagine a more important contribution to economic science."
    —JEFFREY BELL, director of policy for the American Principles Project

"An accurate knowledge of history is critical as we choose our future paths. *Redeeming Economics* fills in many gaps in our collective understanding of the history of economics. My father would have had this book by his chair as I do now, and I hope our political leaders will as well."
    —JAMES P. KEMP, president of the Jack Kemp Foundation

"Mueller turns popular economic myths on their heads. His book unearths a forgotten piece of the puzzle that could prove to be the holy grail of modern economics."
    —EDWIN FEULNER, president of the Heritage Foundation

"At a time when economists around the world are reexamining the way we think about economic decisions, Mueller presents an interesting and daring way to understand the way we make economic decisions and solve the distribution problem notwithstanding the relational dimension of the human person. *Redeeming Economics* is a great contribution and service to economic science. A must read for all of us."
    —MARIA SOPHIA AGUIRRE, associate professor of economics at the Catholic University of America

"At a time as never before when the world turns to economics for advice and wisdom, *Redeeming Economics* shows that all along there has been a hole in economics' soul. Mueller conclusively proves that giving and sharing—which classical, neoclassical, and Marxist economics all consigned to the realm of the 'noneconomic'—is no less than the very center of economic drive."
    —BRIAN DOMITROVIC, author of *Econoclasts*

"Economics and the relationships of humans need to be reintegrated. This is the genius and passion of John Mueller. His book gives history, wholeness, and hope to economics—and to our future."
    —JEFF KEMP, founder of Stronger Families, senior fellow at the Marriage and Family Foundation

REDEEMING ECONOMICS

Culture of Enterprise series

Previously published:

Human Goods, Economic Evils:
A Moral Approach to the Dismal Science
Edward Hadas

Third Ways:
How Bulgarian Greens, Swedish Housewives, and
Beer-Swilling Englishmen Created Family-Centered Economies—
and Why They Disappeared
Allan C. Carlson

A Path of Our Own:
An Andean Village and Tomorrow's Economy of Values
Adam K. Webb

Econoclasts:
The Rebels Who Sparked the Supply-Side Revolution
and Restored American Prosperity
Brian Domitrovic

Toward a Truly Free Market:
A Distributist Perspective on the Role of Government, Taxes, Health Care,
Deficits, and More
John C. Médaille

REDEEMING ECONOMICS

Rediscovering the Missing Element

JOHN D. MUELLER

Wilmington, Delaware

The Culture of Enterprise series is supported by a grant from the John Templeton Foundation. The Intercollegiate Studies Institute gratefully acknowledges this support.

Mueller, John D.
  Redeeming economics : rediscovering the missing element / John D. Mueller.
    p. cm.
  Includes bibliographical references and index.
  ISBN 978-1-932236-94-1
  1. Economics. 2. Economic history. 3. Natural law. I. Title.
  HB171.M84 2010
  330—dc22
                              2010022232

ISI Books
Intercollegiate Studies Institute
3901 Centerville Road
Wilmington, DE 19807-1938
www.isibooks.org

Manufactured in the United States of America

To my wife, Linda Mallon,
and my friend Lewis E. Lehrman,
who know that
"faith is the substance of things hoped for,
the evidence of things unseen" (Hebrews 11:1).

CONTENTS

Introduction: Rediscovering the Missing Element in Economics   1

Part 1
The Birth, Death, and Resurrection of Economics

Chapter 1: Smithology and Its Discontents   11
Chapter 2: Scholastic Economics (c. 1250–1776)   17
Chapter 3: Classical Economics (1776–1871)   49
Chapter 4: Neoclassical Economics (1871–c. 2000)   77
Chapter 5: Neo-Scholastic Economics (c. 2000–)   107

Part 2
Personal Economy

Chapter 6: The "Mother's Problem" and Augustine's Solution   133
Chapter 7: The Success and Failure of Neoclassical Economics   155
Chapter 8: An Empirical Test: Fatherhood and Homicide   175
Chapter 9: The Moral Implications of Scarcity:
The Good Samaritan Paradigm   189

Part 3
Domestic Economy

Chapter 10: Marriage, the "First Natural Bond of
Human Society"   203
Chapter 11: Why Do Parents Give Children "Existence,
Rearing, and Instruction"?   231
Chapter 12: How Neo-Scholastic Economics Explains Our
Life Earnings and Spending   245

Part 4
Political Economy

Chapter 13: Saving America's Infant Industry   275
Chapter 14: The Theory of American Public Choice   283
Chapter 15: Injustice in Exchange: Unemployment   303
Chapter 16: Injustice in Exchange: Inflation   327

Part 5
Divine Economy

Chapter 17: The Three Worldviews   355

Notes   367

Acknowledgments   451

Index   453

Rediscovering the Missing Element
in Economics

The thesis of this book is straightforward. The most important element in economics is missing, and its rediscovery is priming a revolution the likes of which has occurred only three times in more than 750 years.

The Scottish moral philosopher Adam Smith (1723–90) is frequently called the founder of economics. But in fact it was Smith who eliminated this pillar of economic thought. He rendered economic theory incomplete and made it incapable of describing human behavior.

The first revolution in economics had occurred five centuries before Smith, when Thomas Aquinas (1225–74) set forth the basic elements of economic theory. Synthesizing the work of Aristotle (384–322 B.C.) and Augustine of Hippo (A.D. 354–430), Aquinas offered a comprehensive view of human economic actions. All such actions fall into four categories: humans *produce, exchange, distribute,* and *consume* goods (human and nonhuman). Thus the theory Aquinas outlined—known as "Scholastic" economics—had four key elements: the theory of *production,* which explains which goods (and how many of them) we produce; the theory of *justice in exchange,* which accounts for how we are compensated through the sale of goods for our contributing to their production; the theory of *final distribution,* which determines *who* will consume our goods; and finally, the theory of *consumption* (or *utility*), which explains which goods people prefer to consume.

Adam Smith sparked the second economic revolution when he drastically simplified the Scholastic economics he had been taught. He dropped not one but two elements of the four that Aquinas had outlined. He eliminated the Scholastic theories of consumption and final distribution, launching "classical" economics with production and exchange alone. At the same time, he claimed that Aristotle's theory of production could be pared to a single factor: labor.

Most complications in economics result from the fact that Smith's revision was an *over*simplification. In the 1870s, about a century after Smith's *Wealth of Nations*, "neoclassical" economists recognized shortcomings in Smith's theory. They led the third revolution in economics by restoring one of the elements Smith had dropped: Augustine's theory of utility, which describes consumption. But they did *not* reinstitute the other.

The fourth revolution is now upon us and will (I hope) finish what the last one started, by reintegrating the most important original element: the one that accounts for the social relationships that define us, the loves (and hates) that motivate and distinguish us as human beings. In trying to reduce human behavior to exchanges, modern economists have forgotten how these essential motivations are expressed, which is as personal or collective *gifts* (and their opposite, crimes). This book is an effort to outline what difference this makes, not only for economic theory but especially for its practical applications. Only by reintegrating this fourth element can we make economics whole again.

I'm quite fond of the old story about an economist who goes fishing with a Jewish rabbi, a Catholic priest, and a Protestant minister. After they've been sitting in the boat all morning, the rabbi says he thinks he'll stretch his legs, climbs out of the boat, and walks across the water to the shore. The priest and the minister then step out of the boat and walk across the water to join him. Though the economist has always been a skeptic, he resolves to make the leap of faith. He offers up a prayer, steps out of the boat—and promptly sinks to the bottom of the lake. As he comes up sputtering, the rabbi turns to the others and says, "Shall we tell him where the stepping-stones are?"

The stepping-stones of economics are the four essential facets of all human economic decisions, which were integrated at all three levels of human society: personal, domestic, and political. Originally grounded in natural law philosophy, the stepping-stones are the facts of human existence explained with elements originally derived from Greco-Roman philosophy and the Bible. Smith, in effect, got rid of two of the stepping-stones, leaving economists at times to seem all wet.

Knowing the location of stepping-stones certainly doesn't make us smarter than anyone else. On the contrary, what is hidden from the learned and clever is often revealed to the merest children. Yet the knowledge can save a great deal of effort and lead us to search in places where we otherwise wouldn't. Like natural law philosophy itself, economic theory is the product of human reason reflecting on common human experience, and that is the approach followed throughout this book. But economic theory also has a peculiar relationship, both historically and logically, to biblical revelation. In that respect, it resembles modern cosmology, the theory of the origins and development of the universe.

The prevailing big bang theory might in principle have occurred to any physicist. And in the end it will be confirmed or disproved by instrument readings, not quotations from Genesis. But as a matter of historical fact, nearly all scientists in human history who considered the question, including Albert Einstein, began by merely assuming that the universe had always existed. The first physicist open-minded enough to consider that the universe had a beginning in time as an empirically testable hypothesis was a Belgian priest, Georges Lemaître (1894–1966).[1] (He was fortunate enough to learn a few months before his death that astronomers had detected the cosmic background radiation that seems to confirm his thesis.)

In the same way, a logically complete and empirically testable outline of economic theory might in principle have occurred to anyone. Only it didn't. History records that it occurred first to Aquinas, the most famous member of the Order of Preachers, who was trying to puzzle out exactly what is meant by Jesus's distillation of the Torah into the Two Great Commandments, to "love God with all your heart" and "love your neighbor as yourself."[2] For this reason, I've suggested that Aquinas might be called "the preacher as economist."[3]

The peculiar relationship between natural law and biblically orthodox religious faith can be expressed by noting that *economics is essentially a theory of providence*. It mostly concerns human providence, describing how we provide for ourselves and the other persons we love, using scarce means that have alternate uses. From the beginning, however, economic theory has also concerned divine providence. All serious attempts to explain the order in markets (which is a fact, not a theory) have been derived from some theory of divine providence. The most famous, of course, is Adam Smith's renowned "invisible hand." But the earliest and still the most coherent theory was Augustine's, who deliberately avoided the term *invisible hand* and called the order in markets the "hidden equity . . . stamped upon the business transactions of men by the Supreme Equity."[4] Augustine explained why a correct understanding of the relation between human and divine providence is necessary for a correct understanding of economic activity even—or especially—when it contradicts moral or religious norms.

To explain all this, I have divided the book into five parts.

The first part amounts to a brief, structural history of economics. This is necessary for a highly significant but little-known reason: the near-universal abolition, starting in 1972 at the University of Chicago, of the requirement that university students of economics learn its history before being granted a degree. The usual approach to the history of economics in most colleges and universities today is to interpret both past and present economic theories in terms of some modern school of economics. (The University of Chicago's George Stigler called this approach to economics, fittingly enough, "The Economist as Preacher.")[5] In order to restore the balance, I begin in chapter 1 with Joseph Schumpeter's *History of Economic Analysis* (1954); Schumpeter confronted the assumptions of experts, who for a century had regarded Smith as the founder of economics, by highlighting the crucial roles of Aristotle and Aquinas (though Schumpeter ignored Aquinas's dependence on Augustine). In chapter 2 I trace the origins of the Scholastic outline of economic theory, its transmission and dissemination by Protestant or lay Scholastics like Samuel Pufendorf, and its adoption and development by the Founders of the United States.

My chapter on classical economics (3) calls for a reevaluation of Adam Smith. It considers how Smith's revision was motivated by his Stoic pantheism, moral Newtonianism, and Sophistical view of rhetoric. It also explains the predictive failures caused by Smith's "labor theory of value." Karl Marx did not misunderstand this theory, but rather understood it very well, when he claimed that it had turned every exchange from the approximate equality of Aristotle's "justice in exchange" into pervasive *injustice* in exchange, with workers producing all the value while capitalists skimmed much of it for their own profit.

I then move on in chapter 4 to explain how Augustine's theory of utility was reinvented in neoclassical economics to remedy the shortcomings of classical economics. I also describe the problems resulting at every level from the failure to restore Augustine's theory of personal distribution and Aristotle's theory of distributive justice: circular logic, nonverifiability, and empirically false assumptions.

The first part of the book concludes with a chapter (5) predicting that dissatisfaction with the failure of modern neoclassical theory to explain the facts will give way in coming decades to a "neo-Scholastic" phase, in which economists will rewrite economic theory at every level to reintegrate the element missing from neoclassical theory, while retaining the cumulative technical advances achieved in the other elements.[6]

Having considered broadly where economics came from, how it evolved, and where I think it is going, I turn in the next three parts to the theory and practical implications of the neo-Scholastic approach at three different levels—personal, domestic, and political economy.[7] Each corresponds to one essential aspect of human nature—that we are, as Aristotle put it, "rational," "matrimonial," and "political animals."

The second part, on personal economy, begins with a chapter (6) on the "Mother's Problem," described (but not solved) by Philip Wicksteed, and goes on to outline Augustine's solution, which requires both of his main contributions to economic theory: the theory of personal distribution (gifts and crimes) and the theory of utility. The next chapter (7) explains the success of neoclassical economics in reinventing Augustine's theory of utility, but also the failures in the state-of-the-art "economic approach to human behavior" caused by its attempt to explain personal distribution that way. In chapter 8, I show that the strong simultaneous inverse relation between fatherhood and crime gives striking empirical evidence for Augustine's "personal distribution function," while disproving the claim of Steven D. Levitt in the best-selling book *Freakonomics* that legalizing abortion in the 1970s must have reduced crime starting in the 1990s. Finally, in chapter 9, I examine the moral implications of scarcity, including an exchange with utilitarian philosopher Peter Singer, in which his own behavior illustrates Augustine's theory of gifts.

In the third part of this book, I look at domestic economy, arguing that the basic facts of American domestic economy in the twenty-
first century can be explained only with a suitable updating of Aristotle's
theory of the household as amended by Augustine and Aquinas.

In chapter 10, I consider the basic principles of every household,
business firm, charitable foundation, and government, starting from the
simple example of a children's lemonade stand.

In chapter 11, I explain that the same principles can be extended
from the production of property to the (re)production of people, showing that a simple country-by-country neo-Scholastic model of fertility
is more accurate than more elaborate neoclassical models because it
includes the element of final distribution.

In the final chapter on domestic economy (12), I show how average
earnings can be systematically explained with just four factors suggested
by the neo-Scholastic theory of domestic economy (age, education,
sex, and marital status). This approach is confirmed by census data,
which reveal extensive (but so far ignored) intrafamily gifts, particularly
between husbands and wives, parents and children.

In the fourth part of the book, I turn to political economy. This
part draws on the lessons from my ten years as economist and chief
speechwriter for then-Congressman Jack Kemp (1935–2009) while he
and President Reagan made national economic policy—and history—
from opposite ends of Pennsylvania Avenue. But it also draws on my
more recent experience making my living as an economic and financial-
market forecaster and consultant to investment managers and policymakers, more often than not regarding the consequences of economic
policy. Since 2005 I've served also as director of the economics and ethics
program at the nonprofit Ethics and Public Policy Center.

In chapter 13, I offer an overview of the four principles of all economically successful and politically popular economic policy, as well as
outline the biggest challenge facing America in coming decades—avoiding the national decline that has overtaken all developed nations in
Europe and Asia owing to a self-inflicted "baby bust." In chapter 14, I
explain what I call the theory of American public choice, as devised by
the American Founders, which holds that justice is the end of government and that all kinds of income should be treated equally. Data from
the American National Election Studies (ANES) show that this theory

explains—far more accurately than competing theories—why there are two major political parties, who identifies with them, and why unjust economic policies are also unpopular, particularly in presidential elections.

The last two chapters on political economy (15 and 16) explain how the most important instances of "injustice in exchange"—unemployment and inflation/deflation—result from party factions violating the basic principles of economic policy. I show that from the Great Depression of 1929–33 to the Great Recession of 2007–9, all major U.S. financial crises can be traced to the dollar's role as chief official reserve currency—suggesting that to avoid similar future misfortunes, it's urgently necessary to end the dollar's "reserve currency curse."

In the final section of the book I turn to "divine economy" (Aristotle's term for metaphysics), in an effort to explain how and why all the other elements fit together. This part is much shorter than the others because it summarizes the three worldviews expressed in (neo-) Scholastic, classical, and neoclassical economics and shows that the same three worldviews were competing in first-century Athens and Rome, and the United States in both 1776 and at the start of the twenty-first century.

* * *

Though intended for the general reader, this book is not a popular rendering of ideas that are widely shared, or even yet widely understood, among academic specialists. In fact, I decided to write it only after judging that we might have to wait another decade or more for its thesis to emerge from academic scholars. I hope it will contribute to the efforts of two small but important and growing bands of economists and political philosophers working in the natural law tradition.[8]

Few economists in the past two centuries have taken natural law seriously. But that number is growing, and, as I have said, I believe it offers the only solution to the most serious problems with neoclassical economic theory.[9] As historian of economics Henry William Spiegel noted of the "marginal revolution" that ended classical and launched neoclassical economics in the 1870s, "Outsiders ranked prominently among the pioneers of marginal analysis because its discovery required a perspective that the experts did not necessarily possess."[10] The same will be true of the neo-Scholastic revolution.

To redeem means to "fulfill (an earlier promise or pledge)." Since the further progress of economic theory requires it to return to its historical origins, "redeeming economics" is not only possible but also urgently necessary. I offer this book in the hope that others will learn, as I did, that it's possible to avoid thrashing around in the water, once we rediscover the stepping-stones.

Part 1

THE BIRTH, DEATH, AND RESURRECTION OF ECONOMICS

The stone rejected by the builders has
become the cornerstone.

—Psalm 118:22

1

Smithology and Its Discontents

Disaster quietly befell the field of economics one day in 1972, when the University of Chicago's economics department, acting on a motion culminating a long campaign by Professor George J. Stigler (1911–91), abolished the requirement that Ph.D. candidates learn the history of economic theory before being granted a degree. The economics departments at most other major universities quickly followed suit.[1]

This decision has had three far-reaching consequences.

First, for more than three decades, American economists have been educated in substantial ignorance of the history of their discipline.[2]

Second, economics professors not only lost touch with the history of economic theory but were suddenly free—almost invited—to fill the vacuum by creating "Whig histories of economics" and foisting them on their students. A Whig history tries to read history backward. It views the past as a grand ascent to the pinnacle of the present—on which, of course, we ourselves triumphantly stand.[3] A Whig history of economics begins by identifying some modern school of economics—like the Chicago or the Keynesian—as the unsurpassable culmination of economic theory, and it interprets the past in that school's terms. The actual originators of important theories, if recognized at all, are claimed as "forerunners"—as "proto-Chicagoans" or "proto-Keynesians," according to the taste of the historian.

Third, severing the contact between economists-in-training and the history of economic theory greatly narrowed the range of economists' approaches to modern economic problems. Thus, the economics profes-

sion now finds itself in a predicament from which it can be rescued only
by being reconnected to its historical roots—specifically, its Scholastic
heritage. In this chapter, I'll begin to explain why that's the case. The
problem begins with Adam Smith.

When Adam Smith Became "Founder" of Economics

From the mid-nineteenth to the mid-twentieth centuries, economists—
even specialists in the history of economics—had an idea of their subject much like Saul Steinberg's "View of the World from 9th Avenue,"
the famous poster that depicts Manhattan's Ninth, Tenth, and Eleventh
avenues in exquisite detail, right down to the fire hydrants, while the
rest of the world consists of vast blank areas labeled "Jersey" or "Japan."
For years, textbooks would start their discussions of modern economics
with Adam Smith, while in the hazy distance lay the eighteenth-century
"physiocrats" and "mercantilists."

This peculiar historiography of economics began to change radically in 1954, when Joseph Schumpeter's *History of Economic Analysis* was
published.[4] Schumpeter's *History* demolished what we might call "Smythology," the peculiar kind of Whig history of economics that attributes
to Adam Smith mythical achievements, such as being the founder of
economics or one of its essential elements. Schumpeter correctly noted
that it was not until 1848, when John Stuart Mill's *Principles of Political
Economy* was published, that Adam Smith was "invested with the insig-
nia of 'founder'—which none of his contemporaries would have thought
of bestowing on him—and . . . earlier economists moved into the role
of 'precursors' in whom it was just wonderful to discover what nevertheless remained Smith's ideas."[5] Schumpeter concluded: "The fact is that
the *Wealth of Nations* does not contain a single *analytic* idea, principle or
method that was entirely new in 1776."[6]

Analysis literally means "breaking down." We ordinarily use the
word as a synonym for *theory*, because we use theory to break down complicated realities into their simplest elements, and then combine these
elements to build up an explanation that corresponds satisfactorily to
the reality it seeks to explain. But Schumpeter distinguishes economic
analysis, which according to his definition is scientific, from economic
thought, which he describes as mostly uninformed opinion: "the sum
total of all the opinions and desires concerning economic subjects that,

in any given time and place, float in the public mind."[7] According to Schumpeter, "the history of economic thought starts from the records of the national theocracies of antiquity,"[8] but "the history of economic analysis begins only with the Greeks."[9]

Even among the Greeks, says Schumpeter, economic analysis is confined almost entirely to Aristotle,[10] whose work on the subject Schumpeter describes as "decorous, pedestrian, slightly mediocre, and more than slightly pompous common sense."[11] He concludes:

> Aristotle based his economic analysis squarely upon wants and their satisfaction. Starting from the economy of a self-sufficient household, he then introduced division of labor, barter, and, as a means of overcoming the difficulties of direct barter, money—the error of confusing wealth with money duly coming in for stricture. There is no theory of "distribution." This—presumably the extract from a large literature that has been lost—constitutes the Greek bequest, so far as economic theory is concerned. We shall follow its fortunes right to A. Smith's *Wealth of Nations*, the first five chapters of which are but developments of the same line of reasoning.[12]

After Aristotle, there is what Schumpeter calls the "Great Gap," which encompasses the period between the death of Aristotle and the work of Thomas Aquinas in the thirteenth century. Insofar as anyone deserves the title of founder of economics, according to Schumpeter, it was the "Scholastic doctors" of the Middle Ages: that is, professors teaching in the newly established European universities. He singles out Aquinas not so much for his contributions to economic analysis—which Schumpeter describes (wrongly) as "strictly Aristotelian"[13]—as for taking the "earliest and most important step" in establishing the ground rules for modern scientific analysis.[14] Of the later (fourteenth- to seventeenth-century) Scholastics, Schumpeter says that "while the economic sociology of the Scholastic doctors of this period was, in substance, not more than thirteenth-century doctrine worked out more fully, the 'pure' economics which they handed down to laical successors was practically, in its entirety, their own creation. It is within their systems of moral theology and law that economics gained definite if not separate existence."[15]

In particular, "the Aristotelian distinction between value in use and value in exchange was deepened and developed into a fragmentary but genuine subjective or utility theory of exchange value or price for which there was no analogue in either Aristotle or St. Thomas, though there was in both what we may describe as a pointer."[16]

From these beginnings, according to Schumpeter, the Scholastic doctors fashioned all the basic analytical tools that Smith found at hand when he wrote the *Wealth of Nations*. What, then, in Schumpeter's view, was Smith's achievement? "The scholastics and the natural-law philosophers,"[17] he asserts, "had worked out all the elements of" economic analysis; Smith simply undertook "the task of co-ordinating them."[18] He was but one of a growing number of "systematizers" who were working during this period to integrate the inherited tools of economic analysis. But, Schumpeter argues, Smith's synthesis left much to be desired. The analyses of Anne-Robert-Jacques Turgot, Baron de Laune (1727–87) in France and Cesare Beccaria (1738–94) in Italy were both superior to Smith's *Wealth of Nations*. In fact, what is commonly called Smith's labor theory of value turned out to be "a time- and labor-consuming detour"[19] on the way to a workable theory of value and prices.[20]

John Stuart Mill was painfully premature in announcing—at the same time that he was anointing Adam Smith the founder of economics—that "[h]appily, there is nothing in the laws of Value which remains for the present or any future writer to clear up; the theory of the subject is complete: the only difficulty to be overcome is that of so stating it as to solve by anticipation the chief perplexities which occur in applying it."[21] Actually, at the time Mill was writing, what lay ahead were at least two more decades of confusing debate, after which Smith's labor theory of value was finally scrapped and replaced with a modernized version of the Scholastic theory of economic value. As Schumpeter wrote, Smith is to blame "for much that is unsatisfactory in the economic theory of the subsequent hundred years, and for many controversies that would have been unnecessary had he summed up in a different manner."[22] Schumpeter estimated that Smith's scheme actually retarded the development of economic analysis by more than eighty years.[23]

As we will see, Schumpeter's conclusion that "the *Wealth of Nations* does not contain a single *analytic* idea, principle or method that was entirely new in 1776" is sustained by the evidence.[24] Thanks to Schumpeter, it is no longer possible for any serious history of economics to begin with Adam Smith (or his immediate predecessors), thus leaving out Aristotle and the Scholastic doctors.[25]

However, Schumpeter's narrative leaves us with two puzzles. First, if Aristotle's and Aquinas's economic theories were essentially the same, why were there no Aristotelian "economists" after Aristotle, in either ancient Greece or Rome? Conversely, why was there a long and continuous tradition of Scholastic economists after Thomas Aquinas, many coming "nearer than does any other group to having been the 'founders' of scientific economics"?[26] The answer is that Scholastic economics was not, in fact, strictly Aristotelian. Aquinas added something important to Aristotle, something that he found in St. Augustine.[27]

Second, if Adam Smith's synthesis was inferior to that of at least two of his contemporaries, how did Smith become so influential? The answer, I think, is that rather than merely synthesizing the work of previous economic thinkers, as Schumpeter believed, Smith radically *simplified and rearranged* the whole outline of economic theory—in a way that made it easier to develop two of its essential elements but harder or even impossible to develop the others. The simplicity of Smith's theory accounts for his appeal among classical economists; but because it was an *over*simplification, it necessitated another rearrangement of the outline of economic theory, a project begun but not completed by the neoclassical economists who followed.

2

Scholastic Economics (c. 1250–1776)

Scholastic economic theory might be called AAA economics, because its basic formula is Aristotle + Augustine = Aquinas. The best way to understand the relation of these three to one another and to economic theory is to begin with Thomas Aquinas's selection and integration of the basic elements or "first things" of economic theory: his descriptive or "positive" economics. After asking how and why Aquinas's description differs from Aristotle's, we will briefly consider the applications made by later Scholastics, and finally summarize their prescriptive or "normative" Scholastic economic theory.

The Scholastic Outline of Economic Theory

Surprisingly, economic theory is integral to Thomas Aquinas's comprehensive description of the human person.[1] The whole of economic theory can be reconstructed from four elements that Aquinas first gathered together, deriving them from just two sources, Aristotle and Augustine. Aquinas's genius lies in his recognition that an adequate picture of human nature required combining the insights of both men. Furthermore, Aquinas's synthesis contains the first complete statement in history of what is involved in any human economic action, a description that is not only formally complete but also valid at any level—from a single person, to a family, business, or nonprofit foundation, to a nation under a single government, to the entire world economy. It is helpful to state the Scholastic outline of economic theory in three ways: first from the com-

monsense point of view of a noneconomist, then from the point of view
of an economist, and finally from its historical sources.

First, the commonsense explanation: What is economic theory
about? Well, as the title of a delightful children's book asks, *What Do
People Do All Day?*[2] Jesus once noted (as an astute empirical observation,
not divine revelation) that since the days of Noah and Lot, people have
been doing—and presumably will continue to do for as long as there are
humans on earth—four kinds of things. He gave these examples: "planting and building," "buying and selling," "marrying and being given in
marriage," and "eating and drinking."[3] In other words, we human beings
produce, exchange, give (or *distribute*), and *use* (or *consume*) our human
and nonhuman goods.

That's the usual order in action, but not in planning. Thomas Aquinas realized that rather than four *different* acts, these verbs actually constitute four essential aspects of *every* economic act. Whether I want to
consume something (after, in effect, making it a "gift" to myself) or give
it to someone else to consume, I must first produce it or else produce
something else and exchange it for the item I wish to use or give away.
Aquinas integrated these four basic elements of economic theory into a
coherent outline. Moreover, rather than being "strictly Aristotelian,"[4] as
Schumpeter believed, Aquinas subordinated Aristotle's thought on these
matters to Augustine's.

Recall my suggestion in the introduction to this book that *economics
is essentially a theory of providence.* Every human economic action raises
three basic questions: First, *for whom* shall I provide? Second, *what* shall
I provide? And third, *how* shall I provide it? Any adequate economic
theory must answer these three questions. This will require either three
or four answers, depending on whether exchange is involved.

To grasp the logic, take an everyday example: What happens when
someone plans, prepares, and serves a pot-roast dinner for family and
friends? The question "For whom?" must be answered to explain why *these*
particular persons—out of all others—were chosen to consume the dinner. And the answer is that the host prefers them to all others (at least for
this purpose) and expresses that preference by sharing with them this meal.

The question "What?" must be answered in order to explain the
fact that a pot roast, rather than, say, eggplant casserole, is being served.
(The host might well prefer eggplant casserole, if she were cooking only

for herself, but she also knows or guesses the preferences of the people she has invited to share the meal. Hence the pot roast.)

The question "How?" must be answered to explain the otherwise mysterious fact that pot roast actually materializes on the table. But this answer is not as simple as the first two, depending on whether the family has had to produce and exchange other things in order to get the pot roast. If there is no exchange, the household produces out of its own resources not only the total amount but also the exact variety of each good consumed by its members. This might happen, say, on a cattle ranch where potatoes and vegetables are also raised. The "How?" answer would explain where the cow came from, how it was raised and slaughtered, how the meat was dressed, how the potatoes, onions, and carrots were grown, and all the other steps needed to prepare and serve the meal.

But when exchange is involved—as of course it usually is—the family's members first produce something that they think other producers will value more highly than the good that they have produced, and then they exchange the products for mutual benefit. Now, we do not typically barter sides of beef for consulting services. We almost always use money (or claims on it) as our "medium" of exchange. Such exchanges require us to answer a two-step question: first, what goods or services were produced and sold to acquire the money with which to purchase the dinner ingredients that the host family did not itself produce? And second, how did the purchases allow the grocery store to pay its employees, the rancher, the farmer, and everyone else in order that they all might realize their own very different dinner plans for the same evening?

Let's approach each element from the point of view of an economist. We will give a name to each of the four elements of Aquinas's outline of economic theory and describe them concisely, with the benefit of mathematical notation that had not been invented in the thirteenth century.[5] (I will put the economic equations in endnotes so as not to daunt the numerophobic reader, though the math is very elementary.)[6] Although the level of detail and sophistication at which we understand each of the elements has advanced considerably since the Middle Ages, especially since the invention of mathematical calculus in the seventeenth century and its general use by economists since the late nineteenth century, the reason we have a mathematical theory of economics today is that both Aristotle and Augustine recognized from the beginning that the objective aspect of justice and of loving your neighbor with finite goods could be described in mathematical terms.

Since all the elements are simultaneously necessary for a complete economic explanation, the order in which we consider them is somewhat arbitrary. What comes first in logical order may be last in the succession of time, and vice versa. But in describing them here, I will try as far as possible to treat them in logical order.

1. For whom? The theory of "final distribution"[7] describes personal gifts (as well as their opposite, crimes) and their social analogue, distributive justice. The "ends" or purposes of our actions are always persons (including ourselves), whose relative significance (first, second, third, etc.) we express by distributing the use or consumption of our human and nonhuman goods among them.[8] Each person's share in the total use of goods is proportional to that person's significance, relative to all persons sharing in the distribution. His total consumption therefore equals his own income or wealth plus or minus any gifts or other "transfer payments" received or given.[9]

2. What? The theory of *utility* describes how we value (or rank or prefer) the scarce human and nonhuman goods we choose as the means to be used (consumed) by or for the persons who are the end or purpose of our action.[10]

3. How?—A. The theory of *production* explains how we produce such scarce means, by combining the useful services of people ("human capital") and of property ("nonhuman capital"), both of which are usually reproducible.[11]

4. How?—B. The theory of justice in exchange, which economists now call *equilibrium*, explains how the sale of each product provides the compensation of its producers: labor compensation for the workers and property compensation for the property owners.[12]

Though most obviously applicable for an individual person in a single period of time, this general description of economic action is also valid with appropriate modifications for explaining the behavior of any social group over any period. Ordinarily we are not considering a Robinson Crusoe, deprived by shipwreck of spouse and offspring, but rather members of family households within larger political communities integrated by money, specialized production, exchange, and all the social, legal, and political institutions that these entail.

This requires us to revise our account as necessary to suit the particular agent we are describing: an individual person, a family household (or one of its modern offshoots, the business firm and nonprofit foundation), a monetary authority, or a government. For example, while final distribution always involves some kind of "transfer payment," this might be a gift from one person to another, a joint gift from parents to their children, or a tax-funded government benefit authorized by a political community according to its formula of "distributive justice."

We will describe all of these in later chapters. But whatever the change in details, at least three and usually all four elements remain necessary for a complete and accurate description.

To understand the historical development of economic theory, then, it's important to notice several things.

First, the Scholastic system can be described in *a set of economic equations* (though I've followed the advice of Alfred Marshall (1842–1924): "burn the mathematics"—or rather, I've buried it in endnotes for those who wish to test (or possibly teach) the arguments presented.[13]

Second, the system is *logically complete*, which we can verify by observing that there is one equation to explain each unknown variable.[14]

Third, the system is *empirically verifiable:* the dependent variables correspond to measurable realities, like goods consumed and produced, market prices paid, and incomes received.

Fourth, so far it is *purely descriptive* or "positive": it attempts to describe what actually happens, not what *ought* to happen.

Fifth, this system remains *valid at every level* of analysis, from a single person to the entire world economy. To proceed from one level to the next, we simply add together the equations describing all the persons involved.[15]

Finally, since the Scholastic outline is a logically complete description of reality, *the outline itself never changes* in the least. Goods must be produced, exchanged, distributed for final use, and consumed, whether or not economists describe these actions accurately. But when (as frequently happens) economic theorists replace facts with assumptions, their descriptions become empirically false. And when they ignore any element, their descriptions are rendered logically incomplete and unverifiable.

Sources of the Scholastic Outline

Now let's look at the same ideas in historical perspective. Where did the four elements of "AAA" economic theory come from?

Aristotle provided a theory of final distribution pertaining to the social and political distribution of common goods; he assumed rather than stated the theory of utility; and he provided the theories of production and equilibrium. Augustine filled out Aristotle's theory of social and political distribution with a theory of personal distribution, and he also provided a theory of utility as a scale of preferences in the place of Aristotle's sketchy remarks on the subject. Aquinas synthesized the two. Let us take the elements in order.

1. Final distribution. Our evaluation of things, not according to their inherent value but according to their value *to us*, involves the choice of both ends and means. Our ranking of persons as the ends of our economic activity is expressed by our distribution of goods among them for final use, while utility is our ranking of such goods as means.

By what principles do we distribute our wealth? Aristotle noted in his *Ethics* that every human community necessarily has a principle for distributing its *common* goods, which he called its "distributive justice."[16] In each case, the goods are distributed in (geometric) proportion to the relative importance or merit of the persons involved: "All men agree that what is just in distribution must be according to merit in some sense, though they do not all specify the same sort of merit." Aristotle applied this idea mostly to political distribution,[17] noting that "democrats identify it with the status of freeman, supporters of oligarchy with wealth (or noble birth), and supporters of aristocracy with excellence."[18] In other words, Greek democrats wanted equal shares in every public benefit, wealthy citizens wanted shares proportional to the value of their wealth, and the nobility wanted shares according to their social status. This is a fine piece of analysis, because it tells us exactly what we are disagreeing about when we debate (for example) proposals to raise or lower taxes or government spending. We are arguing about two things: first, how much (and from whom) private wealth will be appropriated as common wealth; and second, what share any person shall enjoy of its use. Everyone accepts the basic principle that shares be allocated according to some formula, but people often disagree about what that formula ought to be.[19]

Without a theory of personal distribution, however, the practical value of this analysis is limited, because it cannot explain why or how individual persons form families or join political communities, and (except in communist societies) common political goods ordinarily represent a minority of a community's total wealth. Augustine, on the other hand, provided a theory of personal distribution in observing that every human person, by virtue of his natural interdependence with other persons, also has a principle for distributing the use of his wealth between himself and other persons: the degree of his love for other persons relative to himself.[20]

Augustine was hardly the first to say that persons *ought* to be treated as ends and not merely as means. What sets Augustine apart as an analyst is his observation that every human *does*, as a matter of fact, always act with some *person(s)* as the ultimate end or purpose of action.

Earlier philosophers, including Aristotle, had debated whether happiness lay in making one's highest good wealth or fame or knowledge or moral virtue or pleasure (and each answer defined a different school of moral philosophy). But Augustine sliced through all this. A miser is said to love money as his highest good, noted Augustine—yet he still parts with it to buy bread to continue living, thus showing that his deepest motive is love of self, not money.[21] But it is not the case that every human acts *solely* for him- or herself. That is precisely what each person is free to decide. Every economic choice is therefore a moral choice. In other words, each of us has not only a scale of preferences for instrumental goods as means but also a scale of preferences for persons as ends of our actions.

"Human society is knit together by transactions of giving and receiving,"[22] Augustine noted. But these outwardly similar transactions are of two essentially different kinds: "sale or gift."[23] Generally speaking, we *give* our wealth without compensation to the people we particularly love and sell it to (or *exchange* it with) people we don't.

Augustine began with Aristotle's definition that to love a person means to will him or her some good, but he took it much farther by going on to explain that the share of goods that a person gives to others, relative to the share he retains for his own use, is proportional to his love for those others relative to himself. If there are only two of us, and I love you equally with myself, I will give you the use of half my resources; if

I love you half as much as myself, I will give you a third and keep two-thirds; and so on.

Two persons agree to exchange wealth, on the other hand, when they choose different people as the ends or purposes of their action (for example, I want to provide for *my* family, not yours, while you want to provide for *your* family, not mine) and when the means they have chosen are compatible (I offer something useful to your family to receive something useful for mine). "The specific characteristic of an economic relation [exchange] is not its 'egoism,' but its 'non-tuism,'" as Philip Wicksteed pithily put it—*tu* being Latin for "thou," as *ego* is for "I." "The economic relation [exchange] does not exclude from my mind everyone but me, it potentially includes everyone but you."[24]

Recognizing their mathematical similarity and social complementarity, Aquinas combined Augustine's theory of *personal* distribution with Aristotle's theory of *political* or *social* distribution. At least in principle, the final distribution of the use of all a society's wealth was accounted for.

2. Utility. Aristotle suggested in his *Ethics* that economic value is based on *chreia*.[25] Though sometimes anachronistically translated as "demand," the Greek word connotes use or need. But the economic theory of utility as a mathematical scale of preference was first explicitly described by Augustine in *The City of God*. Each thing's being, and thus its inherent goodness or value, is utterly unaffected by any human's attitude toward it: It is what it is, no more and no less. "This is the scale according to the order of nature," said Augustine, "but there is another gradation which employs utility as the criterion of value."[26]

Utility is the value of any thing considered, not in or for itself, but as a means to some other end or goal, which, ultimately, is always one or more persons. For example, the intrinsic value of a live mouse—a sentient being—is obviously higher than that of a dead plant; yet most of us prefer loaves of bread (which are made from dead plants) to live mice in the house. Why? Because we plan to eat the bread, not the mice. The natures of the mouse and the wheat are the same whether there exist one or a billion specimens of each; but the order of our preference according to utility is affected by the relative scarcity of the two goods. (The world's only specimen of a certain kind of mouse might be worth a lot of "dough." Or if bread and all other substitutes were sufficiently scarce, as in a famine, we might even learn to eat mice.)[27]

Augustine also introduced the fundamental distinction between "private" goods like bread, which inherently only one person at a time can consume, and "public" goods (like a performance in an ancient amphitheater, a modern radio or television broadcast, national defense, or enforcement of justice) that many people can simultaneously enjoy because (at least within certain limits) they are not "diminished by being shared."[28] Most of our discussion of personal and domestic economy will concern private goods, but as we'll see later, both public goods and quasi-public goods (which benefit many but not all citizens) are often central to political economy.

3. Production. We humans not only reappraise but also rearrange the things we find in nature in order to produce combinations we value more highly. Though our decision to produce one kind of good rather than another is dictated by their relative value, production determines the amount of resources actually available for final distribution and use. And since production alters the relative scarcity or abundance of the goods, it will in turn affect our estimates of their relative value.

How are goods produced? Aristotle remarks in his *Politics* that "any piece of property can be regarded as a tool enabling a man to live; and his property is an assemblage of such tools."[29] He notes that some goods are enjoyed or consumed directly, but others indirectly, by helping to produce goods that are consumed directly; furthermore (a point too often overlooked), some goods are versatile enough to serve either purpose. Thus, Aristotle distinguishes final products from the factors that produce them. Aristotle also observes that "tools may be animate as well as inanimate; a ship's captain uses a lifeless rudder [for steering], but a living man for watch; for the worker in a craft is, from the point of view of the craft, one of its tools." In other words, wealth may take either of two forms: what modern economists call human capital (the useful qualities embodied in human persons) and nonhuman capital (the useful qualities embodied in property). To produce more of either kind of wealth usually requires a combination of both.

In Aristotle's day, both people and property were products of the household: a business was simply a merchant's or craftsman's household, just as a government was essentially a king's or chieftain's household. Moreover, some people *were* property: slaves were a significant part of human capital. Over time, the biblical understanding of the human person led first to the replacement of slavery with serfdom and eventually to the widespread abolition of both. The economic functions of the ancient household were also differentiated among more specialized entities—the modern household (which specializes in producing and maintaining human persons); the modern business firm (which specializes in producing and maintaining property owned by the persons in households); and the modern nonprofit foundation (which specializes either in assisting the household's investments in people or in its distribution of charitable benefits to persons outside the household).

4. Equilibrium. Aristotle suggested that the compensation of producers comes from the sale of their product and that the value of the compensation depends on their respective contributions to the value of that product.[30] At least, this is how Thomas Aquinas's teacher, Albert the Great, and all later Scholastics read him.[31] Equality between each product's value and the total income of its producers is necessary for economic *equilibrium*, which Aristotle called "justice in exchange," or "commutative justice," and for the very continuation of the economic system. But actual equality can come about only with a properly functioning monetary system and in the absence of monopoly (because only then can no one party rig market prices to its own advantage) and other obstacles to an effectively functioning market.[32] The price determined under such conditions was once called the just price and is now called the equilibrium price.[33] Aristotle noted that to overcome the disadvantages of multilateral barter we agree to use one commodity as a medium of exchange, and that its roles as standard and store of value are derived from this function.[34]

Watching Aquinas at Work

All four elements of Scholastic economic theory, then, originated with Aristotle and/or Augustine. By integrating them into a coherent system, Thomas Aquinas fashioned a kind of analytical Swiss Army knife that contained all the basic tools necessary to explain any economic event, simple or complex. Economists have been using it ever since.

But far from being the culmination of an integrated Scholastic economic theory, Aquinas represented its beginning. We can date this beginning approximately to the year 1250, when Albert the Great began to lecture on Aristotle's newly recovered and translated *Nicomachean Eth-*

ics at the University of Cologne, assisted by Aquinas as second professor and master of students. Aquinas transcribed Albert's lectures on the subject and later prepared Albert's commentary for publication.[35]

Three of the four elements of economic analysis (the distribution function, the utility function, and the equilibrium conditions) are to be found (and the production function implied or mentioned) in Aquinas's own later commentary on the *Nicomachean Ethics*, while the production function is described in his commentary on Aristotle's *Politics*.[36] The same analysis is also scattered throughout much of his *Summa theologiae*. By comparing his treatment of the material in both places, we can watch Aquinas integrating Augustine's elements with Aristotle's. At the same time, we can begin to understand why Augustine's considerable contribution has been neglected and why Aquinas's economics has been dismissed as "strictly Aristotelian," though its content and organization differ from Aristotle's.

Aquinas describes personal distribution most explicitly in the *Summa theologiae*, where he correctly attributes its mathematical formulation to Augustine.[37] He inserts the same theory (but not Augustine's name) in commenting on Aristotle's theory of friendship in the *Ethics:* "Thus it seems that one person is a friend of another if he acts the same way for a friend as he might for himself"[38] and "a person loves himself more, to the extent that he assigns to himself greater goods."[39] Because the fit is so natural, it is easy to overlook the fact that Aristotle did not exactly say that or that Aquinas is describing the pagan Aristotle's ideas using Augustine's explanation of the Second Great Commandment to "love your neighbor as yourself."

Similarly, when explaining Augustine's theory of utility in the *Summa theologiae*, Aquinas cites its author by name: "As Augustine says . . . the price of things salable does not depend on their degree of nature, since at times a horse fetches a higher price than a slave; but it depends on their usefulness to man."[40] When commenting on Aristotle's sketchy remarks on the subject in the *Ethics*, Aquinas inserts Augustine's scale of utility, along with Augustine's mouse example from *The City of God*: "Articles are not valued according to the dignity of their nature, otherwise a mouse, an animal endowed with sense, should be of greater value than a pearl, a thing without life. But they are priced according as man stands in need of them for his own use."[41]

Why would Aquinas insert Augustine's economic theory into his commentary on Aristotle's *Ethics*? Primarily because Aquinas correctly saw that both Augustine's mathematical theory of personal distribution (gifts and crimes) and his mathematical theory of utility, though not worked out specifically in response to Aristotle, were complements necessary to complete Aristotle's mathematical theories of production, equilibrium (justice in exchange), and distributive justice. He thereby completed Aristotle's account by drawing out implications that Aristotle had overlooked. Aquinas's became the authoritative interpretation of Aristotle's economics, with the ironic result that even as erudite a scholar as Schumpeter could view Aquinas as "strictly Aristotelian" and ignore the critical contributions he had drawn from Augustine. Aquinas similarly received no recognition for replacing Aristotle's division of moral philosophy into ethics and politics (which left discussion of the household floating uncertainly between the two) with the more logical tripartite structure of personal, domestic, and political philosophy (and economy).[42]

So Why the "Great Gap"?

Now we have enough information to solve the puzzle posited by Schumpeter: Why were there no Aristotelian economists after Aristotle? Starting with Albert the Great and Thomas Aquinas, historians are able to trace the transmission of economic theories from teacher to student, and from one "school" to another, right down to the present. But no earlier tradition of a purely Aristotelian economics has been found, even though the Greek Academy continued to operate until A.D. 529.[43] Aristotle's economic ideas were seldom repeated, and not at all developed, until Aquinas integrated them with Augustine's.

An obvious reason for this gap is that Aristotle's outline of economic theory was too incomplete to serve as the platform for universal application to questions like the determination of prices and incomes, which is necessary for solving practical problems like the proper conduct of monetary, fiscal, and regulatory policies. Without Augustine's theory of personal gifts and crimes, Aristotle's theory of distributive justice, which applies only to common goods, left the distribution of most wealth in most societies unaccounted for. And without Augustine's theory of utility it was not possible to work out the reasons for most of the systematic variation of market prices.

Why could Augustine see farther than Aristotle on these points? Two concepts were missing from Aristotle's description of reality but present in Augustine's: "creation" and "person." As a result, also missing from Aristotle's worldview, and therefore lacking in his economic theory, is Augustine's understanding that every person—God or man—is fundamentally motivated to act by love of some person(s), including but not limited to him- or herself.

Both Aristotle's virtuous man and his God were largely self-contained. Aristotle's God was a First Mover but not a Creator; he informed but did not create prime matter. For Aristotle, God was Self-Thinking Thought. He did not actually know things (including humans) outside himself as individual beings, but only collectively, according to their species or concepts. And as far as humans are concerned, Aristotle argued that, since friendship involves a kind of equality, "when one party is removed to a great distance, as God is, the possibility of friendship ceases."[44] In Aristotle's philosophy, God and man could not and did not communicate or share gifts with one another.

The idea that the universe was created from nothing is in itself a philosophical rather than a religious idea. But it simply did not exist in pagan Greek or Roman philosophy. The Christian belief that God had become a particular man could not help but affect even pure philosophy in its view of both God and man. For Augustine, in addition to rational intellect and will, personhood always includes *relationships* to, and love for, other persons. For Augustine and Aquinas, God knows and loves each human person individually. Humans resemble God in being persons who are similarly motivated by love of persons, including one another and God, and who express this love with gifts.[45]

Though he expounded it at greater length in *The City of God*, Augustine first worked out the relation between divine and human providence in a much shorter, earlier work, which he cited twice later in life as a turning point in his own thought on the subject. That work is a letter to his friend Simplician, who had asked Augustine to consider some problems raised by the Apostle Paul's letter to the church at Rome, which seems to indicate God's unequal treatment of different people.[46]

Augustine's response focuses on the fact, and ends with an explanation, of the order in human transactions, including markets. Earlier in the same letter, Paul had contrasted justice in exchange with a gift:

"Now when a man works, his wages are not credited to him as a gift, but as an obligation" (Romans 4:4). These, Augustine suggests, are the paradigms for *all* transactions, not only among men but also between the Creator and his creatures. Creation means that everything (including a man's goodwill) is received as a "free gift of God."[47] This places God in the same relation to his creatures as a creditor to impecunious debtors: "Human society is knit together by transactions of giving and receiving, and things are given and received sometimes as debts, sometimes not. No one can be charged with unrighteousness who exacts what is owing to him. Nor certainly can he be charged with unrighteousness who is prepared to give up what is owing to him. This decision does not lie with those who are debtors but with the creditor. This image or, as I said, trace of equity is stamped on the business transactions of men by the Supreme Equity."[48]

Weakened by sin and having chosen to disobey God, "sinful humanity must pay a debt of punishment to the supreme divine justice. Whether that debt is exacted or remitted there is no unrighteousness." God does not "compel any man to sin when he simply does not bestow his justifying mercy on some sinners, and for that reason is said to harden some sinners." Evil is therefore not a *thing*, but a *disorder*, man's turning from God, the source of all good things, to his creatures, which are lesser goods.[49] God freely offers his grace, without which the sinner, having freely fallen, cannot freely turn back to God. Why some accept this grace, while others do not, remains a mystery. But Augustine has shown at least that God is just, truthful, and free, and that man's will, though foreknown, is not predetermined by God (as the Stoics maintained). The letter to Simplician amounts to Augustine's first draft of the Christian theory of divine providence, which he elaborated in *The City of God*, and which Aquinas follows closely.[50]

The Scholastic Development of Economic Theory

Let us sketch a few of the ways in which the Scholastic economists after Aquinas applied the basic elements of economic theory that Aquinas had integrated. As we'll see more clearly in the next two chapters, since the thirteenth century there has been an unbroken tradition at the highest academic level of teaching two of the four elements of economic analysis (production and exchange) and a third, utility, with less than a century's interruption. Historian Odd Langholm, following what he called "one of the shrewd proposals made by Schumpeter,"[51] undertook the daunting project of tracing the chain of custody of these three elements through the unbroken tradition of Latin Aristotle commentaries from the thirteenth to the seventeenth centuries. His research allows us to follow the Scholastics' analysis of supply and demand, first at the microeconomic level, then on progressively broader and more highly aggregated levels, and finally as it is integrated with a monetary theory that encompassed the whole economy and served as the foundation for modern macroeconomics.

On the "demand" side, Henry of Friemar (d. 1354) advanced the theory of product prices in the late thirteenth and early fourteenth centuries by formally aggregating the concept of need or use, "not of this or that person, but of the whole community."[52] His "common need of something scarce" begins to approach the notion of total market demand for a product. Though many early commentators (apparently because of Aristotle's use of the word "need" for utility) restricted their discussions to the prices of necessities, Jean Buridan made clear in the mid-fourteenth century that demand implies an ability to offer something in exchange, and that the same principles of utility and scarcity explain the prices of luxuries as well as of necessities.

Monetary theory is especially important in every age. Since money forms part of every exchange in a market economy, a monetary theorist is responsible not merely for explaining the labor market or product market or capital market, but also for providing an overview of the entire economy. In the first treatise devoted to money, Nicole Oresme (1320–82) extended Buridan's analysis from a treatment of the total demand for one product in the direction of an analysis of the total or aggregate demand for all products. He also developed the most important implications for government economic policy (which I'll consider shortly in the context of Scholastic normative economics). Oresme's monetary analysis was to be followed by Bernardo Davanzati (1529–1606), Geminiano Montanari (1633–87), and Ferdinando Galiani (1728–87). The macroeconomics of the twentieth and twenty-first centuries grew out of these monetary theories.

Meanwhile, the supply side of value analysis had developed, at first in parallel with the demand side and then finally integrated with it. Aristotle had said in the *Ethics* that "the builder must get from the shoemaker the latter's work" and that if such exchanges were not equal "the arts would be destroyed."[53] Thomas Aquinas's teacher, Albert the Great, interpreted this to mean that if the builder cannot cover his *labor et expensae,* "the art of building would be destroyed"—suggesting that market prices are also regulated by the cost (and thus profitability and scale) of production. Thomas Aquinas retained Albert's idea, and his followers transmitted it to Gerald Odonis, a Franciscan of the early fourteenth century. Odonis was the first to attempt a unified theory of the value of products and their factors or producers; he explained the income of the producer by the demand for his product and the rarity of his skills. St. Bernardino of Siena in the fifteenth century, St. Antonino of Florence and Johannes Mair of Scotland in the sixteenth century, and Johannes Crell (whom Langholm describes as "a Thomist of the German Protestant branch") in the seventeenth century progressively developed this approach.[54]

Langholm's research therefore shows that the Scholastics had proceeded farther and sooner toward an integration of the key economic theories of product value and factor compensation than Schumpeter had been aware. In fact, all the crucial elements in the Scholastic tradition mentioned by Schumpeter had developed much sooner than Schumpeter suggested—within a century of Aquinas's synthesis, by the mid-fourteenth rather than by the sixteenth century—and their development thrived on a clash of different philosophical schools. It was not merely a placid development within a single recognizably Thomist tradition.[55]

The fact that this development occurred nearly two centuries before the Protestant Reformation in the sixteenth century helps explain an otherwise mystifying fact on which Schumpeter and Langholm agree: there is no significant difference on economic theory between Catholics and Protestants after the Reformation.[56] Langholm showed, for example, that the price analysis of the sixteenth-century Protestant Reformer Philip Melanchthon (1497–1560) continued the tradition traceable from Aquinas through Nicolas Oresme and Henry of Friemar, and that Melanchthon's Protestant followers transmitted it basically unchanged into the following century.[57] Historian Henry William Spiegel further traced Scholastic economic ideas to pre-Revolutionary Protestant America, where he discovered that Puritan clergyman John Cotton's (1584–1652) rules of business behavior were "similar to those laid down by the medieval schoolmen."[58]

Though straightforward in retrospect, discerning these lines of development was complicated for two reasons.

First, the invention of movable type seems to have had the curious effect of slowing down or even decreasing the quality of economic analysis—much as the average *quality* of information has dropped since the Internet vastly expanded the *quantity* that is freely available. The information available in electronic form on any subject displaces the printed information sitting in the libraries. Likewise, most of the manuscript economic commentaries written before 1500 were never printed, and therefore sat unknown, while a few newer, printed books filled the demand for such analysis. As a result, we find Grotius and Pufendorf debating aspects of price theory that had been elaborated and settled centuries earlier.[59] And we see Galiani still treating in parallel the Scholastic theories of value concerning the prices of products and of the factors that produce them, though they had been integrated at least two hundred years earlier.

Second, the entanglement of economic discussions with religious controversies, while not changing the analysis, made it much harder to see accurately where certain ideas came from. For example, St. Antonino of Florence was always generous in disclosing the sources of his economic ideas, but in one important case he was able to preserve and hand on the economic analysis of a man accused of heresy only by concealing its source.[60] After the Reformation, similar considerations made it far less likely that a Protestant would correctly attribute ideas originating with Thomas Aquinas or that Catholics would give credit to Protestants for having developed those ideas.

Particularly important for the transmission of Scholastic economic theory to the American colonies and its adoption by key American Founders was Samuel Pufendorf. Writing in the first generation after the Peace of Westphalia ended Europe's brutal religious wars in 1648, Pufendorf had embraced and renewed Augustine's and Aquinas's argument that among citizens who disagree about divine revelation, only reasoning from common human experience—the natural law—can provide a workable basis for government. Though not intended primarily as an economic treatise, Pufendorf's concise and readable compendium of the natural law, *On the Duty of Man and Citizen According to Natural Law*, contains the four basic elements of economic theory, organized according to personal, domestic, and political economy, and integrating descriptive with prescriptive theory by the Two Great Commandments.[61] Pufendorf's work was widely circulated in the colonies and recommended by Alexander Hamilton (1755–1804), who penned two-thirds of *The Federalist* and became the first U.S. secretary of the treasury under George Washington.[62] Also noteworthy are the Founders' extensions of Aristotle's theories of production, faction, and ideology, and Augustine's theory of public goods, into the theory of American public choice, which we will consider as part of normative Scholastic economics and later test empirically in chapter 14.

The Main Analytical Shortcoming in Early Scholastic Economics

The early Scholastic "economists" certainly knew the nature and causes of the wealth of nations. As we will see more clearly when considering domestic economy, their theory contains everything necessary to explain investment and economic growth—which amount to producing human and nonhuman resources faster than they are consumed or used up.[63] But like most economists, they routinely made simplifying assumptions that seemed warranted by experience. They adopted Aristotle's assumption that the population and its average standard of living do not increase—because mankind in general had never experienced a substantial and sustained increase of either.[64] One reason they had not increased was that the average length of a human life had not increased. As we will discover in a later chapter, a key determinant of the rate of investment in both human and nonhuman capital, and therefore of real economic growth, is the length of human life. Average life expectancy in England in the fourteenth and early fifteenth centuries—twenty-four years—was about the same as it had been in Roman Egypt.[65] Since longevity had not increased and a twenty-four-year life span is too short for the average person to acquire much human or nonhuman wealth, average per capita real income was close to the subsistence level, and average annual real economic growth during the whole period was approximately zero. Life expectancy and economic growth appear to have risen in the twelfth and thirteenth centuries, but the Black Death of the fourteenth century reversed this progress, making it seem like an aberration. Another decline in mortality caused life expectancy in England to rise to about thirty-four years, or by almost half, by the mid-sixteenth century.[66] Both the population and the living standard began to grow, though at rates that we would consider very slow. The Scholastics' assumptions (as opposed to their theory) about production and economic growth failed to account for this actual experience.

The Scholastic assumption that economies did not grow was directly relevant to the controversy about interest and usury. Aristotle had argued that charging interest on loaned money is unnatural because money itself is sterile. Unlike crops or livestock, money does not naturally reproduce itself. The Scholastics carefully analyzed the components of interest and resolved them into three: the risk of loss (*damnum emergens*) when the borrower defaults or repays the loan in depreciated money, for example; the opportunity cost of forgoing income from alternative investments (*lucrum cessans*); and the pure interest (*interesse*) excluding these factors. A consensus allowed for the charging of interest to compensate for risk of loss, but it did not allow charging pure interest, while there was disagreement about whether it was right to expect compensation for opportunity cost.

If pure interest is in fact zero, it is hard to argue with Aristotle's point: People shouldn't be charged for what doesn't exist. In that case, interest should be charged only to compensate for risk of loss, because there is no opportunity cost. But pure interest is a matter of empirical fact, not morality, and therefore cannot be settled by theoretical deduction. As Schumpeter pointed out, "The fundamental factor that raises interest above zero is the prevalence of business profits."[67] A stagnant economy, the kind the early Scholastics routinely assumed, rarely produces aggregate business profits, because new production at best replaces goods consumed directly and the human and nonhuman capital used up in the process of production. Those who favored allowing interest in the case of opportunity cost were generally located in cities or regions that were commercial centers experiencing economic growth and aggregate profitability.

Prescriptive or "Normative" Scholastic Economics

It is often helpful to distinguish carefully between "positive" theory, which describes things as they are, and "normative" theory, which prescribes how they ought to be.[68] The descriptive or positive economic theory of the Scholastics was distinct from—but integrated with—their prescriptive or normative economics.[69] And Aquinas followed Augustine in placing the fact of scarcity squarely at the center of moral decision making. Since I will consider normative economics in more detail at the personal, domestic, and political levels, I will offer only a brief overview here.

Personal economy. The virtue of Augustine's "positive" theory of human choice is that it can equally describe the behavior of both the person who observes and the person who violates moral norms. Good and bad persons alike require some wealth to live, both choose among real or imagined goods (not "bads"), and both derive their preferences for such goods from their love for some person or persons. The whole difference lies in the order in which they rank these ends and means. The good man treats at least some person other than himself as an end and only lower things as pure means, while the bad person may rank every person but himself as a mere means.

The moral norm governing preferences for ends and means of economic action consists of the Two Great Commandments: "You shall love God with all your heart, soul, mind, and strength" and "You shall love your neighbor as yourself."[70] According to the Scholastic "natural law," these are not "counsels of perfection" intended only for believing Christians or Jews, but the rule of reason that naturally binds the conscience of everyone, everywhere, always—which, for emphasis, received the sanction of Hebrew and Christian revelation. No commandment, "You shall love yourself," is necessary, explains Augustine, because everyone naturally loves himself. The whole problem is to love ourselves "ordinately"; that is, while observing the proper ranking of persons as ends and instrumental goods as means.

Since love properly means willing some good to some person, said Augustine, what it means to love your neighbor as yourself depends critically on whether the good in question is "diminished by being shared with others"—that is, by whether it is scarce.[71] Augustine, followed by Thomas Aquinas, accordingly distinguished two ways in which we can love our fellow man: *benevolence*, or goodwill, which can be extended to everyone in the world, and *beneficence*, or doing good, which cannot.[72] We can always avoid harming others, which is why there are no exceptions to the prohibitions against murder, theft, adultery, and so on. But the share of one's scarce goods that can be distributed to others is practically limited, because no one, however rich, can share equally with everyone in the world and still leave himself enough to live on.

What is inherently impossible is not morally binding. This means that when scarce goods are involved, loving your neighbor *as* yourself cannot always mean loving your neighbor *equally with* yourself. "Since you cannot do good to all," wrote Augustine, "you are to pay special regard to those who, by the accidents of time, or place, or circumstance, are brought into closer connection with you."[73] The Good Samaritan is the classic case of "loving your neighbor as yourself."[74] He loved the man he found beaten by robbers *as* himself by regarding him *as a person* like himself; but he did not love him *equally with himself,* by dividing his property equally with him. The economic value of the Samaritan's time and the two coins he gave to care for the man probably amounted to half his wages for the week—not for the year or his whole life. This was a generous but also properly human—not superhuman—act, and everyone should be prepared to undertake such a sacrifice in order to prevent the death or extreme misery of a fellow human being.

Domestic economy. According to the Scholastics, the same moral imperative to love your neighbor as yourself applies to decisions at every social level, from the personal to the political; but the practical limits on distribution imposed by the fact of scarcity also apply: The approximate equality of wealth and income that can actually be practiced in a group the size of a household cannot be extended to a whole nation or the world. At the same time, the wide acceptance of the view that a person's eternal salvation depended on treatment of his or her neighbor led to the elaboration of specialized methods of distribution at the domestic level. For example, the endowment of charitable foundations by personal gifts and bequests and the incorporation of charitable distribution into the ordinary functions of guilds and business partnerships. For example, it was not uncommon to create a fund for the poor with part of a company's capital, to pay a proportional share of the dividends as alms, and to make the poor a creditor in the event of bankruptcy.[75]

Political economy. At the political level, a much wider range of questions is raised, questions concerning the whole social order. What right do humans have to appropriate inanimate objects and animals for their own use? Does the right extend to human slavery? Should most or all property be privately owned or held in common? Who should have responsibility for alleviating cases of extreme need? Should restrictions be imposed on economic activity, such as freedom of foreign and domestic trade or allow-

able wages and prices? And how should the government's own finances be
conducted? On these questions Aquinas combines and develops Aristotle's
and Augustine's ideas, and subsequent thinkers built on his foundation.[76]

Right to ownership and use of property. The Scholastics believed
that the right to own and use animals and inanimate objects is rooted
in man's reason, which enables man to make use of them to satisfy his
needs.[77] Unlike Aristotle, the Scholastics viewed slavery as conventional,
not natural.[78]

Purpose of government. Aquinas's theory of the proper role of government is most concisely presented in *On Kingship*.[79] He rejects the idea
that the end of human life is an abundance of wealth. If that were so, "the
knowledge of economics would have the last word in the community's
government."[80] Instead, "men form a group for the purpose of living well
together, a thing which the individual man living alone could not attain,
and good life is virtuous life."[81] To this basically Aristotelian view of society, Aquinas adds the Augustinian proviso: "It is not the ultimate end of
an assembled multitude to live virtuously, but through virtuous living to
attain to the possession of God."[82]

Aquinas's primary concern is with establishing and maintaining
social order. Man is not only an intelligent but also a social animal, and
his social life is integrated in several social institutions, each with a different level of self-sufficiency: the "family of one household," which provides
life itself and satisfies the most basic daily needs; the local community,
which Aquinas views as including and organized around the economic
occupations that sustain the household; the city, which is devoted not
just to living but to "living well"; and the province, in which "still more
self-sufficiency is found . . . because of the need for fighting together and
of mutual help against enemies."[83]

Principles of social order. For an individual human to lead a good
life "two things are required. The first and most important is to act in
a virtuous manner (for virtue is that by which one lives well); the second, which is secondary and instrumental, is a sufficiency of those bodily
goods whose use is necessary for virtuous life."[84] Both are true of community life as well, but every community also has a third vital concern—its
own unity, which, unlike an individual's, is not naturally organic.[85]

Private vs. communal ownership. From this view it follows that a
political commonwealth obviously does require some "common wealth":

common goods administered by government to promote the general common good. But the fact of scarcity requires that most property be privately owned,[86] because in administering scarce goods, private ownership usually has the triple advantage of greater social peace, productivity, and order.[87] Whether or not the government provides such goods itself, it must ensure that there are places of learning, military defense, law courts, markets, places of worship, and the various productive occupations.[88]

Care for the needy. The ownership of wealth does not necessarily coincide with its use: that is the whole point of making decisions about its final distribution. And human arrangements of private property do not supersede the fact that every human being requires property to live.[89] In fact, Aquinas goes so far as to say that in cases of extreme need when there is no other remedy, taking and using another's property to avoid death is not even stealing. This is because the conventions of private property do not take precedence over the fact that some wealth is necessary for everyone to live. But Aquinas immediately points to the fact of scarcity as the reason for placing the general responsibility for the poor, except in emergencies, primarily on individual persons in their various intermediating social relationships rather than the government.[90]

"Globalization" and foreign trade. Aquinas presents a clear-eyed view of the trade-offs involved in pursuing this view of human life and society in the face of "globalization"—which, far from being a new problem, is one of the oldest. After public health and safety, the most essential instrumental goods are food and energy (in his time, vegetation and animal feed, which provided most motive power before the use of steam and internal combustion engines). If a city or nation cannot provide these, it must trade for them, and a broader circle of exchange unambiguously brings a greater abundance of wealth by lowering prices paid for imported goods and increasing prices received for exported goods. However, self-sufficiency in food and energy is militarily safer, since "the city may be overcome through lack of food [and feed]." It's also "more dignified," since foreign trade undermines the unity of civic life insofar as it introduces foreign customs and dependence, promotes vices like greed and venality, and bestows honor on the rich—as the result of which "civic life will necessarily be corrupted." Having noted these problems, Aquinas firmly rejects autarky as impractical.[91] In other words, there are several legitimate reasons for restricting foreign trade, but they exact an economic cost. This balanced discussion fairly captures the pros and cons of "globalization" today and the unsatisfactory nature of insisting on either laissez-faire or autarky.

Regulation of domestic trade. In contrast to foreign trade, the same view argues generally against regulating domestic commerce, except to enforce standard weights and measures and curb unjust uses of monopoly power.[92]

Regulation of monopoly. Following Aristotle, the Scholastics understood that justice in exchange requires that prices be determined in a market free from monopoly or other price manipulation to the benefit of a few.[93] Otherwise, government intervention was justified to correct the injustice. These are among the conditions of equilibrium in modern economic theory. Similarly, the Scholastic thinkers opposed collaborative fixing of prices by guilds as a violation of commutative justice.

Basic principles of monetary and fiscal policy. Partly because his theory had some important gaps and partly because Greek governments had not yet financed government spending on a large scale by issuing money, as later Roman emperors and medieval monarchs were to do, Aristotle did not develop some of the most important economic policy implications of his monetary analysis.[94] Where Aristotle suggested as a *statement of fact*, "Now the same thing happens to money itself as to goods—it is not always worth the same; yet it tends to be steadier,"[95] Aquinas corrected this to the normative principle, "Nevertheless, it *ought to be so established* that it retains the same value more permanently than other things."[96]

Following Aquinas's lead, but with the advantage of three or four generations of further development of supply-and-demand analysis guided by the Thomist framework, Oresme identified monetary debasement resulting from the monetary authority's abuse of its monopoly privilege to issue money as a fundamental cause of "injustice in exchange" or disequilibrium. This takes the form of general price inflation (or less frequently, because usually less lucrative for the government, deflation). As we've seen, justice in exchange or equilibrium entails a near equality in value of the products and services exchanged. This requires that the value of money remain roughly constant over time and also that the total value of products supplied closely equal the total value of products demanded. Practically speaking, the main source of inequality between the two is the issue of money to finance a deficit in the government's budget, which adds to the total demand for goods but not their total supply. Oresme pointed out that money is owned by the people who use it, not the monetary authority that issues it, and he laid down the normative principle that except in extraordinary circumstances like war (when the community's survival is at stake and gives its approval), government must not issue money as a significant source of revenue. This simple precept meant that the government must balance its other revenues with its expenditures over time, though not necessarily every year.[97] If the government has no other significant source of revenue, the current consumption of the goods and services it provides must be financed by taxes on the incomes of workers and property owners. But taxes on production discourage production, and this disadvantage must be weighed against any advantages derived from the expenditure. The distribution of taxation, the use of government-provided goods and services, and the receipt of transfer payments are all governed by the political community's formula for distributive justice.

Modern confusion of justice in exchange and distributive justice. A confusion of commutative and distributive justice has bedeviled both critics and admirers of the Scholastics. Though not as common as it once was among experts, the error remains widespread enough to require mention. On the one hand, a few neoclassical economists ignorant of economics history have dismissed the thought of the Scholastics on the grounds that their concern for distributive justice vitiated their economic analysis.[98] On the other hand, modern admirers of the Scholastics have used the same misunderstanding of the just price to argue for legislation that would regulate maximum prices or minimum-wage rates as a matter of distributive justice.[99]

As Stephen Worland pointed out, this error can be traced to a book by Sir William Ashley that was first published in 1888.[100] Ashley was much taken with the speculation of Sir Henry Maine that society has evolved since ancient times from being based on status to being based on contract.[101] He accordingly misinterpreted a key passage in Thomas Aquinas to mean that the Scholastic just price meant that "the maker [of a product] should receive what would fairly recompense him for his labour, not what would enable him to make a gain, but what would permit him to live a decent life according to the standard of comfort which public opinion recognized as appropriate to his class."[102] Thus, Ashley incorrectly said that the Scholastic just price was a matter of distributive, not commutative, justice, and that it was based upon the social status of the parties to an exchange, rather than on market conditions. According to Ashley, Aquinas "clearly considers that in any particular country or district there is for every article, at any particular time, some one just price: that prices, accordingly, should not vary with momentary supply and demand, with individual caprice, or skill in the chaffering of the market."[103]

But Aquinas said nothing of the sort. In the question Ashley cites, Aquinas clearly states that at any time and place, "the just price of things is not fixed with mathematical precision, but depends on a kind of estimate, so that a slight addition or subtraction would not seem to destroy the equality of justice."[104] He notes that human laws allowed variation of up to "half the amount of the just price of the thing," and that an article's price changes according to "differences in location, time, or the risk incurred in transferring it from one place to another. Neither purchase nor sale according to this principle is unjust."[105] Considering the objection that "it is not lawful, in trading, to sell a thing for a higher price than we paid for it," Thomas responds that while greed is always wrong, "nothing prevents gain from being directed to some necessary or even virtuous end, and thus trading becomes lawful." Among such ends are "trading for the upkeep of his household, or for the assistance of the needy."[106] In other words, the issue in the article Ashley misquoted was whether it is morally justifiable to trade for a profit—not how the price of goods is determined.

The Scholastics, as we have seen, correctly noted that the continuation of the economic system depended on market prices covering the costs of production. This is another key condition of equilibrium in modern economic theory. If a businessman failed to cover his costs under normal competitive conditions, the loss was his, regardless of his need or social dignity. *Distributive* justice required that *common* goods be distributed according to the prevailing social norms, which might take account of the dignity or need of persons. But this did not directly involve the just price of goods or services.

Similarly, Scholastic efforts to enforce standard weights and measures or regulate monopoly have often been misinterpreted as attempts to regulate domestic prices. Anyone who looks carefully while visiting the cathedral in Freiburg, Germany, will find etched into the north wall of the main entrance (under the watchful eyes of the divine judge and Twelve Apostles) the dimensions of bushel baskets used for grain, containers of charcoal, and loaves of bread, against which customers of the nearby market could bring their purchases for immediate comparison. These show that the standard loaves were much smaller during times of dearth (as in 1270 and 1313) and many times larger during years of plenty (as in 1320).[107] Holding the money prices of products constant while the standard size and weight varied with supply was an effective way of policing attempted market fraud while avoiding both the inconveniences of frequent price changes—in an age when most customers were illiterate and market days periodic—and the shortages or surpluses that inevitably result when both money prices and unit sizes are controlled.

In other words, the Scholastics were ordinarily dealing with markets much more imperfect than those to which we are accustomed;[108] yet we do sometimes face cases of imperfect markets, in which Scholastic methods are not only directly relevant but also unconsciously automatic. For example, when wholesale commodity markets were closed after communications were disrupted by the September 11, 2001, terrorist attacks in New York City, several state authorities spontaneously prosecuted wholesale suppliers and gas station owners who charged a price substantially higher than when wholesale markets were last open. This was analytically correct, because there had been no disruption of supplies, only a temporary closing of the market. And it was precisely the method the Scholastics used to govern prices when the markets were closed seven centuries earlier.

Differences over church–state relations. While maintaining remarkable consistency in their natural law philosophy and economic theory, adherents to Scholastic economics differed in their theory of the relation between government and religion. Aquinas presumed the unity of Roman Catholic religion that largely prevailed in western Europe in the thirteenth century, so that authority in purely temporal matters rested with secular rulers, while authority in spiritual matters rested with the pope.[109] Four centuries later, Pufendorf's Protestant version of natural law presumed the principle *cuius regio eius religio:* each nation would have a unified Christian religion, chosen and supported by the secular ruler.[110]

As Seamus Hasson amply and engagingly documented, starting with the *Mayflower*, the first thing every religious minority has done after fleeing to America to escape religious persecution is turn around and persecute members of other religions once in power.[111] In reaction to these earlier models, the American Founders devised a system that treated religious observance as a fundamental human right: any state might establish its own religion, but national religious establishment was prohibited.

American Founders' development of the theories of property, faction, and public goods. We noted that Aristotle's theory of production included both people and property; that according to his theory of distributive justice, any community's use of common goods must be shared according to a geometric ratio; but that in political distribution there is systematic disagreement about the precise ratio depending on each class of citizens' interest. The American Founders developed each of these by broadening the understanding of property, tying it to equal protection of all forms of property, and specifying that true public goods should be defrayed by taxes levied equally on income from all forms of property.

The Founders' theory of government is crystallized in James Madison's *Federalist* No. 10: "From the protection of the different and unequal faculties of acquiring property possession of different degrees and kinds of property immediately results; and from the influence of these on the sentiments and views of the respective proprietors, ensues a division of the society into different interests and parties. The latent causes of faction are thus sown in the nature of man."[112] In this very Augustinian view, factional injustice is inevitable, caused by the twin scourges of ignorance and sin: inordinate self-love.[113] Hence, "different interests necessarily exist in different classes of citizens."[114]

Perhaps because this statement was so compressed, Madison elaborated on it in a 1792 summary, "Property," in which he distinguished "property strictly so called" from "property in the general sense of the word." In the narrower sense, "property means 'that dominion which one man claims and exercises over the external things of the world, in exclusion of every other individual.' [But i]n its larger and juster meaning, it embraces every thing to which a man may attach a value and have a right; *and which leaves to every one else the like advantage.*" Property "strictly so called" therefore includes "a man's land, or merchandize, or money," but property "in the general sense" comprises "his opinions, his person, his faculties, or his possessions"—including "a property of peculiar value in his religious opinions, and in the profession and practice dictated by them. . . . In a word, as a man is said to have a right to his property, he may be equally said to have a property in his rights."[115]

The narrower meaning approximates the classical Roman Stoic notion of absolute *dominium* or *proprietas*, ignores justice, and can be (in fact, was) used to justify slavery.[116] Property "in the general sense" is analytically more comprehensive, but also universally binding prior to any economic transaction (gift or exchange).

Meanwhile, Hamilton distinguished true public goods, which benefit all citizens equally, from quasi-public goods, which benefit many but not all citizens.[117] Combining Madison's theory of faction with Hamilton's distinction between public goods and quasi-public goods, the corresponding theory of American political distributive justice implies that true public goods should be financed by equiproportional taxation of income from all sources of property, but quasi-public goods by taxation on the class of citizens that benefits.

The two definitions of property therefore not only differ, but lead to two different theories of government—as became clear in the decade before the U.S. Civil War.[118] Yet as Lincoln showed so effectively, attempts to enact the narrower definition of property fall apart as soon as it is applied impartially to those who would enforce it on others.[119]

How Later Economists Treated the First Things of Economics

The Scholastic outline of economic theory was both versatile and durable. I have sketched only a few of the main theoretical and practical applications Scholastic economists derived from it. Tracing the later development of each of the four elements—for example, the theory of production or the theory of equilibrium—can be fascinating. So can tracing their combined applications; for example, in the theories of money, interest, international trade, economic development, the household, the business firm, or industry. But in doing so, even in severely truncated form, it is easy for both economists and noneconomists to lose the forest for the trees. That is, the overall *structure* of economic theory, as used by economists, tends to be overlooked.

From the perspective of its structure, the entire history of economic theory thus far may be naturally divided into just three periods: the Scholastic (1250–1776), the Classical (1776–1871), and the Neoclassical (1871–c. 2000). To gauge the net result of the development of economic theory so far, let's make a standing broad jump across more than 750 years of development to the present. What do we find? We find that nearly all modern economists are still using Thomas Aquinas's "Swiss Army knife"—but most seem to be under the impression that it contains only three (in a few cases, only two) tools instead of four. Most modern economists are trained to use mathematical forms of the second, third, and fourth basic elements—utility, production, and equilibrium—but not the first, which I have called final distribution.

This is odd, since Aristotle, Augustine, and Aquinas all provided its mathematical formula. How did this "hole" in theory come about? Well, Adam Smith tried to discard two of the basic elements (final distribution and utility), and he was followed in this effort by most classical economists. This meant that classical economics was logically incomplete, falling two equations short of the number of unknown variables. The classical economists' neoclassical successors have so far restored only one of the omitted elements (utility). But there remains an analytical hole, that left by the omission of final distribution. Most of the difficulties of modern economists can be traced to this very fact.

Table 2–1

The Scholastic 'Map' of the Human Person (and Knowledge) Aristotle vs. Aquinas[120]		
Kind of virtue	*Aristotle* Disciplines determined by human virtue and scope (object studied)	*Thomas Aquinas* Disciplines delimited by virtue, scope and method
Theological	n.a.	Faith, Hope, & Charity: Revealed Theology
Intellectual ('speculative')	Wisdom: Metaphysics (study of being: includes natural theology)	*Same*
Rational	Logic ('analytics'): order of reason	*Same*
Science (= Knowledge of a particular kind of being)	Mathematics: order of being abstracted from matter and motion Physics (science of 'natures'): being abstracted from matter Biology: being abstracted from animate matter	*Same* 'Mixed' (physico-mathematical) sciences *Same* *Same*
Practical: Moral: Active, toward others Active, toward oneself Productive	Moral philosophy (Aristotle's virtues not fully systematic) Politics Ethics Memo: Justice: Distributive Commutative/corrective Liberality Various (not fully systematic) Various (not fully systematic) Mechanical and Fine Arts	*Same* Prudence (= Economy): Political Domestic Individual Justice: Political distributive Domestic distributive Individual: beneficence, commutative justice Fortitude (*re:* aversions) Temperance (*re:* attractions) *Same*

3

Classical Economics (1776–1871)

Adam Smith was not the "founder" of economics. We get off on the wrong foot if we ask, "What did Adam Smith add to economic theory?" Joseph Schumpeter was quite correct to conclude that "the *Wealth of Nations* does not contain a single *analytic* idea, principle or method that was entirely new in 1776."[1]

If Smith added nothing to economic theory, how could he have become so influential? To put it another way, "What did Adam Smith *subtract* from economic theory—and why was this subtraction popular?" Smith tried to subtract two of the four basic elements of the outline of economic theory he inherited—final distribution and utility. His new outline's greater simplicity was what attracted the classical economists who adopted it. His narrowing of the range of economic theory allowed the classical economists to concentrate on developing the implications of the two elements he retained—production and equilibrium. But as we will see in the next chapter, later neoclassical economists found it necessary to abandon Smith's revised outline, mostly because the economists who used it were unable to answer some important questions. This is because they were led to make empirical predictions that turned out to be spectacularly wrong and because Smith's inadequate substitutes for the subtraction directly fostered Karl Marx's disastrously erroneous economic analysis.

Smith *deliberately* revised the basic Scholastic outline of economic theory. He became familiar with it through the works of Hugo Grotius and Samuel Pufendorf, which Smith had been taught by his teacher,

Francis Hutcheson (1694–1746), a predecessor in Smith's Glasgow chair from 1730 to 1746.[2] Hutcheson had followed the tradition of his own predecessor, Gerschom Carmichael, by teaching from an annotated edition of Pufendorf's compendium of the natural law, *On the Duty of Man and Citizen According to Natural Law* (which we noted in the previous chapter on Scholastic economics).[3] The facts that Pufendorf was a German Lutheran (who wrote a critical history of the Catholic Church) and that his theories were taught to Adam Smith at the generally Calvinist University of Glasgow indicate that the Scholastic outline of economic theory was broadly known and generally accepted by both Protestants and Catholics well into the second half of the eighteenth century. Moreover, Pufendorf placed heavy emphasis on a phrase with which Smith was to identify himself: natural liberty. However, Hutcheson also theorized about a supposed "moral sense" and emphasized the contribution of the Stoics to moral philosophy: a combination which Smith would pursue in a new direction.

The Main Problem to Be Solved

Broadly speaking, the central analytical problem for Adam Smith, and even more for his followers, was to explain general and sustained real economic growth, which began to become a reality for the first time in human history at the end of the Middle Ages. This breakthrough required a reexamination of the theory of production. The theory of utility explains which goods people prefer to consume; final distribution determines who will consume them; and equilibrium or justice in exchange equalizes the value of products with the compensation of their producers. But production determines how many and which goods are actually available to exchange, distribute, and consume.

Aristotle's theory of production involves two basic kinds of factors—people and productive property. It was as obvious to the Scholastics as it is to us that an individual person, business, or local community might have different quantities of these factors. Otherwise, no merchant could become rich, and no town or region could ever prosper. But like Aristotle, the Scholastics routinely assumed that the *total* quantities of these two factors were approximately constant—and this had in fact been a pretty good empirical description for most of human history. After the prosperity of the twelfth and thirteenth centuries—the great age of urbanization and cathedral-building—the plagues of the fourteenth century wiped out about one-third of Europe's population, drastically lowered life expectancy, and made the earlier prosperity rather than the later catastrophes seem like the aberration.

But average life expectancy recovered in the fifteenth century and began steadily to increase; this was accompanied by renewed investment in both human and nonhuman capital. By the mid-eighteenth century, life expectancy in England was about thirty-five years—not much higher than in the sixteenth but still considerably above the twenty-four-year average that seems to have prevailed for millennia before the end of the Middle Ages. By the early nineteenth century, it had risen to about forty-one years. Smith and the classical economists were chiefly concerned with the most obvious result: sustained population growth, which accelerated to an unprecedented average of 0.76 percent a year between 1700 and 1820 in what is now the United Kingdom—a rate doubling the size of the population every century.[4] Per capita real income also seems to have increased in the same period, but at a far less noticeable 0.26 percent average annual rate. Thus the total real or price-adjusted size of the economy, once assumed to be static, was doubling about every seventy years—and much faster in some regions, like Adam Smith's native Scotland.

There are three keys to understanding Smith, both as a philosopher and as an economist: his moral Newtonianism, his philosophical Stoicism, and his curious Sophistic view of rhetoric.

Smith wanted to do for moral philosophy what he believed Isaac Newton had done for natural science: to reduce all its phenomena to a single familiar principle, like gravity. He was always aiming, as he put it in a Glasgow university lecture, "to see the phenomena which we reckoned the most unaccountable all deduced from some principle (commonly a well-known one) and all united in one chain."[5] The idea of a system with *four* basic elements rather than one was repugnant to him.

Moreover, Smith, having rejected his Christian baptism well before writing the *Wealth of Nations*, was a wholehearted convert to Stoic philosophy—and Stoics are pantheists.[6] Though it may anticipate our later discussion of divine economy, let us note here the two ways in which the providence of Stoic pantheism differs from that of the biblically orthodox natural law of Augustine and Aquinas, but also from the rationalistic deism with which Smith is sometimes incorrectly identified (as exemplified by Thomas Paine, who was equally anti-Christian).[7] First, the Stoic god is not the creator but rather the world-soul of an eternal and uncreated universe.[8] Second, it necessarily follows that humans are not creatures endowed with reason and free will, but rather appendages of God fated to do everything they do, good or bad. What we humans consider our reason, Smith argues, is ultimately only rationalization of actions we do not in fact understand.[9] The one partial exception is the Stoic sage, who alone understands and submits to the fact that he and everyone else are fated to do what they do.[10] The main problem with this theory is not so much *theo*-logical as merely logical: In Smith's Stoic philosophy, the "vices and follies" as well as the "wisdom or virtue" of mankind are supposed to be equally intended and affected by the Stoic world-soul, and to tend equally to produce order in human society.[11] According to Augustine's more logically consistent theory of providence, the order we observe in markets and society results entirely from the virtue (itself a kind of rational order) that remains even in bad people as long as they exist.

Finally, Smith was much more proficient (and interested) in rhetoric than in logical, systematic analysis. When first hired by the University of Glasgow as professor of logic (shortly before being named professor of moral philosophy), he immediately shifted the course toward rhetoric instead of the prescribed logic and metaphysics.[12] Moreover, as his lectures and unpublished papers make clear, Smith disagreed fundamentally with Aristotle about the nature of rhetoric.

According to Aristotle, the purpose of rhetoric "is not to persuade, but to discover the available means of persuasion in a given case." Why? "In Rhetoric, as in Dialectic, we should be able to argue on either side of a question; not with a view to putting both sides into practice—we must not advocate evil—but in order that no aspect of the case may escape us, and that if our opponents make unfair use of the arguments, we may be able to refute them."[13]

Smith's view of rhetoric, in contrast, resembled that of the Sophists who opposed Aristotle by placing a higher value on whether a statement is useful to the speaker than whether it is an accurate description of reality. "The Rhetoricall [discourse] again endeavours by all means to perswade us; and for this purpose magnifies all the arguments on one side and diminishes or conceals those that might be brought on the side contrary to that which it is designed that we should favour," Smith taught his students.[14] And this, as we will see, is exactly how Smith presents his economic theory.

Smith's moral Newtonianism induced him to oversimplify the economic theory he had inherited. Just as in his earlier *Theory of Moral Sentiments* he had tried to reduce all morality to the single principle of sympathy, Smith attempted in the *Wealth of Nations* to explain all economic behavior by the single principle of labor. Yet he failed to integrate these two.

Smith's philosophical Stoicism accounts for his rejections of some elements of the Scholastic outline of economics and his retention of others.[15] In the *Theory of Moral Sentiments*, Smith rejected the Scholastic theories of final distribution and utility on the grounds that they presume rational, purposive behavior.[16] In Smith's view—and here the pantheism becomes apparent—decisions about ends and means, rather than being decided *by* human beings, are ultimately *dictated to* them by an inscrutable Stoic version of providence, which engages the vast majority of humankind in a "deception" about the "real satisfaction" afforded by economic goods.[17] By systematically manipulating human emotion, the Stoic Author of Nature supposedly "rouses and keeps in continual motion the industry of mankind," luring most people (except the Stoic sage) into vice. The rich are seduced by greed into "selfishness and rapacity," while the "mob of mankind" is corrupted by envy of the rich. Yet all is for the best. To satisfy their "vain and insatiable desires," the rich few must employ the envious mob, and so "they are led by an invisible hand to make nearly the same distribution of the necessaries of life, which would have been made, had the earth been divided into equal portions among its inhabitants"—a strong and empirically questionable claim.[18] In the more famous "invisible hand" passage in the *Wealth of Nations*, Smith claims that this process also necessarily maximizes the value of a nation's total product and income. Each individual "intends only his own gain, and he is in this, as in many other cases, led by an invisible hand to promote an end which was no part of his intention."[19]

Smith's famous "invisible hand," therefore, is not a *summary* of his economic analysis; it is a rhetorical plug that he merely inserts where the two elements of economic analysis that he eliminated are logically required: the Scholastic theories of utility and (particularly) final distribution. But "invisible hand" is a thoroughly apt metaphor: Smith's Stoic version of providence reduces humans to marionette puppets compelled to act by a hidden force manipulating the heartstrings of their moral sentiments.

Smith's Revision of the Scholastic Outline

To understand more fully Smith's revision of the outline of the Scholastic economic theory he inherited, it is helpful to recognize that there were two phases in the development of his ideas. The first is reflected in his lectures at the University of Glasgow between 1751 and 1764, part of which culminated in *The Theory of Moral Sentiments* (first published in 1759). The second is reflected in the *Wealth of Nations*, first published in 1776.[20]

Economists have been both surprised and puzzled since discovering in 1896 that the outline of economic theory Smith taught at the University of Glasgow resembles what later came to be called "neoclassical" economics. That is, its outline contains three of the four basic elements of economic theory—utility, production, and equilibrium—while omitting final distribution. The version in the later *Wealth of Nations* contains only two distinct elements—production and equilibrium.

Recall Joseph Schumpeter's conjecture that Adam Smith's formulation of economic theory in the *Wealth of Nations* retarded the development of a workable theory of value by some eighty years.[21] This may be true, but it would be even more precise to say that most of the eighty-year detour could have been avoided if Smith had simply written the *Wealth of Nations* based on the economic outline presented in his own university lectures—despite its own deficiencies.

However, the lectures also suggest why Smith didn't proceed along these lines. Smith's ingenuity in the *Theory of Moral Sentiments*, first published in 1759, had created major inconsistencies between the ethical theory presented in that book and the economic theory that he still taught at the university in 1762–64.

Recall that the Scholastic theory of final distribution describes how we rationally choose persons as ends or purposes of our action, while the Scholastic theory of utility describes how we choose other goods to serve those persons as means. Smith apparently thought that he could dispense with both rational theories by pointing to some "sentiment or affection of the heart from which any action proceeds."[22] But Smith's Stoicism explains his main disagreement about human nature not only with the Scholastics but also with the Epicurean philosophy of his friend David Hume. Smith's teacher Hutcheson had argued that moral philosophy is based on a direct "moral sense" rather than practical reason, and he reinterpreted benevolence as the fundamental moral sentiment rather than an act of rational will.[23] Hume and Smith agreed with Hutcheson in starting from Hume's premise that "All morality depends upon our sentiments."[24] However, according to Hume, we still reason about means toward ends that are predetermined by sentiment or instinct: "Reason is, and ought only to be the slave of the passions, and can never pretend to any other office than to serve and obey them."[25] In his own search for a single, ultimate, Newtonian moral principle, Smith proposed in the *Theory of Moral Sentiments* to deprive utility of even the purely instrumental role it played in Hume's ethical theory. In Smith's Stoic view, man is able to reach both ends and means directly by sentiment, because Nature herself is reasonable.[26]

Yet the lectures show Smith still teaching an economic theory of value squarely based on the Scholastic theory of utility—the rational choice of means—in his final year at Glasgow, four years after the first edition of the *Theory of Moral Sentiments*. His difficulty in resolving this inconsistency helps explain why it took him another twelve years to publish the *Wealth of Nations*.

Though most of its outline is contained in the university lectures, Smith made some important changes to his economic theory in the *Wealth of Nations*—for better and worse.[27] The most important change for the better is that he tries to make his theory of production more general by following the French physiocrats in accounting for three factors of production—labor, capital, and land—and three corresponding kinds of compensation—wages, profits, and rent—instead of only the wages of labor. The most important change for the worse is that he neutralizes this apparent advance by trying to replace the theory of utility with a theory that the value of all goods is derived from the labor required to produce them (instead of the reverse, as he had previously taught, following the Scholastics). As we will see, this so-called labor theory of value boils down to the (false) assertion that there is always really only one factor of production: labor.

Since Smith typically treats final distribution and utility by omission, it is easy to overlook their significance when we come upon the passages in the *Wealth of Nations* in which their omission is signaled. Let's consider carefully Smith's treatment of both:

Final distribution. Augustine's theory of personal distribution seeks to answer the following question: Once I have acquired wealth through production and/or exchange, to whom do I devote its use? Myself only, or do I share it with others, and in what proportion? Aristotle's theory of distributive justice posed the corresponding question for any social or political community: When I share the ownership of any kind of wealth with others, by what principle do we allocate its consumption or use?

Smith's elimination of Augustine's theory of personal distribution from the outline of economic theory is signaled in the passage that includes his famous declaration: "It is not from the benevolence of the butcher, the brewer, or the baker, that we expect our dinner, but from their regard to their own interest. We address ourselves not to their humanity but to their self-love, and never talk to them of our necessities but of their advantages."[28] In the lectures he had made a more succinct version of the same claim: "The brewer and the baker serve us not from benevolence, but from self-love."[29]

In Augustine's theory, the tradesmen serve their customers *precisely* from benevolence (a point we will consider more closely in chapter 6 on personal economy). The main reason the brewer, the butcher, or baker doesn't serve his customers from *beneficence* is not exclusive self-love, but rather because each is faced with the fact of scarcity. If the baker shared his bread equally with every customer instead of charging for it, he would leave himself and his family too little to live on. Augustine's theory also explains why the brewer or baker shares with his family or friends but not with his business customers: He loves his customers with benevolence (wishing good to them) but his family with both benevolence and beneficence (doing good to them). He sells his product to customers to earn the means to provide for himself and the rest of his family. Augustine's theory of personal distribution explains the essential difference between a gift and an exchange, and it provides an objective measure of how far each of us actually is motivated by self-love and how much by love of neighbor.

Adam Smith discusses both benevolence and beneficence in *The Theory of Moral Sentiments*. But in contrast to Augustine, he fails to distinguish them consistently and is concerned to show that benevolence is only a motivating feeling, not an act of the rational will. Without benevolence or beneficence, Smith argues, society "though less happy and agreeable, will not be dissolved," because "it may still be upheld by a mercenary exchange of good offices according to an agreed valuation."[30] (The sentiment motivating commutative justice, Smith argues, is resentment at injustice.)

By treating self-love as the only essential motive of economic behavior, Smith replaced Augustine's empirically verifiable theory of personal distribution with an arbitrary and often false assumption: that no one ever shares his wealth with anyone else.[31]

In his introduction to the *Wealth of Nations*, Smith himself raised the fact that this assumption is false, noting, "Among the savage nations of hunters and fishers, every individual who is able to work, is more or less employed in useful labour, and endeavours to provide, as well as he can, the necessaries and conveniencies of life, for himself, and such of his family or tribe as are either too old or too young, or too infirm to go a hunting and fishing."[32] His reason for mentioning this behavior was to emphasize the difference between the modern (eighteenth-century) standard of living and the one in a society without a division of labor, in which, he claims, the people are so miserably poor that they are reduced to "abandoning their infants, their old people, and those afflicted with lingering diseases, to perish with hunger, or to be devoured by wild beasts." Smith dwells so heavily on this supposed necessity that he never accounts for the behavior he has just described: that the primitive hunter supports "such of his family or tribe as are either too old or too young, or too infirm to go a hunting and fishing." Smith fails to grapple with the fact that charitable behavior simply does not fit into a theory that reduces all human transactions to self-love. The point of the passage is to introduce the routine assumption that every individual consumes only (and all) the income he or she receives. But Smith never explains why customers *never* expect their dinner from the butcher's beneficence, while the butcher's friends occasionally and his children *always* expect it.[33]

Smith's understanding of distributive justice was related to, and just as radically confused as, that regarding beneficence. He became the first major economic thinker to try to eliminate distributive justice from consideration, by restricting the meaning of justice to commutative justice, or justice in exchange alone; "and he holds this position throughout his career," Smith's biographer Ian Ross notes.[34] As a surviving Glasgow lecture fragment indicates, Smith erroneously taught that "in the Schools" distributive justice meant "doing good according to the most perfect propriety" but that commutative justice (which he correctly defined) "can alone properly be called justice." He apparently realized this significant error only when his manuscript of *The Theory of Moral Sentiments* based on his lectures was close to publication (a predicament with which any author can sympathize). Smith's solution was to retain the incorrect definition of distributive justice as "proper beneficence" in the text (through all six editions) but add a footnote noting that the Scholastic definition of distributive justice derived from Aristotle's was "somewhat different."

Thomas Hobbes had tried to redefine political distributive justice, without changing its substance, by claiming that public property is not actually owned in common by those who are parties to the supposed social contract that brings government into existence but is turned over to an absolute dictator, who is not a party to the social contract.[35] Smith similarly refers to the magistrate or sovereign as something different from the political community. He expresses this notion in the *Wealth of Nations* by defining "political economy" as "a branch of the science of the statesman or legislator" that "proposes to enrich both the people and the sovereign."[36]

Yet, like Hobbes's political theory, Smith's discussion of government economic policy presupposes the reality of distributive justice. He had argued against the British government devoting part of the revenues raised by taxation to a subsidy for particular products on the grounds that it would reduce national wealth. But how could one prove (or disprove) this argument? Only by using Aristotle's theory of distributive justice: that is, by first defining the formula by which the subsidy was granted and paid for, and then relating the subsidy and taxes measured by that formula to some aggregate measure of national income or wealth. Moreover, Smith proposed some sensible rules for financing various kinds of public works—employing the very theory of distributive justice that he had ostensibly abolished.

Thus did Smith eliminate the Scholastic theory of distribution—the element of economic theory necessary for explaining personal gifts as well as domestic and political distribution—before starting the *Wealth of Nations*.

Utility. Aristotle pointed out that what makes different goods similar enough to compare and exchange is their usefulness in satisfying human needs; Augustine described the way in which we compare and choose among them; and Thomas Aquinas integrated these ideas into the Scholastic theory of utility. Shortly after dismissing the Scholastic theory of final distribution with his assertion about universal self-love, Smith dismisses the Scholastic theory of utility by posing what is sometimes called the "paradox of value":

> The word VALUE it is to be observed, has two different meanings, and sometimes expresses the utility of some particular object, and sometimes the power of purchasing goods which the possession of the object conveys. The one may be called "value in use"; the other, "value in exchange." The things which have the greatest value in use have frequently little or no value in exchange; and on the contrary, those which have the greatest value in exchange have frequently little or no value in use. Nothing is more useful than water: but it will purchase scarce any thing; scarce any thing can be had in exchange for it. A diamond, on the contrary, has scarce any value in use; but a very great quantity of other goods may frequently be had in exchange for it.[37]

Without offering a solution to this apparent paradox, Smith rhetorically throws up his hands and abandons discussion of value in use, as if the concept were absurd. This is a clear case in which Smith "endeavours by all means to perswade us; and for this purpose magnifies all the arguments on one side and diminishes or conceals those that might be brought on the side contrary to that which it is designed that we should favour."

In his own university lectures, Smith had posed the same paradox involving diamonds and easily resolved it by proceeding along Scholastic lines. After distinguishing the market price of a commodity or service from its cost of production (which he referred to as the "natural price"),[38] he continued,

> The market price of goods is regulated by quite other circumstances. When a buyer comes into the market, he never asks the seller what expenses he has been at in producing them. The

regulation of the market price of goods depends on the following circumstances:

First, the demand or need for the commodity. There is no
demand for a thing of little use; it is not a rational object of
desire.

Secondly, the abundance or scarcity of the commodity in
proportion to the need of it. If the commodity be scarce, the
price is raised, but if the commodity be more than is sufficient
to supply the demand, the price falls. Thus it is that diamonds
and other precious stones are dear, while iron, which is much
more useful is so many times cheaper, though this depends on
the last cause, viz:

Thirdly, the riches or poverty of those who demand. When
there is not enough to serve everybody, the fortune of the bid-
der is the only regulation of the price.[39]

In other words, Smith had explained the higher price per unit of
diamonds than of water or iron by differences in their utility and (particularly) scarcity. To emphasize the latter he had added, "If for every ten
diamonds there were ten thousand, they would become the purchase of
everybody, because they would become very cheap."[40]

As we will see more clearly in the next chapter, the main difference
between this explanation and the modern economic theory of utility was
the failure to distinguish the *total* value of a certain kind of good—such
as water or diamonds—from its *marginal* utility, the difference in total
value made by adding or subtracting one unit. It is the nature of scarce
goods to have declining marginal utility beyond a certain point: that
is, the value of each additional unit consumed declines as the quantity
increases. When the quantity is large to begin with, adding or subtracting one unit usually makes a small difference in value, but when the
quantity is relatively small to begin with, the change in value from adding or subtracting one unit can be relatively large. Thus, what seemed to
the Scholastics (and the early Smith) to be two principles—utility and
scarcity—can be expressed as a single principle, marginal utility, which
explains both value in use and value in exchange. Even in the *Wealth of
Nations*, Smith inconsistently reverted to the Scholastic theory of utility
to explain the value of precious metals.[41]

Economists eager to interpret Smith as a forerunner of the modern theory of value have variously expressed puzzlement and annoyance at discovering that he had learned and taught the theory of utility before abandoning it. Edwin Cannan, who edited and published the transcript of Smith's university lectures, remarked, "It is not easy to explain why the first two sections were omitted from the *Wealth of Nations*, and the fact will be regretted by those who ask for a theory of consumption as a preliminary to the other parts of political economy." George Stigler similarly described "Smith's rejection of consumption in fixing on a measure of value" as "one of his greatest idiosyncrasies."[42] But as we have seen, this idiosyncrasy is the logical result of Smith's combination of moral Newtonianism, Stoic philosophy, and rhetorical sophistry.

Production. Smith believed that the Scholastic theory of utility could be dispensed with by adopting what is loosely, but somewhat inaccurately, known as the "labor theory of value." More accurately, what Smith did was to substitute a "one-factor" theory of production for the Scholastic version, which always contained at least two factors. This departure would have far-reaching consequences.

After dismissing the theory of utility with the "paradox of value," Smith quickly (but erroneously) asserts that what makes different goods comparable in exchange is not their utility but that all require human labor to produce. "Labour, therefore, is the real measure of the exchangeable value of all commodities";[43] "Labour was the first price, the original purchase money that was paid for all things";[44] and "Labour alone therefore, never varying in its own value, is alone the ultimate and real standard by which the value of all commodities can at all times and places be estimated and compared."[45]

Smith's economic theory in the university lectures was peculiar in containing only one factor of production, labor, and explaining only one kind of income, wages.[46] The *Wealth of Nations* apparently made an important advance by attempting to account for three factors of production—labor, capital, and land. But Smith vitiated this advance by insisting at the same time that the apparent productivity of the other factors is really due to labor alone.[47]

The gist of Smith's "labor theory of value" is set forth as follows:

> In that early and rude state of society which precedes both the accumulation of stock and the appropriation of land, the proportion between the quantities of labour necessary for acquiring different objects seems to be the only circumstance which can afford any rule for exchanging them for one another. If among a nation of hunters, for example, it usually costs twice the labour to kill a beaver which it does to kill a deer, one beaver should naturally exchange for or be worth two deer. It is natural that what is usually the produce of two days' or two hours' labour should be worth double of what is usually the produce of one day's or one hour's labour.[48]

Smith concedes that the value of an hour's work may be different for different workers, but he attributes the difference to the additional time and trouble it must have cost the worker whose labor is more valuable to learn his skills.

As we see here, Smith's economic theory was hampered by his emphatic but inaccurate and inconsistent views about the historical stages that, in his opinion, societies had gone through and must go through in exact sequence: first, hunting and gathering; second, pasturage of livestock; third, agriculture; and finally, manufacture and commerce.

According to Smith in both his university lectures and in the *Wealth of Nations*, the *only* factor of production in the hunter–gatherer stage is labor: "An Indian has not so much as a pick-axe, a spade, or a shovel, nor anything else but his own labour."[49] We might call Smith's labor theory of value more accurately the "bare hands theory of production." If we take him literally, Smith is saying that human existence was once such that natural resources contributed nothing to human production in addition to human labor. According to Smith's argument, there once existed a domestic household that used *no* nonhuman resources, not even the most rudimentary tools. Yet such tools are often the only characteristic by which archaeologists today are able to identify early human remains as precisely human.

Moreover, Smith immediately contradicts his own claim by introducing a nonhuman factor of production—a hunter's bow and arrows.[50] But in doing so, Smith fails to adjust his theory of production to recognize that there are now always at least *two* factors of production, each contributing a different service to the hunter's final product: his labor and natural resources to make his bow and arrows or knife, his labor and the bow and arrows to kill the deer, his labor and a knife to skin it, and so on.

Instead, in Smith's fanciful view, humans began to use tools for the first time only in the "advanced state" of economic development. He assumes that these tools are supposed to be producible by labor alone. Moreover, he assumes that labor and capital belonged from the beginning to different, independent persons, rather than being owned by the same person or household. (His definition of capital is also confusing: It excludes a house if occupied by its owner, but includes it if rented to tenants; includes improvements to land but not the land itself; includes "the acquired and useful abilities of all the inhabitants and members of the society," but not their bodies.[51]

Land becomes a third factor of production, in Smith's view, not when it contributes to production—as we saw it did even in the "early and rude state of society"—but only as the result of its appropriation, a mere change in ownership. In explaining this, Smith reveals the source of his confusion. Because land is owned in common in the "early and rude state," he assumes that both land and its natural fruits are costless.[52] Yet the material from which the hunter made his bow and arrows is *not* common property. He appropriated it for himself, and if it weren't his own, he could not exchange it for other goods, charging it as the cost of the goods he receives in exchange.

The "labor theory of value" is superficially plausible only if there really is only one factor of production. Only on that assumption do the possible combinations of products that can be produced with a given amount of labor trace a straight line, indicating a constant price. If we accept the assumption that game can be killed, prepared, and brought to market without any weapons or tools, and if it takes four hours to trap a beaver and two hours to kill a deer, it is possible to "produce" many different combinations by hunting sixteen hours a week: four beavers and no deer, or two beavers and four deer, or no beavers and eight deer (or any other combination that lies on the same straight line). This simple linear relationship was the main attraction of Smith's "labor theory."

But the linear relationship results from the assumption that there is only one factor of production. It has nothing to do with that factor being labor. Practically speaking, this means that each hunter must chase down the beaver or deer, strangle it with his bare hands, skin it with his teeth, and tan it by chewing the hide. Add another "factor" of production, such as any kind of tool (a bow and arrows, a knife), and the combinations of various quantities of goods that can be produced with available resources no longer trace a straight line, but a curve, indicating a continually varying cost.

For example, by sharing a single knife, two equally talented hunters can bag more game per hour or day than either hunter alone using the same weapon—but not twice as much.[53] (That might be possible if each had his own knife.) This means that with more than one factor of production, the cost of producing any commodity, which Smith claimed is always naturally constant, actually varies with the combination of factors employed to produce it. This fact remains true for every kind of human production, from the most primitive to the most advanced—squarely contradicting the main premise of the "labor theory of value."

Equilibrium. Both the initial triumph and ultimate demise of classical economics resulted mostly from the new interpretation that Smith's revision of the outline of economics gave to the Scholastic theory of equilibrium or "justice in exchange."

The price of any product, Smith correctly noted, is equal to the total incomes of its producers. But his revised theory could no longer explain why this is so. Under the peculiar assumptions of his "labor theory of value," no producer's contribution to the value of the finished product equals the income actually received by that producer. Smith's assumptions turned Aristotle's and the Scholastics' "justice in exchange" into universal "injustice in exchange."

In his university lectures, because he still retained the theory of utility, Smith correctly based the incomes of producers (and thus the cost of production) on the market value of their products, not vice versa. ("When a buyer comes into the market, he never asks the seller what expenses he has been at in producing them.") After distinguishing a good's cost of production (which he called the natural price) from its market price, Smith noted that the two are equated by exchange under conditions of equilibrium:

> However seemingly independent they appear to be, they are necessarily connected. This will appear from the following

considerations. If the market price of any commodity is very great, and the labour very highly rewarded, the market is prodigiously crowded with it, greater quantities of it are produced, and it can be sold to the inferior ranks of people. If for every ten diamonds there were ten thousand, they would become the purchase of everybody, because they would become very cheap, and would sink to their natural price. Again, when the market is overstocked, and there is not enough got for the labour of the manufacture, nobody will bind to it, they cannot have a subsistence by it, because the market price falls then below the natural price.[54]

This also explains how producers decide which and how many goods to produce, and how much. To take Smith's example, if there is only one factor (labor) and it takes all hunters twice as long to trap a beaver as to bag a deer, in a barter economy the so-called natural price of one beaver will be two deer. (With a properly functioning monetary system, the monetary cost of producing a beaver will be about twice the monetary cost of a deer as well.) If the market price of a beaver should rise to three deer (or its equivalent in money), while the labor cost of producing each animal stayed the same, it would pay deer hunters to switch to trapping beavers, since they could then receive more in exchange for the same amount of work. A reduced supply of deer, on the one hand, and an increased supply of beavers, on the other, would eventually restore both goods to their natural price of two deer for one beaver. The converse would be true if the market price should fall below its natural price.

Smith's explanation of equilibrium is close to the one taught by Johannes Mair at the same university two centuries earlier (when it was not the most advanced version available).[55] The Scholastic theory of equilibrium, therefore, was not fatally compromised by Smith's unrealistic one-factor theory of production as long as he retained the theory of utility.

However, by abandoning the theory of utility in the *Wealth of Nations*, Smith turned market prices, in effect, into unexplained random departures from the cost of production; reversed the relationship between prices and incomes; and, most seriously, turned every exchange from an approximate equality into a lopsided inequality.

Instead of arguing that the producers' incomes are derived from the value of their products, as he did in his university lectures, Smith says in the *Wealth of Nations* that the market prices of goods are derived from their cost of production—that is, from their producers' incomes.

Injustice in exchange. The ambiguity introduced into Smith's thinking by the labor–quantity theory is reflected in his constant use of the phrase *resolves itself* in describing the relationship between a product's price and the income of its producers. We can see how Smith turns equilibrium or "justice in exchange" from a tendency toward equality into one of inequality by considering Smith's comparison of each producer's contribution to production with that producer's compensation.

According to the *Wealth of Nations*, in the "early and rude state" of society, "the whole produce of labour belongs to the labourer." This is actually true in the strict sense, but false in the way Smith means it. The whole product of the primitive *hunter* belongs to the *hunter*, and the whole product of the hunter *as laborer* belongs to him *as laborer*—but Smith is wrong in claiming that the hunter's labor accounts for his whole product. The rest is due to the hunter *as proprietor*—that is, as owner of his bow and arrows, the useful service of which is the hunter's ability to bag additional game. Without exchange, this service is compensated by the additional game. The value of the same property service to other hunters is also the basis for the bow's and arrows' value in exchanging property with them.

Smith makes the same mistake in explaining the contribution and compensation of the "capitalist": "As soon as stock [that is, tools or reproducible nonhuman capital] has accumulated in the hands of particular persons, some of them will naturally employ it in setting to work industrious people, whom they will supply with materials and subsistence, in order to make a profit by the sale of their work, or by what their labour adds to the value of the materials."[56] Moreover, "the value which the workmen add to the materials, therefore, resolves itself in this case into two parts, of which the one pays their wages, the other the profits of their employer upon the whole stock of materials and wages which he advanced."[57]

As the price or exchangeable value of every particular commodity, taken separately, resolves itself into some one or other or all of those three parts, so that of all the commodities which compose the whole annual produce of the labour of every country, taken complexly, must resolve itself into the same three parts, and be parceled out among different inhabitants of the country, either as the wages of their labour, the profits of their stock, or the rent of their land. The whole of what is annually either collected or produced by the labour of every society, or what comes to the same thing, the whole price of it, is in this manner originally distributed among some of its different members. Wages, profit, and rent, are the three original sources of all revenue as well as of all exchangeable value. All other revenue is ultimately derived from one or other of these.[58]

This is factually false, for the same reason as in the hunter's case. The sale of the product results in both labor and property compensation. "The whole value which the workmen add to the materials" belongs in justice to the workers, and in a competitive market its sale actually provides the workers' labor compensation. The proprietor's share of total compensation results from the value that the productive property adds to the product, exactly like the hunter's bow and arrows. (Strictly speaking, this property compensation is not "profit." Profit is what's left of the proceeds of the product's selling price after paying both the workers and property owners for their productive services; it compensates the entrepreneur for organizing the whole enterprise.) After denying that people ever used tools in primitive society, Smith claims that in its advanced state, the tools "use" the people: "capital" employs "labor.")

Smith uses similarly flawed reasoning to explain the compensation of landowners. "As soon as the land of any society has all become private property, the landlords, like all other men, love to reap where they never sowed, and demand a rent even for its natural produce." In this case, according to Smith, the laborer "must then pay for the licence to gather [the natural fruits of the earth]; and he must give up to the landlord a portion of what his labour either collects or produces. This portion, or, what comes to the same thing, the price of this portion constitutes the rent of land, and in the price of the greater part of commodities makes a third component part."[59] Because Smith implicitly views land as costless and does not recognize it as a factor of production until it is privately owned, he attributes its product to the workers and views rent as subtracted from the workers' labor compensation rather than compensating for the value that the land adds to the product.

In each case, then, Smith supposes that the workers produce the whole value of the product, when there is really at least one other productive factor. So when the other factors are paid, Smith erroneously asserts that the value of the workers' contribution is greater than their compensation.

Classical Economists Develop Smith's Outline

At first, Smith's economic theory, as presented in the *Wealth of Nations*, attracted followers not only because it was simple but also because it appeared to explain some key features of a market economy with great precision.

David Ricardo (1772–1823) was the first to extend Smith's reasoning about the gains from specialized production and exchange, which Smith had imprecisely called the division of labor.[60] Suppose that there are two hunters, and one hunter is *both* a better deer hunter *and* a better beaver trapper than the other. The better hunter takes three hours to trap a beaver and one hour to bag a deer, while the other takes four hours per beaver and two hours per deer. It might seem (and Smith strongly implied) that the two hunters cannot gain from exchange, since they produce exactly the same products, and the first hunter is absolutely more efficient in both kinds of hunting.

But Ricardo demonstrated that what matters most in exchange is not the absolute advantage, but the relative or "comparative" advantage. Each beaver costs the first hunter the same amount of work as three deer but costs the second hunter the same amount of work as two deer. It will therefore pay the first hunter to exchange some of his beavers for the second hunter's deer, and for the second hunter to exchange some of his deer for the first hunter's beavers. Their gains and total production will be maximized if each hunter, instead of hunting only for himself, specializes in hunting the animal in which he is relatively more productive, and exchanges with the other hunter for the animal in which he is relatively less productive. If each hunter hunted sixteen hours a week, the first hunter would usually bag two beavers and ten deer, while the second hunter would usually bag two beavers and four deer. If the better hunter hunted only deer, while the other hunted only beaver, and the two exchanged some of their game, their combined output would increase. By giving up beaver hunting, the first hunter can increase his bag of deer from ten to sixteen. By giving up deer hunting, the second hunter can increase his bag of beavers from two to four. Their combined total remains at four beavers per week but rises from fourteen to sixteen deer per week. They have two additional deer to split between them, for the same number of hours' work as before.

This, then, was the main attraction to classical economists of Smith's revision of the previous outline of economic theory. It appeared to offer much greater simplicity, while (thanks to Ricardo) yielding insights not previously developed.

It was only after the first flush of success wore off that economists became aware of several drawbacks inherent in Smith's rearranged outline of economic theory. Dropping the theory of utility made it impossible to explain demand adequately, the "labor theory of value" warped the theory of production in peculiar ways, and dropping the theory of final distribution thoroughly confused it with the theory of how producers are compensated, even making them seem arbitrary and unrelated. And this combination of confusions led straight to Karl Marx's theory of communism.

Absence of utility. While the classical theory, as developed by Smith and his successors, tries to explain how much of each good will be produced, without the theory of utility it can't tell us how much of each good will be demanded. For example, why should each hunter in our example of comparative advantage wish to consume two beavers a week, rather than more or less? To answer the question in the real world, we would need to know each hunter's relative preferences for the two goods, not just their relative costs of producing them. And if people produce for the sake of what it ultimately allows them to consume, then even production is not fully explained. For the same reason, the classical theory cannot tell us how the two deer that represent the gains from exchange and specialization will be split between the two hunters.

Without the theory of utility, the classical economists could not explain the exchange value of labor itself; why goods that cannot be reproduced with labor (for example, Old Masters paintings) have any value; nor why the market prices of most goods depart—often widely and for long periods—from the "natural" prices that, in Smith's theory, are supposed to be set by their costs of production.

Arbitrary assumptions about production. Smith's approach led the classical economists, like their Scholastic predecessors, to restrict the theory of production with special assumptions that seemed plausible at first but turned out to be inaccurate.

In general, where the Scholastic thinkers had routinely assumed that the total amounts of human and nonhuman capital are constant, the classical economists routinely assumed that population might vary freely in response to wages, but that the other factors, including land, technology, skills, and tools per worker, are given.[61] Under this set of assumptions, real income per capita cannot permanently rise, because any rise in wages encourages workers to have more children, and the resulting increase in population and in the number of workers causes wages to fall again. "Men multiply like Mice in a barn if they have unlimited Means of Subsistence," wrote Richard Cantillon (c. 1680–1734).[62] This "Mouse Assumption," not economic theory, was the basis of Thomas Malthus's and David Ricardo's supposed "Iron Law of [Unraisable] Wages" and of Karl Marx's theory of the inexorable "immiseration" of workers.

Nothing in the theory of production itself requires the Mouse Assumption. But the classical economists were predisposed to make it because they were following Smith's revised outline of economic theory.

To duplicate the linear relationship of all costs of production assumed by Smith's labor–quantity theory, David Ricardo resorted to lumping quantities of capital and labor together into a standard unit of labor mixed with an average amount of buildings and machinery. This implied that every increase in the supply of labor was automatically matched by a proportional increase in nonhuman capital—thus *prescribing* the nature of economic reality rather than attempting to *describe* it. Ricardo went to his grave searching for an invariant measure of exchange value of the sort that Smith had proclaimed human labor to be.

But the assumption of automatic, proportional increases in productive resources was not remotely plausible in the case of land in densely populated Western Europe (as it might have been, say, in the newly formed United States of America). So Ricardo treated land as a special case: a factor of which the quantity is fixed, while the quantities of labor and capital were assumed to vary, but always in constant proportion to one another. For the first time, classical economists had a theory of production with more than one factor. The result was that, beginning with Ricardo, the classical economists had to admit an important exception to Smith's labor theory of value. As John Stuart Mill summarized the revised theory, "The natural value of some things is a scarcity value: but most things naturally exchange for one another in the ratio of their cost of production, or at what may be termed their Cost Value."[63] According to the revised theory, only rent had a scarcity value because of the limitation of the supply of land, while wages and profits did not, because labor and capital were assumed to be capable of indefinite increase. Therefore, unlike labor and capital, "rent of land is not an element in the cost of production of the commodity which yields it" (as Smith had maintained).[64]

Not until the late nineteenth century would economists reapply the theory of utility to factor compensation and recognize that what seems to make land rent a special case is actually true of the income earned by any factor of production (including human capital and reproducible property), whenever that factor's quantity remains the same while the quantities of the other factors are altered.[65] In fact, this is how the compensation of each factor is determined, as a general rule. But to gain this insight meant abandoning the labor–quantity theory altogether.

The labor–quantity theory of value had actually been proposed by a minor cleric in the fifteenth century, and it was promptly recognized and refuted by his colleagues as a fallacy.[66] It was similarly recognized as a fallacy and refuted by some of Smith's contemporaries and a few dissidents during the classical period. As the Abbé Condillac (1714–80) wrote in 1776, "a thing does not have value because of its cost, as some suppose; but it costs because it has value."[67] Other notable dissidents include Jean-Baptiste Say (1767–1832), Nassau Senior (1790–1864), and Richard Whately (1787–1863). Whately pointed out, "It is not that pearls fetch a high price *because* men have dived for them; but on the contrary, men dive for them because they fetch a high price."[68]

Say is usually regarded as a mere popularizer of Smith, but he immediately pronounced Smith's attempt to replace the theory of utility with a labor–quantity theory of value a mistake. He also objected to Smith's distinction between productive and unproductive labor, his attempt to reduce all factors of production to labor alone, his claim that the contributions of the other factors are due to the division of labor, and his dis-

missal of enterprise as mere bureaucratic management.[69] Say's objections
were noted by John Stuart Mill,[70] but they were not regarded as serious
enough to call into question Smith's revision of the overall outline of
economic theory.[71]

Confusion of compensation and (final) distribution. Before
Smith, the theories explaining final distribution and the compensation of
the factors of production had been recognized as clearly distinct. Factor
compensation was explained by the fact that, just as the value of products
depends upon their utility and scarcity, the producers' compensation is
derived from their contributions to the market value of products. The
theory of final distribution explained how those who receive such factor
compensation decide to allocate, between themselves and other persons,
the current and future consumption made possible by this income.

Smith eliminated Augustine's theory of gifts from personal economy,
and Aristotle's theory of distributive justice from domestic and political
economy, replacing these theories with an assumption that no one who
receives labor or property compensation ever shares it with anyone else.
Smith was intent on proving that despite their vices and follies everyone
is "led by an invisible hand to make nearly the same distribution of the
necessaries of life, which would have been made, had the earth been
divided into equal portions among its inhabitants."

While many laymen objected to the assumption of selfishness on
moral grounds, all economists of the classical period failed to see that
Smith had confused the final distribution of income with the compensation of the factors of production. Essentially, Smith assumed that there
is only one optimal allocation of economic goods. Actually, as we will
see in the next chapter, there is a different "equilibrium" for every possible allocation of wealth or income. Yet by eliminating the theory of
final distribution, Smith had removed the means necessary to investigate such questions.

As a result, classical economists jumped to a dangerously false conclusion: that the distribution of income is essentially arbitrary, and that
government efforts to redistribute income or wealth will leave production
unaffected. Mill summarized the general view of classical economists
when he wrote: "The laws and conditions of the production of wealth,
partake of the character of physical truths. There is nothing optional or
arbitrary about them." But "it is not so with the Distribution of Wealth.

That is a matter of human institution solely. The things once there, mankind, individually or collectively, can do with them as they like. They can place them at the disposal of whomsoever they please, and on whatever terms."[72]

Marx memorably but fairly accurately described the basic premise of the "labor theory of value" by saying that "Regarded as exchange-values, all commodities are merely definite quantities of *congealed labour-time*."[73] Recall that, in Smith's words, "The value which the workmen add to the materials" is split "into two parts, of which the one pays their wages, the other the profits of their employer." Marx named the latter "surplus value."

Normative Classical Economics

Normative classical economics falls into three categories. The first consists of conclusions (for example, the basic ground rules of monetary, fiscal, and trade policies) that generally accorded with Scholastic prescriptions but had to be reformulated because of Smith's change in economic theory. The second comprises prescriptions (notably regarding the feasibility and desirability of charitable aid to the poor) that differed from the normative Scholastic conclusions because of the change in theory. The third consists of Karl Marx's serious challenge, based on logical conclusions from Smith's economic theory that neither Smith nor his mainstream classical followers had anticipated, to the Scholastic justification of the whole organization of society.

Agreement with the Scholastics about means, but not ends. According to Aquinas, the purpose of human life is "through virtuous living to attain to the possession of God." Political economy concerns what is "secondary and instrumental"—"a sufficiency of those bodily goods whose use is necessary for virtuous life." According to Smith, the Stoic world-soul always arranges maximum human happiness without any conscious cooperation by humans, and he says that political economy "proposes to enrich both the people and the sovereign." Despite this basic difference about its purpose, Smith's description of the government's duties is remarkably similar to that of the Scholastics:

> First, the duty of protecting the society from violence and invasion of other independent societies; secondly, the duty of protecting, as far as possible, every member of the society from the

injustice or oppression of every other member of it, or the duty
of establishing an exact administration of justice; and, thirdly,
the duty of erecting and maintaining certain public works and
certain public institutions which it can never be for the interest
of any individual, or small number of individuals, to erect and
maintain.[74]

After observing wartime price inflation during the American Revolutionary War, the French Revolution, and in Great Britain during the
Napoleonic Wars, classical economists came to the same practical conclusion as the Scholastics about monetary and fiscal policy. To ensure stability
in the general price level, it is necessary to avoid financing government by
creating money, which in turn requires balancing government spending
with taxes over time.

Smith's foremost exception to freedom of international trade is the
same as Aquinas's: "when some particular sort of industry is necessary
for the defence of the country."[75] Both men stipulate that national wealth
will be adversely affected by discouraging cheaper imports, because
it entails a reduced market for exports. But for Smith as for Aquinas,
national defense trumps national wealth when the two conflict.[76] Smith
did not think complete freedom of trade likely in England.[77] He advocated duties on foreign goods to match taxes on domestic goods,[78] as well
as tariffs designed to force the lowering of foreign tariffs by retaliation.[79]

Smith's pointed advice to the new United States of America in the
Wealth of Nations, published when the two nations were at war, led to
Alexander Hamilton's "heated agreement" (as my friend Hadley Arkes
likes to put it). Smith argued, in effect, that the United States should
forswear Smith's advice to his own country, by preferring wealth to
American independence: "Were the Americans . . . to stop the impor-
tation of European manufactures," Smith predicted, "they would . . .
obstruct, instead of promoting, the progress of their country towards
real wealth and greatness."[80] Similar arguments were frequently made by
American Loyalists, e.g., Samuel Seabury (1729–96), to whom Hamilton was responding in *The Farmer Refuted* (1775)[81] when he adumbrated
the three main counterarguments of his own later *Report on Manufactures* (1791) and Washington's Farewell Address: national security, infant
industry, and national union.[82] Hamilton became not only the first U.S.

treasury secretary, but also the first treasury secretary to force a change in economic theory, when John Stuart Mill recognized protection for infant industries as a legitimate exception to free trade in his revision of Smith's classical economics.[83] The German-American economist Friedrich List (1789–1846) systematically analyzed the historical evidence supporting Hamilton's theory of economic development and prophesied accurately in 1841 that the United States "will perhaps in the time of our grandchildren exalt itself to the rank of the first naval and commercial power in the world," and following the example of Britain, "[revert] to the principle of free trade and of unrestricted competition in the home as well as in foreign markets."[84]

Disagreement with the Scholastics. According to the Scholastics, both private and public charity are praiseworthy but inherently limited by the fact of scarcity. But according to the classical population doctrine, all such efforts are inherently futile. As John Stuart Mill summarized this view, "It is but rarely that improvements in the condition of the labouring classes do anything more than give a temporary margin, speedily filled up by an increase of their numbers. The use they commonly choose to make of any advantageous change in their circumstances, is to take it out in the form which, by augmenting the population, deprives the succeeding generation of the benefit." Thus, "the most promising schemes end only in having a more numerous, but not a happier people."[85]

Laymen often lampooned this classical population doctrine for its opposition to charity, notably Charles Dickens (1812–70) in "A Christmas Carol" (1843). Upon being told that many poor people would rather die than go to prison or the Poor House, Ebenezer Scrooge responds, "If they would rather die, they had better do it, and decrease the surplus population."

Marx takes Smith's ideas to their logical conclusion. Smith's "labor theory of value" and his fanciful social history not only created difficulties for those later economic theorists who followed Smith's lead; they also directly spawned Karl Marx's (1818–83) theory of "capitalism" and capitalist exploitation of the worker.

V. I. Lenin (1870–1924) would accurately describe Marx's theory as the combination of "German philosophy, English political economy and French socialism."[86] Marx combined David Hume's Epicurean materialism and Hegel's dialectical idealism into a philosophy of dialectical materialism. From the French socialists he adopted the famous slogan, "from each according to his ability, to each according to his needs"[87]—which is a fairly accurate description of distributive justice within the family, but not in "society," to which the socialists mistakenly applied it.

However, these two elements had been politically ineffectual until Marx joined them to his theory of "surplus value," which was a straightforward recounting of Adam Smith's "labor theory of value" as developed by Ricardo. According to Marx,

> surplus value is produced by the employment of labour power. Capital buys the labour power and pays wages for it. By means of his work the labourer creates new value which does not belong to him but to the capitalist. He must work a certain time merely in order to reproduce the equivalent value of his wages. But when this equivalent value has been returned, he does not cease work, but continues to do so for some further hours. The new value which he produces during this extra time, and which exceeds in consequence the amount of his wage, constitutes surplus value.[88]

Marx was thus only applying widely accepted classical theory when he assumed that owners of capital and land could be expropriated and their incomes arbitrarily redistributed by the government without affecting the value of production.[89]

The most important reason for the undeserved political success of communism, therefore, was that Lenin could truthfully write, "Adam Smith and David Ricardo, by their investigations of the economic system, laid the foundations of the labour theory of value. Marx continued their work."[90]

Ironically, the means by which Smith pursued his grand ambition of synthesizing ethics, economics, and politics—his preference for rhetoric over empirical accuracy and logical consistency—caused him to fail to achieve it.[91] The unintended consequences were disastrous.

4

Neoclassical Economics (1871–c. 2000)

Economists of the latter third of the nineteenth century were undoubt-edly embarrassed by Dickensian lampoons of selfish *homo oeco-nomicus*, and they were alarmed by the quite logical conclusions that Karl Marx had drawn from Smith and Ricardo's labor theory of value. But what sealed the fate of classical economics among economists was the spectacular failure of its empirical predictions. According to the "Iron Law of Wages," rising population should have trapped workers permanently at subsistence wages. Mainstream classical economists had ignored Richard Whately's correct observation that this "law" was contradicted by gener-ally rising living standards over long periods. The Iron Law was unmistak-ably routed when annual population growth in what is now the United Kingdom averaged 0.79 percent between 1820 and 1870—slightly faster than from 1700 to 1820—yet per capita real income advanced an average of 1.26 percent per year. This meant that the real size of the economy, once considered static, was now doubling every generation.

This predictive failure resulted in two revisions of the classical assumptions about production, one in the nineteenth century and a sec-ond, much more satisfactory version in the twentieth century. By restor-ing and updating the theory of utility (one version of which updated Augustine's), the so-called neoclassical economists also succeeded in pos-ing—and beginning to answer—questions that the classical economists could not. However, neoclassical economists retained Smith's assump-tion of universal human selfishness. For that reason, they failed to redis-cover the Scholastic theory of final distribution.

The latter failure is related to the general adoption by neoclassi-cal economists of the worldview of Adam Smith's friend, the Epicurean skeptic David Hume. Scholastic natural-law philosophy started from Aristotle's definition of humans as rational animals, while Smith's Stoic pantheism viewed the whole universe, in effect, as one big rational animal that chooses what's best for humans, who are supposed to be individually incapable of choosing either ends or means properly. Hume's estimate of human nature was intermediate between these two views. He famously wrote, "Reason is, and ought only to be the slave of the passions, and can never pretend to any other office than to serve and obey them."[1] In other words, according to Hume, man is essentially not a rational but only a very clever animal. In the Scholastic understanding, reason or intellect consists in the ability to understand universal ideas like "man" or "beauty," rather than merely perceiving a particular man or beautiful object, as do other animals. Hume demoted reason to a highly sophis-ticated calculation of the particular means necessary to achieve ends or purposes that are predetermined by our passions or "sentiments." The practical result was to assume that no one ever chooses to act for anyone but him- or herself—even when one is apparently being altruistic.

Hume's worldview expanded vastly in influence in the mid-nine-teenth century after the French philosopher Auguste Comte (1798–1857) systematized it into what he called the Positive Philosophy, or Positivism.[2] Comte had rejected his family's devout Roman Catholicism and political royalism but consciously imitated Aquinas's synthesis of Scholastic natural law philosophy when constructing the Positive Phi-losophy.[3] Comte added or subtracted disciplines to reflect the change from the Scholastic to the Epicurean worldview, which recognizes no ultimate realities but matter and chance. As reflected in table 4–1 at the end of this chapter, Comte's reclassification of disciplines is first of all a reclassification of what it means to be human. Comte obliterated the virtues and any distinction between natural and moral sciences. He eliminated all disciplines involving immaterial realities (revealed theol-ogy, metaphysics, logic, and moral philosophy: Comte invented sociol-ogy to replace moral philosophy).

Among those influenced by Positivism was John Stuart Mill. But Mill jibbed when Comte accompanied his Positive Philosophy with a Positive Religion: an elaborate French Catholic version of Hume's atheistic materialism (if such a thing is possible), complete with a calendar honoring secular saints like Adam Smith and ritual "Sociolatry" to worship that "immense and eternal Being, Humanity," led by himself as first high priest.[4] Max Weber, like Mill, wanted to keep Comte's Positive Philosophy while rejecting the "Positive Religion." He revised Comte's sociology into what he called an "antipositive" or "value-free" version. However, Weber joined Comte in rejecting the Scholastic worldview and instead adopted Hume's view of human nature, along with Emmanuel Kant's conclusion from it, that rather than understanding and *describing* reality, humans *prescribe* it.[5] Weber thereby burdened the many neoclassical economists who followed him with an extraordinary load of Hume's and Comte's intellectual baggage.

The Neoclassical Revision of Adam Smith's Outline

Neoclassical economists started to revise Smith's revision of economic theory, although not with complete success, beginning around 1871. Let's alter our usual order of the four basic elements (final distribution logically comes first) in order to see how the neoclassical economists, who recognize only three of the four, treat the subject.

    1. Utility. The neoclassical economists began their house cleaning by rejecting Adam Smith's so-called labor theory of value and by reinventing a modernized theory of utility. They did so partly in response to Marx. Perhaps the most cogent answer to Marx came from Philip Wicksteed, but his response also illustrates what is wrong with Smith's version.[6] Marx had argued that "[t]he whole mystery of commodities, all the magic and necromancy that surrounds the products of labour as long as they take the form of commodities, vanishes . . . so soon as we come to other forms of production. Since Robinson Crusoe's experiences are a favourite theme with political economists, let us take a look at him on his island."[7] Wicksteed responded, "I accept this invitation, and proceed to make my own observations on what I see."[8]

    Wicksteed notes that Crusoe has to perform various kinds of useful work, such as making tools or furniture and taming or hunting animals, "and although he does not ever exchange things against each other, having no one with whom to exchange, yet he is perfectly conscious of the equivalence of utility existing between certain products of his labour, and as he is at liberty to distribute that labour as he likes, he will always apply it

where it can produce the greatest utility in a given time."[9] Since his most
urgent need is food, Crusoe devotes his time initially to finding something to eat. Once he has done this, his next most urgent need is shelter,
so he devotes his next hours to devising one. Then he proceeds to satisfy
less urgent wants. Eventually, writes Wicksteed, Crusoe would arrive "at
a state of equilibrium, so to speak, when his stock of each product is such
that his desire for a further increment of it is proportional to the time it
would take to produce it, for when this state of things is realized, equal
expenditures of labour, wherever applied, would result in equal utilities."

Wicksteed then asks Marxists to imagine an ideal communist indus-
trial community—in other words, a system that, like Robinson Crusoe's,
is without exchange—in which it took four days to make a coat, and
half a day to make a hat, but in which there was at first an equal need
of hats and coats. Marx had used such examples extensively in *Capital*.
Under these conditions, the community would prefer to direct its productive resources to producing hats rather than coats, because though
the need for hats and coats was equally urgent, it took only one-eighth
as long to produce a hat as it did a coat. As the supply of hats increased,
the urgency of the need for further hats would decline while the need
for coats would remain the same. But even if the need of hats fell by, say,
half, the community would continue to produce hats rather than coats
because it could still get four times as much value from every hour spent
producing hats as it could from every hour spent producing coats.

At some point, however, the scarcity of hats would decline to the
point at which the value of an additional hat was worth only one-eighth
as much as the value of an additional coat. At this point, a worker could
satisfy equally urgent wants for the community whether he made hats or
coats. "But observe [that] a coat is not worth eight times as much as a hat
to the community, because it takes eight times as long to make it (that
it always did, even when one hat was worth as much to the community
as a coat)—but the community is willing to devote eight times as long
to the making of a coat, because when made it will be worth eight times
as much to it," Wicksteed concluded.[10] Even George Bernard Shaw, a
convinced Marxist at the time, finally admitted that Wicksteed was right
and that the labor theory of value had therefore to be abandoned.[11]

Wicksteed's analysis illustrates the primary theoretical advance
made by the neoclassical economists: the reduction of what had seemed

to the Scholastics to be two principles, utility and scarcity, into a single principle: *marginal* utility. That is, they saw that the exchange value of any good depends not on its total utility, but on the difference in value made by one unit more or less—which, for scarce goods, always declines after a certain point as the quantity increases.

However, the early neoclassical economists disagreed (and some of their modern followers still disagree) about the precise meaning of "utility." The utility theory was independently but almost simultaneously reinvented in 1871–74 by William Stanley Jevons (1835–82) in Manchester, England; Leon Walras (1834–1910), who was French but taught in Lausanne, Switzerland; and Carl Menger (1841–1921) in Vienna, Austria.[12] The three were unaware of one another's work for several years. From them derive the three main branches of neoclassical economics: from Jevons the British school, from Walras the Lausanne school, and from Menger the Austrian school. Though the "schools" quickly proliferated, all later neoclassical theories can be traced to one or more of these three.

Jevons was a disciple of Jeremy Bentham, the founder of philosophical utilitarianism. Bentham's theory, following that of David Hume, was essentially a modern application of the ancient philosophy of Epicurus, who argued that all human action is motivated by pleasure-seeking and avoidance of pain. Bentham certainly didn't invent the theory of utility;[13] rather, his peculiar contribution was to redefine utility as a synonym for pleasure, which he viewed as a purely physiological sensation. The practical result was to change the word's meaning from Augustine's idea of a *relation* (a person's order of preference for different goods) into a *thing*, a hypothetical physiological quantum, which the utilitarians regarded as the ultimate good that everyone wishes to consume and which they confidently believed would soon be isolated by scientists and measured like so many ounces of liquid or volts of electricity. Augustine's version of the idea is known as *ordinal utility* and Bentham's as *cardinal utility*. Generally speaking, early neoclassical English economists adopted the notion of cardinal utility, while early neoclassical economists on the European continent followed Menger and Walras in employing the concept of ordinal utility.

Because they considered utility to be a thing, the Benthamite economists assumed that the marginal utility of any good depended only on the quantity of that good. Yet it soon became apparent that such a view is unrealistic, because people's preferences for any particular good are also related to their preferences for other goods, especially when those goods are complementary (like coffee and sugar) or competing (like coffee and tea). That is, if you like to drink coffee laced with sugar, the desirability of a cup of coffee will depend not only on the quantity of coffee available but also on the available quantity of sugar. Likewise, if you drink either coffee or tea, but not both at a single sitting, your preference for a cup of coffee will depend not only on the availability of coffee but also on the availability of tea.

As Bentham had noted, the capacity for pleasure and pain is common to most animals, so the notion of cardinal utility cannot logically be confined to humans. Moreover, scientists never did discover or quantify the physiological units of pleasure that the Benthamites had confidently expected. Lionel Robbins, among others, pointed out that this meant there is no objective basis for comparing utility (interpreted as pleasure, satisfaction, or welfare) among different humans, much less different animal species.

It took almost sixty years for the English-speaking economists to reach a consensus that the idea of cardinal utility is unscientific because unverifiable. That was the main point of Robbins's classic 1932 definition, "Economics is the science which studies human behaviour as a relationship between ends and scarce means that have alternate uses."[14] Utility is not a *thing*, but a *relation* between a person and a thing. It refers to our order of preference for instrumental goods, just as Augustine had described it fifteen centuries earlier. By the 1930s, most economists had shifted from tools of analysis that depended on cardinal utility to tools that could only be interpreted in terms of ordinal utility.[15] (However, as we will also see, by the 1960s some later neoclassical economists abandoned this hard-won consensus and revived the notion of cardinal utility, with unfortunate results.)

2. Production. The early neoclassical economists also reacted to the failure of the classical predictions of stagnant real wages by revising the theory of production. However, in their eagerness to correct Adam Smith's error of reducing all productive factors to labor alone and to instead focus on the contribution of nonhuman capital, for nearly a century they went to the opposite extreme. Their habit of treating labor and technical progress merely by assumption had the practical result of roughly reversing the

classical economists' assumptions about production: Whereas the classical economists usually assumed that population may vary in response
to wages and that the supplies of other productive resources were inherently limited, the early neoclassical economists routinely assumed that
only investment in reproducible tangible property (like buildings and
machines) varies with its rate of return; the population, its skills, and the
state of technical progress were all treated as "given."

I have called this set of assumptions the stork theory, since it implicitly assumes that adult workers spring from out of the blue, as if brought
by a large stork: in effect, denying Aristotle's observation that humans are
"conjugal" or "matrimonial" animals.[16] Given the stork theory's assumptions, the accumulation of workers' tools—buildings and machines—is
the only possible source of economic growth that can be affected by policymakers, and the total tax burden not only should, but inevitably must,
fall entirely upon the incomes of workers (who under the same assumption cannot avoid such taxes by having fewer or less educated children,
though property owners are assumed to be able to avoid taxes on property income by investing less in property). This empirically false assumption—not sound economic theory—underlies the proposals to abolish
taxes on property income that are perennially advocated by a cottage
industry of (mostly my fellow Republican) economists centered in Washington, D.C. But to be fair, many economists who are liberal Democrats
propound an equally erroneous mirror-image ideology—assuming that
only investment in people, but not investment in property, is adversely
affected by higher tax rates.

Neoclassical economists using the stork theory's assumptions proved
unable to account for over half of the economic growth in advanced
countries like Germany, Japan, and the United States in the twentieth
century, a failure that became increasingly obvious after the Second
World War. In a now famous address given in 1960, economist Theodore
W. Schultz pointed out that this fact was a major challenge to prevailing
neoclassical economic theory: "The income of the United States has been
increasing at a much higher rate than the combined amount of land,
man-hours worked, and the stock of reproducible capital used to produce
the income. . . . To call this discrepancy a measure of 'resource productivity' gives a name to our ignorance but does not dispel it. . . . Unless
this discrepancy can be resolved, received theory of production applied

to inputs and outputs as currently measured is a toy and not a tool for studying economic growth."[17]

Schultz went on to present his own hypothesis. "Investment in human capital is probably the major explanation of this difference. Much of what we call consumption constitutes investment in human capital. Direct expenditures on education, health, and internal migration to take advantage of better job opportunities are clear examples."[18] If Schultz was right, not only the assumptions but also the main thrust of the policy advice associated with the stork theory were wrong: "Laborers have become capitalists not from a diffusion of corporate stocks as folklore would have it, but from the acquisition of knowledge and skill that have economic value."[19]

Schultz's address stimulated new efforts to explain and measure the growth of production and income. Gary S. Becker undertook to refine the microeconomic theory of what Schultz had called "human capital"—the economically useful qualities embodied in human beings. Just as all property income is the return on investment in nonhuman capital, Becker theorized that all labor compensation should be considered the return on investment in human capital.[20] Meanwhile, John W. Kendrick (1917–2009), a pioneer of economic measurement, more comprehensively reformulated Schultz's thesis as the "total capital hypothesis" and set out to test it by careful measurement.

The total capital hypothesis was essentially a restoration and updating of Aristotle's theory of production, in that it recognized the same forms of wealth—people and property—but for the first time in the history of economics allowed all the variables in production actually to vary. It is probable, Kendrick suggested, that the productivity of labor and capital doesn't change much over time, if at all; the apparent increase is due to the fact that these factors aren't measured properly. Neither growth of the labor force nor rising labor productivity owing to technical progress can be assumed, because there can be no growth of the labor force without a prior investment in child-rearing; no increases in income resulting from education, training, health, safety, or mobility without a prior *investment* in education, training, health, safety, or mobility; and no technical progress without prior investment in research and development.

Kendrick was eventually able to show that Schultz's hypothesis had been proved correct: "the total capital approach . . . provides an effective explanation of most of the rate of growth of real (adjusted) GDP."[21] (The word *adjusted* is necessary because Kendrick showed that the official statistics measuring national production and income were—and still are—inconsistent with facts described by the total capital theory in several ways, and on balance seriously understate the total values of national production, investment, and income.) Kendrick showed that, while part of the previously unexplained economic growth could be traced to investment in research and development (intangible property), most was the result of investment in "human capital," just as Schultz had argued. The growth of human capital has consistently accounted for about two-thirds of economic growth in the United States, while growth of nonhuman capital (including intangible investment in research and development as well as tangible investment in buildings and machines) accounts for the rest.

3. Equilibrium. Neoclassical economists also differed among themselves about the meaning, and to some extent even the existence, of *equilibrium*. Walras was the first to work out a theory of general equilibrium: the process by which equality of exchange values comes about for all participants in connected markets. But the most influential English neoclassical economist, Alfred Marshall, routinely assumed only partial equilibrium—holding most things constant—which is usually analytically easier but often seriously misleading. (Partial equilibrium analysis typically focuses on an individual person or business firm, assuming that market prices are unaffected by that agent's behavior. But if we assume that no individual person's or firm's actions are able to affect the market price of any commodity, it means that the actions of *all* individuals together also cannot affect market prices, which is obviously false.) Menger routinely focused on exchange between isolated individuals— for whom the gains from exchange are not necessarily equal or even comparable—and reasoned from this special case that there can be no such thing as equality of exchange value, justice in exchange, or equilibrium. Most of his Austrian-school followers today reject even the mathematical description of economic events. (Mathematical description would show the Austrian system to be even more logically incomplete than the other schools of neoclassical theory, since the Austrian school implicitly uses only two equations to describe the four basic elements of economic theory, while other neoclassical schools use three). Since without mathematical treatment, empirical verification of an economic theory is virtually impossible, despite its impressive beginnings Austrian-school economics has contributed relatively little in recent decades to the development of economic theory, and it has become virtually irrelevant to the formulation of economic policy.

4. Final distribution. The neoclassical economists succeeded in reintegrating utility theory with the early neoclassical theory of production by about 1910. These concepts were linked by the theory of equilibrium. And many believed that economic theory was thereby substantially complete. Marshall, a leader of the British school, famously likened the structure of economic theory to a pair of scissors,[22] with the theory of production ("supply") acting as one blade, the theory of utility ("demand") as the other, and the theory of equilibrium, like the pivot of the scissors, as the principle connecting the two.

It came as a jolt, therefore, when neoclassical economists were forced to recognize that the combination of utility, production, and equilibrium is not a logically complete description of any economic activity. The result is not a single, optimum distribution of economic resources, as economists since Adam Smith had assumed. Instead, there is at least one competitive market equilibrium for every possible distribution of income or wealth. That is, even if we knew the total value of goods that can be produced, and everyone's preferences for those goods, the description would not be complete—the state of equilibrium would not be unique—until we knew which persons would be able finally to consume the goods. Only that would reveal exactly which combination of goods to produce, and at what prices. But the neoclassical economists still had no descriptive theory of final distribution.[23] This hole in modern economic theory is responsible for most of the embarrassments suffered by modern economics. The problem is pervasive at all levels—personal, domestic, and political.

The Current Predicament of Economists

The history of economics I have provided thus far is highly schematic, but it nevertheless allows us to begin to understand the unsatisfactory state of current economic theory. So far, we have seen that the Scholastic outline of economic theory identified the four basic elements necessary for the accurate description of any economic activity: final distribution, utility, production, and equilibrium. The "classical" outline initiated by

Adam Smith retained the Scholastic theory of equilibrium and advanced a lopsided theory of production, and it rejected the Scholastic theories of utility and final distribution. Modern "neoclassical" economics has restored and modernized the utility theory of value, further deepened our understanding of equilibrium, and restored and updated the Scholastic two-factor theory of production. However, economists using this model have been burdened in their work for more than a century with the problems created by the absence of a theory of final distribution. These problems have been multiplied rather than diminished by the many other interesting developments in economic theory, ranging from game theory to the theory of public choice to experimental economics, since each spreads the problem to a new branch (or twig) of theory.

The Mother's Problem

The modern economist's embarrassment can perhaps best be illustrated by observing that the current state of economic theory cannot adequately describe, let alone solve, the simplest economic problem that a typical mother faces—and solves—at least a dozen times each day. The Mother's Problem was first clearly posed in modern economics by Philip Wicksteed in *The Common Sense of Political Economy*[24]—a text with the engaging premise that the best way to learn economic theory is not to begin with the fictional Robinson Crusoe, but rather with the ordinary daily activities of a typical mother.

A remarkable self-taught economist, Wicksteed was also a former Unitarian minister, a leading Dante scholar, and a translator of Aquinas from the Latin and Aristotle from the Greek. Wicksteed recognized toward the end of his life that the next step, logically speaking, was to study Augustine, but he didn't live long enough to do so.[25] And this accounts for his own failure to solve the problem he posed.

Putting the Mother's Problem in its simplest form, Wicksteed asks the reader to imagine how a typical mother (in Edwardian England, circa 1910) might allocate a single scarce commodity—milk—that has alternative uses: "In the usual routine, milk may be wanted for the baby, for the other children, for a pudding, for tea or coffee, and for the cat." The Mother's Problem is simply to determine the amount of milk to allocate to each use. If all the alternatives were for her own personal use, neoclassical economic theory could provide the solution. To make the best use of the milk, the mother should begin with the most urgent use—that is, the use with the highest marginal utility—and, as the urgency of this need is diminished by the application of milk, continue to the next most urgent, and so on, until the incremental benefit from adding or subtracting the same small quantity of milk is equal for every different use.

But the mother's actual problem is quite different, and unanswerable by neoclassical economics, since she is dealing not only with her own preferences but also with the preferences of several other users of milk. Her problem is twofold: not only to estimate the preferences of each user but also to decide how much *weight* to give to those preferences. Should she give the same weight, other things being equal, to her own preferences, those of her husband, each of her own children, a neighbor's child, and the family cat?

After showing that the Mother's Problem cannot be reduced to a matter of exchange, Wicksteed concludes that its solution must lie outside of economic theory. "Now the very widest definition of the economic life, or the range that should be covered by economic study, . . . would not be taken to extend to the administration, or distribution among varied claimants, of personal and inalienable qualities and powers that flow directly towards their ultimate purpose or expression. The widest definition of the scope of Economics would confine their scope to things that can be regarded as in some sense exchangeable, and capable of being transferred according to order and agreement. No one would regard the principles upon which I balance the claims of devotion [to God] against those of friendship, or of either against the indulgence of my aesthetic appetites, as within the range of economic science."[26]

As we have seen, Augustine and his Scholastic followers regarded those principles as the most fundamental in economic theory. Augustine had pointed out that goods are voluntarily "transferable" in two ways, not just one: "by sale or gift." Thus, confining "transferability" to sale (that is, exchange) alone leaves personal and collective *gifts* unexplained.[27]

Many other economists have since taken refuge in the strategy of refusing to face the consequences of the neoclassical omission of final distribution. They simply declare the answer a matter of normative or moral judgments that economists qua economists cannot make. But this is an unacceptable dodge. It leaves economists with a fundamentally analytical or "positive" failure: Neoclassical economics does not provide a coherent, empirically verifiable description of how people actually choose—rightly *or* wrongly—to distribute the use of their resources, whether as individual persons, as members of a family household, or as a whole society under the same government.

All neoclassical economists who have tried to solve the Mother's Problem have tried to deduce final distribution from utility—in effect, to argue that the economic means determine the economic ends, rather than vice versa, and that all apparent gifts are really disguised exchanges. Wherever this method has been applied, the same two problems have emerged: the approach relies on circular logic, and its hypotheses about final distribution are either empirically false or not falsifiable.

The Problem in Political Economy

The failure first became obvious in the field of welfare economics, which initially focused mostly on providing advice to government policymakers.

The early British neoclassical economists began with the high hope that they could produce an unambiguous scientific theory to guide government policymakers. Assuming with Bentham that happiness can be reduced to pleasure; that goods are desirable because they afford pleasure (or the avoidance of pain—viewed as a kind of negative pleasure); that pleasures can be easily measured and simply added up for different persons; and that all pleasures (though not all people) are equal,[28] they viewed welfare economics as a straightforward exercise in bringing about "the greatest happiness of the greatest number." This is essentially how Alfred Marshall and Arthur Pigou of Cambridge University approached the field.

Marshall, as we have seen, laid down the basic premises of early British neoclassical economics. Marshall's successor Pigou proceeded from these premises to argue that "there are many obstacles that prevent a community's resources from being distributed among different uses or occupations in the most effective way." He sought to identify "ways in which it now is, or eventually may become, feasible for government to control the play of economic forces in such wise as to promote the economic welfare, and through that, the total welfare of citizens as a whole."[29]

Note Pigou's use of the word "the": "*the* most effective way," "*the* economic welfare," and "*the* total welfare." Like Adam Smith and Marshall, Pigou simply assumed that there is only *one* possible market equilibrium. He then proceeded to identify the "obstacles" to this optimum with what he called "incidental services" and "incidental disservices": producers' actions with beneficial or harmful effects on others, such as air pollution.[30] (These have since been renamed "external diseconomies and economies" or more generally, "externalities.") To maximize "the economic welfare" and "the total welfare," according to Pigou, it was necessary only to equalize "'private' and 'social' product," which he defined as total national production and income, measured with and without externalities, respectively. Pigou typically focused on negative externalities, interpreted these as evidence of market failure, and concluded that taxes should be imposed in amounts equal to the monetary value of the harm caused, or else subsidies provided equal to the desired positive benefits.

Lionel Robbins's influential critique of cardinal utility led in the 1930s to a "New Welfare Economics," which attempted to avoid the problem of measuring and making interpersonal comparisons of pleasure by restoring Augustine's version of ordinal utility and refocusing on utility as people's order of preferences for goods. The new approach also incorporated Leon Walras's previously neglected demonstration of the fact that, rather than a *single* optimum distribution of wealth or income, market exchanges can achieve at least one efficient equilibrium for any possible distribution.[31] The New Welfare Economics drew attention, among other things, to the existence and nature of "public goods" like air and national defense, "which all enjoy in common in the sense that each individual's consumption of such a good leads to no subtraction from any other individual's consumption of that good."[32] (None of the antagonists in the subsequent debate was aware that the distinction between private and public goods had already been described by Augustine, was part of Scholastic economics, and was further developed by the American Founders and Abraham Lincoln, as we saw in chapter 2.)

Yet without the theory of final distribution, this new approach soon raised problems of its own. The prevailing method in the New Welfare Economics is typically expressed in what Paul Samuelson termed the "individualistic social welfare function." That is, policymakers (advised by economists) are assumed to be able not only to *know* the preferences for all goods in all conceivable social situations of all individuals in a society—*each of whom is assumed to be purely selfish in matters of final distribution*—but also, by somehow adding up these preferences, to be able to determine a more appropriate distribution of wealth or income than that which results from the individuals' own actions. This in turn depends on the assumption that the nature of relations within political society is essentially the same as that of a very large household in which all property is owned in common.[33] The obvious problems are that, except in a communist society, most property is privately owned, and that adding the preferences of different people is not possible without first assigning a weight for each person—which, in matters of final distribution, is exactly the thing to be determined.

To escape this circular logic, the policymaker must either impose his own ideas about distribution or allow everyone to vote. However, as Kenneth Arrow showed, it is usually impossible to find a single solution that will satisfy everyone, or even a majority.[34] Moreover, Amartya Sen demonstrated that the problem is not limited to decisions made by voting: "The failings are 'general'—shared by all rules that make no use of interpersonal comparisons."[35] In particular, Sen showed that the objection applies to the theory of justice put forth by the late John Rawls (1921–2002), which is based on the assumptions of neoclassical New Welfare Economics.[36]

One important response to this objection is the libertarian theory of public choice, which began in the mid-twentieth century with important works by Duncan Black, Anthony Downs, James Buchanan, Gordon Tullock, and Mancur Olson.[37] The theory focuses on voters, politicians, bureaucrats, and lobbyists as rational, self-interested individuals, all seeking to maximize the utility of their own wealth through government, exactly as they are presumed to maximize their utility as individual producers and consumers in the market. As Buchanan put it in a succinct and accessible pamphlet, "The hard core in public choice can be summarized in three presuppositions: (1) methodological individualism, (2) rational choice, and (3) politics-as-exchange."[38] The essence of this contribution, he added, was that "public choice became a set of theories of governmental failures, as an offset to the theories of market failures that had previously emerged from theoretical welfare economics. Or, . . . 'politics without romance.'"[39]

As we'll see in the next chapter, Buchanan's formula does indeed illuminate the essential differences in public choice theories, but only if we use the neo-Scholastic economic theory to correct it. Doing so reveals three disadvantages that greatly outweigh the apparent advantages: The libertarian theory of public choice is (1) logically incomplete and empirically unverifiable in its own terms, chiefly because it omits the theory of distribution at every social level, (2) inapplicable as a theory of *American* public choice, since it contradicts the Founders' theories of human nature, justice, and government (notably omitting the presidency), and (3) as we'll see in chapter 14, empirically false in its main conclusions about the relation between American citizens' economic interests and voting.

While it avoids the error of presuming only a single possible equilibrium, the libertarian version of public-choice theory, like the earlier liberal version, was also unable accurately to describe *any* unique equilibrium. As Buchanan candidly acknowledged, the presuppositions of the libertarian neoclassical public-choice theory depend on circular logic, its immediate applications are "relatively empty of empirical content," and even some of its most important hypotheses "have not been readily falsifiable empirically."[40]

Among modern welfare economists, perhaps Sen has come closest to identifying the nature of the main problem with neoclassical theory: "traditional theory has *too little* structure. A person is given *one* preference ordering, and as and when the need arises this is supposed to reflect his interests, represent his welfare, summarize his idea of what should be done, and describe his actual choices and behavior. Can one preference ordering do all these things?"[41]

The answer is no. As Augustine was the first to point out, all economic choice involves not one but two kinds of preferences: a ranking of persons as ends, which is reflected in the way we distribute the use of our wealth, and a ranking of scarce means, which is reflected in the particular contents of our wealth. No ranking of persons can be deduced by adding the utility of different persons for two reasons. There is no common unit with which to measure them, and any method of aggregation presupposes a ranking of persons. Sen's counterproposal of "meta-rankings," or "rankings of preference rankings," might be said to be a groping toward Augustine's theory of our preference for persons, which *is*, in effect, a "meta-ranking" or "ranking of preference rankings" that explains what the theory of utility alone cannot.

The choice in welfare economics, then, has been between a theory that must logically include the whole animal kingdom yet is not scientifically grounded, and one confined to humans that leads to few practical conclusions. As a result of this impasse, apart from helping economists to clarify their concepts, the new welfare economics turned out to be of remarkably little help to policymakers.[42] This impasse led to two different reactions.

The first was widespread skeptical relativism, especially among economists influenced by the tradition of Leon Walras. Joseph Schumpeter went so far as to exclude the whole of political economy from "pure economics," on the grounds that it provides no valid standard for comparing the economic merits of different political systems: "We may indeed prefer the world of modern dictatorial socialism to the world of Adam Smith, or vice versa, but any such preference comes within the same category of subjective evaluation as does, to plagiarize Sombart, a man's preferences for blondes over brunettes. In other words, there is no objective meaning to the term progress in matters of economic policy or any other policy because there is no valid standard for interpersonal comparison."[43]

The second reaction occurred once the new welfare economics had begun to be widely greeted with such skepticism. Economists whose ideas descended from the British school emerged from their temporary eclipse to reassert the old welfare economics but reach a different policy conclusion. In a famous 1960 paper, Ronald H. Coase attempted to start from the same premises as Pigou but, instead of the sweeping redistributions of income that Pigou and his followers had advocated through government taxes and subsidies, to advocate a sweeping reassignment of property rights and legal liability.[44] As Coase summarized in his 1991 Nobel Prize lecture,

> Pigou's conclusion and that of most economists using standard economic theory was, and perhaps still is, that some kind of government action (usually the imposition of taxes) was necessary to restrain those whose actions had harmful effects on others, often termed negative externalities. What I showed . . . was that in a regime of zero transaction costs, an assumption of standard economic theory, negotiations between the parties would lead to those arrangements being made which would maximize wealth and this irrespective of the initial assignment of rights. This is the infamous Coase Theorem, named and formulated

by Stigler, although it is based on work of mine. Stigler argues that the Coase Theorem follows from the standard assumptions of economic theory. Its logic cannot be questioned, only its domain. I do not disagree with Stigler. However, I tend to regard the Coase Theorem as a stepping stone on the way to an analysis of an economy with positive transaction costs. The significance to me of the Coase Theorem is that it undermines the Pigovian system. Since standard economic theory assumes transaction costs to be zero, the Coase Theorem demonstrates that the Pigovian solutions are unnecessary in those circumstances.[45]

However, as Coase ruefully noted, while the Coase theorem's "influence on legal scholarship has been immense," even after several decades, "its influence on economics . . . has not been immense." Coase argued that this was because economists were "extremely conservative in their methods" and because "the concept of transaction costs has not been incorporated into a general theory." But a deeper reason can be found by asking exactly what Coase meant by "standard economic theory," the logic of which "cannot be questioned." Actually, the Coase theorem's assumptions are not standard for all schools of neoclassical economics or even all members of the Chicago school. Partly because of its own peculiar assumptions, but mostly because of premises it borrowed from "the Pigovian system," the Coase theorem is questionable precisely in its logic and impossible to verify.

We can better understand both problems if, when the Coase theorem is mentioned, we are careful to ask, "*Which* Coase theorem?" Coase was awarded his Nobel in economics for two papers, which proposed hypotheses that, as he frankly admitted, he was unable to combine in a single coherent theory. In a 1937 article, Coase had set out "to discover why a [business] firm emerges at all in a specialized exchange economy." He answered with what might be called Coase theorem I: "The main reason why it is profitable to establish a firm would seem to be that there is a cost of using the price mechanism. The most obvious cost of 'organizing' production through the price mechanism is that of discovering what the prices are."[46] The thesis of his more famous 1960 article might be called Coase theorem II: "If market transactions were costless, all that matters (questions of equity apart) is that the rights of the various parties should be well-defined and the results of legal actions easy to forecast."

Thus, Coase theorem I says that business firms exist *only* because there are transaction costs, while Coase theorem II says that if there were no transactions costs, it wouldn't matter whether the firms inflicting or suffering damage were held legally liable—but in that case, according to Coase theorem I, there would be no business firms. The apparent attraction for Stigler and for many legal scholars appears to have been arguing for Coase theorem II while ignoring Coase theorem I, thwarting what Coase himself saw as his main purpose: to *study* rather than *dismiss* the significance of transactions costs.

Part of the apparent contradiction can be resolved by noting that Coase's theory of information was outmoded. That is, by assuming that everyone in a perfectly competitive market would have the same perfect information about all past, present, and future events, and that such information would be costless, Coase theorem II treats transaction costs, particularly the cost of information, as an anomaly, something essentially different from, say, the cost of transportation. Schultz's total capital hypothesis, first published at almost exactly the same time as the (second) Coase theorem, explained that just as the cost of transportation is the compensation we pay to the workers and owners of property who provide the valuable service of transportation to us, the cost of information is simply the compensation we pay to those who provide valuable information to us. In both cases, a service without any cost to anyone would necessarily mean a service without value to anyone.[47]

However, the (second) Coase theorem's fatal problem is that, far from "undermining the Pigovian system," it depends upon that system's erroneous assumption that there can be only *one* optimum distribution of resources. This is why, when Richard Posner and others used the Coase theorem to try to ground the legal distribution of property rights on "efficiency" (i.e., utility), the effort encountered exactly the same two problems that we have already noted in the new welfare economics and will meet again when we discuss Gary Becker's theory of personal and domestic economy. As Ejan Mackaay concisely puts it: "[E]fficiency cannot be the foundation of the distribution of property rights, since for any distribution, an efficient allocation of resources can be found. Hence the efficiency thesis is circular. . . . A second difficulty is that the efficiency thesis appears to be non-falsifiable. Where an apparently inefficient arrangement is found, hitherto unnoticed costs can be called in to account for it. This may be useful as a heuristic, but as a way of theory testing, it does not pass muster."[48]

The Problem in Personal and Domestic Economy

Only relatively recently have economists considered the Mother's Problem in the way that Wicksteed posed it: as the problem of an actual mother. In the past few decades, economist Gary Becker has claimed to have solved it. Becker focused the attention of economists on the long-ignored realities of everyday domestic life, and he did so with analytical rigor, grace, and humor. Unfortunately, in collaboration with George Stigler, Becker turned for philosophical inspiration not to Aristotle or Augustine but to Jeremy Bentham. Becker adopted Bentham's identification of utility with pleasure, then added the assumption that everyone's fundamental preferences for pleasure are identical. In what he and Stigler called the "economic approach to human behavior," Becker tried to prove that all human behavior can be reduced to a matter of utility so understood.

I must begin my comments on the "economic approach" by emphasizing two things.

First, Gary Becker is an economist whose sandals I am unworthy to untie. I choose Becker's version to illustrate the problem with neoclassical economic theory not because it is the worst, but precisely because it is the best. No other version of neoclassical economic theory has been as coherently or completely thought out. And no economist in the last third of the twentieth century was more ingenious in applying economic analysis to daily human life than Gary Becker. Becker's doctoral dissertation was a study of the economics of discrimination against minorities. He showed that discrimination by a majority group reduces both its own and the minority group's income. In the 1960s, Becker pioneered an analysis of crime and punishment that challenged the conclusion that punishments are ineffective in deterring crime. Also in the 1960s, Becker began a fundamental revision of the theory of the household, based on the recognition that households are producers as well as consumers of scarce goods. This led to further inquiries in the 1970s and 1980s about marriage, fertility, child-rearing, and family dynamics. In the 1990s, Becker applied his analyses to habitual and addictive behavior.

The second thing I must emphasize is that Becker strikes me as a humane, humorous, and gentle man. In his footnotes, Becker often generously acknowledges the source of an inspiration, notes a change in his own earlier view, or illustrates a point with an apt quotation from Dickens or The Forsyte Saga or St. Paul or the Wizard of Id. But Becker's work also illustrates the dangers in choosing the wrong premises or assumptions for one's theory.

Assessing Becker's achievements in historical perspective, we might say that when Becker's colleague Theodore W. Schultz rediscovered Aristotle's theory of the household as a producing unit around 1960, Becker aspired to become its foremost theorist. The strength of the "economic approach" is its treatment of household production, which accounts for the theory's fruitfulness in treating economic topics involving "human capital"—the size and useful skills of the population. But in his view of human nature, Becker resorted to Jeremy Bentham, the founder of modern philosophical utilitarianism. (Surprisingly, however, Becker often begins by assuming that humans are identical asexual animals, or even that they are not animals at all.)[49] That choice of philosophical starting point accounts for the weakness of the "economic approach" whenever final distribution is involved, since it attempts to explain two things— the choice of persons as ends (*final distribution*) and the choice of scarce means (*utility*)—as if both could be reduced to utility alone.

To understand these strengths and shortcomings, we must begin by asking why, in Becker's opinion, economic theory was in need of revision. The "traditional" approach of economists, according to Becker, had been to say that consumers derive satisfaction or "utility" directly from products that they purchase in the market from business firms and that in demanding such goods, consumers seek to maximize their satisfaction subject to three constraints: the relative prices of the goods, the limitations of their budgets (income or wealth), and the "tastes and preferences" by which they rank the various goods.

According to Becker, there were two problems with this approach: First, the assumption that households consume only products purchased from business firms was unrealistic. Economists had been making this assumption in order to focus on the specialized nature of the business firm as a producing unit, but in the process they were neglecting the fact that the household produces as well as consumes—most important, it

produces people, as well as other goods. Second, when economists failed
to find sufficient reason to explain household behavior in changes in the
prices of market goods or in household incomes, they resorted all too
quickly to the assumption that people are irrational, or else they presumed that there had been a change in fundamental "tastes." These were
all-purpose excuses, because the source of tastes and preferences, as of
irrationality, was generally agreed to lie beyond the scope of economics.

Becker proposed to solve the two problems in the following way.
First, economists should look beneath the preferences for marketable
products and assume that the demand for such goods is really derived
from a demand for fewer, more fundamental goods, which Becker called
"basic commodities." If utility is derived directly from market goods, it
would seem difficult to explain anything as simple as why households
purchase more fuel oil or natural gas in the winter, when fuel prices are
higher, than in summer, when prices are lower—except by suggesting
that consumers' preferences shift toward fuel oil every winter and back to
other goods during the summer, or that consumers are irrational. But if
households are really demanding, say, a comfortable home environment,
then their underlying preference remains the same year-round. Second,
Becker argued, economists should recognize that households produce
these "basic commodities" for themselves by combining goods purchased
in the market with nonmarket household resources, such as the time not
devoted to earning a money income. And it is from these "basic commodities" that households derive utility.

Becker began with a theory of the allocation of time, which was
founded on the assumption that households "combine time and market
goods to produce more basic commodities that directly enter their utility
functions."[50] In 1973, he took the fateful step of identifying these basic
commodities with the basic pleasures in Jeremy Bentham's philosophy:

> Jeremy Bentham's *Principles of Legislation* in 1789 set out a list
> of fifteen "simple pleasures" which he argued was "the inven-
> tory of our sensations." These pleasures, which were supposed
> to exhaust the list of basic arguments in one's pleasure (i.e., util-
> ity) functions, are of senses, riches, address, friendship, good
> reputation, power, piety, benevolence, malevolence, knowledge,
> memory, imagination, hope, association and relief of pain. Pre-

sumably these pleasures are "produced" partly by the goods purchased in the market sector.[51]

Becker's embrace of Bentham was a fateful step for three reasons. First, it constituted a foray into metaphysics, in which even a future Nobel laureate economist is no more than an amateur, and which should not be undertaken lightly. By taking Bentham as his starting point, Becker was adopting an entire worldview, including Bentham's ideas about the ultimate nature of reality (there is no God) and human nature (man is not a rational animal, but merely a clever animal). Second, this identification of utility with Bentham's list of pleasures discarded the hard-won consensus among economists, finally achieved about 1930, that the equation of utility with pleasure is gratuitous and without scientific foundation.

Finally, the move failed to solve the economic problem with which Becker was dealing. It did not help explain how people are supposed to allocate their resources to satisfy the various pleasures that Bentham, and now Becker, had said are the whole point of human life. Rather than putting forward a theory about how preferences are formed, Becker complained of the absence of such a theory: "If behavioral responses are attributed to differences in tastes, not much more can be said, since there is no useful theory of the formulation of tastes."[52] In place of such a theory, Becker added two further assumptions: that the preferences for basic pleasures are the same for all persons and that they are the same for each person over time. "In the standard theory all consumers behave similarly in the sense that they all maximize the same thing—utility or satisfaction. It is only a further extension then to argue that they all derive that utility from the same 'basic pleasures' or preference function, and differ only in their ability to produce these pleasures.'"[53] "The combined assumptions of [utility-] maximizing behavior, market equilibrium, and stable preferences, used relentlessly and unflinchingly, form the heart of the economic approach as I see it."[54]

Becker's original theory considered the allocation of time among alternate uses only in the present. But Becker extended the analysis to consider the allocation of time and goods over time, including investments in "human capital" (like education) along with labor-force participation and household production and consumption. In *The Economic Approach to Human Behavior* and his *Treatise on the Family*, Becker went further, applying the same methods "to analyze marriage, births, divorce, division of labor in households, prestige and other nonmaterial behavior with the tools and framework for material behavior."[55] "Indeed, I have come to the position that the economic approach is a comprehensive one that is applicable to all human behavior."[56] In *Accounting for Tastes*, Becker extended his analysis to habits and addictions.[57]

According to Becker, "The economic approach to human behavior is not new, even outside the market sector. Adam Smith often (but not always!) used this approach to understand political behavior. Jeremy Bentham was explicit about his belief that the pleasure-pain calculus is applicable to all human behavior: 'Nature has placed mankind under the governance of two sovereign masters, pain and pleasure. It is for them alone to point out what we ought to do, as well as what we shall do. . . . They govern us in all we do, in all we say, in all we think.'"[58] But as we have seen, both historically and logically, a complete description of economic behavior has always required both a *ranking of persons as ends* of economic activity—the distribution function—and a *ranking of scarce goods as means*—the utility function. The "economic approach" attempts to remove the consideration of persons as ends, thus reducing all human behavior to the choice of means (a maximization of utility); and then to reduce utility to the satisfaction of basic pleasures that are assumed to be the same for everyone and unchanging over time.

The neoclassical system, then, as exemplified by Becker's theory, seems to be missing an equation: the one that specifies the *final distribution* of economic goods among persons.[59] This can be interpreted in two ways. The first interpretation is that Becker's system is logically incomplete, having one more variable than the number of equations can explain. This means the system does not have a unique equilibrium, and so the theory cannot fully describe even the simplest action or behavior. The second interpretation is that Becker's system is logically complete, but some of the equations have not been spelled out. Specifically, it could be interpreted as including all four elements of the Scholastic system, plus an additional assumption, that everyone is always selfish.[60] (Becker sometimes appears to stipulate this—for example, in discussing marriage: "Let me emphasize that these results do not assume that men value wives for their own sake, but only consider the value of the output produced by husbands and wives.")[61] But this very "strong" assumption is not required by the logic of economic theory. Its truth or falsity can be established only through an investigation of the facts.

Under either interpretation, the system has a problem. To solve it, Becker proposed what might be called the "Becker-Stigler-Bentham assumptions," which are these: the "final objects of choice" are identified with the "basic commodities" listed in the utility function; these "basic commodities" are said to include persons (for example, "children"); and "tastes" for these "final objects" are assumed to be constants. Note that the Becker-Stigler-Bentham assumptions mean that humans are not free to choose or alter their fundamental preferences, either for commodities or for persons. These peculiar restrictions are necessary to make up for Becker's missing equation, the distribution function.

Becker's University of Chicago colleague George Stigler recognized that these assumptions, if widely accepted, would revolutionize not only microeconomics but the whole relation between economics and the other social sciences. In a joint manifesto issued in 1977, Becker and Stigler outlined the implications: "On the traditional view, an explanation of economic phenomena that reaches a difference in tastes between people or times is the terminus of the argument: the problem is abandoned *at this point* to whoever studies and explains tastes (psychologists? anthropologists? phrenologists? sociobiologists?). On our preferred interpretation, one never reaches this impasse: the economist continues to search for differences in prices or incomes to explain any differences or changes in behavior."[62] Thus, the economist need never cede the argument to the authority of any other discipline. On the contrary, economics would, as it were, colonize and absorb the other social sciences with its logic. Accordingly, Stigler began to call economics "the imperial science."[63] He wrote, "The prospect that economic logic may pervade the study of all branches of human behavior is as exciting as any development in the history of economics, or, for that matter, in the history of science."[64]

The facts of everyday experience—that different people have different fundamental preferences and that the same person can change his preferences profoundly over time—represent no valid objection to the method, according to Becker and Stigler. They ultimately rested their case not on the logic of their set of assumptions but rather on its fruitfulness: "We assert . . . that no other approach of remotely comparable generality and power is available,"[65] a challenge Becker repeated in his

Nobel Prize address.[66] Indeed, a cross-disciplinary review of the literature by Stigler and Becker's University of Chicago colleague Edward P. Lazear in 1999 concluded that "economic imperialism has been successful," at least as measured by the test that "the analyses of the imperialists must influence others."[67]

Despite its undoubted influence, the same two fundamental problems remain: the theory's circular logic and apparent nonfalsifiability. Stigler and Becker argued that theirs "is a thesis that does not permit of direct proof because it is an assertion about the world, not a proposition in logic."[68] How can a thesis be an assertion about the world and yet "not permit of direct proof"? Does this mean the hypothesis cannot be put to a test that would disprove it? Or does it mean that the hypothesis can be tested indirectly but not directly—much as, say, astronomers detect the nature of distant stars and planets that cannot be physically reached by interpreting the information derived from light from or reflected by those bodies? By hypothesis, the "Becker-Stigler-Bentham assumptions" concern "basic commodities," most of which are not observable. How could anyone verify whether preferences for unobservable entities are constant? Moreover, the "basic commodities" are, by hypothesis, never exchanged. How then should their value be expressed? In Becker's theory, the value of market goods is derived from the value of "basic commodities"; but "basic commodities" are valued in terms of market goods.[69]

The problem mushrooms as Becker tries to explain habits and addictions while continuing to insist that underlying preferences remain strictly unchanged, for to do so he must expand the utility function to include (in addition to the "basic commodities") one's "social capital" and "personal capital." At this point, Becker's utility function becomes exactly what he originally said economic theory needed to get rid of—a laundry list that fails to "separate preferences from resources and is instead a hodge-podge."[70]

Not surprisingly, despite the constantly increasing specificity of Becker's models of behavior, researchers seeking to test them have had increasing difficulty in getting them to generate falsifiable, testable theories. On the contrary, the tendency to throw everything but the kitchen sink into the theory appears to have contributed directly to the decline in its empirical usefulness.[71]

In plain language, Becker's solution to the Mother's Problem means that the mother cares for her children for the same reason that she buys a refrigerator or keeps a cat. The mother is explicitly assumed to regard other persons as "commodities" that provide her with a flow of useful services, such as warm feelings or the prospect of financial support in her old age. To account for the obvious facts of human love and hate, Becker redefines love—he prefers the word "altruism"—as the gaining of utility from someone else's utility, and hate as the diminishment of one's utility by someone else's utility. To support this redefinition, he invented the notion of "social income," which he defines as the total income—whether one's own or others'—from which one derives utility. But this double counting of the same income implicitly denies that the goods in question are scarce.

To understand the problem, take a simple example involving a husband and wife. If both were purely selfish, in Becker's terms, each would derive utility only from his or her own direct use of resources. In this case, therefore, each person's "social income" would equal his or her actual income. But the "social income" of an "altruistic" spouse, who is supposed to derive utility from the other spouse's use of resources as well as from his or her own, would exceed his or her actual use of resources. The limit of altruism, according to Becker, is reached when one spouse receives as much utility from the other spouse's consumption as from his or her own. If this were the case, in his view husband and wife would split their income equally. Thus, in the end, according to Becker's theory, as in early British neoclassical welfare economics, *utility* is supposed to determine *final distribution*.

However, this is where economists' headaches with the problems of circular logic and nonverifiability begin. First, the circularity: If the husband gets utility from the wife's utility, and the wife from the husband's utility, then . . . the husband must get utility from the wife's getting utility from her husband's utility and the wife must get utility from the husband's getting utility from his wife's utility, and so on. As Becker admitted, this is an "infinite regress," and limits must be arbitrarily imposed on the permissible degree of "altruism" to prevent nonsensical results (such as infinite utility).[72] That is why Becker must assume that no one can ever receive more utility from another person's consumption than from his or her own—an assumption that is not obviously true.

The other, related problem is verifiability. How could one possibly test such a theory? We've seen that "social income" is supposed to equal actual, measurable income only if both husband and wife are purely selfish. But when both are altruistic, the appropriate measure of "social income" is up to *twice* their actual income. Similarly, in a family of five, the appropriate measure of "social income" would be between one and *five* times their actual income. And in a family with two parents and twelve children—I grew up in such a family—the appropriate measure of "social income" might be anywhere between one and fourteen times the actual income. For empirical researchers, that way lies madness, because it amounts to denying the fact of scarcity,[73] and such huge uncertainties make statistically valid conclusions impossible.

This confronts us with the basic difference in approach between the Scholastics and all modern neoclassical economists. The Scholastics operated with the premise that economics is the study of a certain aspect of *human* action. Unless it is specified that the ends of human action are always persons, these ends fade into the background and an exclusive focus on the choice of scarce means is not only natural but almost inevitable. With this shift in emphasis, economics becomes essentially the study of an aspect of action common to all animal behavior, whether or not one identifies utility with pleasure, as Becker does.

This point did not escape Becker, who wrote, "We could apply the approach equally well to the division of labor, altruism, and other aspects of the family life of different species." (And, in fact, he has done just that.) A typical textbook, *The Theory of Choice: A Critical Guide*, is prefaced with the statement, "Rationality is . . . a matter of means, not of ends. It is a relation of consistency between preferences, information and action."[74] The text immediately proceeds to misquote what it called "Lionel Robbins' famous definition of economics" as "the science which studies the allocation of scarce resources which have alternate uses." Gone from the definition are Robbins's specification of "*human* behavior" and the words "as a relationship between ends and scarce means." The authors also assert, "If we are to claim that our choices are the product of our rationality, then we should be prepared to admit that rats are rational too."

In sum, despite having made some important advances—restoring and updating the theory of utility and deepening our understanding of the theories of production and equilibrium—modern neoclassical economics has some very serious problems of logical inconsistency and empirical inaccuracy, and these faults bear directly on the question of what it means to be human. In the next chapter, we will consider how economists can (and, I believe, will) resolve these problems in coming decades.

Table 4–1

How Comte Revised Aquinas's 'Map' of the Human Person (and Knowledge)*		
Kind of virtue	*Thomas Aquinas:* Disciplines determined by human virtue, scope and method	*Auguste Comte:* No virtues; disciplines by scope only; all same method
Theological	Faith, Hope, & Charity: Revealed theology	*Eliminated (yet 'Sociolatry' in Comte's 'Positive Religion' is 'Worship of Humanity')*
Intellectual	Wisdom: Metaphysics (order of being; includes natural theology)	*Eliminated: 'All things' presumed material*
Rational	Logic (order of human reason)	*Subsumed in mathematics*
Science (= Knowledge of particular kind of being)	Mathematics (being abstracted from matter and motion)	*Same*
	'Mixed' (physico-mathematical) sciences	*Eliminated (along with not yet mathematized sciences, e.g., geology)*
	Physical sciences (being abstracted from matter), e.g., astronomy	'Physics (proper)' Astronomy Chemistry
	Biology (being abstracted from animate matter)	*Moved (see below)*
Practical:		Biology *[= 'Preliminary Sociology']*
Moral:	Prudence (includes Economy):	
Active, toward others	Political Domestic Individual	'Sociology (Proper)'
	Justice: Political: distributive Domestic: distributive Individual: commutative justice, beneficence	'Morals' *[Three theological and four moral virtues replaced by 18 irrational 'propensities,' 'affections,' and 'instincts']*
Active, toward oneself	Fortitude (*re:* aversions) Temperance (*re:* attractions)	*A 'result,' not a 'virtue'* *Eliminated*
Productive	Mechanical and Fine Arts	*Serve 'Positive Polity'*
* Auguste Comte, *The Catechism of Positive Religion*, 187.		

5

Neo-Scholastic Economics (c. 2000–)

The neoclassical period is ending. We will soon witness the emergence of what, for want of a better term, might be called a school of new natural-law or neo-Scholastic economists. This will happen not because economists will have drawn back in horror at the philosophical implications of their prevailing theory, but simply because the various strains of neoclassical theory fail to explain the empirical facts of human economic behavior. The neo-Scholastic economists will resemble the Scholastics by being the first economists in more than two centuries to integrate all four elements of economic theory, but they will also not hesitate to take advantage of the technical advances that have added to our understanding of each element. The neo-Scholastic approach will retain the modernized theories of (ordinal) utility and (general) equilibrium and the cumulative advances in the theory of production (which recognize human and nonhuman capital, and each in both its tangible and intangible forms). But above all, neo-Scholastic economics will devise a modernized mathematical version of the Scholastic theory of final distribution—specifically, one that incorporates descriptions of personal gifts (and crimes) and of distributive justice in the family, business firm, charitable foundation, and government. Those economists who choose to pursue this project can expect full employment for at least a generation because of the rewriting of existing economic theory that this will require, because of the work of challenging defenders of the status quo to empirical tests, and because of the need to apply neo-Scholastic analysis to public policy.

Economic theory will have to be rewritten at three levels: personal economy, domestic economy, and political economy.

Personal Economy

The conceptual problem with all varieties of the neoclassical approach is that love cannot be based on utility (as Augustine was the first to explain), for the simple reason that utility is derived from love. The neo-Scholastic approach will be based on the premise that all human action is ultimately motivated not by utility but by love for some person or persons. The double nature of love for rational animals is illustrated by G. K. Chesterton's remark that "a man is fortunate in marrying the woman he loves, but he is even more fortunate in loving the woman he marries." The first kind of love is an emotion: a deep or passionate affection. The second kind of love is an act of the rational will, which may coincide with, be unrelated to, or even run contrary to the emotion of affection. What remains the same is the decision to give goods of a certain value to a certain person in proportion to the other person's relative significance to the giver. Only animals can love in the first way, only persons can love in the second way, and only human persons—as rational animals—can love in both ways at once. Neoclassical economic theory can describe only the first kind of love.

An outline of the neo-Scholastic solution to the Mother's Problem should be clear from our earlier discussion of Scholastic economic theory. Instead of always doing only one thing—maximizing the utility to herself of various persons and things—a mother is always doing two things: weighing the importance to herself of persons as ends, and of things like milk as means to serve those persons. She solves the problem of allocating quantities of milk essentially by multiplying the relative significance of each *user* of milk, times her estimate of the value of each *use* of milk to those persons. She distributes milk or other scarce goods only to those who have a positive significance to her, and she does so in proportion to their relative significance. This means that almost everyone in the world receives a zero significance. Rather than *increasing* the mother's utility, her love determines how much value or utility to herself of the scarce means she is willing to *sacrifice*. But her ability to sacrifice is inherently limited, since the more she distributes to others, the scarcer and thus more valuable each remaining unit becomes to herself. Love always involves sacrifice. This not only accords with common sense; it also makes economic theory both simpler and empirically verifiable, since all income is counted only once.

In other words, altruism—understood as the opposite of egoism—is not the same as love, because love of self is always present along with love for other persons, and love for some person is always the source of the value of any goods used by *any* person. As we noted in discussing Scholastic economics, the difference between a gift and an exchange is that the person who receives a gift is the end or purpose of the gift, which expresses the significance of the recipient to the giver. In a pure exchange, the persons who are the ultimate ends or purposes intended by each party do not coincide, but the means the two have chosen to pursue these different ends do coincide. Both parties try to advance their own different ends indirectly, by exchanging scarce means that each considers less valuable for scarce means each considers more valuable—more valuable, that is, to the persons who are the ends of his or her action.

If the neo-Scholastic approach implies a new economic description of everything related to love (such as fertility, worship, bequests, and charitable contributions, etc.), it also suggests a new theory of hate: for example, of crime. The predominant economic approach to crime starts with the assumption that everyone has the same basic preferences but that some people commit crimes because the utility of their prospective rewards for crime happens to outweigh the prospective losses of utility from the probable penalties of getting nabbed. Though rewards and penalties are not insignificant, the existing theory cannot explain why the vast majority of people, even in poor socioeconomic environments, do not commit crimes. And if the theory were true, the crime rate would never change except when the rewards and penalties for crime changed. The hypothesis can be salvaged only by turning it into a tautology: if people don't commit crimes, it must be because they receive a net benefit from abstaining.

The neo-Scholastic hypothesis is that crime, like love, is essentially not a weighing of *utilities* but a weighing of *persons:* thus, it is always a moral decision. If love means distributing some good to some person and selfishness means distributing all of one's goods to oneself (giving everyone else a zero significance in that distribution), a crime consists in depriving some person of a good that belongs to him or her—giving that person a *negative* significance in the distribution of goods. There will be many opportunities to test the two approaches empirically. For example, the neo-Scholastic approach implies that there should be an inverse simultaneous relationship between the birth rate and the homicide rate, since these involve diametrically opposite attitudes toward other persons; the "economic approach to human behavior" predicts no such relationship. (As I will show in part 2, "Personal Economy," the inverse relationship between the birth rate and homicide rate is indeed strong.)

Domestic Economy

The theory of the household and its offshoots (the business firm and non-profit foundation) will have to be rewritten in light of the neo-Scholastic approach to personal economy. The basic idea behind the prevailing economic approach is that the fundamental reason the household exists is to provide for a division of labor. Two adults are assumed to get married or live together (Gary Becker's theory is designed to apply equally to homosexual and heterosexual relationships) because each can thereby increase his or her utility, interpreted as pleasure or satisfaction. If the interests and abilities of the two differ even slightly, according to this theory, it will be of mutual benefit for them to agree that one should specialize in earning cash by providing services outside the household, while the other specializes in providing services directly to the household. The relationship between the two persons is then said to consist of explicit or implicit exchanges of such goods as cash, warm feelings, sex, security, and material benefits. People get divorced or stop living together, in this view, when the utility of the arrangement to each party falls below the utility that could be obtained in some other relationship.

The division-of-labor argument can explain the existence and economics of hotels, brothels, and dormitories, but not the universal prevalence of the family household. The neo-Scholastic theory of the household differs in two ways. First, it begins with the premise that the main economic purpose of the household is the reproduction, education, and maintenance of human beings. This means that the household is essentially an arrangement built around marriage, the union between a man and a woman. If it weren't, all households and persons would cease to exist within a single human lifetime. At any moment, a large fraction of adults live in households without a partner. Though partly due to the increased rate of divorce, this is mostly the result of increased longevity, which causes people to spend more years obtaining a formal education, to marry later, and to survive their spouses, all for many more years than when life was shorter. When viewed over a lifetime, the vast majority of single-person households occur either before or after married life. More than 96 percent of American adults have been married by age sixty-five, and about 90 percent have had children. Neoclassical economics cannot explain why so many people choose to get married, nor can it accurately predict how many children they will have. The latter failure, we will see, results because it is empirically false to assume that everyone's preferences are either the same or purely selfish. Including our preferences for people is logically necessary in a theory of fertility (the reproduction of people), and doing so removes most of the inaccuracy in the existing neoclassical theory of fertility.

Second, the neo-Scholastic view is that marriage is better viewed in economic terms as a series of mutual gifts than as exchanges. Under normal circumstances, it is sometimes difficult to distinguish the two, but the difference becomes obvious when an event occurs that affects married persons unequally—for example, an accident or illness that disables one while leaving the other unimpaired. If the relationship were based solely on utility (even vicarious, altruistic utility), the higher cost of living for one spouse would result in there being relatively fewer real household resources devoted to that spouse. But if the relationship were one of mutual gifts, the unimpaired spouse would naturally reduce his or her own use of resources so far as was necessary to maintain the same proportion in the distribution of real resources as reflected the significance of the other person relative to him- or herself. Once again, the neo-Scholastic theory both agrees with common sense and is empirically testable. In the prevailing theory of the household, domestic life is a series of exchanges, a market; in the neo-Scholastic view, domestic life is recognized as an *oasis* from the market, in which many if not most actions are gifts rather than exchanges.

At the same time, the neo-Scholastic approach will occasion a revised theory of the business firm. Ronald Coase, as we have seen, suggests that business firms exist to minimize the costs of market transactions, and this theory has merit. But like Becker, he has no theory of the household and describes nonprofit foundations as a kind of business firm. The neo-Scholastic approach suggests instead that both the business firm and nonprofit foundation can best be understood as specialized offshoots of the family household. The modern household specializes in producing and maintaining people, the modern business firm in producing and maintaining property, and the modern nonprofit foundation in distributing household gifts beyond the household. Because of these different specific functions, each institution will tend to employ different kinds of transactions. Families use mostly gifts internally (though also externally with nonprofit foundations), but mostly exchange goods and services with business firms.

Political Economy

The theory of political economy will also have to be rewritten. The prevailing theory in welfare economics, as we have seen, is that politicians preside over society in the same way that a parent presides over the household. But the *polis* differs from the household, as Aristotle states on the first page of the *Politics*, "not merely in size but in kind."[1] The fact of scarcity is central to the decisions of both, but the implications are different. Scarcity means that a mother can *not* treat similar persons alike. She cannot possibly feed all hungry children, only a few, which are usually (though not necessarily) her own. The fact of scarcity also means that a politician cannot care for all hungry children, any more than can the mother. He (and, indirectly, a voter) may be able to help those babies who are hungry because neither their mothers nor anyone else is able to provide for them, but justice requires that he must treat them all exactly alike—unlike a mother.

The neo-Scholastic approach offers a principled method of constructively criticizing existing theories of distributive justice. For example, it shows that scarcity creates an asymmetry between what some political scientists call "negative rights" (like the right to remain unharmed in one's own person and property) and "positive rights" (such as the entitlement to a certain level of income, or a guaranteed bundle of services, like health insurance). Enforcement of negative rights is inherently practicable, because to refrain from harming another person incurs no cost; the only cost lies in the actual enforcement. Positive rights, in contrast, can never extend farther than the ability to pay for them: no matter how often or how loudly they are proclaimed, they remain empty if sufficient scarce resources are not actually set aside for the purpose.[2]

The capacity for voluntary and socially organized redistribution of wealth is always limited by the fact of scarcity, as the Scholastic economists recognized. Absolute equality of wealth or income is neither practically possible nor useful to society, since it would require abolishing private property and its advantages (as opposed to communism) of greater productivity, order, and social peace.

What is more significant, the neo-Scholastic approach offers a principled method for deciding what *should* be done. As we have seen, the deepest problem in political economy today is not that prevailing theories are unsatisfactory but rather that no principled theory of public policy is compatible with neoclassical economic theory. Neoclassical economic theory therefore offers no set of principles for deciding the most ordinary political questions affecting income distribution, such as whether the government should tax income or consumption, or whether specific deductions like the personal exemption ought to exist at all and, if so, how large they ought to be. The logical political counterpart to neoclassical economic theory, which attempts to reduce everything to utility, is realpolitik, which reduces everything to raw political power. Policymaking, in this view, is merely the result of the relative balance of power between those political factions which stand to gain or lose from the policy decisions. The theory of "public choice" has made this Hobbesian premise explicit.

The practical consequences can be observed in American government, which I was able to closely observe for ten years as a congressional staffer for the Republican caucus in the U.S. House of Representatives and intermittently since as an adviser to both U.S. and foreign economic policymakers. Both major political parties have theories of economic policy that are often little more than thinly disguised special-interest pleading. Generally speaking, the Democratic Party represents the interests of persons who have significantly more human capital and own less property than average: not just union members and recipients of government benefits but also members of the news and entertainment media, health-care professionals, college professors, government employees, and trial lawyers. The Republican Party tends to represent the economic interests of those who own significantly more property and relatively less human capital than average: not just those with inherited wealth and members of the National Association of Manufacturers but also the thriftiest middle-class families, owners of mom-and-pop small businesses on Main Street, and retirees whose incomes depend on savings invested in stocks and bonds.

Neither party today has a coherent theory for determining economic policy. The practice of each is to tax the constituents of the other party while favoring its own constituents. In the Republican Party, the prevailing theory defines tax neutrality as a tax code that exempts property income while taxing only labor compensation. In the Democratic Party, tax fairness is defined so that any change must increase the progressivity of the tax burden—which, given the nature of income distribution, relatively advantages labor compensation and disadvantages property income.

As we shall see, neo-Scholastic theory offers, in contrast, a principled method for settling economic policy questions. For example, as an adviser to the 1995–96 National Commission on Economic Growth and Tax Reform, I applied the general principles I have described here to argue that since all income originates as either labor compensation or property compensation, on grounds of both equity and efficiency the two ought to be treated alike for tax purposes. Practically speaking, this means that the tax code ought to tax income rather than consumption (as long as the definition of investment is restricted to the purchase of plant or equipment). It also suggests that there ought to be a presumption in favor of the continued existence and size of the standard deductions and personal exemption, since these serve the economic purpose of human maintenance, analogous to the deductions for maintenance of plant and equipment. The same principles also argue in favor of keeping pay-as-you-go Social Security retirement pensions and against replacing the system with private retirement accounts that can be invested only in stocks and bonds. Other policy analysts, of course, are free to challenge both my reasoning and my grasp of the empirical facts. But I maintain that the theory I have described offers a coherent method for deciding such questions, which is absent from modern political economy because of its very premises. We'll explain why this is the case in part 4, "Political Economy."

Having no theory of final distribution, neoclassical economic theory is unable to describe the nature of justice. This is reflected in the confusion over both Pigou's theory of externalities and the Coase theorem. Neither is able to describe the final distribution of wealth before or after the redistribution of property that Pigou proposed to effect through taxes and subsidies and Coase through changes in legal liability. I believe that this is the main reason why, as one survey concluded, "our understanding of the nature and importance of externality has advanced very little over the last 100 years."[3]

Coase illustrated his paper with colorful examples of negative externalities, including one that figured largely in a famous discussion in which Coase convinced twenty other economists to adopt his position. As George Stigler recounted,

> The argument turned on a picturesque example Coase had used. A cattle rancher lives next to a grain farmer, and occasionally the cattle of the rancher invade the fields and damage the grain of the farmer. Does it make any difference in the number of cattle maintained and the amount of grain grown, whether the cattle rancher is responsible for the damage to the grain or the grain farmer is responsible? The Coase answer is: No! One way of making Coase's answer plausible is to ask what will happen if both the grain farm and the cattle ranch are owned by the same person. That single owner should combine the two operations to achieve the largest profit. If, for example, adding another head of cattle raises cattle profits by $100 but lowers grain profits by $120, he won't add that head of cattle. Similarly, he will decide on building a fence only if the savings over the years fully compensate for the cost of the fence. But separate owners of the grain farm and the cattle ranch can achieve exactly this best solution by contract, and they will be led to do so because then they will have a larger pie to divide. The assignment of legal liability for the grain damage will determine who pays whom, but it will not affect the best way to conduct grain farming or cattle ranching.[4]

Coase's example is supposed to show a negative externality—a harm done by the livestock rancher to the grain grower. Actually, it involves both positive and negative externalities, a fact overlooked by all the economists involved in the discussion, including several future Nobel laureates. We can see this by adopting Stigler's suggestion of considering first what we might call the situation's *internalities*—the negative and positive factors affecting profits if there were a single owner of both operations instead of two—before inquiring into the sweeping redistribution of property Coase proposed by a change in legal liability.

According to the essayist Wendell Berry, a similar case involved a farmer named Lancie Clippinger, who purchased a 175-acre farm of which all croppable area had been used by the previous owner to raise a single crop (corn) with equipment like tractors, buildings, and chemical fertilizer.[5] It might seem that such specialization and methods would be the most efficient use of the land (as all economists discussing the Coase case assumed). But Clippinger realized that the farm had failed financially because it was *too* specialized and too dependent on expensive purchased resources for the scale of its operation ever to turn a profit. He therefore converted the same land to raising a diversified selection of livestock (pigs and draft horses) and crops (corn, oats, and alfalfa). Instead of a tractor, he used some of the horses for plowing and planting, part of the crops to feed the livestock, and crop rotation and livestock manure to sharply reduce fertilizer purchases. But most interesting of all was how Clippinger turned what Coase and the other economists assumed to be a "negative externality," or cause of loss, into a "positive internality," or cause of profit:

> Lancie, that year, had planted forty acres of corn; he had also bred forty gilts that he had raised so that their pigs would be ready to feed when the corn would be ripe. The gilts produced 360 pigs, an average of nine per head. When the corn was ready for harvest, Lancie divided off a strip of the field with an electric fence and turned in the 360 shoats. After the shoats had fed on the strip for a while, Lancie opened a new strip for them. He then picked the strip where they had just fed. In that way, he fattened his 360 shoats and also harvested all the corn he needed for his other stock. . . . [I]nstead of harvesting the corn mechanically, hauling it, storing it, grinding it, and hauling it to the shoats, he let the shoats harvest and grind it for themselves. He had the use of the whole hog, whereas in a "confinement operation," the hogs' feet, teeth, and eyes have virtually no use and produce no profit.[6]

In this way, Clippinger soon turned the farm from a substantial loss to a substantial profit.

The example shows that whether livestock eating grain causes economic loss or profit depends on its timing and degree, and does so in ways that, even in this very simple case, a roomful of professors of economics was unable to anticipate. Coase was correct in believing that in his example an error cannot be undone by taxing all livestock ranchers to subsidize corn growers, or vice versa. But he was wrong in thinking that it can be remedied by decreeing that all livestock ranchers should be allowed to sue corn growers for losses, or vice versa.

Unlike the neoclassical theory, the neo-Scholastic approach is able to describe the economic nature of the justice necessary to render to each his or her own, which is based on a proportion between the value of goods and the significance of the persons among whom they are distributed. We employ distributive justice to distribute our common goods, always in proportion to the relative significance of the persons (just as with personal gifts). But we use "rectificatory" justice to distribute our individually owned goods, always "according to arithmetical proportion. For it makes no difference whether a good man has defrauded a bad man or a bad man a good one," as Aristotle observed; "the law looks only to the distinctive character of the injury, and treats the parties as equal."[7] Rectificatory justice may be either voluntary, as in the case of exchanges, or involuntary, as in cases of theft, violence, or negligence.

Pesch's Seminal Half-Step Toward Neo-Scholastic Economics

Heinrich Pesch (1854–1926) profoundly affected the expression of official Roman Catholic social doctrine after it was inaugurated by Pope Leo XIII in his 1891 encyclical *Rerum Novarum*. Yet only excerpts of the German Jesuit economist's major works—*Liberalism, Socialism and Christian Social Order* and *Lehrbuch der Nationalökonomie* (Teaching Guide to Economics)—had been translated into English until the Edwin Mellen Press published full translations between 2000 and 2006. Their publication affords us the opportunity not only to assess Pesch's role in launching, but also glimpse the surprising prospect of completing, the project of realigning modern economics with the Scholastic natural law in which it began.

How can we begin to grasp a corpus exceeding 6,000 pages (the *Lehrbuch* and *Liberalism* are half again longer than Thomas Aquinas's *Summa theologiae* and *Summa contra gentiles*, respectively), the contro-

versy with libertarian economists over Pesch's "solidarist" economic theory, and the fact that Pesch got the original Scholastic economic theory
almost but not quite right? We must start by clearing the ground of debris
strewn by decades of brawling admirers and detractors.

Pesch's admirers are typified by Richard E. Mulcahy, who claimed
in *The Economics of Heinrich Pesch* (1952) that "Pesch is the first theorist
who constructed an integrated economic theory based on Aristotelian-
Thomistic philosophy."[8] Its publisher similarly calls the *Lehrbuch* "a kind
of *Summa Economica*." Actually, as we've seen, the first theorist who constructed an integrated economic theory based on Thomistic philosophy
was Thomas Aquinas, whose outline was taught and developed at the
highest university level for five centuries before Adam Smith. The term
Aristotelian-Thomistic flags the debility that prevented Pesch from producing a modern summary of Scholastic economics: its neglect of a central feature, St. Augustine's theory of personal gifts.

Though extraordinarily fruitful, the Thomistic revival of the late
nineteenth and early twentieth centuries in which Pesch participated was
burdened by a neo-Thomism that viewed Aquinas as restating an essentially Aristotelian philosophy. As I have suggested, the formula of Scholastic economics, is Aristotle + Augustine = Aquinas. The neo-Thomist
formula, on the other hand, is "AA economics": Aristotle = Aquinas
(= Catholic social doctrine. Which raises the obvious question: After
Aristotle, why do we need Aquinas or Catholic social doctrine?). Neo-
Thomism and probably Pesch himself influenced the erroneous state-
ments in Joseph Schumpeter's otherwise valuable *History of Economic
Analysis* (1954) that Aquinas's economics was "strictly Aristotelian" and
that Augustine "[n]ever went into economic problems."

Pesch's most famous detractor was the Viennese economist Ludwig
von Mises (1881–1973), who in 1922 condemned Scholastic economics and modern Christian social reform as irremediable "state socialism,"
singling out Leo XIII, Pius XI, and above all Pesch for obloquy:

> The protagonists of Christian social reform as a rule do not
> regard their ideal Society of Christian Socialism as in any way
> socialistic. But this is simply self-deception. . . . Where private
> property exists, only market prices can determine the formation
> of income. To the degree in which this is realized, the Christian

social reformer is step by step driven to Socialism, which for him can be only State Socialism.[9]

Perhaps the simplest way to adjudge these interpretive differences is to focus on an atypically succinct bit of economics from the *Lehrbuch:*

> In a communistic community, let us say, for example, in a familial community, a portion of the annual product is turned over by the head of the community to the various members so that they may have it for their consumption. Other goods like land, tools, seed, etc., remain in the possession of the head of the family or the family as a whole, however one wishes to view it. . . . In a society with a market economy based on private ownership of the means of production, the owner of such goods, after products are sold, gets to recover out-of-pocket costs along with a return for his own contribution of effort and materials. The portion of return which he uses to support himself as befits his station in life, that represents his consumable property which he may dispose of freely.[10]

As far as it goes, this is a reasonably accurate rendition of Scholastic economic theory. Pesch describes the family as a "communistic community" because like the best economists of his time, he distinguished socialism, a system in which the means of production are collectively owned, from communism, in which the means of both production and consumption are collectively owned. Though stated in prose, the passage could be recast as a system of four simultaneous empirical equations: the first describing Aristotle's theory of production (from the *Politics*); the second (from Aristotle's *Ethics*) describing the exchange by which selling services and products provides the family's labor and property income; the third (also from the *Ethics*) describing the "geometric ratio" of distributive justice by which consumption of common goods is distributed; and the fourth (from Augustine's *City of God*, less explicit here) explaining that market prices of products, and indirectly the compensation of their producers, are derived from the ultimate consumers' preferences ("utility"). Pesch adapts the same "model" to describe government finance, the income of which (in a system based on private property) is derived mostly from taxing households' labor and property income, while goods and services acquired as "common wealth" are distributed by a formula just like the family's. Production, exchange, distribution, and consumption: The four basic elements of Scholastic economic theory first integrated by Aquinas are neatly combined at the domestic and political levels.

In doing so, Pesch points to most of what Adam Smith's classical and modern neoclassical economic theory omitted, and what Catholic social doctrine means by criticizing "collectivism" and "individualism." On the one hand, socialist (especially Marxist) theorists propose to abolish private property (and thus its exchange), collapsing all justice to distributive justice—as if all wealth were common and political, like one big household. That's collectivism. The socialist slogan "from each according to his ability, to each according to his needs" isn't a bad description of family economics; but as Aquinas explained (building on Aristotle), it fails as a method of organizing society by ignoring the fact of scarcity. On the other hand, since Adam Smith's classical economics eliminated the theories of distribution and utility, while later "neoclassical" economists restored only the latter, classical and all schools of neoclassical economics (including Mises's Austrian theory) collapse justice to justice in exchange—as if all wealth were personal and exchanged but never given. That's individualism.

This was the premise of Mises's assertion, "Where private property exists, only market prices can determine the formation of income." This is wrong because of the usually false assumption that any goods produced and exchanged, e.g., by Pesch's head of household, are consumed by that person. Though usually implicit, Mises made this assumption explicit when he wrote, "Where each household is economically self-sufficient, the privately owned means of production exclusively serve the proprietor. He alone reaps all the benefits derived from their employment."[11] It amounts to the claim that there are neither personal gifts nor common goods to be distributed: no families, foundations, governments, or for that matter, business firms. Technically, it also reflects the fact that classical and all schools of neoclassical economics are logically incomplete by having at least one (in Smith's and Mises's cases, two) explanatory equation fewer than variables to explain. Rather than *one* optimal distribution toward which Smith and Mises assumed a free market inevitably tends, there is *at least one* for every possible distribution of wealth or income.

Without a theory of distribution, Smith, Mises, and their followers therefore cannot fully describe but rather can only prescribe reality: so many *Kathederindividualisten*, as it were, as dogmatically obtuse as the *Kathedersozialisten* ("socialists of the [professorial] chair") against whom the early Austrians rightly railed more than a century earlier.

Historian Allan Carlson has described several efforts in the past century to find "third ways" between capitalism and communism, notably including the distributism inspired by the "Chesterbelloc": G. K. Chesterton and Hilaire Belloc.[12] What the distributists grasped clearly, as classical and neoclassical economists who opposed them usually did not, is that a broad distribution of productive property is a prior condition, not the inevitable outcome, of a properly functioning market economy, for which vigorous regulation against monopoly is necessary. Yet Carlson's pessimistic conclusion is that "By the 1990s, the search for a third way economy was over. One reason was that the 'Second Way' of communism had dissolved around the globe. . . . With only one of the mega-combatants still standing, the quest for a Third Way became illogical."[13]

We'll return to the question of exactly what is meant by a "third way" in this book's final chapter on divine economy. Yet the prognosis even for distributism in its original agrarian version, with the slogan "three acres and a cow," may be more hopeful than its own proponents suppose.[14] As we saw in the case of Lancie Clippinger, agricultural efficiency and profitability depend on using methods appropriate to the scale of the operation, and it is quite possible to be *too* specialized and *too* dependent on machinery and other purchased inputs to be profitable. This suggests that as long as laws are not actively biased in favor of large agribusinesses, it should be possible for family farms like Lancie Clippinger's to thrive alongside agribusinesses.

During and after the Second World War a group of European "neo-liberals," notably including Wilhelm Röpke in Germany and Jacques Rueff in France, while agreeing with Mises's and Friedrich Hayek's critical analyses of political socialism and communism, differed sharply from their "methodological individualism" by clearly stating the theory of distributive justice within the family; in fact, they argued that the family is the largest unit in which communism actually works! For example, Rueff wrote:

[N]o human agency can realistically be expected to cope with an economic situation involving a group larger than the average household. For in the family unit the price mechanism does not apply. Here, the father—accurately and constantly informed of the needs of each member of the family, and at the same time fully aware of his resources and, therefore, of the total value of the commodities available in his commonwealth—decides to what extent individual needs may be satisfied. Likewise, his up-to-the-minute knowledge of the productive capacity of the members of his group enables him to apportion the tasks, and the fruits of the joint effort will be pooled and put to the best use in the common interest. At this level, "management" is fairly simple. The head of the family is armed with all the necessary facts, and his undisputed natural leadership ensures that his well-grounded decisions will be respected. It follows, therefore, that the communist system is best suited to the nature and size of the universe over which the family head rules.[15]

Like Pesch and unlike the libertarian Austrians, then, Rueff incorporated Aristotle's theory of distributive justice.

Similarly, Röpke offered a genuine economic theory of what he called "the simplest and most genuine of communities, the Family . . . which derives from monogamous marriage and which is the original and imperishable basis of every higher community."[16] Because of its inherently intergenerational nature, the family is also the primary unit for preserving any tradition or culture. Röpke's theory of distribution was well integrated at the domestic and political levels.[17] In an important passage in *A Humane Economy* he explains, "To be in want means to be in a situation, for whatever reasons, in which we lack the means of subsistence and are unable to procure them by current earnings because we are ill or unemployed or bankrupt or too young or too old. . . . If we think it through carefully, we live in times of need by consuming what someone else produces but does not himself consume. . . . By what title the needy draw on the current flow of production is quite another question."[18] With this simple device Röpke goes on to simply yet comprehensively categorize all such provision for need as either "self-providence" (e.g., saving or insurance) or "extraneous relief," the latter being either "voluntary" (e.g., "borrow or accept charity or the help of my family or some other group") or "compulsory" (e.g., "public old age pensions, health insurance, accident insurance, widows' benefits, unemployment relief"). Since these forms of individual and collective providence are substitutes for one another, Röpke argues, the methods must be preferred in this order to avoid impairing the ability and willingness of persons, families, and other human groups to fulfill their proper responsibilities.[19]

Yet Pesch's, the neoliberals', distributists', and other third-way theories all fell short of theoretical sufficiency, not because they followed Aquinas too closely, as Mises asserted, but because they didn't follow him quite closely enough. We saw that Pesch's "model" involves an indefinite number of households, each comprising one head and usually unspecified other members. But that's a theory of the family without marriage or personal gifts, both of which are central to Scholastic economic theory. Pesch, Rueff, and Röpke do mention wives and mothers, but not their central role in domestic economy. Even if we assumed that each household were headed by a widower who produced all the family's valuable goods and services, while other members were dependent children who only consumed them, these third-way theories would remain incomplete because of the question left unanswered: Where did all the human and nonhuman wealth, the source of the family's labor and property income, come from? Since the family's most valuable asset is the parents' so-called human capital, which is not collectively owned (and thus not explained by distributive justice), the only possible answer is *a personal gift*. As Augustine first systematically explained, all persons are motivated by love, which is essentially a scale of preference for persons, and we human persons express love with gifts distributing our scarce goods in proportion to our love for each person relative to ourselves.

Since no one clearly identified these differences, both sides in the libertarian-solidarist controversy resorted to loose and inaccurate metaphors. The libertarians' were borrowed from physical sciences, such as Mises's assertion of economic "laws" governing a "price mechanism" that powered an "evenly rotating economy"; while Pesch claimed Aquinas's authority for the biological metaphor of society as a "moral organism." Yet Aquinas takes pains to avoid such confusion: his *Commentary on Aristotle's* Nicomachean Ethics and *On Kingship* both dwell on the fact that every purely human society faces the constant threat of disunion precisely because it is a "unity of order" rather than an organism.[20]

Both sides in the controversy were equally handicapped by having developed their theories before Theodore W. Schultz reinvented Aristotle's theory of production, coining the term *human capital* to describe investments in people (particularly formal education) and "nonhuman capital" for investments in property.[21] Chesterton, Belloc, Mises, Hayek, Rueff, and Röpke[22] all became financially comfortable not by investing in property according to their respective economic theories but rather chiefly from the return on investment in their so-called human capital. For example, Chesterton acquired his Beaconsfield suburban villa and Belloc his Kings Land farm through writing, not farming. A complete "neo-Scholastic" economic theory must therefore combine the theory of distribution at the personal, domestic, and political levels with Schultz and Kendrick's updated version of Aristotle's theory of production (along with the theories of consumption and exchange, which are accepted by most versions of neoclassical economic theory).

Neo-Thomism also failed to avoid being contaminated by the welter of nineteenth-century historicist theories of everything, particularly Sir Henry Maine's Whiggish thesis that all human society inexorably progresses from relations of "status" based on family kinship to individual "contract." Maine's thesis was first published three years before Bishop Emmanuel von Ketteler's clarion "The Labor Question and Christianity" (1864), which though rightly critical of individualistic classical economics, uncritically accepted Maine's status-to-contract thesis and attributed its cause to "occupational freedom."[23] As we saw in describing Scholastic economics, Maine's theory also inspired Sir William Ashley to misrepresent Aquinas in 1888 as having based the Scholastic just price on "the standard of comfort which public opinion recognized as appropriate to [each producer's] class." Many libertarian Catholics have claimed the opposite: that the just price is based purely on justice in exchange, interpreted as the market price.

These differences are first of all matters of positive (factually descriptive), not normative (prescriptive) economics. There can have been no inexorable shift from "status to contract" such as Maine asserted, for the simple reason Aquinas gave when he combined Aristotle's and Augustine's insights: All human societies in all ages are based on *both* status *and* contract. In both Augustine's description of personal gifts and Aristotle's description of distributive justice, parties to the transactions may and do receive unequal shares based on differing "status"; but in all exchanges, whether involving shiny-pebble-for-coconut barter or sophisticated modern financial derivatives, both the status of transacting persons and values exchanged are equal in a competitive market. Rereading Pesch's example, we see that the income received by the head of household for his labor and property services is set solely by exchange (commutative justice), but in distributing the goods acquired with that income he can and does take into account everyone's "station in life" (for example, in buying himself business suits that are more expensive than the children's play clothes). Similarly, governments may tax households with higher labor incomes and fewer children to supplement the wages of those with lower earnings and more children; and when properly designed, such a "family wage" doesn't cause unemployment, pace Mises. So the just wage is based neither solely on distributive nor solely on commutative justice: in a competitive market the *pretax* wage is based on commutative justice; but personal love and distributive justice, expressed by personal and family gifts, not just taxes and social benefits, are indispensable (as Pope Benedict XVI noted in the encyclicals *Deus Caritas Est* and *Caritas in Veritate*).[24]

Like Moses, Pesch could lead others to the border of the Promised Land without entering himself. But I predict that in coming decades we will witness a revolution in secular economics like the one that started in the 1870s when three neoclassical economists dissatisfied with failures of classical economics rediscovered Augustine's theory of utility and began reintegrating it with the theories of production and exchange that classical economics had retained. This time, "neo-Scholastic" economists dissatisfied with the many empirical failures of neoclassical theory will complete the restoration of Aquinas's Scholastic outline by reintegrating not only Aristotle's theory of distributive justice, as Pesch did, but also Augustine's theory of personal gifts (and crimes), which Pesch omitted.

Supply-side economics. It would seem odd if I did not mention supply-side economics. After all, my own interest in economics began when I reviewed Jude Wanniski's supply-side manifesto *The Way the World Works* in 1978, and it was my privilege and delight to serve as then-Congressman Jack Kemp's speechwriter and economist during the decade from 1979 through 1988, when he persuaded Ronald Reagan to adopt supply-side tax policies and helped implement them in both Reagan's presidential administrations.[25] (I benefited from following or working with many excellent economists, most of whom served in key positions in the Reagan Treasury, White House, the U.S. Congress or Senate, or in Kemp's circle of advisers.)[26]

Wanniski adapted the term *supply-side economics* from economist Herbert Stein, who coined the term *supply-side fiscalism* to distinguish the theories of economists (notably Robert A. Mundell and Arthur Laffer) who departed from the dominant Keynesian theory, which focused chiefly on total demand rather than supply. Wanniski wrote that supply-side economics is "nothing more than classical economics in modern garb."[27] But like John Maynard Keynes, Wanniski and other supply-siders did not distinguish classical and neoclassical from Scholastic economics according to the clear distinctions I have drawn in this book. As we have seen, Adam Smith's (and Karl Marx's) classical economics abandoned the Scholastic theory of utility and tried instead to rely on the so-called labor theory of value, while all varieties of neoclassical economics use the theory of marginal utility, an updated version of the earlier Scholastic theory. Supply-side economics shares with Smith's classical economics the preoccupation with production and economic growth.[28] But because its theory of incentives relies squarely on the theory of marginal utility, and the leading supply-side economist, Robert A. Mundell, based his own theory explicitly on that of neoclassical economist Leon Walras, supply-side economics is actually a variety of neoclassical, not classical economics.

The theory of American public choice. Finally, neo-Scholastic theory offers a solution to the troubles that have plagued the alternate versions of public-choice economics, beginning with their circular logic and premises, which are either false or nonfalsifiable.

In the first place, neo-Scholastic economic theory allows us to adapt Buchanan's succinct but inaccurate definition of public choice in order to distinguish accurately the various schools of political economy. I'll state them in chronological order, inserting in italics in each description the necessary corrections to Buchanan's definition:

Adam Smith's libertarian classical political economy can be summarized in three presuppositions: (1) methodological individualism, (2) rational choice *of neither persons as ends nor other things as means*, and (3) politics-as-*justice-in*-exchange-*only*.

Marxist classical political economy can be summarized in three presuppositions: (1) methodological *collectivism*, (2) rational choice *of neither persons as ends nor other things as means*, and (3) politics-as-*distributive-justice-only*.

Liberal neoclassical political economy entails (1) methodological *incoherence of* individualism *and collectivism*, (2) rational choice *of nonpersons as means but not persons as ends*, and (3) politics-*ostensibly*-as-exchange *yet applying distributive justice to all goods, e.g., national income.*

The hard core in *libertarian neoclassical* public choice can be summarized in three presuppositions: (1) methodological individualism, (2) rational choice *of nonpersons as means but not persons as ends*, and (3) politics-as-*justice-in*-exchange-*only*.

The theory of American public choice *combines* (1) methodological *personalism, which integrates individual, domestic and political economy,* (2) rational choice *of both persons as ends and nonpersons as means,* and (3) politics-as-*both-distributive-justice-and-justice-in*-exchange.

By comparing these descriptions and theories, it becomes obvious that differences in political economy really boil down to differences about *personal* economy—that is, what it means to be human.

The troubles with libertarian public choice theory result not from assuming that people are rational, but rather from its first and third presuppositions, which conflate rationality with radical selfishness: ruling out *by mere assumption* the existence of personal gifts and common goods (thus distributive justice, which amounts to a collective gift by community members). Though perhaps understandable as a response to Marxism and, to a lesser extent, socialism, which assume that *all* goods are both common and political, the libertarian theory of public choice errs by following Mises in presuming that *no* goods are individually donated, common, or political; in short, assuming that humans are at best *semi-*rational animals—free to choose other things as means but not persons as ends—but neither matrimonial nor political animals.

A definition of economics. Because he was acutely aware that neoclassical economic theory could explain the nature of exchanges but not of gifts, Philip Wicksteed argued that the "broadest conception of Economics includes all dealings with exchangeable things, but does not extend beyond them."[29] The ultimate ends of human action not only should not, but by their nature cannot, be exchanged. If a person is used or exchanged, the mere fact is proof that that person is not the end intended by the action.

Most economists have failed to build upon this insight, choosing instead to follow the lead of Gary Becker and others in assuming that in economics and elsewhere, there is no essential difference between humans and other animals. If this is the case, Becker asks in effect, "Why not reconstruct ethics and politics and all other social sciences from within economics as applications of the theory of marginal utility?"

Well, for at least two reasons. First, as a matter of pure economic theory, not all human action can be reduced to utility, or else utility itself would be unexplained. All human economic action involves a weighing of persons as well as objects, of ends as well as means. This must be expressed in economic theory by recognizing that exchanges and gifts differ in kind. Gifts cannot be reduced to implicit exchanges, or else they are no longer gifts. Second, economic theory has nothing to say about the appropriate weights to be attached to persons and things, other than to point out that scarcity must be taken into account. Moral philosophy has a great deal to say about the appropriate ranking of persons and things. What kinds of things ought to be exchanged, what it means to love one's neighbor in a given situation, and what exactly constitutes distributive justice in a given society are questions the economist qua economist cannot answer. Far from being a vast new empire, economic theory always has been, and will always remain, a colony of moral philosophy.

Personalism vs. individualism. The Scholastics adopted Augustine's method of personalism, which recognizes the moral freedom and responsibility of each person to make free choices about both the ends and means of economic activity. The fact of personal interdependence is expressed above all by the fact that every human person and community has a "distribution function." Utilitarian philosophy adopts a method of individualism, largely ignoring the fact of relationships among different persons and assuming that everyone has the peculiar kind of distribution function in which all goods are distributed to the self. For the same reason, utilitarianism can treat a household or larger community only as if it were a single organism, not a "unity of order" arising from, and explainable by, the choices freely made by persons who recognize and act upon their interdependence.

The modern utilitarians have therefore missed—as Philip Wicksteed did not—the most important lesson that the mother has to teach: *All human action, including economic activity, is done by persons and for persons.* Human economic activity is not ultimately undertaken by "individuals" for "utility."

Lionel Robbins's famous definition of economics needs to be revised to specify the nature of the ends as well as the means of economic action. My suggested redefinition is: "Economics is the science of human providence—personal, domestic, and political—for oneself and other persons, using scarce means that have alternate uses." With this revised definition in mind, the field of economics naturally divides into three parts: *personal economy*, which studies the behavior of persons; *domestic economy*, which investigates the household and its modern offshoots (the business firm and charitable foundation); and *political economy*, which analyzes economic policy, including not only government finances but also the framework for all transactions among persons and social institutions. The next three sections of this book take up each of these areas of economics in depth.

Table 5–1

The Origins and Historical Structure of Economic Theory				
Common-sense meaning	*Gifts (or Crimes) & Distributive Justice*	*Consumption*	*Production*	*Justice in Exchange*
Generic meaning	1. Preference for persons as ends	2. Preference for scarce means	3. Actualization of means: a.	4. Actualization of means: b.
Element of Economic Theory	Final Distribution (social unit described)	Utility (type)	Production (factors typically assumed to vary)	Equilibrium (type)
Source	Augustine, *On Christian Doctrine* I, 26 (person); Aristotle, *Ethics* V, 3 (household, business, government)	Augustine, *City of God* XI, 16 (ordinal: 1st, 2nd, 3rd, ...)	Aristotle, *Politics* 1, 4 (none)	Aristotle, *Ethics* V, 5 (partial)
Period				
Scholastic (1250–1776)	Yes (all: personal, domestic, & political)	Yes (ordinal)	Yes (none)	Yes (partial)
Classical (1776–1871)	No	No	Yes (tangible human)	Yes (partial)
Neoclassical (1871–c.2000) School:	No	Yes	Yes	Mixed
British	"	" (cardinal: ...-1,0,1,2, ...)	" (tangible nonhuman)	Yes (partial)
Austrian	"	" (ordinal)	" (" ")	No (Mises)
Walrasian	"	" (ordinal)	" (" ")	Yes (general)
Chicago (1920–1960: like British)	"	" (cardinal)	" (" ")	Yes (partial)
(1960–)	"	" (cardinal)	" (all: tangible & intangible human & nonhuman)	Yes (partial)
Neo-Thomist (Pesch: 1900–)	Mixed (domestic & political only)	Yes (cardinal)	Yes (all: tangible & intangible human & nonhuman)	Yes (partial)
Neoscholastic (c. 2000–)	Yes (all: personal, domestic, & political)	Yes (ordinal)	Yes (all: tangible & intangible human & nonhuman)	Yes (general)

Part 2

Personal Economy

The more we really look at man as an animal,
the less he will look like one.

—G. K. Chesterton, *The Everlasting Man*

6

The "Mother's Problem" and Augustine's Solution

Classical economists of the eighteenth and nineteenth centuries often tried to pose economic questions in terms of an isolated individual like Daniel Defoe's Robinson Crusoe: an imaginary grown-up who finds himself cast away one day on a desert island without family, friends, or even acquaintances, and is thus dependent entirely on his own resources. Though partly due to a natural desire to strip things to their essentials for easier understanding, there was another reason classical economists used Robinson Crusoe. Adam Smith had revised the outline of economic theory by removing the elements—particularly the theory of personal distribution—most necessary to explain the actions of anyone with social relationships. It is much more instructive to follow the example of Philip Wicksteed by considering the daily activities of a typical mother; that is, someone who comes *loaded* with social relationships and complications.

Wicksteed's *Common Sense of Political Economy*[1] is the most enlightening and engaging, rigorous but nontechnical introduction to neoclassical economics written by any of the economists who played a central role in shaping it. Most economists (and perhaps most mothers) labor under the impression that mothers need to learn from economists, not vice versa. It was Wicksteed's view that the job of the economist is not to *tell* the mother what to do but to *understand* and *explain* what she is doing.[2] And the only way to learn this is to stand aside and watch.

Wicksteed's *Common Sense* therefore begins with examples from the life of a typical English mother circa 1910. We first find her shopping: weighing the advantages of new potatoes against old potatoes, assessing the purchase of a piano against a bicycle (which, among other uses, could take her to piano recitals), deciding whether to serve cod or chicken to her dinner guests (in light of the couple's concern for social standing, the fact that all the women guests know the current prices of cod and chicken, and the aspirations to economize on household expenses so that the couple's children will learn to speak French), and weighing all of these alternatives against an urgent appeal to alleviate famine in India. Then we observe the mother at home, as she blends her market purchases with her own most important resources—her time and attention—in the combinations she thinks will be most valuable to her family. Finally, we watch her distribute the household's goods to the users she had in mind from the beginning: whether serving the milk and potatoes to family or guests, distributing her time and attention among family members, or spending her time on an outside job, unpaid volunteer service, reading great literature, or worshipping God.

According to Wicksteed, the mother is always undertaking the essential task of trying to maximize the value of her household's resources. "Her doings in the market-place and her doings at home are . . . parts of one continuous process of administration of resources, guided by the same fundamental principle; and it is the home problem that dominates the market problem and gives it its ultimate meaning." The fundamental principle is that in all cases, "she is trying to make everything go as far as it will, or, in other words, serve the most important purpose that it can. She will consider that she has been successful if, in the end, no want which she has left unsatisfied appears, in her deliberate judgment, to have really been more important than some other want to which she attended in place of it. Otherwise there has been waste somewhere, for money, milk, potatoes, or attention has been applied to one purpose when they might better have been applied to another."[3]

And yet, when he considers even the simplest of her daily tasks, Wicksteed confesses that his economic theory cannot fully explain what the mother is doing. Consider Wicksteed's aforementioned milk example: "In the usual routine, milk may be wanted for the baby, for the other children, for a pudding, for tea or coffee, and for the cat."[4] Wicksteed explains that the quantity of milk on hand begins with the amount the mother purchases from the daily delivery wagon, which decision is based on the various ways she expects to use milk that day and on its price.[5]

Normally, before any milk goes to the older children, the baby gets to drink until she is full. The older children's cups in turn ordinarily take precedence over milk for the adults' daily tea or coffee, and milk for the adults' coffee or tea normally takes precedence over an occasional pudding or a saucerful for the family cat.

Now what, exactly, is the mother doing here? After saying she is always doing one thing, Wicksteed now describes her as mixing two things: "[T]he housewife's administration of her stores amongst different claimants at home is not a series of acts of exchange, but is a series of acts relating to exchangeable things." Thus does Wicksteed flag for our attention the fact that the mother, by dealing simultaneously with exchangeable things like milk and with nonexchangeable things like the persons she loves, is doing something that cannot be reduced to "a series of acts of exchange" or be fully explained as "maximizing utility." But he never describes exactly what these acts are—only that they are not exchanges.

The passage of time might make Wicksteed's example seem quaint or irrelevant, thus obscuring what is of lasting importance. Today's American mother—my own wife, for example—buys milk in the supermarket instead of having it delivered by milk wagon. She also spends much less time working in the household and much more time working in the labor market than did her counterpart of a century earlier. And when in the household, she spends much less time preparing food and doing laundry, and much more time transporting family members from place to place. Our family's budget can purchase a much larger quantity, a higher quality, and a much larger variety, of goods and services. The particular objects of choice are therefore somewhat different: we consider the purchase of a minivan in the same light the couple of a century earlier viewed a bicycle, for example. Much of the food is at least partially prepared when it is purchased, in order to save on the mother's time. Although today's mother can expect to live twenty or twenty-five years longer than an Edwardian-era woman, the twenty-four hours in a day are one thing that has not increased.

This last fact points beneath what are essentially superficial differences to the fundamental things (in the words of the old song) that still apply as time goes by. Even allowing for changes in income, household technology, and longevity, Wicksteed's examples from the early twentieth century remain perfectly intelligible to an American mother of the twenty-first century. In both cases, the biggest problem the mother faces is not how to distribute milk but how to distribute among many competing uses any scarce resource and, above all, her single most valuable resource—her *time*. To be more precise, her biggest problem is how to use her own valuable human resources in successive periods of time.

Moreover, this problem is not essentially related to the fact that she is a mother. When you think about it, the "Mother's Problem" is actually everyone's problem. We all face it constantly in deciding, for example, whether to spend the next five minutes reading a book for our own enjoyment or profit, returning a friend's phone call, or filling out a school form for one of our children.

Moreover, each of the acts, which Wicksteed had such difficulty describing, is essentially a *gift*. The reason for his difficulty is that modern neoclassical economics has no way to describe gifts except by assuming that they are disguised exchanges.

The mother is a person, not an individual. The most basic similarity, on which Wicksteed rightly insists, is that each of us—even a shipwrecked Robinson Crusoe[6]—is not an *individual*, but a *person*—which means, in part, an intelligent being with relationships to other persons. The mother is not only somebody's wife, but also, in my wife's case, the mother of three other somebodies (not to mention the mistress of three cats). She is someone's daughter, someone else's granddaughter (deceased but not forgotten), and someone's sister, aunt, cousin, and niece. She is someone's friend and someone's neighbor. Part of the time, she is someone's employee, someone's supervisor, and someone's coworker. On any given day, she may have been the room mother at her child's school or the manager of her child's soccer team. She is the customer of many businesses. She volunteers her time for one or two community organizations. She considers herself a daughter of God, worshipping him in church once a week and serving him one evening a month on the church's education committee. When she gets any time to herself, she likes to read books, listen to music, complete crossword puzzles, go to the theater, and travel.

Just to consider this one woman, then, uncovers a complex web of personal, social, and cultural relationships. And these in turn reveal the economic and political organization of the society in which she lives: a neighborhood of similar households, many business firms, charitable and religious institutions, public and private schools, and at least two levels of government.

This exposes another complication: In some cases, the goods of which the mother disposes (like her own talents) are her own personal wealth; in some cases (like the family grocery budget) they are jointly owned with her husband; and in other cases she deals with wealth jointly owned by some other community, like her church or the national or local government. In this section, we will focus on how she disposes of her personal wealth, because we must understand such personal behavior in order to understand how we behave in communities with others.

Augustine's Solution Updated

If we consider her activities closely, we realize that the mother is always asking herself (and always answering) three basic questions: For whom shall I provide? What shall I provide? And how shall I provide it? To understand how she answers these questions, we need to profit from the wisdom of St. Augustine, who considered the problem carefully.[7] Augustine first described the principles by which every human person solves the Mother's Problem by answering the first two questions: For whom? And What? While anticipating Aristotle's answers to the third question—How?—we will leave a detailed discussion until the next section of the book, "Domestic Economy."

So, what can a Christian bishop from fifth-century northern Africa tell us about the economic choices of an American woman of the twenty-first century?

The preliminary distinction of "goods." Augustine's explanation of economic value begins with the broader question of "goods" and "values" in general. It is therefore of interest not only to the economist or historian of economics but also to anyone trying to understand the role that economic choice plays in his or her own life.[8]

Augustine begins by taking a sort of inventory of everything that exists and can be known, and which therefore can be a possible object of value. Everything is obviously a thing, for "what is not a thing is nothing at all,"[9] and "that which is nothing cannot be known." We humans are ourselves among those things. Our intellect is what enables us to know what a thing is. And when we consider things in themselves, we recognize a kind of "scale of being" ascending from inanimate objects to plants to animals to humans to God. Everything's intrinsic value is simply its degree of *be*-ing. Whatever exists, insofar as it exists, is good, in exactly that degree.[10]

But by mentioning intellect, we express an important factual distinction among things. Some things are endowed with intellect and free will—these we call "persons"—and some are not. Humans are, as far as we know, the only animals that are persons. Other animals are like us in having sensation, imagination, memory, affections, desires and aversions, pleasures and pains, and the ability to calculate means—but not in possessing intellect. Animals therefore also have a kind of choice but not free choice: they can choose their means, but not their ends, for those ends are already determined by their natural inclinations.

The human person, on the other hand, writes Augustine, possesses "a rational soul" and therefore "subordinates to the peace of the rational soul all that part of his nature which he shares with the beasts, so that he may engage in deliberate thought and act in accordance with his thoughts."[11] Humans are "rational animals," as Aristotle put it; according to Genesis they are "made in the image and likeness of God." But while all humans are persons, not all persons are human: notably God, whose existence we know both by reason reflecting on experience and by divine revelation, according to Augustine.

Now if we consider a thing not in itself but in relation to ourselves, we consider it as an object of the will, as something to attain, avoid, or ignore. This requires us to rank things, not according to their intrinsic value but according to their value *to us*. Yet we are not *forced* to choose one thing over another, even if we recognize that its intrinsic or moral value is higher. We can choose rightly or wrongly, whether measured by our own or by others' understanding. That's what we mean by "free will." In this light, a thing is viewed not in itself but either as an *end* or among *means* to an end. In Augustine's day, most philosophers made the distinction that an end was to be "enjoyed" for its own sake while a means was to be "used" for the sake of something else. But which things are ends and which are means? What should we enjoy and what should we use?

According to Augustine, "We are said to enjoy something which gives us pleasure in itself, without reference to anything else, whereas we 'use' something when we seek it for some other purpose." This means that "we should use temporal things, rather than enjoy them, so that we may be fit to enjoy eternal blessings, unlike the wicked, who want to enjoy money, but to make use of God, not spending money for God, but worshipping God for money."[12]

1. The choice of persons as ends. The first thing that sets Augustine apart as an economic analyst is his observation that every human does, as a matter of empirical fact, always act with some person(s) as the ultimate end of his action, even if that person is only him- or herself. Others had said—and would continue to say—that persons *ought* to be treated as ends and not merely as means, but Augustine argued that it was unavoidable that the ends of one's action be some person(s) and that to do so, we rank those persons in a certain order (first, second, third, etc.). The problem is that we often love inordinately—and hence tend to overprivilege—ourselves as the end of our activity. This is why the Two Great Commandments—"You shall love God with all your heart, soul and mind" and "You shall love your neighbor as yourself"[13]—are necessary.

But what does it mean to love someone? Augustine started from Aristotle's classic definition: "Let loving be defined as wishing for a person those things which you consider good—wishing them for his sake, not yours—and tending so far as you can to effect them. And a friend is one who loves, and is beloved in return."[14] Thus, love always involves a relationship between persons who are considered good in themselves, and it is expressed by providing intermediate goods as means for those persons. Even the miser, who is supposed to love money above everything, "buys bread for himself—that is, he gives away money that he is very fond of and desires to heap up—but it is because he values more highly the bodily health which the bread sustains."[15] Unlike Adam Smith and the neoclassical economists, Augustine does not assume that every human acts *solely* for him- or herself. That is precisely what each person is free to decide. Every human life is defined by that person's loves; indeed, every human person defines him- or herself by those loves.

2. The choice of means. The second thing that sets Augustine apart as an economic analyst is that he was the first to formulate the theory that economic value and prices are based on utility. His reasoning about the choice of scarce means parallels that involving the choice of persons as ends. Augustine stated the theory of utility as early as A.D. 396 in "On Free Will,"[16] elaborating it at greater length in *The City of God* (begun c.

410) in a chapter titled, "The distinction among created things; and their different ranking by the scales of utility and logic." Augustine points out that market prices often do not reflect the intrinsic value of things, and that there is a good reason for this:

> Now among those things which exist in any mode of being, and are distinct from God who made them, living things are ranked above inanimate objects; those which have the power of reproduction, or even the urge towards it, are superior to those who lack that impulse. Among living beings, the sentient rank above the insensitive, and animals above trees. Among the sentient, the intelligent take precedence over the unthinking—men over cattle. Among the intelligent, immortal beings are higher than mortals, angels being higher than men.
>
> This is the scale according to the order of nature; but there is another gradation which employs utility as the criterion of value. On this other scale we would put some inanimate things above some creatures of sense—so much so that if we had the power, we should be ready to remove these creatures from the world of nature, whether in ignorance of the place they occupy in it, or, though knowing that, still subordinating them to our own convenience. For instance, would not anyone prefer to have food in his house, rather than mice, or money rather than fleas? There is nothing surprising in this; for we find the same criterion operating in the value we place on human beings, for all the undoubted worth of a human creature. A higher price is often paid for a horse than for a slave, for a jewel than for a maidservant.
>
> Thus there is a very wide difference between a rational consideration, in its free judgment, and the constraint of need, or the attraction of desire.[17]

Here we find articulated clearly for the first time the idea of an economic value as a "scale of preference," as distinguished from a metaphysical scale of being or "intrinsic" goodness. In other words, utility is simply the relative value of something, considered not in itself, but as means to the good of some person.

Modern economists call an individual's order of preferences a "scale of values" or "utility function." The notion is fundamental to economic analysis. "It does not require much knowledge of modern economic analysis to realize that the foundation of the theory of value is the assumption that the different things that the individual wants to do have a different importance to him, and can be arranged therefore in a certain order," Lionel Robbins observed. "From this elementary fact of experience we can derive the idea of the substitutability of different goods, of the demand for one good in terms of another, of an equilibrium distribution of goods between different uses, of equilibrium in exchange and of the formation of prices."[18]

3. The decisive importance of scarcity of means. The third thing that sets Augustine apart as an economic analyst is that in outlining the choice of ends and means, he places the fact of scarcity squarely in the center of the discussion. Augustine points out that the order of our preferences, even in loving persons as ends in themselves, is necessarily affected by the scarcity of the means chosen to express this love. Both reason and divine revelation direct us to love God above all else and to "love your neighbor as yourself." But what does it mean, Augustine asks, to love your neighbor *as* yourself? Loving a person means willing him or her some good; but whether loving someone "as" yourself means loving him or her *equally with yourself* depends critically on whether the good which we wish or give to the other person is "diminished by being shared with others"[19]—that is, on whether it is scarce.

When it comes to distributing scarce goods, it is impossible to share equally with everyone else while leaving oneself enough to survive. This means, in point of fact, that we are simply unable to love all persons *equally* with ourselves when that love is expressed by the gift of scarce means. But Augustine said that loving one's neighbor depends on "the observance of two rules: first, do no harm to anyone, and, secondly, to help everyone whenever possible."[20] How is merely refraining from harming someone "loving" that person rather than expressing indifference? Well, refraining from harming someone means, at a minimum, willing that person to continue to enjoy the goods he or she already possesses, whether or not we have provided them. Indeed, most goods are beyond our power to give. But we could, if we chose, rather easily prevent people from enjoying the goods they possess, including life itself. Our refraining from doing so requires us, in effect, to say, "It is good that you exist and that you enjoy these goods." This is why the minimum standard of love is called "goodwill," and the rule about it takes a negative form: "do no harm to anyone."

The positive rule, "help everyone whenever possible," contains the qualifier "whenever possible" because helping everyone with scarce means is often not possible. Differential calculus, which is necessary to describe utility in mathematical terms, would not be invented for some 1,200 years, but Augustine expressed the idea of scarcity and "marginal utility" by posing the problem of an indivisible good: "Suppose you had a great deal of some commodity, and felt bound to give it away to somebody who had none, and that it could not be given to more than one person; if two persons presented themselves, neither of whom had either from need or relationship a greater claim on you than the other, you could do nothing fairer than choose by lot to which you would give what could not be given to both. Just so among men: since you cannot consult for the good of them all, you must take the matter as decided for you by a sort of lot, according as each man happens for the time being to be more closely connected with you."[21]

Thomas Aquinas later characterized and systematized Augustine's observation by saying that in "loving our neighbor as ourselves," we must distinguish between "benevolence," or "goodwill"—wishing others a good without actually providing it—and "beneficence," or "doing good"—actually providing for others out of our own scarce goods. "As regards beneficence we are bound to observe inequality, because we cannot do good to all: but as regards benevolence, love ought not to be thus unequal."[22]

Table 6–1

Augustine's Theory of Love and Hate			
Kind of love	Inner Act	Outer Acts toward: Self	Others
Ordinate	Benevolence (goodwill)	Utility	Beneficence (doing good: gifts)
Inordinate	Malevolence (ill will)	Vice	Maleficence (doing evil: crimes)

What Augustine did, then, was to explain that we scale or rank or value everything in three ways. The first is according to the scale of *being*, by which we classify everything known to exist, judged according to its nature. The second is according to our scale of preferences for *persons*, the much smaller list of ultimate ends or purposes of our action—always including, but not necessarily limited to, the person doing the ranking. The third is according to the scale of *utility*, by which we rank all the means we want to be used by or for those persons. And Augustine has explained that the ranking of both ends and means (and thus market prices) will be affected by the scarcity of the chosen means. This, then, is how basic "values" are related to economic value.

Now let's update Augustine's analysis and use it to describe how the Mother's Problem is solved.

1. The choice of persons as ends: the economic meaning of love and hate. The most fundamental choice anyone makes is to select the person(s) who will be the purpose of his or her actions. Their significance to the acting person is expressed by his or her distribution of scarce goods for final use among them (including him- or herself). The relative significance of the self versus other persons is described in each person's "distribution function."[23]

All economic action involves a gift either to oneself or to some other person. Our love for ourselves is expressed by allowing ourselves to use the things we own, while our love for others is expressed by allowing them to use the things we own. In economic theory, therefore, human love is essentially neither an emotion nor a weighing of utilities (though either or both may also be present) but rather a weighing of persons. If there are only two of us, and I love you equally with myself, then I will give you the use of half of what I own: it's that simple. If I love several people equally with myself, I will divide my property or income equally among all such persons, including myself. But it is not always necessary to love ourselves and others equally. If I consider another person to be half as significant as myself, I will divide my income or wealth into three parts and allocate to myself two-thirds and to the other person one-third. And so on.

Rather than an exchange, love is best described in economic theory as a gift or voluntary "transfer payment"—that is, as a voluntary distribution out of one's resources *not* made in compensation for useful services rendered. The size of the gift or transfer payment is determined by the resources of the distributor and the relative importance of the recipient in the eyes of the distributor.

Figure 6–1

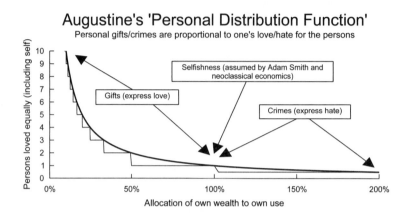

Augustine's 'Personal Distribution Function'
Personal gifts/crimes are proportional to one's love/hate for the persons

Objectively speaking, love always involves sacrifice, regardless of how the person loving *feels* about it. A mother may be happy or sad, willing or resentful, or all of these alternatively. But her love is expressed by what she does, not by what she feels. (It is probably more often the case than not that the feelings follow the doing, not vice versa.)

"Altruism," understood as opposed to "egoism," is not the same as love, because love of self is always present with love of others, and it is the source of the value of any goods used by anyone. The difference between a gift and an exchange is that in exchange, the persons who are the ultimate ends or purposes of those involved in the exchange do not coincide, but the means they have chosen to pursue their respective ends do. As a result, both parties try to advance their own ends indirectly by furthering the ends of the person with whom they are dealing.

Now it is usual for people who love each other to express that love by giving one another gifts, and even to speak of an "exchange of gifts." Though simultaneous gifts sometimes look like an exchange, when we later consider the neoclassical assumption that gifts are *always* disguised exchanges, we will see that there is an important difference between simultaneous gifts and exchanges.

Crime, or any unjust act, is the reverse of love. Rather than a gift or voluntary transfer payment, it is an involuntary transfer payment exacted from its rightful owner. In both cases, the motivation of the transfer depends essentially on a weighing of persons, not a weighing of utilities. In gifts (voluntary transfers), the significance of the other person is either positive (for someone who receives a gift) or zero (for someone who doesn't). In the case of a crime, the criminal gives himself a positive and the victim a negative significance. If I take what belongs to you against your will, I am giving myself a positive significance in a distribution that exceeds 100 percent of my own resources and giving you a negative significance in the "distribution." I may take something from you, or I may destroy something belonging to you. Just as loving one other person half as much as oneself is mathematically equivalent to loving one-and-a-half persons equally, increasing one's wealth by half through stealing from another person is mathematically equivalent to loving "two-thirds of a person" equally with oneself. But the number of persons loved is always greater than zero, because one always loves oneself. Note that this analysis provides an objective basis for defining a crime, one that is unaffected by whether the crime (for example, slavery) is made legal by positive human law. In fact, it provides a formula for measuring the economic harm done by crime or exploitation.

Thus, it is clear that pure selfishness, which has been the assumption of classical and neoclassical economists since Adam Smith, is just that—an assumption, and in fact a special case. It is a single point on a continuum that ranges from great generosity to others to great crimes against others.

2. The mother's choice of scarce means. After deciding the shares by which to distribute her own wealth or income between herself and the other persons she loves, the next question facing the mother is which particular goods she will provide to express her love for herself and the other persons. She orders her preferences for such goods according to their usefulness in satisfying the wants of the persons who are the end or purpose of her action.[24]

The mother is forced to choose among different goods because of their scarcity: Each good has a cost, and her budget of money, time, and other scarce resources is limited. It's obvious that any gift of a scarce good to other persons diminishes the share remaining to her own use. And by reducing the quantity she can consume, such a gift increases the value of each unit of her remaining goods. Therefore, she must choose the combination of goods remaining to herself that she considers most useful or valuable—whether that means using the milk remaining after the children have had their own drinks to mix with her tea or her cereal, or using any time left to herself after helping the children with their homework to read a good book or fill out a crossword puzzle.

When making the gifts to the other persons, she must likewise take into account their own needs and preferences. If she doesn't own the goods she wants to give, she can exchange the goods she does have for the goods she wants to give.

To see how she chooses among goods, let's take the simplest possible example. Suppose that the mother normally buys both bread and milk, and that she plans to spend $5 per day on both goods. She goes into the store one day to find that the price of milk is $1.25 a quart and the price of bread is $1 a loaf. This means she could spend the whole $5 per day on four quarts of milk, but then there would be no bread; or she could buy five loaves of bread, but then there would be no milk. Neither of these extremes is the best choice as long as the mother wants to buy some of both goods. Since the market price means that each quart of milk costs as much as one-and-a-quarter loaves of bread, the mother's best choice must lie somewhere on the straight line between the two extreme positions.[25] Her problem is to choose the one combination of bread and milk costing $5 that has the highest value to herself or her family.[26]

In Figure 6–2, this combination turns out to be two-and-a-half loaves of bread and two quarts of milk per day (Point A). The mother

Figure 6–2

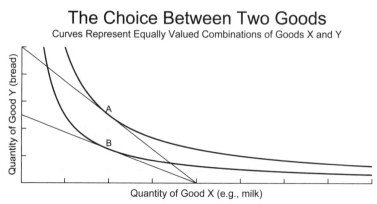

The Choice Between Two Goods
Curves Represent Equally Valued Combinations of Goods X and Y

As cost of Good Y rises, budget shrinks: consumer shifts choice from A to B.

chooses it because, at prevailing prices, any other combination that she considers equally valuable would cost more than her $5 budget. If there were a shortage of milk, the mother might be willing to accept one quart of milk and six loaves of bread as equivalent to two quarts and two-and-a-half loaves, but that combination would cost $7.25; or if there were a shortage of bread she might be willing to accept one loaf of bread and five quarts of milk, but that bundle would cost $7.75. The total value of both goods and the purchasing power of her budget are both greatest when the rate at which the mother is willing to substitute one good for the other is exactly equal to the relative market prices.

The same graph also shows how the mother's choice is affected when the relative prices of the goods change. Suppose, for example, that because of a transportation problem the price of bread doubles the next day from $1 to $2 a loaf, while the price of milk remains $1.25 a quart and her daily budget stays at $5. This change means that the possible combinations of bread and milk that the mother can purchase with her $5-a-day budget shift from the straight line between extremes of four quarts of milk (with no bread) and five loaves of bread (with no milk), to the straight line between extremes of four quarts of milk (and no bread) and two-and-a-half loaves of bread (and no milk). As long as she buys any bread, the purchasing power of her budget has declined because of the increased price of bread. But her problem remains essentially the same: finding the combination of bread and milk costing $5 that has the highest value to her family. As the result of the price change, then, the mother's best choice moves from Point A to Point B. Point B is now the single point, on the highest curve that traces bundles of equivalent value, at which the combination of goods is the same as the market price. In short, the mother ordinarily responds by buying a smaller quantity of the good that has risen in price.

3. The Mother's Problem solved. In solving the Mother's Problem dozens of times each day, the mother combines both sets of preferences described by Augustine: her preferences for persons as ends, which she expresses by distributing her goods among them, and her preferences for other things as means for those persons, which she expresses by her selection of those goods. We can see how she makes this combined choice in the following graphs.

If she were purely selfish, the mother would devote all her own income to her own consumption (Point A' in Figure 6–3). But if she loves one other person equally with herself, she instead limits her own consumption accordingly (Point C' in Figure 6–3), giving away half (the share corresponding to A' minus C').

The combination of goods she would choose in each case is shown in the second chart, which continues the simplifying assumption that her

Figure 6–3

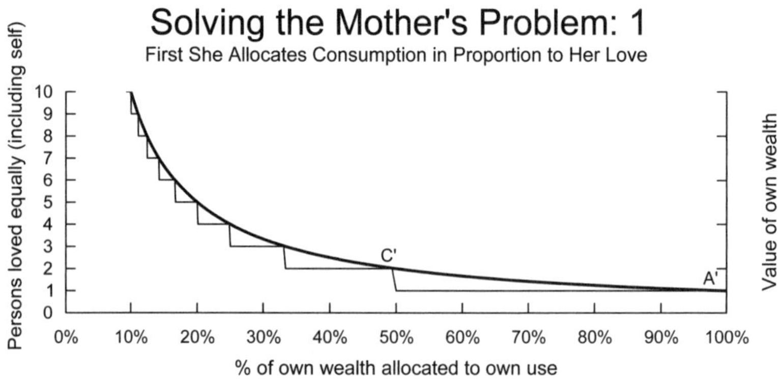

Solving the Mother's Problem: 1

First She Allocates Consumption in Proportion to Her Love

If purely selfish, she would allocate all possible consumption to herself (Point A')
If she loves, e.g., one other person equally with herself, she shares equally (Point C')

food budget is entirely devoted to bread and milk. If she were purely selfish, devoting her whole income to her own consumption, she would have chosen the combination of bread and milk that most closely matches her own preferences (the combination depicted by rectangle A in Figure 6–4). But she instead chooses the combination depicted by rectangle C, giving away the difference. The value of her own consumption (the size of the smaller rectangle) relative to the total consumption she could have afforded herself (the size of the larger rectangle) is the same ratio as her love of self relative to her love of all persons including herself (corresponding to Point C' in Figure 6–3).

Augustine's solution to the Mother's Problem is basically simple. But it requires us to begin by acknowledging the fact that we always act on *two* kinds of preferences: preferences for persons as ends and preferences for other things as means. Let's consider some important implications of Augustine's theory, which will be very useful in explaining several aspects of personal, domestic, and political economy.

Solving the Mother's Problem: 2
Next she chooses which particular goods she will consume.

Consumption of Good Y (bread)

Consumption of Good X (milk)

After making gift of A - C, she chooses to consume combination C instead of A.
Value proportion C/A is determined by choice of C' in Figure 6-3.

How we allocate our time. As we have noted, the most important economic choice that anyone faces is how to allocate his or her time among alternate uses; or, more precisely, how to apply his or her abilities during successive periods from the current moment through the rest of his or her life.

We have seen that the exchangeable wealth actually used by any person may be less or more than he owns, depending on his relationships to other persons. If he loves other persons in an economic sense, he uses less wealth than he commands, because he either gives away or allows others to use part of that wealth; if he hates other persons in an economic sense, he takes or destroys what belongs to them, thus giving himself a positive share and the others a negative share in a distribution exceeding the wealth to which he had a right. Everyone's own human wealth, however, is not "alienable," in the sense that we are always physically present even when it is used by others. Therefore, one voluntarily allocates one's own time between use by oneself and by others in proportion to the relative significance of the persons. Someone who loves only himself allocates 100 percent of his own time to his own use. Someone who loves one other person equally with himself allocates half his time to his own use and the other half to the other person. Someone who loves one other person half as much as himself will devote two-thirds of his time to his own use and the other third to the other person; this is equivalent to loving one-and-a-half persons equally with himself. And where more than one other person is involved, one's time is allocated among all persons in proportion to the relative or marginal significance of each person:

Note that as the share of "time" devoted to other persons rises, the value of each minute or hour remaining to oneself rises. This is why everyone's ability to love other persons by devoting time to them is limited. The value limit is reached when the last unit is sacrificed for others: it is literally true that "No one has greater love than this, to lay down one's life for one's friends."[27]

Figure 6–5

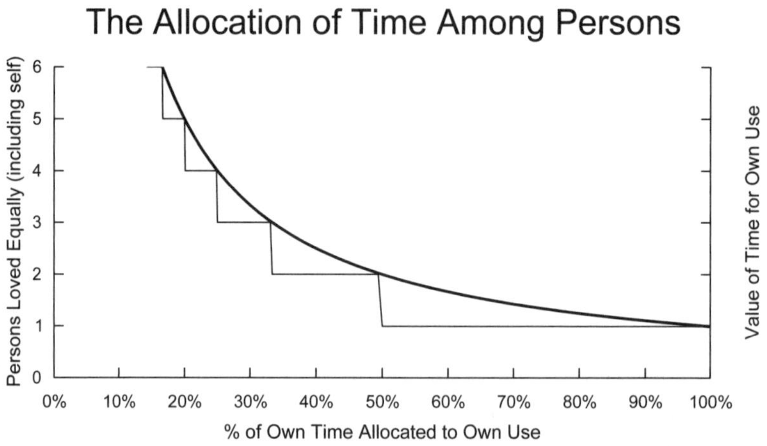

The Allocation of Time Among Persons

The other persons may be physically present or absent. For example, a parent who earns a living to support his family is effectively devoting part of his time to his children even while in the labor market, just as much as another parent who may stay home in their physical presence. How the parents' time is allocated between the household and market economies is a second-order decision, which follows from the first-order choice of whom to love and the means by which this love is expressed. One also devotes time to an absent person when writing a letter to that person, for example. And the persons to whom one devotes one's time may not be living humans: One can devote time to God, for example, in prayer or worship, or to a deceased relative by recalling him or her in memory. To treat such time as if devoted to the self would not explain either the motivation or the fact of the behavior.

A theory of social graces. Augustine's theory of personal gifts suggests a new approach to the whole cluster of theories regarding what some sociologists and economists have termed social, cultural, religious, and spiritual "capital"—terms often used, unfortunately, with greater enthusiasm than precision.[28] (One researcher, for example, started seriously to apply the concept of social capital to natural resource management, but he found it necessary to abandon the effort as impracticable after discovering no fewer than twenty different, largely incompatible definitions and no meaningful way to measure the concept.)[29]

When Theodore W. Schultz coined the term *human capital* to describe economic investments in people, he advanced the term almost apologetically, prefacing his remarks by noting that "our values and beliefs inhibit us from looking upon human beings as capital goods, except in slavery, and this we abhor."[30] But as Schultz's approach proved extraordinarily fruitful, subsequent researchers progressively extended the "capital" metaphor with fewer and fewer inhibitions. Almost the only thing on which theorists can agree is that the various forms of capital are all essentially *produced* by human beings at some cost and in the prospect of some return on the investment.

Yet the human realities that these terms attempt to describe are more properly identified as social, cultural, religious, or spiritual "graces"— that is, something essentially given or received gratis, as free gifts. Augustine's theory of personal distribution therefore provides the indispensable microeconomic foundation that has so far been missing from the discussion. Moreover, whatever its other merits or demerits, each theory remains formally incomplete until it integrates a description of how and why that form of capital may be freely given or received without explicit or implicit compensation.[31]

Consider, for example, the everyday gestures that most of us make when we allow someone we do not know and expect never to meet again to take our rightful, lawful, or customary place—say, allowing that person ahead of us in traffic or when waiting to be served at a store.[32] The facts that such gestures cost us scarce resources and that we do not expect reciprocation from the same persons make these social *graces* rather than investments in social *capital*.[33]

At least as far back as Aesop's ancient fable of the town mouse and the country mouse, it has been observed that the urban population is materially richer, more anxiety-ridden, and less generous than the rural population. The rudeness of New York City's inhabitants to one another and to strangers is legendary. How, then, can we explain outpourings of generosity by New Yorkers, for example, to families whose members perished in the September 11, 2001, terrorist attacks on the World Trade Center?

The answer to this apparent puzzle, I suggest, is that city dwellers are not any less generous on average than country dwellers, but their daily generosity is typically distributed among many more individual recipients. A city dweller who interacts with hundreds or even thousands of other people in the course of a typical day (for example, when commuting to work) simply cannot afford to be as generous to each other individual as a country dweller who devotes exactly the same total time per day to strangers but whose total daily contacts may be numbered on the fingers of both hands. A person who loves three other people equally with himself will devote the same share of his or her scarce resources to the other persons as if he loved three hundred others 1 percent as much or three thousand others one-thousandth as much as himself. This explains how it can be true *both* that the typical city dweller *is* ruder on average to any *one* given stranger he or she meets, *and* no less generous to *all* strangers, than the typical country dweller. Such arithmetic also explains why, when the generosity of a significant share of citizens of a large city like New York is focused on a relatively small number of recipients, like the victims of the terrorist attacks, the average gift received can be extraordinarily large. Unlike the existing theory of social capital, an Augustinian theory of social graces is able to identify each small gift from some specific person to some other specific person, and to explain its reason.

Converse to *social graces* are the little *social crimes* or *robberies* we commit when we usurp other people's places according to right, law, or custom—say, by failing to yield in proper order at a stop sign or in traffic, thus delaying others' commutes to work. Moreover, someone who habitually does so in a crowded urban area often causes as much total economic damage in a single day as a single criminal who may be fined or jailed for inflicting that amount of damage on a single victim.

The same approach might also be extended to religious and spiritual graces, the context in which Augustine originally thought of them. All spiritual or religious experience involves (or is perceived to involve) some kind of gift. This is obvious whether the action is viewed as proceeding from God to man (for example, creation in Abrahamic traditions and redemption and sanctification in Christian traditions); from man to God (gifts of praise, adoration, sacrifice, and thanksgiving in most religious traditions); or from human to human (such as sacramentally "giving and being given in marriage,"[34] making charitable donations, or doing volunteer work out of religious motivation).

Augustine's theory of personal gifts sheds important light on the nature of spiritual graces, one peculiarity of which is that they are subject to scarcity on the human side but not from the side of God. While "spiritual capital" and "religious capital" have been conceived as something essentially *produced* by humans, of their nature religious and spiritual graces must be conceived as something essentially *received* by humans.

Thus, Augustine provided the first and second elements necessary to explain personal economy—the theories of personal distribution and utility. By combining them, we can understand how to solve the Mother's Problem, which describes the essence of our economic decisions as individual persons, and we can also outline a theory of social, cultural, religious, and spiritual graces. In the next two chapters, we will consider the success of neoclassical economists in developing Augustine's theory of utility and their failure to develop his theory of personal distribution.

7

The Success and Failure
of Neoclassical Economics

Neoclassical Success: Reinventing the Theory of Utility

Though neoclassical economists failed to rediscover Augustine's theory of personal distribution, they reinvented and have systematically developed a fundamental insight implicit throughout his theory of utility. In valuing goods, we are always considering the difference in value when one or more units are added to or subtracted from what we already own: their "marginal" utility.

Ordinarily, goods have declining marginal utility, which means that we usually consider a larger quantity of any good to be worth more than a smaller quantity, but that the value of each *additional unit* gets smaller as the total quantity grows larger. We can see this in both small and large ways.

For example, the value of a glass of milk depends not only on how much we like milk but also on how long it's been since we last drank any. If we've just had two glasses, the value we place on a third glass will be lower than if we haven't had any since yesterday. This is why a baby, when she is hungry, drinks the first half of the bottle of milk more eagerly than the second half, and at some point simply becomes full. If she drinks too much, she may wish she had had less. Too much of a "good" can turn into a "bad." In that case, the total value of milk does not merely rise at a slower rate but actually falls as the quantity consumed increases. But when the baby feels better and gets hungry again, the milk turns back into a "good." Furthermore, we must be careful to remember that utility is not the pleasure the child receives in consuming milk but simply the relative value she places on the units she consumes, whether or not pleasure is involved.

Figure 7–1 shows what this means to both the total and "marginal" value: At first, value increases at an accelerating rate (rising marginal utility), then continues to rise but at a slower rate (decreasing marginal utility), then reaches a peak (zero marginal utility), and finally declines (negative marginal utility).

Figure 7–I

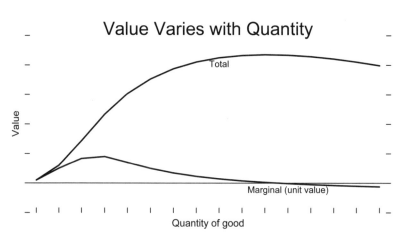

Value Varies with Quantity

While declining marginal utility is the rule, it sometimes applies only "after a certain point." Up to that point, it's possible for each extra unit to rise in value as the quantity increases. I recall having to adjudicate a lunchtime dispute between our (then) fifteen-year-old son and twelve-year-old daughter over the last can of chicken soup. I should explain two things: First, because no water is added, one can of soup equals either one large bowl or two small bowls; and second, the usual rule in our house is to divide the last of any such resource equally between those who want it. My daughter therefore argued that the only fair thing to do was to split the soup into two small bowls. My son insisted that this was not as fair as flipping a coin for the whole can—or even as no one getting the soup. (I dismissed this last alternative, since I suspected that it involved the calculation of getting all the soup when his sister wasn't around. The choice for both of them was not between soup and nothing at all for lunch, but rather between soup and something else—say, a sandwich—that neither of them valued as highly at the moment as soup.) The key fact was that to my son, a 50 percent chance of a full can of soup was more valuable than the 100 percent certainty of half a can. This meant that the second half of the can of soup was more valuable to him than the first half; while for my (smaller) daughter, the first half was more important than the second. She faced a declining marginal utility of soup, but he faced an increasing marginal utility of soup. But the marginal value of soup for my son must decline after the first can, because I've never known him to consume more than one can when more is available. (By the way, I ruled that they should split the soup equally: Fairness trumps utility in our family. However, I didn't think at the time to ask whether they would have been satisfied with a different split.)

The mother (or father) is always matching the marginal significance of each good with the terms on which it is offered—that is, with its price, broadly understood. She goes shopping with a list that is a first approximation, based on the uses to which she expects to put her purchases and the prices she expects to pay for them. But what she actually does buy will be affected by the prices she actually finds in the market. If the prices of the items are substantially higher or lower than she had expected, she may change her plans on the spot, deciding to satisfy more or less urgent needs, depending on the price.

For example, if she found that she could procure only a single cupful of milk a day (say, because of a delivery truck drivers' strike), she might pay 79 cents for it (the equivalent of $3.15 a quart or $12.60 a gallon), so that at least the baby could have enough milk for one feeding a day (see Figure 7–2). If only one quart per day were available, she might be willing to pay, say, $2.30 for it, and it might suffice for the baby's daily feedings, smallish glasses for the older children, and a couple of teaspoonfuls for the adults' tea or coffee. She would pay, say, $1.43 for a second quart per day, in order to give all the children full portions, provide for the adults' tea or coffee, and also for the adults' breakfast cereals. And if she found milk on sale for 75 cents a quart, she might buy a third quart a day, to give the children chocolate milk for their snacks, to offer a daily treat to the cat, and to make some cakes or puddings. She might accept

a fourth quart a day if it were free, but the danger is that it would spoil
before a sensible use could be found.

Let's say the actual price of milk today is $1.29 a quart. The mother
buys two quarts, because the marginal significance of the second quart
in all her family's uses ($1.43) slightly exceeds the market price, but the
marginal significance of a third quart would be only 77 cents. So instead
of paying $1.29 for a third quart of milk, she buys something else—say,
a first head of lettuce—the value of which she judges to be greater than
that of a third quart of milk. Notice that at $1.29 for both quarts of milk,
the total cost she pays for milk is less than its total significance to her
family (which started at $3.15 a quart for the first cupful, and declined to
$1.43 a quart for the last ounce of the second quart).

Figure 7–2

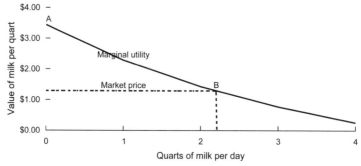

Total Value Highest When Price = Marginal Utility

Our apparently simple example turned out to contain more complications than first appeared. Though we ostensibly considered a single
good with different uses, we had to refer a number of times to the importance of other goods, used either as substitutes (juice or baby formula)
or as complements (tea, coffee, chocolate syrup, and pudding and cake
mix). Therefore, the marginal significance of milk turned out to depend
not only on the quantity of milk but also on the quantities of many other
goods—and potentially of all other goods valued by the members of the
household. The mother has all of these in the back of her mind when she
goes shopping.

In every case, what matters is the relative value of different goods or different units of the same good, not their absolute money values. If the money prices of all goods were multiplied or divided by 10 or 100 or 1,000, it would make no difference, as long as the price of each good in terms of every other remained unchanged. The main reason we use money is that when there are many goods and their relative prices are constantly changing, it's easier to compare the values of different goods against that of some familiar common good, namely money. What always matters is that a quart of milk had the same significance or market price as eighteen eggs or seven-sixteenths of a box of crackers yesterday, and as thirteen and a half eggs or thirty-five sixty-fourths of a box of crackers today. But most of us find it easier to remember the price of each good in terms of money: that milk was 99 cents a quart yesterday and $1.29 today, eggs $1.49 a dozen yesterday and $1.19 today, and crackers $3.59 a box yesterday and $2.99 today. (At least, this is easier as long as the value of the monetary unit remains more constant than the value of any other individual good. When it doesn't, as in the case of hyperinflation, people switch to a different standard.)

The mother also learns to think, not in terms of absolute quantities of goods, but in terms of their *rates* of use or supply: not just so many quarts of milk in the abstract, but so many quarts *per day, week, month,* etc. Otherwise, how could she weigh, say, the purchase of two quarts of milk at $1.29 a quart against that of a new piano that costs $5,000? If the piano will last ten years with constant use, the piano's cost, spread out over 3,652 days, is about $1.37 per day. Thus, at current prices, the family's daily cost of owning a new piano is a little more than buying a third daily quart of milk for the next 10 years. Or put another way, at current prices and rates of use, the cost of the piano is about the same as five and a half years' worth of milk for her family.[1]

Marginal Utility and Risk

We can see the consequences of declining marginal utility on a much larger scale by considering how we regard the risk of losing all or part of our wealth.[2] This is essentially what we have to do when making investments on which the return is known to vary. Though most of us don't use the term *risk aversion*, we all know what it means. The idea is captured in the adage "A bird in hand is worth two in the bush." To be risk averse means that the prospect of losing a dollar you already own weighs more heavily than the chance of gaining a dollar you don't yet own.[3]

It is easy to find out whether you are risk averse. For example, let's say that we agree to flip a coin. If the coin comes up tails, you lose half your wealth—half the value of your bank accounts, stocks, bonds, house, car, and other assets; and also half of what you will earn for the rest of your life. If the coin comes up heads, you win an equal dollar amount. A "risk-neutral" investor—one who neither seeks nor avoids risk—would just accept this bet, because it is "actuarially fair." The odds of winning or losing are equal, and so are the potential gains and losses. If you would not accept the bet, you are "risk averse." To be averse to risk indicates that your total wealth has declining marginal utility for you. And if so, you are not alone. Risk aversion is the rational response to the human condition. None of us lives long enough or has enough resources to try risky things an infinite number of times. The decision to invest is a lot like our example of the coin toss. The risk of an investment is typically measured by the variability of its return: How much above or (more important) below average does the return tend to fluctuate?

Almost no one would risk half his wealth on a coin toss for the prospect of an equal gain. But there are many degrees of aversion to risk. Most people would accept the bet if it were modified, so that the risk of loss was smaller, the promised payoff larger, or the odds of winning better. It's possible to measure your degree of aversion to risk by comparing how large a gain, and at what odds, would induce you to risk losing some specified share of your wealth.[4] The following graph (Figure 7–3) shows the actual results of an experiment involving a wager like the one just described—along with an attempt to describe mathematically the three basic attitudes toward risk that seem to be suggested by the results.

The evidence seems to indicate that for the typical person, a bird (or a dollar) in hand is indeed worth two in the bush (or in the stock market)—at least, if the number of birds or dollars at stake is not too large compared with the number one starts with. That is, to balance the chance of losing 1 percent of his wealth, the typical person requires an equal chance of gaining about 2 percent. A more conservative investor appears typically to require an equal chance of gaining about 3 percent. A relatively speculative investor seems to require only a 1.5 percent gain. But this still shows an aversion to risk, because an investor indifferent

Figure 7–3

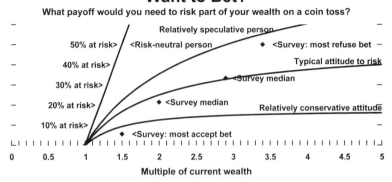

Want to Bet?

Survey: MacCrimmon & Wehrung (1988), 110.

to risk would risk losing 1 percent for an equal chance of gaining 1 percent. What this means, mathematically, is that the value a typical person places on each extra dollar of wealth varies inversely with the square of his wealth.[5] For the conservative investor, this "marginal utility" of wealth varies inversely with the cube of his wealth. But as the size of possible losses increases, each investor requires more than just one and a half or two or three times the gain to accept the bet.

Ordinarily, however, we are not considering only units of a single good like milk or thinking about our wealth as a whole, as if it were such a good, but comparing units of one good against units of another. For example, when we considered the mother's decision whether to buy one quart of milk and six loaves of bread for $7.25, or two quarts of milk and two and a half loaves of bread for $5, or one loaf of bread and five quarts of milk for $7.75, it meant that she was quickly calculating whether the total value would be greater, the same, or less each time a quart of milk was added while a loaf of bread was subtracted. We are often choosing among hundreds of possible alternatives that would take an economist a system of equations with hundreds of variables to describe. But in making these decisions, the mother doesn't need to know the mathematics. All she needs to know are the prices of the goods she wants to buy, the size of her budget, and her order of preference for different combinations of quantities of those goods: that is, which combinations she would consider more valuable, less valuable, or equivalent in value.

Augustine first described the theory of utility, it was developed by Scholastic economists, and after its abandonment by classical economists following Adam Smith, later neoclassical economists returned to it to achieve these further insights. But they have neglected his insight that our more fundamental preference is for persons, not instrumental goods. In the next chapter, we'll see that the controversial relationship of fertility and crime provides a decisive empirical test of the neoclassical and neo-Scholastic economic theories.

The Neoclassical Failure to Solve the "Mother's Problem"

The psychologist Abraham Maslow famously observed, "It is tempting, if the only tool you have is a hammer, to treat everything as if it were a nail."[6] This is the basic problem with all existing varieties of neoclassical economic theory regarding questions of distribution. If the only aspects of human economic behavior that an economist recognizes are the choice, realization, and exchange of scarce means—in economic jargon, the utility function, the production function, and the equilibrium conditions—then he or she naturally assumes that all human behavior can be reduced to utility alone and that humans interact only by treating one another as commodities. What is forgotten is the most important aspect of economic choice: the choice of persons who are always the ends or purposes of economic activity, which we express by our distribution of wealth or income among them.

We have already considered Augustine's successful solution to the Mother's Problem, which explains how we go about choosing persons as ends and other things as scarce means of our actions. In this chapter and the next, I will describe the failure of the most sophisticated version of neoclassical theory to solve the same basic problem. First, I will present as clearly as possible the fundamental difference between the two theories, focusing on the way in which people who love respond to hardship. Then I will propose a factual test of the two theories that involves their respective predictions about the relationship between the rates of "economic fatherhood" and homicide.

Consider the following cases, all drawn from life:

1. My wife's grandfather Glenn was a born salesman with a heart of gold. My wife and I still have the rug he accepted from somebody during the Great Depression in lieu of money for insurance premiums on a pol-

icy he had sold. Glenn was always the guy who organized the hilltop Easter sunrise service for his church, conducted Sunday school, and visited those who were sick or in the hospital. When Glenn was in his eighties but still in good health, he went into the hospital for an operation to clear an artery of built-up plaque that was dangerously threatening to cause a stroke. But a piece of plaque broke loose during the operation, and Glenn suffered a stroke immediately. He lived for a couple of years after that but could no longer speak (though he could sing hymns) and was confined to a wheelchair. My wife's grandmother Lucy responded by taking care of her husband. Among other things, that meant getting up several times every night to see to his needs. The whole thing wore her out and probably hastened her own death by several years. But Lucy (after whom my wife and I named our daughter) refused to have it any other way.

2. My friend Dave and his wife, Karen, had two active, intelligent children, Katie and Geoffrey. Their third child, Greg, was born with Down syndrome. Greg is my godson. He is the sweetest, most loving child imaginable. He is a real character, a ham on any occasion. But Greg is also a handful for his parents. Most parents find that the time they devote to each child tapers off as the child becomes progressively more able to take care of him- or herself. If all goes well, the child becomes completely self-supporting, as Geoffrey and Katie are well on their way to doing. But caring for Greg at every age has always been much more costly in money and time for Karen and Dave, partly because of the medical complications that typically afflict those with Down syndrome. That's true even though Katie and Geoffrey have been pitching in to help care for Greg since he was born. Greg may never be able to live completely on his own. Dave, Karen, Katie, and Geoffrey have all responded to this unexpected burden with charity and humor.

3. My father died several years ago after a long battle with esophageal cancer—a particularly nasty variety. Our family is rather unusual, in that I'm one of twelve children. Looking back, I can see that the biggest trick my parents pulled off was making us feel that growing up in such a large family was perfectly normal. (Who can possibly invite you over to dinner?) What's more, my parents somehow managed to instill in each of us the secret belief that we were the "special" child. When my father's final decline began, several of us children were able to take care of him in rotation, applying the useful skills we had severally obtained as

nursing home orderly, physical therapist, intensive care nurse, financial planner, and paralegal professional. Such an arrangement would not have been possible in a smaller family. Because nearly every one of us also had his or her own family to take care of, often with young children, the burden was still significant. But when my turn came, it always seemed a small return for all that my father had done for me.

I raise these examples for two reasons. First, all are perfectly ordinary experiences. Almost everyone either has experienced or will experience a similar event in the course of his or her life. What all the cases have in common is that the "cost of living," in the broad sense, suddenly got very expensive for one person. Since all humans are mortal, that will happen to every one of us, sooner or later. Second, in each case, those involved did not respond in the way that neoclassical economic theory says they should have.

The Neoclassical View of Human Nature

As we noted in chapter 4, neoclassical economic theory is based on a different view of human nature from either Scholastic or classical economic theory. In the Scholastic view, every human is a rational animal—with equal emphasis on both words. Because we are animals, we have emotions, experience pleasure and pain, reproduce, raise offspring, grow old, and die. But because we are rational, unlike other animals we can understand universal concepts, freely choose both ends and means, and act when necessary against our feelings. In Adam Smith's Stoic worldview, the whole universe is rational, but individual humans rationally choose neither their ends nor their means. Neoclassical economics is based on a third alternative that might be said to be halfway between the Scholastic and classical theories. In neoclassical economic theory, man is a semi-rational or *clever* animal, adept at calculating means but having no choice about the single presumed end of self-gratification, since "reason is, and ought only to be, the slave of the passions," as David Hume put it.[7]

Though this worldview is usually ignored or left implicit, a few economic thinkers have worked out this view of human action explicitly and systematically. One of the most influential was the Austrian economist Ludwig von Mises, whose views we had occasion to consider in chapter 5. According to Mises, "Action is based on reason, action therefore which is understood by reason, knows only one end, the greatest pleasure of the

acting individual. The attainment of pleasure, the avoidance of pain—
these are its intentions." He added that pleasure or satisfaction must be
construed broadly enough to embrace all action.[8] But if we accept this
premise, it follows that all human action is a kind of exchange.[9] Even
the actions of an isolated individual, according to Mises, are a form of
exchange: an exchange of one state of pleasure for another that he values
more highly.[10]

Moreover, it follows from the same theory that humans have no
choice about the persons they choose as the end of their actions. "The
power to choose whether my actions and conduct shall serve myself or
my fellow beings is not given to me," Mises maintained.[11] Presumed to
have no choice of persons as ends, humans are therefore presumed to
arrange all goods on a single comprehensive scale of preference, rather
than on separate scales for persons as ends and other things as means, as
in Scholastic economics.[12] According to Mises, "Nothing that men aim
at or want to avoid remains outside of this arrangement into a unique
scale of gradation and preference."[13]

The Neoclassical Explanation of Love

When Kenneth Arrow considered the nature of "altruism," he posed three
interpretations, all based on utility interpreted as a feeling of satisfaction:

> (1) The welfare of each individual will depend both on his own
> satisfaction and on the satisfaction obtained by others. We here
> have in mind a positive relation, one of altruism rather than
> envy.
>
> (2) The welfare of each individual depends not only on the
> utilities of himself and others but also on his contributions to
> the utilities of others.
>
> (3) Each individual is, in some ultimate sense, motivated by
> purely egoistic satisfaction derived from the goods accruing to
> him, but there is an implicit social contract such that each per-
> forms his duties for the other in a way calculated to enhance the
> satisfaction of all.[14]

The only difference among these three explanations is what *kind* of
feeling is supposed to explain altruism—satisfaction derived from *per-*

ceiving others' satisfaction, from *contributing to* others' satisfaction, or from feeling more secure in one's own possessions as the result of pursuing "enlightened self-interest." Arrow added, "This classification is not exhaustive, or even exclusive"; but he did not suggest that there is an explanation based on any principle other than utility.

The notion that calculations of utility explain all human action lies at the heart of Gary Becker's "economic approach to human behavior." By reducing all human behavior to utility, his approach requires that each person treat other persons for economic purposes only as objects, much the way the mother in the Mother's Problem regards the milk. Becker argues that people get married or have children "because they expect to increase their utility." He says that "if more is voluntarily spent on one child than on another, it is because the parents obtain additional utility from the additional expenditure. . . ."[15] As some of Becker's students put it, a mother "extracts utility from the number of her children (n) and the quality, or well-being (z), of each one of them."[16] According to Becker, one has a "taste" for children, not totally unlike the witch in *Hansel and Gretel*. He recognizes that there is "altruism" within a household, but he explains it as a case of Arrow's (1) or (2): the satisfaction derived either from perceiving or contributing to the satisfaction of others.[17]

Even some economists who rebel at the notion of reducing all human relations to utility accept that this is what economic theory in fact teaches.[18] And some economists of a utilitarian or positivist stripe argue that no alternate explanation is even logically possible.[19] But the neoclassical explanation simply doesn't cover the facts.

Consider the mother's apportionment of milk. Does the baby get first claim on the milk because the mother derives more "utility" at the moment from the baby—say, has warmer feelings toward it—than the other children? Only the mother can tell us, but it is more likely that she loves the children more or less equally (there's the ranking of persons) but judges the urgency of the baby's need for a marginal thimbleful of milk and a marginal minute of the mother's time to be greater than that of the older children (there's the ranking of means). Of course, the older children were once that young and required the mother's care in the same way, just as the mother's mother had to care for her as a baby. So let's consider their needs over a lifetime. This doesn't remove the difficulty of trying to explain love as a matter of utility. The average boy/man eats considerably more than the average girl/woman over his lifetime. Apart from any difference in activities, this is simply the result of the fact that the average man weighs more than the average woman, and therefore requires more food to maintain his body weight. If the cost of food and other costs like education were equal for both sexes, then the lifetime cost of raising a boy must be higher than the cost of raising a girl. If so, does this mean that the parents gain more utility from boys than from girls? Are boys of higher "quality" than girls? Or are girls more "productive" of utility per dollar spent than boys? (If that were so, why wouldn't parents spend more on girls?) Becker's approach can't tell us.

And what about the cat? Does the mother apportion the least amount of milk to the cat because she loves the cat least? Or does she love the cat as much as the children but judge its needs to be the least urgent? Does she recognize that the cat sees the marginal utility of milk as high, but she ranks the cat lower than the other members of the household? Normally it's the last explanation. There are of course people who mistake their pets for persons. We've all heard of the oddball widow who leaves her estate to pet Puffy. (And as we will see, philosopher Peter Singer, who shares with Becker essentially the same utilitarian philosophy, considers many nonhuman animals to be persons.) But the usual case is that parents don't believe that the persons already in the household can afford to divide their scarce goods more or less equally with another person, and a mother feeds a cat rather than another child because the cat costs far less to maintain than a child (the cat won't be attending college). The marginal significance of the saucer of milk may be relatively high to the cat, but the sharply lower upkeep of the cat relative to a human is of the same order of magnitude as the cat's sharply lower relative importance in the household compared with the human persons. Puffy is a good old cat and will be sorely missed when she is gone, but in a sane household she ranks considerably below the humans (though above the plants).

The problems of circularity and nonverifiability are also involved in Becker's effort to explain altruism and crime in terms of utility. We must therefore disentangle these problems in order to derive an empirical test of the "Becker-Stigler-Bentham assumptions."

Becker, as we have seen, tries to explain all human acts as a maximization by their users of the satisfaction of various "basic wants or commodities." Other persons can enter this framework only as "basic commodities." ("Household-produced commodities are numerous and include the quality of meals, the quality and quantity of children, prestige, recreation, companionship, love, and health status.")[20] He argues that people get married or have children "because they expect to increase their utility."[21] He says that "if more is voluntarily spent on one child than on another, it is because the parents obtain additional utility from the additional expenditure, and it is this additional utility, which we call higher 'quality.'"[22]

Person i is an altruist, according to Becker, "when i's utility function depends on j's welfare."[23] Becker also assumes that the head of each household has sufficient economic power so that his or her preferences will override the preferences of all other members. If the head of household happens to be an "altruist," his or her preferences *include* the utility functions of the other members. Likewise, if the other family members arc altruists, their utility functions will include that of the head of household. When both are altruists, the result is a "hall of mirrors": A's utility increases B's utility, which in turn increases A's utility, which increases B's utility, and so on.

Becker concedes that these overlapping and interacting utility functions entail an "infinite regress."[24] He argues that with sufficiently restrictive assumptions about the degree of altruism, the interactions need not involve actually infinite utility. But such restrictive assumptions do not solve the problem of nonverifiability.

In stating the "Becker-Stigler-Bentham assumptions" above, we noted that in Becker's system, the utility of scarce goods is not uniquely assigned to the persons who actually use the goods. Altruism is supposed to multiply what Becker calls "social income" beyond what is actually observed. Observable consumption of, say, food, is the proper measure only when all parties involved are selfish. In that case, each person receives utility only from the food he or she consumes, so that total consumption equals 100 percent of observed consumption. But in describing "caring and sharing" between a husband, M, and wife, F, Becker says, "M's income . . . exceeds his own consumption because of the utility he gets from F's consumption. . . . [W]ith mutual and full caring, the combined incomes of M and F would then be double their combined output: all of M's and F's consumption would be jointly consumed."[25] In other words, depending on the degree of "altruism," the appropriate measure of Becker's "social income" ranges between 100 percent and 200 percent of observed consumption for households of two persons, between 100 percent and 300 percent for households of three persons, between 100 percent and 400 percent for households of four persons, and so on.

Like the "individualistic social welfare function" in welfare economics, Becker's household utility superfunction mixes the utility function (the scale of preferences for economic goods, which are the means of economic action) with the distribution function (which expresses the scale of preferences for persons, who are the ultimate purpose of economic action). Becker and Stigler refer to both kinds of preferences indiscriminately as "tastes."

The Neoclassical Explanation of Hate

Just as modern economists have tended to explain love in terms of utility, many have tried to explain crime and other antisocial behavior in terms of utility. The difference between love and hate in neoclassical theory is that in the case of love, the welfare of the other person increases one's utility, while in the case of hate, an increase in the welfare of the other person decreases one's utility. Gary Becker was the leader in expounding this theory as well.[26] According to Becker, "a person commits an offense if the expected utility to him exceeds the utility he could get by using his time and resources at other activities. Some persons become 'criminals,' therefore, not because their basic motivations differ from that of other persons, but because their benefits and costs differ."[27] In addition, according to Becker, "there is a function relating the number of offenses by any person to his probability of conviction, to his punishment if convicted, and to other variables, such as the income available to him in legal and other illegal activities, the frequency of nuisance arrests, and his willingness to commit an illegal act."[28] Becker's entire discussion centers on the probabilities and magnitudes of gain and punishment, not the "willingness to commit an illegal act." This willingness, he and Stigler later argued, is actually the same for everyone; all that differs from person to person are the relative costs and benefits of crime.

The problem is that this explanation doesn't account for the fact that most people do not commit crimes, even though doing so would increase their wealth (after allowing for the probability of punishment), thus raising the expected total utility of their wealth. To argue that most people must receive utility from *not* committing crimes reduces the theory to a tautology; it is unscientific, because it renders the theory unfalsifiable.

In contrast to Becker's "economic approach to human behavior," the main tradition of economic theory has always been based on Augustine's *human* approach to economic behavior. The logic of economic theory is quite clear that love cannot be based on utility, for the simple reason that utility is derived from love. To love a person for his or her own sake is precisely to treat him or her as an end; and it is only because there is such an end that the means selected to serve that end (like milk or college tuition) have any value. To say that love is based on utility is therefore circular.

In other words, loving someone does not increase one's utility. Rather, our estimate of other persons' importance, relative to our own, determines how much we are willing to *lower* our own utility to love them. Likewise, utility doesn't cause the gift; rather, the gift affects the utility of remaining wealth. With the declining marginal utility of wealth, the gift raises the total but lowers the marginal utility of wealth on the part of the recipient, while lowering the total but raising the marginal utility of wealth to the donor. We have no grounds for assuming that the utility of the gift to the recipient equals the loss of utility it represents to the giver, because there is no common absolute unit of utility in which to express them.

Likewise, mutual love (as ideally exists in marriage) is not essentially an exchange of utilities, though of course a mixture of gift and exchange is possible. Mutual love is best viewed as a simultaneous pair of gifts or voluntary transfer payments, of which there is no reason to believe that any equality in gifts should apply—except in the special case in which the resources of each person and their respective estimates of the importance of the other person happen to be exactly identical. But even in this case, the utility of the two gifts for their recipients cannot be assumed to be equal.

For Better or Worse

Mutual gifts between adults who are capable of supporting themselves are often hard to distinguish from exchanges; statistically speaking, it's much easier to detect a gift from a parent to a child, because the child ordinarily cannot make an equal return. But the fact that a gift differs fundamentally from an exchange becomes clear whenever a disaster affects one adult more than the other or prevents a child from achieving a normal degree of self-sufficiency as an adult. And this brings us back to the examples with which I opened the chapter.

If people loved each other because they gained "satisfaction" or utility from doing so, as utilitarian neoclassical economists theorize, the analysis ought to be essentially the same as in our example of the mother choosing how much bread and milk to buy. This would be true even for "altruists," who are described by utilitarians as taking the utility of other persons into account in making their own decisions.[29] The only difference is that instead of having preferences for various combinations of bread and milk, people would have preferences for the use of wealth by themselves and by the persons they love. Instead of the price of bread doubling while the price of milk stays the same, the graph in Figure 7–4 shows the "cost of living" doubling for the person who suffers the hardship, while the cost remains the same for the other person. The "budget line" before the disaster shows that the initial wealth or income could be used entirely by one person or the other, or apportioned anywhere in between. The graph is drawn as if the Lover loved the Loved One equally with him- or herself, the fifty-fifty division of the use of wealth being shown at Point A. But the analysis would hold with any other division. If the utilitarian view were right, a hardship concentrated on one person should have the same result as a rise in the price of bread while the price

Figure 7–4

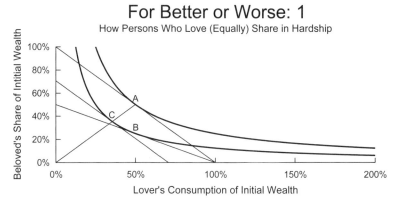

For Better or Worse: 1

How Persons Who Love (Equally) Share in Hardship

As Lover shares in Beloved's hardship, both go from A to C, not B (as neoclassical theory predicts).

of milk stays the same: The optimal choice is supposed to go from Point A to Point B, meaning that the higher cost would be absorbed by the person directly affected by the disaster. If preferences for goods are stable and the price of only one good rises, the rational response is to devote fewer resources to that good. And if this is what happens in the case of a disaster like the ones we have described, the "love" is revealed to be indeed based purely on utility—which depends, as Augustine pointed out, on love of self.

Yet, in each of the four cases we considered, instead of allowing such a thing to happen, those persons who were not directly affected by the hardship, but who loved the person directly affected, responded by giving their own scarce time and other resources to that person. The mix of consumption went from Point A to Point C in Figure 7–4, meaning that in each case the Lover shared in the hardship proportionally with the Loved One. This is exactly what one would predict from Augustine's theory that our most fundamental preferences are for persons, not for economic goods. In fact, unlike utilitarian theory, Augustine's theory allows us to predict how much wealth the Lover will devote to the Loved One. A Lover who seeks to maintain the same relative importance for the Loved One will always devote the same share of total real wealth or income to that person, after adjusting for the change in the Loved One's cost of living, just as if the Lover also were directly affected by the price change.[30] The Lover's choice will always fall at the point where a ray

Figure 7–5

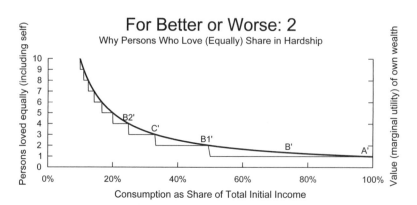

Unequal hardship lowers total from A' to B': Beloved from B1' to B2'; Lover stays at B1'.
If Lover shares equally in hardship, both go to C': same shares as before (C'/B' = B1'/A').

from the origin, tracing the same proportion for every level of wealth, intersects the appropriate price-adjusted "budget line." The ray represents constant shares in the Lover's "distribution function," which allocates the use of wealth between him- or herself and the Loved One, as reflected in Figure 7–5.

"Indifference curve" analysis is useful for explaining the choices that each person makes regarding wealth intended for his or her own use, but inappropriate for describing the economic aspect of love—simply because people who love are not indifferent to the welfare of their loved ones. For that purpose, the prevailing neoclassical approach is either superfluous[31] or else empirically false. In all such cases, we must use Augustine's "distribution function" as well as his utility function, because the distribution function describes the weighing of persons that always precedes the weighing of instrumental goods.

The updated Augustinian description of love that I have put forward explains why the people I mentioned earlier responded as they did when a birth defect or an accident or a terminal illness was suffered by a loved one: The lover sought to maintain the parity of persons, not to maximize his or her utility. This required the lover to sacrifice his or her own utility so as to share proportionally in the hardship. In most cases, the people who make such a sacrifice don't consider it a gift, because the sacrifice is simply required to preserve their relationship to the person they love. As we'll see when we consider domestic economy, the same principles that explain personal gifts apply to distributive justice within the family; in fact, the family's distributive justice originates in the personal gifts of husband and wife. Neoclassical economic theory does not understand and cannot explain this; but Augustine did, and that is an important reason that a neo-Scholastic economic approach is now necessary.

8

An Empirical Test:
Fatherhood and Homicide

When economics professor—and, later, *Freakonomics* author—Steven Levitt and law professor John J. Donohue claimed in 2001 that "legalized abortion appears to account for as much as 50 percent of the recent drop in crime,"[1] both sides in the ensuing controversy saw it as another phase in American society's ongoing controversy regarding moral norms. Levitt and Donohue, on the other hand, protested that "ours is a purely positive, not a normative analysis, although of course we recognize that there is an active debate about the moral and ethical implications of abortion."[2]

Actually, the episode revealed precisely a crisis in "positive analysis"—that is, it revealed the great trouble neoclassical economic theory has in providing an accurate description of reality, particularly when personal gifts or their opposite, crimes, are involved. The Donohue–Levitt paper is a straightforward application of George Stigler and Gary Becker's "economic approach to human behavior," which uses a highly restrictive set of assumptions to reduce human behavior to the choice of means—a maximization of "utility"—but also gratuitously redefines utility as a synonym for pleasure. The neo-Scholastic alternative to this approach, which goes back to Aristotle and Augustine, might be called the "human approach to economic behavior." It supplies the crucial element missing from neoclassical theory—the one that describes how we distribute the use of our wealth based on our preferences for persons—and correctly describes utility as our order of preference for economic goods as means for those persons.

An empirical test of the two approaches can be found precisely in the relation of fertility and crime. According to the Becker-Stigler-Bentham assumptions, "some persons become 'criminals' . . . not because their basic motivations differ from that of other persons, but because their benefits and costs differ."[3] The same assumption is made of altruistic or selfish behavior: what supposedly varies are not people's basic motivations, but only the benefits and costs they face. According to the economic approach, therefore, the current fertility rate and the current crime rate should be unrelated. This is why the Donohue–Levitt paper depends critically "on the assumption that there will be a fifteen- to-twenty year lag before abortion materially affects crime."[4]

According to the "human approach"—that is, the neo-Scholastic, Augustinian one I have been outlining in this book—some people make gifts, while others are purely selfish, and still others commit crimes, precisely because "their motivations differ." Moreover, this difference can be explained only by different preferences for oneself relative to other persons. The human approach therefore predicts that the *current* crime rate should be inversely and strongly related to the *current* birth rate. To be more precise, the current crime rate should move opposite to the current rate of "economic fatherhood": the number of children economically supported by the average man. And this is what sixty-five years of evidence shows. Moreover, when this contemporaneous relationship between fertility and crime is accounted for, the statistical effect of lagged abortions claimed by Donohue and Levitt doesn't merely vanish, but reverses. That is, more abortions today, by diminishing economic fatherhood, are accompanied by a higher crime rate, not only almost immediately but also fifteen to twenty years later.

Donohue and Levitt's Argument

Earlier versions of Donohue and Levitt's paper included a "model" making explicit the premise of the economic approach, which is that we treat other persons as objects affording utility to ourselves: "a woman aborts [her child] . . . if the utility of having a baby is more negative than the cost of an abortion."[5] In the final version, this premise is only implicit, and Donohue and Levitt's thesis on abortion and crime begins with the fact that the demographic characteristics of people arrested for crimes differ from those of the general population—particularly by age. As the chart in Figure 8–1 shows, while the general population is fairly evenly distributed by age, the age of persons arrested for crimes peaks between ages twenty and twenty-four.

Figure 8–1

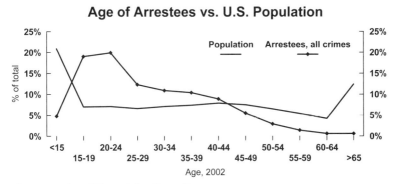

Source: arrestees, FBI; population, Census Bureau

Donohue and Levitt interpret this fact to mean that crime is essentially a function of the "high-crime late adolescent years."[6] But they fail to note that persons arrested for crime are heavily underrepresented in the ages below fifteen and over forty-five, and overrepresented between ages fifteen and forty-five—the ages at which most people have children. This is an important fact to which we shall return.

Pursuing their "adolescent criminal" thesis, Donohue and Levitt argue that legalized abortion must reduce crime rates in two ways. First, it directly causes smaller "cohorts" (the number of persons born in the same year), and by implicitly but incorrectly assuming that most arrestees are between the ages of fifteen and twenty-five, Donohue and Levitt argue that a reduction in crime rates should have become apparent about that many years after abortion was legalized. Second, Donohue and Levitt argue, the first effect is magnified because the abortion rate is higher than average among certain socioeconomic groups—particularly African Americans—who are also disproportionately represented among criminals.[7]

In other words, the Donohue–Levitt explanation of crime, like the economic approach generally, is essentially "environmental." It does not begin by asking why anyone chooses to commit a crime, even in the

highest socioeconomic groups, nor why relatively few people at *any* age
or in *any* socioeconomic group become criminals. Instead, Donohue and
Levitt restrict their focus to the fact that an above-average share of criminals are adolescents or come from the lowest socioeconomic classes.

Donohue and Levitt contend that the rise in legal abortions, which
began in several states in the late 1960s and was extended nationwide by
Roe v. Wade in 1973, explained about half the fall in the crime rate during the late 1990s. To test this thesis, Donohue and Levitt compared the
lagged abortion rate with the current crime rate, using data from all fifty
states for the period 1985–99. The authors also included other variables
intended to capture the effect of rewards and punishments for crime—
such as police per capita, the unemployment rate, per capita income, the
poverty rate, the level of welfare payments, laws permitting concealed
weapons, and per capita beer consumption—but found none of these to
be statistically significant, except the share of the population in prison.

Donohue and Levitt's study has been criticized by researchers who
accept their basic reasoning about the relationship between abortion and
crime but question its results on other, often reasonable but highly technical, grounds.[8] As the debate has become engrossed in increasingly complicated discussions about data, the main point has been obscured. There
is a basic flaw that the Donohue–Levitt study and its neoclassical critics' objections share: they contain no general explanation of why people
commit crimes, nor do they contain an empirically valid explanation of
what causes the crime rate to vary.

Perhaps more significant than the criticisms of other researchers was
Donohue and Levitt's *own* discovery that much of their data failed to
support their paper's reasoning or its conclusion. To obtain results that
supported their theory, Donohue and Levitt restricted their study to a
relatively short snippet of the available data. Comprehensive annual data
on most crime rates begin in 1957; on most violent crimes, in the 1930s;
on homicide rates, in 1900. Moreover, data exist for legal abortions since
the later 1960s, while the number of legal abortions before legalization
was, of course, zero. But the authors tried to explain only the change in
crime rates beginning in the mid-1980s. This choice ignores the commonsense question: What had caused crime rates to rise sharply in the
first place? Crime rates had fallen sharply in the 1930s through 1950s,
risen sharply in the 1960s and 1970s, peaked in the 1980s and early

1990s, and by 2000 had dropped back only to about the same levels as in 1970. This fact alone casts doubt on the theory that legal abortion could have caused the decline in the crime rate in the 1990s, because that theory cannot account for the substantial earlier variation when abortion was illegal. If Donohue and Levitt had used even a slightly longer time period—one including even *part* of the earlier rise in crime rates—they would have been forced to abandon their theory.

Moreover, even within the time period chosen, Donohue and Levitt arbitrarily discarded any evidence indicating a contemporaneous relation between abortion and crime rates. The authors explain:

> An important limitation of the data is that state abortion rates are very highly serially correlated. The correlation between state abortion rates in years t and t + 1 is .98. The five-and ten-year correlations are .95 and .91, respectively. One implication of these high correlations is that it is very difficult using the data alone to distinguish the impact of 1970s abortions on current crime rates from the impact of 1990s abortions on current crime rates; if one includes both lagged and current abortion rates in the same specification, standard errors explode due to multicollinearity. Consequently, it must be recognized that our interpretation of the results relies on the assumption that there will be a fifteen-to-twenty year lag before abortion materially affects crime.[9]

In other words, Levitt and Donohue discovered both contemporaneous and lagged statistical relationships between abortion and crime rates, and their results were statistically similar whether they used 1970s or 1990s abortion rates to try to explain 1990s crime rates. But when both were included, the models went statistically haywire ("standard errors explode due to multicollinearity").

This fact is highly significant. Other researchers have objected to Levitt and Donohue's method on the basis of omitted or misspecified variables within (reduced forms of) the three elements of neoclassical theory. But the neo-Scholastic approach suggests a whole promising new research program: that multicollinearity is a symptom of the circular logic that necessarily results from omitting one or more of the four basic elements of economic theory: not just variables, but whole equations.

After failing to find any statistically valid evidence to support either a twenty-year lag or no lag, Donohue and Levitt decided simply to omit the contemporaneous data, on "the assumption that there will be a fifteen-to-twenty-year lag before abortion materially affects crime." This move reveals a fatal flaw in the Donohue–Levitt analysis, for two reasons.

First, it indicates that the Donohue–Levitt paper is based on "spurious" or "nonsense" regressions: that is, on apparently high statistical correlations that arise not because the variables are related to *each other*, but because each variable's value in any year is closely related to its *own* value in earlier and later years.[10] (Both crime and abortion rates, as Donohue and Levitt put it, are "highly serially correlated.") In such cases, statisticians have found, "the *only conclusion that can be reached is that the equation is mis-specified . . .*" (though it is not explained how).[11]

Second, there is a strong, *positive* contemporaneous relationship between abortion and crime rates. This obviously contradicts Donohue and Levitt's critical assumption that there can be no such relation. To defend this assumption, Donohue and Levitt argue, "Obviously, recent abortions will not have any direct impact on crime today since infants commit little crime."[12] But this is not obvious. What they overlook is the fact that crimes are committed disproportionately not by survivors of abortion, but by men who are the age of the *fathers* of aborted children.[13]

Consider the evidence. In the most recent statistics available when I undertook the analysis, 77 percent of all persons arrested and 93 percent of all convicted prisoners were men.[14] Moreover, as shown in the next chart, the age distribution of persons arrested matches the age distribution of women having abortions quite closely.[15] This is especially apparent after allowing for the fact that young men fathering children are typically two years older than their female sexual partners.[16] As Figure 8–2 shows, this relation between abortion and crime rates is strong for all crimes, but stronger for violent crimes and strongest for the most violent crime of all, homicide.

This suggests that to understand the impact of legal abortion on crime, we don't require convoluted speculations about what crimes a small portion of African American children might commit a couple of decades from now, if they are permitted to be born. The relation between abortion and crime is much more direct. Most violent crimes are committed by men the age of the fathers of aborted children; and it stands to

Figure 8–2

Age Distribution of Women Having Abortions
vs. Arrestees for Murder

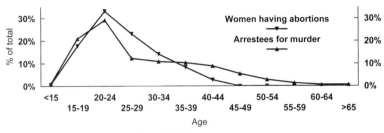

Arrestees (2001), FBI; abortion (2000), CDC. Note: most murder arrestees are men.

reason that a man who has been party to killing his own child, and is not constrained by the bonds and obligations of fatherhood, is much more likely to harm other human beings.[17]

Still, by itself this is only a correlation. It does not necessarily indicate a causal relationship. What is the underlying reality?

The Human Approach to Economic Behavior

Our alternate explanation of crime focuses not on the socioeconomic "environment," but rather on the decisions of potential criminals. Love of neighbor, love of self, and hate all involve a weighing of oneself vs. other persons. Such a weighing of persons is the essence of all moral decisions. The three behaviors differ, however, in the importance given to the self relative to others. A person who loves others along with himself gives all those persons including himself a positive significance and a positive share in the use of his or her scarce resources. A purely selfish person gives himself a positive and all other persons a zero significance, and keeps all scarce resources to him- or herself. A person who hates others gives himself a positive and others a negative significance, and so takes or destroys what belongs to others. This explanation applies equally to everyone we have considered: a mother who bears her child, a mother who aborts her child, a father or mother who supports a child after its birth, a pure egoist, and a criminal who harms others.[18]

We know from everyday experience that people's behavior toward others differs from person to person and often changes over time. If there is a general change among a large enough number of people within soci-ety, we ought to be able to detect general shifts in indicators that measure social or antisocial behavior. Indicators of "prosocial" behavior should move in the same direction, and so should indicators of antisocial behav-ior. But indicators of "prosocial" and antisocial behavior should move in opposite directions.

If the Becker-Stigler-Bentham assumptions were right, then all economic choices would be essentially amoral: Both social and antiso-cial behavior would be the result of "tastes" that are not only natural but essentially unrelated. But if this were true, the aggregate time and resources devoted to social or antisocial behavior would never change, except insofar as behavior responded to exogenous changes in the relative costs of such actions, such as punishments for crime.

The alternate understanding I am proposing holds that every eco-nomic choice necessarily involves a weighing of persons as ends as well as a weighing of utilities of economic goods as means. In other words, all economic choices are moral choices. If so, we should find that all forms of action that involve weighing the self against other persons are system-atically related, even after changes in the relative costs of the alternatives are accounted for. Specifically, those behaviors which involve lowering the importance of the self relative to other persons (as in marriage, fertil-ity, and worship) should be positively correlated with one another. And those behaviors which involve raising the significance of the self relative to other persons (crime and other antisocial behavior) also should be positively correlated with one another. But the two kinds of behavior should be inversely related. For example, the aggregate crime rate should fall whenever the aggregate fertility rate rises, and vice versa.

At the extremes, we should see the largest opposite shifts in the most opposite kinds of behavior, between giving life and taking it—that is, between the birth rate and the homicide rate. To be more pre-cise, since the vast majority of homicides are committed by men, and because not all biological fathers take responsibility for their children, we should see the largest opposite shifts in the rates of *economic father-hood* and homicide. Finding such a correlation would, at one and the same time, support the reality of the "distribution function" described by Augustine, disprove the Becker-Stigler-Bentham assumptions, and, incidentally, cast the strongest doubt on the Donohue–Levitt thesis that legalizing abortion in the 1960s and early 1970s reduced crime rates in the 1990s.

What do we mean by "economic fatherhood"? Economic fatherhood is defined by provision for one's children. As a first approximation, we can begin with the total fertility rate, or TFR, which measures how many children each woman would bear in her lifetime based on the experience of women of all ages in that year.[19] Though the TFR is a ratio of children born per woman, because it takes exactly one man and one woman to produce each child[20] the TFR is also a fairly accurate measure of the number of births to each adult couple (though of course multiple births, births by different partners, etc., are possible and are included in the statistic). Therefore, with appropriate care, the TFR can also be used as a measure of lifetime births per man. Practically speaking, the first half of our hypothesis is that a decision to have children is a decision to devote time to them, and since time is a scarce resource, devoting more time to children means devoting that much less time to oneself.

However, the total fertility rate is only a first approximation to the rate of "economic fatherhood," because not all biological fathers take economic responsibility for their offspring, while some support other people's offspring. Ideally, we would wish to remove from the numerator children who are not supported by their fathers, and from the denominator men who do not provide for their children. Though the necessary data are lacking to do so exhaustively, data are available for the two largest classes of such children and men: children supported by government welfare payments (which are an economic substitute for fatherhood) and men in prison (most of whom are unable to provide economic support for their children, even if they wished to do so).

The final necessary adjustment is to match the social groups used to calculate the rate of "economic fatherhood" with the social mix of men arrested and convicted of the crimes we are trying to predict. This social mix has changed over time. In the 1920s, more than three-quarters of men admitted to prison were white and less than a quarter nonwhite; but in recent years, the shares of white and nonwhite prison admissions have roughly equalized, while the share of those of Hispanic origin has grown rapidly. Adjusting the total fertility rate for both race and Hispanic origin would be desirable, but the necessary data on Hispanic origin begin only in 1990. Practically speaking, therefore, for the period in question we are limited to the categories "white" and "nonwhite" for both the TFR and for prison admissions. We will adjust the mix of the components in the aggregate total fertility rate to be the same as the composition of men admitted to federal or state prison.

To summarize, our measure of "economic fatherhood" will be the total fertility rate, with fertility rates for white and nonwhites mixed in the same proportion as among men admitted to prison, removing children on welfare from the numerator and men in prison from the denominator.

The other half of our hypothesis, as we noted above, is that the time devoted to committing crimes against others is a subset of time not devoted to helping them. This does not mean that everyone who is selfish actually harms other persons; rather, it suggests that crime is a peculiar form of selfishness with that result. The time devoted to harming others should therefore be a small but roughly constant proportion, not of time in general, but of time not already devoted to helping others.

The longest period for which data are available for all factors necessary for this calculation starts in 1936. (Annual data on the homicide rate go back to 1900,[21] on white and nonwhite age-specific fertility rates back to 1917,[22] and on federal and state prisoners back to 1925;[23] but data for children supported by welfare begin in 1936.)[24] The chart in Figure 8–3 compares the annual time series for the national total fertility rate, the rate of "economic fatherhood" just described, and the annual homicide rate.[25] It shows that, as predicted, there is a strong inverse relation-

Figure 8–3

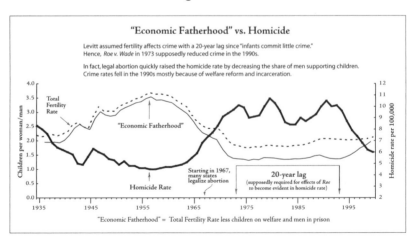

"Economic Fatherhood" vs. Homicide

Levitt assumed fertility affects crime with a 20-year lag since "infants commit little crime." Hence, Roe v. Wade in 1973 supposedly reduced crime in the 1990s.

In fact, legal abortion quickly raised the homicide rate by decreasing the share of men supporting children. Crime rates fell in the 1990s mostly because of welfare reform and incarceration.

"Economic Fatherhood" = Total Fertility Rate less children on welfare and men in prison

ship between the homicide rate and the total fertility rate, and an even stronger inverse relationship between the homicide rate and the rate of "economic fatherhood."

What does this relationship mean in commonsense terms? Recall that the total fertility rate measures how many children would be born to each woman in her lifetime, if her experience were the same at each age as the average of all women in the group surveyed during a single year. Economic fatherhood is a measure of how many economically dependent children each man would support in his lifetime, if his experience were the same at each age as the average of all men during a single year. Recall also our hypothesis that the amount of time devoted to harming others is a constant share of the time not devoted to helping others. What we ought to observe, therefore, should closely resemble the "distribution function" for the allocation of time, which we discussed in chapter 6. Specifically, the crime rate should be inversely proportional to the number of dependent children. And this is in fact what we find: over the sixty-five years for which we have data, there is a 90 percent inverse tradeoff between the current homicide rate and the current rate of economic fatherhood.[26] (See Figure 8–4.)

Moreover, a closer analysis reveals that economic fatherhood and homicide stand in a special kind of relationship known as "cointegration." Economists discovered cointegration when devising statistical tests to detect spurious or nonsense regressions. Cointegration is a "very spe-

Figure 8–4

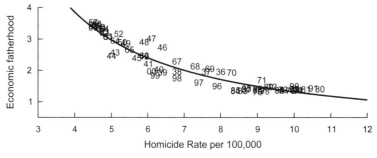

Fatherhood vs. Homicide: 90% Tradeoff
1936-2000

R-square = 0.904   # pts = 65   Label = year (e.g., 70 = 1970)
y = 19.6x^-1.17

cial case" involving variables that may differ in the short run but "are tied together in the long run."[27] Examples of cointegration include "births and deaths in an area with no immigration or emigration, cars entering and leaving the Lincoln Tunnel, patients entering and leaving a maternity hospital, or houses started and houses completed in some region," as well as "series for which a market ensures that they cannot drift too far apart, for example interest rates in different parts of a country or gold prices in London and New York."[28] The statistical tests for cointegration are quite strict,[29] and the correlation of economic fatherhood and homicide passes them.[30]

Taken together, the "multicollinearity" detected by Donohue and Levitt in their own results and the "cointegration" shown when the neo-Scholastic framework was used instead are important for three reasons.

First, they provide very strong evidence for Augustine's theory of personal distribution, particularly in its most important application: the allocation of time. Augustine's theory says that humans devote scarce resources like time to themselves and to other persons in proportion to their love for each person relative to themselves. In our empirical test, economic fatherhood measured the number of children loved equally— in the economic sense of giving them scarce resources—by the average man in his lifetime. At the same time, we showed that the time that men are able to devote to crime is a small but roughly constant share of the time remaining after devoting time to others. Economic fatherhood and crime are cointegrated because we can devote our time to any of four purposes—supporting ourselves, supporting others, harming ourselves, or harming others—and when scarce time is involved, a decision to do one of these things is necessarily a decision not to do the others.[31]

Second, the result shows why the Donohue–Levitt study on legal abortion and crime was statistically invalid. The data were trying to tell the authors that the basic theory was wrong, but they responded by abandoning the data that disagreed with the theory on the basis of a false assumption. Our analysis has just shown that there is the strongest possible *contemporary* relationship between fertility and crime, or at least the most extreme form of crime, homicide.[32]

Finally, the analysis shows that neoclassical economic theory, as exemplified by Stigler and Becker's economic approach to human behavior, is essentially a special case of Augustine's more comprehensive human approach to economic behavior—the case in which everyone is perfectly selfish. Of course, some people *are* always perfectly selfish, and for such persons, the rewards and the punishments for crimes may be the most important factors affecting behavior. However, our empirical test has shown that for the U.S. population as a whole, this special case is empirically false—because, as a matter of fact, most people share their valuable resources with other people they love, especially their children, while a small but equally regular share of all adult time is used for criminal behavior. The relation of "economic fatherhood" and crime rates is only one of many possible ways in which this can be proven. Yes, both Augustine's and Becker's theories can explain the behavior of people who are selfish, but only Augustine's can explain the behavior of people who aren't.

9

The Moral Implications of Scarcity:
The Good Samaritan Paradigm

Augustine's theory of economic choice can be applied to saint as well as sinner (and everyone in between). The difference consists not in how they go about choosing, but in the order of goods in their scales of value. What distinguishes the good man from the bad is his ordering of these values, beginning with the order of preferences for persons. Even a thoroughly evil person prefers what he or she considers "goods," not "bads." As Augustine writes, "[T]he *choice* of evil is an impressive proof that the *nature* [of all things chosen] is good."[1]

Augustine's insight is crucial in understanding the implications of scarcity for moral choice: What does it mean, he asks, to "love your neighbor as yourself"? Loving someone means willing that person some good. What this involves depends crucially on whether the good involved is "diminished by being shared with others"[2]—that is, on whether it is scarce. Though all goods with a material dimension are finite, some are normally so abundant (for example, fresh air at the earth's surface) that we loosely speak of them as being "free." But we realize that this is not literally the case when we consider exactly what is involved in providing sufficient air to astronauts in outer space, or to divers or submariners under the sea, or to miners far below the earth's surface. Even at the earth's surface, fresh air can be diminished by pollution. To be literally free, a good would have to be infinite. As a Christian, Augustine could conceive of infinite goods such as the love of God. And he argued that all men can and should love one another equally in wishing other persons such goods. But Augustine also pointed out that we cannot actually give others such a good, only wish it for them. Moral philosophers follow-ing Augustine have traditionally called this kind of love *benevolence*, or "goodwill." If love is taken to mean actually sharing one's scarce goods (which include one's time and affections), Augustine says that it is flatly impossible to love every other human equally. Moral philosophers fol-lowing Augustine have traditionally called this kind of love *beneficence*, or "doing good." It is possible to avoid harming everyone, and so the prohibition against harming others has no exceptions.

Augustine's sensible position is that no one is morally obliged to do what is impossible. Thus, Augustine puts the fact of scarcity squarely at the center of moral decision making. And all the Scholastic "econo-mists" followed him in explaining what it means to "love your neighbor as yourself." For example, Thomas Aquinas, after noting that the word "neighbor" denotes the reason for loving—"because they are nigh to us, both as to the natural image of God, and as to the capacity for glory"—concludes, "The mode of love is indicated in the words *as thyself.* This does not mean that a man must love his neighbor equally as himself, but in like manner as himself."[3]

By way of illustration, consider the famous story of the Good Samaritan, the classic case of "loving one's neighbor as oneself."[4] On the road from Jerusalem to Jericho, a Samaritan came upon a Jew beaten by robbers and left for dead. A priest and a Levite—that is, two reli-gious officials of the same faith and nationality as the beaten man—had already seen the man and passed him by. A Samaritan in the first century A.D. had roughly the same relation to a Jew as a Palestinian Arab does to a modern Israeli or as a member of an Afghan Taliban to a modern American. Yet the Samaritan stopped, treated the man's wounds as best he could, and transported him to an inn. We are told that the Samaritan paid about two days' wages in cash to the innkeeper to look after the victim, and promised to pay any further costs on his return. He must have lost at least another half-day's wages stopping to help. The decision therefore cost him at least half a week's wages, or 1 percent of his annual income, on the spot (less, if as seems likely, the merchant earned more than a day laborer). For someone earning $50,000 a year today, that would be equivalent to handing out about $500 in cash for a stranger. The Good Samaritan loved his neighbor "as himself" in the sense that, unlike those who robbed and beat him or passed him by, he treated him *as a person* like himself. But the gift represented at most half his income for the week, not the year or the rest of his life. He loved his neighbor *as* himself, but not *equally with* himself.

The parable of the Good Samaritan is interesting not just as a moral but also as an economic paradigm. It illustrates all possible economic transactions described in Augustine's theory of personal distribution, as well as their corresponding evaluations of other persons relative to ourselves. The robbers gave themselves a *positive* and the victim a *negative* significance, expressing their objective hatred by robbing him for their benefit of his property, health, and (they thought) life. The priest and Levite each gave the victim a *zero* significance, expressing their indifference by leaving him to die. The Samaritan and innkeeper gave each other a *hypothetically but not actually positive* personal significance when the Samaritan purchased goods and services from the innkeeper; expressing a love of benevolence but not beneficence toward each other, receiving as much as they gave with neither exploitation nor gift. Finally, the Samaritan gave the victim a *positive* personal significance, expressing his beneficent love of neighbor by distributing a share of his own scarce resources to the victim. The specific mention of the approximate value of this gift shows that the point of the story is not that loving your neighbor as yourself ordinarily demands some impossibly heroic act, but rather that on occasion, it requires merely overcoming one's personal prejudices to do what is decent and quite doable.

The reduction of all human action to calculations of utility defines all forms of utilitarianism. But utilitarians often disagree on questions of distribution. Right-wing utilitarians tend to view the status quo distribution of wealth, whatever it may be, as somehow divinely ordained; as if it were wrong (or, in their terms, utility-diminishing) to try to help the less fortunate. As a technical matter, however, economic theory affirms that there is a unique equilibrium for every possible distribution of wealth or income.

But there is also a brand of left-wing utilitarianism that favors distributions of wealth that are, practically speaking, impossible. Many different arguments are advanced here. Some take absolute equality of wealth as the ideal when advocating the personal, social, or political redistribution of income. Some also view society platonically as if it were one large household, ignoring the fact that a household differs from a nation, as Aristotle pointed out, "not merely in size but in kind."[5] Some treat utility as a thing, a kind of sensation that they claim (without any evidence) to be the same for everyone. But the error chiefly consists of combining two simple errors: regarding all wealth as common political wealth, when most is personal and/or domestic, and ignoring the fact of scarcity in deciding upon distribution of any wealth.

As a norm for personal giving, this view has been put in its purest and most cogent form by the Australian philosopher Peter Singer. Singer has taken many controversial positions, but all of them, as far as I can see, rest on two simple claims. The first is that there is no essential difference between humans and other animals. Singer preaches a version of the Golden Rule in which one's neighbor is potentially not every other human but every other animal. Most of the obvious objections to Singer's position on this have often been made. Singer makes a second claim, however, which, as far as I can tell, has never been challenged. It amounts to saying that the commandment to love your neighbor *as yourself* means loving everyone *equally with yourself*, even when scarce goods are involved. Though he believes that governments of affluent countries should be distributing more foreign aid to poorer nations, Singer does not advocate a political redistribution to equalize incomes, because he recognizes that forced redistribution on a large scale might seriously undermine the size of the world economy. But Singer does argue that at least for the foreseeable future, everyone has a moral obligation to bring about such a redistribution by voluntary means.

Singer puts forward both a "strong version" and a "moderate version" of his argument. The "strong version" is that "if it is in our power to prevent something bad from happening, without thereby sacrificing anything of comparable moral importance, we ought, morally, to do it." The "moderate" or "qualified" version is that "if it is in our power to prevent something very bad from happening without thereby sacrificing anything morally significant, we ought, morally, to do it." Singer notes that "the uncontroversial appearance of the principle just stated is deceptive. If it were acted upon, even in its qualified form, our lives, our society, and our world would be fundamentally changed. For the principle takes, first, no account of proximity or distance. . . . Second, the principle makes no distinction between cases in which I am the only person who could possibly do anything and cases in which I am just one among millions in the same position."[6]

Singer's explanation makes it clear that he is also ignoring the fact of scarcity. He explains that the "strong version" means that "we ought to give until we reach the level of marginal utility—that is, the level at which, by giving more, I would cause as much suffering to myself or my dependents as I would relieve by my gift. This would mean, of course, that one would reduce oneself to very near the material circumstances of a Bengali refugee." And he writes, "I can see no good reason for holding the moderate version of the principle rather than the strong version."[7]

Writing on the occasion of a famine in India, Singer argued that the particular emergency or its precise causes were not the issue; rather "the whole way we look at moral issues—our moral conceptual scheme—needs to be altered."[8] Specifically, he wrote, "Unfortunately for those who like to keep their moral responsibilities limited, instant communications and swift transportation have changed the situation. From the moral point of view, the development of the world into a 'global village' has made an important, though still unrecognized, difference to our moral situation."[9]

Whether Singer recognizes it or not, this is essentially an attack on Augustine. Singer is saying that "instant communications and swift transportation" invalidate Augustine's injunction to "pay special regard to those who, by the accidents of time, or place, or circumstance, are brought into closer connection with you." But Singer ignores the reason Augustine actually gave for ranking persons unequally with ourselves, which is not based on the fact that we have less information about those who are farther removed from us, but rather on the fact of scarcity—"you cannot do good to all."

There are several causes of extreme need. Much depends on recognizing whether it is caused by natural disaster or some similar misfortune beyond the control of those affected; by a failure to accept appropriate personal or family responsibility; or by a failure of political or social administration. The appropriate remedy will differ in each case. Moreover, it is necessary to recognize that economic resources, though scarce, are not fixed; and in particular, that the bulk of wealth in a modern economy is embodied in human beings, not inanimate objects.

Singer correctly quotes Thomas Aquinas, who observes that "whatever a man has in superabundance is owed, of natural right, to the poor for their sustenance."[10] But Singer does not note that Aquinas immediately proceeds to raise the problem of scarcity: "Since, however, there are many who are in need, while it is impossible for all to be succored by means of the same thing, each one is entrusted with the stewardship of his own things, so that out of them he may come to the aid of those who are in need."[11]

By ignoring the fact of scarcity, Singer goes far beyond Augustine's or Aquinas's traditional understanding of the Golden Rule. According to his logic, failing to help someone needier than oneself and actively harming that person are always morally equivalent. Singer writes, "for a utilitarian philosopher like myself—that is, one who judges whether acts are right or wrong by their consequences—if the upshot of the American's failure to donate the money is that one more kid dies on the streets of a Brazilian city, then it is, in some sense, just as bad as selling the kid to the organ peddlers."[12] But for those like Aquinas who recognize the force of Augustine's argument, the two are not always equivalent.[13] The major difference between the two is that Aquinas, like Augustine but unlike Singer, is always conscious of the moral implications of the fact of scarcity.

While the Golden Rule is typically illustrated by the story of the Good Samaritan, to illustrate his moral theory Singer often uses his own colorful parable about an imaginary fellow named Joe who parks his sole possession, an uninsured antique Bugatti automobile worth $250,000, on an unused railroad siding. Suddenly Joe notices a train barreling down the main track toward a child playing on the rails. A nearby switch gives Joe the choice of either allowing the child to die or else shunting the train down the siding to plow into his Bugatti—thus reducing Joe himself to destitution. Singer says that as long as there is extreme need in the world, this is the essentially the choice that Americans face in choosing between their affluent way of life and reducing their standard of living to that of a Bengali refugee. In Augustine's terms, Joe should throw the switch and destroy his Bugatti, because he is the only one able to save the child. The child is given to Joe to save, as Augustine would put it, "by a sort of lottery." (Besides, Joe still has his "human capital," not to mention, presumably, the expectation of Social Security or welfare payments. So he won't die as a result.) But contrary to Singer, Joe does not have an obligation to save every threatened child in the world, just as the Good Samaritan did not have an obligation to help every robbery or beating victim. That would be impossible because of scarcity.

What would happen if you or I ignored Augustine, Thomas Aquinas, and common sense and tried to share our scarce goods equally with everyone? There were about 6.6 billion people on Earth in 2007.[14] The American economy produced about $13.8 trillion worth of goods and services the same year, or about $45,000 per capita.[15] (Median family income for a four-person family was about $61,000; half of all four-person families had higher, and half lower, incomes.)[16] If one American with an income of $45,000 shared it equally, each person in the world (including himself) would receive $0.0000069, or about seven ten-millionths of a penny. He would starve to death. If all Americans did so, American per capita income would fall from $45,500 to about $2,075, or by about 95 percent. A large fraction of Americans would starve to death.

What if we tried to commandeer the whole world's resources to force equality of incomes? The world economy produced about $66 trillion worth of goods in 2007, measured in dollars of the same buying power. Dividing this amount by 6.6 billion people would yield a per capita income of about $10,000, which would cut the average American's standard of living by more than three-quarters (about equal to the U.S. poverty level for a single adult, but slightly above it for larger households). Yet if we tried to liquidate even a fraction of that amount, it would be necessary first to undo the vast network of specialization and exchange of private property that makes such a high income possible. How might this be accomplished? As a first approximation, we would need to change the individual and corporate income tax codes to apply a flat 100 percent marginal tax rate to all gross income, except for a modest personal exemption. That would be a simple, flat tax. But few Americans would voluntarily earn more than this threshold, since they could not either use it themselves or share it with their loved ones. And many poorer non-Americans would stop working, because they could receive the transfer of wealth merely for having incomes below the threshold. So most of the wealth wouldn't be there to distribute—and most of the people would not survive the attempt. This last fact is overlooked by those who ignore the difference in kind between a household and a nation—let alone the whole world.

Common sense and simple arithmetic tell us that Augustine was right: The number of human beings with whom it is possible to share one's scarce goods *equally* is limited for most of us to the fingers of two hands (or even one hand). For most people, substantially equal sharing is limited to their immediate relatives. But it need not be so. It would be entirely feasible for an otherwise unattached person with an average income to share it equally with five close friends, or with five strangers, rather than with five family members. People do it all the time—when they join a religious community, for example. Moreover, most of us can and do voluntarily contribute something to help those in need to whom we are not related. Christians are told that that their lives will be judged on this basis. "If you do good only to those who do good to you, what virtue is there in that? Even sinners do the same."[17] Most Americans also support the organized social or political redistribution of income to the most needy. How much is the right amount? The general answer is, "More than you're doing right now." But because the capacity for such giving is always inherently limited, and differs by situation, how much is given, and to whom, are necessarily matters of personal and political judgment, not derivable from any a priori rule.

When I presented this argument at Princeton University, I invited Peter Singer to hear my critique of his views, and he graciously attended (as did Professor Robert P. George, who instituted the Madison Program and has often debated Singer about ethics).[18] Singer objected to my presentation, apparently because he thought I was trying to discourage people from giving to the needy. But as luck would have it, the next day I had the chance to clarify our differences when Singer spoke before a Princeton audience at a rally to raise money for the United Nations Children's Fund. After presenting the story of Joe and his Bugatti, Singer was asked by a member of the audience how much money he gave away. Singer replied that he had begun as a graduate student in 1971 giving away 10 percent of his income, and now gave 20 percent to 25 percent. When he said that, I saw an opportunity to crystallize the issue of scarcity in moral choice in a way that was immediately relevant to the Princeton students who made up the audience.

On the one hand, I wanted to reinforce Singer's point that we do indeed have an obligation to help persons in extreme need, even on the other side of the planet, and that real-life grownups take this obligation seriously by giving to organizations like UNICEF. On the other hand, I wanted to show the students that a serious person is not morally obliged to reduce himself to penury in doing so, as Singer had maintained for thirty years.

I raised my hand and noted that my wife and I had also begun, at about the same age as Singer, with the goal of giving away 10 percent of our income outside our family but that in the course of raising three children, the oldest of whom was then a college freshman, our giving outside the family had fallen to about 3 percent. I asked Singer whether my wife and I had made the right moral choice in sending our artistically talented oldest son to the Rhode Island School of Design, which costs almost as much as Princeton, instead of giving the tuition money to UNICEF.

It emerged in his answer that, living in Australia, Singer and his wife had not had to pay out of after-tax income for the college educations of their own three children. (Taxes were presumably higher in Australia as a result, but Singer has been a resident of the United States for years.) After first suggesting that Princeton students might consider attending nearby Rutgers instead, and giving away the difference in tuition to the poor, Singer agreed that he probably would have made the same choice that we, and almost everyone else in the audience, had made. (He added that we should impress on our son his moral obligation to use the investment in his education to help others.)

In a follow-up exchange of e-mails, I said, "Augustine is still right: You cannot do good to all." Singer responded: "But I don't have to try to do that—that's why I objected to your calculation of how much I could give to every person in the world. I could just give to, say, 100 people, each of whom lack the means of subsistence, and for each of whom the amount that I can give would bring them enough to subsist. There's no point in spreading your donation so thinly that it does no perceptible good to anyone." I pointed out that this is exactly Augustine's point and that Singer described himself as having exactly the kind of "distribution function" that Augustine talked about. Though Singer might "just give to, say, 100 people," he did not divide his income equally among 102 people including himself and his wife, leaving each about 1 percent. The actual weights in his "distribution function" for after-tax income were, say, 38 percent to 40 percent each for himself and his wife, and 0.2 percent or 0.25 percent each for 100 other persons, making up the remaining 20 percent to 25 percent. That's relatively generous to persons outside the family—but still not as much of a sacrifice as sharing the same family income equally with even one dependent child.

What our exchange showed, I think, is that both of us made proper moral choices, given the different concrete social settings in which we have lived. But a percentage for giving outside the family that is appropriate for a real-life Australian with three children who moves to America is not appropriate for a real-life American with three children who lives in America. And for the 85 percent or so of Americans who will have children, giving away 20 percent or even 10 percent of their income on top of their family responsibilities is, practically speaking, impossible (at least until after the children leave home).

In a sense, I believe Peter Singer feels that he owes somebody the cost of three college educations. But this noble feeling cannot form the basis of a workable moral theory, any more than the same philosophy provided a workable economic theory of personal gifts or crimes.

I was struck by the same disparity between utilitarian theory and the behavior of utilitarian theorists when researching a review of *Freakonomics*, which was coauthored by Gary Becker protégé Steven Levitt and freelance journalist Stephen Dubner.[19] One of the most engaging features of the original *New York Times Magazine* article on which the book was based, written before the two authors became business partners, consisted of examples of Levitt's behavior that, Dubner correctly saw, contradicted Becker's "economic approach to human behavior." The most poignant examples followed the unexpected loss of the Levitts' first child, Andrew, from undiagnosed pneumococcal meningitis. Dubner wrote of Levitt, "He is said to be at the top of every economics department's poaching list. But the tree he and Jeanette planted when Andrew died is getting too big to move." Dubner also noted that Becker taught Levitt's undergraduates while he grieved.

The question in both cases is, why? In Benthamite theory, all of us are selfish, sociopathic freaks, maximizing utility (interpreted as physiological satisfaction) whether having a child, planting a tree to mourn his or her loss, or donating time to allow a younger colleague to grieve for the child. Altruism is similarly defined as a feeling of satisfaction gained from another's satisfaction. So Becker's satisfaction is supposed to depend on assisting the Levitts' "satisfaction," which in turn is supposed to depend on their perceiving or assisting Andrew's satisfaction. But Andrew could gain no feeling of satisfaction from the tree his parents planted, and (as Dubner noted) its planting reduced his parents' economic mobility. According to the Benthamite philosophy expressed in the "economic approach to human behavior," therefore, everyone's behavior was either irrational or purely self-indulgent (or both).

Augustine's theory seems able to explain Singer's, Becker's, and Levitt's behavior where Singer's, Becker's, and Levitt's theories cannot. According to Augustine, the main point of a gift is not to please the giver or even the recipient, but objectively to express the beneficiary's significance to the giver, regardless of feeling. Peter Singer's charitable contributions follow Augustine's rule of concentrating the benefits on a few people rather than everyone equally because "you cannot do good to all." Becker's sacrifice of a Nobel laureate's scarce time similarly expressed his love for the Levitts by putting them, as recipients, in a small minority of persons on the planet. The Levitts' planting of a tree that now cannot be moved, for a child who cannot now sense it, was a thoroughly rational, deeply human gesture, because it expressed the hole in the Levitts' lives far less inadequately than a more "efficiently" portable potted plant.

These examples strikingly illustrate a fact often noted by the late Pope John Paul II: Far from being *Christian* or even specifically *religious*, the "law of the gift" described by Augustine is a universal human phenomenon, more deeply rooted in our human nature than even selfishness or ignorance.[20] *This* is the "nature" to which "natural law" chiefly refers. The religious scribes of old were faulted for failing to practice the moral truths they still rightly taught.[21] But the modern teachers of Benthamite philosophy and economics—to their great credit as persons, though not as teachers—prove, by practicing it, the truth about human behavior that they no longer teach!

In our discussion of personal economy, we have focused on the Mother's Problem in its essence—not on the mother specifically as mother, but as a person rich in relationships to other persons, and who constantly expresses those personal loves with various gifts. Our most fundamental personal relationships begin in the family, and specifically in marriage. Our discussion therefore naturally raises the question, "How do we provide specifically for these family responsibilities?" We turn to that question next in considering domestic economy.

Part 3

Domestic Economy

The business done in the home is nothing less than the shaping of the bodies and souls of humanity. The family is the factory that manufactures mankind.

—G. K. Chesterton, "The Policeman as a Mother"

10

Marriage, the "First Natural Bond of Human Society"

The Greek root words of "economics"—*oikos* and *nemein*—literally mean "to manage a home (or household)." In other words, economics has its roots in *domestic* economy. In this chapter we'll elaborate on the neo-Scholastic theory of the family household and apply it to modern American marriage; in the next, we'll compare the modern neo-Scholastic explanation of why parents have children with that of the prevailing theory of fertility; and in chapter 12, we will see why the neo-Scholastic economic view best explains the peculiar pattern of what we earn, spend, and donate over our lifetimes.

A few basic facts of domestic economy remain as true in twenty-first-century America as when Aristotle enumerated them in his *Nicomachean Ethics* in fourth-century B.C. Athens:

> Between man and wife a natural friendship seems to exist, for they are more inclined by nature to conjugal than political society. This is so because the home is older and more necessary than the state, and because generation is common to all animals.
>
> Only to this extent do animals come together. Men, however, cohabit not only to procreate children but also to have whatever is needed for life. Indeed, from the beginning, family duties are distinct; some are proper to the husband, others to the wife. Thus mutual needs are provided for, when each contributes his own services to the common good.

Therefore, this friendship seems to possess both utility and pleasure. But it can exist for the sake of virtue if the husband and wife are virtuous, for each has his proper virtue and they can delight in it.

Children seem to be a bond of union. Hence sterile [childless] couples separate more readily, for children are a common good of both parties; and what is common maintains friendship.[1]

In observing that humans are by nature not only "rational" and "political" but also "matrimonial" (or "conjugal") animals, Aristotle combines biological, social, and metaphysical truths. First of all, his observation concerns the nature not just of human society in general but of each human *person*. Not everyone will marry and have children or even a heterosexual orientation (though the overwhelming majority does in all three cases). But every human being originates from the union of exactly one mother and one father.[2] If humans ever stopped sexually reproducing, all persons and households would disappear within a single lifetime.

Second, while involving animal biology, our "matrimonial" nature cannot be reduced to it. Like most animal mating, marriage has elements of pleasure and utility; but what makes it also rational and specifically human is the virtue that each spouse exercises as "friend" or "lover" of the other, which Aristotle defines as "one who wills and does what is good (or apparently good) for the sake of his friend."[3]

Third, beyond merely pursuing their individual goods, the man and woman through their complementary roles acquire, produce, and share *common* goods, about which they must decide jointly according to "distributive justice." Distributive justice is the "geometric ratio" describing how "common goods . . . are to be apportioned to people sharing in social community . . . as one person as compared with another may have an equal or unequal share . . . according to a certain merit." Distributive justice may be considered a joint or collective gift, analogous for any human community to the personal gifts we discussed in part 2.

Finally, the most important common good the married couple produces is children, for whom they provide the fundamental goods of "existence, rearing, and instruction."[4] All other kinships are derived from these original marital and/or parental relationships.[5]

Having sketched the theory of the nuclear family household in his *Ethics*, Aristotle tried more ambitiously but less successfully in the later *Politics* to adapt his theory to explain also the contemporary Mediterranean slave-holding agricultural estate and the basic principles of social order. He started once again with two basic household relationships, but rather than "husband and wife" and "parents and children," as in the *Ethics*, these were now "a man and a woman" and the more generic "ruler and ruled." This last relationship he variously identified as the principle of order between an animal's body and soul, between male and female animals, between rational humans and irrational animals, between the human intellect and emotions, between husband and wife, between master and slave, and between political ruler and subject.

Aristotle proceeded from the nuclear family household to the slave-owning agricultural estate by classing the former's livestock with the latter's human slaves as "slaves by nature";[6] and by this reasoning he purported to have found in the slave-owning agricultural estate three rather than the previous two "natural" human relationships: "the first, smallest parts of the household are master and slaves, husband and wife, and father and sons."[7] In each of these relationships, according to Aristotle, the male householder naturally provided the ruling principle of order: over the wife by analogy to the "aristocratic" rule of human reason over the passions, and over the slave by analogy to the "despotic" rule of the soul over the body. Equally crucial to his argument was the assertion that human nature means man only at his combined mental, physical, and moral peak.[8]

Aristotle had criticized his teacher Plato (not without justice) for assuming that "associations differ only in size, not specifically. For example, they suppose that the fathers of families rule few persons, household managers more persons, and statesmen and kings still more persons, as if there were no difference between a large household and a small political community."[9] Yet Aristotle's descriptions of the husband-wife and master-slave micro-communities went on to make essentially the same mistake, by treating both in effect as large *persons*.

The flaw in such analogies, as Aquinas pointed out, is that while every animal (rational or irrational) has an inherent natural unity—which is why we don't worry, for example, that we'll lose an arm or leg if we run—"the whole which the political group or the family consti-

tutes has only a unity of order, for it is not something absolutely one."[10]
Treating purely human communities as "organic unities" or "organisms"
is misleading because, as "unities of order," such communities are constantly threatened by dissolution *precisely through loss of members.*[11]

The failure of Aristotle's body/soul analogies blew several holes in
the more elaborate *Politics* version of his household theory, since that
theory could not really explain why a marriage, family, or household
forms in the first place, gains or loses members, or continues through
time. It is true, for example, that "children are a common good" for
their natural parents and (as we will see) that "childless people part more
easily." But this common good cannot *bring* the parents together, since
it is a result rather than a cause of their association. And if the biological urge to procreate were all that were common to husband and wife,
there would be no essential difference between human marriage and
other animal mating, as Aristotle had previously maintained in the *Nicomachean Ethics*—nor could we explain why even many married couples
with children divorce (albeit less frequently than childless couples). Nor
could their common good bring or keep master and slave together since,
as Aristotle said, "the authority of master over slave is exercised primarily for the benefit of the master and only incidentally for the benefit of
the slave."[12]

Slavery was no less prevalent in Augustine's than Aristotle's day.
Both men started from the same understanding of man as a rational,
matrimonial, and political animal. Both also treated family, slavery, and
political relationships in the same discussion.[13] But Augustine emphati-
cally disagreed with Aristotle on two crucial, related points: that there
could be anything natural about the enslavement of one rational creature
by another, and that we should consider natural powers only "as things
have them by nature and not in corrupt forms."

For Augustine, the general explanatory principle is not "ruling and
being ruled" but "peace, the tranquility of order." "In fact, even when
men wish a present state of peace to be disturbed they do not do so
because they hate peace, but because they desire the present peace to
be exchanged for one that suits their wishes." In Augustine's view, the
root of slavery (as of all sin or vice) is "pride, . . . a perverted imitation of
God," which causes those who would master others to fail first of all to
master themselves. Rather than obeying the innate human reason that

stamps them with the image of their Creator, would-be masters become enslaved to their own passion to dominate others.

Moreover, descriptive realism requires us to explain human behavior not only when it is reasonable but also—especially—in its "corrupt forms." Augustine seeks constantly to contrast and explain the best in parallel with the worst human behavior. For example, where Aristotle emphasizes that man is a social and political animal, Augustine says instead, "the human race is, more than any other species, at once social by nature and quarrelsome by perversion."[14] And in doing so he emphasizes the interconnection of behavior at the personal, domestic, and political levels:

> Even in the extreme case when [men and women] have separated themselves from others by sedition, they cannot achieve their aim unless they maintain some semblance of peace with their confederates in conspiracy. Moreover, even robbers, to ensure greater efficiency and security in their assaults on the peace of the rest of mankind, desire to preserve peace with their associates.
>
> Indeed, one robber may be so unequalled in strength and so wary of having anyone share his plans that he does not trust any associate . . . ; yet even so he maintains some kind of peace, at least with those whom he cannot kill, and from whom he wishes to conceal his activities. At the same time, he is anxious, of course, to be at peace in his own home, with his wife and children and any other members of his household; without doubt he is delighted to have them at his beck and call. For if this does not happen, he is indignant; he scolds and punishes; and if need be, he employs savage measures to impose on his household a peace which, he feels, cannot exist unless all the other elements in the same domestic society are subject to one head; and this head, in his own home, is himself. Thus, if he were offered the servitude of a larger number, of a city, maybe, or a whole nation, on the condition that they should all show the same subservience he had commanded in his household, then he would no longer lurk like a brigand in his hide-out; he would raise himself on high as a king for all to see—although the same greed and malignity would persist in him.

We see, then, that all men desire to be at peace with their
own people, while wishing to impose their will on other people's lives. For even when they wage war on others, their wish
is to make those opponents their own people, if they can—to
subject them, and to impose on them their own conditions of
peace.[15]

Augustine contrasts this degenerate semblance of peace with that in
the transcendent City of God, which lives side by side on earth, and so far
as possible seeks cooperation on purely temporal affairs, with members of
the Earthly City who do not share this view.[16]

This is where domestic peace starts, the ordered harmony about
giving and obeying orders among those who live in the same
house. . . . But in the household of the just man "who lives on the
basis of faith" and who is still on pilgrimage, far from that Heavenly City, even those who give orders are the servants of those
whom they appear to command. For they do not give orders
because of a lust for domination but from a dutiful concern for
the interests of others, not with pride in taking precedence over
others, but with compassion in taking care of others.[17]

Aristotle's formulation of "ruling and being ruled" does not work as
the general principle of social order, because merely giving or receiving
orders does not create order. The resulting nature and degree of order
depend critically on the assessments of oneself vs. the other on the parts
of both the speaker and hearer.

Against what Aristotle seems to argue in the *Politics*, Augustine
therefore traced the household's origin to marriage alone and slavery to
the human convention of positive law rather than natural right. Augustine succinctly stated that "the first natural bond of human society is
man and wife" and that in all cases marriage combines two inseparable
elements—sexual fidelity and acceptance of resulting children—with a
third (sacrament) pertaining only to baptized Christians.[18] To Christian
slaves unable to gain their legal freedom, Augustine recommended the
Apostle Paul's advice to suffer the injustice and serve their masters will-
ingly, thereby avoiding enslavement to their own passions for revenge and

exceeding their masters in both internal freedom and happiness in this life and the next.

In his commentaries on Aristotle's *Ethics* and *Politics*, Aquinas recognized that Augustine's contributions had made it possible to disentangle Aristotle's theory of the household from the latter's apparent justification of slavery. He also saw that Augustine had made it possible to integrate a complete and coherent theory of personal, domestic, and political economy.

Aquinas used Augustine's theory of personal economy to turn the theory of love or friendship from what had seemed an incidental, superfluous, or conflicting feature of Aristotle's philosophy into its simplifying and unifying core. The ultimate principle of social order is neither physical nor social coercion nor yet supposedly superior masculine cleverness, but the personal love (for oneself and other persons) that is always ordered to the good of the beloved person; and this remains true whether the act is intended to be basically altruistic, indifferent, or even predatory.

Moreover, Aristotle had seemed to suggest that what unites any human association is simply *sharing the benefit of one or more common goods*. Without denying this (and while correcting Aristotle's error on slavery), the Scholastic theory initiated by Thomas Aquinas follows Augustine by saying that what unites any human community above all is *common sacrifice of goods*, which is always motivated by love and expressed through personal and/or collective gifts.

Lessons of a Lemonade Stand

To apply this theory, we must first state it in a form capable of empirical verification (or falsification), and then compare it with the evidence. I noted when presenting the Scholastic outline of economic theory in chapter 2 that with appropriate modification it can describe any economic unit from a single person to the world economy and that it contains all the theory necessary to explain investment and real economic growth. I left the elements of production and exchange in the background while discussing personal economy in order to focus on the theories of personal distribution and consumption. The reason is now apparent: Our inherently "matrimonial" nature means that an economic event, whether simple or complex, consisting entirely of isolated and unrelated individuals is not only unsustainable; it's unexplainable. It would require that everyone be, literally, "self-made" men and women—which have never existed anywhere, despite the assumptions of modern economic theory.

To see how these elements must be combined and integrated, let's begin with the simplest possible example: a child's lemonade stand. The prerequisites of such an enterprise are a product (lemonade), a supply of potential customers (say, the people entering or leaving a hiking trail or bike path on a warm day), and a purpose (say, using half as personal spending money and donating the other half for disaster relief). To produce lemonade, as with almost any other product, it is necessary to combine the services of some person or persons (so-called human capital) with those of productive property ("nonhuman capital"). To keep track of their contributions, we will suppose that a brother and sister are involved: One supplies only the labor (mixing the ingredients, setting up the stand, making a sign, waiting on or soliciting customers), while the other supplies only the property (say, a folding table, a pitcher, a cooler, a mixing spoon, glasses, poster board, and marker or crayons for a sign) and the raw ingredients (lemonade mix, water, and ice).[19]

Beyond these prerequisites, the success of the business is largely a matter of price. Because customers ordinarily value the first glass of lemonade more highly than the fifth, the demand for lemonade varies inversely to its price. If the price were set too low (say, a penny a glass), the supply of lemonade would be quickly exhausted: Customers would have to be turned away, yet the stand would fail to cover its cost of raw materials, much less provide any income for the children. Economists call this "excess demand." If the asking price were too high (say, $100 a glass), there would be no customers and, again, no income: a case of "excess supply." Somewhere in between is the price that equalizes supply and demand, maximizing income for the sellers and conforming most closely to the preferences of customers. Ordinarily, this optimum price cannot be predicted in advance but requires a certain amount of trial and error.

Anyone who has observed this process in real life realizes that it is necessary to take into account the demand for lemonade, not only from potential customers but also from the "worker" and "proprietor" of the stand. In calculating quantities to produce and the selling price, the sellers will want to allow for the possibility of drinking some of the lemonade themselves, especially if it promises to be a long, warm day. If demand is slack and the price received from customers is below a certain point, the sellers may prefer to drink the stuff themselves; on the other hand, if demand is brisk and the price higher, they may curb their own consumption in order to increase the stand's cash sales and their own compensation.

Now, how should the revenues from the sale of lemonade be divided? It might seem that a fifty-fifty split makes the most sense, and if the children contributed equally to starting the enterprise, this is a reasonable way to split any profits. But this does not help in figuring out the compensation of the worker and proprietor, because their services constitute most of the costs. A little experience reveals that what is fair compensation varies, ultimately depending on how sales revenue responds to changes in the relative contributions of the two parties. For example, suppose that on two successive days, all conditions but one were the same—same number of passersby, same weather, same quantity of lemonade produced and offered for sale—except that on the first day, the lemonade stand's worker puts in four hours, and on the second day, five hours. It is obvious in this case that the additional revenue must be due to the worker's additional effort. Alternatively, suppose that the number of hours worked and all the other factors are the same on both days, except that on the first day, the "proprietor" forgets the cooler that keeps the lemonade from becoming lukewarm, while on the second day he brings it, thus allowing the advertised "ice cold lemonade" to be sold chilled throughout the day. In this case, the increase in sales on the second day is attributable to the provision of the cooler.

In principle, the entire proceeds from the sale of lemonade can be divided in this way, between the child who provides only labor and the child who provides only the use of property. The children will notice that, just as the value of an additional glass of lemonade to a customer varies inversely with the quantity the customer has already consumed, the value of the worker's and proprietor's incremental services varies inversely with the value already provided. For example, the amount of extra sales realized when the worker works one hour is obviously larger than when he works none, and that, in turn, is ordinarily larger than the extra sales realized when the worker works for two hours instead of one, three hours instead of two, and so on. Similarly, the increase in sales will normally be larger after the first dozen ice cubes are added to the pitcher than after the second dozen. So, if the children accurately perceive what is happening, they should be able to divide the income with a reasonable degree of objectivity, in proportion to the share of the proceeds traceable to the contributions of each. It is often difficult in the real world to disentangle all the variables, especially for an isolated business. But it is much easier to see under conditions of competition—for example, with one or more competing lemonade stands in the vicinity—because the change of a single feature by one business firm results in its capturing a larger share of the market, thus forcing the other competing firms either to offer the same feature or else to lose customers and ultimately go out of business.

In describing the lemonade stand, we have sketched the general description of a business firm that produces one kind of good (in this case, lemonade) with two kinds of factors or producers (people and property). And for many purposes—for example, explaining the distribution of family income or the effect of fiscal policy on unemployment at the national level—we will find that the whole economy can fruitfully be viewed as if it were one large stand producing a single composite product, GNP or GDP, instead of lemonade. This is because the analysis can take the absolute number of workers and the absolute size of the "nonhuman capital" stock as given. (The unemployment rate measures the share of workers employed or unemployed rather than their absolute numbers.)

So, if we left the analysis here, we would be able to explain both how products and their producers' incomes originate and what causes the producers to be employed or unemployed—but not where the producers themselves or their productive property came from. Yet without accounting for that, we would have nothing to say about fertility or population and little to say about what causes income and output to grow. In our example, where did the "proprietor's" property—the table, pitcher, cooler, and so forth—come from? These items must have been produced by a process essentially similar to the children's production of lemonade: by combining the services of people and property, possibly within the children's family but more probably by a business firm from which the family purchased them. Moreover, in every lemonade stand in my experience, the productive property has been borrowed from the children's parents without compensation: that is, it has been received as a gift.

Both facts apply to the children themselves. First, the children were produced (or "reproduced") by their parents in a way analytically similar to the children's production of lemonade or the business firm's production of the cooler. As G. K. Chesterton put it, "The family is the factory that manufactures mankind."[20] Second, the endowments of human and nonhuman goods with which the children began life were also received as gifts.

Thus, to have a truly general theory embracing fertility as well as the production of property, income distribution, and employment, we must be able, when necessary, to regard the two kinds of factors, human and nonhuman, as also being two kinds of reproducible goods, human and nonhuman. The analytical distinction between producer and product typically depends not so much on their inherent qualities as on how humans treat them: Just as we can use the same computer either to play games or run a business, or drive the same car either for business or pleasure, we can also use our own human faculties for work or recreation (or for activities like worship, which is neither). What's just as important, we can't have a fully adequate theory of production, even for an enterprise as simple as a lemonade stand, without taking into account the overlapping generations involved in any family.

Recall from our discussion of Scholastic economics that any economic activity can be fully described in four brief sentences, to which correspond four mathematical equations. Whatever the change in details, all four elements remain necessary for an accurate and complete account. But the analysis must be rewritten in order to suit the particular agent in question: an individual person, a married couple, a business firm, a charitable foundation, or a government. This time the description is restated so that we can more easily measure its predictions using government statistics on income and output, and so that we can apply it to the theory of fertility, which concerns the (re)production of people.[21]

1. For whom: "Final Distribution." We express the significance of the persons who are the "ends" or purposes of our actions (including ourselves) by distributing the use of our goods among them.[22] Each person's actual consumption of goods (after accounting for differences in timing) equals the total wealth or income to be distributed, multiplied by that person's significance relative to all the persons sharing in the distribution. It is therefore equal to that person's factor income plus any net "transfer payments" received or given.[23] While labor and property compensation are received for contributing to current production, transfer payments comprise any income *not* received as compensation for contributing to current production. These naturally fall into three categories: personal, domestic, and political.

1a. Personal gifts (and their opposite, crimes). At the personal level, transfer payments include the gifts of scarce resources that people make to one another, while crimes depriving others of life or property amount to involuntary transfer payments from the victim to the criminal.[24] Among the most fundamental examples of personal gifts are the ones a man and a woman make when they marry, which establish their household and provide its initial stock of common goods.[25]

1b. Domestic "distributive justice." Henceforth, the married couple determines the distribution of the family's income or wealth jointly, according to its formula of familial distributive justice. Such domestic "transfers" include not only those made to or received jointly from each individual spouse to their marriage partnership but also the gifts that parents jointly make to their children (for example, by paying for their living and education expenses before they can support themselves),[26] or conversely, the gifts that adult children later make to support aged parents.[27] Because, as already noted, some of the ancient household's functions have been specialized by its modern offshoots, the business firm and charitable foundation, "domestic" transfers now also include benefits paid by business firms to former, retired, or disabled workers and their dependents, as well as payments made by persons to charitable foundations and the grants made by such foundations to others on behalf of those donors.

1c. Political "distributive justice." Just as with personal gifts and domestic distributive justice, political distributive justice determines the shares in using a political community's common wealth, according to the relative significance of the persons.[28] It is also effected by transfer payments, which include government benefits and taxes,[29] the former amounting to transfers to the beneficiaries from, and the latter amounting to transfers from the taxpayers to, the political "common wealth."[30] We will discuss these in more detail later in considering political economy, but we must also take them into account here, because domestic and political transfers often serve similar or competing purposes.[31]

2. What: "utility" (consumption). We value (or rank, or prefer) scarce economic goods, like lemonade, as the means we intend to be used by or for the persons who are the ultimate purposes or "ends" of our activity.[32] Scarcity implies both that as the quantity of a good increases, the value of each additional unit declines,[33] and also that part or all of the goods produced are "used up"—that is, rendered unusable, by consumption.

3. How: "production." We produce such scarce goods by combining the useful services of people ("human capital") and of property ("nonhuman capital").[34] Generally speaking, the modern household specializes in producing and maintaining people,[35] while the modern business firm specializes in producing and maintaining property.

4. How: "equilibrium" (justice in exchange). The sale of each product provides the compensation of its producers: labor compensation for the workers and property compensation for the property owners.[36] The income is thus wholly divided between labor and property compensation. In a competitive market, each factor is compensated in proportion to the share it contributes to the total value of the final product.[37]

We can see how these elements are integrated over a lifetime for one person with a stylized illustration that, though simple, is surprisingly versatile and empirically verifiable. Figure 10–1 treats the typical life as divided into four phases: childhood, parenthood, the "empty nest," and old age. These four phases are the time periods between five pivotal life events, three of which are absolutely, and the other two nearly, universal: one's own birth; the end of instruction; the birth of a first child; the

Figure 10–1

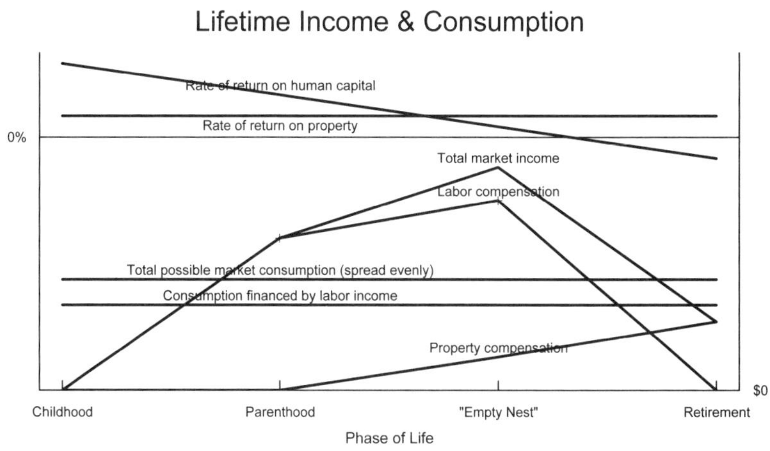

Lifetime Income & Consumption

last child's departure from the household; and death. The "matrimonial" nature of the human person is indicated by the inherently intergenerational pattern.

All four elements of economic theory are combined in and necessary to explain this pattern. For example, the theories of production and exchange are simultaneously reflected in the fact that all income originates as labor or property compensation and that each is equal (in a competitive market) to the value contributed to current production. The theories of production, exchange, and consumption are reflected in the fact that the rate of return on human capital varies inversely with the age of the person in whom it is embodied, but the same is ordinarily not true of nonhuman capital—an important fact. The theories of consumption, exchange, and distribution are reflected partly in the fact that lifetime consumption and production are equal except for any net transfer payments made or received. And the central role of personal and intrafamily gifts is reflected in the fact that each person's production/income usually *doesn't* match that person's consumption in each phase of life—the difference equaling net gifts (or other transfer payments) given or received. For example, the combined excess of total current income over current consumption during the parenthood and "empty nest" phases equals the combined excess of current consumption over income in childhood and old age.

The importance of these elements will be easier to see as we apply them, starting with marriage.

Is Marriage Disappearing?

What unites any human community is not just the common *enjoyment* but especially the common *sacrifice* of goods, which is always motivated by love and expressed through gifts. Applied specifically to marriage, this premise of neo-Scholastic theory predicts that the strongest marriages will share three characteristics: First, the mutual gift of goods that the spouses otherwise could have used for themselves, including the literal self-giving that normally results in the parents' first gift to their children, their existence; second, the parents' cooperation in the joint sacrifices necessary for the gifts that ordinarily follow, the rearing and instruction of the child; and third, the common sacrifice of shared worship. In purely human and empirical terms, the theory says only that couples sharing all three elements—mutual personal gifts, joint gifts to others (especially their children), and the common sacrifice of shared worship—will be more likely to stay or get married than those missing one or more elements.

In considering the evidence for this theory, we at once face an apparently fatal objection: Isn't this an idealized version of marriage that has seldom existed in reality and, insofar as it did, has all but disappeared? And if so, doesn't that make neo-Scholastic theory of domestic economy irrelevant? Doesn't it rather confirm the prevailing neoclassical theory, which starts by assuming one-person households for which marriage is not essential?

Consider the hard facts. First, barely one-third of the world's population even lives in societies in which monogamy is the only legal and/ or culturally accepted form of marriage. In fact, sociological and anthropological research has indicated that some 80 to 85 percent of all known human societies in history have allowed polygamous marriage.[38]

Second, in 1960 about 85 percent of American households were family households (meaning related persons living together), with 75 percent headed by a married couple and 44 percent comprising such couples living together with their own minor children. Yet by 2000 the share of American family households had shrunk by one-fifth from 85 to 68 percent, the share headed by married couples by nearly one-third from 75 to 52 percent, and married couples living with their minor children by nearly half, from 44 to 24 percent—less than one-quarter of all households. Meanwhile the share of family households with unmarried male or (more often) female heads had risen by more than half, from less than 8 to more than 12 percent. Most striking of all, the share of *non*-family households, consisting almost entirely of adults living alone, had more than doubled from 15 to 32 percent and was not only overtaking married couples with children but surpassing *all* families with children. Extrapolating those rates of change suggested that the last American households consisting of married couples with children would disappear by 2050; the last married-couple households by 2100; and the last families of *any* kind with children by 2150.

Thus, it is argued, the apparent strength and stability of American marriage and family constituted a rare and isolated cultural-historical exception that is now being inexorably supplanted.

This claim is based on a misreading of the facts. First, in cultures where polygamy is legal or socially accepted, about 80 percent of all

Figure 10–2

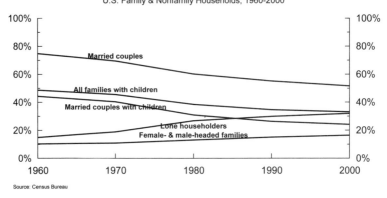

Are Marriage and Family Disappearing in America?
U.S. Family & Nonfamily Households, 1960-2000

Source: Census Bureau

marriages still involve only one husband and one wife.[39] As a result, 89 percent of adults in the world in 2000 had married by age forty-nine— exactly the same as in the United States.[40] Nor does the evidence suggest that the relative experience was ever substantially different.[41] Second, the most important factor driving the changes in American household composition is sharply increased longevity. For most of recorded history, average life expectancy at birth was about twenty-four years. In the United States, this had risen by about half, to thirty-seven years, by 1850; nearly doubled to forty-seven years by 1900; nearly tripled to sixty-eight years by 1950, and by 2000 averaged seventy-seven years (eighty for women and seventy-five for men). If (as some now project) mortality continues to decline at about the same rate as in the latter half of the twentieth century, U.S. life expectancy at birth will rise to eighty-seven years by 2050 and to ninety-eight years by 2100—more than quadruple the historical norm.[42]

This rapid increase in longevity has radically changed the typical course of human life. For most of history the twenty-four-year average life span meant many (possibly even a majority of) people ever born experienced at most the first two stages of life we have described: dependent childhood and active parenthood. These phases must have been of approximately equal average length, and children must have made the transition to adulthood and parenthood much younger than is now

Figure 10–3

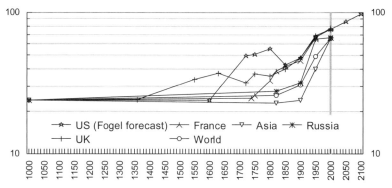

Life Expectancy in the US, UK, France, Asia, Russia, & World
Years of life expected at birth (both sexes)

Source: Maddison 2001, Fogel 2004

typical. Anyone fortunate enough to escape infectious disease and other mortal dangers might still live the biblical span of threescore years and ten, but only a tiny minority actually did. Thanks to increased longevity, most people can now expect to experience all four life stages: dependent childhood, active parenthood, the "empty nest," and retirement. For the average American born in 2000, these phases can be expected to be of roughly of equal length: say, twenty-one years for women, somewhat less for men.

Increased longevity has affected all five pivotal events that define the four life stages. First, because most children now survive to adulthood, parents have been having fewer children than when this was far less likely. Second, by increasing the economic rate of return on instruction of all kinds (since the associated increase in annual earnings can be realized for many more years), increased longevity has prolonged the periods of instruction and dependent childhood. Third, as instruction and dependent childhood have lengthened, people have been marrying later and the period of active parenthood has lengthened commensurately.[43] Fourth, most parents now live long enough to see their children leave home and start families of their own: the "empty nest." This—not a larger proportion of married couples remaining childless—accounts for the larger share of married couples living without children. Finally, widows and widowers—not those choosing "alternative lifestyles"—account for most of the sharp increase in the number and share of householders living alone. (There are about twice as many widows as widowers due to women's greater longevity.)

Perhaps the simplest way to grasp these patterns is to begin with the two essential elements of marriage identified by Augustine: marital fidelity and fertility. Demographers, economists, and sociologists can look at both by "period" or "cohort." The period is typically a year and summarizes the experience of those of all ages, while a cohort comprises those born in the same period. We must combine the period and cohort approaches, because some marital or fertility characteristics are common to a particular age regardless of the year in which one is born (for example, everyone is born "never married," and people have children only after reaching sexual maturity). But whether and when one marries, divorces, or has children is also profoundly affected by major events that affect different cohorts at different ages. For example, the Second World War had a much more profound effect on the marital and fertility decisions of those born in 1925 than on those born in 1956, while the reverse was true of the legalization of abortion by several states beginning in the late 1960s and nationwide by the U.S. Supreme Court's 1973 *Roe v. Wade* decision. Few of those born in 1925 had already married or had children when America's 1941 entry into the war disrupted the plans of tens of millions of Americans, while the fertility of women in that cohort had ended before legalization of abortion. Conversely, the 1956 cohort was born fifteen years after America's entry in the war, and most had not yet married or begun having children in 1973.

If we consider marital status by sex and age in the year 2000, we are implicitly combining the period and cohort approaches, but with relatively limited information about the cohorts. For example, those who were seventy-five years old in 2000 were born in 1925, while those who were forty-four years old were born in 1956. But it is not immediately obvious from such a snapshot whether, say, the fact that far fewer of those seventy-five or older were currently divorced than those forty to forty-four years old was due to being over seventy-five rather than forty to forty-four years old, or to differences resulting from having been born in or before 1925 rather than from 1956 to 1960.

Even so, the "matrimonial" aspect of human nature is demonstrated by men's and women's complementary marital status at every age. Almost

Figure 10–4

Marital Status by Age and Sex, 2000

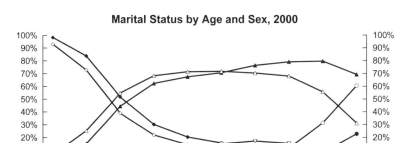

equal shares of men and women below age forty-five were currently married in 2000. But for those above age forty-five, far higher shares of currently married men were mirrored by far higher shares of currently widowed women, mostly because nearly all had been married, but men hadn't lived as long as women.

Only 11 percent of Americans aged forty-nine or over had not married by 2000. If we observe successive cohorts, we find that this was also almost exactly the same percentage for all American cohorts back to the 1840s—though Americans born from the 1910s to 1950s married at significantly higher rates, peaking at an apparently unprecedented 96 percent (98 percent of women and 94 percent of men) of those born in the 1920s and 1930s.

However, these figures take into account only those who had already survived to age fifteen. If we count everyone, the shares of "never marrieds" rise and "ever marrieds" fall substantially in proportion to higher mortality. For example, about 92 percent of American adults born in the 1890s who reached at least age fifteen had married by age fifty; but including those who died sooner, the share of ever marrieds drops to 69 percent. The same respective numbers are 96 percent/83 percent for those born in the 1920s, and 96 percent/88 percent for those born in the 1930s. For those born in the 1950s, an average of about 88 percent of those who attained age fifteen married by age forty-nine. This was lower than for the cohorts born from the 1910s through the 1940s. But when *everyone* born in the 1950s is included, the share of ever marrieds is actually higher than for all earlier cohorts.

Figure 10–5

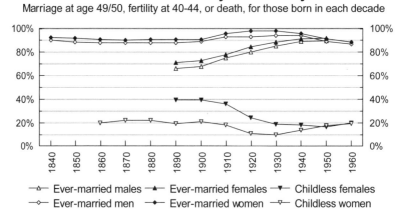

U.S. Marital and Fertility Status by Cohort
Marriage at age 49/50, fertility at 40-44, or death, for those born in each decade

—△— Ever-married males —▲— Ever-married females —▼— Childless females
—◇— Ever-married men   —◆— Ever-married women —▽— Childless women

Americans born from the 1910s through the 1950s were also exceptional in having children, compared with earlier and later cohorts. Contemporary changes in household composition are *not* the result of an unusually large share of American women having remained childless. Most variation in American fertility rates has resulted from the number of children parents choose to bring into the world (which we will consider in the next chapter), not whether they have had children at all. The share of childless American women dropped below 10 percent for those born in the 1930s, but for those born in the 1950s and 1960s it appeared to be stabilizing near the 20 percent average experienced by American cohorts born from the 1860s to the first decade of the twentieth century. As with marital status, the share of women having children or remaining childless is profoundly affected by mortality. After we make the same mortality adjustment in the figures for fertility as we did for marital status, the cohorts born in the 1950s appear to have had the lowest percentage of childless females.

From all available data, we can conclude with reasonable confidence not only that a larger share of Americans had married or had children at the end of the twentieth century than a century earlier but also that the shares never married or remaining childless were the lowest in American history.[44] Thus, the evidence indicates that far from being increasingly rare exceptions, getting married and having children remained the rule rather than the exception for Americans at the start of the twenty-first century. Mortality aside, nine-tenths seems to be the historical norm for marriage, and four-fifths to nine-tenths for the share of Americans having children.

These facts raise two important points:

First, though overwhelmingly practiced, it is neither necessary nor even socially desirable that absolutely everyone marry and/or have children. In fact, that would make many socially useful and necessary occupations impossible. The lives of many of the greatest saints in history would have been inexplicable or at least less admirable if giving up marriage were not a major sacrifice. Many others who choose or are unable to marry and/or have children exhibit the same self-giving demanded of spouses toward each other and their natural children—actually or figuratively becoming adoptive or spiritual parents for those who otherwise would be abandoned.

Second, though at least nine-tenths of each generation of Americans have ultimately gotten married, how can neo-Scholastic theory account for their increasing difficulty in *staying* married, and for the divergent recent experience of such subgroups as African Americans?

The answer has two parts. First, because marriage can ordinarily end in only two ways—by the death or voluntary separation of one or both partners—the rising divorce rate is intrinsically related to the falling death rate. Moreover, the neo-Scholastic theory we have examined explains who stays married and who gets divorced. Second, recent legal changes that separated the two essential elements of marriage, fidelity and fertility—above all, legalized abortion—have not only increased the divorce rate but also reduced the marriage rate most sharply among subgroups in which the abortion rate is highest, for exactly the reason given by Aristotle: "childless couples part more easily."

On the first point, while the impact of divorce as a social pathology ought not to be minimized, too little heed has been given to the observation by Paul H. Jacobson in 1959: "It is widely believed that the disruption of family life in the United States has been increasing at a rapid rate for many years. This view probably has its origin in the marked upward trend of the divorce rate, but it errs by omitting from the reckoning the counterbalancing effect on family life of the decline in the death rate."[45] Jacobson credited Walter Wilcox for being the first American demographer to recognize (in 1891) that "a marriage ends either 'naturally' by the death of either spouse or 'civilly' by divorce or annulment." But, he noted, "no one, apparently, has considered quantitatively the total effect on the family of the long-term upward trend of divorce and the downward course of mortality. In other words, what has been the trend of the combined rate of marital dissolutions resulting from death and divorce?"[46] Jacobson undertook to answer that question with calculations that I have reproduced and updated in the chart seen in Figure 10–6.

Figure 10–6

U.S. Marital Dissolution by Death & Divorce
Shares of existing marriages

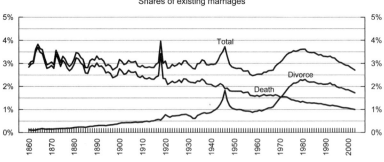

Source: Jacobson 1959, Census Bureau, National Center for Health Statistics

As the chart shows, the rate of marital dissolution by divorce has had a steady uptrend since the Civil War, while the rate of dissolution by death has had a steady downtrend. But since the rate of marital dissolution by death has fallen faster than the rate of dissolution by divorce has risen, the *total* rate of marital dissolution was actually lower at the start of the twenty-first century than at any time in the nineteenth century, when divorce was far less prevalent. Moreover, the total rate of marital dissolution would be at an all-time low but for the bulge in the divorce rate coinciding with the legalization of abortion.

While a few neoclassical economists have used Jacobson's calculations to extend the history of divorce statistics, they have managed to do so while either ignoring or dismissing the other half of his calculation (marital dissolution by death) and the main point he was making: that the divorce and death rates are inherently related.[47] The main reason for this oversight is that no version of neoclassical economic theory contains the Scholastic "distribution function" that is necessary even to describe the problem in question accurately.

The connection will become clearer when we turn to the second point, which concerns recent legal changes, especially legalized abortion, that have reduced the marriage rate and increased the divorce rate by separating marital fidelity from marital fertility.[48] The legalization of abortion did far more than simply grant women an "option" that they did not have before. As George A. Akerlof and Janet L. Yellen of the Brookings Institution have written, it contributed to a retreat from marriage: "Although many observers expected liberalized abortion and contraception to lead to fewer out-of-wedlock births, in fact the opposite happened because of the erosion of the custom of 'shotgun marriages.'"[49] By making the birth of a child the choice of the mother, Akerlof and Yellen pointed out, the legalization of abortion had the unanticipated result of making acceptance of the responsibilities of marriage and child support also a choice of the

Figure 10–7

US Marriage, Divorce, Live-Birth, and Abortion Rates
Ratio to Total Population

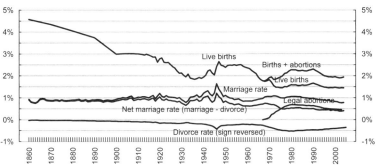

father, not the unavoidable consequence of a previous choice. While the number and rate of abortions soared and the live birth rate declined immediately after *Roe v. Wade*, over time the number and proportion of both out-of-wedlock pregnancies and out-of-wedlock births also rose sharply.

The loosening of divorce laws and restraints on contraception at about the same time abortion was legalized seems to make sorting cause from effect difficult. But the driving role of legal abortion is clear when the rise in the abortion rate is compared with the net marriage rate (the marriage rate minus the divorce rate), as shown in Figure 10–7.

As the chart shows, there was a boom in the rate of children conceived from the late 1960s through the 1990s, one that nearly matched the baby boom from the mid-1940s to mid-1960s in its effect on American population growth. But as the chart also shows, as soon as 24 to 30 percent of the baby boomers' own children were aborted each year, the marriage rate stalled and declined instead of rising with the population of young adults, and the divorce rate mirrored the rate of legal abortions. As a result, the net marriage rate fell by 35 percent between 1968 and 1976, exactly the period of the most rapid increase in the abortion rate. Since 1976, the net marriage rate has fallen further below the rate in 1968, before abortion was legalized.[50]

The rate of out-of-wedlock births soared at the same time as the abortion rate rose and the net marriage rate fell. Excluding miscarriages (for which data are not available before 1976, but which occur in about 13 percent of all pregnancies), 91 percent of conceptions in 1967 resulted in live births to married women, the remaining 9 percent being live births to unmarried women. By 1980, the former share had dropped to less than 60 percent, and by 1995 to 52 percent. Before 1980, most of the decline of live births was the result of legal abortions. About 84 percent of abortions are performed upon women who are not married.[51] But over time, the number of live births to unmarried women has also risen, from 339,000 in 1967 to 1,257,000 in 1997; the proportion of pregnancies resulting in live births to unmarried mothers rose from 9 percent to 23.8 percent between 1967 and 1996. Thus, the proportion of pregnancies resulting in either live births or legal abortions to unmarried women rose from 9 percent in 1967 to 45.8 percent in 1996.

Research has confirmed Akerlof and Yellen's surmise that legal abortion affected these trends by bringing about the decline of the "shotgun marriage." A 1999 survey of women who had been fifteen to twenty-nine years old at the birth of their first child showed that from 1960–64, 10.3 percent of first births were premarital; the rest were born to married women, but 15.5 percent were premaritally conceived, leaving 74.3 percent to be conceived after marriage. By 1975–79, 25.7 percent of first births were premarital, 12 percent premaritally conceived, and 62.2 percent postmaritally conceived. In 1990–94, 40.5 percent of first births were premarital, while 12.3 percent were conceived before marriage and 47.2 percent after marriage. All of this indicates that among women who became pregnant before marriage, the share marrying before birth dropped from 60 percent in 1960–64 to 31.8 percent in 1975–79 to 23.3 percent in 1990–94.[52] The trend was sharpest in those parts of the population for whom the abortion rate was highest, particularly among African Americans, though the same trend can now be seen among recent immigrants of Hispanic origin.

Despite all these changes, the neo-Scholastic theory of marriage with which we began this section reliably predicted who would divorce and who would remain married. According to that theory, couples sharing three characteristics—mutual personal gifts, joint gifts to others (especially their children), and the common sacrifice of shared worship—will be overwhelmingly likely to stay married, while those missing one or more element will be commensurately more likely to divorce or not marry in the first place.

One of the theory's advantages is ironing out existing contradictions in basic assumptions between neoclassical economic theory and other disciplines. Table 10–1 shows the findings of one study by sociologists. This study analyzed the characteristics of American couples that stay married rather than divorce or separate.[53] The study tested three dimensions of religious behavior—affiliation, orthodoxy of belief, and rate of attendance at worship—along with important factors that can coincide with or move independent of those religious categories. I have recategorized these as adverse rearing (having divorced parents), maturity (measured by wife's age at marriage), fidelity (marital duration, attitude toward nonmarital sex, and previous divorce), fertility (recent birth), marital happiness, and the husband's attitude toward employment/family balance. Numbers greater than one indicate the factors increasing, and numbers less than one those reducing, the frequency of divorce.

Table 10–1

Religious and Other Influences on Odds of Separation/Divorce				
Effects multiply, e.g. liberal Protestant couple with divorced parents plus new infant has about 43% the likelihood of divorce (1.000 x 1.556 x 0.276 = 0.429) as same couple without those characteristics, i.e. about 0.8% (=0.429 x 0.0185).				
Characteristic	Dissolution rate		Model	
Affiliation:	Husband	Wife	1	2
None	3.6%	3.2%	1.621	1.301
Mixed	n.a.	n.a.	1.390	1.035
Protestant: Liberal (reference)	1.7%	2.0%	1.000	1.000
Moderate	2.0%	1.7%	1.100	0.895
Conservative	2.1%	2.3%	1.186	0.945
Catholic	1.8%	1.9%	1.141	1.069
Jewish	1.6%	1.0%	0.654	0.861
Other	1.7%	2.3%	0.811	0.862
Worship attendance (0–6: never, once, several times yearly, once, several times monthly, weekly, more than weekly)	Husband		0.955	1.016
	Wife		0.882*	0.920*
	Difference		1.141*	1.132*
Orthodoxy of religious belief (1–5: strongly agree, agree, neither, disagree, strongly disagree)	Husband		1.062	1.069
	Wife		0.862*	0.820*
	Difference		1.052	1.026
Other factors: Adverse rearing	Parents divorced when age 14 (either spouse)		-	1.556*
Previous divorce	Either spouse		-	1.505*
Maturity	Wife's age at marriage (per year vs. age 25)		-	0.946*
Fidelity	Marital duration (per year)		-	0.921*
"	Wife's disapproval of nonmarital sex		-	0.811*
Fertility	Recent birth		-	0.276*
Marital satisfaction/ happiness	Husband		-	0.830*
	Wife		-	0.725*
Employment/ family attitude	Husband		-	0.916
Chi-square [Higher = more robust model]			83.04	465.6
df [Higher = more robust model]			13	22
Based on Call and Heaton 1997	* Significant (probability of chance < .05)			

The results show that while divorce rates differ by religious affiliation, nearly all denominational differences become insignificant in predicting who will divorce or stay married once we look at behavioral factors—factors that are not specific to one religion but correspond to what nearly everyone regards as decent marital behavior. These behavioral factors map almost exactly onto the three criteria mentioned above.

The most fundamental element in today's neoclassical economics is the theory of utility, which explains how we value economic goods as means according to our relative preferences for them. But the neoclassical outline omits the Scholastic theory of distribution, which describes our most fundamental scale of preferences, which is for persons as ends, not means.

This is why the neo-Scholastic theory can explain, while neoclassical theory cannot, exactly what connects skipping church on Sunday (or synagogue on Saturday), the choice of a married couple not to have children, and a significantly greater likelihood of divorce. Neoclassical economics answers that we simply prefer lying in bed to worship and divorce to marriage, just as I prefer butter pecan to strawberry ice cream. But this is because neoclassical economics assumes that we have always already made our choice of persons and chosen "number one": ourselves. This is a false assumption. The behaviors that affect divorce rates are inherently connected because they all express our preferences for persons, including ourselves, our spouse, children, and God. In general, people who get divorced are differentiated from those who do not in part by the way they prefer themselves over others.

The main serious threats to American family stability are relatively recent and mostly traceable to the legalization of abortion. The data clearly suggest that returning abortion law to its status quo ante would raise the net marriage rate, reduce the rate of illegitimacy, and increase the birth rate, just as quickly as those indicators moved in the other direction once abortion was legalized. Moreover, as we will see later, abortion is single-handedly responsible for the prospective imbalances in Social Security, and its restriction would both defuse the immigration issue and permit the United States to avoid the demographic implosion that has started to engulf the developed nations of Europe and Asia. But to understand such problems we must answer the question posed in the next chapter: "Why do parents give children existence, rearing, and instruction?"

11

Why Do Parents Give Children "Existence, Rearing, and Instruction"?

> The best way that man could test his readiness to encounter the common variety of mankind would be to climb down a chimney into any house at random, and get on as well as possible with the people inside. And that is essentially what each one of us did on the day that he was born.
>
> —G. K. Chesterton, "On Certain Modern Writers and the Institution of the Family"

The sharp decline in mortality has profoundly affected American family life. In this chapter, we will consider how it has affected the first of the three gifts from parents to their children enumerated by Aristotle: their existence, upon which the later gifts of rearing and instruction depend.

In a sense, the demographic history of the world has been recapitulated within the territory of the United States over the past two centuries.[1] The average life expectancy at birth for most of recorded history was about twenty-four years. It fluctuated near that average from the peak of the Roman Empire until the fourteenth and fifteenth centuries A.D. in those regions from which most modern Americans' ancestors migrated.[2] Average life expectancy for black Americans in 1850 was twenty-three years, little more than half that for white Americans; yet the life expectancy of white Americans was also much lower than average in eastern cities and in the South, and twenty-three years had also been the average life expectancy for Londoners in 1800.

The average life span was so short because of high mortality, and parents typically respond to higher mortality rates, particularly in infancy, with higher fertility. Fertility is therefore positively related to mortality and inversely related to life expectancy. Since American female fertility typically extends as long as age fifty, completed fertility for any woman or cohort cannot be known with certainty until the woman or women

Figure 11–1

The U.S. "Demographic Transition"

Years of life expected at birth and Total Fertility Rates (net = ex mortality)

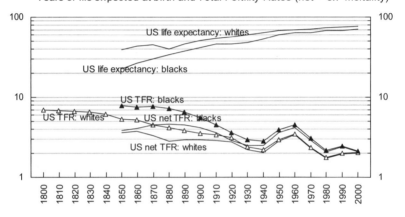

in question are at least that old. A good measure to use, then, is the total fertility rate (TFR), which combines the experience of women at all ages each year as if they were a single composite woman over her lifetime.[3]

Since the total fertility rate counts births but not deaths, to see the relation between fertility and mortality, we must use modified measures that count both. These metrics include the net reproduction rate (NRR) and the net total fertility rate (NTFR).[4] For example, the total fertility rate in 1860 was about 7.6 for black and 5.2 for white Americans. But after accounting for mortality, the net total fertility rates of these two groups were about the same—3.8 for white and 4.1 for black Americans. These net fertility rates were also close to the ones that were seen a century later near the peak of the post–World War II baby boom, thanks to a sharp decline in mortality at all ages, particularly in infancy.[5]

Precisely because the TFR rises or declines with the infant mortality rate (IMR), many researchers have relied heavily on the IMR to "explain"

Figure 11–2

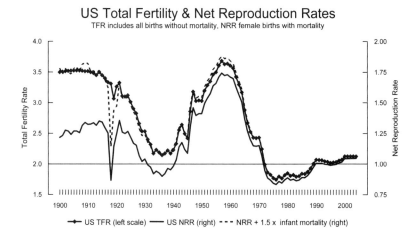

US Total Fertility & Net Reproduction Rates
TFR includes all births without mortality, NRR female births with mortality

fertility. Falling mortality also figures largely as an explanation of falling fertility in the theory of "demographic transition." But this high correlation is due simply to the fact that the two variables are not independent.[6] This might seem to be an obscure technical point, but as we'll see, it reveals a deeper explanatory problem: The modern economic theory of fertility can at best tell us *whether* people reproduce themselves. It cannot explain *why*.

Our updated version of Scholastic theory offers such an explanation. It suggests that after describing the elements of production, exchange, and consumption, which are recognized in some fashion by most schools of neoclassical economic theory, the decision to have children boils down to two motives: People have children either because they love the children for their own sakes, or else because they love themselves and expect some personal benefit from the children (or some combination of these motives).

To the extent that people have children for the first reason—the children's sake—fertility will not be affected by the availability of other forms of saving or social insurance, because the resources devoted to the children take the form of a gift, not an exchange. But to the extent that people have children for the second reason—for the benefits they personally receive from the children—both private saving and government social insurance will reduce fertility. This is because in the latter case, both private saving and government social insurance act as economic substitutes for children. It is quite possible to have a child solely for the benefits received, as if having the child were essentially the same as buying a refrigerator or investing in a security.[7]

The existing neoclassical theory of fertility cannot explain or even distinguish these motives, because neoclassical economic theory omits the "distribution function"—which describes how we share our human and nonhuman resources based on our scale of preferences for persons. The problems created by this gap in neoclassical theory are illustrated in two recent papers that attempted to describe and test the leading variants of the neoclassical economic theory of fertility.[8]

The first paper, by economist Zeyu Xu, surveys both the theories of the family upon which current theories of fertility rest and the evidence for these assumptions. It discovers two problems, one in theory and one in the evidence. The problem with the theory is its logical inconsistency:

> In neo-classical family economics, the household is the unit of study. . . . However, it is the welfare of individuals that should be the fundamental concern. Earlier unitary household models had to reconcile the single utility framework with the presence of multiple individuals. To do so unitary household models assume that family members' utility functions can be systematically aggregated, that individual budget constraints can be combined, and that household production can be unified. To make such aggregations household members are either assumed to have homogeneous preferences, or have an altruistic household head that has all the power within the household.[9]

In other words, neoclassical theory cannot coherently reconcile the economic theories of the individual person and the multiperson household (the very problem that stumped Aristotle). The neoclassical theory of fertility responds simply by assuming either that everyone's behavior is identical or else that each household is characterized by an implausibly asymmetrical pattern of individual behavior. The leading (Becker–Barro) variant assumes, in effect, that every household is a "dynasty" governed by a single founder, who is supposed to be altruistic, farsighted, and able to influence the behavior of all future generations, but that none of this patriarch's descendants exhibit any of these qualities. Another variant (Boldrin–Jones) assumes, in effect, that all parents are essentially selfish toward their children, while all children are essentially altruistic toward their parents.

The Xu paper also surveyed alternative theories that see the family as a place of conflict and intrahousehold bargaining rather than altruism— assuming, in effect, that everyone is purely selfish or even predatory. A further problem is that all the underlying theories presuppose cardinal utility, the notion that utility is a thing that can be added up among different persons like their weight, rather than referring to people's order of preference for economic goods, which cannot meaningfully be so added. The empirical problem, Xu found, is that the factual data appear to support none of these a priori assumptions.[10]

The second paper, by economist Michele Boldrin and his colleagues, argues that the Boldrin–Jones set of assumptions fits the empirical facts about fertility and saving better than the Becker–Barro assumptions. Yet its authors acknowledge that their attempts to test either theory depend heavily on additional assumptions made for at least *nine* intermediate variables, that the predictions vary widely with these alternative assumptions, and that the wide variation in predicted results affects precisely the two elements most important for policymakers: the effects of pay-as-you-go retirement pensions and private national saving on the total fertility rate.[11]

The accuracy of these models does not inspire much confidence for making major policy changes in the United States. For example, the Boldrin–Jones version predicted a total fertility rate for the United States of 2.2 in 1950, when the actual TFR was 3.0, while the model's best fit for the year 2000 was 1.82, when the actual TFR was 2.05—a smaller error, but still the difference between a significantly declining and an approximately stable population. In order to "calibrate" their model to predict the values actually observed, the researchers found it necessary to make assumptions that the authors themselves found questionable, because they were contrary to previous empirical research. "This seems to point to a lack of richness of the models overall," they concluded.[12]

Yet these are not the only problems. Such studies have confined their focus to countries representing a relatively small share of the world's population and cultures (Europe and its cultural offshoots), despite the claim of proponents of the underlying "economic approach to human behavior" that the theory is applicable everywhere and at all times.[13]

In short, the neoclassical economic theory of fertility is in disarray.

Despite their disagreements, these competing theories share one common characteristic. They begin by assuming that the people they study have no freedom of choice about the most fundamental feature of every economic decision, the choice of persons for whom they intend to provide. The problems just recounted are the inevitable result of attempting to explain anything so fundamental as fertility—the reproduction of human persons—without the element of economic theory that describes one's preferences for persons.[14]

Fortunately, if we follow Scholastic theory in including this element from the beginning, the result is not only a major simplification of the theory of fertility but also a major improvement in the clarity, applicability, and accuracy of its empirical predictions.

Figure 11–3

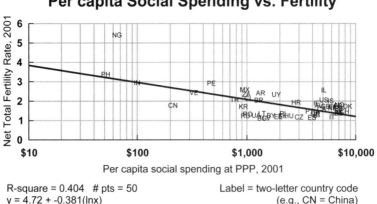

Per capita Social Spending vs. Fertility

R-square = 0.404   # pts = 50   Label = two-letter country code
y = 4.72 + -0.381(lnx)   (e.g., CN = China)

We can see this by comparing the net total fertility rate, or NTFR, with per capita government social spending and per capita national saving for the fifty countries (listed in Table 11–1), containing about two-thirds of the world's population, for which data on all variables were available. Both per capita social spending and per capita national saving were measured at purchasing power parity (PPP), a technique that adjusts for the different purchasing powers of the various currencies in which the original data are expressed.[15]

Figure 11–4

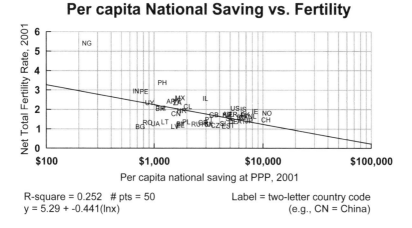

Per capita National Saving vs. Fertility

R-square = 0.252   # pts = 50
y = 5.29 + -0.441(lnx)

Label = two-letter country code
(e.g., CN = China)

As Figures 11–3 and 11–4 indicate, per capita social spending and per capita national saving are both inversely proportional to the net TFR, by about the same proportions.[16]

Those countries with total fertility rates remaining little higher than one, regardless of differences in social spending and national saving, are nearly all currently ruled by, or for a long time previously suffered under, totalitarian governments. Including a variable for totalitarian government is highly statistically significant regardless of the other variables. Yet all three factors together are not sufficient to raise the accuracy of a model beyond the results achieved (albeit with a vastly more complicated model) by Boldrin, De Nardi, and Jones.

Now, what if neoclassical economic theory's failure to account for people's fundamental preferences for persons is responsible for the ambiguity of its findings about fertility? Because of this failure, neoclassical theory substitutes identical assumptions for every individual's prefer-ences, even though these preferences systematically differ, as we know simply from observing people's behavior, but also from the strong and systematic evidence for Augustine's "personal distribution function" that we considered in chapter 8. In the neo-Scholastic framework, on the other hand, whether we are selfish or unselfish we always allocate our scarce resources between ourselves and others in proportion to the rela-tive significance of each person to ourselves.

As Augustine's analysis pointed out, the Two Great Command-ments—you shall love God above all else and your neighbor as your-self[17]—are not only normatively or prescriptively but also positively or descriptively valid, even for those who disobey them. That is, even those who steal from rather than exchanging or sharing with others resist hav-ing their own goods stolen and enjoy receiving gifts. The Two Great Commandments are intimately empirically related, because the decision to devote scarce resources (such as time or money) to another person is essentially the same whether the other person is God or another human being. In both cases, the decision entails sacrificing scarce goods that could otherwise have been used for oneself, and so elevating the other person relative to oneself in one's scale of preferences for persons.

Thus, the choice to have children because we love them rather than because of the benefits they confer upon us should be positively related to the frequency of worship in all cultures. If Gary Becker were correct that everyone's preferences are identical and that these preferences are identical in all cultures, we should find that frequency of worship makes no difference to the total fertility rate. Instead, we find that the rates of weekly worship and fertility are always positively related across countries, with relatively minor variation by religious denomination.[18] On average, in countries where the rate of weekly worship is close to zero, the TFR is approximately 1.25. The relationship in all countries suggests that 100 percent weekly worship is associated with a net TFR of about 2.1 chil-dren higher than that, or about 3.4. Since 2.1 children are necessary for each couple to reproduce itself (the additional 0.1 accounts for typical modern mortality between ages at birth and childbearing), this suggests that after purely selfish factors are accounted for, acting on belief in God and some kind of afterlife makes the crucial difference as to whether peo-ple reproduce themselves. It suggests that the personal gift of time and

Figure 11–5

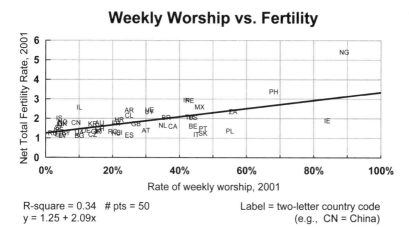

Weekly Worship vs. Fertility

R-square = 0.34   # pts = 50
y = 1.25 + 2.09x

Label = two-letter country code
(e.g., CN = China)

resources involved in worship is closely systematically associated with the personal gift of having children for their own sake rather than for the pleasure and utility of the parents.

Thus, the theory of fertility makes another good test case of the two ways—neo-Scholastic and neoclassical—of explaining people's most fundamental preferences.[19] A simple neo-Scholastic model includ-

Figure 11–6

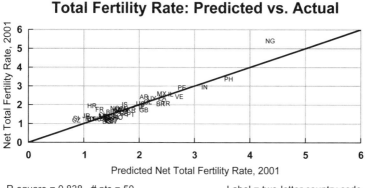

Total Fertility Rate: Predicted vs. Actual

R-square = 0.838   # pts = 50
y = 5.23e-014 + 1x

Label = two-letter country code
(e.g., IN = India)

Table 11–1

NET TOTAL FERTILITY RATE: Predicted vs. Actual, 2001			
Region	Country	Net TFR predicted	Actual net TFR, 2001
America: North	United States	2.05	2.05
	Canada	1.74	1.60
	Mexico	2.42	2.60
America: South	Argentina	2.10	2.42
	Brazil	2.33	2.06
	Chile	2.18	2.15
	Peru	2.80	2.93
	Uruguay	2.26	2.35
	Venezuela	2.77	2.44
Europe: Northern	Denmark	1.64	1.73
	Estonia	1.45	1.20
	Finland	1.68	1.70
	Iceland	1.76	2.01
	Ireland	2.07	1.89
	Latvia	1.55	1.13
	Lithuania	1.35	1.36
	Norway	1.56	1.81
	Sweden	1.75	1.53
	United Kingdom	2.12	1.72
Europe: Western	Austria	1.31	1.39
	Belgium	1.47	1.61
	France	1.26	1.75
	Germany	1.40	1.38
	Netherlands	1.60	1.65
	Switzerland	1.33	1.47
Europe: Eastern	Belarus	1.10	1.26
	Bulgaria	1.43	1.12
	Czech Republic	0.87	1.18
	Hungary	1.24	1.24
	Poland	1.65	1.36
	Romania	1.65	1.33
	Russian Federation	1.07	1.25

Table 11–1 (continued)

	Ukraine	1.34	1.27
Europe: Southern	Croatia	1.17	1.93
	Slovak Republic	1.49	1.24
	Greece	1.43	1.33
	Italy	1.57	1.18
	Portugal	1.85	1.48
	Slovenia	0.87	1.28
	Spain	1.46	1.15
Africa	Nigeria	4.34	5.46
	South Africa	2.34	2.37
Asia/Oceania	Australia	1.63	1.76
	China PR	1.76	1.79
	India	3.17	2.97
	Israel	2.57	2.56
	Japan	1.01	1.41
	Korea (South)	1.85	1.72
	Philippines	3.68	3.39
	Turkey	2.50	2.08

ing these three factors (weekly worship, social benefits, and national saving per capita, along with a legacy of totalitarian government) explains more than 80 percent of the variation in the net TFR for the countries surveyed. These results could doubtless be improved if the available data were more detailed or available for more countries.[20] But the same model explains the American net TFR exactly: 2.05 predicted and actual in 2001.[21] The results by country are listed in Table 11–1.

Unlike the rival models used by neoclassical economists, our neo-Scholastic model of fertility indicates the main reasons that the birth rates in the developed countries of Europe and Asia have fallen sharply below the level that will reproduce each generation. First, insofar as they benefit the parents rather than the children, both high per capita government social benefits and high per capita private saving act as economic substitutes for children, diminishing fertility. Second, countries like China, Russia, and those in Eastern Europe that have been long governed by totalitarian governments have birth rates depressed further by an average of about 0.6 children per couple. (This could be because totalitarian government is associated with lower rates of weekly worship, which are positively related to fertility in a linear fashion. Also, abortion rises exponentially as rates of weekly worship decline.) Finally, after taking all these economic and political factors into account, countries in which the population regularly worships God tend to reproduce themselves, while those that don't, don't.

This model is not the last word on the theory of fertility. I offer it as a first effort in what promises to be a fruitful new program of research. The first way in which it could be extended is by gathering the data necessary to include all countries and 100 percent of the world population. A second is to gather the data necessary to test the influence of different kinds of social benefits on fertility. For example, I made a preliminary effort to test social benefits with and without benefits targeted to families with children, anticipating that this might show a positive effect on fertility from such programs. I found instead that the statistical fit of both the model and the variable for social benefits worsened when family benefits were excluded; but this could have been because of the poorer quality of disaggregated data. A third improvement would be to extend the model of fertility through time. The model is designed to compare all countries at the same time; but it should in principle also explain variation in the total fertility rate for one country (or all countries) through the years. The data would appear to be available for the United States at least back to 1929, and possibly farther. A fourth improvement would be to combine two or more of the first three approaches. For example, to test the impact on fertility of newly established or maturing pay-as-you-go retirement pension systems like Social Security, and to predict the result of any proposed reforms, it would be necessary to measure not only current benefits received by current retirees from current workers but also any net benefits received from (or paid to) earlier or later generations. The version of the model presented here did not attempt this, and current expected intergenerational transfers in the United States are small in relation to the past. But as Figure 11–7 indicates, they would have to be taken into account in explaining the changing U.S. birth rate during the first couple of generations covered by Social Security, which coincided with the baby boom.

Figure 11–7

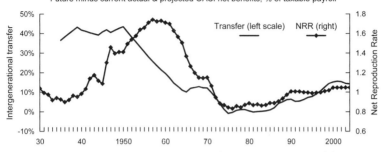

US Social Security Transfer vs. Net Reproduction Rate
Future minus current actual & projected OASI net benefits, % of taxable payroll*

*Transfer lagged by age at first marriage and adjusted for ratio of working to retirement age population.

Our simple analogy of the "Aristotelian lemonade stand," then, has illustrated the basic theory of domestic economy. Its application helped us correct a serious flaw in the prevailing neoclassical approach to the theory of fertility, and it helped us explain why, at the start of the twenty-first century, the birth rate in the United States was just reproducing the existing American population. Later, in the section on political economy, we'll consider what is likely to happen to the American total fertility rate over the next seventy-five years under currently projected U.S. fiscal policy.

In the next chapter, we will see that the same neo-Scholastic theory helps us explain the otherwise puzzling economic pattern of people's lives in modern America after they receive their parents' second and third gifts: rearing and instruction.

12

How Neo-Scholastic Economics Explains Our Life Earnings and Spending

In the previous chapter we analyzed the reproduction of human beings, which is at one and the same time what Aristotle called the first gift from parents to their children and the most obvious form of investment in "tangible human capital." We saw that reduced mortality is typically followed by lower fertility rates. In this chapter we will extend the analysis to show that the same increase in longevity also greatly stimulates investment in the "intangible human capital" of those born—their rearing and instruction—especially formal education and training, but also health, safety, and mobility.[1] We'll see that the peculiar pattern of modern domestic economic life can be explained fully only by combining all four elements of Scholastic economics, above all the one missing from modern neoclassical economics: the theory of distribution, which describes personal gifts and familial distributive justice. In doing so, we'll also find that our incomes and spending are systematically determined by just four factors—age, education, sex, and marital status—and that while most transactions outside the family are exchanges, most transactions within the family are gifts. This truth is beyond the ken of neoclassical economic theory.[2]

Earnings by Age

Consider the lifetime pattern of market income and consumption shown in Figure 12–1. For simplicity, the graph shows purchases of market goods as being the same in each phase of life. This is not necessarily the case—for example, the costs of "human maintenance" tend to rise with age—but it's certainly the case that consumption is much more even than income over a human lifetime.[3] Figure 12–1 indicates that (1) during our childhood dependency, we have no labor market earnings. And, unless we have inherited property, we have no property income either. Any expenses necessary for our consumption of market goods are paid by our parents. This allows us to invest time (for example, in school) in acquiring the skills and qualities that will support us through most of life. The graph also indicates that (2) by the start of active parenthood, the investment in our "human capital" during childhood has begun to earn a return, as we supply our labor services in exchange for labor compensation. The rate of return on our earlier investment in human capital is still high during this stage, and our labor income rises rapidly. Mostly out of their labor income, parents must pay for the consumption of and any investment in market goods by both themselves and their children. For most families, this requires some borrowing—for example, in the form of home mortgages or auto loans or education loans—from lenders who either have inherited more nonhuman wealth or are already in the next, "empty nest" stage.

Figure 12–1

Lifetime Income & Consumption

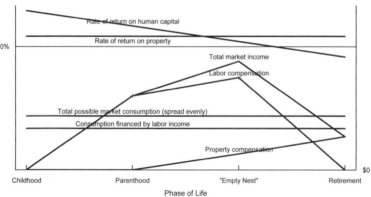

Figure 12–1 reveals two more things: (3) During the "empty nest" stage, though the expected rate of return on human capital is lower than during active parenthood, our absolute labor market earnings rise to

reach their lifetime peak. After children have left home, parents' current expenses also go down, allowing them to repay earlier borrowing and to begin saving significantly for their own retirement. They do this usually by investing as much as possible in the market for nonhuman capital (since the rate of return on further investment in their own or their children's human capital, as we have seen, is now much less attractive). And (4) finally, in retirement, parents leave the labor market, which causes their labor income to cease. To pay for current living expenses, they use current income from previous investments in nonhuman capital, along with any government and business pensions to which they became entitled during their working years. Note that in the absence of other "transfer payments," the difference between current income and current consumption at each stage of life necessarily implies extensive gifts from parents to their dependent children and from adult children to their aged parents.

Figure 12–2

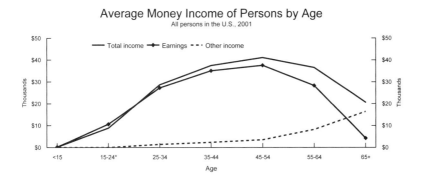

reach. Average Money Income of Persons by Age
All persons in the U.S., 2001

*Ages 15-24 for total money income, 18-24 for labor income

Data on intrafamily gifts are still relatively meager, but we can see how well our simple "model" of family economics explains reality by comparing it with census data on total money income and labor market earnings by age (Figure 12–2).[4] Generally speaking, the pattern of actual income and earnings is quite similar to the one we have described: Labor market earnings rise rapidly until about age thirty, continue rising (but less rapidly) to a peak at about age fifty, and then decline to almost zero after retirement age. All other sources of income are virtually nil at an early age but rise sharply after about age fifty, and they constitute nearly all of total income over age sixty-five.

Earnings by Education

We can see the economic return on rearing and instruction most clearly by considering the effect of investment in formal education—one of the most important kinds of investment in "human capital"—in increasing labor compensation (see Figures 12–3 and 12–4).

Figure 12–3

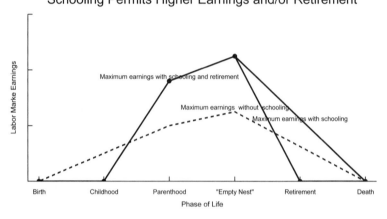

Schooling Permits Higher Earnings and/or Retirement

Differences in earnings may be due either to differences in rates of pay or in the number of hours worked. At each age, the cost of further education includes not only paying tuition expenses but also forgoing current earnings in the labor market instead of going to school. On the other hand, the additional education increases the student's future earning ability. The gain in earning ability is best seen by considering the annual earnings of full time, year-round workers (see Figure 12–5). In interpreting the figures, it must be recognized that due to schooling and retirement, only a small fraction of persons under twenty-five or over sixty-five now work full time and year-round. This makes the averages for those age groups less reliable.

Figure 12–4

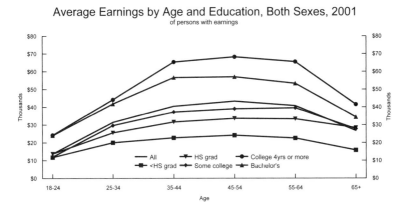

Average Earnings by Age and Education, Both Sexes, 2001
of persons with earnings

Figure 12–5

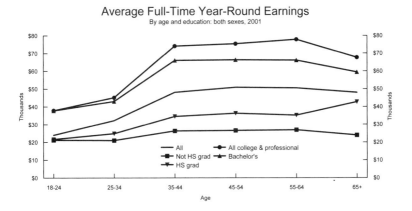

Average Full-Time Year-Round Earnings
By age and education: both sexes, 2001

Perhaps the most striking implication of the data is the difference in earnings between four years of high school and four years of college. The full time, year-round earnings of workers with a high school diploma (or its equivalent) are about half again as high as the average earnings of those who did not graduate from high school. In other words, earning ability increases by approximately the same ratio as the years of education: twelve against eight, or three to two. But when we compare the earning ability of workers with a high school diploma against that of workers with a bachelor's degree, the additional four years of schooling—a one-third increase—correspond to a near doubling of average annual earnings. One comprehensive survey calculated the gross rate of return in 1999–2000 for both men and women in the United States on the time and money invested in a college education to be about 19 percent—that is, about 16 percent beyond inflation.[5] This suggests that there is under-investment not only in human capital in general but in college education in particular—a circumstance that has been true, and noted as such, for nearly half a century.[6]

All this provides a sound economic reason to help explain why most parents pay for their children's rearing and education first—instead of, say, leaving their children uneducated and investing the tuition money on their behalf in the stock market. It's also the main economic reason that most parents (if they cannot afford both) pay for raising and educating their children before saving substantially for their own retirement. In other words, families invest in "things" only after they've run out of attractive investments in people. Most American families run out of resources before the return on additional investment in their dependent children falls below the market return on nonhuman capital (although this minority exception is larger than it used to be).

But now let's consider why the rate of return on investing in people declines much more rapidly than the rate of return on investing in property. At every age, there is a limit to how much economically valuable education any one person can absorb. Most of us can't concentrate on learning more than one thing at a time, so doubling the ratio of teachers to pupils, for example, won't double the amount of learning. At the same time, with each extra year (or dollar) invested in acquiring valuable skills, the "cost" of giving up current labor market earnings increases, while the additional future earnings that one could expect from further education get smaller. The same study I cited earlier calculated that the rate of return on investment in college education for men falls to about 9 percent at age forty, 7 percent at age forty-five, and less than 4 percent at age fifty (all before adjustment for inflation). After about age fifty, human capital depreciates in value. Most of us lose physical and mental energy and economic productivity, which lowers both the rate of remuneration and the likelihood of continued employment. But even if our annual earning ability did not decline with age, as it does for most people, our lifetimes are finite, because we all die. So as we get older, the total value of any additional earnings that we could expect from further investment in education diminishes with our remaining life expectancy. Nonhuman capital also depreciates, but as we will see in "Political Economy," unlike human capital, an allowance for this property depreciation is already accounted for in calculating business profits and the market rate of return on investment property.

When the rate of return on investing further in human capital falls below the market rate of return that can be realized by investing in property, families start to invest in the latter. By the same token, families with a large amount of wealth after paying for their children's upbringing have little practical choice but to invest most of it in property rather than in their family's own "human capital."

We have seen that human and nonhuman wealth are analytically similar in several ways. Both are usually "reproducible"; that is, new examples can be produced by a combination of existing human and/ or nonhuman resources. Both may exist in tangible or intangible form.[7] Both must be properly maintained in order to remain productive. The economic value of both kinds of investment can also depreciate: Machines wear out in use, or their services lose value because of market changes; the same is true of people. Finally, both human capital and nonhuman capital earn a return on investment, in the form of labor or property compensation, respectively.

The two kinds of wealth differ fundamentally, however, in two extremely important respects. Human wealth is embodied in mortal human persons, and since the abolition of American slavery in 1863 there is no longer—fortunately—a market for buying and selling human beings, as there are markets for buying and selling all kinds of property. These differences have a consequence that is not immediately obvious but is highly significant for the economics of the family household: The rate of return on human capital ordinarily varies inversely and substantially with the age of the person in whom it is embodied, while, as long as machines are substantially interchangeable, the rate of return on investment in property ordinarily does not. For example, for most families with dependent children, the average rate of return on investment in "human capital," such as child-rearing and education, is significantly higher than the market rate of return on investment in property. But the economic returns on investment in humans diminish much more rapidly than, and later in life fall below, the rate of return on investment in nonhuman wealth.

What is the reason for this difference? In an organized, competitive market, a relative scarcity of one kind of productive property will tend to raise the share of the total value of the production resulting from one more unit of such property, and therefore its share of the additional income generated by the sale of the product. This raises its rate of return on such investment property relative to that on other kinds. Similarly, a relative abundance of one kind of property will tend to lower its relative rate of return. Investors seeking the highest return on investment will therefore tend to shift from investing in the kinds of property which are relatively abundant into those which are relatively scarce. This regulates the amount of investment among the different kinds of property, so as to equalize their rates of return (taking into account any expected differences in risk of loss, maturity of the investment, and so on). Thus, when investing in, say, the stock market, the amount invested by any one person or family does not appreciably lower the rate of return—at least, not until one is investing many billions of dollars, and even then, not by much. If investors bid up the prices of stocks, while current and expected stock dividends remain the same, the rate of return on stocks falls relative to other investments, like bonds or real estate.

We are used to thinking in such terms about investments in property, but not about investments in human beings. Yet in economic terms, the basic principle is the same: What will I receive in the future, in return for the cost of investment today? The difference in return, compared with the original cost, is the rate of return. For example, formal education or training has a cost, both in terms of direct expenses for books and tuition (which pays for teachers' salaries and for the use of school facilities) and in terms of the income that a student could be earning by working in the labor market instead of going to school. The return on investment in education is the additional earnings that are made possible by the additional education. This rate of return is affected not only by the absolute cost of the investment and by the absolute increase in annual earnings it makes possible but also by how many years the student could expect to receive those higher earnings.

However, there is no organized market for buying and selling "human capital"—at least, not since slavery was abolished in the nineteenth century. To protect human dignity, the government forbids the ownership of other human beings, as well as labor contracts that amount to "indentured servitude." Everyone may "own" the "property" of his or her own person, as it were, but not anyone else's. That's a good thing, as well as a big change from most of human history. But it also means that if someone cannot afford the cost of additional education, even if that education would increase his or her lifetime earning ability by a much larger amount, the workings of the free market alone cannot be relied upon to remedy the situation. Public schools, tuition subsidies, scholarships, and subsidized education loans all help to relieve the problem, at least in primary and secondary education. But for most families with dependent children, the real rate of return on investing time and money in child-rearing and education (in terms of higher lifetime labor compensation for their children) is still much higher than the average return that can be received from investing in the stock market. For example, the long-run, inflation-adjusted average rate of return on the stock market is about 5 to 7 percent (or about 8 to 10 percent before subtracting the tax on business profits). Estimates of the average rate of return on the costs of child-rearing and education are consistently about five percentage points higher than this.

Earnings by Sex

Our discussion so far has focused on those factors—age and education—which are similar for men and women. The census data on income are averages for all men and women in each age group. But a closer look shows that while the general lifetime pattern of earnings is similar for men and women, beginning around age twenty-five, the labor compensation of men rises above, and remains higher than, that of women. Data from the U.S. census and the Social Security Administration indicate that average lifetime market labor compensation for men is about twice as high as the lifetime labor compensation for women (see Figure 12–6). What explains this difference? It cannot be claimed, as it might have been in the past, that the difference is due mostly to different educational opportunities or discrimination against women. If anything, young women now receive more formal schooling than young men. Yet

Figure 12–6

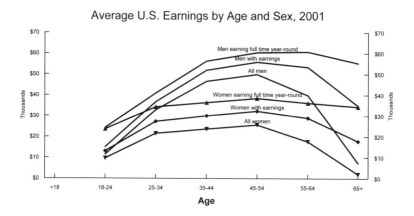

Average U.S. Earnings by Age and Sex, 2001

these differences are apparent even among men and women with identical education levels.

By focusing on the relationship between parents and children, and on phases of life that are common to men and women, we have left in the background another important economic fact of family life. Husband and wife are, in a sense, partners in a small business; and to make the most of their household resources, most married couples work out a coordination of their economic roles. (In a moment, I will ask whether *specialization*, a term often used by economists to describe this relationship, is really the best description.) One spouse—usually, but not necessarily, the husband—concentrates more on earning cash income for the family by working in the labor market. The other spouse—usually, but not necessarily, the wife—concentrates on supplying services directly to the household. The exact balance they agree upon between labor-market and household work depends on their relative education, skills, desires, and aptitudes (which may be influenced by the expectations, social attitudes, and mores of the culture in which they live).

This coordination of roles affects the labor-market earnings of both spouses. The persistent difference in earnings between men and women is partly due to the fact that specialization in the labor market results in higher market labor compensation for the spouse (usually the husband) who so specializes, and partly because the value of the services of the spouse working within the household (usually the wife) does not

Figure 12–7

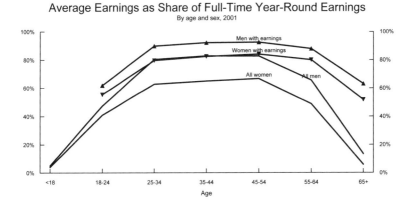

Average Earnings as Share of Full-Time Year-Round Earnings
By age and sex, 2001

show up in government statistics, which are usually restricted to market income.

We can get an idea of the general extent of this coordination of the economic roles of men and women by considering their average labor market employment and participation and how it has changed over time. Someone who is unemployed is still in the labor market rather than the household economy, because the definition requires that the person not just want a job but be actively looking for one. Overall labor-market participation by adults rose from about 59 percent in 1950 to almost 67 percent in 2000. Put another way, the share of adults in the labor market increased from about three-fifths to about two-thirds. But the labor-market participation of women rose from about 34 percent to 60 percent, while the participation of men fell from about 86 percent to 74 percent.

There is a difficulty in describing this relationship as "specialization," as if it were merely another example of the "division of labor" described by Adam Smith, akin to different workers in a pin factory specializing in different processes in the manufacture of pins in order to increase total daily production. There is an important difference between the kind of cooperation involved in producing property and in producing people. If these were merely different examples of the same principle of specialization, it would be difficult to explain the continued difference in earnings of men and women without concluding that equally qualified women are simply not as good as men at earning labor-market income. But the weight of evidence is on the other side: If anything, women are more diligent than men at earning income. And the coordination of roles in the human household also involves more than merely biological specialization. It is obvious that there is biological specialization between men and women—as between the sexes of almost all higher animals. Women bear children and men don't.

But a purely human factor works in the opposite direction. The rising importance of education, which we have already discussed, makes brainpower (in which women have no general disadvantage) relatively more valuable in economic terms than brawn (in which most men have an advantage over most women). And as Chesterton shrewdly observed, since a human is a *rational* animal—that is, one whose nature it is to be mentally omnivorous, to seek to grasp what is universal and not only (like other animals) what is particular in things—the economic aspect of the union between a man and a woman is best described not as the cooperation of two "specialists" but rather as the joining "of special talent and of general sanity."[8] This, he said, is a basic requirement of raising children, "who require to be taught not so much anything as everything. Babies need not to be taught a trade, but to be introduced to a world. . . . I will pity Mrs. Jones for the hugeness of her task; I will never pity her for its smallness."[9]

Coordination of parents' economic roles increases the real value of household economic resources in two ways: first, by increasing the labor compensation earned by its members and, second, by reducing the costs of producing goods within the household and of products that must be purchased in the market.

How do husbands and wives jointly decide how much of their time to devote to working in the labor market and how much to working in the household, in order to maximize their resources? To answer that question, we have to say more about household production. We've already noted that until relatively recently, most households produced both people and property, and that most businesses were in fact conducted within family households. We also said that the modern business firm, historically speaking, is an offshoot of the household that specializes in producing property while the household specializes in "producing" and sustaining people. But this doesn't mean that households no longer produce any property or that all property is now produced by businesses. Specialization is always a relative term. Even though the final "product" of the modern household is complete human persons, to perform this function, the household must still provide itself with a number of "intermediate" products, like family meals.

When producing such "intermediate" goods, the mother undertakes a process of production that combines human and nonhuman resources, just like a business firm. Economists use the term *production function* to describe what the mother simply calls a "recipe." Let's begin with the example of a fairly labor-intensive dinner (though nowadays such a dinner is likely to be reserved for a special occasion) because the example makes it easier to grasp what's going on. Let's say that Sunday dinner will consist of roast beef cooked with carrots and onions, served with mashed potatoes and gravy. A hundred years ago, a typical family might have grown its own carrots, onions, and potatoes, and in many cases even its own cattle. Thus the "production function," or "recipe," would actually have included the whole process of agriculture and animal husbandry. Nowadays, what the mother would consider "raw ingredients" are actually purchased in a relatively highly processed form from more highly specialized producers. Even so, the "raw" beef still has to be seasoned, cooked, sliced, and served. The "raw" carrots, onions, and potatoes have to be pared, sliced, or mashed before cooking.

In doing all this, just as when she goes to the supermarket, the mother weighs marginal significances; but now she is considering the marginal significances of the elements required to produce a good, not just (as with milk) the marginal significance of the finished good itself. Preparing the mashed potatoes requires the mother's labor and the use of certain tools. Both the person and the tools contribute something to the final result. In fact, each contributes a service that, though qualitatively different, could (within certain limits) be quantitatively substituted for the other. If the mother is preparing the potatoes, she normally might use a peeler to remove the skin, a knife to slice the potatoes, a pot and water to boil them, and a masher to mash them. If she is missing any of the tools, she might still accomplish the same task by working longer at it (and then she may not be as satisfied with the result). On the other hand, if she had several of each kind of tool, the process might not go much (if at all) faster than if she had only one of each kind, if she can use only one tool at a time—unless perhaps she can enlist the help of someone else, thus increasing the quantity of labor services along with the services of the tools.

In other words, just as the mother usually finds that the marginal significance of a good declines as the quantity consumed increases, she also usually finds "diminishing returns" in production when she increases the quantity of one productive ingredient while holding the others constant. In other words, she can probably produce more meals using two pots than using one, with the same amount of effort in both cases—but not twice as many; and she can probably produce more using the same tools and twice the effort—but not twice as much. To produce twice as much generally requires not only twice the effort but also twice the tools. In deciding how much to pay for acquiring each tool or how much of her effort to expend in one use rather than another, the mother implicitly considers the price in relation to the value of the services she expected it to contribute to the value of the "intermediate" good of meals. And she finds that the family's resources are greatest when the price paid for each productive ingredient corresponds to the value it has contributed to the final product.

The mother of 100 years ago spent much more time than does her modern counterpart preparing meals, cleaning house, and laundering clothes, and much less time working in the labor market or transporting family members from place to place. As increased longevity has increased the economic value of education, and increased education raised men's and women's labor-market earning ability, rising earnings have also increased the typical family's ability to pay for precooked foods, washing and drying machines, automobiles, and microwave ovens—all of which economize on the use of the mother's valuable time. For example, families began buying condensed soups in cans, which needed only the addition of liquid and heating on a gas or electric stove, rather than making their own soups from raw ingredients cooked using a wood- or coal-burning stove. More recently, they began buying soups that were already fully mixed and heating them in seconds using microwave ovens rather than gas or electric stoves. Of course, even today, the mother normally does not take the groceries home from the supermarket and dump them on the table. But she devotes less time to meal preparation.

The same principles that we found to govern our choices about purchasing and consuming goods also apply when we produce and sell them. In the section on personal economy, we saw that our preferences for purchasing and consuming any scarce good are subject to diminishing returns. That is, the greater quantity of any good that we have already used, the less we value one additional unit. This "marginal significance" or "marginal utility" ultimately governs exchange value.

We saw that when there is one good, its total significance or utility in all uses is greatest when its marginal significance or utility is the same in every different use. And we saw that the marginal significance of a mother's spending on that good is greatest when this marginal utility is equal to the market price. If the price is "given," as for example in a supermarket, the mother adjusts the marginal significance of the good by altering the quantity of goods in her family's possession. With declining marginal significance, adding to the quantity reduces the marginal significance, while reducing the quantity increases the marginal significance.

A habitual consumer of milk for whom milk has a low value can normally increase its "marginal significance" (or value to himself) relative to other goods by buying and consuming less of it in a given period, and a consumer for whom milk has a high value can reduce its marginal significance by buying and consuming more of it. But in both cases, the same exchange is having the opposite effect on the producer/seller as on the buyer/consumer. The purchase of milk for money, while decreasing the marginal significance of milk to the buyer (by increasing his quantity), is at the same time increasing the marginal significance of milk to the seller (by reducing his quantity).

But what about someone who both produces and consumes a commodity? For example, let's suppose that our family lives on a dairy farm and also likes to drink milk. As with most other families, the first quart or two of milk per day is more valuable to the family than its market price. But such a family does not merely stop buying milk when its marginal significance falls to the market price. To earn its living, the family sets out deliberately to produce far more milk than it could possibly consume for its own use, on the expectation that it will be able to sell the surplus to others for whom milk stands higher in its scale of preferences than on the scale of the producing family. Just as a mother will buy milk only if its marginal significance to her family equals or exceeds the market price, a family producing milk will sell it only if the selling price of milk exceeds its marginal significance for the family's own use. The producing family sells the commodity in order to purchase other things that stand higher in its scale of preferences. Thus, both the quantity of the milk that the dairy-farm family sells, and the quantity that it keeps for its own use, are a single continuous function of the marginal significance of milk to the family, relative to the market price.

"But what about the 'supply curve' that usually figures as a determinant of price, co-ordinate with the demand curve?" asked Philip Wicksteed. "I say it boldly and baldly: There is no such thing. When we are speaking of a marketable commodity, what is usually called the supply curve is in reality the demand curve of those who possess the commodity; for it shows the exact place which every successive unit of the commodity holds in their relative scale of estimates. . . . The separating out of this portion of the demand curve and reversing it in the diagram is a process which has its meaning and its legitimate function, . . . but is wholly irrelevant to the determination of price."[10] In other words, a change in the price of milk today may cause milk producers to increase or reduce production and sale of the good, in which case the quantity on hand may be higher or lower tomorrow. But at every moment, it remains true that there are two basic economic facts for each good: the quantities owned by potential consumers and the marginal significances for each potential consumer, including those consumers who are also producers.

It is part of the definition of a "perfect" or "competitive" market that no single consumer or producer can significantly affect the price of a commodity. But every individual purchaser or seller in a competitive market *does* affect the market price, if only imperceptibly. This is why all consumers together, and all producers together, *can* affect the price noticeably. The process by which all the parties adjust their holdings of certain goods, through exchange, in light of prevailing market prices is what makes the market as a whole tend toward "equilibrium"—a state in which everyone in the community *who owns any of the desired and exchangeable goods* comes to share *exactly the same relative preferences*. If that point were ever achieved, exchange would cease, because no one could further improve his position by exchanging goods that he values less at the prevailing market price for goods that he values more. But because most human needs are dynamic (however sated we become by eating and drinking, everyone gets hungry and thirsty again sooner or later), most markets never reach that point, but rather are always tending toward it.

Since very few households nowadays produce milk, the foregoing example may seem of little practical use. But nearly every household both produces and consumes the most widely used economic good in any economy: the labor services that are a necessary ingredient in almost every product of any business firm or household. In this way, almost every household is therefore in the same position as the dairy family that both produces and consumes milk. Each family is constantly faced with the choice whether to sell its services in the labor market in order to earn a wage or salary or else to apply the same services directly to various productive uses within the household. Should we clean our own clothes or hire a housekeeper or pay a commercial launderer to do so? Should we change the motor oil in our car ourselves or pay a service station to do so? Should we prepare our own dinner at home tonight or order a pizza to be delivered or else go out to a restaurant? Should we rebuild the back deck of our home as a do-it-yourself project or pay a professional contractor to do so? All of these choices are interrelated. But in each choice, however complicated, the allocation of the family's total labor services between sale in the labor market and direct use in the household is determined by comparing the marginal significance of the services to the family with their market "price"—i.e., the wage or salary (adjusted for any related costs, including taxes). The household will consume directly those services of which the net value to the family exceeds the net market price and sell those services of which the net market price exceeds the net value to the family.

In families with young children or in which the husband can earn a significantly higher salary or wage than the wife, it is typically the case that the father earns the majority of the family's outside income and the mother provides the majority of adult time devoted directly to the family. But in households where the wife's salary-earning ability more nearly equals or exceeds the husband's, and especially in which there are no young children or other dependents to care for, the couple is much more likely to decide that the amount of the wife's time spent working in the labor market should approach or exceed that of her husband.

Earnings by Marital Status

We have just considered the impact of a couple's marriage on their labor-market earnings. But marriage also affects their "cost of living" in terms of goods purchased in the market with those earnings. To get an idea of the economic consequences of marriage, we can begin by considering what happens when a man and a woman divorce after marrying. Living together, their income is combined into one household; after divorce, their income is split between two households. The difference is more than merely mathematical, however, because a married couple can live in one household much more cheaply than they can in two separate households. The official poverty level in 2000 for an adult living alone was $8,959; for a household of two adults it was $11,531, far less than the poverty level for two separate households, which would be $17,918.[11] Thus, with the same income in both cases, the combined standard of living declines by at least $6,387 after a couple divorces or fails to marry, even if they have no children. (The difference in the cost of living will normally be larger for those above the poverty line, so this estimate represents the minimum change.)

The decline in living standards hurts the woman more than the man, because average lifetime earnings for men are about twice as high as for women. For those born in 1955, the average married man can expect lifetime earnings to average about $31,491 in 2000 dollars; the average married woman, $15,544. Together, the couple can expect combined average annual lifetime earnings of $47,035.[12] For two unmarried people with the same age and education, average expected lifetime earnings are $28,122 for the man and $16,676 for the woman, a total of $44,798. The differences are due to the fact that married men work more hours than unmarried or divorced men, while unmarried or divorced women work more hours in the labor market than married women. The net effect is to reduce average lifetime earnings for the couple by $2,257, or about 4.8 percent. Taking both effects into account, as the result of failing to marry or getting a divorce, the average annual lifetime standard of living of such a couple would decline by at least $8,624, or 18 percent.

The problem is especially acute for households headed by divorced or unmarried mothers. The average American man and woman (including the unmarried) now have almost exactly two children in a lifetime. The poverty threshold for a married couple with two children in 2000 was $17,463. For the same four people split into two households, the combined poverty threshold was $22,833, assuming $8,959 for a man living alone and $13,874 for a mother with two children, which is the most frequent arrangement. The woman's earnings are a little higher than when married because she is forced to work more hours in the labor market, but her share of the family's cost of living is substantially higher. In this example, the mother and children typically go from a household with income equal to 269 percent of the poverty level to a household with income only 120 percent of the poverty line.

All these reasons explain why the poverty rate is much higher for female-headed households than for married-couple households or for households headed by unmarried men. In many cases, compensation from the father is either nonexistent or poorly enforced. But even enforcement of child support or alimony, or any division of income, cannot prevent a decline in this family's combined standard of living, which falls by at least $7,607, or 16.2 percent of the family's initial income.

Intrafamily Gifts and Their Substitutes

Much of the economic planning of the typical American family has to do with the fact that in each phase of life, each person's market income is different from the current spending on market goods actually used by that person. During active parenthood and the "empty nest" stages, the couple's current income exceeds their current spending on market goods for their own use. But for the dependent child and the adult in retirement, current spending on market goods usually exceeds current market

Figure 12–8

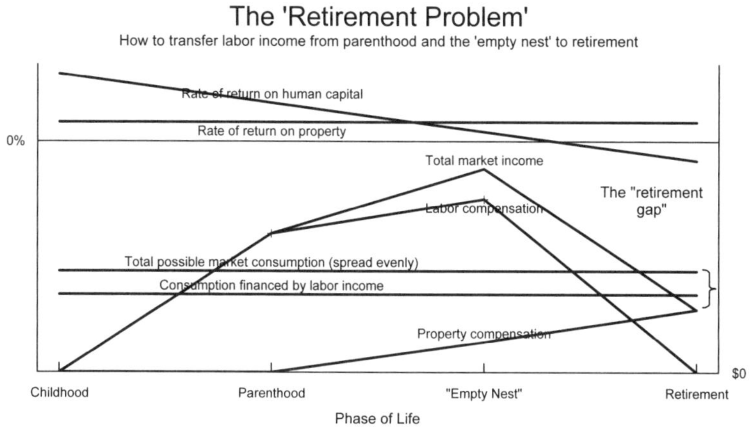

The 'Retirement Problem'

How to transfer labor income from parenthood and the 'empty nest' to retirement income. So at each stage, the person (or the family on his or her behalf) requires a strategy for bridging that gap. In the child's case, the gap is bridged by the parents spending some of their own current surplus upon the child's needs. But in the case of the retiree, current spending exceeds current market income, after counting all sources of income. The "retirement problem," essentially, is how the adults can transfer part of their current surplus from the "empty nest" stage into "retirement," when their "human capital" will be depreciating—ultimately, at death, to zero.

The problem is not due to poor planning; on the contrary, it results precisely from their planning and acting at each stage of life to take maximum advantage of those investments which offer the highest return— and therefore the highest possible lifetime wealth for themselves and their children—and to smooth consumption to be as even as possible over their lifetimes.[13]

We've already noted that the combined consumption of each parent and child is likely to exceed the parent's income during the stage when the child is concentrating on investing in a good education. This requires most parents to borrow when their children are small and to repay such loans during the "empty nest" stage, after the children have left home. Borrowing requires paying rather than receiving interest. The solution might seem simple: to invest in enough nonhuman capital— which, unlike one's own "human capital," can be indefinitely replaced when it wears out. The trouble is that in order to have enough nonhuman wealth to satisfy all current expenses in retirement, it would be necessary to invest less in human capital in the earlier ages of life when the rate of return on human capital is much higher than on nonhuman capital. A strategy of planning to live in retirement entirely out of property income (or the sale of previously accumulated property) would therefore lower the total amount of wealth that each person would enjoy throughout his or her lifetime.

Historically, there have been two strategies for solving the retirement problem. The first was for those too old to work to become dependent on their still-working adult children. Thus, parents would support their children when the children were young but be supported by their children when the parents were aged and the children were adults. When mortality was much higher, most people did not live long enough to reach the "empty nest" stage, let alone today's normal age of retirement.

On the other hand, for those who did live long enough to be too old to work, there was a high probability that the children might die before the parents or suffer some disability that severely reduced their ability to generate income. The second way of solving the "retirement problem" has been pay-as-you-go Social Security retirement pensions, which were established in 1936. It has been argued by opponents of the pay-as-you-go system that it discourages both the private saving available through the private capital markets and traditional intergenerational transfers within families.

After initially sharing that opinion, I changed my mind, finding upon investigation that pay-as-you-go Social Security retirement pensions provide a valuable form of retirement security that the private market cannot duplicate. Here is why: As we have seen, the average rate of return on human capital (particularly investment in "tertiary" or college education) is much higher than the rate of return on nonhuman capital. The fundamental reason is that human capital is embodied in human persons, and protecting human dignity requires forbidding some kinds of security for lenders or investors that are common when investing in property. For example, when you take out a mortgage to buy a house, or an auto loan, the lender receives the right to sell your house or car to satisfy the debt should you default on the payments.

To provide similar security for investment in human capital, the investor would require property in the borrower—which, indeed, Milton Friedman proposed when he first suggested abolishing Social Security: "The device adopted to meet the corresponding problem for other risky investments is equity investment plus limited liability on the part of the shareholders. The counterpart for education would be to 'buy' a share in an individual's earning prospects; to advance him the funds needed to finance his training on condition that he agree to pay the lender a specified fraction of his future earnings. In this way, a lender would get back more than his initial investment from relatively successful individuals, which would compensate for the failure to recoup his original investment from the unsuccessful. There seems no legal obstacle to private contracts of this kind, even though they are economically equivalent to the purchase of a share in an individual's earning capacity and thus to partial slavery."[14]

Actually, there *is* a legal obstacle, as I discovered in the mid-1990s, when I met some entrepreneurs who had been inspired by Friedman's proposal and were trying to set up a family of "human capital mutual funds" on Wall Street. Their main problem, they explained, was to repeal or amend state laws that prohibit "indentured servitude"—the "partial slavery" to which Friedman alluded. That didn't stop a couple of enterprising young people from trying more recently to sell slices of their lifetime earnings to investors in return for tuition money on the Internet auction site eBay. Their entries were removed for violating eBay's policies, not state laws. But such contracts would seem to be unattractive to investors for the same reason raised by the entrepreneurs I met. They are unenforceable—and rightly so.[15]

In another form, the same problem has always confronted any parent who expected to be supported by his children in old age as a quid pro quo for the parent's investment in the child's "human capital." Not only does the parent have no legal way to enforce such an agreement; he also faces the problem of being unable to diversify his risk. A stock market investor avoids "putting all his eggs in one basket" by investing in a portfolio or mutual fund containing the shares of many different companies and industries. It's generally agreed that effective diversification requires at least twenty different companies, but the typical family nowadays has two children. Pay-as-you-go Social Security solved the "retirement problem" of transferring labor compensation from parenthood and the "empty nest" to retirement by serving in effect as a highly diversified mutual fund invested in labor compensation—the return on investment in rearing and instruction. However, a well-administered pay-as-you-go retirement system must not grow so large that paying for it makes it too expensive for families to raise children.

Adding It All Up: From Lemonade Stand to National Income Accounts

It's time to retrace our steps and literally "add it all up": not only to summarize the elements of domestic economy that we have identified but also to see that in the process we have learned how the familiar yet often confusing measures of total national output and income are composed.

Although "matrimonial" human nature is inherently intergenerational, in this chapter we have largely confined ourselves, for the sake of clarity, to how the age, education, sex, and marital status of individual persons affect their lifetime earning and spending. Having analyzed these basic elements, we can now proceed in the other direction, measuring the total income of any community from a single family household up to the whole national or world economy, simply by adding up the incomes of its members.

Allowing for the basic differences between men and women we have already identified, we can represent each generation with an aver-

Figure 12–9

Personal and Family Income of Couples in Overlapping Generations
With replacement fertility and constant education (hence little or no real income growth)

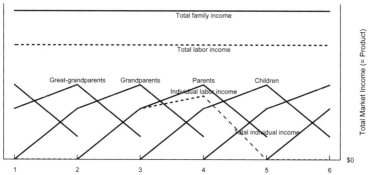

age of the incomes of representative couples. Even though each person's lifetime income and spending generally follow the rising-then-falling pattern we have identified, we would find that the total income of all family members would be constant through time, as long as each couple replaced itself with children on average and as long as it consumed as much human and nonhuman capital as it produced in its lifetime. Such a situation is depicted in Figure 12–9.

But this constancy of total income, under the assumption of constant total human and nonhuman resources, would conceal some important and interesting income dynamics.

First, both the level and sources of annual income among individual family members would be stratified according to individual persons' ages, because in each period we would be adding together the incomes of individuals in four successive generations at four different life stages: children without any current labor or property income; their active parents whose labor income was still rising quickly though below its lifetime peak, and who earned no net property income (after subtracting interest paid on borrowing through mortgages, tuition loans, etc.); their "empty nest" grandparents, whose labor income was at its lifetime peak but whose net property income was still rising; and their retired great-grandparents, whose labor income had ceased and whose total income came entirely from previous investments in property. With life phases of equal length and rates of return on human capital higher than on nonhuman capital in the first two but lower in the last two life phases, between three-quarters and four-fifths of total family income would be labor income. Moreover, among living family members, the great-grandparents would be net owners of most of the family's property.

Second, we've already discussed three of the most important factors raising real family income from one generation to the next: the growth of population through net fertility (or immigration); the effect of investment in education and other kinds of productive assets in raising the average real value that each person can contribute to production and therefore receive as compensation; and bequests, or gifts, willed by those dying in each phase, namely, the grandparents. The effect of the first in increasing the number of family members is obvious, as is the effect of bequests in increasing total property income. The effect of rising education can be seen if, instead of lining up the average incomes at each age by education in the same year as we did earlier, we stagger the same figures as if each successive generation invested more time and income in a higher average level of formal education and other kinds of instruction (see Figure 12–10).[16] In this case, rather than remaining constant,

Figure 12–10

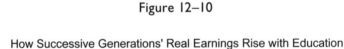

How Successive Generations' Real Earnings Rise with Education
Based on average earnings by age and education, both sexes 2001 (persons with earnings)

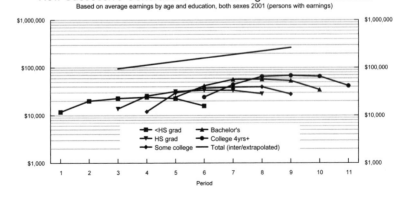

total real family income would rise from generation to generation by the combination of a larger number of members and a higher level of per capita income.

In calculating total national output or income, government agencies in effect make the same kind of calculation for the whole country as we did earlier for a single business firm (the lemonade stand) and just now for a single intergenerational family. The three pairs of lines in Figure 12–11 depict U.S. national production and income since 1890, indexed in each case to the starting values. In the bottom pair, the upper line shows the adult population and the lower line the number of adults employed in productive activities; their difference therefore indicates the rate of adult unemployment. In the middle pair, the upper line is "potential real GDP," which is an estimate of the maximum "real" or price-adjusted output and real income that could be achieved if all American workers and productive property were employed; the lower line of that pair is actual total national production income; and the difference, corresponding to the unemployment rate, is sometimes called the "national income gap." The upper pair of lines is simply the middle pair expressed in current dollars: national output and income without the "real" adjustment for annual inflation (or deflation) of the general price level.

What is true of the purchase of a single product from a single firm by a single person or family remains true (allowing for the small fraction of international payments) if we add up all the purchases by all persons and families of all products from all firms in the country: namely, total factor

Figure 12–11

U.S. Population, Employment, and Output/Income
1890-2009, 1890 = 1

compensation is equal to total spending on final products.[17] The national
income and product accounts attempt to add up all individual transactions as total spending on final products (gross domestic or national
product: GDP or GNP) and as total labor and property compensation received by producers (gross domestic or national income: GDI or
GNI).[18] Looking at the income side, considered before the effect of taxes
and government benefits, about two-thirds of gross national income (the
counterpart to gross national product, or GNP) consists of labor compensation (wages, salaries, and fringe benefits), while about one-third is

Figure 12–12

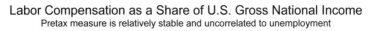

Labor Compensation as a Share of U.S. Gross National Income
Pretax measure is relatively stable and uncorrelated to unemployment

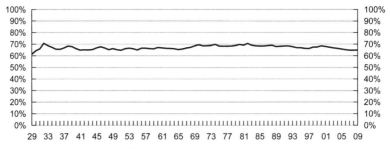

The ratio is equivalent to pretax "real unit labor costs."
Source: Commerce & Labor Depts.; calculated by LBMC LLC

property compensation (dividends, retained profits, interest, rents, and
royalties, Figure 12–12). This ratio implies that workers contribute about
two-thirds and owners of productive property about one-third, on average, of any additional output.

Yet as with the intergenerational family we considered, this remarkably stable average conceals exactly the same systematic differences we
found in the levels and sources of labor and property compensation of
American families. We can see this by considering shares of gross national
income ranked by percentile of family income. For about 80 percent of
American families, about 80 percent of income before taxes and personal
transfers originates as labor compensation, and the remainder as property

compensation. But this share falls to about 60 percent for the top 20 percent of families ranked by income, and the share of property income rises steadily to about 60 percent for the top 1 percent of families (Figure 12–13).[19]

Thus, the basic principles of domestic economy we have outlined in this section would allow any diligent reader (in theory) to calculate and (within limits) even predict the American population and potential real

Figure 12–13

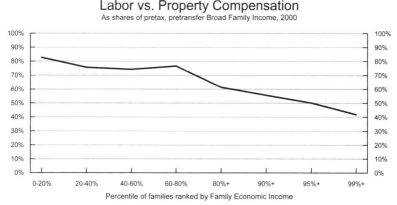

Labor vs. Property Compensation
As shares of pretax, pretransfer Broad Family Income, 2000

Percentile of families ranked by Family Economic Income

Source: U.S. Treasury, Office of Tax Analysis

national output and income. Explaining the causes of unemployment and inflation will require some further discussion, but as we will discover, the basic principles of neo-Scholastic political economy build on the principles of domestic economy. Indeed, in the next section we will see how neo-Scholastic economics can be used to solve the most pressing problem likely to face the United States over the next century: avoiding the combination of shrinking population and high unemployment rates that has engulfed the developed nations of Europe and Asia.

Part 4

POLITICAL ECONOMY

That men may protest against law, it is necessary that they should believe in justice; that they may believe in a justice beyond law, it is necessary that they should believe in a law beyond the land of living men.

—G. K. Chesterton, *Christendom in Dublin*

13

Saving America's Infant Industry

A single coherent tradition links all economically and politically successful American economic policy from George Washington through Abraham Lincoln, Franklin Delano Roosevelt, and Ronald Reagan. Tracing its origins and development will help us understand why the success of the American experiment at first critically depended—and depends now in a more literal sense—on promoting the nation's "infant industry."

The main tradition of American political economy can be distilled into four basic principles, all derived ultimately from the American Founders' understanding of what Aristotle had called (political) distributive justice and justice in exchange.[1] The first principle, established under Washington's administration, is that the federal government's policies to promote national defense, unity, and economic development[2] must be financed by taxation, not money creation. The second, established under Lincoln during the Civil War, is that the most efficient and popular way to raise the general revenues that pay for public goods like justice and national defense, which benefit all classes of citizens equally, is a broad-based, low-rate income tax, levied on both labor and property income. The third principle, first established under FDR, is that any quasi-public benefits more narrowly confined either to workers or property owners must be financed with dedicated taxes on labor or property income respectively, not general revenues. The fourth, associated with Reagan, is that the size and methods of government, particularly social benefits, must be limited to avoid both general unemployment and disinvestment

in people or property.[3] Here, I want to consider the neo-Scholastic application of these principles, particularly to the biggest economic question
facing America in coming decades: whether it will maintain its hard-won
global preeminence or follow the developed nations of Europe and Asia
in committing demographic suicide.

Simply to raise this outcome as a real possibility challenges conventional wisdom among American demographers. For example, one American demographer and political economist whom I highly respect, Nicholas
Eberstadt, has written that "U.S. demographic exceptionalism is not only
here today; it will be here tomorrow, as well. It is by no means beyond the
realm of the possible that America's demographic profile will look even
more exceptional a generation hence than it does today. If the American

Table 13–1

Actual and Projected Population and Relative Size, 1950–2050				
Year	U.S.	Russia	Japan	Germany	U.K.
Population (millions)					
Two figures are given for the U.S. due to changes in U.S. Census Bureau estimates.					
1950	152.3	101.9	83.8	68.4	50.1
2000	282.2/311.6	146.7	126.7	82.2	59.5
2050e	439.0/386.5	109.2	93.7	73.6	64.0
Relative size (world rank)					
1950	3	4	5	7	9
2000	3	8	10	13	22
2050e	3	17	19	22	27
Population growth (annual average %)					
1950–2000	1.2%	0.7%	0.8%	0.4%	0.3%
2000	0.9%	-0.4%	0.2%	0.3%	0.2%
2000–2050	0.8%	-0.6%	-0.6%	-0.2%	0.1%

Source: U.S. Census Bureau, International Data Base[5]

moment passes, or U.S. power in other ways declines, it won't be because
of demography."[4] This complacent view is based on current official projections—for example, those produced by the U.S. Bureau of the Census.

However, official forecasts for the United States rely on the assumption that the U.S. total fertility rate will remain at or above the replacement rate of 2.1. Moreover, the existing neoclassical economic model of
fertility, as we saw earlier, makes inaccurate predictions because it omits

a theory of distribution. As a result, at best it gives contradictory answers on the effects of fiscal policy on fertility. My analysis suggests instead that American "demographic exceptionalism" will soon end unless substantial changes are made to American law and economic policy.

Like successful fiscal policy, the formula for demographic suicide is quite simple; in fact, it consists largely of flouting the basic principles we have considered. The first step is to legalize abortion (as Japan did in 1948, twenty-five years before the United States, aborting over 40 percent of Japanese pregnancies by the late 1950s;[6] Europe now ends over half its known pregnancies by abortion, and the United States about one-quarter, down from over 30 percent). Second, when foreigners line up at the borders to fill this demographic void, try to shut off immigration. Most immigrants are in their twenties, and the annual number of legal and illegal immigrants to the United States (about 1.5 million) is almost exactly equal to the annual number of abortions twenty to twenty-five years earlier. Third, when the fiscal system totters on its shrinking demographic base, raise the tax burden on couples of childbearing age, thus preventing them from having children. This is what Europe has already done—and what both Democratic and Republican legislators now propose.

As we have seen, couples the world over have children for two basic reasons: because they love the children for their own sakes, or because they love themselves and expect some advantage from the children, or for some combination of these two factors. This is why just four factors explain most variation in birth rates among the fifty countries (comprising about two-thirds of the world's population) for which data are available. The birth rate is strongly and about equally *inversely* proportional to per capita social benefits and per capita national saving, both of which measure the average adult's provision for his or her own current and future well-being. A history of totalitarian government further reduces the birth rate by about 0.6 children per couple after such economic variables are taken into account.

Finally, we saw that fertility is strongly and *positively* related to the rate of weekly worship; in other words, people's behavior regarding the Two Great Commandments, to love God and neighbor, is empirically linked: Those who devote scarce resources like time and money to worship also devote such resources to children for the children's sake. The world over, weekly worshippers have about 2.1 more children per couple than those who don't worship, with relatively little variation by religion or denomination.

As we'll see in chapter 15, the factor most likely to depress the U.S. birth rate in coming decades is the projected doubling of social benefits (mostly Social Security, Medicare, and Medicaid) as a share of national income over the next seventy-five years, according to the U.S. Congressional Budget Office.[7]

Since the United States was almost exactly at the replacement birth rate of 2.1 children per family at the start of the twenty-first century, the empirical relationships suggest that with currently projected increases in absolute income and the prospective share absorbed by social benefits (Social Security and especially Medicare and Medicaid), the U.S. birth rate will decline over the next several decades from 2.1 to about 1.6, even if religious observance does not decline and the per capita savings rate does not increase.

However, because legal abortion has reduced American fertility since the early 1970s by an average of 0.6 to 0.7 children per couple, the United States could still avoid a declining population by ending legal abortion. Failing this, continued immigration at about 1.5 million a year will be nearly impossible to prevent.

The outline of a comprehensive economically and politically possible solution is straightforward. It requires reforms of the federal income and payroll taxes, social benefits, and monetary policy, most of which are desirable for reasons other than demography.

Income tax reform. First, as I suggested in 1995 as an economic adviser to the National Commission on Economic Growth and Tax Reform,[8] the income tax should be reformed to balance the annual cost of general government (that is, excluding social benefits) at the lowest possible tax rates on both labor and property income. As I will explain in more detail in the next chapter, this could be achieved if a single tax rate were imposed on all labor and property income. All deductions, exemptions, and credits would be eliminated except for a single credit based solely on family size, which would refund the income and payroll tax rates on an amount exceeding the poverty level.

For administrative simplicity, the tax should be levied as part of the cost of goods and services purchased (including new investment property) rather than on the same income when received by workers and owners of productive property. This means the income tax would be collected only from several million businesses rather than from more than 130 million households. This reform would also mean the end of the alternative minimum tax and similar tax monstrosities. Estates would not need to be taxed separately as long as the tax rate was applied to all realized capital gains. As is the practice with most of our trading partners, to be consistent and avoid multiple taxation of the same income, the tax would be levied on imports and rebated on exports. If Republicans wanted to bribe workers to acquire financial assets (and thus become Republicans), they would have to pay for such subsidies with dedicated taxes on property or property income—for example, by dedicated taxes on capital gains, estates, or dividends, all of which many of my fellow Republicans want to abolish.

Reform of social benefits. Second, to prevent fertility from declining as it is doing in most of Europe and Asia, total social benefits must not be permitted to increase as a share of national income beyond the 2001 level. Each program must be balanced annually on a pay-as-you-go basis (thus eliminating both near-term trust fund surpluses and expected deficits).

As Ronald Reagan correctly saw, Social Security's problems are not due to the program's pay-as-you-go *structure* but rather the prospective *size* of promised benefits. The program's main problems have always arisen from its *not* being kept on a pay-as-you-go basis. The dominant faction in each party seeks to "cure" this problem by actually increasing the current and prospective imbalances, even though such cross-subsidization is always politically unpopular as well as economically inefficient. Since about 1990, Social Security has been collecting about 25 percent more from workers in payroll taxes than necessary to pay current retirement benefits. In other words, workers have been subsidizing from their labor income general government operations that ought to be paid for with an income tax on both labor and property income. Yet over the next couple of decades, the situation is expected to reverse so that annual benefits will exceed annual payroll tax revenues by a similar proportion. Democrats have proposed to "solve" this problem by raising income and estate taxes, thus forcing property owners to pay for workers' benefits. As I will show in chapter 15, this would necessarily raise the cost of hiring and the unemployment rate, just as it has done in Europe. Meanwhile, Republicans want to divert the surplus payroll taxes from Social Security to subsidize property ownership through tax-advantaged financial accounts paid for with general revenues. By further reducing families' after-tax labor income, this could only reduce the birth rate—again, just as it has done in Europe.

The simplest solution for Social Security is to adapt the suggestion of former Republican actuary Robert Myers (1913–2010) to cut payroll taxes immediately by about 25 percent, thus returning the current trust fund surplus to American working families. They could then invest this surplus without restriction in raising and educating their children or in corporate stocks and bonds, depending on their family situation. Prospective deficits would be removed by phasing in a reduction of equal proportion in promised benefits, prorated for the number of years a worker received the payroll tax cuts. (Increasing the retirement age would have a similar effect on the budget, but it would disproportionately penalize those with lower incomes, which are linked to shorter longevity.)[9] New imbalances would then be prevented by automatically adjusting benefits in inverse proportion to the birth rate and average life expectancy.[10]

At the same time, Medicare and Medicaid would be reformed by linking each program's benefits to prior payroll contributions and by maintaining overall annual balance in the same way as for Social Security. Rather than allowing current spending per recipient to drive the programs' shares of national income, the calculation must be reversed by starting with the current total shares of social benefits in national income and dividing by the number of eligible beneficiaries.

Monetary reform. Finally, to end the repeated episodes of commodity-price inflation and the chronic federal budget and U.S. balance-of-payments deficits, the federal government must negotiate an end to the dollar's official role as a reserve currency, as will be described in chapter 16.

As with the George Washington administration's first efforts to establish it, America's continued global preeminence depends on using economic policy to promote its "infant industry." In 1950, the United States was the third most populous country in the world after China and India, but it had the largest economy. Today it is still third in population behind those same countries, and it still has the largest economy. However, it is now expected that in fifty years the United States, while still third in population (but behind India and China rather than vice versa), will be slipping rapidly in both relative population and economic size.[11]

"At what point, then, is the approach of danger to be expected?" Abraham Lincoln asked in 1838. "I answer, if it ever reach us it must spring up amongst us. It cannot come from abroad. If destruction be our lot, we must ourselves be its author and finisher. As a nation of freemen, we must live through all time, or die by suicide."[12] The developed nations

Table 13–2

The Four Principles of Successful (and Popular) Economic Policy
1. Current peacetime consumption of goods and services should be funded by current taxation, not money creation, with borrowing to fund only government-owned investments of equal or lesser duration (Washington/Hamilton).
2. Current consumption of public goods—e.g., defense and administration of justice—should be funded by taxing labor and property income equally (Lincoln).
3. More narrowly targeted "quasi-public" goods require dedicated funding (FDR). This means that:
a. Personal transfer payments—e.g., Social Security, Medicare, and Medicaid—should be financed by payroll taxes, not income or property taxes;
b. Subsidies to property owners—e.g., product subsidies, tax-free savings accounts—should be financed by taxes on property income, not payroll or income taxes.
4. Government's size and methods must be limited to prevent either general unemployment or disinvestment in people or property (Reagan).

How Each Party's Dominant Faction Violates the Four Principles
1. Each party relies on government deficit spending for current consumption,
2. Financed by money creation (Federal Reserve and especially foreign official dollar reserves): causing chronic episodes of commodity-led inflation and federal budget and international trade deficits;
3. Each party diverts payroll-tax surpluses (labor income) to fund public goods, instead of using income taxes (on both labor and property income): Democrats to increase spending, and Republicans to give tax loopholes, for favored constituents.
4. Republicans seek to shift burden of general government from all income to only labor income; Democrats seek to subsidize personal social benefits (e.g., Social Security, welfare, Medicare) with income tax and/or taxes on property income.

of Europe and Asia have adopted demographically suicidal policies, and currently projected fiscal policies are likely to lead to a similar result in the United States. Yet there is still time for the United States to avoid that fate, by renewing the basic principles of American political economy to protect its "infant industry."

In the next three chapters, we'll apply the neo-Scholastic theory of American public choice to explain in greater detail why these modern applications of political distributive justice and justice in exchange are the most just, politically popular, and economically efficient way to rise to this challenge.

14

The Theory of American Public Choice

They began with the fact of sin—a fact as practical as potatoes.
—G. K. Chesterton, *Orthodoxy*

Implicit throughout the history of American political economy is what I call the "theory of American public choice." This theory, originated by the American Founders, maintains (as James Madison put it) that "justice is the end of government";[1] that "as a man is said to have a right to his property, he may be equally said to have a property in his rights";[2] and that "the most common and durable source of factions, has been the various and unequal distribution of property."[3] By contrast, among the competing theories of public choice that we surveyed in chapter 5, the leading libertarian neoclassical version holds (as Anthony Downs put it) that, rather than justice, "the goal of government is attaining the income, power, and prestige that go with office"[4] and that partisan voting is unrelated to voters' economic interests.[5] As such, all these competing theories boil down to little more than the application of Stoic pantheism or Epicurean materialism to economic matters. In this chapter, I will show with empirical tests that only the neo-Scholastic version fully explains certain fascinating questions of American political life, including why there are two major American parties, who identifies with them, and how American voters' views of political distributive justice are reflected in the federal budget.

An Empirical Test of Public Choice Theories

As we will see in considering divine economy in chapter 17, the differences in worldview among the Scholastic natural law, Stoic pantheism, and Epicurean materialism are *not* matters about which reasonable people can disagree, because those differences concern precisely whether (and to what degree) humans are rational. In the same way, the corresponding differences among the Scholastic, classical, and neoclassical economic theories cannot be settled within either classical or neoclassical economic theory, because their logical incompleteness renders both unfalsifiable. Yet these differences can be settled empirically to any reasonable person's satisfaction by applying the neo-Scholastic economic theory, because it is both logically complete and empirically verifiable.

In the realm of political economy, the American National Election Studies (ANES) are reasonably well suited to test the alternative theories, since they have surveyed American voters' economic and demographic characteristics, the issues they consider most important in national elections, and their national voting back as far as 1948 or 1952, depending on the question.[6] Also, the survey ranks voters' characteristics such as family income according to percentiles derived from a normal curve, according to which just over two-thirds of any population should fall within one standard deviation above or below the mean.

Because the libertarian theory of public choice presumes that voters' issue concerns are essentially identical apart from random variation, it treats voters' concerns as essentially random and therefore argues that these interests should be "peaked"—that is, clumped—around the mean. But if they are not random, voters' interests should at least clump around *some* pronounced maximum or minimum, without which, according to the libertarian theory, no stability of government is possible.

The theory of American public choice, which is intuitively grounded in neo-Scholastic insights, distinguishes among public goods properly so called, which concern everyone about equally regardless of income or party affiliation; and quasi-public goods, about which voters' interests should vary systematically, particularly according to the allocation of their family income between labor and property compensation. Moreover, those objectively grounded differences in voters' issue concerns should explain the continuity in partisan ideologies under the American federal system, because the fact that each party needs a majority to win the White House or either house of Congress will force the parties to adjust the positions of their dominant faction in order to win.

If we begin with the single issue that voters identify as most important in each election, looking cumulatively over the whole period for which data are available, we find that voters' issue concerns can be categorized rather neatly under the categories suggested by the theory of American public choice. First, there are public goods like national defense and domestic public order, for which concern is nearly identical regardless of family income. And second, there are quasi-public goods of which the appeal varies systematically both by voter family income and by party affiliation. Concerning quasi-public goods, there is interest at each income level, but issues involving social welfare programs and labor issues are linearly and inversely related to income, while those involving such broadly economic issues as taxation, business, agriculture, consumer safety, and natural resources are linearly and positively related to voter family income (Figure 14–1).

Thus, American voters' concern for both domestic and international public goods behaves according to the theory of American public choice, which suggests that everyone will support public goods that benefit everyone in almost equal proportion, but in being almost absolutely flat rather than "peaked," it contradicts the prediction of the libertarian theory of public choice.

Figure 14–1

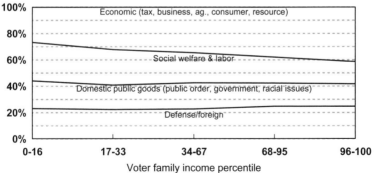

Most Important National Issue "Cluster" by Voter Family Income

Source: American National Election Studies, 1948-2004 cumulative

When we range voters according to their identification with political parties rather than family income, a similar pattern is revealed. The interest of Democrats, Republicans, and independents in both domestic and international public goods is nearly identical regardless of family income, while Democrats are more interested in quasi-public goods involving social welfare and labor issues, and Republicans more interested in all other quasi-public goods, with independents in between (Figure 14–2). Yet voters at every income level and of every political party affiliation are interested in all of these goods, and perhaps surprisingly, voters' interests appear to differ somewhat more by income level than by partisan self-identification. This suggests that rather than viewing each voter as having a single dominant interest, all voters are best viewed as sharing the same interests to about the same degree for public goods, but

Figure 14–2

Most Important Issue "Clusters" by Voter Party ID

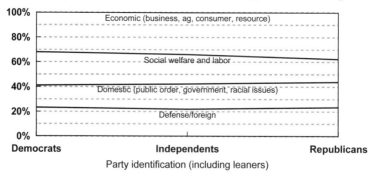

Source: American National Election Studies, 1948-2004 cumulative

for quasi-public goods in degrees that differ systematically with the level and source of their family income.

While casting serious doubt on the claims of the libertarian neoclassical theory of public choice, particularly its presuppositions about the supposed randomness of voters' views; and while supporting one feature of the neo-Scholastic theory of American public choice—its distinction between public goods and quasi-public goods—the evidence just presented is far from confirming the latter theory. For one thing, the neo-Scholastic version emphasizes not the relative *levels*, but the relative *sources* of family income, which the ANES data do not provide. For another, looking at all American voters' behavior cumulatively in postwar national elections ignores how voters' views and behavior change from election to election. Finally, it reveals no discernible influence of the presidency, let alone of individual presidential candidacies or administrations.

The first shortcoming can be remedied by combining the ANES data for voter family income with methods (described in the next section of this chapter) that trace all family income to its sources in labor and property compensation. The percentiles of income obviously stay the same even when absolute incomes change.[7] Combining the two confirms a hypothesis of James Madison's (which he derived from Aristotle): "Different interests necessarily exist in different classes of citizens,"[8] and "the most common and durable source of factions, has been the various and unequal distribution of property."[9] As Figure 14–3 indicates, the data confirm that the Democratic Party attracts voters whose income (before taxes and transfer payments) is disproportionately labor compensation— the return on their investment in "human capital." The Republican Party, on the other hand, attracts voters whose income is disproportionately property compensation—the return on investment in nonhuman capital. The family incomes of independent voters, meanwhile, have been between those of Republican and Democratic voters.

The same chart indicates why, even though the dominant faction in each major party is constantly lobbying for preferential treatment—for labor compensation in the Democratic Party and for property compensation in the Republican Party—the failure of such policies to win voter approval has forced both parties' leadership repeatedly back toward policies that treat labor and property income alike.

As Figure 14–3 indicates, Democratic vs. Republican partisan self-identification parallels the shares of labor vs. property compensation in voter family income before taxes and transfer payments. Yet partisan economic programs do not result from a kind of osmosis. Instead, they are initiated primarily by candidates for president, since the holder of that office will be at the same time the nation's chief executive and (if an effective president) the undisputed leader of a major political party. The ANES data reflect the importance of this dual role if we view shifts in partisan allegiance over time and policies initiated by pivotal presidents.

Figure 14–3

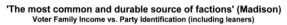

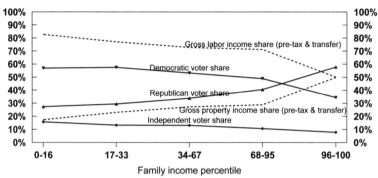

'The most common and durable source of factions' (Madison)
Voter Family Income vs. Party Identification (including leaners)

Source: ANES (1952-2004 cumulative), Treasury, BEA

Pivotal presidential elections typically are won by small majorities or plu-
ralities (e.g., Lincoln, Kennedy, Reagan), while successful first terms are
rewarded by a step change in voter partisan allegiance beginning with
that president's reelection.

The ANES data cover the Eisenhower, Kennedy–Johnson, and
Reagan eras. Eisenhower was a popular Republican president at a time

Figure 14–4

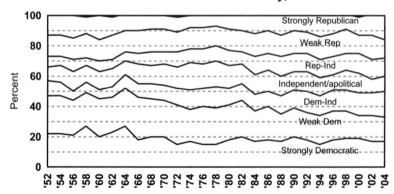

American Voter Party Self-Identification
American National Election Survey, 1952-2004

when nearly 55 percent of all American voters identified themselves as Democrats and only 34 percent as Republicans. After Kennedy's 1960 election, Democrats lost about 1 percentage point and Republicans about 2 percentage points, while the ranks of independents grew nearly 3 percentage points. Reagan's policies caused over 3 percent of voters to stop identifying themselves as Democrats and 4 percent to identify themselves as Republicans, while the share of independents fell slightly. Under Bill Clinton and George W. Bush, Democratic Party self-identification fell another 1 percent and Republican self-identification rose 3 percent, while independents fell 2 percent (Figures 14–4 and 14–5).[10]

Figure 14–5

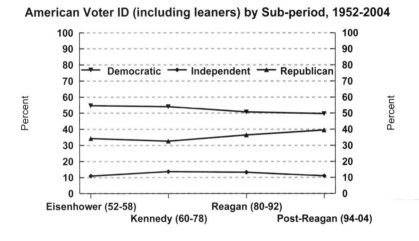

Thus, at the start of the twenty-first century, about 50 percent of American voters identified themselves as Democrats, about 40 percent as Republicans, and about 10 percent as independents, and identified themselves slightly more with Democratic than Republican positions on economic issues (while being more secular than either as measured by the rate of religious worship). Our empirical comparison therefore strongly rejects the predictions of the libertarian neoclassical theory of public choice (that voters' interests should vary randomly and be unrelated to partisan ideology). At the same time, it confirms three important hypotheses of the theory of American public choice: first, that voters' interests and opinions vary systematically with the shares of labor and property compensation in family income; second, that voters respond positively to economic policies that treat labor and property income equally, notwithstanding the extreme reluctance of the dominant factions in both the Democratic and Republican Parties to offer such policies; and finally, that the president, as the only official elected by a national majority of voters, plays a decisive role in the delicate balance of American political power, and presidents have achieved greatest political success by proposing and enacting such policies.

Partisan Ideology and Income Measurement

This exercise provides insight not only into Americans' voting habits but also into the nature of partisan ideology. It is surprisingly difficult to get straightforward facts about the distribution of income after taxes and transfer payments, even though those facts are the crux of the debates over income-tax and Social Security reform. The reason is a constant partisan tug-of-war to bias the statement of facts to support policies favored by the predominant factions in the two major political parties.

A good way to see how partisan ideology skews the presentation of facts regarding justice is to consider the abrupt changes between the administrations of Democratic President Bill Clinton and Republican President George W. Bush in the definition of the measure of family income used by the U.S. Treasury. The Clinton Treasury's "family economic income" was the broadest measure of income employed by any U.S. government agency. The solid lines in Figure 14–6 show how its basic components are divided among labor compensation, cash transfers to persons, and net property income. The broken lines indicate income sources omitted from the calculations, which are of two kinds. On the one hand, property income included the imputed value of owner-occupied residential, which is real but received "in kind," not as a cash payment like a paycheck or dividend. Including it would predispose policymakers to tax such property income. But the same calculation omitted in-kind personal transfers, including Medicare and Medicaid benefits, which approximately doubled total income for the bottom fifth of families. On the other hand, family economic income omitted the value of capital consumption allowances that had already been deducted from property income.

Also shown in Figure 14–6, for comparison, is the poverty level of income for a four-person family. Omitting in-kind transfers made it appear that the bottom fifth of taxpayers were below the poverty line after taxes and transfers; in fact, the transfers had raised those families well above the poverty line (which depends on family size). But the use of several different official measures of poverty meant that some low-income workers were paying taxes to subsidize those who didn't work yet were receiving higher incomes.

Figure 14–6

Ideology: Their Own Set(s) of Facts
Under Democrats, about 1/2 personal transfers ignored; Republicans, 1/4 property income.

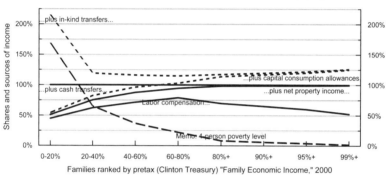

Author's calculations based on U.S. Treasury OTA; BEA; Ways & Means; JCT

The Treasury under President George W. Bush, a Republican president enjoying Republican control of both houses of Congress until 2006, abandoned "family economic income" and deferred to the ostensibly bipartisan Congressional Budget Office, which used a family income measure with roughly the opposite bias from the Clinton Treasury's family economic income measure: property income was now confined to cash payments, yet the imputed value of in-kind personal transfers was included. (The Congressional Joint Committee on Taxation used yet another less-than-consistent measure.)

How can we sort out this tangle? The key is to measure all income consistently. We saw in considering domestic economy that the peculiar pattern of lifetime income and consumption results from the facts that all income originates as labor or property compensation and that prospective returns on investing in people typically exceed those on property below about age forty but fall below them after that age. Early in life, income is mostly labor compensation, which starts at zero and increases as we acquire valuable skills; rises rapidly between childhood and the mid-thirties as we enter and gain experience in the labor market; rises more slowly to peak at around age fifty; then drops finally to zero in retirement. Property income starts close to zero early in life (for those with little or no inherited property), but becomes increasingly significant as the expected rate of return on investment in human capital falls below the rate on investment in property. And for those who acquire significant wealth from any source—whether inheritance, talent, luck, or hard work—the only practical way to save it is in the form of claims on property (stocks, bonds, etc.). These facts of everyday life account for the distribution of income among American families. But to interpret them, we must reconsider the meanings of *income, consumption,* and *investment.*

In the same article in which Theodore Schultz coined the term *human capital,* his first policy conclusion was this: "Our tax laws everywhere discriminate against human capital. Although the stock of such capital has become large and even though it is obvious that human capital, like other forms of reproducible capital, depreciates, becomes obsolete, and entails maintenance, our tax laws are all but blind on these matters."[11] What he meant was that labor and property income—the returns on investment in human and nonhuman capital, respectively—are measured inconsistently. Before property income is ever taxed, the costs of maintaining the property in working order are excluded, and a further allowance for the property's depreciation in use is deducted. Only what is left over after these calculations is taxed. But labor compensation is taxed without regard to its maintenance costs or depreciation. A farmer who buys a $50,000 tractor to increase the productivity of his operations will eventually deduct that full cost as well as maintenance and repairs from his income. Should he spend the same amount sending his daughter to an agriculture school to become an expert manager of the family's property, he will enjoy no similar deductions.

Surprisingly little has changed since Schultz wrote those words. It might be argued that the combination of standard tax deductions, personal exemptions, earned income and child tax credits, etc., which aim to exempt a poverty-level income from taxation, amount to a rough equivalent of minimal "human maintenance" costs. But to say so is to admit that the apparent progressivity of income is an artifact of the inconsistent measurement of labor and property compensation. There is no allowance for the depreciation of human capital (which, since we all die, is always 100 percent). Therefore, a much larger share of labor than property compensation is subject to tax. The political process has clumsily and inefficiently responded by imposing progressive tax rates and multiple layers of taxation on property income.

The simplest way to measure all income properly and to treat all income equally is to add back the allowance for property depreciation to property income and to tax this larger amount, while subtracting a poverty-level income ("human maintenance") from labor compensation before taxing this smaller total. We can call the resulting measure "broad family income." At least 75 percent of gross income for the lowest four-fifths of families is labor income, but the share falls to about 40 percent for the top 1 percent of families (Figure 14–7).

The same issues and ideologies are involved in the debate over income-tax reform. "Consumption"-tax advocates inconsistently define *investment* to mean investment in *property* but not in *people,* and *consumption* as *using up* (of property) but *enjoyment in using* (property by people). By taxing "consumption," they essentially mean taxing only labor compensation (Figure 14–8). For instance, in the example above, the tractor expenses would be treated as investment, the agriculture school expenses as "consumption" (which is why I put the word "consumption" in quotation marks). I call this worldview the economic stork theory, because it begins with the assumption that people and their skills arrive from out of the blue, as if delivered by a large stork. Dick Armey's and Steve Forbes's flat-tax plan of the 1990s would ultimately have eliminated taxation of property income by exempting from taxation both investment in productive property (through "expensing" of plant and equipment) and the personal income that is the return on that property (interest, dividends, rents, and capital gains).

After a transition period, the result would have been to exclude all property income from the tax base—leaving, in effect, a glorified payroll tax. (A national sales tax would get the same result immediately.) Since property income is about one-third and labor income two-thirds of total national income, such a tax reform would require a tax rate at least 50 percent higher than an income tax to raise the same revenue (or a much larger deficit, if you wanted to avoid imposing a tax increase on most workers). Exempting a poverty-level income from taxation through increased standard deductions, personal exemptions, or tax credits can prevent a tax increase on lowest-income taxpayers, but about twice as many middle- and upper-income taxpayers would get a tax hike as a tax cut.

Figure 14–7

Shares of Broad Family Income in "Pure" Tax Bases
After subtracting poverty-level "human maintenance"; property maintenance already deducted

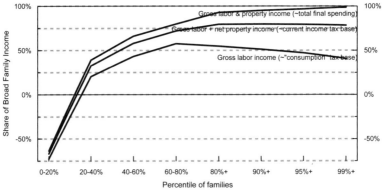

Figure 14–8

Tax Burden with Flat Tax Rate, Different Tax Bases
Raising the same Federal revenue and exempting a poverty-level income in each case, 2000

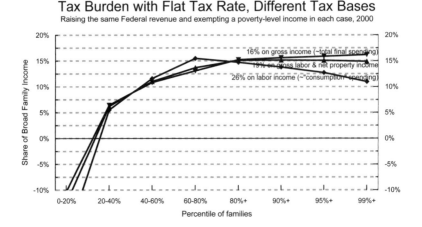

Thus, it didn't take a crystal ball when I warned my former boss, Jack Kemp, on the first day of hearings by the National Commission on Economic Growth and Tax Reform in 1995 that all the "consumption" taxes would politically self-destruct when it became apparent that any revenue-neutral version would represent a tax increase for working families. And that's exactly what happened to the Armey–Forbes plan in the 1996 Republican presidential primaries.[12] As Figure 14–9 shows, any revenue-neutral version would have raised the total federal tax burden for 99 percent of taxpayers, both in the first year and when fully phased in.

Figure 14–9

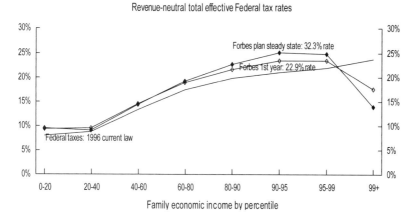

'Consumption' Tax Paradigm: Why the 'Flat Tax' Failed
Revenue-neutral total effective Federal tax rates

Forbes plan steady state: 32.3% rate

Forbes 1st year: 22.9% rate

Federal taxes: 1996 current law

Family economic income by percentile

In the process, I learned that the easiest way to dispose of such a politically unrealistic tax plan is simply to take it seriously. I did so several years later for the author of one of the many "consumption" taxes (the so-called fair tax). Assuming that all federal income, payroll, estate, and gift taxes would be replaced—and poverty-level "human maintenance" exempted (as he proposed)—it turned out that the tax rate on "true consumption" was to be a flat 61 percent (or 43 percent inclusive of the tax, as income tax rates are usually calculated).

The FAST Federal Budget Balancing Plan

From these considerations, it becomes obvious that the apparent progressivity of an income tax results merely from the inconsistent definitions of labor and property income. When maintenance and depreciation of property are deducted from property income but human maintenance and depreciation are not deducted from labor income, the distribution of income *seems* progressive. But when both are treated alike, nearly identical "progressivity" of the tax burden is achieved simply by applying a flat tax rate to properly defined income (Figure 14–10).

The fairest, simplest, and most efficient way to reform the tax code, therefore, would involve not only treating labor and property income exactly alike but also simplifying the means of collection so that taxes were filed mostly by employers (business, government, nonprofit, or the self-employed) rather than by individuals. This would be a radical simplification for the tens of millions of people who would no longer have a personal relationship with the IRS every April, but it is a less radical proposal than it may at first sound. It would simply treat all income in the same way that President George W. Bush proposed in 2003 for dividends alone: nondeductible when paid by businesses, but nontaxable when received by individuals.

Figure 14–10

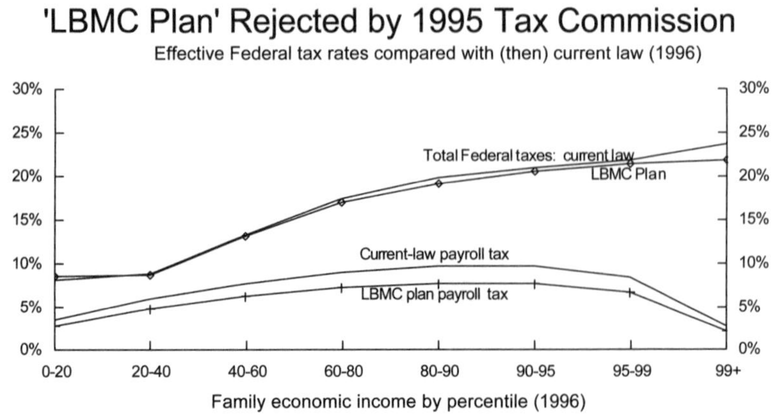
'LBMC Plan' Rejected by 1995 Tax Commission
Effective Federal tax rates compared with (then) current law (1996)
30%
25%
20%
15%
10%
5%
0%
Total Federal taxes: current law
LBMC Plan
Current-law payroll tax
LBMC plan payroll tax
0-20
20-40
40-60
60-80
80-90
90-95
95-99
99+
Family economic income by percentile (1996)

Let's say that a family purchases a new car or computer. The business pays out the money entirely as income to its employees, investors, and creditors. Under our current system, the business deducts all that compensation (except some dividends) from its taxable income, and the government taxes the recipients' income. If instead the compensation paid by the business (or other employer) were nondeductible, the existing corporate and personal income taxes would be superfluous, because the tax on all that labor and property income would already have been "prepaid." There would, however, be a per-person rebate for the income and payroll taxes paid by the employer on income below the poverty line ("human maintenance").

If a flat tax rate were applied to such a properly defined income tax base, there would be three interesting results. First, the tax code's complexity would disappear. Most families would have no contact with the IRS except to receive their rebates. Instead of the IRS having to collect taxes from more than 100 million taxpaying entities, it would have to track only a few million employers. Second, both the tax code and the economy would be vastly more efficient. At the time, I estimated that the same amount of total revenue as raised by both the current corporate and personal income tax codes could be raised with a flat rate of about 16 percent, less than half the current code's top rate. To balance non–Social Security federal spending and eliminate the current deficit, a rate of 18 percent would be required. There would be no double taxation of any income, nor would there be any incentive to make decisions for tax reasons other than economic efficiency. Third, the tax burden under such a system would be about as "progressive" as the current tax code. This is because even though both corporate and personal income taxes with their progressive tax rates would be replaced, all property income now excluded from the tax base would be taxed, while the subpoverty line "human maintenance" costs contained in labor compensation would not be taxed.

The same economic facts of life also explain the economic and political logic of Social Security reform. While income varies according to the lifetime pattern described above, we all need to be fed, clothed, sheltered, and transported, whether or not we earn income. Our income typically exceeds consumption during parenthood and the "empty nest," while consumption exceeds income during childhood and retirement. This last fact creates what I call the "retirement gap." When people retire, labor compensation falls to zero, yet consumption is usually much higher than the property income from earlier saving. The basic problem is how to fill this gap without forgoing retirement, suffering a sharp fall in consumption during retirement, or lowering total lifetime earnings and consumption (which is what happens if early in life one invests more in lower-yielding property and less in higher-yielding human capital).

Without government, the retirement gap can be bridged only by love—a gift from someone (most often one's adult children) whose own consumption is thereby reduced. Pay-as-you-go Social Security solved the retirement problem by providing an asset that the private financial markets cannot. While a financial account is essentially a claim on property, a pay-as-you-go Social Security retirement pension amounts to a share in a diversified human capital mutual fund. Social Security makes it possible for workers, by pooling a fraction of their income, to transfer labor compensation from their working years to retirement, and to surviving dependents after their deaths. However, once pay-as-you-go benefits have closed the retirement gap, any further expansion of benefits necessarily comes at the expense of lower investment in either children or productive property.

Today, any Social Security reform plan must start with a simple fact: Social Security's expected future deficits are entirely the result of lower birth rates (owing above all to three decades and counting of legal abortion). If that trend were reversed, the deficits would be easily surmounted (Figure 14–11).

Figure 14–11

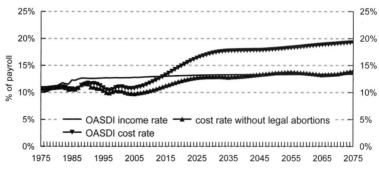

Impact of Legal Abortion on Social Security
OASDI income and cost rates, SSA intermediate projections

From John D. Mueller, "The Socioeconomic Costs of Roe v. Wade," *Family Policy*, April 2000

But if not, options for filling the retirement gap are still much broader than have so far been considered. What's clear is that plans to replace pay-as-you-go Social Security with compulsory individual financial accounts are based on the same stork theory as the consumption tax—and they would worsen the demographic problem. As the redoubtable Martin Feldstein, the GOP's preeminent "stork theorist," has explained, "The essential feature of the transition to a funded program of retirement benefits is a period of reduced consumption by employees during the early years of the transition so that a dedicated capital stock can be accumulated. This dedicated capital is then used to finance retirement benefits, thereby permitting lower taxes and more consumption by employees in later years."

Note that in Feldstein's view, "capital" means "nonhuman capital": Education, training, and child-rearing are classed as "consumption," not as investment in human capital. The analysis takes the population and its skills as given, and only by virtue of this false neoclassical assumption does it come to the equally false conclusion that taxes on property income not only *should* but inevitably *must* be shifted to workers. As the demographic implosions in Europe and Japan suggest, heavily shifting to "consumption" taxes causes a sharp decline in investment in human capital.

When the pay-as-you-go system started, its rate of benefit return on payroll tax contributions was much higher than the stock market, because there were many workers supporting few retirees; but in the long run, the average rate of return on pay-as-you-go Social Security is equal to the rate of economic growth (which over the past seventy-five years has been higher than the average yield on government bonds). Replacing pay-as-you-go pensions with individual financial accounts, as Feldstein forthrightly acknowledges, requires the start-up process to go into reverse: those in the first generation to work under the new regime must continue paying the benefits for their parents' generation while saving for their own retirement.

The size of this transition tax was strikingly illustrated when the author of the leading plan to divert Social Security taxes into private accounts had the plan estimated by Social Security's chief actuary. Until then, its proponents had argued, with apparent plausibility, that the transition cost might be financed by borrowing several trillion dollars, halving discretionary spending, and reaping increased tax revenues from increased investment in plant and equipment. But Social Security chief actuary Stephen C. Goss's estimates made three unpleasant features of the plan explicit. First, general-revenue "transfers to the Trust Fund would . . . not be contingent on achieving these [cuts] in actual federal spending." Second, there would be no net increase in plant and equipment, economic growth, or revenue "feedback" if the cost were financed by federal borrowing. And third, replacing the payroll taxes diverted from the Trust Fund without additional borrowing would require tax increases, mostly on individual and corporate income, lasting several decades and ranging up to more than 7 percent of taxable payroll (Figure 14–12).

Figure 14–12

The Range of Social Security Options
Social Security (OASDI) Tax and Cost Rates, % of Payroll

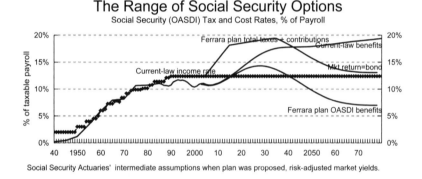

Social Security Actuaries' intermediate assumptions when plan was proposed, risk-adjusted market yields.

Proponents armed with millions in lobbying dollars but few popular votes assumed that this plan would be endorsed by President Bush, brought by Republicans to the House and Senate floors, and adopted by majorities in both chambers. I thought it highly unlikely that any one of these would happen, let alone all three. I didn't see how President Bush could possibly endorse such a plan, because it violated his two basic principles for Social Security reform: that any accounts must be voluntary, and that they must involve no tax increase. The private accounts aren't voluntary, because if you forgo the private account option, you must still pay the government's cost of funding everyone else's account. And that would mean a much larger and earlier tax increase than would result merely from leaving the system on autopilot and raising payroll taxes to cover promised benefits.

The earlier Feldstein plan of 1999 had died in *Republican*-controlled committees, when dismayed GOP lawmakers discovered the "essential feature": a 75 percent "clawback" tax on all money withdrawn from personal retirement accounts—after which the plan still wasn't fiscally balanced. They had a similar shock in 2005 when they discovered the huge income-tax "clawback" in the newer Ferrara-Ryan-Sununu version.

The Social Security reform that my business partners and I proposed to the 1995 national tax commission is a variation of a plan long advocated by former Republican Social Security chief actuary Robert Myers. It would cut payroll taxes immediately, thus getting rid of the Social Security "surplus," which Congress has simply been using to fund deficits in the rest of the federal budget. In exchange, there would be a matching reduction in the level of future retirement benefits (prorated for the share of working years that each worker received the tax cut), eliminating expected future deficits. Families would be free but not required to put the payroll tax-cut money into financial retirement accounts; for most families with children, education would be a more pressing (and higher-yielding) investment.

Since the plan reduces current payroll taxes and future benefits in the same proportion, the rate of return per dollar of payroll contribution would be higher than under any of the other alternatives, which involve tax increases *and* benefit cuts. The plan also depends far less than the other plans on the accuracy of forecasts for economic growth and financial asset returns. If economic growth is as slow in the future as the actuaries have been projecting, then families will be prepared and the system will be kept in balance with relatively small adjustments. But if economic growth outperforms the actuaries' projections, the system will be in surplus and payroll taxes can be cut again, the benefit reductions halted, or both.

In short, a simple, low, flat-rate income tax combined with a workable plan to balance the pay-as-you-go Social Security pension system without income-tax funding remains eminently doable. And it is the way to continue the just, efficient, and popular fiscal legacy linking George Washington, Abraham Lincoln, Franklin Roosevelt, and Ronald Reagan. The party that implements it will realize Reagan's partisan goal of not "a temporary uneasy alliance, but the creation of a new, lasting majority." The only remaining question is which party will accomplish that.

Yet it is not sufficient to explain the positive case for this approach to fiscal policy. We must also understand the economic consequences of the violations of justice in exchange that result when factions pursue objectively unjust partisan agendas. That is what we will explain in chapters 15 and 16, the last two chapters on political economy.

15

Injustice in Exchange: Unemployment

Jacques Rueff was the first modern economist to demonstrate empirically how the instruments of economic policy—taxes, product subsidies, personal transfer payments, and money creation—cause two of the three main problems of *disequilibrium* or *injustice in exchange* in modern economies, unemployment and inflation.[1] The third such problem—a "baby bust" or "demographic winter"—became manifest in developed Europe and Asia only after Rueff's death in 1978. But it too results from factional injustice in exchange, typically because government transfer payments to persons substitute for personal and joint gifts within families among husbands and wives, parents and children. In this chapter, therefore, we will consider the causes and cures of unemployment and a baby bust.[2] In the next, we will consider the causes and cures of inflation and deflation.

Figure 15–1 shows key indicators for the first two problems in the periods for which data are available: the rate of consumer price inflation since 1800; the rates of GDP price inflation and unemployment since 1890; and the "national income gap" (the shortfall of total national output/income below the level possible at full employment) since 1929.

To make our discussion of employment comprehensive, we must account for everyone who could possibly be employed or unemployed. Practically speaking, this means all adults, now defined as everyone sixteen years and older. (Before 1947, the definition included those fourteen years and older.)[3] The first practical distinction we must draw is between those within and those outside the labor market, often errone-

Figure 15–1

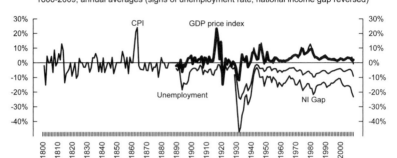

Disequilibrium: U.S. Inflation, Unemployment & Income 'Gap'
1800-2009, annual averages (signs of unemployment rate, national income gap reversed)

ously described as those "working" or "not working." A great deal of work and production occurs outside the market. At one time, nearly *all* work and production occurred outside the market, and even today the production of many goods, as well as of people, occurs within the household. So, it is more accurate and fruitful to distinguish between those working in the labor market and those working outside the labor market in the household economy. For reasons that will become apparent, all unemployment occurs within the labor market. We can therefore further exhaustively describe all adults in the labor market as being employed civilians, employed in the military, or unemployed (Figure 15–2).

Figure 15-2

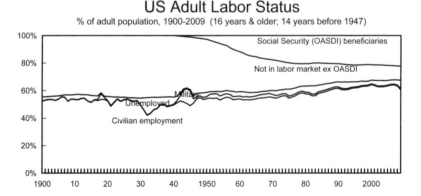

US Adult Labor Status
% of adult population, 1900-2009 (16 years & older; 14 years before 1947)

There are two basic facts to explain. First, what accounts for the unemployment rate, both as a share of the civilian labor force and as a share of the total adult population? Second, what accounts for people's decision to participate in the labor market and, particularly, the increased share of the adult population in the labor market since the Second World War? A closer look reveals a further complication: The labor market employment of men has steadily declined, while the labor market employment of women has steadily increased. So the rising employment/population ratio has resulted from the share of adult women employed in the labor market having risen by more than the labor market employment of men has declined (Figure 15–3).

Figure 15–3

U.S. Labor Force Status
% of adult civilian noninstitutional population, 1950-2009

If we can account for both facts, we will have explained the variation in the (generally increasing) share of the adult population employed in the labor market, and the (generally declining) share outside the labor market. Let us deal with the problem of unemployment first.

Unemployment as Disequilibrium: Rueff's Law

Unemployment is a case of market *dis*equilibrium. That is, when we say that a certain percentage of the civilian labor force is currently unemployed, it means that that proportion of workers is actively seeking a job in the labor market but unable to find employment at the prevailing level of labor compensation. The quantity of labor demanded by business firms falls short of the quantity offered by workers in that proportion.

Rueff was the first to demonstrate empirically that variations in unemployment are closely linked to the relative price of labor and offer an explanation for its variation. The relation between the two was found to be so strong that it became known in the 1930s and 1940s as "Rueff's Law." Rueff showed that the reason for the unprecedented appearance of chronically high unemployment in England in the 1920s was a rise in the relative price of labor (Figure 15–4).[4] He traced its cause to the combination of the new (instituted in 1911) unemployment "dole," which was fixed in nominal terms (that is, so many shillings a week), and a sharp post–Great War decline in the price level (which resulted from Britain's decision to return to the gold standard at the pound's prewar gold value despite more than a doubling of the general price level).

Figure 15–4

U.K. Wages & Prices, 1919-1938
1913=100

Source: Rueff, 2 *Oeuvres Complètes* 2: 265-266, Plon, 1979

Rueff's study caused a sensation when an updated version was reported upon in the *London Times* in 1931, just after British unemployment had risen most sharply (Figure 15–5).[5] Following Rueff's lead, other researchers found a similarly strong relationship between the relative price of labor and unemployment in at least a dozen other countries.[6]

John Maynard Keynes's *General Theory* implicitly depends on Rueff's Law, with the additional assumption that wage rates are fixed in nominal but not real terms.[7] Yet while assuming downward "stickiness" of money wages, Keynes did not acknowledge Rueff's explanation for it: the unemployment "dole," which, at the time (like chronic unemployment), was almost unique to the United Kingdom. Modern followers of Keynes similarly ignore the fact that indexing of such benefits fixes wages in real terms, thus invalidating Keynes's main assumption. As a result, Keynesian economists' exaggerated hopes for a Keynesian Restoration in economic theory, after several decades of eclipse, are likely to be as unavailing as those for the nineteenth-century restoration of the Bourbon monarchy in France, about which Talleyrand presciently remarked, "They have learned nothing, and forgotten nothing."[8]

Figure 15–5

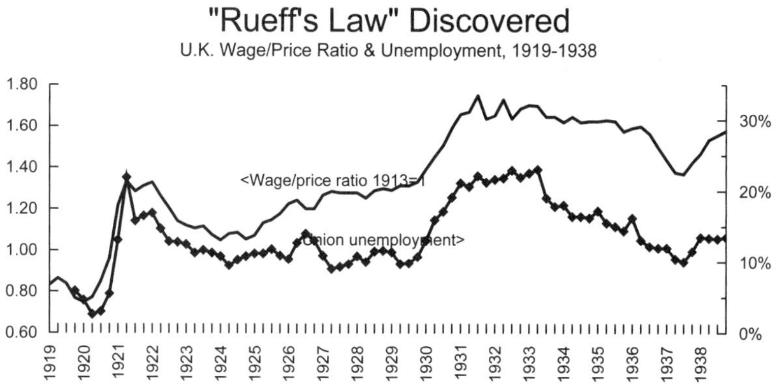

"Rueff's Law" Discovered
U.K. Wage/Price Ratio & Unemployment, 1919-1938

Source: Rueff, 2 *Oeuvres Complètes* 2: 265-266, Plon, 1979

Rueff's Law Forgotten and Rediscovered

For various reasons, Rueff's Law was almost universally forgotten by economists after World War II. But the theory continues to explain variations of unemployment in economies as large as the United States[9] and as small as Puerto Rico,[10] once its measurement is updated.

To understand Rueff's Law, we must draw out the underlying relationships implied in our earlier discussion of domestic economy. That discussion implied that unemployment is a direct function of the "price" of labor. But what, exactly, *is* the relative price of labor? Obviously it has to do with the level of labor compensation. But like all prices, labor compensation has a meaning only in relation to other prices. From the point of view of a worker, whether a wage of $5 an hour is decent or lousy depends, for example, on whether a glass of lemonade costs $5 or 25 cents. And for the prospective employer, whether it is profitable to employ a worker to produce the lemonade also depends on whether the glass of lemonade can be sold for $5 or 25 cents. So the relative price of labor has to take both pay and prices into account.

The cost of labor is also affected by labor productivity. If a business firm could double the quantity of goods produced with an hour of labor while wage rates and prices remained the same, it would effectively cut the cost of labor in half. But in a competitive market, all units of labor (and capital) are paid incomes equal to what the last unit adds to output. If labor productivity suddenly doubled while product prices stayed the same, businesses would find that to maximize their profits they would need to keep hiring more workers until real wage rates had doubled, at which point the relative price of labor would have risen back to its initial level.

To a prospective employer, therefore, the effective "price" of labor is the labor compensation or wage agreed with the worker, adjusted for two things: the selling price of the finished product and the worker's productivity. This is sometimes called the "efficiency wage." The higher the efficiency wage, the lower the demand for workers; the lower the efficiency wage, the higher the demand to hire employees.

As we noted in chapter 12, what is true of the purchase of a single product from a single firm remains true if we add up all the purchases of all products from all firms: namely, total factor compensation is equal to total spending on final products. This means that, just as we could view the purchase of lemonade either as spending on a product or as compensation to its producers, we can view the whole economy either as total spending on final products or as the total income of their producers.[11] The national income and product accounts attempt to add up all individual transactions as total spending on final products (gross domestic or national product: GDP or GNP) and as total labor and property compensation received by producers (gross domestic or national income: GDI or GNI).[12]

In doing the calculations for the whole national economy, we discover that the relative price of labor, or "efficiency wage," is the same as the share of labor compensation in total national income.[13] This is a great convenience in calculation, since it means that we can measure the economy-wide relative price of labor without actually knowing the average hourly wage rate, the number of hours worked, the level of productivity, or total real output. All we need to know is total labor compensation and total national income.

Before taxes and government benefits, gross labor compensation typically makes up about two-thirds, and property compensation about one-third, of gross national income, and those shares are remarkably constant over time. This is presumably because workers consistently contribute about two-thirds, and productive property about one-third, the value of gross output.[14] While this gives us a comprehensive overview of labor costs, the income shares calculated in this way do not have a particularly close correlation with the unemployment rate. This is because the cost of labor has been calculated without taking into account three important realities: taxes, transfer payments (including social benefits), and (non-human) capital consumption. In particular, taxes and benefits must be included because they affect people's behavior. Perhaps ignoring them might have been justifiable seventy or eighty years ago, when both were relatively small in relation to the total economy. But not today.

Parental "Economic Policy" and the Lemonade Stand

To understand the effects of fiscal policy on (un)employment, we must return to our analogy of the lemonade stand and put ourselves in the place of the children's parents, who, after observing the children's efforts, decide to try to help them without taking over the operation.

1. Price regulation. The quantity of a product demanded by customers diminishes as the price increases, and there is generally only one price at which the quantity demanded equals the quantity supplied. What would happen if the parents overruled the children about the price at which they had found they could sell all their lemonade—say, telling them they must sell lemonade for 50 cents rather than 25 cents a glass? This is essentially what the government does when it attempts to regulate the prices of products. If the selling price were already at the level at which the quantity of lemonade demanded just equaled the quantity offered for sale, raising the selling price would cause the quantity demanded to fall short of the quantity supplied, thus creating an unsellable surplus of lemonade. Likewise, lowering the selling price below the "equilibrium" price would increase the quantity demanded but not the quantity supplied, thus creating a shortage of lemonade. In both cases, the amount actually sold would not be equal to the amount demanded. The same principle explains why government price controls, if enforced, always cause either a shortage or a surplus in a competitive market. Below-market rent controls create a housing shortage, below-market interest ceilings a credit shortage, and below-market gasoline price controls a gasoline shortage.

2. Regulation of compensation. Since the compensation is ultimately determined by the product's price, similar effects occur when the government attempts to set the rates of compensation of the productive factors. The most important example of a regulatory control on factor compensation is the minimum wage. This would be like the parents insisting that the child who supplied only labor be compensated at a certain rate per hour. If the minimum rate is set at a relatively low level, say $1 an hour when the children's analysis had indicated the rate should be at $2 an hour out of revenues of $3 an hour, the regulation has no effect. But if the rate were set above the level that would equalize the demand for and supply of labor—say $3 an hour—labor compensation would absorb all revenues, causing the child "proprietor" to take all the property home. The result would be a labor surplus—in other words, unemployment—but without providing any alternate source of income to the worker, who would be unemployed as a result. The minimum wage makes it illegal, in effect, to hire unskilled workers at what their skills are currently worth, and thus to improve their skills and earn a higher wage. So they remain unemployed and unskilled. By removing the unskilled from the labor market, the minimum wage may raise the wages of skilled workers (which is probably why it is championed by labor unions), but it reduces the income of all workers as a group: a good example of economic policy motivated by faction.[15]

3. Product subsidies. Government subsidies or benefits paid to producers can also create shortages or surpluses, but with an important difference compared with price controls. In this case, the surplus created by an above-market price is purchased by the government—rather like parents who insist that the children set the price of lemonade higher (say, 50 cents a glass when most customers are willing to pay only 25 cents) but offer to buy any lemonade that remains unsold at that price. That way, the children's income would be increased at the expense of the parents. However, the benefit or subsidy would also encourage the children to produce more lemonade, thus making it potentially very expensive to the parents.

In the same way, farm price supports increase farmers' incomes but also create government-owned "lakes" of milk or wine and "mountains" of unsold butter, cheese, cotton, sugar, and wheat. The surplus products cannot be sold by the government without driving the market price below the level that it is the whole point of the policy to support. To avoid this, an alternative method might be to offer to pay the children 25 cents for every glass they manage to sell at any price. The subsidy might induce the children to make so much more lemonade that they had to lower the price to customers to 10 cents a glass to sell it all, but the children would receive 35 cents a glass. (However, this would undercut the price of any other lemonade stands in the vicinity, which is analogous to the effect of agricultural subsidies in developed nations upon agriculture in less developed nations.)

4. Transfer payments to persons. Something analogous to government subsidies for products happens in the labor market when the government offers social benefits or "transfer payments" to workers. But the economic consequences depend largely upon conditions on which the payments are granted. Personal transfer payments involve basically three kinds of conditions, with three different results on the employment and income of workers. The first category requires people to be in the labor force but be unemployed to qualify. This would be like the children's parents offering to pay the child "worker" whenever he was not working at the lemonade stand, but at a rate near what the child could earn by so working. This category includes unemployment insurance and welfare payments to the able-bodied that, after paying costs of commuting, etc., exceed the value of labor compensation available from a private job. The result is a surplus of labor that cannot be sold to private employers at the going wage, but that the government, in effect, chooses to purchase at a higher rate, which causes a reduction in market employment and an equal increase in *un*employment.

The second category requires the recipient to be outside the labor force. Such benefits include pay-as-you-go pensions conditioned on retiring from the labor force, as well as disability insurance, which also requires the recipient to be fully or partially disabled from working. This would be like the children's parents offering to pay them, say, to do their homework instead of running the lemonade stand. The result may be a reduction in labor market employment but not an increase in unemployment, since to receive the benefit recipients must leave the labor force.

The third category requires the recipient to be employed. This category includes an earned income tax credit or "workfare." Such benefits are analogous to an arrangement by which one of the parents donated part of his or her own salary to pay the child "worker" an extra dollar an hour in addition to any compensation the child derived from making and selling lemonade. This kind of benefit neither reduces employment nor increases unemployment. Instead, income is transferred from employed workers with higher incomes to employed workers with lower incomes.

Thus, the problem of unemployment is inextricably linked to the question of the overall distribution of income between workers and property owners—and particularly to the policies adopted by modern governments to affect that distribution. The updated version of Rueff's Law sheds a great deal of light on pinpointing which social policies, ostensibly intended to help the poor and particularly low-income workers, actually do so—and which policies actually worsen the situation of those they are supposed to help.

To calculate the relative price of labor accurately, we must therefore make three adjustments.

First, taxes on workers should be subtracted from net labor compensation (and taxes on property income from net property compensation). Second, transfer payments to persons add to the net cost of labor compensation (since the payments are not received by owners of property), while any subsidies to property owners should be added to net property compensation. Third, capital consumption must be subtracted, because using up wealth requires investing current income to replace it. Subtracting capital consumption (and sales taxes) from gross national income (GNI) leaves net national income (NNI).[16]

In other words, though all net income is originally produced and earned by two factors—workers and owners of productive property—the income is finally split three ways: part goes to workers as take-home pay after taxes and transfers to employed workers; part goes to property owners as property compensation after taxes and subsidies; and part is transferred to persons who do not contribute to current output. Under these circumstances, the net cost of labor is no longer the share of income actually received by employed workers but rather the share of total net income *not* received by owners of property—which is equal to employed workers' take-home pay plus net transfer payments to persons.[17]

To estimate the relative price of labor on this basis, I went to the national income and product accounts and calculated pretax labor compensation (including fringe benefits and the government's estimate of self-employed labor income, which had to be reconstructed before 1947), plus after-tax transfer payments to persons, minus personal and payroll taxes on labor compensation.

Including taxes and government transfer payments reveals that the actual change in workers' take-home pay as a share of national income is often quite different from the share as conventionally calculated without the adjustments.[18] For example, take-home pay generally rose from 2000 to 2009 as a share of national income, while the conventional calculation showed the labor share declining—a fact that was made the basis of much ill-informed controversy and many well-intended but misguided policy recommendations (Figure 15–6).

Moreover, unlike the gross measure, the net cost of labor calculated in this way is highly correlated with the unemployment rate. The chart in Figure 15–7 shows the relationship for the United States since 1929 (the earliest year for which sufficiently detailed statistics are available).

Figure 15–6

Labor Cost Before and After Taxes and Transfers

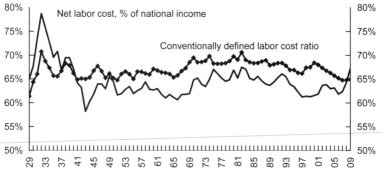

Net labor cost = (pretax labor compensation + transfer payments to persons - taxes on labor)/national income.
Conventional labor cost ratio = pretax labor compensation/GDP

Figure 15-7

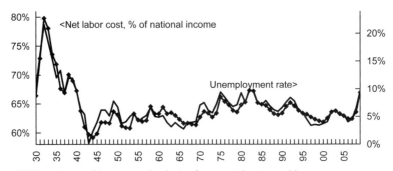

U.S. Net Labor Cost vs. Unemployment
Actual, 1930-2009

Net labor cost = gross labor compensation plus transfer payments less taxes on labor.
Source: Commerce & Labor Depts.; calculated by LBMC LLC

The higher the net labor cost, the higher the unemployment rate. Labor's share of actual national income reached 78 percent at the depth of the Great Depression; at the same time, unemployment peaked at nearly 23 percent.[19] The lower the net labor cost, the lower the unemployment rate. But again, as theory predicts, there is a limit, set by full employment, below which labor's net share of national income has never fallen. The lowest net labor share of national income since 1929 was about 59 percent and coincided with the lowest unemployment rate on record: 1 percent at the peak of the World War II boom in 1943. Since then, labor's share of national income has always been higher and has been mirrored by changes in unemployment.

Yet while labor's net share of national income, including transfer payments, has risen since World War II, the share received by employed wage earners has declined. The entire difference is due to transfer payments to persons who are not employed in the labor market.

If we plot unemployment against the total net labor cost for all years, we have the updated version of Rueff's Law—in effect, the demand curve for labor services in the United States (Figure 15-8).

On average over the whole period, each 1 percentage point change in net labor cost, as a share of national income, has been associated with a 1.1 percentage point change in the rate of employment in the opposite direction, and in the unemployment rate in the same direction.

Figure 15–8

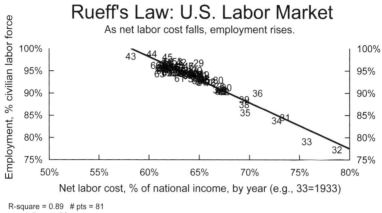

Rueff's Law: U.S. Labor Market
As net labor cost falls, employment rises.

R-square = 0.89   # pts = 81
y = 1.6 + -1.03x

Net Labor Costs and National Output/Income

Since both workers and productive property are necessary for any increase in production, in approximately constant proportions, every increase in unemployment is associated with a proportional decline in output relative to the level that could be achieved if all workers were fully employed.[20] This difference is often described as the "GDP gap," but for our purposes it makes more sense to express it in terms of the "national income gap" (Figure 15–9).

Figure 15–9

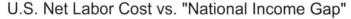

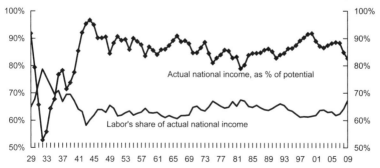

U.S. Net Labor Cost vs. "National Income Gap"

"National income gap" is CBO's GDP gap, adjusted to national income instead of GDP.
Source: CBO, Commerce & Labor Depts; calculated by LBMC LLC.

If we plot the relationship between the net cost of labor and the "national income gap" for all years, we find that the two series trace a relationship quite similar to that between the net cost of labor and the unemployment rate (Figure 15–10). This is not surprising, since the gap is estimated in relation to some measure of full employment. The only difference is that the change in real national income is twice as large as the change in employment. The main reason is that national income includes both labor and property compensation, and property compensation varies by a multiple of the corresponding change in labor compensation.

Figure 15–10

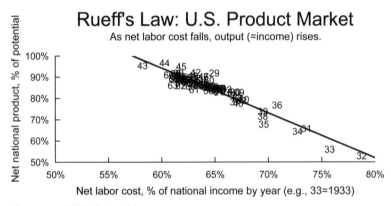

Rueff's Law: U.S. Product Market
As net labor cost falls, output (=income) rises.

R-square = 0.892   # pts = 81
y = 2.21 + -2.11x

Over the period since 1929, every 1 percentage point rise in the U.S. net labor cost has been associated with about a 2.2 percentage point decline of national income below its potential at full employment.

The Net Effect on Real Labor Income

We have found that economic policies (or any other circumstances) that alter the net shares of total national income between workers and property owners have two effects, which work in opposite directions. On the one hand, reducing the relative income share received by property owners necessarily increases the relative remaining share, which goes to employed workers and recipients of transfer payments. (I will call this combined share "net labor cost" for simplicity.) On the other hand, reducing the relative share of net income received by property owners raises the unemployment rate and lowers total actual national income, including the labor compensation of employed workers, in absolute terms.

Thus, not only the cost of labor and employment but also total output and income are all tied in a unique relationship. Labor's net share of income is inversely related to employment, but employment is positively related to output and income (including labor income). Total labor income including take-home pay and transfer payments is positively related to national income and inversely related to labor's share of national income.

Why is this? For any given equipment, organization, and technology, each extra hour of labor has less equipment to work with, and so adds less to output than the previous hour. Therefore, total employment, output, and national income increase in absolute terms; but the "efficiency wage"—the share of labor compensation in total national income—must fall. However, labor's share of income must stop falling when full employment is reached since, if no more labor is forthcoming, labor's relative contribution to extra output cannot decline any further. Similarly, labor's income share rises with unemployment, because the last unit of labor hired has more capital to work with; but real labor income falls, because employment and national income are cut back.

It is crucial, therefore, to know the net result of both effects; for this will determine whether workers, as owners of "human capital," are

Figure 15–11

Labor Cost vs. Actual & Potential National Income

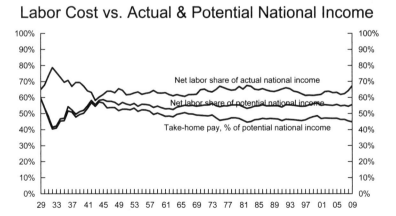

better or worse off if they seek a larger share of lower national income or a smaller share of a larger national income. And we can answer this by comparing the shares of actual national income with potential national income, which is the total national income that would be realized if all workers were employed (Figure 15–11).

The comparison cannot be taken as precise, but it does indicate the general order of magnitudes involved. The most significant fact is that while net labor income (take-home pay plus net transfer payments) has never fallen *below* 58 percent of *actual* national income (when unemployment approached its all-time low of 1 percent in 1944), it also has never *exceeded* 60 percent of *potential* national income if all workers were fully employed. (It fell to a record low of about 42 percent of potential national income in 1932, when unemployment hit an all-time high of nearly 23 percent.)[21] What this means is that under the best of circumstances, the *gains* in net labor income due to a larger *share* of national income have never significantly exceeded the absolute *losses* caused by the associated fall in national income; yet the losses of net labor income associated with higher unemployment have often significantly exceeded the gains from an increased share.

This answers the question about whether workers as a group can increase their real income by ceasing to be employed in the labor market and instead collecting transfer payments while unemployed or remaining outside the labor force. The analysis strongly indicates that most transfer payments are inherently funded by reducing the take-home pay of employed workers. It also points to the central importance of measures that will add to earning ability, particularly increased education.

Different Transfer Payments, Different Effects on Shares of Income

The same analysis permits us to break the net cost of labor down into its components and thereby see the different economic results of various tax-and-transfer programs. When we look at transfer payments, we should find that transfer payments to the unemployed raise labor's share of national income, while transfer payments to persons outside the labor force are matched by a reduction in take-home pay as a share of national income. (Both should reduce labor market employment and lower market production and real national income.) And this is in fact what the data tell us.

Figure 15–12

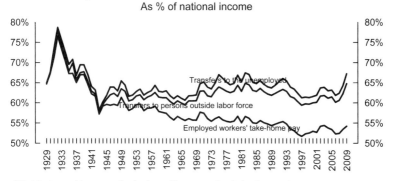

Components of U.S. Net Labor Cost
As % of national income

Note: Labor income = labor compensation, less taxes on labor compensation, plus transfer payments.
Source: Commerce & Labor Depts.; shares calculated by LBMC LLC .

Figure 15–12 shows that apart from cyclical variations, the changes in labor's share of income since the Second World War are approximately equal to the change in benefits to the unemployed (mostly unemployment insurance and welfare to the able-bodied), while the fall in take-home pay is equal to the rise in benefits to persons outside the labor force (mostly transfers to the aged and disabled).

Although the effect of fiscal policy on unemployment is unambiguous, its effect on overall labor-market participation is not. This is because government transfer payments to persons are in some measure substitutes for transfer payments between men and women within the household. We have seen that marriage involves a specialization of roles. Generally, each couple's choice depends on each partner's labor-market earnings ability and whether the couple is currently raising dependent children. Since men's average lifetime labor market earnings are on average about twice as high as women's,[22] it is usually the husband who works more in the labor market than the wife. The covariation in transfer payments as a share of national income and men's and women's labor-market employment suggests that without any government transfer payments to persons, the labor-market employment of men would be about 89 percent and the labor-market employment of women would be about 25 percent.

As the share of government transfer payments in national income has grown, the labor-force participation of men has fallen, while the labor-

Figure 15-13

U.S. Transfer Payments vs. Labor Market Employment
% of adults unemployed or not in the labor force, 1950-2009

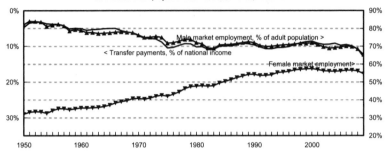

force participation of women has risen (Figure 15–13). The employment/ population ratio for men has fallen about 2 percentage points for each 1 percentage point increase in transfer payments as a share of national income. But for women, the relationship is more complicated. As with men, the employment/population ratio has fallen about 2 percentage points with each 1 percentage point increase in transfer payments conditioned on being unemployed (mostly unemployment insurance and welfare to the able-bodied). But women's employment/population ratio has risen about 4 percentage points for each 1 percentage point increase in transfer payments to persons outside the labor force. This is partly because the rise of transfer payments has lowered take-home pay for all workers as a share of national income. Unless they are disabled, most married women under age sixty-five do not qualify for such transfer payments, but many have entered the labor force to help make up for the relative decline of earnings by husbands—a decline, however, which is reinforced by the increased supply of highly educated women in an economy based increasingly on knowledge rather than physical strength.

Thus, we have our answers to the two questions that we set out to answer about the effects of fiscal policy on employment. First, the variation in the unemployment rate is almost entirely explained by the variation in the net cost of labor as a share of national income. Fiscal policy increases unemployment when transfer payments to persons increase the net labor share of national income, and this can occur in two ways: first, when transfer payments are conditioned on not being employed in the labor market (as with unemployment insurance and welfare for the able-bodied), and second, when transfer payments to persons are funded by taxes on property income rather than labor income. Second, the overall labor-force participation and the employment/population ratio have risen because the labor force participation of women has risen over the past half century by more than the labor-force participation of men has fallen. The labor-force participation of women has risen and the labor-force participation of men has fallen for the same reason: the rise in government transfer payments to persons, which substitute for the transfers that occur within the household between married men and married women.

How Will Projected Economic Policy Affect American Fertility and Employment in Coming Decades?

Our neo-Scholastic economic investigation so far has shown the basic principles by which fiscal policy affects employment and fertility. We discovered that most variation in the total fertility rate is explained by just three basic factors: per capita social benefits, per capita national saving, and frequency of worship. And we have just seen how unemployment is a function of the net cost of labor, which is the same as workers' take-home pay plus government benefits to persons as a share of total national income.

What does all this tell us about the future impact of fiscal policy upon the American worker? We can suggest the general answer by applying the same analysis to the course of federal fiscal policy projected over the next several decades under current law. As is well known, total fed-

Figure 15–14

Actual & Projected Federal Taxes and Spending
% of GDP, 1950-2083

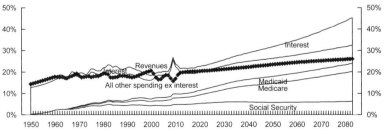

A 125-Year Picture of the Federal Government's Share of the Economy, 1950-2075 (CBO 2002, updated June 2009)

Figure 15–15

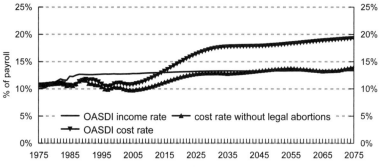

Impact of Legal Abortion on Social Security
OASDI income and cost rates, SSA intermediate projections

From John D. Mueller, "The Socioeconomic Costs of Roe v. Wade," *Family Policy*, April 2000

eral spending as a share of the economy is expected to increase by about one-half (even beyond the sharp spike during the recession of 2007–9), entirely the result of three basic programs: Social Security retirement and disability benefits, Medicare health benefits for persons over age sixty-five, and Medicaid for the indigent (Figure 15–14). At the same time, total federal revenues (apart from Medicare premiums) are expected to remain close to their average since about 1960, or 20 percent of GDP. Because federal spending is expected to rise faster than revenues, interest payments are expected to add more than 10 percentage points, with total federal spending reaching about 45 percent of GDP by 2083.

What effects are these developments likely to have for the fertility and employment of the American worker? There are three basic implications.

First, the United States can either continue its experiment with legal abortion or have a balanced social insurance system, but not both. As I showed in a paper published in 2000, projected Social Security imbalances are due entirely to the reduction in population resulting from legal abortion (Figure 15–15).[23]

Moreover, by applying the model of fertility developed earlier, we can anticipate that if social benefits double as a share of national income as projected, the American TFR will most likely decline from the replacement rate of about 2.1 in the first decade of the twenty-first century to about 1.9 by 2025, 1.8 by 2050, 1.7 by 2075, and 1.6 by 2083 (see column 1 in Table 15–1). That would fall between the Social Security Administration's Trustees' intermediate and high-cost assumptions from 2025 through 2050 and be worse than the high-cost assumptions thereafter. Without immigration, the U.S. population would shrink, but the decline in fertility could be expected to increase the inflow of immigrants (though also the resistance by anti-immigrant political factions). But if legal abortion were ended, the TFR would be likely to rise almost immediately to about 2.8 and remain above the replacement rate at least through 2083 (see column 2 in Table 15–1).[24]

Table 15–1

Current & Projected U.S. Total Fertility Rate					
Year	(1) U.S. Total Fertility Rate (TFR): CBO projected benefit shares and incomes	(2) U.S. TFR: same as (1) without legal abortion	(3) Memo: U.S. TFR, 2009 SSA Trustees "Intermediate" Assumptions	(4) U.S. TFR, Trustees "Low-Cost" Assumptions	(5) U.S. TFR, Trustees "High-Cost" Assumptions
2005 actual	2.08	2.75	2.08	2.08	2.08
2025 est.	1.93	2.57	2.03	2.23	1.82
2050 est.	1.76	2.38	2.00	2.30	1.70
2075 est.	1.67	2.34	2.00	2.30	1.70
2083 est.	1.64	2.26	2.00	2.30	1.70

In this respect, America is not a demographic exception, neither now nor in the future. What would be true of the United States in the future is true already of the rest of the world. Weighing each country equally (e.g., the Netherlands equals China), the most recent total fertility rate for all fifty countries I studied is about 1.8; without legal abortion, it would be 2.3. Weighted by population, the TFR of all countries is now about 2.2 (India is higher, China lower); without abortion, the world TFR would be about 2.7 (Table 15–2).

Second, the relationships we have found between transfer payments and labor market employment suggest that as the share of trans-

Table 15–2

U.S. & World Total Fertility Rates vs. Abortion					
Year	(1) U.S.A. (1) without abortion	(2)	(3) 50 countries (2/3 world) equally weighted	(4) (3) without abortion	(5) 50 countries (2/3 world) population weighted	(6) (5) without abortion
2005 actual	2.08	2.75	1.83	2.29	2.15	2.70
2083 est.	1.64	2.26	n.a.	n.a.	n.a.	n.a.

fer payments in national income rose, the labor-market employment of men would continue to decline from about 65 percent in 2009 (already reduced in the 2007–9 recession) to about 52 percent by 2083. But the labor-market employment of women would very likely increase from just under 55 percent in 2009 to about 67 percent by the 2030s before leveling off (Figure 15–16).

Third, under current law, the net labor cost in the American economy is likely to decline until about 2015 but then rise steadily thereafter. The rise in the net labor cost is due to the projected increase in transfer payments as a share of the economy, which under current law is expected to be funded by borrowing. This suggests that the unemployment rate,

Figure 15–16

U.S. Transfer Payments vs. Labor Market Employment
Transfer payments actual and projected

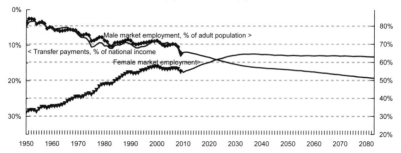

Figure 15–17

U.S. Net Labor Cost vs. Unemployment
Actual & projected, 1930-2080

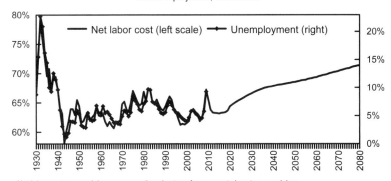

Net labor cost = gross labor compensation plus transfer payments less taxes on labor.
Source: Commerce & Labor Depts.; calculated by LBMC LLC

which had risen from a low of 4 percent in 2000 and spiked to 10 percent during the recession of 2007–9, would fall again at first because of cyclical recovery but then resume rising to minimum levels of about 6 percent in 2025, 9 percent in 2050, and about 11 percent in 2080.

If social benefits increase as a share of national income as projected, whether funded by borrowing, by the income tax, or by taxes on property income, at the same time as the unemployment rate rises as it has in Europe, U.S. national income will fall further below its productive capacity (Figure 15–18).

Figure 15–18

U.S. Net Labor Cost vs. "National Income Gap"
Actual & projected labor share of net national income

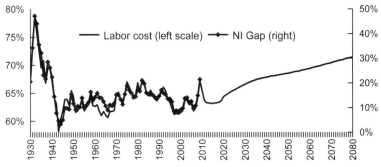

"National income gap" is CBO's GDP gap, adjusted to national income (instead of GDP) at zero unemployment.
Source: Commerce & Labor Depts. & CBO; labor share calculated by LBMC LLC.

Thus, to avoid both a substantial increase in the unemployment rate and the "demographic winter" that has struck developed Europe and Asia, either legal abortion must be ended or else social benefits, rather than doubling, must not increase at all from 2001 levels as a share of U.S. national income. In either case, social benefits must be financed by taxes on labor income, while general government is funded by an income tax that falls equally on labor and property income.[25]

To conclude, we have seen that both unemployment and a baby bust result from violating the basic principles of political distributive justice, which are reflected in the theory of American public choice, and that currently projected U.S. fiscal policy would repeat the combination of policies that has been the recipe for high unemployment and "demographic winter" throughout developed Europe and Asia. The good news is that, precisely because it is a choice, there is nothing inevitable about the outcome, and the American political system was designed to offer the best chance for a good one.

Table 15–3

Year	Transfer payments to persons, share of national income	Men employed in labor market	Women employed in labor market	Net labor cost, current law	Unemployment rate, actual & projected with current law
2000 actual	8.8%	71.9%	57.5%	62.6%	4.0%
2005 actual	9.8%	69.6%	56.2%	63.1%	5.1%
2009 estimated	11.6%	65.3%	54.6%	65.8%	9.3%
2025 projected	13.6%	61.8%	63.1%	64.6%	6.7%
2050 projected	15.9%	57.2%	64.3%	67.7%	9.8%
2075 projected	17.7%	53.5%	63.5%	70.0%	12.4%
2080 projected	18.1%	52.3%	65.6%	70.5%	12.9%

In the next and final chapter on political economy, we will consider the role that monetary policy plays in abetting the injustice in exchange promoted by partisan faction, and the monetary reforms necessary to prevent it.

16

Injustice in Exchange: Inflation

Money: Ending the Reserve Currency Curse

To complete our basic understanding of justice in exchange, we must consider the uses of money. Specifically, we must consider the general injustice in exchange or "disequilibrium" caused by inflation (or, as the recession of 2008–9 reminded us for the first time since the 1930s, deflation), which results primarily from violating the Hamiltonian first principle of American political economy: that the federal budget must not be financed through money creation. Nowadays, this means federal borrowing from central banks, including not only the Federal Reserve but also foreign monetary authorities for which the dollar serves as the world's chief official "reserve currency." Our investigation will explain why the main imperative for American monetary policy is to end what Lewis Lehrman and I have called the dollar's "reserve currency curse."[1]

We hold our wealth in three forms: money, current goods (including services), and securities (which are in effect claims on goods in the future). The main purpose of money is to help us compare and exchange these scarce means, which we provide to express our love for ourselves and other persons. All modern economies are based on highly specialized production for exchange (more colorfully but less accurately described by Adam Smith as "division of labor"), which is impossible without money. Money serves at once as the common reference for comparing the value of other exchangeable goods, a means of exchanging them, and a store of value between the sale of one good and purchase of another. To fulfill these functions, the value of money must be reasonably stable relative to the goods it is supposed to help us evaluate and exchange. Since the prices of different goods ultimately depend on people acting upon their relative preferences for the goods, absolute stability in the value of money against all other goods is neither possible nor desirable. Achieving it would require that all prices be frozen, thus eliminating the valuable information they contain about the relative scarcity of particular goods, and that people be deprived of their freedom to act upon their preferences. Yet a high degree of stability in the value of money against other goods in general is highly desirable. Moreover, history shows that such stability is practically achievable.

The stability of the U.S. dollar has varied widely in its history. This variation can be explained by two factors: changes in the monetary standard chosen for the dollar and whether other countries have simultaneously used the dollar as their own monetary standard. While the first is straightforward, the second is poorly understood and dangerously ignored even by American monetary authorities, notably before and during the Great Depression of 1929–33 and the Great Recession of 2008–9.

The United States has alternated between two kinds of standard money: inconvertible paper money and some precious metal (first silver, then gold). The dollar was an inconvertible paper money during and after the Revolutionary War (1776–92), the War of 1812 (1812–17), and the Civil War (1862–79), and again from 1971 to the present. It was effectively defined as a weight of silver in 1792–1812 and 1817–34, and as a weight of gold in 1834–61 and 1879–1971.[2] The dollar was not used by foreign monetary authorities as a reserve currency before 1913, but it has been an official "reserve currency" for many since 1913, and for most since 1944.

According to these two criteria, the monetary history of the United States since 1776 is divided into ten distinct phases, which are reflected in Figure 16–1. We can compare their results by examining the variation in the producer price index (which has been reconstructed back to 1720); the consumer price index (reconstructed back to 1800); or the price index for the broadest estimate of U.S. output, GDP (reconstructed back to 1890) (Figure 16–2).[3]

Figure 16–1

U.S. Monetary Standards & Producer Prices
All commodities (1967=100), 1720-2009

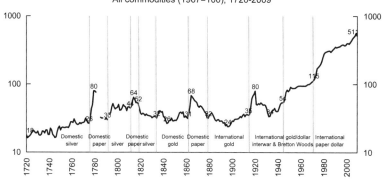

Figure 16–2

U.S. Monetary Standards, CPI & GDP Prices, 1800-2009
Both U.S. & foreign monetary standards affect U.S. prices (1967=100)

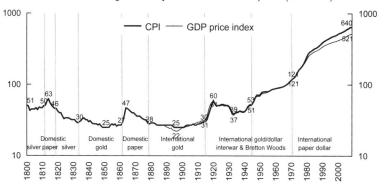

The GDP price index is the most comprehensive of the three indexes; the PPI's history is longest; but since the CPI extends back much farther than the GDP price index and its volatility approximates the GDP price index much more closely than the PPI, we'll use the CPI to rank the performance of these various monetary regimes. Our comparison, which is shown in Table 16–1, combines two simple measures: long-term CPI stability, measured by its annual average change from beginning to end of each monetary standard, and short-term CPI volatility, measured by the standard deviation of annual CPI changes during the period.[4]

Table 16–1

U.S. Consumer Price Index, Long-term stability and short-term volatility, By period and monetary system: 1800–2009	Long-run stability (average annual change)	Short-run volatility (standard deviation annual change)	Memo: Maximum price change (High vs. low)	Stability rank (weighing both criteria equally)
1800–1834: Domestic silver standard (interrupted 1812–17 by domestic paper standard)	-1.5%	5.2%	76%	4
1834–1861: Domestic gold standard	-0.4%	3.5%	36%	2
1862–1879: Domestic paper standard	+0.1%	8.8%	74%	3
1879–1914: International gold standard	+0.2%	2.2%	20%	1
1914–1944: Interwar international gold-dollar-sterling standard	+1.9%	7.2%	99%	5
1944–1971: Bretton Woods international gold-dollar standard	+3.1%	3.1%	130%	4
1971–2009: International paper dollar standard (1971–1981 1981–2009)	+4.5% (+8.5%) (+3.1%)	2.8% (+2.7%) (+1.2%)	432% (125%) (137%)	4

If we considered only the average annual price change, the greatest price stability occurred (by a narrow margin) during the Greenback era of 1862–79, since the CPI rose an average of 0.1 percent from the beginning to the end of the period. But by itself this would be misleading, because that period included a 74 percent rise in consumer prices between 1861 and 1864, followed by a long price deflation back to the original level; as a result, the Greenback era was actually the most volatile American monetary regime (8.8 percent).

Weighing both criteria equally, the period of greatest American monetary stability occurred between 1879 and 1914, when the United States joined most other major countries on the international gold standard and the dollar was not yet used by other countries as an official "reserve currency." The CPI rose an average of 0.2 percent per year—just 20 percent from its lowest to highest points—and the volatility of annual price changes up or down (2.2 percent) was the lowest of any period. This performance is all the more remarkable because the consumer price index in those days consisted almost entirely of food, the price of which is far more volatile than the rest of the modern CPI; because the U.S. financial system was much less sophisticated; and also because our measure of volatility, by weighing price declines more heavily than price increases, stacks the comparison in favor of regimes in which the CPI only rises and never falls—thus favoring not steady prices but *steady depreciation* of the dollar against other goods.[5]

By the same two criteria, the worst period overall occurred between the First and Second World Wars under the first international gold-exchange standard, when the dollar itself was defined as a weight of gold (as under the classical gold standard) but many other countries' monetary authorities used dollar-denominated securities as official monetary reserves—a feature that, for reasons we will shortly consider, causes much larger price swings both up and down. Prices rose an annual average of 1.9 percent, while volatility averaged 7.2 percent per year.

The period since 1971 has been the worst in American history in terms of long-term price stability: The CPI has more than quintupled so far, rising at a 4.5 percent average annual average rate, though its volatility (2.8 percent) compares favorably with all monetary regimes other than the international gold standard. Again weighing long-run stability and short-run volatility equally, this performance matches that of the Bretton Woods gold-exchange standard that preceded it, when inflation was somewhat lower (3.1 percent) but volatility somewhat higher (3.1 percent). But this measured stability partly reflects the fact that the CPI (like the rest of the U.S. economy) has become more heavily oriented toward services, the prices of which are less volatile than commodities and many of which (e.g., the imputed rental value of owner-occupied housing) are estimated rather than directly measured; and partly the fact that low volatility by itself indicates steadiness of average price *inflation*—that is, dollar depreciation—not the average price *level*.

In light of these facts, the obvious question to be answered is whether it is possible to replicate the success of the international gold standard in minimizing both the average rate and volatility of American price changes. Or are we effectively stuck with the current monetary system, which has produced the worst long-term price stability in American history, and repeated episodes of sharp commodity price hikes?

I answer that it is not only feasible but imperative, since the same feature of the current monetary system that produced the worst inflation recently also caused the severe price deflation during the Great Depres-

sion and more recently the financial crisis of 2008. To explain why, we
must understand the basic principles of monetary policy.

The Neighborhood Yard Sale

To grasp the basic relation between money and the price level, let's begin
with the simple case of a neighborhood yard sale, to which everyone brings
some articles to sell and/or some cash for making purchases.[6] Even in such
a simple setting, all kinds of transactions are possible: You might buy
someone else's goods; sell some of your own; use the proceeds from your
first sales to purchase still other goods; change your mind and resell some
of the first purchases; use those proceeds to buy some more; and so on. You
might barter some goods instead of using money, or borrow money from
a neighbor, promising to repay him later. Yet however numerous or complicated your transactions, one thing always remains true: If you bought
goods of greater total monetary value than you sold, you left with less cash
in your wallet than you brought; and if you sold goods of greater total
value than you bought, you walked away with more cash in your wallet.

The important principle that emerges is that to increase your cash
on hand, you have to sell that much more than you buy, while to reduce
your cash holding, you have to buy that much more than you sell. An
economist would say that an "excess supply" of money necessarily means
an "excess demand" for nonmonetary wealth. And the same is true even
when we consider any money you borrowed; because in that case, you
sold in effect (and your neighbor purchased) a "bond" or "security,"
which is what a promise of future repayment amounts to. The total value
of your net purchases of goods and securities must be equal to but opposite from the change in cash you hold.

What would happen if everyone came to the yard sale intending to
sell more than he bought, thus increasing his cash on hand? Assuming
that no additional goods were brought to market and no new money were
added, that would be physically impossible. But under those circumstances, an effort by everyone to sell more than he bought would tend to
lower the average *prices* at which the same goods were bought and sold.
Though the number of dollars remained the same, the fall in the average
price level would continue until the money required to handle the total
value of transactions was reduced by an amount equal to the desired
increase in cash holdings. In other words, the fall in prices would increase

the buying power or "real" value of the existing dollars. Conversely, if everyone tried to reduce his or her cash holdings, the average prices of goods would rise, which would reduce the buying power of each dollar. And the rise in prices would stop only when the aggregate value of goods exchanged had increased by an amount equal to the "real" decline in cash holdings that people were trying to bring about before prices changed.

Similar reasoning holds for any change in the quantity of goods offered for sale as the result of new production. To envision this, we might think of our children's lemonade stand as having been stationed within such a yard sale. An increased total supply of goods—e.g., lemonade—offered for sale would have an effect similar to an increase in the demand for money of equal proportion while the supplies of goods and money remained the same. There would be a general tendency for prices to fall until the reduced demand for money occasioned by the lower average price level matched the increased total demand for money caused by the additional goods brought to market.

It is not as easy to use the yard sale realistically to illustrate the effects of a change in the total supply of money, since the total amount of cash typically isn't controllable or even knowable. Nevertheless, the results of any change in total money supply are symmetrical to any change in the demand for money. For example, if the money supply were to increase while everyone were content with the amount of cash he or she already held, the result would be the same as if everyone were trying to reduce his or her cash holding by that proportion while the money supply were actually fixed: The price level would tend to rise until the money not desired at existing prices was "absorbed" by the additional money that would be required to accommodate the larger monetary value of transactions after prices had risen. Similarly, a reduction in money supply while people were content with their cash holdings would have the opposite effects. This would cause no problem as long as prices were free to adjust; but as we saw in considering Rueff's Law, any factor that delays or prevents price adjustment can cause at least a temporary increase in unemployment of productive resources of which the relative price rises as a result. This makes clear that proper monetary policy affects the stability not only of prices but also of employment and real output.

The basic problem of monetary policy can therefore be summarized fairly simply. Changes in the general price level result from differences between the total supply of and demand for money.[7] The total demand for money is derived from the total monetary value of nonmonetary wealth, which comprises not only current goods but also such securities as government or corporate bonds.[8] The whole task of monetary policy is to maintain overall "justice in exchange" by matching as closely as possible the total supply of money to the total demand for it, and thus the total supply of and demand for nonmonetary wealth. The total supply of money, however, is determined by the way in which the monetary authority responds to this demand. By "monetary authority" today we mean the consolidated functions of the Treasury and central bank, e.g., the U.S. Federal Reserve. This requires further discussion.

Commodity money. The remarkable record of American price stability under the international gold standard in 1879–1914 is explained by the way in which that system accommodated the total supply to the demand for money, in not only the United States but all countries on the gold standard. Gold is a kind of "commodity money," meaning one valued also as a useful commodity—roughly as if people at the yard sale agreed to use pint bottles of lemonade as their currency. Under the gold standard, each nation defined its currency as a weight of gold. For example, the dollar was initially about one-twentieth of an ounce of fine gold, making the dollar "price" of gold $20.67 an ounce; the British pound sterling was defined as 77s 9d, resulting in an exchange rate of about $4.80 per pound; and so on. The gold money in circulation increased when citizens brought gold to the mint to be coined at the official rate, and it decreased when gold coins were exported or put to nonmonetary uses—for example, melted down for production and use as jewelry.

The international balance of payments. Apart from terminology, the payments of whole countries are not much different from the people at the yard sale we have considered. In fact, we might think of the world economy under the gold standard as operating like an international yard sale; only instead of Federal Reserve notes in everyone's pockets or purses, each country's monetary authority kept gold reserves for settling international payments. Just as any person at the yard sale may exchange cash for either current goods or claims on future goods, a country's payments and receipts for nonmonetary wealth are classified under three categories: the "current account," which tracks payments for trade in current goods, services, and unilateral transfers (mostly personal gifts or government foreign aid); the "capital account," which tracks private payments for securities; and the official reserve account. The total balance of payments comprises the current and private capital accounts combined; it must be equal to and opposite to any net change in official reserves. A net rise in a country's official monetary reserves in any period means that the country had a surplus of receipts over payments during that period; a fall in reserves means a deficit of total nonmonetary receipts against payments.

The "equilibrium" gold price level. Under the international gold standard, the general price level was regulated by the facts that people demand money in roughly stable proportion to their other wealth and that gold mining requires scarce human and nonhuman resources. When the prices of other goods rose, so did the cost of gold mining, diminishing its profitability and discouraging gold production. Similarly, when other prices fell, so did the cost of mining; but defining currencies in gold meant that its "price" alone remained constant while other prices were falling, thus increasing the profitability of gold mining. Part of world gold production provided the increase in the world's total supply of gold money. Countries that (unlike the United States) had no gold mines could obtain any gold they required by exporting other goods, ultimately to the gold-mining countries. All countries together therefore had a current account (trade) surplus equal to the total exports from gold-producing countries, which provided the increase in gold money of countries without gold mines. The periods of gently falling prices in 1879–96 and gently rising prices in 1896–1914 were due to the fact that the total supply of gold money and total output of other goods did not rise at exactly the same rate. But the fact that gold mining was stimulated by falling and discouraged by rising prices of other goods served not only as a means of restoring the same "equilibrium" price level but also as a kind of counter-cyclical accelerator or brake for real output.

Banking. Though even most economists (who should know better) carelessly refer to bank deposits as "money," banking leaves the monetary analysis unchanged.[9] The growing general use of banknotes and deposits did not affect the equilibrium price level under the gold standard, because while it reduced the demand for gold money, the forces just described also reduced its supply in equal proportion. Without the privilege of "legal tender" (the legally enforceable requirement that anyone accept its debts in payment), no bank under any monetary standard can "create" money; it can only borrow and lend it. Every bank borrows money from its depositors, just as households and businesses borrow money from the bank. The bank tries to profit by lending to borrowers at a higher rate than it pays its depositors and holders of its banknotes. To stay in business, it must keep a reserve of money sufficient to pay any liabilities presented for payment; which requires that the value of its assets (money reserves and loans) exceed the value of its liabilities (notes and deposits), the difference being the equity of the bank's shareholders or other owners.[10] If a private bank literally could "create" or "print" money, none would ever go bankrupt—as many did under the gold standard and still do under a paper money standard.

The same is true even of monetary authorities: national treasuries and central banks. Federal Reserve notes and deposits served along with Treasury notes and subsidiary coins as close substitutes for gold money as long as they remained convertible upon demand into gold. But each time U.S. gold convertibility was suspended, only the legal-tender privilege permitted the Treasury and Federal Reserve to avoid bankruptcy. Though no U.S. gold coins were minted for several decades after 1933 (even their ownership by U.S. citizens was prohibited until 1975), U.S. and foreign monetary authorities continued to settle international payments with bars of gold: in effect, very large gold coins. Each monetary authority purchased and sold gold upon demand at the official "price." When gold convertibility was suspended also for foreign monetary authorities (de facto in 1968 and officially in 1971), the dollar became inconvertible paper money again. Despite the looseness of their terminology, economists acknowledge the distinction between money and bank credit by classifying money itself as "high-powered money" and bank deposits payable in money as "low-powered money."[11] The money is called "high-powered" because it permits private banks to expand their lending by a multiple of their reserves; when reserves decline, bank lending has to contract by a similar multiple.

Relative size. So much is true of any country sharing the same monetary standard. But size also matters, since the larger a country's economy, the smaller the relative importance of its transactions with the rest of the world. In the limiting case of a country that included the whole world, foreign transactions would be zero. Monetary authorities of countries with larger economies can therefore afford to keep a smaller ratio of internationally accepted money to back their domestic high-powered money. In the limiting case of a country comprehending the world economy, there would be no foreign monetary reserves, and all monetary assets and liabilities would be domestic. The credit policy of a sufficiently large country can therefore affect the world price level. In the limiting case, its price level *is* the world price level. However, without some external monetary "anchor" like the gold standard, there can be no equilibrium price level.

The monetary authority of a nation with a smaller or more open economy, on the other hand, needs to hold larger international reserves in relation to its own domestic liabilities. Its credit policy cannot appreciably affect the world price level or level of interest rates, since the prices of its products and securities are limited by those in the rest of the world, adjusted by the exchange rate.[12] An expansion of domestic loans has little effect on the foreign or domestic price level, since it mostly results in increasing the share of domestic loans and reducing the share of foreign monetary reserves backing the domestic currency. If its domestic credit is too expansive, such a monetary authority will lose all its international reserves and/or be forced to devalue the exchange rate of its national currency.

Reserve currencies. Jacques Rueff famously called the reserve currency system the "monetary sin of the West,"[13] and spent much of his career trying to end it. Today's monetary system has the same potentially fatal instability as the post–World War I and post–World War II gold-exchange standards. The dollar's official reserve-currency role is implicated in all the main pathologies evident in today's world economy: the "hot money" flows that inflate (and deflate) stock, bond, and real estate prices; the sharp rises in commodity (especially energy) prices; Congress's growing fiscal irresponsibility; and the ever-mushrooming U.S. deficit in international trade and payments.

Confusion is almost inevitable when discussing official reserve currencies, because relatively few of the monetary instruments described by that term are actually currency in the common sense of the term, and none, strictly speaking, is a reserve, meaning an asset withheld from current use. That, in fact, is the main problem.

To appreciate what it means that the dollar is the official "reserve currency" for the world, imagine that all the people at the yard sale not only accepted your personal check but also started carrying your uncashed checks around in their wallets along with (or instead of) Federal Reserve notes and Treasury coins. This would have two effects on your personal finances. First, you'd no longer need to carry any cash, just your checkbook. Second, when you received your bank statement every month, you'd find a lot more money in your checking account than you had actually saved. The extra money would equal the value of checks you had written to make purchases and investments yet were still floating around uncashed. Under this arrangement, your purchases and investments would no longer be limited by your savings, only by other people's willingness to hold your checks. For everyone at the yard sale, the total money supply would now equal the total amount of cash in people's pockets *plus* your uncashed checks.

This is roughly what being an official reserve currency country means for the United States. The fact that other nations' monetary authorities hold securities payable in dollars to back their currencies means that our own doesn't need to hold much, if any, foreign money in reserve; it also ensures that the United States makes more investments and purchases of goods and services abroad than are made in the United States—the difference equaling the amount of dollar reserves acquired by foreign central banks.

Without a change in foreign dollar reserves, a U.S. current account (mostly trade) deficit would have to be financed by borrowing from foreign private investors; likewise, a U.S. current account surplus would be used entirely to invest in other countries. In either case, total U.S. payments and receipts would balance, since Americans would in effect simply be exchanging current goods for promises of future goods, or vice versa. However, when foreign monetary authorities invest their reserves in U.S. securities, the inflow of official funds substitutes for an equal amount of private investment and trade. A rise in foreign official dollar reserves therefore not only *permits* but *requires* residents of the United States to have a balance-of-payments deficit with foreigners. This excess of "hot money" flows back to the rest of the world as net purchases of foreign goods and/or securities. In effect, the reserve currency privilege allows the United States to have *negative* net reserves and so run a chronic balance-of-payments deficit of the same amount. Hot money represents a demand for nonmonetary wealth (goods and/or securities) without a matching supply, and so necessarily bids up the price of such wealth. But its withdrawal involves a supply of such wealth without a matching demand, driving down its prices.

Rueff's analysis of reserve currencies had two parts, the first devoted to what constitutes sustainable monetary policy within any individual country and the second to the nature of an international monetary system that would make such a policy simultaneously possible in all countries.

Rueff and Charles Rist, then deputy governor of the Bank of France, were the first economists in a major nation to advise policymakers that after a price inflation as severe as occurred in most countries during and after the First World War (France's price level had sextupled), price deflation and unemployment should be avoided by reducing the currency's gold value before resuming convertibility, in inverse proportion to the previous rise in the price level.[14] The French reform was successful.[15] In contrast, Britain's 1925 return to gold at the prewar parity resulted in price deflation, a rise in British unemployment, and ultimately abandonment of sterling's gold convertibility. Similarly, as President Herbert Hoover bitterly complained in his memoirs, U.S. Treasury Secretary Andrew Mellon "had only one formula: 'Liquidate labor, liquidate stocks, liquidate the farmers, liquidate real estate.'"[16] In other words, allow the price and wage deflation to run its course.

At the same time, Rueff warned that adjusting currency exchange rates alone was insufficient to cure the main cause of the deflation: the system of reserve currencies. From a pre–First World War expedient limited to colonial India, British economists had expanded this practice through a recommendation of the 1922 Genoa conference, which League of Nations economists quickly adopted to rewrite banking laws to encourage substitution of sterling and dollar securities for gold in all European nations. British experts had hoped by this means simultaneously to maintain the prewar gold value of the pound, maintain British prices at the level to which they had risen during World War I, and forestall the imminent repayment of Britain's war debts.[17]

But Rueff captured the essence of the problem: "the gold-exchange standard increase[s] . . . the money supply in the receiving market, without reducing in any way the money supply in the market of origin." This also meant that a decline in foreign exchange reserves *reduces* the money supply in one country without increasing it in another. "The

gold exchange standard dissociates credit movements from gold movements," he said in a 1933 public lecture. "For instance, in 1927 and 1928
it enabled large amounts of capital that had been exported to the United
States and Britain to flow back to Continental Europe, without the bul-
lion reserves of these countries being in any way affected. In this way it
not only operated to loosen the link between credit and gold, it severed
it altogether. Thus it contributed to prolonging and accentuating the
abnormal distribution of gold, since the net result was that capital could
flow back without any flowback of gold.

"By the same token," Rueff continued, "the gold-exchange standard
was a formidable inflation factor. Funds that flowed back to Europe
remained available in the United States. They were purely and simply
increased twofold, enabling the American market to buy in Europe without ceasing to do so in the United States. As a result, the gold-exchange
standard was one of the major causes of the wave of speculation that
culminated in the September 1929 crisis. It delayed the moment when
the braking effect that would otherwise have been the result of the gold
standard's coming into play would have been felt."[18]

The intimate connection before and during the Great Depression
between the rise and fall of foreign dollar deposits and both the U.S.
stock market and the U.S. consumer price index is illustrated by Figures
16–3 and 16–4.[19]

As Figure 16–3 shows, the U.S. stock market rose and fell in the
late 1920s and early 1930s step for step with the rise and fall in foreign

Figure 16–3

Foreign Dollar Deposits & U.S. Stock Market, 1920-1932

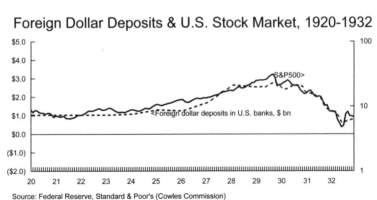

Source: Federal Reserve, Standard & Poor's (Cowles Commission)

Figure 16–4

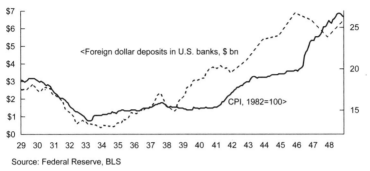

Foreign Dollar Deposits & U.S. Consumer Prices
1929-1948

Source: Federal Reserve, BLS

dollar deposits invested in New York. At their peak in 1929, such deposits added the equivalent of nearly 40 percent to what most economists
consider high-powered U.S. money: domestic currency and commercial
bank reserves. Foreign official dollar reserves were, of course, only one
factor in the relation between the total supply of and demand for money
that we have discussed. But the chart shows that before and during the
Depression, they were large enough to play a decisive role.

As Figure 16–4 indicates, the liquidation of foreign dollar reserves
between 1929 and 1934 and their reexpansion after 1934 also was a
potent force in both the deflation and subsequent reinflation of U.S.
consumer prices in the 1930s and 1940s. Until the late 1930s, there was
little delay between the two; but after the suspension of domestic gold
convertibility, which had directly linked the U.S. gold and money markets, variation in the U.S. price level began to lag the change in foreign
dollar deposits by more than two years (a lag that has continued to the
present).

Rueff's disagreement with other economists. Rueff's explanation
of the Great Depression and of monetary policy differs from the understanding of U.S. monetary authorities, which rests on the "domestic monetarism" of Milton Friedman. In *A Monetary History of the United States*,
Friedman and economist Anna Schwartz held that the Great Depression
was primarily the result of domestic monetary policy mismanagement by
the U.S. Federal Reserve.[20] As succinctly summarized by Ben Bernanke,

a Princeton economist who specialized in the Depression before becoming a governor and ultimately chairman of the Federal Reserve, Friedman's theory held that

> the economic repercussions of a stock market crash depend less on the severity of the crash itself than on the response of policymakers, particularly central bankers. After the 1929 crash, the Federal Reserve mistakenly focused its policies on preserving the gold value of the dollar rather than on stabilizing the domestic economy. By raising interest rates to protect the dollar, policymakers contributed to soaring unemployment and severe price deflation. The U.S. central bank only compounded its mistake by failing to counter the collapse of the country's banking system in the early 1930s. . . . Without these policy blunders by the Federal Reserve, there is little reason to believe that the 1929 crash would have been followed by more than a moderate dip in U.S. economic activity.[21]

This amounts to a belated recognition of Rueff's first point, which concerned precisely "stabilizing the domestic economy." But it ignores Rueff's second point: What had destabilized the domestic economy in the first place?

Rueff and Friedman agreed with such other eminent economists as Robert Triffin and Robert Mundell (and disagreed with John Maynard

Figure 16–5

Sources of the World Dollar Base

Official monetary liabilities, relative to potential output (2% per capita trend), 1967=100

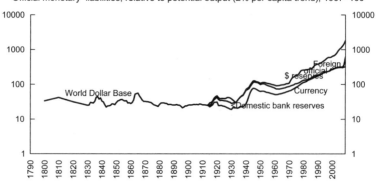

Keynes) that the Depression was chiefly the result of faulty monetary policy. But Rueff differed with the others on a simple point of profound practical consequence. Friedman's "domestic monetarism" considered gold and foreign exchange reserves important chiefly as backing for each nation's high-powered domestic money supply—currency and domestic bank reserves—which in turn was supposed to influence broader measures of low-powered money and ultimately that nation's price level. Mundell's "global monetarism" went beyond Friedman by arguing that the total domestic money supplies of *all* countries affected the world price level.[22]

Rueff pointed out, in contrast to both, that each monetary authority's liabilities to other monetary authorities are an equally potent form of high-powered money, since this borrowing permits expansion or contraction of domestic credit by that much in excess of any change in the domestic money supplies.[23] This means that there are three rather than two basic forms of high-powered dollars: U.S. currency in circulation, commercial-bank deposits held with the Federal Reserve, and the dollar-denominated securities held by foreign central banks (Figure 16–5). The sum of all three is what I call the world dollar base.[24] It is a single measure of money that adapts to the changing domestic and international monetary systems, and it explains the behavior of the U.S. price level over the past two centuries, despite major changes in the monetary system and stability of the general price level.

The financing of federal debt helps explain the appalling growth of federal deficits, as well as the main source of opposition to sensible fiscal and monetary reform. C. Northcote Parkinson famously theorized that "work expands so as to fill the time available for its completion."[25] Though often misinterpreted as advice on time management, "Parkinson's Law" was the history professor's attempt to explain the inexorable growth of bureaucracy along the lines of the neoclassical libertarian theory of public choice. At the suggestion of Milton Friedman, Ronald Reagan had adopted what might be called "Parkinson's fiscal corollary": that public spending expands to absorb all available tax revenues.[26] But Friedman's allowance analogy failed in practice by overlooking what might be called "Parkinson's debt corollary": Public borrowing expands to absorb all available means of finance.[27] If tax revenues are Congress's "allowance," then purchases of Treasury securities by government trust funds

Figure 16–6

Assets Backing the World Dollar Base
Relative to potential output (2% per capita trend), 1967=100

and the banking system are its "credit cards" (Figure 16–6). And the congressional teenager's spending won't be fazed by a cut in allowance, unless the indulgent parents also cut up the credit cards. Those "credit cards" consist, first, of the government trust funds accumulated ostensibly as "reserves" for Social Security and other supposedly self-financing programs, and second, purchases of Treasury debt by the banking system, especially central banks, which use such debt as official monetary "reserves."

Consider the striking evidence for Parkinson's debt corollary depicted in Figure 16–7. At the end of fiscal year 2009, the U.S. public debt stood at some $11.9 trillion, equal to about 90 percent of GDP (a leap of more than 20 percentage points in two years). But of this total, only about $2.2 trillion, or 19 percent, was held by the nonbank public, including foreigners. Some $5.3 trillion was held by federal, state, and local governments—mostly pension funds like Social Security, the necessary reform of which we considered in chapter 15. The remainder—about $4.1 trillion—was held by the banking system. Of that amount, about $769 billion was held by the Federal Reserve and $122 billion by U.S. commercial banks and other depository institutions, but $3.6 trillion by foreign monetary authorities: $2.085 trillion lent directly to the U.S. Treasury, $763 billion to government-sponsored agencies, and $709 billion indirectly through other official monetary liabilities. The latter

Figure 16–7

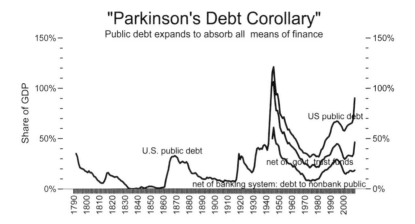

expansion of means of financing U.S. public debt has driven the expansion of high-powered money; and since the Civil War, almost all this credit has been extended to the U.S. Treasury.

All this demand for nonmonetary wealth without a matching supply necessarily pushes up the prices of securities or commodities—usually both in succession. Prices of stocks, bonds, and real estate are bid up immediately, and the real economy receives a temporary boost about a year later. If the process stopped there, the only permanent effect would be a rise in commodity prices, which typically (since the 1930s) takes about two and a half years.

As Figure 16–8 indicates, most of the commodity-led price surges in American history, including 1973–74, 1979–80, 1990–91, and 2005–8, were set in motion by the previous massive expansion of the world dollar base. By observing the growth of such high-powered dollars, my firm was able to predict the 1990–91 episode starting in 1988,[28] in 2005 that gasoline prices would top $3 a gallon and the price of crude oil $100 a barrel by the end of 2007, and to warn investors to shift from equities to Treasury bills before the crashes of 2001–2 and 2008–9.

So if we ask why consumer prices have more than quintupled since 1971, the nontechnical answer is that the banking system has "monetized" more than $4 trillion in federal debt since then. And if we ask why federal deficits have mushroomed in the meantime, the answer is that

Figure 16-8

The World Dollar Base & Consumer Price Inflation
Annual change, 1830-2009

Note: World Dollar Base relative to 2.0% per capita trend, lagged two years since the late 1930s.

our legislators have gotten used to a monetary system that permits public debt to be monetized on such a vast scale. In a word, the banking system has issued new money to the Treasury to finance its deficits without an associated production of new wealth, increasing demand without supply and setting off a secular, worldwide inflation.

The same asymmetric process also works in reverse: When official dollar reserves are sold, the result is deflation of securities and/or commodities proportional to the size of the sale of high-powered dollars relative to the supply of nonmonetary wealth (goods and securities).

Finally, there was the spread first of inflation, then of deflation to real estate. Since relatively little Treasury debt is actually held by private investors and thus available for purchase by monetary authorities, central banks engaged after 2000 in heavy buying of mortgage-backed securities issued by federal-chartered agencies—just as congressional committees charged with oversight of the financial industry insisted on reducing the quality of loans to encourage homeownership. Had central banks hung on to these securities, there wouldn't necessarily have been a housing "bubble," just permanently higher real estate prices. But the sale of nearly $300 billion of such securities helped trigger a deflation of U.S. real estate in 2007–9—exactly as in the United States after 1928 and Japan after 1989.

But deflation cannot always be predicted as far in advance as inflation, because it may be caused not only by an earlier decrease in the

Figure 16–9

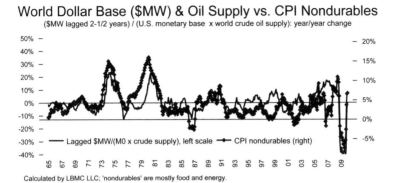

World Dollar Base ($MW) & Oil Supply vs. CPI Nondurables
($MW lagged 2-1/2 years) / (U.S. monetary base x world crude oil supply): year/year change

— Lagged $MW/(M0 x crude supply), left scale —◆— CPI nondurables (right)

Calculated by LBMC LLC; 'nondurables' are mostly food and energy.

supply of, but also a sharp increase in the current demand for, high-powered money. That's what happened in 2008–9 when the Federal Reserve slashed short-term interest rates almost to zero to expand commercial bank reserves, more than doubling the supply of domestic high-powered dollars, as indicated in Figure 16–9.

At a conference in their honor, Bernanke addressed Friedman and Schwartz in these words: "Regarding the Great Depression. You're right, we [the Federal Reserve] did it. We're very sorry. But thanks to you, we won't do it again."[29] If "it" means causing price deflation, foreign central banks played a larger role in precipitating the Great Depression than the Federal Reserve, contradicting Friedman's thesis that only domestic official monetary liabilities matter. But if "it" means being surprised at large changes in the U.S. price level resulting from central bank policies with disastrous political consequences, the Federal Reserve has done "it" again repeatedly.

Both price deflation and commodity-led price inflation are politically deeply unpopular. For example, voter approval of the incumbent president varies in inverse proportion to the consumer price of gasoline; and the approval rating of the president who appointed Bernanke as the Federal Reserve chairman is shown in Figure 16–10.

The gleeful use of this relationship by President George W. Bush's political opponents rested on what we have just demonstrated to be a fallacious assumption: that all or most of the major changes in energy prices are due to "supply shocks," which conspiracy theorists further suppose

Figure 16–10

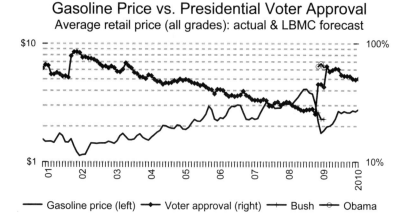

Gasoline Price vs. Presidential Voter Approval
Average retail price (all grades): actual & LBMC forecast

── Gasoline price (left) ──◆── Voter approval (right) ─┼─ Bush ──○── Obama

to be manipulable by American Republican presidential administrations in concert with American oil companies. The plain fact of the matter is that Republican administrations have been almost exactly as clueless as Democratic administrations about the large energy price changes, which result primarily from episodes of massive monetization of U.S. securities by foreign central banks. This is proven not only by equally futile impositions of price controls under the Republican Nixon and Ford and Democratic Carter administrations, but also by the fact that almost exactly ten years apart, under the administrations of Democrat Bill Clinton in 1996 and Republican George W. Bush in 2006, the U.S. Treasury instituted investigations into price-fixing by oil companies.

Thus, both Republicans who dismissed the relationship between gasoline prices and presidential voter approval as a coincidence promoted by "Bush-haters" and Democrats who expect that future Democratic administrations will be immune to the problem will be rudely surprised if nothing is done to correct the dollar's use as an official reserve currency. American voters will continue to express their displeasure at the polls at any future president, Republican or Democrat, under whose administration American families suffer commodity price gyrations like those suffered under President Nixon, President Carter, and both Presidents Bush.

Perhaps the most decisive evidence is to consider how U.S. international trade has swung from a chronic surplus in the early 1960s to a chronic and growing deficit ever since. Increased American consumption and reduced saving have caused an increasing U.S. current-account deficit, and therefore an equal surplus in countries that acquire official dollar reserves. These international imbalances consist almost entirely of goods and services purchased from foreign producers, ultimately paid for by federal deficit spending and financed largely by U.S. official borrowing from foreign monetary institutions. Yet as Figure 16–11 shows, the U.S. *private* balance of payments—the money U.S. residents owe to and are owed by foreigners apart from official monetary authorities—actually was in a net *surplus* at the end of 2009 worth about 7 percent of GDP. This proves that the dollar's official reserve-currency status and the federal deficit spending it has financed, rather than American consum-

Figure 16–11

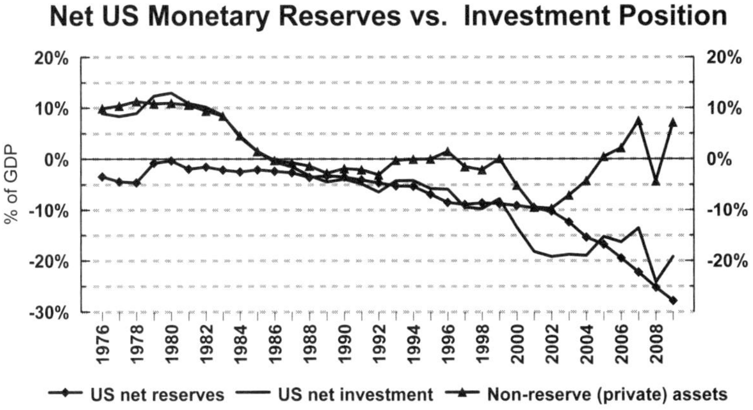

Net US Monetary Reserves vs. Investment Position

ers' private profligacy, are the driving force behind U.S. international-payments deficits.

How to fix the "reserve currency curse." The essential requirement for restoring a stable international monetary system is that the major countries agree to replace all official foreign-exchange reserves with an independent monetary asset that is not ultimately some particular nation's liability. Many standards are possible in theory, but monetary authorities still hold nearly 900 million ounces of gold,[30] and the simplest, most effective, most tested solution is a modernized international gold standard without foreign exchange reserves. This would require changes in U.S. law and an international monetary agreement.

There are two primary conditions for the success of such a reform. First, the gold values of all national currencies must be properly chosen to preclude the deflation of wages and prices that occurred in the 1920s and 1930s. Second, existing official foreign-exchange reserves must be removed from the balance sheets of monetary authorities by consolidating them into long-term government-to-government debts that would be repaid over several decades—much as the Washington–Hamilton administration funded the domestic and foreign Revolutionary War debt.

Similar proposals have been made repeatedly—in the 1920s, in the 1960s,[31] and in the 1980s[32]—but in each case they were rejected by "experts" who predicted that raising the gold "price" (from $20 to $35 in the 1920s, from $35 to $70 in the 1960s, or, still later, from $300 to $500 in the 1980s) would be wildly inflationary. The deflationary collapse of the 1930s, the inflationary collapse of the Bretton Woods system in 1971, and the recent financial crisis were all consequences of this shortsightedness. The gold price soared from $35 in 1971 to nearly $200 by the end of 1974, more than $1,000 an ounce in March 2008, and more than $1,100 by November 2009.

The proposed reform would bring many advantages. First, as we have already seen, convertibility of major currencies to gold produced by far the best performance of price stability in American history. From 1879 to 1914, average annual CPI inflation was 0.2 percent, with average annual volatility (up or down) of only 2.2 percent. No other standard comes close in combining low average inflation with low volatility. The volatility in the period from 1971 to the present (2.8 percent) is a close second to the classical gold standard, but it has had the worst average inflation: 4.5 percent. The 1862–79 Greenback period had the lowest average inflation (0.1 percent) but the worst volatility (8.8 percent). The first (interwar) gold-exchange standard had the worst combined record.

Second, the plan would provide at appropriate times not just an American but a vast worldwide countercyclical "stimulus package"—one not financed by yet more government debt—since when all other prices declined, the gold "price" would stay constant, stimulating gold mining (in which America now rivals South Africa). Third, relieved of its reserve-currency burden of being the world's "spender of last resort," America would see the competitiveness of U.S. industry quickly restored and the chronic U.S. trade deficit quickly return to chronic surpluses.

Fourth, since the whole world would have what amounts to a trade surplus with itself, equal to the increase in official gold reserves, pressure for trade protectionism would diminish sharply. Fifth, the chaos of floating currencies would end along with the reserve-currency curse. The gold standard best integrates the world trading system by bringing about prompt adjustment of balance-of-payments deficits.[33]

Sixth, the reform would halt the proliferation of debt resulting from the current currency system. Not the least benefit would be to recapitalize the balance sheet of the Federal Reserve System itself. In the course of its massive bailout of private institutions in 2008, the Federal Reserve's loan-to-capital ratio rose to about 50 to 1—worse than the troubled major private banks it was trying to save! Revaluing U.S. gold reserves from the current $42.22 to at least $1,000 an ounce could bring this ratio down to 7 to 1, providing the liquidity necessary to deal effectively with the crisis. (The exact appropriate price would have to be calculated when the reform was to take effect.)

Finally, ending the dollar's reserve-currency "privilege" and its inflationary financing of the federal budget would make it not only necessary to limit budget deficits—which could no longer be financed by foreign central banks—but also for the first time politically and economically practicable to do so. The best strategy would be to combine a low-rate, broad-based income tax with a balanced, pay-as-you-go Social Security system.

Neither reforming the international monetary system nor balancing the federal budget could be done without serious national and international discussion. But the technical problems have been long studied and are relatively straightforward. The main action item is for the president to put the reserve-currency addiction on the way to extinction before— not after—its congressional and foreign monetary codependents irreparably harm themselves and all the innocents they have heedlessly placed in harm's way.

Doing so would require overcoming objections from the dominant factions in both parties. Yet putting the common good ahead of political expediency is what distinguishes a great president from a mediocre one. The challenge is great, but so is the reward for doing the right thing.

Part 5

Divine Economy

Take away the supernatural,
and what remains is the unnatural.

—G. K. Chesterton, "Christmas and the Aesthetes"
(in *Heretics*)

17

The Three Worldviews

When the Apostle Paul preached in the *agora*, or marketplace, of Athens (probably in A.D. 51), he prefaced the Gospel with a biblically orthodox version of natural law adapted from Greco-Roman philosophy.[1] The evangelist Luke tells us that "some Epicurean and Stoic philosophers argued with him" (Acts 17:18). This confrontation contains an abiding philosophical significance.

Why these three, out of all possible worldviews? After all, Marcus Terentius Varro (116–27 B.C.) had summarized several centuries of debate among Greek and Roman philosophers by calculating that fully 288 schools of philosophical thought were possible, depending on one's notion of the Highest Good.[2]

The reason is that the same three worldviews that Jews, Romans, and Greeks disputed in Athens in A.D. 51 and northern Africa in 410, and Americans in 1776 in Philadelphia and into the twenty-first century, are the three logically alternative theories of human and divine nature: biblically orthodox natural law, Stoic pantheism, and Epicurean materialism. The structures of (neo-) Scholastic, classical, and neoclassical economic theory examined in this book correspond to the same three philosophical alternatives. Having considered their elements separately, in this final chapter let us summarize and compare these three worldviews, by reasoning from commonly accessible human experience.

In 2009, nearly two millennia after Paul's debate, Pope Benedict XVI succinctly summarized the same choice among these three worldviews in the economic encyclical *Caritas in Veritate:* "For believers, the world derives neither from [Epicurean] blind chance, nor from strict [Stoic] necessity, but from God's plan . . . living as a family under the Creator's watchful eye."[3]

But it is not only those who accept the biblical account by faith who have concluded that we live in a created world. Thomas Paine was about equally as anti-Christian as Adam Smith, and like Smith, Paine was trying to emulate Isaac Newton's physics.[4] Yet unlike Smith, Paine recognized that God's existence can be known with certainty through metaphysical reasoning.[5] Precisely because Paine was so violently opposed to all revealed religion, particularly Christianity, his reasoned argument that we live in a created world is important; after all, several authors recently have renewed the old claim of nineteenth-century freethinkers to have disproved God's existence on the same basis.[6]

Paine argued that "everything we behold carries in itself the internal evidence that it did not make itself. . . . [A]nd it is the conviction arising from this evidence, that carries us on, as it were, by necessity, to the belief of a first cause eternally existing, of a nature totally different to any material existence we know of, and by the power of which all things exist, and this first cause man calls God."[7] I have been unable to trace how Paine came upon this argument, but he is using the third, and most decisive, of Thomas Aquinas's five proofs for the existence of God, summarized more than five centuries earlier.[8]

Like most biblically orthodox thinkers before the thirteenth century, Augustine believed that faith and reason are fundamentally compatible, but he sometimes failed to distinguish clearly between what he believed on the basis of faith and what he knew based on reasoning from experience. However, a community of thinkers gradually emerged who grappled with that distinction and the implications of creation for philosophy. Each was an outstanding philosopher who sought to reconcile Aristotle and Plato, as well as a firm believer in orthodox Muslim, Jewish, or Christian faith. Even though no two were contemporary, I call them a "community" because they learned from one another in a sort of "spiral" fashion: Aquinas learned from Maimonides and Avicenna; Maimonides from Avicenna and Alfarabi; and Alfarabi and (according to Maimonides) Avicenna from earlier Greek and Syriac Christian scholars, who sought to answer objections to their faith raised by Greek pagan philosophers.[9] All shared the view that they ought to be able to agree on whatever could be demonstrated by reason and experience. No pseudo-philosophy should be accepted merely because it happened to agree with the tenets of their own faith. Their thought is therefore of special importance to Americans of the twenty-first century, for whom, exactly as at the Founding, the natural law provides a common basis of conversation and debate among those who disagree about divine revelation.

By far the most influential piece of "Smythology"—Smithology as mythology—was Milton Friedman's linking in *Free to Choose* of "two sets of ideas—both, by a curious coincidence published in the same year, 1776 . . . the economic principles of Adam Smith . . . and the political principles expressed by Thomas Jefferson."[10] I found Friedman's argument compelling and incorporated it into my own worldview for many years, as did many others far more significant than I. The masthead of the *Wall Street Journal*'s editorial page proclaims, "We speak for free markets and free people, the principles, if you will, marked in the watershed year of 1776 by Thomas Jefferson's Declaration of Independence and Adam Smith's 'Wealth of Nations.'"[11] But the evidence clearly shows that the "choice of 1776" was actually a divergence, not a convergence—and of three, not two, worldviews. For the third coincidence of 1776 was the death of Smith's friend, the Epicurean skeptic David Hume.[12]

We saw that each basic outline of economic theory corresponds to a certain theory of human nature. According to the Scholastic outline, humans are rational but also "matrimonial" and political animals, who choose both the ends and means of their actions. According to Adam Smith's revised outline, which served as the basis for classical economics, humans choose neither the ends nor the means. In the neoclassical outline, humans choose the means but not the ends of their actions.

Strictly speaking, these are not differences about which reasonable people can disagree—because the disagreement is precisely about whether or to what extent humans are reasonable. We have seen that both classical and modern neoclassical economics are defined by their omission of the theory of distribution at every level. (They differ in that classical economics also omits the theory of consumption.) In place of the original Scholastic theory of personal distribution, which describes personal gifts (and their opposite, crimes), the classical and neoclassical theories simply but inaccurately assume that every personal gift or crime is a disguised form of consumption, production, and/or exchange.

Though these worldviews differ chiefly about immaterial things, such as the existence of God or the soul, we have found repeatedly that the classical, neoclassical, and (neo-) Scholastic theories make different empirically testable predictions about human behavior. Perhaps the most striking result at the personal level was the 90 percent inverse relationship between economic fatherhood and crime—above all homicide—since it provided direct evidence of Augustine's "personal distribution function" while disproving the neoclassical and supporting the (neo-) Scholastic prediction. Yet it was almost as striking to find that even the behavior of the foremost champions of the neoclassical "economic approach to human behavior"—Gary Becker and Steven Levitt—accorded with the (neo-) Scholastic theory, as did that of the utilitarian philosopher Peter Singer, with whom I had the exchange about Augustine's theory of personal gifts. The (neo-) Scholastic theory also offers a new theory of social and spiritual "graces" to balance the neoclassical theory's one-sided emphasis on all the "capitals"—human, social, religious, and spiritual—which fails to grasp the gratuitous nature of much human life.

We found the same difference apparent in domestic economy, which is impossible to explain without personal gifts. The absence of the theory of domestic distributive justice compounded the problem, making it impossible for neoclassical economic theory accurately to describe modern marriage, fertility, or lifetime income and spending. Yet the (neo-) Scholastic approach suggested a new approach to the theory of fertility and showed how the lifetime pattern of earnings and consumption can be explained only as the result of extensive personal gifts from parents to their dependent children and later from adult children to their aged parents.

Moreover, the gaps in neoclassical theory at the personal and domestic levels make it impossible for neoclassical political economy theory accurately to predict some of the most important results of economic policy—particularly the effects of government taxes and social benefits, which often substitute for personal and joint gifts among family members. Neo-Scholastic theory can tell us the relative effects of private saving and social benefits on fertility, but the neoclassical version cannot. This is a serious problem when policymakers are contemplating sweeping reforms of the income-tax, Social Security retirement, or health insurance systems. And neoclassical theory has a similar problem explaining the effects of economic policy on employment and unemployment. Neoclassical theory has, we found, attempted to incorporate political behavior, but the theory cannot explain American political economy.

I confidently predict that in coming decades, neoclassical economists now advocating the "economic approach to human behavior" will become—or be supplanted by—"neo-Scholastic" economists, who understand the original "human approach to economic behavior" of Aristotle, Augustine, and Aquinas. I don't underestimate the time or effort it will take, but it will happen, because each development in economics since Adam Smith has been to restore a major component of the original Scholastic outline of economics. The whole neoclassical era has been essentially the reintegration of Augustine's theory of utility along with the theories of production and exchange that Smith's classical outline had retained. What John W. Kendrick called Theodore Schultz's "total capital hypothesis" was a reinvention of Aristotle's and Augustine's theory of household production. And even the struggle between the Chicago and Keynesian schools in the second half of the twentieth century is instructive.

The first lesson is that truth matters. In fact, in the long run, the truth is irresistible.

The second is that mere criticism of a wrong theory is useless. George Stigler was quite correct in arguing that "it takes a theory to beat a theory: if there is a theory that is right [only] 51 per cent of the time, it will be used until a better one comes along. (Theories that are right only 50 per cent of the time are less economical than coin-flipping.)"[13]

The third lesson is that of two theories with equal explanatory power, the simpler one is better. This has an important "sociological dimension" for which Stigler has not received proper credit.

Milton Friedman likened economic theory to an "analytical filing system."[14] To adapt that idea, economic theory should be considered a set of three vertical filing cabinets—corresponding to personal, domestic, and political economy—each with four drawers, corresponding to final distribution, consumption, production, and exchange. The trouble is that Adam Smith and neoclassical economists locked the drawers containing the most important files: final distribution and consumption in Smith's case, and final distribution for neoclassical economists.

In 1955, just as Stigler was elaborating his new theory of "the Economist as Preacher," there was a flurry of comment for and against the mathematization of economics, apparently pitting "mathematical" against "literary" economists. Stigler's brief comment in this exchange has received little notice, but it explains the main reason for the victory of the Chicago over the Keynesian school in the next few decades. It also underscores why neo-Scholastic economics will emerge in coming decades: a simpler theory and simpler mathematics are better when it comes to accurate description, as long as what we're looking at is described properly.

Anyone's knowledge of economics, Stigler argued, may be ranked from "Zero, or less" for the Poet, to "Some," to "Much" (the last including Adam Smith), and mathematical ability from "None" (including both the Poet and Adam Smith) to Algebra, Calculus, Matrices, to "Vast." This resulted in a table of fifteen classifications, from the Poet ("None" on both scales) to the "Well-Balanced" (including Stigler and Keynes) to the "Scholar." Stigler argued that "there are hundreds of millions of people in the Poetic class but as yet not one Scholar." He concluded, "The Factual, the Well-Balanced and the Scholar may be rivals or partners in reaching their goal. . . . Meanwhile we can all scold the Poetic type."[15]

Yet the Poet may have the last laugh. Stigler's table included only mathematical ability and knowledge of markets (that is, exchange), when the most important dimension of human nature is our choice of persons, which is expressed by personal and collective gifts—and this is where the Poet shines. Thus, economists armed with only modest or average mathematical abilities can yield superior results with the inherently more accurate (neo-) Scholastic economic theory. If we combine Friedman's and Stigler's insights with the neo-Scholastic outline of economics, the result is a "filing system" like that depicted in Figure 17–1.

Modern economists can be rescued from their current predicament by relearning what all "economists" knew before Adam Smith. This will call for restoring the requirement that students of economics learn its history. Any university economics department, but especially those with a strong background in liberal arts, will gain an advantage by doing so, because its students will better understand the basic concepts to be applied, and with such a background, more students will be able to produce cutting-edge research without requiring mathematical pyrotechnics.

Finally, we have seen that all theories of the order in markets are frankly theological. Each traces the order in markets back to the order implanted by God in man's nature (though Smith's version also involves

Figure 17–1

The 'Filing Cabinet' of Economic Theory:
How the 'Poet's' Knowledge May Exceed Adam Smith's

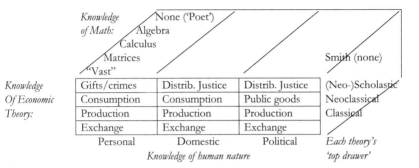

Knowledge of Math:	None ('Poet') Algebra Calculus Matrices "Vast"			Smith (none)
Knowledge Of Economic Theory:	Gifts/crimes	Distrib. Justice	Distrib. Justice	(Neo-)Scholastic
	Consumption	Consumption	Public goods	Neoclassical
	Production	Production	Production	Classical
	Exchange	Exchange	Exchange	
	Personal	Domestic	Political	*Each theory's*
		Knowledge of human nature		*'top drawer'*

According to George Stigler, Adam Smith and the 'Poet' have the same math skills: "none" (back of cabinet). But the (Neo-)Scholastic outline shows that the Poet or Philosopher may grasp two more elements of economics (indicated by a 'top drawer' two levels higher) and broader knowledge of human nature (more vertical cabinets).

and requires an ongoing divine "deception" about economic value). In St. Augustine's theory, God's providence and human free will are compatible rather than mutually exclusive. Smith's "invisible hand" is simply the Stoic theory of providence, according to which God is the soul of an uncreated universe and humans are, in effect, God's puppets. The Epicurean view does not formally have a theory of providence, because it holds that God does not exist and everything is governed by chance. But Epicurean philosophy is implicitly pantheistic, making Nature the ultimate cause of everything. In fact, *Natura* was a mythical goddess.

The theory of natural selection is inherently unable to address the question of creation one way or the other. "Evolution is either an innocent scientific description of how certain earthly things came about; or, if it is anything more than this, it is an attack on thought itself," G. K. Chesterton sanely observed. "If evolution simply means that a positive thing called an ape turned very slowly into a positive thing called a man, then it is stingless for the most orthodox; for a personal God might just as well do things slowly as quickly, especially if, like the Christian God, he were outside time. But if it means anything more, it means that there is no such thing as an ape to change, and no such thing as a man to change into. It means that there is no such thing as a thing."[16] The Stoics and Augustine even agreed on a principle that they would apply to the theory of natural selection: They spoke of "seminal reasons" or "seminal causes" implanted in nature, which causes things to develop as they do. But the Stoics used the idea to explain the endlessly repeated cycles of an eternal, uncreated cosmos, while Augustine used it to explain how new things could appear after creation out of nothing. Adaptive evolution, like seminal causes, may offer a theory about how the universe has developed but can say nothing about its origin. Even if the universe were eternal in time—and all the scientific evidence is against that view—its existence would still have to be accounted for. This is not a question that the scientific method can answer, since we can't get outside the universe to observe it. Therefore, adaptive evolution is not a third alternative. The universe either was created out of nothing or it wasn't—there is no third possibility. Someone who believes that matter is the ultimate reality is, for all practical purposes, a pantheist.

Stanley Jaki (1924–2009), a historian of science, and Étienne Gilson (1884–1978), a historian of philosophy, both argued that the idea of creation was necessary for the successful emergence and development of exact sciences. According to Jaki, "There can be no more fundamental difference than the one between a world which is in no need of being created and a world that owes its existence to the Creator. That difference lies at the root of the invariable stillbirths of science in all the ancient cultures."[17] Common to all ancient philosophies, he argues, was an essentially pantheistic view of the universe; this pantheism prevented any order in the universe from being complete. Because God was not considered to transcend sensible reality, he always, so to speak, got in the way when it came to explaining sensible reality. For example, to make his theory of physics work, Aristotle had to suppose two different kinds of matter: a special, immutable kind for the celestial bodies (which Aristotle thought were animated by eternal intelligences attracted to God, the Unmoved Mover) and another, "ordinary" kind of matter for sublunary bodies. A single theory that explained astronomy, mechanics, and the basic elements was therefore impossible.

Something similar happened to economics, and for the same reason. Economics was born with Aristotle, but it was stillborn, resulting in what Schumpeter called the "Great Gap" in economic theory between the fourth century B.C. and the thirteenth century A.D. Aristotle had provided the theory of *production* and the theory of justice in exchange or *equilibrium*. But he assumed rather than stated the theory of *utility*. And his theory of *final distribution* was limited to (mostly political) distribution of *common* goods. Aristotle had discussed friendship as a "sharing" and had even suggested that the practical possibility of sharing among friends is limited by the fact of scarcity.[18] But he never stated the principle of *personal* distribution, by which we decide how much of our scarce goods to allocate to ourselves and how much to others. Aquinas saw that Aristotle's philosophy and economic theory were incomplete, and supplemented them with Augustine's. Aquinas replaced Aristotle's sketchy preliminary remarks on economic value with Augustine's theory of *utility*, and he completed Aristotle's theory of *social and political distribution* with Augustine's theory of *personal distribution*.

In itself, creation is a philosophical rather than a religious idea, but the idea did not exist in Greek or Roman philosophy until after its encounter with Christianity. Among the premises of Augustine's theory are that God knows and loves each human person individually and that human persons are also motivated by love of persons, including themselves, each other, and God. Thus, a single theory of action could embrace God and man—and make the first logically complete economic theory practically possible.

Chesterton is often misquoted as having said, "The first effect of not believing in God is to believe in anything." (Despite considerable effort, Chesterton scholars have been unable to find it in his writings.)[19] But the most frequent alternative to believing in the God of Abraham, Isaac, and Jacob is not to believe in *nothing* but rather to believe in *everything*. That is, the main alternative to biblically orthodox faith is not atheism but pantheism. Our culture is so steeped in pantheism that we do not recognize it when we hear it (for example, the theme of the *Star Wars* movies: "Use the Force, Luke!").

This is a problem especially for economists. The order in markets is not a theory; it's a fact. The question is where the order comes from. Augustine says that the order comes from the conscious choices of humans. But ultimately, in his view, "this image or, as I said, trace of equity is stamped on the business transactions of men by the Supreme Equity."[20] Yet for many if not most economists of my generation, the argument from design does not point to a Creator. What was it, I finally began to wonder, that unites Marxists, libertarians, and even some of my fellow supply-siders—who couldn't agree on anything else—in their exaggerated admiration for Adam Smith? It's the mating call of pantheism, I concluded. The only thing they disagree about is which collective body—Marx's proletariat, the libertarian's unfettered market, or the supply-sider Jude Wanniski's "global electorate"—best expresses the mind of God. We are dealing with a genuine but misguided religious impulse.

The idea that "all men are *by nature* equal" is an old one. We find it in exactly, or almost exactly, those words in Plato,[21] Zeno of Citium (the founder of Stoicism),[22] Thomas Hobbes,[23] Algernon Sidney,[24] and John Locke.[25] But to say "all men are *created* equal" was a much more specific, and one might say inspired, formulation.

Thomas Jefferson's countrymen differed in religion, but it was their general sense that God exists, that he is a Creator, and that human beings are creatures living in a created world.[26] This means that Friedman's effort to equate Smith's Stoic philosophy with the Declaration of Independence is untenable. As we saw, Smith generally avoids calling God a "creator," and when he cannot avoid it, he never uses the term to mean creation out of nothing, only in the looser sense of "shaping" or "fashioning." This was precisely the root of Smith's difference with Augustine about providence, human choice, economic analysis, and everything else. Augustine's view that we live in a created world is compatible with the Declaration of Independence, but Adam Smith's Stoic philosophy is not, because Smith's Stoic God is not a Creator, and Smith's human beings are not creatures.

On such a matter, therefore, we are *not* "free to choose." We can have *either* Adam Smith's Stoic "invisible hand," deceiving and manipulating humans as God's puppets by the heartstrings of their "sentiments," *or* "all men . . . created equal," as it says in the Declaration of Independence—but not both. All men cannot be free to choose the persons their economic actions are intended to benefit unless they are created equal; and all men are not created equal unless all men are created.

Table 17–1

Worldview Implicit in Each Outline of Economic Theory			
Economic theory:	(Neo-)Scholastic	Classical	Neoclassical
Philosophical worldview:	Biblically orthodox natural law	Stoic pantheism	Epicurean materialism
Ultimate cause:	God	Uncreated animate matter	Uncreated inanimate matter
Governing principle:	Logos (Reason)	Fate (Necessity)	Chance
View of God: Is He immanent? Transcendent?	Creator (ex nihilo) Yes Yes	World-Soul Yes No	Doesn't exist No No
View of man: Personal soul? Free choice of ends and means?	Rational animal Yes Yes, both (though weakened by sin)	God's puppet No Neither: both driven by 'sentiments' (Adam Smith)	Clever animal No Means, not ends: reason 'slave of passions' (Hume)
Theory of knowledge	Moderate realism: Creation rational, hence knowable	Nominalism: Divine 'deception' (Adam Smith)	Nominalism: No 'real connection' of things (Hume)

Notes

Introduction

1. Abbé G. Lemaître, "The Expanding Universe," *Monthly Notices of the Royal Astronomical Society* 91 (March 1931): 490–501.

2. Deuteronomy 6:5; Leviticus 19:18 (noted in Matthew 22:37–39).

3. John D. Mueller, "The Preacher as Economist vs. The Economist as Preacher." Remarks delivered to a conference on "Faith and the Challenges of Secularism," Princeton University, October 11, 2003: retrieved from http://www.eppc.org/publications/pubID.2263/pub_detail.asp 24 January 2010; also John D. Mueller, "The Preacher as Economist vs. The Economist as Preacher: Economics, Secularism, and Faith," A Faith and Law Lecture, Washington, DC, 30 May 2008, retrieved from http://www.eppc.org/publications/pubID.3416/pub_detail.asp on 24 January 2010.

4. Augustinus Aurelius, "To Simplician—On Various Questions," book 1, q. 2 a. 16, in *Augustine: Earlier Writings*, [c.397], 398, selected and translated with introductions by John H. S. Burleigh (Philadelphia: Westminster Press, 1953). In another letter Augustine explains why he avoids terms like *hands of God* as metaphors for divine providence: Most people take the expressions too literally. *Letter to Fortunatianus*, Letter 148 (A.D. 413), chap. I and IV, at http://www.newadvent.org/fathers/1102148.htm, retrieved 1 September 2009.

5. See chap. 1, note 2 below.

6. I hesitated to use the term neo-Scholastic, partly because in theology it has the (often deserved) connotation of retaining the outward form of Scholastic thinking while altering the substance, yet I seek the reverse, to restore the substance of Scholastic theory while updating its form; and partly because there is nothing so quickly dated as a theory called "neo-" anything. Outweighing these apparent disadvantages, "Scholastic" and "neo-Scholastic" make a natural parallel with the widely used titles "classical" and "neoclassical" for the intervening

periods in the history of economics—and as Aristotle noted, language follows
the usage of the multitude. Thus a warning to theologians: "neo-Scholastic" has
nearly opposite meanings in theology and economics. In nineteenth- and twentieth-century theology it essentially meant equating Aquinas with Aristotle and
removing Augustine's fundamental insight that all persons (human or divine)
are motivated by love for some person(s), and all personal love is expressed with
a gift. In twenty-first-century economics "neo-Scholastic" theory restores that
insight to its central role. In chapter 5 I also distinguish "neo-Scholastic" from
"neo-Thomist" economic theory.
7. Thomas Aquinas suggested this division to replace Aristotle's into ethics and
politics. St. Thomas Aquinas, *The Summa Theologica [Theologiae]*, translated by
the Fathers of the English Dominican Province (New York: Benziger Brothers,
1948 [1268–73]); II-II Q47 A11 contra and corpus, and Q50, introduction.
8. Since about 1950, but especially since 1980, there has been a renaissance
of "natural lawyers," as political philosophers in the natural law tradition are
called. As will be apparent from the book, I have learned much from them. But I
also found that they disagree about a question that is central to economic theory
and therefore to this book: the nature of value. Much of the disagreement takes
the form of an apparently abstract debate as to whether all human goods are
"commensurable": basically, whether we should or do treat persons and other
things in the same way. All natural lawyers agree in sharply opposing those who
claim, in effect, that we *should* treat persons the same as impersonal things. But
they disagree about describing how we *do* treat them. A good introduction to
this debate can be found in William E. May, *An Introduction to Moral Theology*,
revised edition (Huntington, IN: Our Sunday Visitor, 1994). In writing this
book, I not only could not avoid the issue, but also was forced to offer a solution,
which comes from St. Augustine. If Augustine's solution is heeded, it should
soon be possible for the first time in the modern era for moral and political
philosophers to agree with economists on a consistent theory that works equally
well in personal ethics, mathematical economics, and politics. Moreover, many
questions now widely regarded as irreconcilable matters of opinion will be settled not merely as matters of logic and theory, but also as matters of fact.
9. Several economists deserve special mention, both in order to acknowledge and
recommend their work and to explain how my approach may differ: Stephen
T. Worland, *Scholasticism and Welfare Economics* (Notre Dame, IN: University
of Notre Dame Press, 1967); Alejandro Chafuen, *Christians for Freedom: Economic Thought of the Late Scholastics* (San Francisco: Ignatius Press, 1986) and
Faith and Liberty: The Economic Thought of the Late Scholastics (Lanham, MD:
Lexington Books, 2003); Jennifer Roback Morse, *Love and Economics: Why the
Laissez-Faire Family Doesn't Work* (Dallas: Spence Publishing, 2001); Maria
Sophia Aguirre, "The Family and Economic Development: Socioeconomic Rel-
evance and Policy Design," in *Family and Policy*, ed. Scott Love (World Family
Policy Center, 2004) and "Marriage and the Family in Economic Theory and

Policy," 4 *Ave Maria Law Journal* 2 (June 2006): 435–65; Alberto M. Piedra, *Natural Law: The Foundation of an Orderly Economic System* (Rowman & Littlefield, 2004); Andrew Yuengert, *The Foundations of Technique: Ordering Positive and Normative Concerns in Economic Research* (Lanham, MD: Lexington Books, 2004); and John C. Médaille, *The Vocation of Business: Social Justice in the Marketplace* (New York: Continuum Publishing, 2007). Most have tried to show the essential complementarity of the natural law philosophy with some school of modern neoclassical economic theory. My own 1996 essay, though inspired by Scholastic theory, was still formally neoclassical: John D. Mueller, "Taxation," in *Natural Law and Contemporary Public Policy*, ed. David F. Forte (Georgetown University Press, 1998), 219–79. Yet each (including me) found something important in Scholastic natural law that failed to fit into neoclassical economic theory. I hope in this book to provide coherence and direction to these efforts by precisely identifying the main missing element and suggesting how it might be reintegrated. Especially since this book was accepted for publication in October 2004, Aguirre and Morse in particular have already begun the necessary rewriting of the neoclassical economic theory of the family.
10. Henry William Spiegel, *The Growth of Economic Thought* (Duke University Press, 1971), 507.

Chapter 1

1. "In 1972, he [Stigler] successfully proposed that the history of thought requirement be dropped at Chicago. Most other economics departments later followed suit . . . At the same meeting Stigler unsuccessfully proposed that the economic history requirement also be dropped." Robert Leeson, "The Chicago Counter-Revolution and the Sociology of Economic Knowledge," Working Paper 159, Economics Department, Murdoch University, Murdoch, WA, Australia, July 1997, endnote 62. This paper later became a chapter in Robert Leeson, *The Eclipse of Keynesianism: The Political Economy of the Chicago Counter-Revolution* (New York: Palgrave Macmillan, 2001).
2. Stigler had been taught what I call below the "New Yorker's Eye View" of the history of economics by Jacob Viner (1892–1970) and Frank H. Knight (1888–1972), the cofounders of the University of Chicago's economics department. Stigler had first built his reputation precisely as a historian of economics, largely based on his doctoral thesis (George J. Stigler, *Production and Distribution Theories: The Formative Period* [New York: Macmillan, 1941]), and a series of historical essays (most reprinted in *Essays in the History of Economics* [Chicago: University of Chicago Press, 1965], and *The Economist as Preacher and Other Essays* [Chicago: University of Chicago Press, 1982]). But Joseph Schumpeter's *History of Economic Analysis* (described below) not only revolutionized the history of economics, by expanding its timeline from two to either seven or twenty-three centuries (depending on whether we consider the first fully inte-

grated economic theory to have begun with Aristotle, as Schumpeter supposed, or Thomas Aquinas, as the thesis of this book suggests), it also slashed Stigler's relative expertise by between seven and nine tenths. This precipitated a reversal of Stigler's attitude to Adam Smith, the nature of science, and the nature of originality in economics. Stigler expressed these views in a review of Schumpeter's *History* (George J. Stigler, "Schumpeter's *History of Economic Analysis*," *Journal of Political Economy* 62:4 [August 1954]: 344–45); in an essay the following year (George J. Stigler, "The Nature and Role of Originality in Scientific Progress," *Economica* New Series 22:88 [November 1955]: 293–302, reprinted in Stigler's *Essays in the History of Economics*, 1–15); in a famous article advocating abolition of teaching the history of economics to economists-in-training (George J. Stigler, "Does Economics Have a Useful Past?" *History of Political Economy* 1 [Fall 1969], reprinted in *The Economist as Preacher and Other Essays*, 107–18); in his Nobel lecture (George J. Stigler, "Nobel Lecture: The Process and Progress of Economics," *Journal of Political Economy*, vol. 91, Issue 4 [August 1983]: 529–45); and in his memoirs (George J. Stigler, *Memoirs of an Unregulated Economist* [New York: Basic Books, 1988] 191–220). Ironically, also stimulated by Schumpeter's *History*, Viner meanwhile went on at Princeton University to a second career as a historian of ideas, in which he explored the role of Scholastic economics and was among the few historians of economic theory to recognize Augustine's crucial technical role in treating both justice and utility as scales of preference (Jacob Viner, *The Role of Providence in the Social Order: An essay in intellectual history*, Jayne Lectures for 1966 [Philadelphia: American Philosophical Society, 1972]; and [especially] Jacob Viner, *Religious Thought and Economic Society: Four Chapters of an Unfinished Work*, ed. Jacques Melitz and Donald Winch [Duke University Press, 1978]).

3. The term was popularized by Herbert Butterfield, *The Whig Interpretation of History* (New York: W. W. Norton & Co., 1931). Butterfield meant "the tendency of many historians to write on the side of Protestants and Whigs, to praise revolutions provided they have been successful, to emphasize certain principles of progress in the past and to produce a story which is the ratification if not the glorification of the present" (page v). The approach is typical of Thomas Babington Macaulay, who saw all of history as leading up to British parliamentary democracy of the nineteenth century. But the fact that the essence of a Whig history lies not in religious or party affiliation, but rather in the interpretation of the past in terms of the present, can be gathered from the fact that the only historian specifically criticized by Butterfield was Lord Acton, who was a staunch Catholic (John Dalberg-Acton, 1834–1902).

4. Joseph Schumpeter, *History of Economic Analysis*, edited from manuscript by Elizabeth Boody Schumpeter (New York: Oxford University Press, 1954). Schumpeter had died in 1950, but his wife, who was also an economist, edited the unfinished manuscript for publication.

5. Schumpeter, *History*, 194.

6. Schumpeter, *History*, 184.
7. Schumpeter, *History*, 38.
8. Ibid.
9. Schumpeter, *History*, 52.
10. Schumpeter, *History*, 9. Schumpeter does not call Aristotle the "founder" of economics, because in his view all sciences emerge and develop by "slow accretion," thus making it "in general impossible to date—even by decades—the origins, let alone the 'foundation,' of a science as distinguished from the origin of a particular method or the foundation of a 'school.'"
11. Schumpeter, *History*, 57.
12. Schumpeter, *History*, 60. Though it's not immediately obvious, Schumpeter has just wrongly described Aristotle's economics as essentially identical to modern neoclassical economics. Schumpeter's view of the history of economics is determined by adopting the viewpoint of one particular school of modern economics, which descended from the neoclassical economist Leon Walras. Schumpeter's mention of "distribution" reveals an important but often confusing issue. As we will see in chapter 2, Aristotle most certainly had a theory of distribution, which he called "distributive justice." It describes the way in which the use of goods owned in common (for example, by a family or by the citizens under a single government) is shared by the owners. And as we will also see, it was a first-class bit of economic analysis, describing in mathematical terms exactly what people argue about when they disagree (for example) about taxation, government spending, and government benefits. But Schumpeter uses the term *distribution* with quite a different meaning, adopted by classical economists following Adam Smith, to describe what is more properly called "compensation"—that is, how the proceeds from the sale of a product are paid out as income to its producers or "factors," the workers and owners of the property that cooperated to produce it. We'll describe and distinguish compensation from final distribution in the next chapter.
13. Schumpeter, *History*, 93.
14. According to Schumpeter, "the earliest and most important step in methodological criticism" was taken by Aquinas: "the exclusion of revelation from all sciences except *sacra doctrina* [revealed theology] was coupled by St. Thomas with the exclusion of appeal to authority as an admissible *scientific method*." Schumpeter, *History*, 8n. Schumpeter himself remained deeply ambivalent about choosing between Aristotle and Aquinas's "realist" theory of knowledge and the "nominalist" version proposed by Schumpeter's colleague Max Weber (described below in chapter 4). In the "realist" theory of knowledge, humans *recognize* a pre-existent order inherent in things, while in the "nominalist" version, humans must *impose* their own order upon an inherently chaotic nature. Schumpeter attempted to be "nominalist" in theory and "realist" in practice but was struggling to reconcile these two opposite theories when he died, leaving his manuscript unfinished; his wife and editor simply combined what Schumpeter

had written about the two theories without reconciling them coherently. Upon reading Schumpeter's *History*, Stigler adopted Schumpeter's nominalist version of science in both theory and practice.

15. Schumpeter, *History*, 97. Preceding or coinciding with Schumpeter in his thesis about the Scholastics, but generally ignored until his *History* stimulated interest in the subject, were Bernard W. Dempsey, "Just Price in a Functional Economy," *American Economic Review*, 25 (September 1935): 471–86, and *Interest and Usury*, American Council on Public Affairs, Washington, DC (1943); and Raymond de Roover, "Monopoly Theory Prior to Adam Smith: A Revision," *Quarterly Journal of Economics* 65 (November 1951): 492–524; also "Scholastic Economics: Survival and Lasting Influence from the Sixteenth Century to Adam Smith," *Quarterly Journal of Economics* 69 (May 1955): 161–90.

16. Schumpeter, *History*, 98. In the chapter on Scholastic economics, I show that Thomas Aquinas's "pointer" was Augustine's theory of utility, which he integrated with Aristotle's sketchy remarks on economic value.

17. Schumpeter, *History*, 182.

18. Schumpeter, *History*, 183.

19. Schumpeter, *History*, 97, 308–11. As we'll see in chapter 3 on classical economics, Smith's so-called labor theory of value is actually a theory of production assuming only one productive factor, labor.

20. Schumpeter, *History*, 188.

21. John Stuart Mill, *Principles of political economy with some of their applications to social philosophy* (Boston: C. C. Little & J. Brown, 1848), book III, chap. I.

22. Schumpeter, *History*, 308.

23. Schumpeter, *History*, 249.

24. Schumpeter, *History*, 184.

25. The degree and rate of acceptance of Schumpeter's broad thesis by historians of economics can be roughly gauged by comparing three standard textbooks: Marc Blaug's *Economic Theory in Retrospect*, first published in 1962, eight years after Schumpeter's *History* (Cambridge University Press, Fifth Edition, 1997); Henry William Spiegel's *The Growth of Economic Thought*, which first appeared in 1971 (Duke University Press, *Revised and Expanded Edition*, 1983); and Roger Backhouse's *The Ordinary Business of Life*, first published in 2002 (*The Ordinary Business of Life: A History of Economics from the Ancient World to the Twenty-First Century* [Princeton University Press]). Blaug devotes a slim opening chapter to what he calls "pre-Adamite economics," almost entirely concerned with eighteenth-century ideas. Spiegel and Backhouse devote fully *one-third* of their texts to the "pre-Adamites"—about the same as Schumpeter. Blaug's main reaction to Schumpeter was a two-page "afterthought" on Scholastic influences and, as the volume of research into the "pre-Adamites" swelled over the years, some increasingly defensive endnotes. The text of the fifth edition in 1997 remained essentially unchanged.

26. Schumpeter, *History*, 97.

27. All Schumpeter says about Augustine is that the Christian thinkers of his period "lacked nothing in refinement and did develop techniques of reasoning—that partly hailed from Greek philosophy and from the Roman law—for the subjects that seem to them worth while. Yet neither Lactantius (260–340) nor Ambrosius (340–97) . . . nor Chrysostomus (347–407) nor St. Augustine (354–430), the accomplished author of the *Civitas Dei* and of the *Confessiones*—whose very obiter dicta reveal analytic habits of mind—ever went into economic problems though they did go into the political problems of the Christian state." Schumpeter, *History*, 71–72.

Chapter 2

1. Aquinas's economics is embedded within a broader philosophy that seeks to comprehend all human knowledge, with a place for everything and everything in its place, as summarized in Table 2–1. The Scholastic framework outlines what it means to be a "rational," "matrimonial," and "political animal" by describing the theological, intellectual, and practical virtues. The latter pertain either to action (moral virtue) or production; the moral virtues discipline the senses according to reason and are oriented either toward oneself (temperance to curb inordinate attractions and fortitude to overcome inordinate aversions to human goods) or toward other persons (beneficence and commutative justice between individuals and distributive justice in any domestic or political society). The whole of human knowledge and action can be outlined in a single table. Thomas Aquinas, *The division and methods of the sciences*, translated by Armand Maurer, Fourth Revised Edition (Toronto: Pontifical Institute of Medieval Studies, 1986 [1255–59]); Thomas Aquinas, *Commentary on Aristotle's* Nicomachean Ethics, translated by C. I. Litzinger, (Henry Regnery Company, 1964 [1271–72]); Foreword by Ralph McInerny (Notre Dame, IN: Dumb Ox Books, 1993, [1271–72]); Lecture I, 1–3; Jacques Maritain, *The Degrees of Knowledge* (Notre Dame, IN: University of Notre Dame Press, 1995 [1932]).
2. Scarry, Richard, *What Do People Do All Day? Written and Illustrated by Richard Scarry* (New York: Random House, 1968).
3. Luke 17:27–28.
4. Schumpeter, *History*, 93.
5. I first presented the (neo-) Scholastic outline of economic theory as an empirically verifiable system of four simultaneous equations in a paper presented at Princeton University's James Madison Program in American Ideals and Institutions: John D. Mueller, "The End of Economics, or, Is Utilitarianism Finished?" April 15, 2002, available at http://www.eppc.org/docLib/20050216_mueller_apr02.pdf (retrieved 16 May 2006). I'm grateful that Professors Robert P. George and Peter Singer of Princeton graciously agreed to join the discussion. That paper outlined in greatly condensed form the argument presented in this book, especially chapters 2, 3, 4, 6, 7, 8, and 9.

6. All of the actions described are understood to have the dimension of time—
for example, consumption C should be understood as $C/\delta t$, or consumption per
unit of time—the notation for which is usually omitted here for simplicity. By
abstracting from differences in timing, we leave until later our consideration of
investment, which is essentially providing for future consumption by producing
more than we currently consume.

7. I say "final" distribution, because, as we will see, Adam Smith started a
long tradition among economists of using the term *distribution* to conflate
distribution properly defined (personal gifts/crimes and distributive justice)
with *compensation*—the explanation of how the incomes of the factors of production are determined, which Aristotle and the Scholastics called justice in
exchange.

8. (1) $C_{Ki} + C_{Li} = Y_i D_{ii}/\Sigma D_{ij}$ [final distribution function],
where $C_{Ki,}$ and C_{Li} represent the use ("consumption") by Person i of the services
of his or her human capital, L_i, and nonhuman capital, K_i; Y_i is total compensation (labor and property income) of Person i; D_{ii} is the significance of Person i
to himself, and ΣD_{ij} is the significance of all persons to Person i.

9. For clarity and simplicity later on, we will define
(5) $Y_i = rK_i + wL_i$
meaning that Y_i is the total net factor compensation (labor and property income)
of Person i; and
(6) $Ti = Y_i - Y_i D_{ii}/\Sigma D_{ij}$.
By substituting (5) and (6), (1) may therefore be restated as
(1a) $C_{Ki} + C_{Li} = Y_i - T_i$.
This makes clear that the difference between Person i's total consumption, C_{Ki}
+ C_{Li}, and total compensation, Y_i, is equal to T_i—(net) personal, domestic, and
political "transfer payments" from Person i to other persons. Transfer payments
comprise any income *not* received as compensation for contributing to current
production. "Net" means that personal gifts made are offset by gifts received,
while taxes are treated as transfers paid to the government and balanced against
government transfers received.

10. (2) $U_i = f(C_{Ki}, C_{Li})$ [utility function],
where U_i is the ranking by Person i ("utility") of C_{Ki}, and C_{Li}, the units consumed in use by Person i of the services of his or her nonhuman goods, K_i,
and human capital, L_i, respectively. In reality, K and L are not two goods but
two classes of goods consumed: $(K_1, K_2, \ldots, K_n)$ and $(L_1, L_2, \ldots, L_n)$. Scarcity
implies that the value of each unit consumed declines as the number of units
increases ($\delta U/\delta C < 0$: "declining marginal utility") and that goods are "used
up"—that is, rendered unusable—by consumption (for example, $C_{Ki} = -\Delta Ki$).

11. (3a) $\Delta K_i = f_1(K_i, L_i)$ [production function for nonhuman capital];
(3b) $\Delta L_i = f_2(K_i, L_i)$ [production function for human capital];
where ΔK_i is the change in the stock (production) of nonhuman goods and ΔL_i
the change in the stock of "human capital," owned by Person i.

12. (4) $P_K \Delta K_i + P_L \Delta L_i = rK_i + wL_i$, where P_K and P_L are the unit prices of K and L, respectively, w labor compensation per unit of L, r property compensation per unit of K. (P_L is a market price only in a slave-owning society, like ancient Athens or the antebellum American South.)

13. Economics is (and has been since Aristotle) a mathematical as well as moral discipline. But Alfred Marshall once gave another economist this excellent advice: "(1) Use mathematics as a shorthand language, rather than an engine of inquiry. (2) Keep to them till you have done. (3) Translate into English. (4) Then illustrate by examples that are important in real life. (5) Burn the mathematics." In other words, mathematics cannot say any more than can be said in English. "Twice two equals four" means the same as "2 x 2 = 4." But the math does serve some very useful purposes: checking whether a theory is logically complete, discovering its implicit assumptions, and quantifying and testing its predictions. Once you realize this, math loses any mystique and becomes no more exciting (though it remains no less necessary) than proper spelling and grammar. The practicing economist is a man of simple pleasures, like Charles Dickens's Mr. Micawber: "Annual income twenty pounds, annual expenditure nineteen nineteen six, result happiness. Annual income twenty pounds, annual expenditure twenty pounds ought and six, result misery." Or rather, for the practicing economist: four unknowns, four equations, result happiness. Four unknowns, three equations, result misery. As an empirical practitioner, I began to suspect that most of the misery in modern economics results from the simple error of starting with more unknown variables than explanatory equations. All varieties of modern neoclassical economics have no more than three kinds of equations to explain the four essential facets of human economic decisions. Each missing equation or explanation forces economists either to resort to circular logic (thus making their descriptions unverifiable) or else to replace missing variables with assumptions (and thus to prescribe and falsify rather than describe the facts). The explanatory equation missing from classical and neoclassical economics is the one that describes gifts (and their opposite, crimes) at the personal level and distributive justice at all social, e.g., family and political, levels. Marshall to Bowley, 27 February 1906, in *Memorials of Alfred Marshall*, edited by A.C. Pigou (London: Macmillan, 1925), 427.

14. The known variables include the D's and U, which describe preferences for persons and nonpersonal wealth that are independently (freely) determined by Person i; also the variables resulting purely from simplifying definitions (Y and T). For realism, the system described includes two goods consumed (C_K and C_L) and two factors (K and L). As a result, there are two equations in the production function instead of one, while two equations were added to define Y and T. But to show its logical completeness and consistency (though at the cost of losing empirical realism), the system could be reduced to one containing only one good and one factor, for example, by eliminating L, C_L, and P_L, while Y and T could be eliminated without changing the substance. In doing so, it becomes

clear that there are only four equations with four unknowns (C_K, P_K, r, and K) and that for each additional unknown variable an equation was added.

15. If we analyze a single person's actions, we are not considering how that person's actions will affect other persons, and vice versa. For example, market prices are taken as given. This would be a partial equilibrium analysis. As we add more persons, our perspective changes from a partial toward a general equilibrium analysis. A truly general equilibrium approach requires adding other economic agents (a monetary authority and a government, for example), which we do later in the book.

16. *The Nicomachean Ethics of Aristotle*, translated and introduced by Sir David Ross (Oxford: Oxford University Press, 1954) [c. 350 B.C.], book V, chap. 3; 112–14; retrieved from http://www.constitution.org/ari/ethic_05.htm on 27 January 2010.

17. Aristotle says that "the distribution is made from the common funds of a partnership . . . according to the same ratio which the funds put into the business by the partners bear to one another." Ibid., 114. But this is not necessarily the case. The shares may be and often are the result of investments made (or other compensation for goods and services), but businesses also can and do make "transfer payments" to persons who do not contribute to current production.

18. Ibid., 112–13.

19. As we'll see in part 4 on political economy, it's possible to determine the appropriate formula for political distributive justice with a reasonable degree of objectivity; the main obstacle to its achievement is partisan factions seeking unjustly to prevent it.

20. Augustine, *On Christian Doctrine*, I, 28 (Grand Rapids, MI: Christian Classics Ethereal Library [CCEL]), 396–97. Retrieved on 27 January 2010 from http://www.ccel.org/ccel/augustine/doctrine.xxviii.html.

21. *On Christian Doctrine*, I, 26, ibid. Retrieved from http://www.ccel.org/ccel/augustine/doctrine.xxv.html on 27 January 2010. Note that the chapter divisions differ slightly: Augustine's chapter 26 is here numbered 25.

22. To Simplician—On Various Questions," book 1, question 2, article 16 in *Augustine: Earlier Writings* [A.D. 397], selected and translated with introductions by John H. S. Burleigh (Philadelphia: Westminster Press, 1953), 398.

23. Augustine, *On Free Will*, in *Augustine: Earlier Writings* [A.D. 396–97], edited by John H. S. Burleigh (Philadelphia: Westminster Press, 1953), 131.

24. Philip H. Wicksteed, *The Common Sense of Political Economy* [1910], edited with an introduction by Lionel Robbins (London: Routledge & Kegan Paul, 1933), vol. I, 174.

25. *Ethics* V, 5, retrieved from http://www.constitution.org/ari/ethic_05.htm on 27 January 2010.

26. Augustine, *The City of God*, XI, 16. *Concerning the City of God Against the Pagans*, trans. H. Bettenson, ed. J. O'Meara. (New York: Penguin Classics,

1984) 413–26/427; available online in a different translation at http://www. newadvent.org/fathers/120111.htm, retrieved 27 January 2010.

27. Among modern economists, only Jacob Viner (late in his career) seems correctly to have identified Augustine's main technical contribution to economic theory, distinguishing separate scales of preference for persons (love and justice) and nonpersons (utility), and both of these from the absolute metaphysical scale of being: Augustine deals "simultaneously with three scales of value, relating to order of nature, utility, and justice." Jacob Viner, *The Role of Providence in the Social Order*, 55.

28. "In the case of corporeal things, that is, things we perceive with the bodily senses, when we cannot both perceive them together but must do so severally, it is due to the fact that we make them completely ours by consuming them and making them part of ourselves, like food and drink of which you cannot consume the same part as I do. . . . It is therefore evident that things which we perceive with the bodily senses without causing them to change are by nature . . . common to us both, because they are not converted and changed into something which is our peculiar and almost private property. By 'peculiar and private property' I mean that which belongs to each of us alone, which each of us perceives by himself alone, which is part of the natural being of each of us severally. By common and almost public property, I mean that which is perceived by all sensitive beings without thereby being affected and changed." Augustine, *On Free Will*, viii, 19, in Burleigh, ed., 146. Private goods are sometimes now called "rival" goods. The formulation "diminished by being shared" is from Augustine's *On Christian Doctrine*, I, 1, retrieved from http://www.ccel.org/ccel/augustine/doctrine.iv.ii.i.html on 27 January 2010.

29. Aristotle, *The Politics*, book I, chap. 4 [c. 350 B.C.]. Trans. T. A. Sinclair (Baltimore: Penguin Books, 1962).

30. *Ethics*, book V, chap. 5, retrieved from http://www.constitution.org/ari/ ethic_05.htm on 27 January 2010.

31. Odd Langholm, *Price and Value in the Aristotelian Tradition: A study in scholastic economic sources* (Bergen: Universitetsforlaget, 1979), 61ff.

32. Aristotle analyzed monopoly in *The Politics*, book I, chap. 11 [c. 350 B.C.]. Ed. T. A. Sinclair (Baltimore: Penguin Books, 1962), 47–49.

33. As we will see, the notion that the medieval just price was supposed to be determined by distributive rather than commutative justice, and specifically by social status rather than by market conditions, is an error that can be traced to a late-nineteenth-century British historian. The immediate relevance of "justice in exchange" in a modern economy has been underscored by the economic damage to consumers, investors, and workers that results from abuses of monopoly, insider trading, self-dealing and fraudulent business accounting—all of which violate justice in exchange.

34. Aristotle, *The Politics*, book I, chap. 9; 42. This means that each person's

money, K_{Mi}, must be included among the goods produced, used, exchanged, and donated (or stolen).

35. James A. Weisheipl, OP, "Albert the Great and Medieval Culture," *The Thomist* (October 1980): 481–501.

36. Thomas Aquinas, *Commentary on Aristotle's* Nicomachean Ethics, translated by C. I. Litzinger, OP, foreword by Ralph McInerny (Notre Dame, IN: Dumb Ox Books, 1993), 1271–72; book V, lectures IV-IX, 293–318. The social "distribution function" is described on 294, the "equilibrium conditions" on 294–96 and 297–99, and the "utility function" and analysis of money on 312–15; the "production function" in Thomas Aquinas, *Commentary on Aristotle's* Politics, trans. R. J. Regan (Indianapolis and Cambridge: Hackett Publishing, 2007), 1271–72; book I, chap. 4; 6–7.

37. *Summa theologiae* II-II Q26 A6. Retrieved from http://www.newadvent.org/summa/3026.htm#article6 on 27 January 2010.

38. Commentary on *Ethics* IX, 4, 548.

39. Commentary on *Ethics* IX, 8, 567.

40. Thomas Aquinas, *Summa theologiae* II-II Q77 A2 ad3. In the same article, Aquinas combines utility with scarcity by noting that value will be affected by "the difference in supply"; II-II Q77 A2 ad2. Retrieved from http://www.newadvent.org/summa/3077.htm#article2 on 27 January 2010.

41. Thomas Aquinas, *Commentary on Aristotle's* Nicomachean Ethics, translated by C. I. Litzinger, OP, foreword by Ralph McInerny (Notre Dame, IN: Dumb Ox Books, 1993), 312; book V, lecture IX.

42. Ibid., 1271–72; lecture I; 1–3.

43. Josef Pieper noted that the date is symbolic because the monastery of Monte Cassino was founded the same year: Greek philosophy was subsumed, handed on, and enriched by the Schoolmen; "Scholasticism," *Encyclopedia Britannica*, Fifteenth Edition, 16:352.

44. Aristotle, *Nicomachean Ethics*, VIII, 7, retrieved from http://www.constitution.org/ari/ethic_08.htm on 27 January 2010.

45. Thus Aquinas says, in contrast to Aristotle, "there is a communication between man and God, inasmuch as he communicates His happiness to us," and defines the chief theological virtue of charity as "the friendship of man for God." *Summa theologiae* II-II Q23 A1, retrieved from http://www.newadvent.org/summa/3023.htm#article1 on 27 January 2010.

46. Augustinus Aurelius, "To Simplician—On Various Questions," in *Augustine: Earlier Writings* [c. 397], selected and translated with introductions by John H. S. Burleigh (Philadelphia: Westminster Press, 1953). Simplician had been instrumental in Augustine's conversion and would succeed Augustine's mentor St. Ambrose as bishop of Milan. Among the examples of unequal treatment by God are the twin brothers Jacob and Esau ("Jacob I loved, but Esau I hated"), and God's apparent causing of some men to sin (as when God is said "harden" Pharaoh's heart to continue Israelite slavery: Romans 9:10–29).

47. Augustine, "To Simplician—On Various Questions," ibid., 391, 394.

48. Augustine, "To Simplician—On Various Questions," book 1, question 2, article 16; ibid., 398.

49. "Every creature of God is good. Every man is a creature as man but not as sinner. God is the creator both of the body and of the soul of man. Neither of these is evil, and God hates neither. He hates nothing which he has made. But the soul is more excellent than the body, and God is more excellent than both soul and body, being the maker and fashioner of both. In man he hates nothing but sin. Sin in man is perversity and lack of order, that is, a turning away from the Creator who is more excellent, and a turning to the creatures that are inferior to him. God does not hate Esau the man, but hates Esau the sinner." Augustine, "To Simplician—On Various Questions," book 1, question 2, article 16; ibid., 398.

50. Aquinas's metaphysics of existence would radically recast (and improve) Augustine's philosophical description of the nature of God, both in Himself and in relation to His creatures. Etienne Gilson, *The Unity of Philosophical Experience* [1937] (San Francisco: Ignatius Press, 1999); *Being and Some Philosophers* (Toronto: Pontifical Institute of Medieval Studies, 1952). Aquinas also corrected Augustine's occasional Platonic tendency to describe human nature as "a soul using a body" (the phrase occurs in *On the Moral Behavior of the Catholic Church*, I, 27, 52, cited in Vernon J. Bourke, ed., *The Essential Augustine* [New York: Mentor-Omega Books, 1964], 67) and rejected his argument that man requires special divine illumination for the ordinary use of his natural reason. But all this had the effect of putting Augustine's social, economic, and political theory on a firmer philosophical foundation. On all questions of order—the nature of evil (*Summa theologiae* I-II Q18 A1: http://www.newadvent.org/summa/2018.htm#article1; I-I Q48 A4: http://www.newadvent.org/summa/1048.htm#article4; I-I Q49 A1: http://www.newadvent.org/summa/1048.htm#article4; I-I Q49 A2 ad2: http://www.newadvent.org/summa/1049.htm; I-II Q92 A1: http://www.newadvent.org/summa/2092.htm; I-II Q93 A6: http://www.newadvent.org/summa/2093.htm#article6), God's providence (*Summa theologiae* I-I Q22 A2-A4: http://www.newadvent.org/summa/1022.htm), the ineradicability of natural law from human nature (*Summa theologiae* I-II Q94 A6: http://www.newadvent.org/summa/2094.htm#article6), and the real but imperfect order in human society (*Summa theologiae* I-II Q91 A4: http://www.newadvent.org/summa/2091.htm; *Summa Contra Gentiles* III, XX: University of Notre Dame Press, 1975. [S.C.G.])—Aquinas follows Augustine closely. The distinction between Augustinians and Thomists, often useful in revealed theology, does not apply to economics, because regarding justice in exchange and distributive justice Augustine was already Aristotelian and Aquinas (unlike Aristotle) was thoroughly Augustinian. As F. C. Copleston put it, "What [Aquinas] did was to express Augustinianism in terms of Aristotelian philosophy." F. C. Copleston, *Aquinas* (New York: Penguin, 1991), 33.

51. Odd Langholm, *Price and Value in the Aristotelian Tradition: A study in scholastic economic sources* (Bergen: Universitetsforlaget, 1979), 32.
52. Ibid., 108.
53. *Ethics*, book V, chap. 5, retrieved from http://www.constitution.org/ari/ethic_05.htm on 27 January 2010.
54. Odd Langholm, *Price and Value* (1982 [1979]), 160.
55. Odd Langholm, *Price and Value in the Aristotelian Tradition: A study in scholastic economic sources* (Bergen: Universitetsforlaget, 1982 [1979]); also *Wealth and Money in the Aristotelian Tradition: A Study in Scholastic Economic Sources* (Bergen: Universitetsforlaget, 1983); *The Aristotelian Analysis of Usury* (Bergen: Universitetsforlaget, 1984); *Economics in the Medieval Schools: Wealth, Exchange, Value, Money and Usury According to the Paris Theological Tradition, 1200–1350* (Bergen: Universitetsforlaget, 1992); and *The Merchant in the Confessional: Trade and Price in the Pre-Reformation Panitential Handbooks* (Leiden-Boston: Brill, 2003).
56. Notwithstanding the famous debate about usury, which was essentially a disagreement about economic assumptions, not faith and morals.
57. Odd Langholm, *Price and Value*, 120.
58. William Henry Spiegel, *The Rise of American Economic Thought* (Philadelphia: Chilton Company, 1960), 5–8.
59. Odd Langholm, *Price and Value*, 104–5.
60. Ibid., 153–54.
61. Samuel Pufendorf, *On the Duty of Man and Citizen According to Natural Law*, translated by Michael Silverthorne, edited by James Tully (Cambridge: Cambridge University Press, 1991 [1673]): Personal distribution, 64–67; social and political distribution, 32 and 61–63; utility, 94–96; production of and by human and nonhuman factors, 84–89; society organized around family household, 120–31; justice in exchange or equilibrium equating product values and factor compensation, 31 and 94–95; the Two Great Commandments integrating description and prescription, 11–12.
62. Alexander Hamilton, "The Farmer Refuted" (1775), *The Works of Alexander Hamilton*, vol. I, ed. H. C. Lodge (New York: G. P. Putnam's Sons, 1904). Retrieved from http://oll.libertyfund.org/Home3/Book.php?recordID=0249.01 on 30 June 2009. Hamilton read Pufendorf when loaned by his employer in 1771–72 and again at the King's College (New York; now Columbia University) when Hamilton was enrolled in 1773–74. Broadus Mitchell, *Alexander Hamilton: A Concise Biography* (Oxford: Oxford University Press, 1976), 16, 25.
63. Net investment in human and nonhuman resources occurs when $\Sigma \Delta L_i >$ ΣC_{Li} and $\Sigma \Delta K_i > \Sigma C_{Ki}$. Other things equal, this leads to increased total annual labor and property compensation.
64. In terms of the system of equations outlined above, this amounts to adding the assumptions $\Sigma \Delta L_i = \Sigma C_{Li}$ and $\Sigma \Delta K_i = \Sigma C_{Ki}$. In other words, total investment in people and property equals their total consumption.

65. Angus Maddison, *The World Economy: A Millennial Perspective* (Paris: OECD, 2001), 29.

66. The decline in mortality that was chiefly responsible for the rise in life expectancy was due to improved public hygiene, increasing medical knowledge, and improved nutrition. On the last, see Robert William Fogel, "Economic Growth, Population Theory, and Physiology: The Bearing of Long-Term Processes on the Making of Economic Policy," Nobel lecture, December 9, 1993, available at http://nobelprize.org/nobel_prizes/economics/laureates/1993/fogel-lecture.html, retrieved on 11 July 2007.

67. Schumpeter, *History*, 105.

68. For example, in an influential essay, Milton Friedman has written, "Positive economics is in principle independent of any particular ethical position or normative judgments"—which is true—but then asserts that "fundamental differences in basic values [are] differences about which men can ultimately only fight"—a gratuitous and unsubstantiated denial of Aristotle's reasoned observation that humans are rational animals. (If "men can ultimately only fight" about basic values, they are not just fallible but fundamentally irrational.) Milton Friedman, "The Methodology of Positive Economics," in *Essays in Positive Economics* (Chicago: University of Chicago Press, 1953), 3–43; 4, 5. Friedman appears to confuse scientific and metaphysical truth.

69. Historically, normative economics preceded and stimulated the development of positive economics. "They wrote for many purposes but principally for the instruction of confessors." Schumpeter, *History*, 102. A council of 1215 had greatly stimulated the demand for economic analysis by establishing the (still current) church law that everyone must confess his sins to a parish priest at least once a year. To give proper advice, the priests had to understand what was being confessed.

70. Deuteronomy 6:5 and Leviticus 19:18; Matthew 22:37–39 and Mark 12:29–31.

71. *On Christian Doctrine*, I, 1, retrieved from http://www.ccel.org/ccel/augustine/doctrine.iv.ii.i.html on 27 January 2010.

72. Aquinas draws the terms *benevolence* and *beneficence* from Aristotle's *Ethics*, IX, 5 and IX, 7, but as we'll see in chapter 6, his distinction between the two based on the scarcity of the good willed to the other person is from Augustine. "Perfection for man consists in the love of God and of neighbor," says Aquinas. "For a man to love thus, he must do two things, namely, avoid evil and do good. Certain of the Commandments prescribe good acts, while others forbid evil deeds. And we must know that to avoid evil is in our power; but we are incapable of doing good to everyone. Thus, St. Augustine says that we should love all, but we are not bound to do good to all." "Explanation of the Ten Commandments" in *The Catechetical Instructions of St. Thomas Aquinas* (New York: Joseph F. Wagner, Inc., 1939); reprinted by Sinag-Tala, Manila (no date), 101.

73. *On Christian Doctrine*, I, 28, retrieved on 27 January 2010 from http://www.ccel.org/ccel/augustine/doctrine.xxviii.html.

74. Luke 10:29–37.

75. Armando Sapori, *The Italian Merchant in the Middle Ages*, translated by Patricia Ann Kennen (New York: W. W. Norton & Co., 1970), 21–28.

76. See the excellent discussion in Stephen T. Worland, *Scholasticism and Welfare Economics* (Notre Dame, IN: University of Notre Dame Press, 1967), especially 27–50.

77. Aristotle had grounded the human right to own property in nature: "Getting a living in this self-supporting way is clearly given by nature herself to all her creatures," *Politics*, I, 8, 39. And "we must believe that plants exist for the sake of animals, second, that all other animals exist for the sake of man." Ibid. 40. Augustine and Aquinas agreed with this, but where Aristotle refers to nature for the hierarchy of being (plants, animals, man) that justifies man's ownership of property, Aquinas cites "the divine intellect, which is the source of natural things." Thomas Aquinas, *Commentary on Aristotle's* Politics, translated by Richard J. Regan (Indianapolis: Hackett Publishing Co., 2007), prologue, 1.

78. In his *Commentary on Aristotle's* Politics, Aquinas says we study Aristotle's views on slavery not only so that we can learn about ancient slavery or Aristotle but also that "we can thereby understand matters better than what ancient peoples thought about mastery and slavery." Commentary on book I, chap. 2; ibid., 22.

79. Thomas Aquinas, *On Kingship: To the King of Cyprus*, translated by Gerald B. Phelan, revised with introduction and notes by I. Th. Eschmann (Toronto: Pontifical Institute of Medieval Studies, 1982; first published 1949). As the editor explains in the introduction, it is important to note that *On Kingship*, known in the Middle Ages as *De regno*, is an authentic work of Aquinas, but another, longer "apocryphal compound," called *On the Governance of Rulers* (*De regimine principium*), also circulated under Aquinas's name and was widely used well into the twentieth century. The latter was "welded together by an unknown compiler" in the early fourteenth century using a mangled version of *De regno* and other, inauthentic fragments "profoundly different in scope and even contradictory in doctrine" (ibid., ix-xxvi).

80. *On Kingship* II, 3; 59.

81. Ibid.

82. *On Kingship* II, 3; 60.

83. *On Kingship* I, 1; 9.

84. *On Kingship* II, 3; 65.

85. "Therefore, to establish virtuous living in a multitude three things are necessary. First of all, that the multitude be established in the unity of peace. Second, that the multitude thus united in the bond of peace, be directed to acting well. For just as a man can do nothing well unless unity within his members be presupposed, so a multitude of men of men lacking the unity of peace will be hindered from virtuous action by the fact that it is fighting against itself. In the

third place, it is necessary that there be at hand a sufficient supply of the things required for proper living, procured by the ruler's efforts." Ibid., 65.

86. "While property up to a point should be held in common, the general principle should be private ownership." *Politics* II, 5; Sinclair, ed., 63. Aquinas appropriates Aristotle's argument, adding that "possessions be private as to ownership, but common as to their use." Thomas Aquinas, *Commentary on Aristotle's* Politics (2007 [1271–72]), trans. R. J. Regan, book 2, lesson 6.

87. Aristotle pointed out the first two general advantages of private property over Plato's proposed communal ownership of all property: greater social peace and productivity. "If the responsibility for looking after property is distributed over many individuals, this will not lead to mutual recriminations; on the contrary, with every man busy with his own, there will be increased production all round." Aristotle, *Politics* II, 5; Sinclair, ed., 63. Aquinas added the third, greater order resulting from the efficient use of specialized knowledge: peace ("a more peaceful state is ensured to man if each one is contented with his own"), productivity ("every man is more careful to procure what is for himself alone than that which is common to many or all"), and order ("human affairs are conducted in more orderly fashion if each man is charged with taking care of some particular thing himself, whereas there would be confusion if everyone had to look after any one thing indeterminately"). *Summa theologiae* II-II Q66 A2, retrieved from http://www.newadvent.org/summa/3066.htm#article2 on 27 January 2010.

88. *On Kingship*, 57. Some of these functions are public goods and some quasi-public goods, a distinction made below.

89. "Now according to the natural order established by Divine Providence, inferior things are ordained for the purpose of succoring man's needs by their means. Wherefore the division and appropriation of things, which are based on human law, do not preclude the fact that man's needs have to be remedied by these very things." And "whatever a man has in super-abundance is owed, of natural right, to the poor for their sustenance." *Summa theologiae*, II-II Q66 A7; retrieved from http://www.newadvent.org/summa/3066.htm#article7 on 27 January 2010.

90. "Since, however, there are many who are in need, while it is impossible for all to be succored by means of the same thing, each one is entrusted with the stewardship of his own things, so that out of them he may come to the aid of those who are in need." Ibid.

91. "Still, trade must not be entirely kept out of a city, since one cannot easily find any place so overflowing with the necessaries of life as not to need some commodities from other parts. Also, when there is an overabundance of some commodities in one place, these goods would serve no purpose if they could not be carried elsewhere by professional traders. Consequently, the perfect city will make a moderate use of merchants." Aquinas, *On Kingship*, 75.

92. "Now the relations of one man with another are twofold: some are effected under the guidance of those in authority; others are effected by the will of pri-

vate individuals," wrote Aquinas. "And since whatever is subject to the power of an individual can be disposed of according to his will, hence it is that the decision of matters between one man and another, and the punishment of evildoers, depend on the direction of those in authority, to whom men are subject. On the other hand, the power of private persons is exercised over the things they possess: and consequently their dealings with one another, as regards such things, depend on their own will, for instance in buying, selling, giving, and so forth." *Summa theologiae* I-II Q105 A2; retrieved on 27 January 2010 from http://www.newadvent.org/summa/2105.htm.

93. Besides the works of Dempsey and de Roover cited in the previous chapter, see also Raymond de Roover, "The Concept of the Just Price: Theory and Economic Policy," *Journal of Economic History* 18 (December 1958): 418–34; and Stephen T. Worland, "Justum Pretium: One More Round in an 'Endless Series,'" *History of Political Economy* 9 (Winter 1977): 504–21.

94. Aristotle lived about as close to the first coinage of money in Greece as we are to the American Revolution. Coinage was introduced in Lydia in the seventh century B.C. and in Greece in the sixth, only about 150 years before Plato and Aristotle analyzed the nature of money.

95. *Ethics* V, 5, Ross, ed., 120; retrieved from http://www.constitution.org/ari/ethic_05.htm on 27 January 2010.

96. Thomas Aquinas, *Commentary on Aristotle's* Nicomachean Ethics, V, v, Lecture IX, §987, "Money," 314.

97. Government borrowing is advantageous if it finances investment in government-owned assets, as long as the advantage of investment exceeds the cost of borrowing. But the debt's repayment with interest will still require taxation.

98. A typical example is Todd G. Buchholz, *New Ideas From Dead Economists: An Introduction to Modern Economic Thought*, Revised Edition (New York: Penguin Putnam, 1999), 5–6.

99. John A. Ryan, *A Living Wage: Its Ethical and Economic Aspects* (London: Macmillan, 1906); *Distributive Justice: The Right and Wrong of Our Present Distribution of Wealth* (New York: Macmillan, 1916).

100. Stephen T. Worland, *Scholasticism and Welfare Economics* (Notre Dame, IN: University of Notre Dame Press, 1967), 290n.

101. Henry Sumner Maine, *Ancient Law: Its Connection with the Early History of Society, and Its Relation to Modern Ideas*, Third American from fifth London Edition (New York: Henry Holt and Company, 1888 [1861]).

102. Thomas Aquinas, *Summa theologiae*, II-II, Q77; Sir W. J. Ashley, *An Introduction to English Economic History and Theory* (London: Longmans, Green and Co., 1923 [1888]), vol. I, 138.

103. Ashley [1888], vol. I, 146.

104. Thomas Aquinas, *Summa theologiae*, II-II, Q77 A1 ad1, retrieved on 27 January 2010 from http://www.newadvent.org/summa/3077.htm#article1.

105. Thomas Aquinas, *Summa theologiae*, II-II, Q77 A4 ad2. (Dempsey's translation, Bernard W. Dempsey, "Just Price in a Functional Economy," *American Economic Review* 25:3 (September 1935): 471–86; 481.

106. Thomas Aquinas, *Summa theologiae* II-II Q77 A4; retrieved on 27 January 2010 from http://www.newadvent.org/summa/3077.htm#article4.

107. Pictures may be found in Konrad Kunze, *Himmel in Stein: Das Freiburger Mánster* (Herder, Freiburg, 1980), 109–10.

108. David D. Friedman, "In defense of Thomas Aquinas and the just price," *History of Political Economy* 12 (Summer 1980): 234–42.

109. "[J]ust as the king ought to be subject to the divine government administered by the office of the priesthood, so he ought to preside over all human offices, and regulate them by the rule of his government." *On Kingship* I, 15. "[T]he ministry of this kingdom [of Our Lord Jesus Christ] has been entrusted not to earthly kings but to priests, and most of all to the chief priest, the successor of St. Peter, the Vicar of Christ, the Roman Pontiff." *On Kingship* I, 14.

110. "It is . . . the duty of the sovereign . . . to ensure that the pure and sincere Christian doctrine flourishes in the state, and that the public schools teach dogmas consistent with the purpose of states." Samuel Pufendorf, *On the Duty of Man and Citizen*, book II, chap. 11, 4.

111. Kevin Seamus Hasson, *The Right to Be Wrong: Ending the Culture War Over Religion in America* (Encounter Books, 2005).

112. James Madison, *Federalist* No. 10, in George W. Carey, *The Federalist* (The Gideon Edition), edited with an Introduction, Reader's Guide, Constitutional Cross-reference, Index, and Glossary by George W. Carey and James McClellan (Indianapolis: Liberty Fund, 2001), 43. Accessed from http://oll.libertyfund.org/title/788/108577/2273715 on 11 September 2009.

113. "As long as the reason of man continues fallible . . . he is at liberty to exercise it . . . and the connection subsists between his reason and his self-love . . . , his opinions and his passions will have a reciprocal influence on each other." James Madison, *Federalist* No. 10, ibid.

114. James Madison, *Federalist* No. 51, ibid., 270. Accessed from http://oll.libertyfund.org/title/788/108659/2274491 on 11 September 2009.

115. James Madison, "Property," *The Papers of James Madison* 14 (March 29, 1792): 266–68. Edited by William T. Hutchinson et al. (Chicago and London: University of Chicago Press, 1962–77), vols. 1–10; (Charlottesville: University Press of Virginia, 1977–), vol. 11. Available at http://press-pubs.uchicago.edu/founders/print_documents/v1ch16s23.html (emphasis in original).

116. F. Pringsheim, "The Unique Character of Classical Roman Law," *Journal of Roman Studies* 34:1 & 2 (1944): 60–64.

117. Among true public goods, for which government is instituted, Hamilton listed in *Federalist* No. 31 "the duties of superintending the national defence, and of securing the public peace against foreign or domestic violence" (ibid., 151). Accessed from http://oll.libertyfund.org/title/788/108619/2274086 on

11 September 2009. In *Federalist* No. 34 he added also what might be called "quasi-public goods," which benefit many but not all classes of citizens equally: "the encouragement of agriculture and manufactures." Such public and quasi-public goods "will comprehend almost all the objects of state expenditure. "Alexander Hamilton, *Federalist* No. 34, ibid., 165. Accessed from http://oll.libertyfund.org/title/788/108625/2274123 on 11 September 2009.
118. "Slavery is founded in the selfishness of man's nature—opposition to it, in his love of justice. These principles are an eternal antagonism. . . . [R]epeal the [D]eclaration of [I]ndependence—repeal all past history, you still can not repeal human nature." Abraham Lincoln, Speech at Peoria, Illinois, October 16, 1854. *Collected Works of Abraham Lincoln*, vol. 2: 271, ed. Roy P. Basler (1953). The significance of this passage is noted in Lewis E. Lehrman, *Lincoln at Peoria: The Turning Point* (Mechanicsburg, PA: Stackpole, 2008), 218.
119. This principle is "[s]o plain that no one, high or low, ever does mistake it, except in a plainly selfish way; for although volume upon volume is written to prove slavery a very good thing, we never hear of the man who wishes to take the good of it, by being a slave himself." Fragment on slavery [April 1, 1854?] according to Lincoln's secretaries, but possibly from 1858 or 1859, according to the editors of the *Collected Works*.
120. The sources for this table are listed in endnote 1 in this chapter.

Chapter 3

1. Schumpeter, *History*, 184.
2. Ian Simpson Ross, *The Life of Adam Smith* (Oxford: Clarendon Press, 1995), 53–54.
3. Samuel Pufendorf, *On the Duty of Man and Citizen According to Natural Law*, trans. Michael Silverthorne, ed. James Tully (Cambridge: Cambridge University Press, 1991 [1673]). Carmichael's annotated version, from which Hutcheson taught Adam Smith, is contained in Gershom Carmichael, *Natural Rights on the Threshold of the Scottish Enlightenment: The Writings of Gershom Carmichael*, ed. James Moore and Michael Silverthorne (Indianapolis: Liberty Fund, 2002). Accessed from http://oll.libertyfund.org/title/1707 on 14 September 2009.
4. Angus Maddison, *The World Economy: A Millennial Perspective* (2001), Table B-13.
5. Adam Smith, *Lectures on Rhetoric and Belles Lettres* [hereafter *LRBL*], ed. J. C. Bryce, vol. 4 of the Glasgow Edition of the Works and Correspondence of Adam Smith (Indianapolis: Liberty Fund, 1985 [1762]). Lecture XXIVth. Accessed from http://oll.libertyfund.org/title/202/55538/918007 on 30 November 2009. Smith's audience understood that this was what he was attempting. As one former student summarized: "His Theory of Moral Sentiments founded on sympathy, a very ingenious attempt to account for the principal phenomena in the moral world from this one general principle, like that of gravity in the natural

world." Adam Smith, *The Theory of Moral Sentiments* [hereafter *TMS*], ed. D. D. Raphael and A. L. Macfie, vol. I of the Glasgow Edition of the Works and Correspondence of Adam Smith (Indianapolis: Liberty Fund, 1982 [1759]), 3. Accessed from http://oll.libertyfund.org/title/192/200027/3301044 on 21 August 2009. See also Norriss S. Hetherington, "Isaac Newton's Influence on Adam Smith's Natural Laws in Economics," *Journal of the History of Ideas* 44:3 (July–September 1983): 495–505. Though it was generally agreed that Smith's attempt was ingenious—it involved redefining sympathy from the usual sense of compassion to the ability to imagine and judge the feelings of others—it was not generally agreed that Smith had succeeded. "I conceive this meaning of the word Sympathy is altogether new & that if one had not a hypothes[is] to serve by it he would never have dreamed that it is Sympathy that makes us blush for the impudence and rudeness of another," remarked Thomas Reid, who succeeded Smith as professor of moral philosophy at Glasgow. J. C. Stewart-Robertson and D. F. Norton, "Thomas Reid on Adam Smith's Theory of Morals," *Journal of the History of Ideas* 45 (1984): 314. Smith's conception of humans as a-religious social atoms would have a decisive influence on the French Revolution's effort to eradicate all "mediating" social institutions—above all the Christian church and its clergy—as mortal threats to individual liberty. Thomas C. Kohler, "The Notion of Solidarity and the Secret History of American Labor Law," April 1, 2006, Boston College Law School, Boston College Law School Faculty Papers, Paper 137, 10–26, available at http://lsr.nellco.org/bc/bclsfp/papers/137, retrieved 11 July 2007; also published in *Buffalo Law Review* 53:3 (2005): 883–924. The American Founders chose instead to encourage the proliferation of such institutions, as described by Alexis de Tocqueville in 1 *Democracy in America* 300–314, Phillips Bradley, ed., Random House, New York, 1990 [1835].

6. As the editors of Smith's *Theory of Moral Sentiments* observe, "Stoic philosophy is the primary influence on Smith's ethical thought. It also fundamentally affects his economic theory"; "Stoicism never lost its hold over Smith's mind"; Smith, *TMS* (1976 [1759]), Raphael and Macfie, eds., 5, 6. Accessed from http://oll.libertyfund.org/title/192/200027/3301053 on 14 September 2009. The sixth and final edition of *TMS* (1790) begins with an advertisement featuring its expanded explication of "that famous sect"; ibid., 3, http://www.econlib.org/library/Smith/smMS0.html; accessed 15 September 2009; Emma Rothschild's contrary opinion about the significance of Smith's Stoicism (in "Adam Smith and the Invisible Hand," *American Economic Review* 84:2 [May 1994]: 319–22, subsequently expanded in *Economic Sentiments: Adam Smith, Condorcet, and the Enlightenment* [Cambridge, MA: Harvard University Press, 2001]) often ignores the plain sense of Smith's writing and contemporary accounts. This follows the pattern Jacob Viner had noted among professors of economics and of ethics: "If perchance Adam Smith is a hero to them, they follow one or the other of two available methods of dealing with the religious ingredients of Smith's thought. They either put on mental blinders, which hide from their

sight these aberrations in Smith's thought, or they treat them as merely traditional and in Smith's day fashionable ornaments to what is essentially naturalistic and rational analysis, especially where economic matters and the *Wealth of Nations* are in question" (Jacob Viner, "The Invisible Hand and Economic Man," in *The Role of Providence in the Social Order*, 55–85; 81–82). By the time he wrote the *Wealth of Nations*, Smith was openly hostile to the Christian faith in which he had been baptized. In a letter dated August 14, 1776, which he caused to be published, Smith wrote: "Poor David Hume is dying very fast, but with great chearfulness and good humour and with more real resignation to the necessary course of things, than any Whining Christian ever dyed with pretended resignation to the Will of God." Smith, *TMS*, Raphael and Macfie, eds. (1976 [1759]), 19. Accessed from http://oll.libertyfund.org/title/192/200035/3301093 on 14 September 2009. Moreover, Smith's opinion was recognized by those who knew him well. James Boswell recorded that "it was strange to me to find my old Professor in London, a professed infidel with a bag wig" (Ross, *The Life of Adam Smith*, 251).

7. "[E]verything we behold carries in itself the internal evidence that it did not make itself. . . . and it is the conviction arising from this evidence, that carries us on, as it were, by necessity, to the belief of a first cause eternally existing, of a nature totally different to any material existence we know of, and by the power of which all things exist, and this first cause man calls God." Thomas Paine, *The Age of Reason*, in Thomas Paine, *Collected Writings* (The Library of America, 1955), 688. Though I have been unable to trace Paine's arrival at this argument, it is the third and most decisive of the five rational proofs for the existence of God summarized by Thomas Aquinas: "The third way is taken from possibility and necessity, and runs thus. We find in nature things that are possible to be and not to be. . . . [I]f at one time nothing was in existence, it would have been impossible for anything to have begun to exist; and thus even now nothing would be in existence—which is absurd. . . . . Therefore we cannot but postulate the existence of some being having of itself its own necessity, and not receiving it from another, but rather causing in others their necessity. This all men speak of as God." Thomas Aquinas, *Summa theologiae*, I A2, (1981 [1265–1272]). Accessed from http://www.newadvent.org/summa/1002.htm, 26 September 2009.

8. In Stoic philosophy, as Smith put it in an early but posthumously published manuscript, "the whole of Nature" was believed "to be animated by a Universal Deity, to be itself a Divinity, an Animal, . . . whose body was the solid and sensible parts of Nature, and whose soul was that aetherial Fire, which penetrated and actuated the whole." Thus the Stoic god was "the Vital Principle which animated the Universe," "the infinite essence of this almighty Jupiter," while "all inferior intelligences were detached portions of the great one" and "all of which would again, at a fated time, be swallowed up in a like conflagration, again to be re–produced, and again to be redestroyed, and so on without end." Smith,

Essays on Philosophical Subjects. (1982 [1795]), 120, accessed on 19 August 2009 at http://oll.libertyfund.org/title/201/56020/916315.

9. "When by natural principles we are led to advance those ends, which a refined and enlightened reason would recommend to us, we are very apt to impute to that reason, as to their efficient cause, the sentiments and actions by which we advance those ends, and to imagine that to be the wisdom of man, which in reality is the wisdom of God." *TMS*, II.ii.3.5, 87. Accessed from http://oll.libertyfund.org/title/192/200110/3301456 on 19 September 2009.

10. "A wise man never complains of the destiny of Providence," says Smith, "He does not look upon himself as a whole, separated and detached from every other part of nature, to be taken care of by itself and for itself. He regards himself in the light in which he imagines the great genius of human nature, and of the world, regards him. He enters, if I may say so, into the sentiments of that divine Being, and considers himself as an atom, a particle, of an immense and infinite system, which must and ought to be disposed of, according to the conveniency of the whole."*TMS* VII.ii.1.20, Raphael and Macfie, eds., 276. Accessed from http://oll.libertyfund.org/title/192/200171/3301881 on 15 September 2009.

11. "The ancient stoics were of opinion, that as the world was governed by the all-ruling providence of a wise, powerful, and good God, every single event ought to be regarded, as making a necessary part of the plan of the universe, and as tending to promote the general order and happiness of the whole: that the vices and follies of mankind, therefore, made as necessary a part of this plan as their wisdom or their virtue; and by that eternal art which educes good from ill, were made to tend equally to the prosperity and perfection of the great system of nature." Smith, *TMS* I.II.24, Raphael and Macfie, eds., 36, http://www.econlib.org/library/Smith/smMS1.html#I.II.24

12. Smith began as a professor of logic in 1751, took the chair of moral philosophy in 1752, and continued lecturing until early 1764. *TMS*, Introduction, Raphael and Macfie, eds., 5, 23–24. Accessed on 12 February 2010 from http://oll.libertyfund.org/title/192/200027/3301042. According to John Millar, a former student, "In the professorship of Logic, to which Mr. Smith was appointed on his first introduction to this University, he soon saw the necessity of departing widely from the plan that had been followed by his predecessors, and of directing the attention of his pupils to studies of a more interesting and useful nature than the logic and metaphysics of the schools. Accordingly, after exhibiting a general view of the powers of the mind, and explaining so much of the ancient logic as was requisite to gratify curiosity with respect to an artificial method of reasoning which had once occupied the universal attention of the learned, he dedicated all the rest of his time to the delivery of a system of rhetoric and *belles lettres*. . . ." Introduction to *Lectures on Justice, Police, Revenue and Arms delivered in the University of Glasgow by Adam Smith, reported by a student in 1763* (hereafter *LJ[B]*), edited and with an introduction and notes by Edwin Cannan (Oxford: Clarendon Press, 1896 [1763]), xiii. These notes apparently

are based on Smith's lectures in 1763–64 though possibly reedited for sale and dated 1766. Another set of student lecture notes (hereafter *LJA*) was found and published around 1960 and seems to date from 1762–63. Taken together, *LJ(A)*, *LJ(B)*, and *LRBL* represent Smith's final two years' lectures at the university. *LJ(A)* and *LJ(B)* (and an early draft of *Wealth of Nations*) are available at Adam Smith, *Lectures on Jurisprudence*, ed. R. L. Meek, D. D. Raphael, and P. G. Stein, vol. V of the Glasgow Edition of the Works and Correspondence of Adam Smith (Indianapolis: Liberty Fund, 1982 [1762]). Accessed from http://oll.libertyfund.org/title/196 on 12 February 2010.

13. Aristotle, *Rhetoric I, 1*; *The Rhetoric of Aristotle* [335–22 B.C.], translated by Lane Cooper (New York: Appleton-Century-Crofts, 1932), 6.

14. Adam Smith, *LRBL* (1985 [1762]), 62, retrieved from http://oll.libertyfund.org/title/202/55525/917785 on 11 February 2010.

15. The history of the "Adam Smith problem"—scholars' puzzlement over how the same man could have written the *Theory of Moral Sentiments* and *Wealth of Nations*—is summarized in Ingrid Peters-Fransen, "The Canon in the History of the Adam Smith Problem," in *Reflections on the Classical Canon in Economics: Essays in Honor of Samuel Hollander*, ed. Evelyn L. Forget and Sandra Peart (London and New York: Routledge, 2000), 168–84.

16. *TMS* IV.1, 179–87. http://www.econlib.org/library/Smith/smMS4.html; accessed 15 September 2009.

17. *TMS*, IV.I.9, ibid., 183. http://www.econlib.org/library/Smith/smMS4.html#IV.I.9, accessed 15 September 2009.

18. *TMS*, IV.I.10, ibid., 184–85. http://www.econlib.org/library/Smith/smMS4.html#IV.I.10 accessed 15 September 2009.

19. Adam Smith, *Wealth of Nations*, IV.ii.9, accessed on 19 September 2009 from http://www.econlib.org/library/Smith/smWN13.html#IV.2.9.

20. Adam Smith, *An Inquiry into the Nature and Causes of the Wealth of Nations* (London: W. Strahan and T. Cadell), 2 vols. Facsimile published by Augustus M. Kelley Publishers, New York (1966 [1776]). The definitive Cannan edition is available online: Adam Smith, *An Inquiry into the Nature and Causes of the Wealth of Nations*, ed. Edwin Cannan (Library of Economics and Liberty, 1904 [1776]). Retrieved 15 April 2009 from http://www.econlib.org/library/Smith/smWN.html. In citations of *Wealth of Nations*, page numbers refer to the first edition, but variations of the text in subsequent editions are noted in the Cannan edition.

21. Schumpeter, *History*, 308.

22. *TMS*, I.i.24, at http://www.econlib.org/library/Smith/smMS1.html; accessed 15 September 2009.

23. Francis Hutcheson, *An Inquiry into the Original of Our Ideas of Beauty and Virtue in Two Treatises*, ed. Wolfgang Leidhold (Indianapolis: Liberty Fund, 2004 [1726]), II.III.1. Accessed on 13 February 2010 from http://oll.libertyfund.org/title/858/65996.

24. David Hume, *A Treatise of Human Nature*, III.ii.5, ed. L. A. Selby-Bigge (Oxford: Clarendon Press, 1965), 517. First Edition (1888 [1739]). *TMS* VII. iii.2.9. Accessed from http://oll.libertyfund.org/title/192/200184/3301992 on 13 February 2010.

25. David Hume, *A Treatise of Human Nature*, II.iii.3, 415.

26. "With regard to . . . the favourite ends of nature, she has constantly . . . not only endowed mankind with an appetite for the end which she proposes, but likewise with an appetite for the means by which alone this end can be brought about, for their own sakes, and independent of their tendency to produce it" (i.e., utility). *TMS* II.i.5.10n, http://www.econlib.org/library/Smith/smMS2. html#n2.

27. Smith's development of his ideas on the "division of labour" beginning near the end of his Glasgow period is recounted in Ronald L. Meek and Andrew S. Skinner, "The Development of Adam Smith's Ideas on the Division of Labour," *Economic Journal* 83:332 (Dec. 1973): 1094–116. A comparison of *LJ(A)* in 1762–63 and *LJ(B)* in 1763–64 is complicated by the fact that "LJ(A) . . . stops short about two-thirds of the way through the [relevant] 'police' section of Smith's lectures, whereas LJ(B) continues right through to the end of the course" (*LJ* Introduction, paragraph 73; accessed from http://oll.libertyfund. org/title/196/55550/919704 on 12 February 2010); but "it is perhaps significant that there is no trace in LJ(A) of the statement in LJ(B) that 'labour, not money, is the true measure of value.'" (*LJ* Introduction, paragraph 127; accessed from http://oll.libertyfund.org/title/196/55550/919758 on 12 February 2010).

28. *Wealth of Nations*, vol. I (1966 [1776]), 17; *Wealth of Nations*, I.2.2, retrieved from http://www.econlib.org/library/Smith/smWN1.html#I.2.2 on 30 November 2010.

29. *LJ(B)*, 169. Accessed from http://oll.libertyfund.org/title/196/55650/920606 on 12 February 2010.

30. Adam Smith, *TMS* II.ii.iii.2. Accessed from http://oll.libertyfund.org/ title/192/200110 on 17 October 2009.

31. Eliminating the distribution function (equation [1.1] in the previous chapter) altogether would make Smith's system logically incomplete. Smith's categorical statement appears instead to add the restriction $D_{ii}/\Sigma D_{ij} = 1$, collapsing the equation

(1.1) $C_{Ki}+C_{Li} = Y_i D_{ii}/\Sigma D_{ij}$ [final distribution function], to:

(1.1b) $C_{Ki}+C_{Li} = Y_i$.

This would mean that no one shared any income with anyone else. The logic of the system would require, for example, that every child beget and rear itself.

32. Smith, *Wealth of Nations*, Introduction; vol. I (1966 [1776]), 2. Accessed from http://www.econlib.org/library/Smith/smWN1.html#I.I.4 on 15 September 2009.

33. In a fascinating book (published two years after this one was submitted for publication), Deirdre McCloskey renames the seven Scholastic virtues the

"bourgeois virtues" and erroneously includes Smith in a "septet, Plato, Aristotle, Cicero, Aquinas, and at the very end, before Kant, Adam Smith," who supposedly "built on each other's thought a great engine of analysis." Deirdre N. McCloskey, *The Bourgeois Virtues: Ethics for an Age of Commerce*, (Chicago: University of Chicago Press, 2006), 313. McCloskey asserts, "A bourgeois version of the virtues deriving ultimately from Aristotle + Augustine = Aquinas is also called liberalism. The bourgeois moment is Smith, whom I have claimed as something like a secular Aquinian . . ." (500). This thesis ignores the testimony of Smith himself, presented in this chapter, that he was rejecting Christianity and Scholastic philosophy in favor of Stoicism. McCloskey does qualify the thesis to concede, "Adam Smith, a late writer in the tradition, stands four-square on five of them—trimmed, as I said, of faith and hope" (373); and notes that Smith's "master virtue" is neither charity nor prudence but Stoic "self-command" (306–7), which Smith had accurately described as motivated ultimately by "self-applause" (Adam Smith, *The Theory of Moral Sentiments*, IV. I. 23; accessed from http://oll.libertyfund.org/title/192/200139/3301669 on 13 February 2010.) After an excellent explanation of the failure of neoclassical economics to reduce love to utility (108–16), McCloskey ultimately follows Smith by omitting Augustine's theory that personal love is always expressed by a gift, and, like sociologist Marcel Mauss, chooses instead "to think of the gift, too, as a sort of exchange" (310).

34. A highly significant fragment from Smith's university lectures predating the *Theory of Moral Sentiments* survives to reveal his early and consistent reduction of all justice to justice in exchange alone, omitting distributive justice. The fragment is discussed by Raphael and Macfie in appendix II of *TMS* (382–401; accessed from http://oll.libertyfund.org/title/192/200192/3302081 on 16 September 2009); but is summarized succinctly by Ross: "The lecture fragment indicates [erroneously] that 'doing good according to the most perfect propriety' is known 'in the Schools,' i.e., in the medieval Scholastic tradition thought of as descending from Aristotle, as 'distributive justice.' *TMS* at VII.ii.I.10 shows how Smith had qualified this bald view. He added a footnote, citing the *Nicomachean Ethics* (5.2), to make clear that the 'distributive justice of Aristotle is somewhat different . . . [consisting] of the distribution of rewards from the public stock of the community.' In the fragment, Smith expresses the view that commutative justice can 'alone properly be called Justice,' by which he means the negative form of not harming a neighbour in person, estate, or reputation; and he holds this position throughout his career." Ross, *The Life of Adam Smith*, 119.

35. "To speak properly, commutative justice, is the justice, of a contractor. . . . And distributive justice, the justice of an arbitrator; that is to say, the act of defining what is just." Thomas Hobbes, *Leviathan: or the Matter, Forme and Power of a Commonwealth Ecclesiastical and Civil*, edited by Michael Oakeshott with an introduction by Richard S. Peters (New York and London: Collier Books, 1962 [1651]), 117–18.

36. Smith, *Wealth of Nations* IV, Introduction, vol. II (1966 [1776]), 1. Accessed from http://www.econlib.org/library/Smith/smWN12.html#IV.I.1 on 12 February 2010.

37. Smith, *Wealth of Nations* I, IV; vol. I (1966 [1776]), 34. Accessed from http://www.econlib.org/library/Smith/smWN1.html#I.4.13 on 12 February 2010.

38. "A man then has the natural price of his labour, when it is sufficient to maintain him during the time of labour, to defray the expenses of education, and to compensate the risk of not living long enough, and of not succeeding in the business. When a man has this, there is sufficient encouragement to the labourer, and the commodity will be cultivated in proportion to the demand." *LJ(B)*, 176. Accessed from http://oll.libertyfund.org/title/196/55650/920616 on 12 February 2010.

39. Ibid., 177. Accessed on 12 February 2010 from http://oll.libertyfund.org/title/196/55650/920617, http://oll.libertyfund.org/title/196/55650/920618, and http://oll.libertyfund.org/title/196/55650/920619.

40. Ibid., 178.

41. "These qualities of utility, beauty and scarcity, are the original foundation of the high price of those metals, or of the greater quantity of other goods for which they can everywhere be exchanged." *Wealth of Nations* I. XI; I, 215. Accessed from http://www.econlib.org/library/Smith/smWN5.html#I.11.83 on 13 February 2010.

42. Cannan, Editor's Introduction, *LJ(B)*, xxvii. "The Successes and Failures of Professor Smith," *Journal of Political Economy* 84 (1976). Reprinted in George J. Stigler, *The Economist as Preacher and Other Essays* (Chicago: University of Chicago Press, 1982), 154.

43. Smith, *Wealth of Nations* I, V; vol. I (1966 [1776]), 35. Accessed from http://www.econlib.org/library/Smith/smWN2.html#I.5.1 on 13 February 2010.

44. Ibid., 36. Accessed from http://www.econlib.org/library/Smith/smWN2.html#I.5.2 on 13 February 2010.

45. Ibid., 39. Accessed from http://www.econlib.org/library/Smith/smWN2.html#I.5.7 on 13 February 2010.

46. Thus replacing (1.3a) and (1.3b) with
(1.3 c) $\Delta K = f_1(L_i)$, and
(1.3d) $\Delta L_i = f_1(L_i)$,
ignoring "nonhuman capital" K_i.

47. This amounts to dividing nonhuman capital K into land (K_T) and reproducible capital (K_R). But assuming that both K_R and K_T can be produced with labor L alone amounts to replacing equations (1.3a) and (1.3b) with
(1.3e) $\Delta K_{Ri} = f_1(K_{Ri}, L_i, K_{Ti})$ and
(1.3f $\Delta L_i = f_2(L_i)$ and
(1.3g) $\Delta K_{Ti} = f_3(L_i)$.
Thus any version of Smith's production function is always a linear function of labor alone, exactly as in his imaginary "rude state of society" in which he

supposed there was only one factor, labor. The same result could be reached by assuming that there are in fact three different factors, but that each is infinitely substitutable for the other. This means that a worker could become a useful machine or chemical, or vice versa, whenever necessary.

48. Smith, *Wealth of Nations* I, VI; vol. I (1966 [1776]), 56. Accessed on 13 February 2010 from http://www.econlib.org/library/Smith/smWN2.html#I.6.1.

49. *LJ(B)*, 223. Accessed from http://oll.libertyfund.org/title/196/55650/920693 on 13 February 2010.

50. *LJ(B)*, 169–70. Accessed from http://oll.libertyfund.org/title/196 /55650/920615 on 13 February 2010; *LJ(A)*, March 30, 1763. Accessed from http://oll.libertyfund.org/title/196/55633/920200 on 13 February 2010; and *Wealth of Nations* I, II; vol. 1 (1966 [1776]), 18. Accessed from http://www. econlib.org/library/Smith/smWN1.html#I.2.3 on 13 February 2010.

51. Smith, *Wealth of Nations* II, I; vol. I (1966 [1776]], 335; (1981 [1776]). Accessed on 13 February 2010 from http://www.econlib.org/library/Smith/ smWN6.html#II.1.17.

52. "As soon as the land of any society has all become private property, the landlords, like all other men, love to reap where they never sowed, and demand a rent even for its natural produce. The wood of the forest, the grass of the field, and all the natural fruits of the earth, which, when the land was in common, cost the labourer only the trouble of gathering them, come, even to him, to have an additional price fixed upon them." *Wealth of Nations* I.VI, vol. I, 59. Accessed from http://www.econlib.org/library/Smith/smWN2.html#I.6.8 on 13 February 2010.

53. At least, not while using the same procedures.

54. *LJ(B)*, 178. Accessed from http://oll.libertyfund.org/title/196/55650/920624 on 13 February 2010.

55. Ross, *The Life of Adam Smith*, 116. For a description of Mair's synthesis of market prices and factor compensation, see Odd Langholm, *Price and Value in the Aristotelian Tradition*, 157–59.

56. Smith, *Wealth of Nations* I, VI; vol. 1, 56. Accessed from http://www.econlib.org/library/Smith/smWN2.html#I.6.5 on 14 February 2010.

57. Ibid., 57–58. Accessed from http://www.econlib.org/library/Smith/ smWN2.html#I.6.5.

58. Ibid., 63. Accessed from http://www.econlib.org/library/Smith/smWN2. html#I.6.17 on 14 February 2010.

59. Ibid., 60. Accessed from http://www.econlib.org/library/Smith/smWN2. html#I.6.8 on 14 February 2010.

60. David Ricardo, *On the Principles of Political Economy and Taxation*, Third Edition (London: John Murray, 1821); First Edition (1817).

61. Ricardo and the other classical economists routinely equated human capital L_n with population n, another assumption restricting the production function: (3i) $\Delta L_n = f(\Delta n)$.

This meant that each person's intangible human capital (such as education, skills, and health) is constant. The combination of (3h) and (3i) meant that per capita income could never permanently rise.

62. Richard Cantillon, *Essai sur la Nature du Commerce en Général* [c. 1730], edited with an English translation by Henry Higgs (New York: Augustus M. Kelley, 1964), 83.

63. John Stuart Mill, *Principles of Political Economy, With Some of Their Applications to Social Philosophy* (London: Longmans Green & Co., 1911 [1848]), 291.

64. Ibid.

65. For example, $\delta\Sigma K_i/\delta\Sigma L_i = w\Sigma L_i/P_{Ki}\Sigma K_i$ and $\delta\Sigma K_i/\delta\Sigma K_i = r\Sigma K_i/P_K\Sigma K_i$.

66. Odd Langholm, *Price and Value in the Aristotelian tradition: A study in scholastic economic sources* (Bergen: Universiteitsforlaget, 1979), 72ff.

67. Étienne Bonnot, Abbé de Condillac, *Le Commerce et le Gouvernement considérés relativement l'un à l'autre, À Amsterdam, et se trouve à Paris* (Chez Jombert & Cellot, 1776).

68. Richard Whately, *Introductory Lectures on Political Economy*, Second Edition (1832). Reprints of Economic Classics (New York: Augustus M. Kelley, 1966), 253.

69. Jean-Baptiste Say, "Critical Notes on the Wealth of Nations" [1789–1802] in *On the Wealth of Nations: Contemporary Responses to Adam Smith*, edited and introduced by Ian S. Ross (Bristol: Thoemmes Press, 1998), 188–202. Also, *Traité d'économie politique, ou simple exposition de la manière dont se forment, se distribuent, et se consomment les richesses* (Paris: Deterville, 1803); published in the United States as *A Treatise on Political Economy*, trans. C. R. Pinsep, ed. Clement C. Biddle (Philadelphia: Lippincott, Grambo & Co., 1855); and R. R. Palmer, *J.-B. Say: An Economist in Troubled Times* (Princeton: Princeton University Press, 1997).

70. John Stuart Mill, *Principles of Political Economy, With Some of Their Applications to Social Philosophy* (London: Longmans Green & Co., 1911 [1848]), 28.

71. Although differential calculus, which makes it possible to advance systematically from the theory of "utility and scarcity" to marginal utility, had been developed to the point of usefulness in the seventeenth century, neither the Scholastics nor dissident classical economists like Say, Senior, and Whately possessed the notion of marginal utility. But at least one contemporary of Smith, Daniel Bernoulli (1700–82), had applied it to economic reasoning in 1738: Daniel Bernoulli, "Exposition of a New Theory on the Measurement of Risk," *Econometrica* 22 (1954 [1738]), 23–36. Several French and German writers did so during the period of classical economics, including Arsène Jules Etienne Dupuit (1804–16) and Antoine Augustin Cournot (1801–77), both in France, and Johann Heinrich von Thuenen (1780–1850) and Hermann Heinrich Gossen (1810–58), both in Germany. But their contributions were entirely ignored (until being rediscovered after 1870, when the "Marginalist Revolution" had already begun), because the theory of utility was widely supposed to have been

refuted by Smith. A good survey of contributions to the theory of utility during the classical and neoclassical periods can be found at http://cepa.newschool. edu/het/essays/margrev/phases.htm, accessed 25 August 2009.

72. John Stuart Mill, *Principles*, 123.

73. Karl Marx, *Critique of Political Economy*, 1859; http://www.marxists.org/ archive/marx/works/1859/critique-pol-economy/ch01.htm, accessed 1 May 2006.

74. Adam Smith, *Wealth of Nations* IV, 9, 51; http://www.econlib.org/library/ Smith/smWN19.html#IV.9.51. While including education in the third category, Smith disagrees with Aquinas about what should be taught. (Smith disparages metaphysics and any religious instruction involving an afterlife.)

75. Adam Smith, *Wealth of Nations* IV, II; vol. 2 (1976 [1776]), 44; http://www. econlib.org/library/Smith/smWN13.html#IV.2.24.

76. Discussing Britain's Navigation Acts, which protected British commercial shipping and sailors, Smith concludes, "By diminishing the number of sellers, therefore, we necessarily diminish the number of buyers, and are thus likely not only to buy foreign goods dearer, but to sell our own cheaper, than if there were perfect freedom of trade. As defence, however, is of much more importance than opulence, the act of navigation is, perhaps, the wisest of all the commercial regulations of England." Ibid., 46; http://www.econlib.org/library/Smith/ smWN13.html#IV.2.30.

77. "To expect, indeed, that the freedom of trade should ever be entirely restored in Great Britain, is as absurd as to expect that an Oceana or Utopea should ever be established in it. Not only the prejudices of the public, but what is much more unconquerable, the private interests of many individuals irresistibly oppose it." Ibid., 54; http://www.econlib.org/library/Smith/smWN13.html#IV.2.43.

78. "There may be good policy in retaliations of this kind, when there is a probability that they will procure the repeal of the high duties or prohibitions complained of." Ibid., 46–47; http://www.econlib.org/library/Smith/smWN13. html#IV.2.39.

79. "The second case, in which it will generally be advantageous to lay some burden upon foreign for the encouragement of domestic industry is, when some tax is imposed at home upon the produce of the latter." Ibid., 51; http://www. econlib.org/library/Smith/smWN13.html#IV.2.31.

80. Smith, *Wealth of Nations*, book II, chap. 5; http://www.econlib.org/library/ Smith/smWN9.html#II.5.21.

81. *Works of Alexander Hamilton*, vol. 1, ed. Henry Cabot Lodge, Federal Edition (New York: G. P. Putnam's Sons, 1904) at http://oll.libertyfund.org/ Home3/Book.php?recordID=0249.01.

82. First, "Not only the wealth, but the independence and security of a Country, appear to be materially connected with the prosperity of manufactures." Second, economic policy must also take into account the country's stage of economic development. Defense apart, free trade was in Hamilton's view ordinarily

advantageous if a country had either no or a highly developed manufacturing capacity. But "[b]etween the recent establishments of one country and the long matured establishments of another country, a competition on equal terms . . . is in most cases impracticable . . . without the extraordinary aid and protection of government." In such cases, Hamilton argued, protective manufacturing tariffs combined with domestic "bounties" (producer subsidies) "are productive, when rightly applied," and "particularly in the infancy of new enterprises indispensable." Finally, "Mutual wants constitute one of the strongest links of political connection, and the extent of these bears a natural proportion to the diversity in the means of mutual supply." *Works of Alexander Hamilton*, vol. 4, available at http://oll.libertyfund.org/Home3/HTML-voice.php?recordID=0249.04; accessed 19 April 2007.

83. Mill, *Principles* (1911 [1848]), 556.

84. Friedrich List, *The National System of Political Economy*, first published 1841 but first translated by Sampson S. Lloyd, 1885 (London: Longmans Green & Co., 1909); available at http://www.econlib.org/library/YPDBooks/List/lstNPE.html.

85. Mill, *Principles* (1911 [1848]), 100.

86. V. I. Lenin, "The Three Sources and Three Component Parts of Marxism," *Prosveshcheniye* 3 (March 1913). Reprinted in *Lenin Collected Works*, vol. 19 (Moscow, USSR: Progress Publishers, 1977), 21–28. Accessed 18 April 2006, http://www.marxists.org/archive/lenin/works/1913/marx01.htm.

87. Karl Marx, *Critique of the Gotha Program*, I.3 (written 1875 but first published in *Die Neue Zeit*, vol. I, no. 18, 1890–91). Retrieved from http://www.marxists.org/archive/marx/works/1875/gotha/ch01.htm on 14 February 2010.

88. Karl Marx, *Capital: A Critique of Political Economy*, vol, I, 1867; First English Edition. (Moscow: Progress Publishers, 1887). Retrieved on 15 February 2010 from Marx/Engels Internet Archive (marxists.org) 1995, 1999; http://www.marxists.org/archive/marx/works/1867-c1/index.htm. However, the succinct English translation of this passage is from Henri Chambre, "Marxism," *The New Encyclopedia Brittanica Macropedia*, vol. 11, Fifteenth Edition (Chicago, 1974), 555.

89. "Capital, therefore, it not only, as Adam Smith says, the command over labor. It is essentially the command over unpaid labor." Marx, *Capital*, vol. I, chap. 18; retrieved on 15 February 2010 from http://www.marxists.org/archive/marx/works/1867-c1/ch18.htm.

90. V. I. Lenin.

91. "It is highly significant that A[dam] Smith found it impossible to do what [his teacher] Hutcheson had done as a matter of course, namely, to produce a complete system of moral philosophy and social science at one throw." Schumpeter, *History*, 142. Smith abandoned his plan, promised in the *Theory of Moral Sentiments*, of writing a treatise on jurisprudence and government, as well as planned treatises on science and art.

Chapter 4

1. David Hume, *A Treatise of Human Nature, Reprinted from the Original Edition in Three Volumes*, ed. L. A. Selby-Bigge (Oxford: Oxford University Press, 1888 [1739]), 415.

2. *Auguste Comte and Positivism: The Essential Writings, with a New Introduction and Postscript by the Editor*, ed. Gertrud Lenzer (New Brunswick and London: Transaction Publishers, 1998); *The Positive Philosophy of Auguste Comte*, Harriet Martineau (Trübner, 1875); August Comte, *A General View of Positivism*, translated by J. H. Bridget (London: G. Routledge, 1908); Mary Pickering, *Auguste Comte, An Intellectual Biography, Volume I*, (Cambridge: Cambridge University Press, 1993).

3. Comte had been a student and for several years secretary to the French socialist philosopher Saint-Simon (Claude Henri de Rouvroy, Comte de Saint-Simon [1760–1825]); "August Comte," *Encyclopedia of World Biography*, 2004, at www.encyclopedia.com, retrieved 22 August 2008.

4. Auguste Comte, *The Catechism of Positive Religion, or, Summary Exposition of the Universal Religion*, trans. Richard Congreve (London: John Chapman, 1858 [1852]), 160, 315. As the agnostic Thomas H. Huxley wrote in 1869, "Comte's ideal . . . is Catholic organization without Catholic doctrine, or, in other words, Catholicism minus Christianity," *Fortnightly Review* (February 1869): 141–42; cited in Mary Pickering, *Auguste Comte: An Intellectual Biography*, (Cambridge: Cambridge University Press, 1993), 14.

5. Hume argued that humans "are nothing but a bundle or collection of different perceptions, which succeed each other with an inconceivable rapidity." David Hume, *Treatise of Human Nature*, I, iv, 6; ibid., 252. Comte similarly described reason as a kind of instinct, "a faculty that is, by its nature, common to all animal life . . . Thus the famous Scholastic definition of man as a *reasonable animal* offers a real no-meaning, since no animal, especially in the higher parts of the zoological scale, could live without being to a certain extent reasonable, in proportion to the complexity of its organism." August Comte, *Cours de Philosophie Positive* I.6, *Auguste Comte and Positivism: The Essential Writings, with a new introduction and postscript by the editor*, ed. Gertrud Lenzer (New Brunswick and London: Transaction Publishers, 1998), 187. I treated the relation of Comte and Weber to neoclassical economics in a couple of book reviews: John D. Mueller, "Review of 'Calculated Futures: Theology, Ethics, and Economics,'" *The Journal of Markets and Morality*, vol. 12, no. 1, spring 2009, http://www.acton.org/publications/mandm/jmm_review_12.php# and http://www.eppc.org/publications/pubID.3939/pub_detail.asp, 14 September 2009; John D. Mueller, "Economics Deconstructed," Review of *The Dismal Science: How Thinking Like an Economist Undermines Community*, by Stephen A. Marglin, *The Family in America*, vol. 24, no. 1, winter 2010, http://www.familyinamerica.org/index.php?rid=11&cat_id=6. James W. Ceaser applied

a similar analysis to Comte's influence on modern American politics in "The Roots of Obama Worship: Auguste Comte's *Religion of Humanity* finds a 21st-century savior," *The Weekly Standard,* January 25, 2010, vol. 15, no. 18, http://www.weeklystandard.com/articles/roots-obama-worship.

6. Philip Wicksteed, "The Marxian Theory of Value," To-Day, vol. II, New Series (October 1884): 388–409; reprinted in *The Common Sense of Political Economy,* Vol. II, 705–33.

7. Karl Marx, *Capital: A Critical Analysis of Capitalist Production,* edited by Friedrich Engels, translated from the third German edition by Samuel Moore and Edward Aveling (New York: International Publishers, 1967 [1867], 76.

8. Wicksteed, 716.

9. Ibid.

10. Ibid., 718.

11. Herford, 208.

12. William Stanley Jevons, *The Theory of Political Economy* (London: Macmillan, 1871); Carl Menger, *Principles of Economics* [*Grundsätze der Volkswirtschaftslehre*] (1871); Leon Walras, *Elements of Pure Economics, or the Theory of Social Wealth* [*Éléments d'économie politique pure, ou théorie de la richesse sociale*] (1874).

13. As George Stigler incorrectly suggested in his 1950 essay on the subject: George J. Stigler, "The Development of Utility Theory—I," *Journal of Political Economy* 58:4 (August 1950): 307–27, 308–11. This essay was continued in "The Development of Utility Theory—II," *Journal of Political Economy* 58:5 (October 1950): 373–96.

14. *An Essay on the Nature and Significance of Economic Science,* Second Edition (London: Macmillan, 1935), 16.

15. The main new tool was the "indifference curve," which traces all the combinations of different goods that a person values equally, and thus to which he or she is "indifferent." A "family" of indifference curves can express the person's order of preferences without requiring the use of an absolute unit of utility. This technique originated with Francis Ysidro Edgeworth (1845–1926), who like Jevons conceived utility in the Benthamite sense: F. Y. Edgeworth, *Mathematical Psychics: an Essay on the Application of Mathematics to the Moral Sciences* (London: Kegan Paul, 1881). But the method was recognized and adopted by others as a useful way to describe ordinal utility without making those questionable claims. We will use it in explaining personal economy.

16. John D. Mueller, "The Stork Theory of Economics: Why Economists Want Moms on the Payroll," *Family Policy,* vol. 14, no. 1 (January-February 2001). Available at http://www.eppc.org/publications/pubID.2265/pub_detail.asp.

17. Theodore W. Schultz, "Investment in Human Capital," *American Economic Review,* vol. LI, no. 1 (March 1961): 1–17, 6.

18. Ibid., 1.

19. Ibid., 3.

20. "Particularly in developed economies but perhaps in most, there is suffi-cient investment in education, training, informal learning, health and just plain child-rearing that the earnings unrelated to investment in human capital are a small part of the total. Indeed, in the developmental approaches to child-rear-ing, all the earnings of a person are ultimately attributed to different kinds of investment made in him." Gary S. Becker, *Human Capital*, Third Edition (Chi-cago: University of Chicago Press, 1994), 111; First Edition (New York: Columbia University Press for the National Bureau of Economic Research, 1964). Yet, sur-prisingly, Becker's theory begins by assuming that humans reproduce asexually (see discussion of domestic economy below in this chapter).

21. John W. Kendrick, assisted by Yvonne Lethem and Jennifer Rowley, *The Formation and Stocks of Total Capital* (New York: National Bureau of Economic Research, 1976); updated in John W. Kendrick, "Total Capital and Economic Growth," *Atlantic Economic Journal*, vol. 22, no. 1 (March 1994): 1–18, 16.

22. "We might as reasonably dispute whether it is the upper or the under blade of a pair of scissor that cuts a piece of paper, as whether value is governed by utility or cost of production." Alfred Marshall, *Principles of Economics: An Intro-ductory Volume*, book five, chap. three, "Equilibrium of Normal Demand and Supply" (London: Macmillan, 1920 [First Edition, 1890]).

23. To summarize: The neoclassical economists restored the utility function (equation [2] in chapter 2 on "Scholastic Economics" above). They restored the two-factor production function (3a) and (3b). But until about 1960, they interpreted both human and nonhuman capital as being limited to tangible factors. The neoclassical economists followed Adam Smith in ignoring the dis-tribution function in theory, but in practice they have assumed that everyone is purely selfish, thus adding the restrictive assumption $D_{ij}/\Sigma D_{ij} = 1$. As with Adam Smith, this special assumption collapses equation (1) into:

(1b) $C_{Ki} + C_{Li} = Y_i$.

It also means of course that there are no personal gifts, crimes, common goods, or distributive justice:

(6a) $T_i = 0$.

24. Philip H. Wicksteed, *The Common Sense of Political Economy*, edited with an introduction by Lionel Robbins (London: Routledge & Kegan Paul, 1933 [1910]).

25. "'Many lines converge to make me see that Augustine must come next, or soon, in any course of study,' he wrote in 1911, while still deep in the Aris-totle-Aquinas sequence. But . . . this larger plan remained in abeyance." C. H. Herford, *Philip Henry Wicksteed: His Life and Work*, in *Collected Works of Philip Henry Wicksteed*, edited and introduced by Ian Steedman, vol. 5; 299. Wicksteed is best known among modern economists for his contribution to the "theory of marginal productivity," which is essentially an updating of Aristotle's "justice in exchange" (*Ethics* V, v), describing how workers and property owners are compensated for their contributions to the value of products.

26. Wicksteed, *Common Sense*, 160.

27. By restricting the scope of economics in this way, Wicksteed was following the lead of Nassau Senior, who had defined wealth as "all those things, and those things only, which are transferable, are limited in supply, and are directly or indirectly productive of pleasure or preventive of pain; or, to use an equivalent expression, which are susceptible of exchange" Nassau Senior, *Political Economy*, 2.2.

28. "The utility of all these arts and sciences,—I speak both of those of amusement and curiosity,—the value which they possess, is exactly in proportion to the pleasure they yield. Every other species of preeminence which may be attempted to be established among them is altogether fanciful. Prejudice apart, the game of push-pin is of equal value with the arts and sciences of music and poetry. If the game of push-pin furnish more pleasure, it is more valuable than either." Jeremy Bentham, *The Rationale of Reward*, book 3, chap. 1.

29. Arthur Cecil Pigou, *The Economics of Welfare*, Fourth Edition (London: Macmillan, 1932). *Chapter I: INTRODUCTORY*. Accessed from http://oll.libertyfund.org/title/1410/31974/1468902 on 31 August 2009.

30. Arthur Cecil Pigou, *The Economics of Welfare*, Fourth Edition (London: Macmillan, 1932). II, IX, 10. Accessed from http://oll.libertyfund.org/title/1410/31990 on 31 August 2009.

31. An equilibrium from which it is impossible by redistributing resources to move to another that everyone would prefer is known as "Pareto-optimal," after Vilfredo Pareto (1848–1923), a leader of the Lausanne school whose insights were central to the new welfare economics: *Manual of Political Economy*, trans. Ann Stranquist Schwier and Alfred Nye Page (New York: Macmillan, 1971 [first Italian edition, 1906]).

32. Paul A. Samuelson, "A Pure Theory of Public Expenditure," *The Review of Economics and Statistics* 36:4 (November 1954): 387–89. Also "A Diagrammatic Exposition of a Theory of Public Expediturer," *The Review of Economics and Statistics* 37:4 (November 1955): 350–56. In subsequent debate, further distinctions were drawn between "rival and nonrival," "excludable and nonexcludable" goods, resulting in four possibilities: not only typical private goods like bread, which are rival and excludable; typical public goods like defense and air that are public and nonexcludable; but also nonexcludable common goods like water, fish, and game; and "club goods" like cable television, which are nonrivalrous and excludable. The net result was to confirm the existence and importance of public goods while increasing the room for debate about how best to supply them.

33. "What we have been calling a family is after all but a disguised version of society itself—i.e., a collection of more than one person." Paul A. Samuelson, "Social Indifference Curves," *The Quarterly Journal of Economics*, vol. 70, no. 1 (February 1956): 1–22.

34. Kenneth Arrow, *Social Choice and Individual Values*, Cowles Foundation (New Haven, CT: Yale University, 1951); *Social Choice and Justice, Collected*

Papers of Kenneth J. Arrow, vol. I (Cambridge, MA: Harvard University Press, 1983).

35. Amartya K. Sen, "Social Choice and Justice: A Review Article," *Journal of Economic Literature*, vol. 23, issue 4 (December 1985): 1764–76. This review of Arrow's articles on the subject provides an accessible description of the problem.

36. John Rawls, *A Theory of Justice* (Cambridge, MA: Harvard University Press, 1971); *Justice as Fairness: A Restatement* (Cambridge, MA: Harvard University Press, 2001); Amartya Sen, "The Impossibility of a Paretian Liberal," *Journal of Political Economy*, vol. 78, issue 1 (January-February, 1970): 152–57.

37. Duncan Black, "On the rationale of group decision making," *Journal of Political Economy* 56 (1948): 23–34; James M. Buchanan and Gordon Tullock, *The Calculus of Consent: The Logical Foundations of Constitutional Democracy* (Ann Arbor, MI: University of Michigan Press, 1962); Anthony Downs, "An Economic Theory of Political Action in a Democracy," *Journal of Political Economy* 65:2 (April 1957): 135–50; and *An Economic Theory of Democracy* (New York: Harper, 1957); Mancur Olson, *The Logic of Collective Action* (Cambridge, MA: Harvard University Press, 1965); Gordon Tullock, "Problems of Majority Voting," *Journal of Political Economy* 67 (December 1959): 571–79; and "The Welfare Costs of Tariffs, Monopolies, and Theft," *Western Economic Journal* 5 (June 1967): 224–32.

38. James M. Buchanan, "Public Choice: The Origins and Development of a Research Program," Center for Study of Public Choice (George Mason University, 2003), 1. Available at http://www.gmu.edu/centers/publicchoice/pdf%20 links/Booklet.pdf.

39. James M. Buchanan, "Public Choice: The Origins and Development of a Research Program," 6.

40. "Our analysis was normative in its fundamental individualistic presuppositions but positive in its examination of the workings of alternative rules within those presuppositions," James M. Buchanan, précis of *The calculus of consent*, in *Current Contents* 2 (January 11, 1988): 16; James M. Buchanan, "Public Choice: The Origins and Development of a Research Program," 9.

41. Amartya K. Sen, "Rational Fools: A Critique of the Behavioral Foundations of Economic Theory," *Philosophy and Public Affairs*, vol. 6, issue 4 (summer 1977): 317–44; 335–36. Emphasis in original.

42. A good overview of the parties to the debate over the New Welfare economics can be found at http://cepa.newschool.edu/het/essays/paretian/pareto-social.htm#swf (accessed 27 September 2006).

43. Schumpeter, *History*, 40.

44. Ronald H. Coase, "The Problem of Social Cost," *Journal of Law and Economics* 3 (October 1960): 1–44.

45. Ronald H. Coase, "The Institution Structure of Production," Prize Lecture, the Sveriges Riksbank Prize in Economic Sciences.

46. Ronald H. Coase, "The Nature of the Firm," *Economica* 4 (November

1937): 386–405; reprinted in R. H. Coase, *The Firm, the Market and the Law* (Chicago: University of Chicago Press, 1988), 37–38.

47. This was the point of George J. Stigler's pioneering article "The Economics of Information," *Journal of Political Economy* 69:3: 213–25. Yet it was Stigler who dubbed and promoted Coase theorem II. George J. Stigler, *Memoirs of an Unregulated Economist* (New York: Basic Books, 1988), 75–80.

48. Ejan Mackaay, *History of Law and Economics*, in Bouckaert, Boudewijn and De Geest, Gerrit (eds.), *Encyclopedia of Law and Economics, Volume I. The History and Methodology of Law and Economics* (Cheltenham: Edward Elgar, 2000), 77–80.

49. For example, in discussing "division of labor in households and families," Becker begins by assuming that "a person lives forever, does not age . . . faces a stationary environment," and "[a]11 persons are . . . intrinsically identical." Gary S. Becker, *A Treatise on the Family*, enlarged edition (Cambridge, MA: Harvard University Press, 1991 [1981]), 32. Similarly, in discussing "the equilibrium inequality of income," Becker and Nigel Tomes "assume that children have the same utility function as their parents and are produced without mating, or asexually. A given family then maintains its identity indefinitely, and its fortunes can be followed over as many generations as desired. Asexual reproduction could be replaced without any effect on the analysis by perfect assortative mating: each person, in effect, then mates with his own image." Gary S. Becker and Nigel Tomes, "An Equilibrium Theory of the Distribution of Income and Intergenerational Mobility," *The Journal of Political Economy* 87:6 (December 1979): 1153–89. As reprinted in *A Treatise on the Family* (201–37), "we assume" is softened to the conditional forms, "even if all families were," "all families would maintain," "if each person produced children without mating," and "when each person mates with someone having the same endowment" (ibid., 203), but without altering the analysis.

50. Gary S. Becker, "A Theory of the Allocation of Time," *Economic Journal* 75:299 (September 1965): 493–517. Reprinted in Gary S. Becker, *The Economic Approach to Human Behavior* (Chicago: University of Chicago Press, 1976), 89–114.

51. R. T. Michael and Gary S. Becker, "On the New Theory of Consumer Behavior," *The Swedish Journal of Economics* 75:4 (1973). Reprinted in Gary S. Becker, *The Economic Approach to Human Behavior* (Chicago: University of Chicago Press, 1976), 131–49.

52. Ibid., 145.

53. Ibid.

54. Gary S. Becker, *The Economic Approach to Human Behavior* (Chicago: University of Chicago Press, 1976), 5.

55. Gary S. Becker, *A Treatise on the Family*, enlarged edition (Cambridge, MA: Harvard University Press, 1991 [1981]), ix.

56. Gary S. Becker, *The Economic Approach to Human Behavior*, 8.

57. Gary S. Becker, *Accounting for Tastes* (Cambridge, MA: Harvard University Press, 1996).

58. Gary S. Becker, *The Economic Approach to Human Behavior*. Becker cites Bentham's *An Introduction to the Principles of Morals and Legislation* (New York: Hafner, 1963).

59. (1) $C_{Ki} + C_{Li} = Y_i D_{ii}/\Sigma D_{ij}$ [distribution function], where C_{Ki} and C_{Li} represent the use ("consumption") by i of the services of human capital, L, and nonhuman capital, K; Y_i is total compensation of Person i; D_{ii} is the significance of i to himself, ΣD_{ij} the significance to i of all persons.

60. This would add the restrictive assumption $D_{ii}/\Sigma D_{ij} = 1$, meaning that all income earned or received is distributed to oneself.

61. "Polygamy and Monogamy" in *Treatise on the Family*, 96.

62. George J. Stigler and Gary S. Becker, "De Gustibus Non Est Disputandum," *American Economic Review* 67:2 (1977): 76–90. Reprinted in Gary S. Becker, *Accounting for Tastes* (Cambridge, MA: Harvard University Press, 1996).

63. George J. Stigler, "The Imperial Science," *Memoirs of an Unregulated Economist* (New York: Basic Books, 1988), 191–205. Stigler may have borrowed the term from G. Raditzky and P. Bernholz, *Economic Imperialism: The Economic Method Applied Outside the Field of Economics* (New York, 1987).

64. *Memoirs of an Unregulated Economist*, 203.

65. Ibid., 25.

66. Gary S. Becker, "The Economic Way of Looking at Life," revised version of Nobel lecture, delivered December 9, 1992, in Stockholm, Sweden, originally published in *Journal of Political Economy* 101:3 (June 1993): 385–409. Reprinted in Becker, *Accounting for Tastes*, 139–61.

67. Edward P. Lazear, "Economic Imperialism," Hoover Institution and Graduate School of Business (Stanford University, May 1999), 7.

68. Stigler and Becker, 25.

69. "A Theory of the Allocation of Time," 93–94.

70. R. T. Michael and Gary S. Becker, "On the New Theory of Consumer Behavior," 146.

71. "Within any modeling framework, specifying the potential causal links among and between them and indicators of attainment increases exponentially as the domain of relevant determinant variables expands. While skilled draftsmen may be able to draw the spaghetti-like lines of exogenous effects and causal and simultaneous interdependence in such complex models, the constraints imposed by sample sizes, data reliability, correlation among the variables, and available econometric techniques for causal modeling make estimation of the magnitude of these relationships problematic." Robert Haveman and Barbara Wolfe, "The Determinants of Children's Attainments: A Review of Methods and Findings," *Journal of Economic Literature* XXXIII, No. 4 (December 1995): 1829–78.

72. Gary S. Becker, "A Theory of Social Interactions," *Journal of Political Economy* 82:6 (1974): 1063–91. Reprinted in Gary S. Becker, *The Economic*

Approach to Human Behavior (Chicago: University of Chicago Press, 1976), 253–81, 270n.
73. The argument implicitly reclassifies private goods (which cannot be consumed by more than one person at the same time) as public goods (which can). But if the goods are in fact private, as most consumption goods are, this assumption is empirically false.
74. Shaun Hargreaves Heap et al., *The Theory of Choice: A Critical Guide* (Oxford: Blackwell Publishers, 1992), vii.

Chapter 5

1. Aristotle, *Politics*, book 1, chap. 1, 25.
2. This explains the weakness in Rawls's apparently plausible "maximin" principle (the ground rule that no action shall be permitted unless it improves the lot of the least advantaged person in society), which is the cornerstone of the liberal theory of distributive justice. It is entirely possible to enforce a rule that no action shall *harm* the least advantaged person. And even the positive version would be entirely practicable if the least advantaged person meant literally that—a single person, or a relatively small group. The main flaw in the maximin principle is that like all efforts to reduce justice to political distributive justice alone, it ignores the fact of scarcity. As redistribution continues in pursuit of the principle, the least advantaged person embraces an ever-increasing share of the population. Strictly interpreted, it demands absolute equality of income distribution. This is inherently impossible, because the principle would outlaw most ordinary economic activity long before the stated goal was attained. And a moral precept that is inherently impossible is not morally binding.
3. A. H. Barnett and Bruce Yandle, "The End of the Externality Revolution." *Social Philosophy and Policy*, 26, 130–50.
4. George J. Stigler, *Memoirs of an Unregulated Economist* (New York: Basic Books, 1988), 76–77.
5. Wendell Berry, "A Good Farmer of the Old School," *Home Economics* (San Francisco: North Point Press, 1987), 152–61.
6. Berry, 152–53.
7. Aristotle, *Nicomachean Ethics*, book V, chap, 4, 114–15.
8. Richard E. Mulcahy, SJ, *The Economics of Heinrich Pesch* (Henry Holt, 1952).
9. Ludwig von Mises, *Socialism: An Economic and Sociological Analysis* (Indianapolis: Liberty Fund, 1981), first published 1922 in German; II.15.33. Available at http://www.econlib.org/library/Mises/msS6.html, accessed 13 March 2008.
10. *Heinrich Pesch on Solidarist Economics: Excerpts from the Lehrbuch der Nationaloekonomie*, trans. Rupert J. Ederer (University Press of America, 1998), 141.
11. Ludwig von Mises, *Human Action: A Treatise on Economics*, Fourth Edition, ch. XXIV, 683–84. Available at http://www.mises.org/humanaction/chap-24sec4.asp, last accessed 13 March 2008.

12. Allan C. Carlson, *Third Ways: How Bulgarian Greens, Swedish Housewives, and Beer-Swilling Englishmen Created Family-Centered Economies—and Why They Disappeared* (Wilmington, DE: ISI Books, 2007).

13. Ibid., 180.

14. G. K. Chesterton, *What's Wrong with the World* (New York: Dodd, Mead and Co., 1910), 84; Hilaire Belloc, *The Servile State* (London: T. N. Foulis, 1912). The phrase "three acres and a cow" was popularized in the 1880s by earlier British agrarian reformers, including Jesse Collings (1831–1920). A. W. Ashby, "Jesse Collings," in *Oxford Dictionary of National Biography*, vol. 12 (Oxford: Oxford University Press, 2004), 668–69.

15. Jacques Rueff, *The Age of Inflation*, trans. A. H. Mecus and F. G. Clarke (Chicago: Regnery Gateway, 1964), 58–59.

16. Wilhelm Röpke, *The Moral Foundations of Civil Society* (New Brunswick, NJ: Transaction Publishers, 1996), 133 [First Edition, William Hodge & Co, 1948].

17. I discussed Röpke's theory of distribution and his philosophical differences with Mises and Hayek and some similarities with distributism in John D. Mueller, "What Have We Learned About—and From—Wilhelm Röpke?" Remarks to the Intercollegiate Studies Institute's 2008 National Leadership Conference, Indianapolis, IN, 12 April 2008. Available at http://www.eppc.org/programs/economics/publications/programID.41,pubID.3355/pub_detail.asp.

18. Wilhelm Röpke, *A Humane Economy: The Social Framework of the Free Market* (South Bend, IN: Gateway Editions, 1960), 173.

19. Ibid., 174–75.

20. The only society organically united without its members losing individual freedom is the mystical Body of Christ: As Augustine summarized the theologies of John and Paul, "What the soul is to the human body, the Holy Spirit is to the Body of Christ, the church"; but the scope of this book is limited to reasoning from common human experience. In an unpublished 1958 dissertation discovered recently by Thomas C. Kohler, J. E. S. Hayward perceptively commented that as Christendom abandoned this self-conception, "the vacuum left by the retreat of religion was provisionally occupied by the laic dogma of 'Solidarity.'" Thomas C. Kohler, "The Notion of Solidarity and the Secret History of American Labor Law," Boston College Law School Research Paper no. 92, *Buffalo Law Review* 53:3 (2005): 883–924.

21. Theodore W. Schultz, "Investment in Human Capital," *American Economic Review*, vol. LI, no. 1 (March 1961), 1–17, 6. John W. Kendrick later generalized Schultz's insight into the "total capital hypothesis," which comprehensively describes investments in human and nonhuman capital, both tangible and intangible, and showed that it is empirically true. John W. Kendrick, *The Formation and Stocks of Total Capital* (New York: National Bureau of Economic Research and Columbia University Press, 1976). "Total Capital and Economic Growth," *Atlantic Economic Journal*, vol. 22, no. 1 (March 1994): 1–18.

22. In his extremely readable economics textbook, Röpke had said that when population increases in proportion to production, labor productivity and the standard of living remain unchanged "if we ignore certain incidental influences on production, such as inventions, etc." Wilhelm Röpke, *Economics of the Free Society*, Ninth Edition (Henry Regnery, 1963), 59. First Edition, *Die Lehre von der Wirtschaft* (Vienna: Julius Springer, 1937). But in the Schultz-Kendrick total capital hypothesis, the research that produces such inventions is not incidental but rather the main factor raising living standards over long periods.

23. Wilhelm Emmanuel Freiherr von Ketteler, *Sämtliche Werke und Briefe* [*Complete Writings and Letters*] 1:368–455, ed. Erwin Iserloh (Mainz: von Hase & Koehler Verlag, 1977); translated selections at http://germanhistorydocs.ghi-dc.org/sub_document.cfm?document_id=471, accessed 24 June 2008. Belloc's acceptance of the "status-to-contract" thesis, which was influential on many Distributists, is described in Hilaire Belloc, *The Crisis of Civilization: Being the Matter of a Course of Lectures Delivered at Fordham University, 1937* (Rockford, IL: TAN Books and Publishers, 1992), 113ff.

24. Pope Benedict XVI, *Deus Caritas Est*, Libreria Editrice Vaticana, 25 December 2005, at http://www.vatican.va/holy_father/benedict_xvi/encyclicals/documents/hf_ben-xvi_enc_20051225_deus-caritas-est_en.html. Pope Benedict XVI, *Caritas in Veritate*, Libreria Editrice Vaticana, 29 June 2009, at http://www.vatican.va/holy_father/benedict_xvi/encyclicals/documents/hf_ben-xvi_enc_20090629_caritas-in-veritate_en.html. I noted Benedict's Augustinian inspiration and emphasis on gifts in John D. Mueller, "A Return to Augustinian Economics," *First Things*, 19 August 2009, at http://www.firstthings.com/onthesquare/2009/08/a-return-to-augustinian-economics and http://www.eppc.org/publications/pubID.3910/pub_detail.asp.

25. The Economic Recovery Tax Act of 1981 (ERTA) originated as the Kemp–Roth bill, which was first introduced by Kemp in 1977 with Senator Bill Roth. The Republican congressional prototype for what became the bipartisan Tax Reform Act of 1986 (TRA) was the Kemp–Kasten bill, which Kemp introduced with Senator Bob Kasten in 1984. Other key prototypes were the Bradley–Gephardt bill introduced by Democratic Senator Bill Bradley and Rep. Dick Gephardt, and the 1985 Treasury "Blueprints for Tax Reform."

26. The literature by and about my supply-side colleagues is too voluminous to summarize here, but the first scholarly history of supply-side economics gives an excellent overview: Brian Domitrovic, *Econoclasts: The Rebels Who Sparked the Supply-Side Revolution and Restored American Prosperity* (Wilmington, DE: ISI Books, 2009). Though part of the history is well-known, Domitrovic's book is unusual in giving proper weight to the influence of Jacques Rueff, whose theories we will consider in greater detail in chapters 15 and 16. My own summary of Reagan's economically and politically successful fiscal strategy, Kemp's role in shaping it in the 1970s and 1980s, and its subsequent abandonment by the Republican Party in the 1990s, can be found in part 3 of John D. Muel-

ler, "Infant Industry: The Past and Future of the American System," Lehrman American Studies Center, Princeton University, (17 June 2008): 12–20, available at http://www.eppc.org/publications/pubID.3926/pub_detail.asp; and in chapter 14.

27. Jude Wanniski, *The Way the World Works*, Introduction to Second Edition (Washington, DC: Regnery Gateway, 1998 [1978]), 345.

28. "Supply-side economics it was, though a less catchy title might have been 'neo-classical' for the [supply-siders] . . . understood well that they were basically returning to pre-Keynesian understandings." Robert L. Bartley, Introduction to Third Edition of *The Way the World Works*; ibid., 368.

29. *The Common Sense of Political Economy*, 163.

Chapter 6

1. Philip H. Wicksteed, *The Common Sense of Political Economy*, edited with an introduction by Lionel Robbins (London: Routledge & Kegan Paul, 1933 [1910]).

2. The *Common Sense* begins with a quotation from Goethe, "*Ein jeder lebt's, nicht vielen ist's bekannt*," which means, "Everyone lives it, but not many are aware of it."

3. Ibid., 20.

4. Ibid., 88.

5. In Wicksteed's example, and in this section of the book, we are not inquiring how the milk was produced, whether its production was subsidized, how the milk got from the dairy to the shopkeeper or milkman who sold it to her, whether, how, and how much it was taxed, nor how the mother and her husband acquired the means to purchase it. Such questions will be addressed in "Domestic Economy" and "Political Economy."

6. Even before meeting Friday, Robinson Crusoe spent part of each day in communication with another person: in daily prayer and Scripture reading. "July 4. . . . . This was the first time I could say, in the true sense of the words, that I prayed in all my life; for now I prayed with a sense of my condition, and a true Scripture view of hope, founded on the encouragement of the Word of God; and from this time, I may say, I began to hope that God would hear me. . . ." Daniel Defoe, *Robinson Crusoe* [1719], chap. X, available (with N. C. Wyeth's illustrations) at http://www.deadmentellnotales.com/onlinetexts/robinson/crusoe2.shtml, accessed 19 September 2007.

7. Augustine's economic theory was the byproduct of his concerns as a philosopher and Christian bishop. His economic theory is sprinkled throughout his works but can be found especially in two earlier works, "On Free Will," *De Libero Arbitrio* in *Augustine: Earlier Writings*, edited by John H. S. Burleigh, Library of Christian Classics, Ichthus Edition (Philadelphia: The Westminster Press, 1953), 102–217; and "On Christian Doctrine" (*De doctrina christiana,*

On Christian Doctrine, in Four Books, by St. Augustine, <http://www.ccel.
org/a/augustine/doctrine/doctrine.html>, accessed 9 January 2002), as well as
in his magnum opus, *The City of God*, Augustine, *Concerning the City of God
Against the Pagans*, translated by Henry Bettenson with an introduction by John
O'Meara (New York: Penguin Classics, 1984).

8. It is also important to note that Augustine conceives our judgments about
reality, our choice of persons as ends, and our valuation of the means used by or
for those persons, in mathematical terms. "Do not hesitate to attribute to God as
its maker everything which you see has measure, number and order. When you
take these things completely away nothing at all will remain. Wherever measure,
number and order are found there is perfect form." *On Free Will*, II, xx, 54, in
Augustine: Earlier Writings, edited by John H. S. Burleigh, Library of Christian
Classics, Ichthus Edition, (Philadelphia: The Westminster Press, 1953), 169.

9. *De doctrina christiana*, I, 2. Augustine also notes that some things are signs,
that is, things that are used to indicate something else; but here he is considering things in themselves.

10. This does not mean that objects fade into or out of existence like Lewis
Carroll's Cheshire Cat. As Aquinas noted, any creature's being is the combined
result of its essence or nature (what it is) and its actual existence (whether it
is). Everything therefore either exists or it doesn't, but the degree of its being
is determined by the excellence of its nature. Thomas Aquinas, *On Being and
Essence*, in *Selected Writings of St. Thomas Aquinas*, translated by Robert P.
Goodwin (Englewood Cliffs, NJ: Prentice Hall, 1965), 31–70; also, Etienne
Gilson [1956], *The Christian Philosophy of St. Thomas Aquinas* (Notre Dame,
IN: University of Notre Dame Press, 1994), 59–83.

11. Ibid., 873.

12. *City of God*, XI, 25; 458.

13. Deuteronomy 6:5 and Leviticus 19:18; Matthew 22:37–39.

14. *The Rhetoric of Aristotle*, trans. Lane Cooper (New York: Appleton-Century-
Crofts), 2.4: 102–3.

15. *On Christian Doctrine, in Four Books*, by St. Augustine, <http://www.ccel.
org/a/augustine/doctrine/doctrine.html>. Accessed 9 January 2002.

16. "Reason has a different standard of judgment from that of utility. Reason
judges by the light of truth, and correctly subordinates lesser things to those
that are greater. Utility, guided by experience of convenience, often attributes
a higher value to things which reason convinces us are of lesser rank. Reason
sets a vast difference of value between celestial and terrestrial bodies, but what
carnal man would not prefer that several stars should be wanting in the heavens,
than one shrub should be lacking in his field or one cow from his herd." On Free
Will 17, 180–81.

17. *City of God*, book XI, chap. 16.

18. *An Essay on the Nature and Significance of Economic Science*, Second Edition,
revised and extended (London: Macmillan and Company, 1945 [1933]), 75.

19. *On Christian Doctrine*, I, 1.

20. Ibid.

21. Ibid.

22. *Summa theologiae*, II-II, Q26, a6.

23. The "distribution function" was described in chapter 2 on Scholastic economics, as equation (1) $C_{Ki} + C_{Li} = Y_i D_{ii}/\Sigma D_{ij}$ [distribution function], where C_{Ki} and C_{Li} represent the use ("consumption") by Person i of the services of human capital, L, and nonhuman capital, K; Y_i is total compensation of Person i; D_{ii} is the significance of Person i to himself; ΣD_{ij} and is the significance to i of all persons. For clarity and simplicity we defined

(5) $Y_i = rK_i + wL_i$

meaning that Y_i is the total factor compensation of Person i; and

(6) $Ti = Y_i - Y_i D_{ii}/\Sigma D_{ij}$,

making clear that the difference between Person i's total consumption and total compensation is equal to T_i—(net) personal, domestic, and political "transfer payments" from i to other persons. By "net" I mean that personal gifts made are offset by gifts received, while taxes are treated as political transfers paid and balanced against political transfers received.

24. (2) $U_i = f(C_{Ki}, C_{Li})$ [utility function],

where U_i is the ranking by Person i ("utility") of units of C_{Ki} and C_{Li} the units consumed in use by Person i of the services of nonhuman goods, K, and human capital, L, respectively. In reality, C_{Ki} and C_L are not two goods but two classes of goods consumed: $(K_1, K_2, \ldots, K_n)$ and $(L_1, L_2, \ldots, L_n)$. Ordinarily, $\delta U/\delta C < 0$ ("declining marginal utility": the value of each unit consumed declines as the number of units increases).

25. Economists call this the "budget line" or "budget constraint."

26. Economists call the curve tracing all the different combinations or "bundles" of goods that a purchaser considers to have equal value an "indifference curve." It's like a topographical map that tries to suggest three dimensions on a two-dimensional (flat) surface, by using contour lines that represent the same height above sea level, thus depicting the elevation as well as the location and distance between places. So a set of indifference curves is like a hill rising out of the page but increasing in height as you move away from the origin. All points on a single indifference curve are valued equally, but all points on a curve that is further from the origin are preferred to all the points on a lower indifference curve. The curves are concave, that is, bowed toward the origin, because of the assumption that each good's marginal significance declines as its quantity increases. But the precise shape depends on, because it tries to describe, the preferences of a unique real person.

27. John 15:13.

28. A good introduction to the origins and limitations of the idea of social capital may be found at http://www.socialcapitalgateway.org (last accessed 17 October 2006). The term *social capital* was apparently coined by French sociologist

Pierre Boudrieu, *"Ökonomisches Kapital, kulturelles Kapital, soziales Kapital," in Soziale Ungleichheiten (Soziale Welt, Sonderheft 2)*, edited by Reinhard Kreckel (Goettingen: Otto Schartz & Co., 1983), 183–98; English translation available at http://www.viet-studies.org/Bourdieu_capital.htm, accessed 24 October 2006. The term was developed by James S. Coleman, "Social Capital in the Creation of Human Capital," *American Journal of Sociology* 94 (1988): S93ff; and popularized by Robert D. Putnam, in *Bowling Alone: The Collapse and Revival of American Community* (New York: Simon & Schuster, 2000). Gary Becker assimilated social capital into his "economic approach to human behavior" by positing it as yet another "basic commodity" produced to provide utility, understood as Benthamite pleasure or satisfaction to its consumers, in Gary S. Becker, *Accounting for Tastes* (Cambridge, MA: Harvard University Press, 1996).

29. Tristan Claridge, "Definitions of Social Capital," http://www.gnudung.com/literature/definitions.html, last accessed 17 October 2006.

30. Theodore W. Schultz, "Investment in Human Capital," *American Economic Review* (March 1961): 1–17; 2.

31. As we saw in the discussion of neoclassical economics, welfare economics has admitted since the 1930s, and the theory of the household since the mid-1970s, that the three basic elements of neoclassical economics—production, utility, and equilibrium—cannot fully describe economic behavior, because there is at least one unique equilibrium for every possible distribution of wealth or income. This means that at each level, from a single person to the world economy, the final distribution of wealth or income must be specified or else there will be fewer explanatory equations than variables to be explained. Such specification is the purpose of Augustine's theory of personal distribution and Aristotle's theory of distributive justice.

32. By mentioning roads or other public accommodations, we implicitly introduce the principle of distributive justice, which governs the distribution of common goods and which we will consider later when describing domestic and political economy. But whether the objects given and received are originally acquired by exchange, personal gifts, or domestic or political distributive justice, social graces are essentially little personal gifts.

33. Such gestures might still be social graces even if we should later receive similar gifts from those same persons, but I have chosen the example of unrequited gifts because they are much easier to distinguish from exchanges.

34. Matthew 24:38 and Luke 17:27.

Chapter 7

1. Of course, in both cases, there are other related costs, such as refrigeration for the milk, and maintaining the proper atmosphere and tuning for the piano. The daily cost of the piano may turn out to be less than $1.37 if the piano can

be sold for something at the end of its useful life. If she judges that the family would use a piano for less than its useful life, she may consider renting the piano for a shorter period—usually at a higher daily rate—rather than buying it outright. Finally, alternate uses of the money today always include investing it to increase the future buying power of the money. We'll consider these complications in their proper place.

2. The following four paragraphs are adapted from a study on Social Security reform, John D. Mueller, "Can Financial Assets Beat Social Security? Not in the Real World," Lehrman Bell Mueller Cannon Inc., October 1997, at http://www.eppc.org/docLib/20050916_Mueller13.pdf, accessed 25 May 2006.

3. This insight is usually attributed to Daniel Bernoulli (1738). An interesting but philosophically quirky history of risk theory can be found in Peter L. Bernstein, *Against the Gods: The Remarkable Story of Risk* (New York: John Wiley & Sons, 1996). For a brief and readable but slightly more technical introduction, see "The Measurement of Utility and the Economics of Risk," in Donald N. McCloskey, *The Applied Theory of Price* (New York: Macmillan, 1985), chap. 2.

4. A brief but comprehensive overview of the theory and research in this field can be found in Kenneth R. MacCrimmon and Donald A. Wehrung, *Taking Risks: The Management of Uncertainty* (New York: The Free Press [Macmillan], 1988), 44–50. MacCrimmon and Wehrung's own study includes an experiment like the bet just described (shown for comparison in the graph). The authors describe flaws in the study's design from the point of view of the original purpose (120). Most conservative investors accepted the smallest bet and refused to gamble on the largest, so results of the smallest bet were skewed toward the most risk-averse investors and the largest bet was skewed toward the least risk averse. For the purpose of our discussion, this was fortunate, however, because it suggested three distinct subgroups with different attitudes toward risk, rather than just a single average.

5. The utility functions used in the graph have the advantages of fitting the facts—in controlled experiments as well as in observed investment returns—while being intuitively appealing. Marginal utility declines inversely to Person i's wealth ($W_i = K_i + L_i$) raised to some power (s, $s>0$): $U'(W) = W^{-s}$. Then total utility is $U(W) = (1 - s)^{-1}aW^{1-s} + c$, where a and c are scaling constants. (Since utility is a scale of preference, what matters is greater and less, not the absolute numbers.)

6. Abraham Maslow, *The Psychology of Science: A Reconnaissance* (New York: Harper & Row, 1966), 15–16.

7. David Hume, *A Treatise of Human Nature*, II, III, iii, http://www.gutenberg.org/dirs/etext03/trthn10.txt.

8. "The modern concept of pleasure, happiness, utility, satisfaction and the like includes all human ends, regardless whether the motives of action are moral or immoral, noble or ignoble, altruistic or egotistical." Ludwig von Mises, *Socialism*, II.5.6, available at http://www.econlib.org/library/Mises/msS3.html#Part%20IICh.5, accessed 11 March 2008.

9. "All human action, so far as it is rational, appears as the exchange of one condition for another. Men apply economic goods and personal time and labour in the direction which, under the given circumstances, promises the highest degree of satisfaction, and they forego the satisfaction of lesser needs so as to satisfy more urgent needs. This is the essence of economic activity—the carrying out of acts of exchange." Ibid., II.5.9.

10. "It is true that if an isolated man is 'exchanging' labour and flour for bread within his own house, the considerations he has to take into account are not different from those which would govern his actions if he were to exchange bread for clothes on the market. And it is, therefore, quite correct to regard all economic activity, even the economic activity of isolated man, as exchange." Ibid., II.5.18.

11. Ludwig von Mises, *Socialism*, IV.27.7, available at http://www.econlib.org/library/Mises/msS10.html#Part%20IVCh.29, last accessed 11 March 2008.

12. "Unity of action can exist only when all ultimate values can be brought into a unitary scale of values," Ludwig von Mises, *Socialism*, IV.27.13, available at http://www.econlib.org/library/Mises/msS10.html#Part%20IVCh.29, last accessed 11 March 2008.

13. Ludwig von Mises, *Human Action: A Treatise on Economics*, Fourth Revised Edition (San Francisco: Fox & Wilkes, 1996 [First Edition, 1949]), 1. Available at http://www.mises.org/humanaction/introsec1.asp#p1, accessed 28 March 2008.

14. Kenneth J. Arrow, "Gifts and Exchanges," *Philosophy and Public Affairs*, vol. I, issue 4 (Summer 1972): 343–62; 348. Arrow thanked philosopher Thomas Nagel for the formulation.

15. Gary S. Becker, "An Economic Analysis of Fertility," *Demographic and Economic Change in Developed Countries* (Princeton: Princeton University Press for the National Bureau of Economic Research, 1960). Reprinted in *The Economic Approach to Human Behavior*, 173.

16. Assaf Razin and Efraim Sadka, *Population Economics* (Cambridge, MA: The MIT Press, 1995), 14.

17. Moreover, Becker writes, "Many economists, including myself, have excessively relied on altruism to tie together the interests of family members." Gary S. Becker, "The Economic Way of Looking at Life," revised version of Nobel Lecture, delivered December 9, 1992, in Stockholm, Sweden, originally published in *Journal of Political Economy*, 101, No. 3 (June 1993): 385–409. Reprinted in Becker, *Accounting for Tastes* (Cambridge, MA: Harvard University Press, 1996), 139–61.

18. "Economic theory focuses on people as hedonists who want to maximize pleasure and minimize pain." Charles K. Wilber, "Can a Christian Be an Economist?" http://www.nd.edu/~cwilber/pub/recent/acexrist.html, 7.

19. Lawrence Boland, "On the Futility of Criticizing the Neo-classical Maximization Hypothesis," *American Economic Review* 71:5 (December 1981): 1031–36.

20. Gary S. Becker, "A Theory of Marriage," *Economics of the Family: Marriage, Children, and Human Capital,* edited by Theodore W. Schultz (Chicago: University of Chicago Press, 1975). Reprinted in Gary S. Becker, *The Economic Approach to Human Behavior* (Chicago: University of Chicago Press, 1976), 207.

21. Ibid.

22. Gary S. Becker, "An Economic Analysis of Fertility," *Demographic and Economic Change in Developed Countries* (Princeton: Princeton University Press for the National Bureau of Economic Research, 1960). Reprinted in *The Economic Approach to Human Behavior* (Chicago: University of Chicago Press, 1976), 173.

23. Gary S. Becker, "A Theory of Social Interactions," *Journal of Political Economy* 82:6 (1974): 1063–91. Reprinted in Gary S. Becker, *The Economic Approach to Human Behavior* (Chicago: University of Chicago Press, 1976), 253–81, 264.

24. Gary S. Becker, "A Theory of Social Interactions," *Journal of Political Economy* 82:6 (1974): 1063–91. Reprinted in Gary S. Becker, *The Economic Approach to Human Behavior* (Chicago: University of Chicago Press, 1976), 253–81, 270n.

25. Gary S. Becker, "A Theory of Marriage," *Economics of the Family: Marriage, Children, and Human Capital,* edited by Theodore W. Schultz (Chicago: University of Chicago Press, 1975). Reprinted in Gary S. Becker, *The Economic Approach to Human Behavior* (Chicago: University of Chicago Press, 1976), 236.

26. Gary S. Becker, "Crime and Punishment: An Economic Approach," *Journal of Political Economy* 76:2 (March/April 1968): 169–217. Reprinted in Gary S. Becker, *The Economic Approach to Human Behavior* (Chicago: University of Chicago Press, 1976), 39–85.

27. Ibid., 46.

28. Ibid., 47.

29. This is how Gary Becker describes "caring." Gary S. Becker, "A Theory of Marriage," in *Economics of the Family: Marriage, Children, and Human Capital,* edited by Theodore W. Schultz (Chicago: University of Chicago Press, 1975). Reprinted in Gary S. Becker, *The Economic Approach to Human Behavior* (Chicago: University of Chicago Press, 1976), 205–50; 233f.

30. This analysis removes Paul Samuelson's objection that constant proportions are an inappropriate "shibboleth" because "when we change one or more of those prices, the different members [of a family] will be affected differently." Paul A. Samuelson, "Social Indifference Curves," *The Quarterly Journal of Economics,* vol. 70, no. 1 (February 1956): 1–22, 11. Samuelson's objection applies to the neoclassical but not the neo-Scholastic approach.

31. Indifference-curve analysis would be superfluous, but not false, if a disaster always affected people in proportion to their share of total consumption or use of wealth. Becker makes this special assumption, for example, in "A Theory of Marriage," so he never confronts Samuelson's anticipation of the basic flaw in his analysis.

Chapter 8

1. John J. Donohue III and Steven D. Levitt, "The Impact of Legalized Abortion on Crime," *Quarterly Journal of Economics*, vol. CXVI, issue 2 (May 2001): 379–420 (cited hereafter as *QJE*). Earlier versions had been widely circulated, including "Legalized Abortion and Crime," Stanford Public Law and Legal Theory Working Paper No. 1, June 24, 1999, and "The Impact of Legalized Abortion on Crime," National Bureau of Economic Research, Working Paper No. 8004, Cambridge, MA, November 2000 (hereafter cited as NBER). Levitt further promoted the claim in a book he coauthored with Stephen J. Dubner, *Freakonomics: A Rogue Economist Explores the Hidden Side of Everything* (New York: William Morrow [HarperCollins], 2005), 117–44.

2. Donohue and Levitt, *QJE*, 382–83.

3. Gary S. Becker, "Crime and Punishment: An Economic Approach," *Journal of Political Economy* 76:2 (March/April 1968): 169–217. Reprinted in Gary S. Becker, *The Economic Approach to Human Behavior* (Chicago: University of Chicago Press, 1976), 39–85.

4. Donohue and Levitt, *QJE*, 402. The assumption is often repeated: "There should be no effect of abortion on crime between 1973–1985." Ibid., 401.

5. Donohue and Levitt, *Stanford*, 15 and Figure 4.

6. Donohue and Levitt, *QJE*, 381.

7. "Through a purely mechanical relationship, the 5.4 percent overall postlegalization decline in cohort size . . . translates into a 5.4 percent reduction in homicide. Fertility declines for black women are three times greater than for whites (12 percent compared with 4 percent). Given that homicide rates of black youth are roughly nine times higher than those of white youths, racial differences in the fertility effects of abortion are likely to translate into greater homicide reductions." Donohue and Levitt, *QJE*, 390.

8. Especially worthy of note are John R. Lott Jr. and John Whitley, "Abortion and Crime: Unwanted Children and Out-of-Wedlock Births," Working Paper #254, Program for Studies in Law, Economics, and Public Policy, Yale Law School, May 27, 2001, subsequently published in *Economic Inquiry*, vol. 44, no. 4 (2006). Ted Joyce, "Did Legalized Abortion Lower Crime?" National Bureau of Economic Research Working Paper 8319, May 2001. Christopher L. Foote and Christopher F. Goetz, "Testing Economics Hypotheses with State-Level Data: A Comment on Donohue and Levitt (2001)," Federal Reserve Bank of Boston Working Paper 05–15. Lott and Whitley agree that "abortion may prevent the birth of 'unwanted' children, who would have . . . a higher probability of crime," but rightly point out that Donohue and Levitt ignored research showing that legalized abortion also eroded the socioeconomic environment by making out-of-wedlock births and single motherhood vastly more common (George A. Akerlof, Janet L. Yellen, and Michael L. Katz, "An Analysis of Out-of-Wedlock Childbearing in the United States," *Quarterly Journal of Economics*

[May 1996]: 277–317). Joyce also accepted the Donohue–Levitt theory but found flaws in the Donohue–Levitt methodology, "little evidence to support the claim that legalized abortion caused the reduction in crime," and suggested an epidemic of crack cocaine use as an alternate explanation. Foote and Goetz found that "the actual implementation of [Donohue and Levitt's] statistical test . . . differed from what was described" and that after correcting the error, "evidence for higher per capita criminal propensities among the youths who would have developed, had they not been aborted, vanishes."

9. Donohue and Levitt, *QJE*, 402.

10. C. W. J. Granger and P. Newbold, "Spurious Regressions in Econometrics," *Journal of Econometrics* 2 (1974): 111–20. Spurious relationships are characterized by high "autocorrelation" of residual forecasting errors, which can usually be detected by a statistical test known as the Durbin-Watson (d) statistic. Ideally, d should be close to a value of 2, but autocorrelation is reflected in a low d (e.g., 0.5).

11. Ibid., 117; emphasis in original.

12. Donohue and Levitt, *QJE*, 394.

13. Women and men are arrested in equal numbers only for crimes requiring brains rather than force, such as fraud, embezzlement, and disposing of stolen property.

14. Statistical Abstract of the United States: 2006, Tables 339 and 313.

15. Arrest rates by age and sex from *Sourcebook of Criminal Justice Statistics*, various issues, available at http://www.albany.edu/sourcebook/, last accessed 15 August 2006. Ages of women having abortions from Laurie D. Elam-Evans et al., "Abortion Surveillance—United States, 2000," Centers for Disease Control Surveillance Summary SS12 (November 28, 2003): 1–32, available at http://www.cdc.gov/mmwR/preview/mmwrhtml/ss5212al.htm, last accessed 10 August 2006.

16. Fathers older than the age at which women are typically fertile are about eight years older than the mothers. *Statistical Abstract of the United States: 1998*, 112.

17. This obviously does not apply to a father who is unaware of his child's abortion, but most fathers of aborted children are aware of the fact.

18. The difference is described by each person's "distribution function," as explained in chapters 2 and 6. Each person's use of economic goods is proportional to that person's significance relative to all persons sharing in the distribution:

(1) $C_{Ki} + C_{Li} = Y_i D_{ii}/\Sigma D_{ij}$ [distribution function],

where C_{Ki} and C_{Li} represent the use ("consumption") by Person i of the services of human capital, L, and nonhuman capital, K; Y_i is total compensation of Person i; D_{ii} is the significance of i to himself, ΣD_{ij} the significance to Person i of all persons.

For a purely selfish person, the distributive share $D_{ii}/\Sigma D_{ij}$ is 100 percent;

...

for a person who makes gifts to others, less than 100 percent; for a criminal, more than 100 percent; and for the victim of crime (or abortion), less than zero percent.

19. The TFR corresponding to the "replacement rate" is about 2.1: the average woman must have two children to replace each man and woman, while the extra fraction is necessary to offset the ordinary mortality of women through the end of the childbearing years. The TFR is especially useful for our purposes because it is not affected by changing proportions of women in each age group.

20. This is true also in cases of "cloning" one human being from another: both are, in effect, identical twins with the same biological parents.

21. National Center for Health Statistics, Vital Statistics, reported by Bureau of Justice Statistics (available at http://www.ojp.usdoj.gov/bjs/glance/tables/hmrttab.htm, accessed 16 August 2006).

22. Total fertility rate calculated from U.S. population by single year of age, sex, and race (since 1900, U.S. Census Bureau), age-specific fertility rates (since 1940 from annual *National Vital Statistics Reports* and beginning 1917 from Office of Population Research at Princeton University, available at http://opr.princeton.edu/archive/cpft/).

23. Data on persons arrested, starting in 1932, and admissions to federal and state prisons, starting 1926, are from *Historical Statistics of the United States from Colonial Times to 1970*, part 1, U.S. Department of Commerce, U.S. Government Printing Office, 1975, updated in annual *Statistical Abstract of the United States* (available at http://www.census.gov/compendia/statab/, accessed 23 August 2006) and in Ann L. Pastore and Kathleen Maguire, eds. *Sourcebook of Criminal Justice Statistics* [Online]. Available at http://www.albany.edu/sourcebook/ [22 August 2006].

24. Children on public assistance before 1970 from *Historical Statistics*, part 1, 356; more recent statistics from U.S. Department of Health and Human Services, *Temporary Assistance for Needy Families (TANF), Sixth Annual Report to Congress*, November 2004, available at http://www.acf.hhs.gov/programs/ofa/annualreport6/ar6index.htm, accessed 23 August 2006.

25. The chart is reprinted with permission from Elliott Banfield and the *Claremont Review of Books*, where it appeared in John D. Mueller, "Dismal Science," *Claremont Review of Books* 6:2 (Spring 2006): 47–48.

26. The regression tested is log(homicide rate) = c_1 + c_2 * log(economic fatherhood).

	Coefficient	Standard error	t-statistic	Prob.
c_1	2.480789	0.022910	99.59044	0.0000
c_2	-0.771135	0.031829	-24.22761	0.0000

Adjusted R^2 = 0.903073   D-W = 0.487996   F-statistic = 586.9769   Prob(F-statistic) 0.000000

27. C. W. J. Granger, "Some Properties of Time Series Data and Their Use in Econometric Model Specification," *Journal of Econometrics* 16 (1981): 121–30, 127, 129. A cointegrated pair of data series may have a low Durbin-Watson

(*d*) statistic, but unlike a spurious regression, the two series never drift apart because they are tied in a functional relationship.

28. Ibid., 128.

29. Cointegration can be detected with the Augmented Dickey-Fuller (ADF) test, which tests the likelihood that the two series will ever drift apart. While a "good" regression is one that holds at least 19 times out of 20, the ADF test must exceed 99 cases out of 100.

30. The ADF Test Statistic for the unit root test on the residuals of the regression of economic fatherhood on homicide is -3.752339; the Mackinnon critical value for the hypothesis of a unit root at the 1 percent level is -3.5380. (At the 5 percent level the critical value is -2.9084, and at the 10 percent level the critical value is -2.5915.) Therefore, the series for economic fatherhood and homicide are cointegrated.

31. The homicide rate is relatively high and the suicide rate relatively low in the United States, compared with Japan and some Western European countries, in which the homicide rate is relatively low and the suicide rate relatively high.

32. A general theory of crime in all its forms is beyond my purpose. But I was able to test the explanatory power of several variables most frequently cited in the analysis of homicide, by including them in statistical regressions along with the rate of economic fatherhood: the share of the population aged 15–24 (which is deemed the most crime-prone), the share of the adult male population incarcerated by the criminal justice system (removing opportunity and providing deterrence), the probability that a murder will be followed by the murderer's execution (deterrence), the civilian unemployment rate (economic environment), the share of U.S. children supported by public welfare programs (economic environment), and the rate of legal abortions lagged 16 years (social environment). In every case, economic fatherhood was by far the most significant variable tested. Three of these variables were not statistically significant: the unemployment rate, the share of the population aged 15–24, and the share of all U.S. children on welfare. The other three variables were statistically significant: the share of the adult male population incarcerated, the probability of a murderer's execution, and the abortion rate lagged 16 years. When all the statistically significant variables were included in a single regression on the homicide rate, the results indicated that a 1 percent increase in the rate of economic fatherhood lowers the homicide rate by 0.72 percent; a 1 percent increase in the share of the adult male population in prison reduces the homicide rate by 0.25 percent; a 1 percent increase in the probability of a murderer's execution reduces the murder rate by about 0.029 percent; and a 1 percent increase in the rate of legal abortions 16 years earlier raises the homicide rate by 0.084 percent. The equation was $\log(\text{homicide rate}) = c_1 + c_2*\log(\text{economic fatherhood}) + c_3*\log(\text{share of adult males in prison}) + c_4*\log(\text{probability of murderer's execution}) + c_5*\log(\text{abortion rate lagged 16 years})$. The results for the period 1936–2000 were as follows:

	Coefficient	Standard error	t-statistic	Prob.
c_1	1.702962	0.149331	11.40391	0.0000
c_2	-0.716678	0.043065	-16.64170	0.0000
c_3	-0.250365	0.059984	-4.173842	0.0001
c_4	-0.029457	0.006867	-4.289775	0.0001
c_5	0.083556	0.022365	3.735970	0.0004

Adjusted $R^2 = 0.933842$ D-W= 0.743068   F-statistic=226.8471   Prob(F-statistic) 0.000000

ADF Test Statistic= -5.154528   Mackinnon critical values for hypothesis of unit root:

1% Critical Value –3.5380   5% Critical Value –2.9084   10% Critical Value -2.5915

The ADF test shows that the equation, due to its inclusion of economic fatherhood, is cointegrated with the homicide rate. Similar or stronger relationships (not reported here) were found when using the same variables to explain the overall, violent, and property crime rates, as well as the rate of violent death (the combined homicide and suicide rates) for the same period. The main difference was the relative importance of each explanatory variable. However, periods of at least fifty years were necessary to satisfy the tests for cointegration.

Chapter 9

1. *City of God*, XI, 17; 448.
2. *On Christian Doctrine*, I, 1.
3. *Summa Theologiae*, II-II, Q44, A7.
4. Luke 10:29–37.
5. *Politics*, I, 1.
6. Peter Singer, "Famine, Affluence and Morality," *Philosophy and Public Affairs*, vol. 1 (Spring 1972): 229–43. Reprinted in *Writings on an Ethical Life* (New York: Ecco Press, 2000), 107.
7. Ibid., 115.
8. Peter Singer, "Famine, Affluence and Morality," *Philosophy and Public Affairs*, vol. 1 (Spring 1972): 229–43. Reprinted in *Writings on an Ethical Life* (New York: Ecco Press, 2000), 106.
9. Ibid., 108.
10. *Summa Theologiae*, II-II, Q66, A7.
11. Ibid.
12. Peter Singer, "The Singer Solution to World Poverty," *New York Times Magazine* (September 5, 1999). Reprinted in *Writings on an Ethical Life* (New York: Ecco Press, 2000), 119.
13. "Perfection for man consists in the love of God and of neighbor," Aquinas says. "For a man to love thus, he must do two things, namely, avoid evil and do good. Certain of the commandments [the Third and Fourth] prescribe good acts, while others forbid evil deeds. And we must know that to avoid evil is in our power; but we are incapable of doing good to everyone. Thus, St. Augustine says that we should love all, but we are not bound to do good to all. But among

those to whom we are bound to do good are those in some way united to us." *The Catechetical Instructions of St. Thomas Aquinas*, Joseph F. Wagner, New York City, 1939; The Fourth Commandment.

14. Population Reference Bureau, *2007 World Population Data Sheet*, available at http://www.prb.org/pdf07/07WPDS_Eng.pdf, accessed 23 October 2009.

15. "Gross domestic product, 2007," *World Development Indicators* database, World Bank, Washington, DC, revised 24 April 2009, available at http://www. scribd.com/doc/16386220/World-Bank-World-GDP-2009-PPP.

16. Carmen DeNavas-Walt, Bernadette D. Proctor, and Jessica C. Smith, U.S. Census Bureau, Current Population Reports, P60–235, *Income, Poverty, and Health Insurance Coverage in the United States: 2007*, U.S. Government Printing Office, Washington, DC, Table 1, "Income and Earnings Summary Measures, Selected Characteristics: 2006 and 2007," 7, available at http://www.census. gov/prod/2008pubs/p60–235.pdf.

17. Luke 6:32.

18. John D. Mueller, "The End of Economics, or, Is Utilitarianism Finished?" seminar presentation, James Madison Program in American Ideals and Institutions, Princeton University, 15 April 2002; available at http://www.eppc.org/docLib/20050216_mueller_apr02.pdf, accessed 23 October 2009. The population and income figures in that paper referred to what was then the most recent year of actual data, 1999, but the comparisons were similar to those based on more recent data cited in this text.

19. John D. Mueller, "Dismal Science," *Claremont Review of Books*, vol. VI, no. 2 (Spring 2006): 47–48.

20. George Weigel, *Witness to Hope: The Biography of Pope John Paul II* (HarperCollins, 1999), 136.

21. Matthew 23:3.

Chapter 10

1. Litzinger's translation, from St. Thomas Aquinas, *Commentary on Aristotle's* Nicomachean Ethics, translated by C. I. Litzinger, OP, foreword by Ralph McInerny (Notre Dame, IN: Dumb Ox Books, 1964), 520. I use this translation because the elements of economic theory originated not from the "Greek" but the "Latin Aristotle": Aristotle as known in Latin translation and first interpreted by Albert the Great and especially his student Thomas Aquinas.

2. This would be true even if it were possible for one human person to be "cloned" from another, since no matter how far apart in time they were born, the two would remain identical twins with the same mother and father.

3. *Nicomachean Ethics*, book IX, chap. 4, trans. Litzinger, 547.

4. Aristotle mentions this triple parental benefit in *Nicomachean Ethics*, book VIII, both chapters 11 and 12. W. D. Ross translated the terms in chapter 11 as "existence," "nurture," and "upbringing" (trans. Ross, 211), in chapter 12 as

"being," "nourishment," and "education" (ibid., 214); C. I. Litzinger, chapter 11 as "existence, "rearing," and "instruction" (515), chapter 12 as "existence," "upbringing," and "training" (ibid., 519); Aquinas's paraphrase of chapter 11, "by generation, . . . existence," "by upbringing, . . . rearing," and "instruction" (ibid., 517); in the Introduction, as "generation," "nourishment," and "instruction" (ibid., 2). According to the *American Heritage Dictionary, education* connotes formal academic and *training* non-academic instruction; *teaching* the broadest term for instruction; *rearing* caring-for, which is much broader than *nourishment*; and *upbringing* the combination of rearing and training. The most precise and concise translation into modern American usage would therefore seem to be "being, rearing, and teaching," to which Litzinger's translation of chapter 11 comes closest.

5. *Nicomachean Ethics*, book VIII, chap. 12 (trans. Litzinger), 519.

6. "It was out of the two associations of men and women and master and slaves that the first household arose. And the poet Hesiod rightly said that the first household consists of a wife and an ox for plowing, since the ox is the poor man's slave." *Politics*, book I, chap. 1; 4–5.

7. *Politics*, book I, chap. 2; ibid., 19.

8. "But we should consider natural powers as things have them by nature and not in corrupt forms. And so we should consider those human beings who are both physically and mentally best disposed, those in whom the powers are clearly present. For the body will seem very often to rule over the soul of the diseased and the wicked, since they are disposed wrongly and contrary to nature. *Politics*, book I, chap. 3; ibid., 25.

9. *Politics*, book I, chap. 1; ibid., 4.

10. Aquinas, *Commentary on the Nicomachean Ethics*, Introduction, 2.

11. The one community to which the organic analogy properly applies is the description of the Christian church as the "mystical body of Christ." But since this is a matter of revealed theology, it is beyond the scope of the current book, which is confined to reasoning from sensible and empirically verifiable experience.

12. *Politics*, book I, chap. 3, vi, ed. Sinclair, 188.

13. *City of God*, book XIX, chap. 12–17; 866–79.

14. *City of God*, book XII, chap. 28; ibid., 508.

15. Ibid., 866–67.

16. "The peace of the body, we conclude, is a tempering of the component parts in duly ordered proportion; the peace of the irrational soul is a duly ordered repose in the appetites; the peace of the rational soul is the duly ordered agreement of cognition and action. The peace of body and soul is the duly ordered life and health of a living creature; peace between mortal man and God is an ordered obedience, in faith, in subjection to an everlasting law; peace between men is an ordered agreement of mind with mind; the peace of a home is the ordered agreement among those who live together about giving and obeying orders; the peace of the Heavenly City is a perfectly ordered and perfectly har-

monious fellowship in the enjoyment of God, and a mutual fellowship in God; the peace of the whole universe is the tranquility of order—and order is the arrangement of things equal and unequal in a pattern which assigns to each its proper position." Ibid., 870.

17. Ibid., 874.

18. "The good of marriage throughout all nations and all men stands in the occasion of begetting, and faith of chastity: but so far as it pertains unto the People of God, also in the sanctity of the Sacrament. . . . All these are goods, on account of which marriage is a good: offspring (*proles*), faith (*fides*), sacrament (*sacramentum*)." Augustine of Hippo, "Of the Good of Marriage," (de Bono Conjugali), http://www.newadvent.org/fathers/1309.htm, accessed 2 February 2005.

19. We might also recognize a third productive factor, enterprise. Whose idea was the lemonade stand; who chose the time, location, organization, etc.? We could also begin, as we will later, by distinguishing tangible and intangible forms of capital, between capital consumption and maintenance—as many distinctions as necessary. Since our purpose in this section is basically to understand the nature of production and the relation between a product's price and the compensation of its producers, I will ignore such complications for now and treat profits as if they were a part of property compensation. To avoid fallacies like Smith's "labor theory of value," it is sufficient merely that there be at least two productive factors.

20. G. K. Chesterton, "The Policeman as a Mother," *The New Witness* (November 14, 1919); cited in Alvaro de Silva, G. K. Chesterton on *Men & Women, Children, Sex, Divorce, Marriage & the Family* (Ignatius Press, 1990), 141.

21. Equations beginning with "1" denote the "two-factor, one-good" model, and those beginning with "2" denote the "two-factor, two-good" model. We can typically use the first for the discussion of employment, but the second is necessary for the discussion of fertility. All the actions described are understood to have the dimension of time; for example, consumption, C, should be understood as $\delta C/\delta t$, or additional consumption *per unit of time*—the notation for which is usually omitted in this presentation for simplicity.

22. (1.1) $C_{Qi} = Y_i D_{ii}/\Sigma D_{ij}$ [final distribution function], where C_{Qi} represents the use ("consumption") by Person i of the good Q; Y_i is total compensation of Person i; D_{ii} is the significance of i to himself; ΣD_{ij} is the significance to i of all persons.

(2.1) $C_{Ki} + C_{Li} = Y_i D_{ii}/\Sigma D_{ij}$ [final distribution function], where C_{Ki} and C_{Li} represent the use ("consumption") by Person i of the services of "human capital," L, and "nonhuman capital," K; Y_i is total compensation of Person i; D_{ii} is the significance of Person i to himself; and ΣD_{ij} is the significance to Person i of all persons.

23. For clarity and simplicity, we will define:

(1.5) and (2.5) $Y_i = rK_i + wL_i$,

meaning that Y_i is the total factor compensation of Person i; and
(1.6) and (2.6) $T_i = (1 - Y_i) D_{ij}/\Sigma D_{ij}$.
By substituting (1.6) and (2.6), (1.1) and (2.1) may be restated as
(1.1a) $C_{Qi} = Y_i - T_i$ and
(2.1a) $C_{Ki} + C_{Li} = Y_i - T_i$,
making clear that the difference between Person i's total consumption, C_{Qi} or $C_{Ki} + C_{Li}$, and total compensation, Y_i, is equal to T_i—(net) personal, domestic, and political "transfer payments" from Person i to other persons.
By "net," I mean that personal gifts made are offset by gifts received, while taxes are treated as political transfers paid and balanced against political transfers received. Equations (1.1) and (2.1) are the simplest and most general forms of the final distribution function for an individual person. The refinements necessary to specifically describe gifts within marriage, from parents to children and vice versa, as well as accounting for taxes and government benefits, are considered below.
24. Such personal transfers are described in equations (1.1) and (2.1).
25. In the passage cited at the beginning of this chapter (*Nicomachean Ethics*, 214), Aristotle notes that a household, say, J_1, is created by the marriage of a man, M_1, and a woman, F_1, and that its wealth, W_{J1}, is initially acquired by their "throwing their peculiar gifts into the common stock" of household wealth: $W_{J1} = K_{M1} + K_{F1} + L_{M1} + L_{F1}$. This means that each spouse, M_1 and F_1, starts marriage with an initial personal gift or transfer, $T_{M1:J1}$ and $T_{F1:J1}$, to the new joint family partnership, J_1, consisting of all his or her human and nonhuman wealth:
(1.6a) $T_{M1:J1} = K_{M1} + L_{M1}$.
(1.6b) $T_{F1:J1} = K_{F1} + L_{F1}$.
For the marriage partnership to continue and flourish, the initial gifts must be followed by a series of gifts by which any new income realized separately by each spouse (particularly from "human capital," since it is not alienable) is put into the "common stock":
(1.6c) $T_{M1:J1} = Y_{M1}$, and
(1.6d) $T_{F1:J1} = Y_{F1}$.
according to a new joint family distribution function, D_{J1}. For example, the woman's share in the use of total current family income becomes:
(1.1b) $C_{QF1} = Y_{J1} D_{J1:F1}/\Sigma D_{J1:i}$ and
(2.1b) $C_{KF1} + C_{LFi} = Y_{J1} D_{J1:F1}/\Sigma D_{J1:i}$
A similar formula applies to every other family member—and, in fact, to everyone else in the world, for most of whom the distributive share in the family's resources is zero.
26. For example,
(1.6e) and (2.6e) $T_{J1:M2} = (1 - Y_{J1}) D_{J1:M2}/\Sigma D_{J1:i}$,
which means that the gift or transfer from the parents, J_1, to dependent son, M_2, is determined by his relative significance, $D_{J1:M2}/\Sigma D_{J1:1}$, out of his parents' total distributed income, Y_{J1}.

27. (1.6f) and (2.6f) $T_{M2:J1} = (1 - Y_{M2}) D_{M2:J1}/\Sigma D_{M2:i}$,
which means that the gift or transfer from (now adult) son, M_2, to the parents, J_1, $T_{M2:J1}$, is determined by their relative significance, $D_{M2:J1}/\Sigma D_{M2:i}$, out of all the people among whom the son distributes his income, Y_{M2}.
We note that the son's gift at time t_n yields a quasi-rate of return on the parents' gift to the son at time t_0 equal to $(T_{M2:J1(t0)}/T_{M2:J1(tn)})^{1/n} -1$.
28. For example,
(1.6g and 2.6g) $T_{Li} = (1 - Y_{G1}) D_{G1:i}/\Sigma D_{G1:j}$.
That is, a transfer payment from a government, $G1$, to Person i, T_{Li}, is determined by that person's significance relative to all persons who share in the distribution of such transfers.
29. By including typical taxes and government transfer payments, (1.1) and (2.1) become
(1.1b) and (2.1b), $C_{Qi} = D_{ii}(1 - \tau)[(1-p)wL_i + (1 - \tau)(1 - k)rK_i + T_i]/P_Q D_{ij}$,
where C_{Qi} is Person i's consumption of economic goods (Q), of which the price is P, $T_{G1:i}$ is net government transfer payments received by Person i, τ is the income tax rate, p is the payroll tax rate and k is the tax rate on property income. D_{ii} is the significance of Person i to himself or herself, and ΣD_{ij} is the significance of all persons to Person i, including himself or herself.
For realism and simplicity, we should also redefine Y_i as Person i's disposable (rather than gross) income:
(1.5a) and (2.5a) $y_i = (1 - \tau)[(1 - p)wL_i + (1 -\tau)(1 - k)rK_i + T_i]/P$, thus preserving the essential simplicity of
(1.1) $C_{Qi} = Y_i D_{ii}/\Sigma D_{ij}$ and
(2.1) $C_{Ki} + C_{Li} = Y_i D_{ii}/\Sigma D_{ij}$.
30. Apart from debt service, government outlays are devoted to current consumption of goods and services, investment, and transfer payments, while government cash flow includes tax receipts (which consist, in the United States, chiefly of the personal and corporate income taxes and the payroll tax), borrowing, and creation of fiat money:
(1.7) and (2.7) $C_G + \Delta K_G + T_L + T_K = \tau(w\Sigma L + r\Sigma K) + pw\Sigma L + kr\Sigma K + \Delta B_G + \Sigma K_{GMi}$ [government budget], where C_G is current consumption (including capital consumption) of government goods and services, T_L is government transfer payments to persons, T_K is government subsidies to property owners, τ is the income tax rate (assumed to be equal for labor and property income), p is the payroll tax rate, k is the tax rate levied only on property income, B_G is government debt, and $\Sigma \Delta K_{GMi}$ is the issue of government fiat money. As we will see in the section on political economy, to maximize both fairness and economic efficiency, the sources and uses of government funds should be paired and restricted in this way: government should not be funded by fiat money creation; general consumption of government-provided goods and services should be funded by an income tax falling equally on labor and property income; transfer payments to persons funded by payroll taxes and subsidies to property owners by taxes

on property income; all of which further implies that government borrowing should be confined to funding investment in government-owned assets. That is, $\Sigma\Delta K_{GMi} = 0$; $\Sigma C_{Gi} = \tau(w\Sigma L_i + r\Sigma K_i)$; $\Sigma T_{Li} = pw\Sigma L_i$; and $\Sigma T_{Ki} = kr\Sigma K_i$; implying $\Sigma\Delta B_{Gi} \leq \Sigma\Delta K_G$.

31. As in the case of transfers between parents and children, the implicit rate of return on payroll taxes paid at time t_0, $pwL_{(t0)}$, that fund pay-as-you-go retirement pensions to persons received at time t_n, $T_{L(t=n)}$, is $(T_{L(t=n)}/pwL_{(t=0)})^{1/n} -1$.

32. (1.2) $U_i = f(C_{Qi})$ [utility function],
where U_i ("utility") is the order of preference of Person i for units of his or her own consumption of the class of goods Q, C_{Qi}.

(2.2) $U_i = f(C_{Ki}, C_{Li})$ [utility function],
where U_i is the ranking by Person i ("utility") of units of C_{Ki}, and C_{Li} the units consumed in use by person i of the services of nonhuman goods, K, and "human capital," L, respectively. In reality, C_{Ki} and C_{Li} are not two goods but two classes of goods consumed: $(K_1, K_2, \ldots ,K_n)$ and $(L_1, L_2, \ldots ,L_n)$.

33. $\delta U_i/\delta C_i < 0$.

34. (1.3) $\Delta Q_i = f(K_i, L_i)$ [production function]
That is, Person i's production of Q is a function of his or her "nonhuman" (K_i) and "human capital" (L_i). As we will see, for the market economy as a whole, the two factors are combined in roughly constant proportions: $\Delta\Sigma Q_i = \Sigma K^a \Sigma L^{1-a}$, where a is the share of the total marginal product, $\Sigma\Delta Q_i$, contributed by all "nonhuman capital," ΣK_i, and $1 - a$ is the share contributed by all "human capital," ΣL.

(2.3a) $\Delta K_i = f_1(K_i, L_i)$ [production function for "nonhuman capital," especially a modern business firm];

(2.3b) $\Delta L_i = f_2(K_i, L_i)$, [household production function for "human capital," especially a household],
where ΔK_i is the change in the stock (production) of nonhuman goods, and ΔL_i is the change in the stock of "human capital," owned by Person i.

35. Each child is unique and uniquely related to its biological parents. The "original" production function for the initial human capital endowment (L^*), of a boy, M_2, whose biological father is M_1 and whose biological mother is F_1, may therefore be written:

(2.3g) $L^*_{M2} = f(L_{M1}, L_{F1}, K_i)$.
In other words, though the "nonhuman capital" that is necessary to bring a child into being does not have to belong to its biological parents, the "human capital" does. Once the child is in the world, many other persons, besides its parents, can and do make additions to this initial endowment, as described by the general "production function" for "human capital" (2.3b). Yet, it remains true that, until the child becomes an adult, the bulk of such investments are typically made by or at the direction of the child's biological parents.

36. (1.4) $P_Q\Sigma\Delta Q_i = w\Sigma L_i + r\Sigma K_i$ [equilibrium condition],
where P_Q is the price level (ideally corresponding to the GNP deflator), $\Sigma\Delta Q$ a measure of total output corresponding to real GNP, ΣL_i total hours worked in

the labor market, w labor compensation per unit of L_i, and r the rate of return per unit of "nonhuman capital" K. $w\Sigma L$ is therefore total labor compensation, and $r\Sigma K$ total property compensation.

(2.4) $P_K\Delta K_i + P_L\Delta L_i = rK_i + wL_i$ [equilibrium condition],

where P_K and P_L are the unit prices of K and L, respectively, w is labor compensation per unit of L, r is property compensation per unit of K. P_L is a market price only in a slave-owning society, like ancient Athens or the antebellum American South.

37. For example, $\delta\Sigma Q_i/\delta\Sigma L_i = w\Sigma L_i/P_Q\Sigma Q_i$ and $\delta\Sigma Q_i/\delta\Sigma K_i = r\Sigma K_i/P_Q\Sigma Q_i$.

38. A succinct marshaling of research and data on the incidence of monogamous marriage with bibliography may be found at http://en.wikipedia.org/wiki/Incidence_of_Monogamy (last accessed 26 October 2007). The entry was apparently compiled by Andrey Korotayev, author of *World Religions and Social Evolution of the Old World Oikumene Civilizations: A Cross-Cultural Perspective* (Mellen Press, 2004).

39. George P. Murdock, *Atlas of World Cultures* (Pittsburgh, PA: University of Pittsburgh Press, 1981); Douglas R. White, "Rethinking polygyny: Co-wives, codes, and cultural systems," *Current Anthropology* 29: 568–72; White-Veit EhnoAtlas, available at http://eclectic.ss.uci.edu/~drwhite/ethnoatlas/nindex.html, last accessed 2 November 2007.

40. United Nations, *World Fertility Report 2003* (New York, 2004), last accessed 27 October 2007 at http://www.un.org/esa/population/publications/worldfertility/World_Fertility_Report.htm.

41. One reason suggested by sociologists is that to attract multiple wives, a would-be polygamous husband must achieve sufficient wealth and status, and most men fail to do so. G. K. Chesterton gave a more commonsense, less materialistic answer: most men have difficulty handling one wife, and few women stand for polygamy, in *any* culture: "Variability is one of the virtues of a woman. It avoids the crude requirement of polygamy. So long as you have one good wife you are sure to have a spiritual harem." G. K. Chesterton, "The Glory of Grey," in *Alarms and Discursions* (London, 1910).

42. Angus Maddison, *The World Economy: A Millennial Perspective* (OECD, 2001), Tables 1–4 and 1–5a. Robert William Fogel, *The Escape from Hunger and Premature Death, 1700–2100: Europe, America, and the Third World*, (Cambridge, MA: Cambridge University Press, 2004), Table 1.1, 2. Michael Haines, "Fertility and Mortality in the United States," EH.Net Encyclopedia, edited by Robert Whaples (January 22, 2005). URL http://eh.net/encyclopedia/article/haines.demography.Though in broad agreement over long periods and since 1900, these sources often differ in detail. The chart combines what seems the most sensible and consistent combination: Maddison before 1700, Fogel from 1700 until 1850, Haines since 1850, and Fogel's forecast.

43. Yet thanks to improved nutrition (apparently accelerated by absence of natural fathers during female development), the age of sexual maturity has declined

two to three years in the past century, causing a mismatch between social and sexual maturity with consequences for marital stability. See Peter D. Gluckman and Mark A. Hanson, "Evolution, development and timing of puberty," *Trends in Endocrinology & Metabolism* 17:1 (January 2006): 7–12; and "Changing times: The evolution of puberty," *Molecular and Cellular Endocrinology* 254–55 (25 July 2006): 26–31; Robert J. Quinlan, "Father absence, parental care and female reproductive development," *Evolution and Human Behavior* 24 (2003): 376–90.

44. Consistent data series were constructed from Patrick Festy, "Canada, United States, Australia and New Zealand: Nuptiality Trends," *Population Studies* 27:3 (November 1973): 479–92; Donald W. Hasting and J. Gregory Robinson, "A Re-Examination of Hernes' Model on the Process of Entry Into First Marriage for United States Women, Cohorts 1891–1945," *American Sociological Review* 38:1 (February 1973): 138–42; Robert Schoen, William Urton, Karen Woodrow, and John Baj, "Marriage and Divorce in Twentieth Century American Cohorts," *Demography* 22:1 (February 1985): 101–14; Joshua Goldstein and Catherine T. Kenney, "Marriage Delayed or Marriage Foregone? Cohort Forecasts of First Marriage for U.S. Women," *American Sociological Review* 66:4 (August 2001): 506–19; Robert Heuser, "Fertility Tables for Birth Cohorts by Color: United States, 1917–1973," DHEW Publication No. (HRA) 76–1152, National Center for Health Statistics (April 1976); and Jane Lawler Dye, "Fertility of American Women: June 2004," Census Bureau (2005).

45. Paul H. Jacobson, *American Marriage and Divorce* (New York: Rinehard & Co., 1959), 138.

46. Ibid., 143.

47. See, for example, Betsey Stevenson and Justin Wolfers, "Marriage and Divorce: Changes and Their Driving Forces," published as NBER Working Paper No. 12944 and at http://knowledge.wharton.upenn.edu/papers/1335.pdf, accessed 28 November 2007. Despite a more thorough effort, Samuel H. Preston and John McDonald, in "The Incidence of Divorce Within Cohorts of Marriages Contracted Since the Civil War," *Demography* 16:1 (February 1979): 1–25, 15, 16, also relied on Jacobson's figures while dismissing his argument about mortality, and abandoned an effort to test for factors affecting the divorce rate owing to "multicollinearity and measurement problems." These, we saw in the case of Steven Levitt's theory on fertility and crime in chapter 2.3, are symptoms of "misspecification" errors resulting from neoclassical economic theory's omission of the "distribution function." Divorce is obviously another field inviting reexamination and new research based on the more comprehensive neo-Scholastic model.

48. This section draws on John D. Mueller, "The Socioeconomic Costs of *Roe v. Wade*," *Family Policy* 13:2 (March–April 2000): 1–20, available at http://www.eppc.org/publications/pubID.2288/pub_detail.asp.

49. George A. Akerlof and Janet L. Yellen, "An Analysis of Out-of-Wedlock Births in the United States," Policy Brief #5, The Brookings Institution (August

1996). The original article appeared as George A. Akerlof, Janet L. Yellen, and Michael L. Katz, "An Analysis of Out-of-Wedlock Childbearing in the United States," *Quarterly Journal of Economics* 111:2 (May 1996): 277–314.

50. U.S. National Center for Health Statistics, *Vital Statistics of the United States*.

51. National Center for Health Statistics, "United States Health, 1999, With Health and Aging Chartbook," Hyattsville, MD (1999).

52. Amara Bachu, *Trends in Premarital Childbearing: 1930 to 1994*, Current Population Report P23–197, U.S. Census Bureau, Washington, DC (1999).

53. Vaughn R. A. Call and Tim B. Heaton, *Journal for the Scientific Study of Religion* 36:3 (September 1997): 383–92. Converting the original results to the simpler form shown in the table occasionally required some minor recoding of respondents' answers, e.g., when the original coding was "0" or "1" (since the logarithm of zero is undefined).

Chapter 11

1. The model of fertility in this chapter was first published in John D. Mueller, "How Does Fiscal Policy Affect the American Worker?" *Notre Dame Journal of Law, Ethics, and Public Policy* 20:2 (Spring 2006): 563–619, http://www.eppc. org/docLib/20060725_MuellerNDJLEPP.pdf, accessed 12 July 2007.

2. Angus Maddison, *The World Economy: A Millennial Perspective*, OECD (2001); Table 1–4.

3. The TFR's advantage of timeliness is partly offset by its somewhat greater variability than measures of average cohort fertility, but this can be largely mitigated by making reasonable assumptions about the most recent cohorts in the most recent years. Robert Schoen, "Timing Effects and the Interpretation of Period Fertility," *Demography* 41:4 (November 2004): 801–19; Norman B. Ryder, "Observations on the History of Cohort Fertility in the United States," *Population and Development* 12:4 (December 1986): 617–43.

4. The total fertility rate (TFR) calculates how many live births the average woman would have in her lifetime if her experience at each age were the same as the average for women of all ages in that year. The gross reproduction rate (GRR) is calculated in the same way as the TFR but typically counts only the number of daughters born (though it could also be calculated for fathers and sons). The net reproduction rate (NRR) adjusts the GRR for mortality as well as fertility at each age. The net total fertility rate (NTFR) is the total fertility rate after taking mortality of both sexes into account. At least for twentieth-century America, the NRR and NTFR can be closely approximated by subtracting 1–1/2 times the infant mortality rate (IMR)—deaths during the first year of life—from the gross reproduction rate or total fertility rate. This is how the rate was calculated when more detailed data were unavailable.

5. Author's calculations based on Michael Haines, "Fertility and Mortality in the United States," EH.Net Encyclopedia, edited by Robert Whaples (January 22,

2005), available at URL http://eh.net/encyclopedia/article/haines.demography.
6. Since infant mortality is typically defined as death within the first year of life, when using annual data, about half of this year's infant deaths are included in this year's births, and the rest in last year's or next year's.
7. As we found when describing the basic theory above, raising children who may support one in old age, investing in one's own human capital to receive future labor income, investing in property to receive future property income, and government transfer payments funded by dedicated taxes can all be expressed as a rate of return on the initial outlay. For example, a son's gift at time t_n yields a quasi-rate of return on the parents' gift to the son at time t_0 equal to $(T_{M2:J1}(t_0)/T_{M2:J1}(t_n))^{1/n-1}$. The return on Person i's previous investment in nonhuman capital, Ki, is r/ Ki; on his human capital, w/ Li; the implicit rate of return on payroll taxes paid at time t_0, $pwL(t_0)$, that fund pay-as-you-go retirement pensions to persons received at time t_n, $T_L(t_n)$, is $(T_L(t_n)/pwL(t_0))^{1/n-1}$. People will therefore tend to maximize those investments yielding the highest rates of return.
8. Michele Boldrin et al., *Fertility and Social Security*, National Bureau of Economic Research, Working Paper No. 11146 (2005); Zeyu Xu, A Survey on Intra-Household Models and Evidence (May 2004) http://www.columbia.edu/~zx20/Papers/A%20Survey%200n%20Intra-Household%20Models%20 (submitted).pdf.
9. Xu, 2.
10. "Empirical support for the existence of altruistic motives is not overwhelming. Indeed, some of the most influential studies have reached mixed conclusions, possibly favoring 'exchange' rather than altruism as a motive for intrafamily transfers." Ibid., 3.
11. "What varies substantially, and sometimes dramatically, with the preference parameters are the levels of both fertility and the capital-output ratio, and this sensitivity in levels is common to both models." Boldrin et al., 32.
12. Ibid.
13. Moreover, Boldrin, De Nardi, and Jones follow many other researchers in relying heavily on the infant mortality rate (IMR) as an independent explanatory variable to explain the total fertility rate (TFR), with the problems described above in the text. The same study also uses per capita GDP as an independent variable, but this has a similar problem, because per capita GDP is highly correlated with longevity. People who expect to live longer invest more in human and nonhuman capital than those who don't, because the returns can be expected for a longer period; conversely, people with higher incomes tend to afford better health care and so live longer. Both problems can be avoided by excluding the IMR and per capita GDP as independent variables and using the NRR or NTFR instead of the TFR as the thing to be explained.
14. Aristotle's and Augustine's "final distribution function," which describes personal love and hate and domestic and political distributive justice, is found in equations (1.1) and (2.1) of the model outlined in chapter 10.

15. Gross national income per capita at purchasing power parity (PPP) and national saving per capita are from World Bank 2003. Social spending per capita at PPP, calculated from the same sources, comes mostly from OECD 2004.

16. The adjustments for infant mortality and life expectancy do not significantly affect the statistical relationships, allowing us to take infant mortality into account without artificially skewing the results.

17. Deuteronomy 6:5; Leviticus 19:18 (noted in Matthew 22:37–39). As Augustine carefully explained, "as yourself" cannot always mean "equally with yourself" when scarce goods are involved. But it does always mean "as a person" like yourself.

18. The data for weekly worship come from the World Values Survey, *The Values Surveys* (2001), http://www.jdsurvey.com:8080/bdasepjds/wvsevs/PrinDocumentation.jsp.

19. The equation was net TFR (total fertility rate-infant mortality rate, 2001) = c_1 + c_2*(rate of weekly worship) + c_3*(% Protestant population) + c_4*(% Jewish population) + c_5*(totalitarian legacy) + c_6*log(social spending per capita at PPP/life expectancy, 2001) + c_7*log(national saving per capita at PPP/life expectancy, 2001). The results were as follows:

	Coefficient	Standard error	t-statistic
c_1	3.3988	0.3286	10.3443
c_2	1.3537	0.2677	5.0555
c_3	1.5908	0.4364	3.6455
c_4	0.8857	0.1851	4.7840
c_5	-0.5851	0.1152	-5.0808
c_6	-0.2914	0.0069	-4.2125
c_7	-0.2820	0.1067	-2.6422

Adjusted R^2 = 0.80847   n=50.

20. I updated the model based on the most recent actual data available for TFRs in 2009 (usually 2005) in a paper presented at the Fifth World Congress of Families, and the fit was improved from 0.808 to 0.849. John D. Mueller, "How Do Nations Choose 'Demographic Winter'? Is America Doing So?" Panel on Family and Demography, Fifth World Congress of Families, Amsterdam, available at http://www.eppc.org/programs/economics/publications/programID.41,pubID.3911/pub_detail.asp. These data are used later in chapter 15 for projecting the future TFR. But since no newer data were available by country for some variables including the most important, weekly worship, for consistency in this chapter, the model is tested based on the simultaneous data for all variables in 2001.

21. Including a detailed breakdown of each country's population by religious affiliation showed that, for any rate of weekly worship, adding the shares of these populations that are Jewish or Protestant is statistically significant but that adding the Catholic, Orthodox, Muslim, and Hindu shares is not.

Chapter 12

1. Investment in such intangible forms of nonhuman capital as research and development is also stimulated.

2. The comprehensive system of classification presented in this chapter was first outlined in John D. Mueller, "Winners and Losers from 'Privatizing' Social Security," Washington, DC (March 1999), a study commissioned by the National Committee to Preserve Social Security and Medicare but undertaken in cooperation with the Employee Benefit Research Institute (EBRI) and Policy Simulation Group; a summary of findings was presented at a hearing on "Investing in the Private Market" before the Subcommittee on Social Security of the Committee on Ways and Means of the U.S. House of Representatives on March 3, 1999; Serial 106–113, Committee on Ways and Means, U.S. Government Printing Office; http://bulk.resource.org/gpo.gov/hearings/106h/57507.pdf, retrieved 29 November 2007. The text only of the summary is available at http://www.eppc.org/publications/pubID.2369/pub_detail.asp, retrieved 5 December 2007.

3. Most people value wealth used in even increments more highly than the use of the same total wealth bunched unevenly over time. This is not only because most people value consumption right now more highly than the promise of the same consumption in the future. Most people also weigh the prospect of a given loss of wealth more heavily than they would value an equal gain. This is known as being "risk averse."

4. There are a number of inconsistencies in the census definition of income, but we are using it here only to grasp the general pattern of earnings and income by age, not as a precise measure of income. Later on, we'll develop and apply a more precise comprehensive measure of income.

5. S. Bloendal, S. Fickel, N. Girouard, and A. Wagner, "Investment in Human Capital Through Post-Compulsory Education and Training," Organization for Economic Cooperation and Development (Paris, 2001): 10. As with business property, when taxes and the social costs of subsidies for investment are taken into account, the "social rate of return" is somewhat lower—but the comparison still shows a significantly higher rate of return on investment in "human capital" than on business property.

6. Gary S. Becker, "Underinvestment in College Education?" *American Economic Review*, Proceedings L (1960), 346–54.

7. Tangible human capital consists in people's bodies, while intangible human capital consists in their education, other learned skills, health, safety, and mobility. Tangible nonhuman capital includes land and other natural resources, and reproducible property like buildings and machines. Intangible nonhuman capital includes the technology embodied in reproducible property, which results from investment in research and development and may be owned in the form of a patent.

8. G. K. Chesterton, *What's Wrong With the World,* in *Collected Works: Vol. IV* (San Francisco: Ignatius Press, 1987), 118.

9. Ibid., 118–19.

10. Philip H. Wicksteed, "The Scope and Method of Political Economy in the Light of the 'Marginal Theory of Value and Distribution,'" *The Economic Journal,* vol. XXIV, no. 93, London (March 1914): 1–23. Presidential address to Section F of the British Association, Birmingham, 1913. Reprinted in *The Common Sense of Political Economy,* vol. II: 772–96, 785.

11. U.S. Census Bureau and U.S. Department of Labor, Current Population Survey, March 1998 Supplement.

12. These examples are derived from U.S. census data as described in John Mueller, "Winners and Losers from 'Privatizing' Social Security."

13. The value of maximizing total income or wealth may be obvious, while the advantage of smoothing consumption may not be. It seems to be the case for nearly everyone that the value, not only of any particular good but also of total wealth, is subject to diminishing returns. Another way of saying this is that people value the gain of a significant quantity of wealth less highly than the loss of an equal quantity. If so, the total value of a given quantity of wealth that is consumed highly unevenly over time will be lower than the same quantity spread more evenly. This is because the loss of value during those periods when the quantity consumed is significantly lower will outweigh the gains in value of the quantity consumed during periods when that quantity is larger.

14. Milton Friedman, *Capitalism and Freedom* (Chicago: University of Chicago Press, 1962), quotation from 1982 paperback edition, 103.

15. A copy of nineteen-year-old Ron Steen's 2006 eBay sales offer can be found at http://www.pankaj-k.net/archives/eBay%20Entry%20—%20Ron%20 Steen%27s%20Future%20Earnings.pdf. Twenty-three-year-old Terrance Wyatt's similar effort is recounted at http://blogs.ajc.com/get-schooled-blog/2009/08/20/ college-student-selling-his-future-for-10000-on-ebay/. Both accessed 1 September 2009.

16. Since all the figures are actually from the same year, the chart in effect shows the resulting increase in real incomes, since we don't have to make the usual adjustments for inflation in comparing dollar amounts from different years. Moreover, the inflation-adjusted figures for each level of education have actually been nearly constant since the Census Bureau's figures began. To see this in a time series, both changes in the price level and the changing proportions of persons at each age must be taken into account.

17. National income and product data pertain only to "final" products, since including the value of raw materials and intermediate goods, as well as finished goods, would result in multiple counting of the same "value added" in production.

18. "National" refers to the production actually owned and received as income by a country's residents, while "domestic" refers to the income generated by production *within* a country, without regard to whether the income is ultimately

received by residents or by foreigners. If our purpose is to maximize the incomes of the country's residents, then the appropriate measures are gross or net *national* product (GNP or NNP) and their counterparts, gross or net *national* income (GNI or NNI). "Gross" means before, and "net" means after, subtracting the value of capital consumed in production, as well as indirect (sales) taxes.

19. This estimate of pretax, pretransfer broad family income was derived from the most comprehensive, reasonably consistent measure of family income used recently by U.S. government agencies, "Family Economic Income"; Julie-Ann Cronin, "U.S. Treasury Distributional Analysis Methodology," OTA Paper 85, Office of Tax Analysis, U.S. Treasury (September 1999). As noted in the section on political economy, "Family Economic Income" has some anomalies but was suitable at least for obtaining a measure of family income that closely approximated gross national product, with the addition of capital consumption allowances (which were excluded from that family economic income), obtained from the Bureau of Economic Analysis. Capital consumption was allocated by income in proportion to other property income.

Chapter 13

1. I gave an overview of the historical discovery of these four principles in a longer version of this chapter that was presented as a seminar at the Lehrman American Studies Center's summer institute at Princeton University: John D. Mueller, "Infant Industry: The Past and Future of the American System," Princeton University, 17 June 2008, available at http://www.eppc.org/publications/pubID.3926/pub_detail.asp; accessed 1 September 2009.

2. Virtue ranked in between, but under the Constitution was effectively left to the states.

3. As mentioned already in chapter 10, the government's budget may be written: (1.7 and 2.7) $C_G + \Delta K_G + T_L + T_K = \tau(w\Sigma L_i + r\Sigma K_i) + pw\Sigma L_i + kr\Sigma K_i + \Delta B_G + \Sigma K_{GMi}$,

where C_G is current consumption (including capital consumption) of government-owned goods and services, T_L is government transfer payments to persons, T_K is government subsidies to property owners, τ is the income tax rate (assumed to be equal for labor and property income), p is the payroll tax rate, k is the tax rate levied only on property income, B_G is government debt, and $\Sigma \Delta K_{GMi}$ is the issue of government fiat money. As explained in more detail in the next three chapters, the four basic policy principles described in the text amount to pairing and restricting the sources and uses of government finance in this way:

$\Sigma \Delta K_{GMi} = 0$ [no government fiat money finance];

$\Sigma C_{Gi} = \tau$ $(w\Sigma L_i + r\Sigma K_i)$ [current consumption of public goods financed by income tax];

$\Sigma T_{Li} = pw\Sigma L_i$ and $\Sigma T_{Ki} = kr\Sigma K_i$ [social benefits financed by current payroll taxes, and subsidies for property ownership from taxes on current property income];

$\Sigma T_{Li} / w\Sigma L_i \leq (\Sigma T_{Li} / w\Sigma L_i)_{t=2001}$ [social benefits not to exceed 2001 share of labor income].

4. Nicholas Eberstadt, "Born in the USA," *The American Interest* (Summer 2007), available at http://www.aei.org/publications/filter.all,pubID.25988/pub_detail. asp, retrieved 1 September 2009. See also "America the Fertile," *Washington Post* (May 6, 2007): B7, available at http://www.washingtonpost.com/wp-dyn/content/article/2007/05/04/AR2007050401891.html, retrieved 15 May 2007.

5. U.S. Census Bureau International Database, available at http://www.census.gov/ipc/www/idb/ranks.php, retrieved 1 September 2009.

6. William Robert Johnston, "Abortion statistics and other data," is an extensive, thorough, and judiciously analyzed source of data for the United States and other countries: Johnston's Archive, http://www.johnstonsarchive.net/policy/abortion/index.html, last accessed 5 December 2007.

7. Congressional Budget Office, "A 125-Year Picture of the Federal Government's Share of the Economy, 1950–2075" (July 3, 2002), available at http://www.cbo.gov/showdoc.cfm?index=3521; updated in "The Long-Term Budget Outlook" (June 2009), available at http://www.cbo.gov/ftpdocs/102xx/doc10297/06-25-LTBO.pdf, retrieved 1 September 2009.

8. John D. Mueller, *The LBMC Plan for Tax Reform*, Memo to the National Commission on Economic Growth and Tax Reform (September 26, 1995); and "'LBMC Plan' Menu of Tax Reform Choices" (September 27, 1995). For an updated discussion, see John D. Mueller, "Taxes, Social Security & the Politics of Reform," *The Weekly Standard* (November 29, 2004): 24–29; available at http://www.eppc.org/publications/pubID.2268/pub_detail.asp.

9. John D. Mueller, "Winners and Losers from 'Privatizing' Social Security," appendix C.

10. See James C. Capretta, "Building Automatic Solvency into Social Security: Insights from Sweden and Germany," *The Brookings Institution* (1 March 2006), available at http://www.eppc.org/publications/pubID.2692/pub_detail.asp.

11. U.S. Census Bureau International Data Base, Population Division/International Programs Center, available at http://www.census.gov/ipc/www/idbrank.html, accessed 1 September 2009.

12. *Collected Works of Abraham Lincoln, Volume 1,* available at http://showcase.netins.net/web/creative/lincoln/speeches/lyceum.htm.

Chapter 14

1. James Madison, *Federalist* No. 51, 271.

2. James Madison, "Property," *The Papers of James Madison* 14 (29 March 1792): 266–68, edited by William T. Hutchinson et al. (Chicago and London: University of Chicago Press, 1962–77), vols. 1–10; (Charlottesville: University Press of Virginia, 1977), vol. 11; available at http://press-pubs.uchicago.edu/founders/print_documents/v1ch16s23.html (emphasis in original).

3. James Madison, *Federalist* No. 10, 44.
4. Ibid., 150.
5. "In reality party ideologies probably stem originally from the interests of the persons who found each party," Downs conceded. "But, once a political party is created, it takes on an existence of its own and eventually becomes relatively independent of any particular interest group." Anthony Downs, "An Economic Theory of Political Action in a Democracy," *Journal of Political Economy* 65:2 (April 1957): 135–50, 142n. Presumed randomness is reflected in the theory's prediction that voters' interests will follow the "normal" (i.e., bell-shaped) curve associated with random variations: according to Downs, "stable government in a two-party democracy requires a distribution of voters roughly approximating a normal curve. When such a distribution exists, the two parties come to resemble each other closely." Anthony Downs, "An Economic Theory of Political Action in a Democracy," ibid., 143.
6. American National Election Studies (ANES), Stanford University and the University of Michigan, with funding by the National Science Foundation, http://www.electionstudies.org/, retrieved 4 September 2009.
7. For example, the ANES data indicate that 13 percent of American voters in 1948 and 11 percent in 2004 were in the 96th–100th percentile of family income; rather than proving that income inequality was greater in those years, they merely reflect the fact that those were the smallest samples. The shares of family income originating as labor and property compensation are based on figures for the year 2000. The total shares of labor and property compensation in gross national income can be determined from the National Income and Product Accounts, and are quite stable from year to year, for reasons explained in chapter 12 and chapter 15.
8. James Madison, *Federalist* No. 51, 270.
9. James Madison, *Federalist* No. 10, 44.
10. The ANES data for the 2006 and 2008 elections were scheduled for release after publication of this book. But according to exit polls, the decisiveness of economic issues in defeating Republicans suggests that the results will confirm rather than disprove the connection between sources of family income and partisan voting. "Campaign 2008," www.pollingreport.com, retrieved 1 September 2009.
11. Schultz, 13, 15.
12. In making that prediction, unlike the staff and other outside advisers to the tax reform commission, I had the considerable advantage of having thoroughly analyzed the prototype of the DuPont, Armey, and Forbes flat "consumption" tax plans, which had been devised in 1981 by Robert E. Hall and Alvin Rabushka of the Hoover Institution, as described in their book *The Flat Tax* (Hoover Institution, 2006): http://www.hoover.org/publications/books/3602666.html. Apart from the Democratic Party's Bradley–Gephardt plan, Hall–Rabushka was the first proposal I considered when tasked to devise

the personal side of what became the Kemp–Kasten tax plan of 1984, which became the GOP prototype for the 1986 tax reform act. Despite its admirable simplicity, I had to reject the Hall–Rabushka plan because it skewed the tax burden toward workers as explained in this chapter. With support from my business partners, Lewis E. Lehrman, Jeffrey Bell, and Frank Cannon (all with Kemp political connections), former Kemp congressional chief of staff David Smick, and a briefing book of supporting data, I argued to the tax reform commission that the plan's disparate treatment of labor and property income was bad economics and politically suicidal. Ending the roughly equal treatment of labor and property income would dissolve the glue that held the Reagan coalition together and jeopardize many of the party's positions on noneconomic issues with independent voters. I offered several alternatives that were equally simple but without the adverse distributional effects. I was therefore deeply chagrined when Kemp (for whom I retained undiminished affection) went along with the majority of the tax commission in supporting, and Steve Forbes (whom I also like and admire) ran in 1996 as a GOP candidate for president on, a plan that in my view is not economically or politically viable for any presidential candidate or party in a national election. Bell and Smick came to similar conclusions in their subsequent books: Jeffrey Bell, *Populism and Elitism: Politics in the Age of Equality*, (Washington, DC: Regnery Gateway, 1992), 65–66; and David M. Smick, *The World Is Curved: Hidden Dangers of the World Economy*, (New York: Penguin, 2008), 237–40. The latter was also a well-timed warning about the monetary crisis described below in chapter 16. And Bell extends his provocative, sweeping historical and political analysis in Jeffrey Bell, *Social Conservatism: The Movement that Polarized American Politics*, Encounter Books, forthcoming.

Chapter 15

1. My friend and senior business partner, Lewis E. Lehrman, knew Rueff well, and the Lehrman Institute published Rueff's complete works in his native France (though unfortunately not yet in English). My use of the "world dollar base" is one of many analytical tools that were inspired by Rueff's work. Rueff was both a theorist and a successful practitioner of economic policy. He gave the earliest accurate diagnosis of the two biggest economic policy problems of the twentieth century: chronic unemployment and chronic inflation. He used that diagnosis to engineer several successful reforms of national economic policy, and his analysis is just as valid today as when it was developed in the 1920s. Rueff also contributed to the philosophy of the "social market economy" and of what became the European Union. And he understood the critical link between economics as a science and economic policy as a branch of moral or political philosophy. I have tried to outline these important contributions in a monograph, "Jacques, Rueff: Political Economist for the 21st Century?" *The LBMC*

Report, Lehrman Bell Mueller Cannon Inc., Arlington, VA (January 28, 2000), available at http://www.eppc.org/publications/pubID.2261/pub_detail.asp.

2. Though originally drafted for this book, owing to the vagaries of its publication, this section was first published as part of John D. Mueller, "How Does Fiscal Policy Affect the American Worker?" *Notre Dame Journal of Law, Ethics and Public Policy* 20:2 (Spring 2006): 563–619, available at http://www. eppc.org/publications/pubID.2671/pub_detail.asp. This chapter adds several years of data and projections by the Congressional Budget Office and the Social Security Administration's Trustees. The updated demographic projections were presented at the Fifth World Congress of Families: John D. Mueller, "How Do Nations Choose 'Demographic Winter'? Is America Doing So?" Remarks to the World Congress of Families V, Panel on "Family and Demography," Amsterdam, Netherlands (11 August 2009), available at http://www.worldcongress.org/wcf5.spkrs/wcf5.mueller.htm and http://www.eppc.org/publications/pubID.3911/pub_detail.asp.

3. See U.S. Department of Commerce, *Historical Statistics of the United States* (1975): 121–26.

4. Jacques Rueff, "Les Variations du Chômage en Angleterre," *Revue Politique et Parlementaire* 32 (1925): 425 [hereinafter "Les Variations"].

5. Sir Josiah Stamp, "Work and Wages: I.—Fettered by the Dole: A French Theory," London *Times* (June 11, 1931): 17; "Work and Wages: II.—The Ban on Unemployment: A System Out of Gear," London *Times* (June 12, 1931): 17. "The astonishing thing is not that this relationship exists," Rueff modestly remarked in his memoirs, "but that it should astonish anyone." Jacques Rueff, *De l'Aube au Crépuscule: Autobiograhie* (Paris: Plon, 1977), 96.

6. Jean Denuc, "Les Fluctuations Comparées du Chômage et des Salaires dans Quelques Pays de 1919 à 1929 [Comparative Fluctuations in Unemployment and Salaries in Several Countries from 1919 to 1929], *Bulletin de la Statistique Générale de la France* (1930) (Fr.).

7. Keynes cited Rueff's wage/price calculations to support his assumption of downward "stickiness" of wages: "Yet it might be a provisional assumption of a rigidity of money-wages, rather than of real wages, which would bring our theory nearest to the facts. For example, money-wages in Great Britain during the turmoil and uncertainty and wide price fluctuations of the decade 1924–1934 were stable within a range of 6 percent, whereas real wages fluctuated by more than 20 percent." John Maynard Keynes, *The General Theory of Employment Interest and Money* (1936): 276. Keynes and Rueff debated many times, but Rueff summarized his objections to Keynes's *General Theory* in Jacques Rueff, "The Fallacies of Lord Keynes General Theory," *The Quarterly Journal of Economics* 61:3 (May 1947): 343–67.

8. Charles Maurice de Talleyrand-Perigord (1754–1838), *Chevalier de Panay* (letter to Mallet du Pan, January 1796).

9. John D. Mueller, "The Answer to Three Puzzles: Welfare Reform Lowered

Unemployment," *The LBMC Report* (July 23, 1999), available at http://www.
eppc.org/publications/pubID.2367/pub_detail.asp.
10. John D. Mueller and Marc A. Miles, "More Similar Than Different," Lehrman Bell Mueller Cannon Inc., Arlington, VA (July 1998), a study commissioned by the Government Development Bank of Puerto Rico. Though the
government declined to publish the study (which had demonstrated among
other things that the Section 936 tax exemption had not increased the incomes
of Puerto Rico's residents), some of its key findings were featured in Alexander
Odishelidze and Arthur Laffer, *Pay to the Order of Puerto Rico* (Fairfax, VA:
Allegiance Press, 2004).
11. National income and product data pertain only to "final" products, since
including the value of raw materials and intermediate goods, as well as finished
goods, would result in multiple counting of the same "value added" in production.
12. "National" refers to the production actually owned and received as income
by a country's residents, while "domestic" refers to the income generated by production *within* a country, without regard to whether the income is ultimately
received by residents or by foreigners. If our purpose is to maximize the incomes
of the country's residents, then the appropriate measures are gross or net *national*
product (GNP or NNP) and their counterparts, gross or net *national* income
(GNI or NNI). "Gross" means before, and "net" means after, subtracting the
value of capital consumed in production, as well as indirect (sales) taxes.
13. Why is this? The relative price of labor is derived by dividing the rate of
labor compensation per hour by both product prices and labor productivity. Let
w be labor compensation per hour, L the number of hours worked, P the index
of product prices, and Q net output. Then the "product wage" is w/P, and labor
productivity (output per hour) is Q/L. So the relative price of labor is $(w/P)/$
$(Q/L) = wL/PQ$. But wL is total labor compensation, and PQ is the value of
total output. PQ (net of nonhuman capital consumption and indirect taxes) is
also equal to national income. Therefore the relative price of labor is the same
as labor's share of national income. As long as we know the aggregate value of
labor compensation (wL) and national income (PQ), we can measure the relative price of labor without actually knowing w, L, P, or Q.
14. $\Sigma Q = \Sigma K^a \Sigma L^{1-a}$, where a is the share of total product value contributed by
all nonhuman capital ΣK, and $1 - a$ the share contributed by all human capital
ΣL; empirically, $a \cong 0.3–0.4$, so $1 - a \cong 0.6–0.7$.
15. The same issues are raised by efforts to regulate the financial markets and
the compensation of wealthy bankers as by regulation of prices or the minimum wage. No matter how sophisticated the financial instruments, financial
regulation is not rocket science. It almost always boils down to enforcement of
the exceptionless commandments "Thou shalt not steal" and "Thou shalt not
bear false witness." (In fact, most infractions involve lying in order to steal.) Yet
it is fatuous to believe that federal regulation alone could have prevented the
financial crises of 1929–33 or 2007–9. As we will see in chapter 16, both events

originated in the massive "injustice in exchange" that resulted from violating the Hamiltonian first principle of economic policy: not financing the federal budget through American or foreign monetary authorities. The error is all the more patent when such regulation is imposed by congressmen and senators who themselves rely upon and personally benefit from the factional injustice.

16. However, as noted above, the government calculates the consumption of nonhuman but not human capital, which is equally real.

17. $L/L_{pot} = c_1 + b(1 - \tau)[(1 - p)wL + T_L]/(PQ - C_K)$; that is, employment as a share of the labor force is a function of labor's net share of national income, where c_1 is a constant, L is actual employment, and L_{pot} is the labor force (maximum potential employment), so $L_{pot} - L$ is the number of (hours or workers) unemployed and $1 - L/L_{pot}$ is the unemployment rate. When unemployment is eliminated, $L = L_{pot}$. Since actual employment can never exceed potential employment and actual employment is a function of labor's share of total income, labor's net share of total income can never fall below $1-a \cong 0.6–0.7$. No matter how "greedy" employers are, their greed will cause them to hire workers, thus raising workers' incomes, as long as it is profitable to do so. It stops being profitable when $L = L_{pot}$.

18. E.g., Paul Gomme and Peter Rupert, Federal Reserve Bank of Cleveland, Measuring Labor's Share of Income (2004), available at http:// www.cleveland-fed.org/Research/PolicyDis/N07Nov04.pdf; Michael R. Pakko, Labor's Share, Nat'l Econ. Trends (August 2004), available at http://research. stlouisfed.org/ publications/net/ 20040801/cover.pdf.

19. As currently calculated. Before World War II, workers employed on public works projects were counted as unemployed, which raised the peak rate reported at the time to about 25 percent.

20. $NI/NI_{pot} = c(L/L_{pot})$; empirically, $c \cong 2$. When expressed in terms of GDP, this relationship is sometimes called "Okun's Law." The output gap is derived from that of the Congressional Budget Office, which is based on CBO's estimate of the non-accelerating inflation rate of unemployment, which has frequently changed. The measure used here is based instead on output if all workers were employed: zero unemployment.

21. The officially reported unemployment rate at the time was more than 25 percent, but workers employed on public works projects were counted as unemployed.

22. This estimate is from John D. Mueller, "Winners and Losers from 'Privatizing' Social Security," Washington, DC (March 1999), a study commissioned by the National Committee to Preserve Social Security and Medicare, undertaken in cooperation with the Employee Benefit Research Institute (EBRI) and Policy Simulation Group; a summary of findings was presented at a hearing on "Investing in the Private Market" before the Subcommittee on Social Security of the Committee on Ways and Means of the U.S. House of Representatives on March 3, 1999; Serial 106–113, Committee on Ways and Means, U.S. Govern-

ment Printing Office; http://bulk.resource.org/gpo.gov/hearings/106h/57507.
pdf, accessed 29 November 2007. The text only of the summary is available
at http://www.eppc.org/publications/pubID.2369/pub_detail.asp, accessed 5
December 2007.
23. John D. Mueller, "How Abortion Has Weakened Social Security," *Family Policy* (March–April 2000), available at http://www.eppc.org/publications/
pubID.2267/pub_detail.asp.
24. John D. Mueller, "The Socioeconomic Costs of *Roe v. Wade*," *Family Policy* 13:2 (March–April 2000): 1–14, available at http://www.eppc.org/
docLib/20050328Mueller3.pdf.
25. I have not referred in this book specifically to energy use and policy, except
for discussing in chapter 2 the trade-off between free trade and national security
pointed out by Thomas Aquinas, and noting in chapter 3 that this reasoning
was also followed by Adam Smith, Alexander Hamilton, and Abraham Lincoln. As Lewis E. Lehrman concluded in a comprehensive survey of U.S. energy
use and policy, "Employment is the only factor with a one-for-one relationship
to total energy use over the whole period since 1950." Therefore, "if energy
use keeps step with employment, U.S. energy efficiency will continue to climb
as in the past 20 years—but total U.S. energy use will also rise. Those Malthusians who favor an absolute reduction in U.S. energy and hydrocarbon use
haven't yet spelled out to the American public what that would mean: namely,
a corresponding decline in employment, a decline in the standard of living
from what Americans would otherwise enjoy, and ultimately, a decline in U.S.
population." Lewis E. Lehrman, "Energetic America: The energy policy the
U.S. needs," *The Weekly Standard*, September 29, 2003, vol. 9, no. 3, 25–29;
retrieved 29 April 2010 from http://www.weeklystandard.com/print/Content/
Public/Articles/000/000/003/143kzyec.asp?pg=2.

Chapter 16

1. John Mueller, "The Reserve Currency Curse," *Wall Street Journal* (September 4, 1986), available at http://www.eppc.org/publications/pubID.2424/
pub_detail.asp; Lewis E. Lehrman and John Mueller, "The Curse of Being a
Reserve Currency," *Wall Street Journal* (January 4, 1993). Parts of this section
were incorporated into Lewis E. Lehrman and John D. Mueller, "Go Forward
to Gold: How to lift the reserve currency curse," *National Review* (15 December 2008); available at http://www2.nationalreview.com/monetary.html and
http://www.eppc.org/publications/pubID.3634/pub_detail.asp, accessed 8
December 2008.
2. Though the dollar was nominally on a bimetallic standard, changes in the
mint ratio or relative market prices of gold and silver caused one metal to predominate.
3. The CPI and PPI series back to 1913 are from the Bureau of Labor Statis-

tics, http://stats.bls.gov/data/; GDP data back to 1929 from the Bureau of Economic Analysis, http://www.bea.gov/; both before 1913 from *Historical Statistics of the United States*.

4. Long-term price stability is measured as the geometric annual average change, short-term price volatility by the average *absolute* annual change, and maximum price change as the percent difference between the lowest and highest levels, of the consumer price index during the period.

5. The measure of volatility I use is the standard deviation of the log difference in the consumer price index. For example, the log of an increase of 5 percent (1.05) is about 5.1 percent, and the log of a decline of 5 percent (0.95) is about 4.9 percent.

6. My example of the neighborhood yard sale adapts Rueff's analytically identical example of the village market, which was (and remains) far more common in Europe than America; Jacques Rueff, *The Age of Inflation*, trans. A. H. Mecus and F. G. Clarke (Chicago: Regnery Gateway, 1964), 20–23.

7. $P_Q = f(M_S, M_D)$.

8. $M_D = P_{K,L}(\Sigma K + \Sigma L) \cong f(P_Q Q, r)$: the demand for money is a function of total wealth, which may be approximated by total output, Q, e.g., GDP and the rate of return on productive assets, r.

9. For a discussion clarifying the crucial distinction between money and bank credit, see Charles Rist, *History of Monetary and Credit Theory from John Law to the Present Day*, trans. Jane Tabrisky Degras (New York: Macmillan, 1940), 31–43.

10. $\Sigma M_B + E = \Sigma K_M + \Sigma A$: bank liabilities, ΣM_B, plus the bank's equity, E, equal the bank's reserve of money (here assumed to be commodity money, K_M, plus bank loans, A_B.

11. "High-powered" money currently includes not only legal-tender Federal Reserve notes but also Federal Reserve deposits, which, though not legal tender, are considered a close substitute because they are convertible upon demand into such legal tender. However, as the discussion in the text indicates, nearly all foreign official dollar reserves are also high-powered for exactly the same reason.

12. $P_{Qdom} = P_{Qrow}e$. The domestic price level, P_{Qdom}, equals the price level in the rest of the world, P_{Qrow}, times the exchange rate, e.

13. Jacques Rueff, *The Monetary Sin of the West*, trans. Roger Glémet (New York: Macmillan, 1972), available at http://mises.org/books/monetarysin.pdf.

14. Rueff described the franc stabilization and his own role in Jacques Rueff, "Sur un point d'histoire: le niveau de la stabilization Poincaré," 69 *Rev. d'écon. Pol.* 168–78 (1959); and his preface to Émile Moreau, *The Golden Franc: Memoirs of a Governor of the Bank of France The Stabilization of the Franc (1926–1928)*, trans. Stephen D. Stollar and Trevor C. Roberts (Boulder, CO: Westview Press, 1991 [1954]), 1–10.

15. Kenneth Moure, "Undervaluing the Franc Poincaré," *Economic History Review* 69 (1996): 137–53.

16. Herbert Hoover, 3 *The Memoirs of Herbert Hoover* (New York: Macmillan, 1953), 30.

17. R. G. Hawtrey, *The Gold Standard: Theory and Practice* (London: Longmans, Green, 1931), 94.

18. The full text of the lecture, "Défense et illustration de l'étalon-or," may be found in 3 *Oeuvres Complètes* 105–27, and a translation in Rueff, *The Age of Inflation*, 30–61. This translated excerpt is from Rueff, *The Monetary Sin of the West*, 18–19.

19. Federal Reserve statistics do not distinguish official from private dollar deposits until the late 1930s, but most of the deposits during the 1920s and 1930s were apparently official. *Banking and Monetary Statistics, 1914–1941*, Washington, 1943: Board of Governors of the Federal Reserve System; *Banking and Monetary Statistics, 1941–1970*. Washington: Board of Governors of the Federal Reserve System, 1976. Then *Annual Statistical Digest*, various issues. More recent data on foreign dollar reserves from *Monthly Treasury Bulletin*, various issues; since 1996 at http://fms.treas.gov/bulletin/backissues.html.

20. Milton Friedman and Anna J. Schwartz, *A Monetary History of the United States, 1867–1960* (Princeton: Princeton University Press, 1963).

21. Ben S. Bernanke, "A Crash Course for Central Bankers," *Foreign Policy* 120 (September–October 2000): 49.

22. I offered a *précis* of Mundell's thought in John Mueller, "Nobel-Prize Winner Robert A. Mundell: An Appreciation," *The LBMC Report*, Lehrman Bell Mueller Cannon Inc., Arlington, VA (29 December 1999), available at http://www.eppc.org/publications/pubID.2262/pub_detail.asp, accessed 16 October 2009. Mundell presents his monetary theory most fully in Robert A. Mundell, *International Economics* (New York: Macmillan, 1968); and Robert A. Mundell, *Monetary Theory: Interest, Inflation and Growth in the World Economy* (Pacific Palisades, CA: Goodyear, 1971). Mundell outlined his differences with Rueff in his review article, "The Economic Consequences of Jacques Rueff," *Journal of Business* (June 1973). "The 'monetary sin of the West' is not the development of the gold-exchange standard, as Rueff argues, since the only real alternative to it was the dollar standard. The monetary 'sin' was, rather, the failure to establish a world currency at the time of Bretton Woods, leaving the vacuum to be filled by the dollar. Our present problems of using a purely national currency as an international standard all stem from this omission"; 394. In other words, Mundell favors a paper currency issued by a world central bank, which Keynes had unsuccessfully proposed in 1943. "To be pedantic, let G, R, C, M and L represent, respectively, gold weight, international reserves, currency, money, and total liquidity, and let p^* be the price of gold expressed in, say, the dominant currency. [Mundell uses "money" throughout in the looser sense that usually means bank deposits or "low-powered" money.] Then the different assets are related to one another by their reserve ratios as follows: $p^*G = a_0R$; $R = a_1C$; $C = a_2M$; $M = a_3L$. Thus $p^* = a_0a_1a_2a_3L/G$. A pure gold-specie system would

set a_o a_1 a_2 (and perhaps even a_3 equal to unity. To reintroduce such a system would require a fantastic increase in the price of gold [from $42.22] to over $1,000 an ounce!. . . . Rueff's compromise . . . [leaves] only a_o = 1, which carries the proposal into the political ball park. The fact of political feasibility does not, however, conceal the thin intellectual foundations of the basic argument." Ibid., 392. However, the system that Rueff proposed was the one that actually existed and maintained world price stability for nearly a century despite numerous monetary innovations and upheavals in individual countries. The lasting value of Mundell's article is in the analytical difference with Rueff that it reveals. According to Mundell's "global monetarism," there is a single world price level, P_{Qw}, determined by the ratio of total world domestic money supplies, M, to total world output, Q_W: P_{Qw} = f(M/Q_W). But in this view, official dollar reserves, R_s (= R - p*G), are important only insofar as they influence M; which requires that the reserve ratios a_o, a_1, and a_2, as well as all exchange rates, remain fixed. All but one of these special assumptions are unnecessary in Rueff's simpler and empirically more accurate theory: the U.S. price level, P_{US}, is a function of the world dollar base, consisting of the U.S. domestic monetary base, C_{US}, plus foreign official dollar reserves, R_s, to U.S. output, Q_{US}: P_{US} = f([C_{US} + R_s]/Q_{US}); the price level in any other country, say, Britain, P_{GB}, equals the U.S. price level times the sterling/dollar exchange rate, $e_{GB/US}$: P_{GB} = $P_{US}e_{GB/US}$. Rueff's theory remains true whether or not the dollar is convertible into gold and whether the exchange rate is fixed, managed, or allowed to float. But as actually happened under the international gold standard, P_{US} fluctuates around the same equilibrium level as long as a_0 = 1; that is, if there are no reserve currencies. As Jude Wanniski summarized in late 1985, "There's little support for returning to a dollar-centered Bretton Woods arrangement, politically unstable. Supply-siders divide over the alternatives, a multilateral standard of gold convertibility or an IMF-centered system of 'paper gold,' with a 'collective exercise of sovereignty.' . . . My tendency is to think along these [Mundellian] lines, rather than the Rueffian approach of Lehrman's. But both seem technically sound.'" Jude Wanniski, "The Kemp-Bradley Monetary Conference," *Polyconomics*, Morristown, NJ, November 20, 1985. In subsequent discussions in Kemp's congressional office and at the Lehrman Institute in New York, Kemp's monetary advisers came to an agreement in principle on a "plan [that] calls for a gold standard without reserve currencies in the United States, Europe, and Japan; nonindustrial countries would be free to choose gold or foreign exchange reserves": John Mueller, memo to Jack Kemp, "Supply-side Plan for International Monetary Reform," 17 April 1986; Jude Wanniski letter to Jack Kemp, 11 April 1986.

23. $M_S = \sum M_{Bdom} + \sum M_{Brow} + E = \sum K_M + \sum A_{Brow} + \sum A_{Bdom}$: the total money supply, M_S, equals domestic monetary liabilities, $\sum M_{dom}$, plus foreign monetary liabilities, $\sum M_{row}$, plus the central bank's equity, E; which equals commodity, e.g., gold money, $\sum K_M$, plus foreign loans, $\sum A_{row}$, plus domestic loans, $\sum A_{dom}$. In a modern monetary system, $\sum M_{dom}$ typically comprises legal tender currency

held by the public, plus commercial bank reserve deposits with the central bank, plus government deposits, while A_{dom} comprises loans to the government and the private banking system and A_{row} monetary reserves in foreign currencies.

24. John Mueller, "The World's Real Money Supply," *Wall Street Journal* (March 5, 1991); available at http://www.eppc.org/publications/pubID.2437/pub_detail.asp. There have been few academic studies on the subject so far. Among them are Oliver Fratscher, "The World Dollar Base and Causality," University of Montreal (May 1990); and "Monetarism Revisited: The World Dollar Base; Some theoretical and empirical evidence for an international monetary indicator," Harvard University (May 1991).

25. C. Northcote Parkinson, "Parkinson's Law," London *Economist* (November 1955); available at http://alpha1.montclair.edu/~lebelp/ParkinsonsLaw.pdf, accessed 17 February 2008.

26. "I have long favored cutting taxes at any time, in any manner, by as much as possible as the only way of bringing effective pressure on Congress to cut spending," Friedman explained. "Like every teenager, Congress will spend whatever revenue it receives plus as much more as it collectively believes it can get away with. Reducing spending requires cutting its allowance." Milton Friedman, "If Only the United States Were as Free as Hong Kong," *Wall Street Journal* (July 8, 1997), available at http://www.hoover.org/publications/digest/3522326.html. Ronald Reagan borrowed Friedman's reasoning in a 1980 presidential campaign debate and a 1982 budget speech: "John [Anderson] tells us that first, we've got to reduce spending before we can reduce taxes. Well, if you've got a kid that's extravagant, you can lecture him all you want to about his extravagance. Or you can cut his allowance and achieve the same end much quicker. But Government has never reduced[.] Government does not tax to get the money it needs. Government always needs the money it gets." The Anderson-Reagan presidential debate (September 21, 1980), Commission on Public Debates, available at http://www.debates.org/indexphp?page-september-21-1980-debate-transcript, accessed 7 July 2010. "Increasing taxes only encourages government to continue its irresponsible spending habits. We can lecture it about extravagance till we're blue in the face, or we can discipline it by cutting its allowance." Ronald Reagan, "Remarks at the Annual Policy Meeting of the National Association of Manufacturers," http://www.reagan.utexas.edu/archives/speeches/1982/31882c.htm, accessed 17 February 2008.

27. After leaving office, Reagan assessed the result this way: "With the tax cuts of 1981 and Tax Reform Act of 1986, I'd accomplished a lot of what I'd come to Washington to do. But on the other side of the ledger, cutting Federal spending and balancing the budget, I was less successful than I wanted to be. This was one of my biggest disappointments as president. I just didn't deliver as much to the people as I'd promised." Ronald Reagan, *Ronald Reagan: An American Life* (New York: Pocket Books, 1990), 355.

28. John Mueller, "CPI at 7%? Bet Your Reserve Dollar," *Wall Street Journal*

(February 24, 1989); "Recession's Coming—Will We Learn?" *Wall Street Journal* (June 29, 1989).

29. "Remarks by Governor Ben S. Bernanke, at a conference to honor Milton Friedman, University of Chicago, November 8, 2002," available at http://www.federalreserve.gov/BOARDDOCS/SPEECHES/2002/20021108/default.htm.

30. "Gold Reserves, tones, 1948–2008, major official gold holders," World Gold Council, http://www.research.gold.org/reserve_asset/; accessed 16 October 2009.

31. Jacques Rueff, *Balance of Payments: Proposals for Resolving the Critical World Economic Problem of Our Time*, (New York: Macmillan, 1967).

32. *Report to the Congress of the Commission on the Role of Gold in the Domestic and International Monetary Systems*, vol. II, annex A, "Supplementary and Dissenting Views" (March 1982), available at http://www.goldensextant.com/library.html, accessed 8 December 2008. On June 29, 1984, Jack Kemp introduced H.R. 5986, the Gold Standard Act of 1984, which would have defined the dollar as a fixed weight of gold, restored gold convertibility of Federal Reserve notes and deposits, and provided for gold coinage: 130 Congressional Record-House 20314–317. Both Kemp's explanatory statement, "Lower Interest Rates and Economic Growth by Restoring a Golden Rule," and Lewis E. Lehrman's op-ed column in the *Wall Street Journal* of that day, "Golden Antidote to High Interest," which Kemp inserted into the Congressional Record, remain valid.

33. The data in Figure 16–11 are from "U.S. Net International Investment Position at Yearend 2009," Bureau of Economic Analysis, BEA 10–32, 25 June 2010, http://www.bea.gov/international/.

Chapter 17

1. On the date, see William A. McDonald, "Archeology and St. Paul's Journey in Greek Lands: Athens," *The Biblical Archaeologist* 4:1 (February 1941): 1–10.

2. St. Augustine, *The City of God*, XIX.2, 843–44.

3. Benedict XVI, encyclical letter *Caritas in Veritate* (29 June 2009), http://www.vatican.va/holy_father/benedict_xvi/encyclicals/documents/hf_ben-xvi_enc_20090629_caritas-in-veritate_en.html. This choice of alternatives casts a different light on the long quest, especially among my fellow Roman Catholics, for a "third way" in economics, an effort that we considered in chapter 5. Pope John Paul II cautioned against doing so in his 1987 encyclical *Sollicitudo rei socialis:* "The Church's social doctrine is not a 'third way' between liberal capitalism and Marxist collectivism nor even a possible alternative to other solutions less radically opposed to one another: Rather, it constitutes a category of its own" (*SRS*, 41); http://www.vatican.va/holy_father/john_paul_ii/encyclicals/documents/hf_jp-ii_enc_30121987_sollicitudo-rei-socialis_en.html. The notion of a third way between capitalism and communism misconceives the alternatives, not merely in terms of revealed religion but also metaphysics and economic theory. The first way of biblically orthodox natural law is philosophi-

cally irreconcilable with the second way of pantheist Stoic necessity and the
third way of Epicurean "matter and chance," because the latter two exclude
Creation. In effect, Adam Smith was reverting to Stoic pantheism, which views
the universe "to be itself a Divinity, an Animal" (as Smith put it in an early but
posthumously published essay) and conceives of God as the immanent World
Soul, manipulating humans as puppets who choose neither their ends nor means
rationally, since "every individual . . . intends only his own gain . . . and is led by
an invisible hand to promote an end which was no part of his intention." Liberal
capitalism as described by Smith and Marx's communism are thus obverse sides
of Stoic pantheism. The main difference is that Smith tries to reduce all justice
to justice-in-exchange while Marx tries to reduce it to political distributive justice. John D. Mueller, "A Return to Augustinian Economics," *First Things* (19
August 2009), http://www.firstthings.com/onthesquare/2009/08/a-return-to-
augustinian-economics and http://www.eppc.org/publications/pubID.3910/
pub_detail.asp, retrieved 29 October 2009.
4. *The Age of Reason* "in essence . . . is an application of reason to the Bible, in
the light of the Newtonian principles of science." Editor Philip S. Foner, *The
Complete Writings of Thomas Paine*, vol. I, 460; retrieved 28 October 2009 from
http://www.thomaspaine.org/contents.html. Paine argued that "the story of
Christ is of human invention, and not of divine origin," and inveighed against
"the stupid Bible of the church." He noted wryly of the Apostle Thomas (the
"doubting Thomas" in whose name Paine was christened), "it appears that
Thomas did not believe the resurrection; and, as they say, would not believe
without having ocular and manual demonstration himself. *So neither will I*, and
the reason is equally as good for me, and for every other person, as for Thomas."
Theological Works of Thomas Paine, ed. Calvin Blanchard (Kessinger Publishing, 2003). Of course, according to John 20:28, the Apostle Thomas was convinced by what he considered "ocular and manual demonstration."
5. What Aristotle called the "divine science" of metaphysics is the rational discipline that studies the ultimate nature of reality and our knowledge about it.
(Aristotle, *Metaphysics* I [A], 2; in *A New Aristotle Reader*, ed. J. L. Ackrill,
[Princeton: Princeton University Press, 1987], 259). Aristotle coined the term
"metaphysics," which means roughly "beyond physics," and described it as "a
science which investigates being as being." He explained, "Now this is not the
same as any of the so-called special sciences, for none of these deals generally
with being as being. They cut off a part of being and investigate the attributes of
this part." Aristotle, *Metaphysics* [IV], 1; in *Aristotle Selections*, ed. W. D. Ross
(New York: Scribner, 1927), 53.
6. Sam Harris, *The End of Faith: Religion, Terror, and the Future of Reason* (New
York: W. W. Norton, 2004); Daniel Dennett, *Breaking the Spell: Religion as a
Natural Phenomenon* (New York: Penguin, 2006); Richard Dawkins, *The God
Delusion* (Houghton Mifflin Harcourt, 2006); and Christopher Hitchens, *God Is
Not Great: How Religion Poisons Everything*, (New York: Twelve, Hachette, 2007).

Meanwhile, David Kinnaman and Gabe Lyons document "the increasingly negative reputation of Christians, especially among young Americans. . . . They are perceived as being judgmental, antihomosexual, and too political," in *unChristian: What a New Generation Really thinks About Christianity . . . and Why It Matters* (Grand Rapids, MI: Baker Books, 2007); jacket summary. Logan Gage and Patrick Fagan have ably summarized and documented the scholarly evidence contradicting Dawkins's claim that "there's not the slightest evidence that religious people in a given society are any more moral than non-religious people." Logan Paul Gage, "Staying Power: Does Religion Really Poison Everything?" *Touchstone*, January/February 2008. http://touchstonemag.com/archives/article. php?id=21-01-062-r, retrieved 27 April 2010; Patrick Fagan, "Why Religion Matters Even More: The Impact of Religious Practice on Social Stability," 18 December 2006, http://www.heritage.org/research/reports/2006/12/why%20 religion%20matters%20even%20more%20the%20impact%20of%20religious%20practice%20on%20social%20stability, retrieved 27 April 2010.

7. Thomas Paine, *The Age of Reason*, in Thomas Paine, *Collected Writings*, The Library of America (1955): 688.

8. "The third way is taken from possibility and necessity, and runs thus. We find in nature things that are possible to be and not to be. . . . [I]f at one time nothing was in existence, it would have been impossible for anything to have begun to exist; and thus even now nothing would be in existence—which is absurd. . . . . Therefore we cannot but postulate the existence of some being having of itself its own necessity, and not receiving it from another, but rather causing in others their necessity. This all men speak of as God." Thomas Aquinas, *Summa theologiae*, I, A2, available at http://www.newadvent.org/summa/1002. htm, accessed 26 September 2009. Aquinas offered five proofs of God's existence, most of which had been given in a different form by Aristotle: from motion or change, which, with the impossibility of an infinity of causes, points to a First Mover, which we call God. Aquinas similarly offers proofs by Efficient Cause, from Necessary Being, from the Degrees of Being, and from the Final Cause. But in all of them, Thomas may be said to have transformed Aristotle with a new proof, the proof from existence. *Summa theologiae*, I, A3, ibid.

9. Étienne Gilson, *History of Christian Philosophy in the Middle Ages* (New York: Random House, 1955), 651.

10. Milton and Rose Friedman, *Free to Choose: A Personal Statement* (New York and London: Harcourt Brace Jovanovich, 1979), 1–2.

11. It continues, "So over the past century and into the next, the Journal stands for free trade and sound money; against confiscatory taxation and the ukases of kings and other collectivists; and for individual autonomy against dictators, bullies and even the tempers of momentary majorities." http://online.wsj.com/ public/page/news-opinion-commentary.html, retrieved 12 May 2009.

12. Hume is wrongly supposed by some to have demolished metaphysical reasoning, but he did demolish some very bad metaphysical reasoning. After a

string of philosophers, notably René Descartes (and before him Saint Anselm), had tried to prove the *existence* of God and of the external world from their *concepts* of God and the external world, Hume responded that while we can reason necessarily from one concept to another, and perceive the existence of external objects, we cannot possibly reason from the mere *concept* of one external object to the *existence* of another. "In short there are two principles which I cannot render consistent; nor is it in my power to renounce either of them, viz. *that all our distinct perceptions are distinct existences*, and *that the mind never perceives any real connection among distinct existences,*" Hume says in his *Treatise of Human Nature*. David Hume, *A Treatise of Human Nature: Being an Attempt to introduce the experimental Method of Reasoning into Moral Subjects* (Oxford: Clarendon Press, 1888 [1739]), 636: appendix. And thus far, Hume's argument is absolutely correct. In his own way, Hume was pointing to the peculiar fact of existence, which is what makes anything real or actual but cannot be *deduced* from any concept about it.

13. George J. Stigler, *The Theory of Price: Third Edition* (London: Macmillan, 1966), 6.

14. Milton Friedman, "The Methodology of Positive Economics," *Essays in Positive Economics* (Chicago: University of Chicago Press, 1953), 3–43. Friedman curiously insisted that the filing system's organization need not—in fact, *should not*—reflect the structure of the economic behavior it describes, because he followed Max Weber's confused notion that all classification is a falsification rather than a distillation of reality.

15. E. B. Wilson and George Stigler, "Mathematics in Economics: Further Comment," *The Review of Economics and Statistics* 37:3 (August 1955): 297–300.

16. G. K. Chesterton, *Orthodoxy* (London: John Lane, The Bodley Head, 1909), 58–59.

17. Stanley L. Jaki, *Bible and Science* (Front Royal, VA: Christendom Press, 1996), 107.

18. *Nicomachean Ethics*, VIII, 6; IX, 10.

19. American Chesterton Society (ACS) Quotemeister (1997), retrieved from http://chesterton.org/qmeister2/any-everything.htm on 29 October 2009.

20. *Questions for Simplicianus*, I.II.16; translation by Herbert A. Deane, *The Political and Social Ideas of St. Augustine* (Columbia University Press, 1963), 97.

21. "All men are by nature equal, made all of the same earth by one Workman; and however we deceive ourselves, as dear unto God is the poor peasant as the mighty prince."

22. "All men are by nature equal, and virtue alone establishes a difference between them."

23. "Men by nature equal." *Leviathan*, chapter 13.

24. "All are equal, and equals have no right over each other." Algernon Sidney, *Discourses Concerning Government*, Revised edition, foreword and ed. by Thomas G. West (Indianapolis: Liberty Fund, 1996), 3:33:511.

25. "All men are by nature equal . . . in that equal right that every man hath to his natural freedom, without being subject to the will or the authority of any other man; . . . being equal . . . no one ought to harm another in his life, health, liberty or possessions." John Locke, *Second Treatise on Government* (1698), chap. 2, section 6.

26. Ironically, the first African American president sided with Stephen Douglas against Abraham Lincoln on the Founders' understanding of the truth. According to Barack Obama, "It's not just absolute power that the Founders sought to prevent. Implicit in its structure, in the very idea of ordered liberty, was a rejection of absolute truth, the infallibility of any idea or ideology or theology or 'ism,' any tyrannical consistency that might lock future generations into a single unalterable course, to drive both majorities and minorities into the cruelties of the Inquisition, the pogrom, the gulag, or the jihad. The Founders may have trusted in God, but true to the Enlightenment spirit, they also trusted in the minds and senses that God had given them. They were suspicious of abstraction and liked asking questions, which is why at every turn in our early history theory yielded to fact and necessity." Barack Obama, *The Audacity of Hope: Thoughts on Reclaiming the American Dream* (New York: Random House, 2006), 144. But Lincoln argued, "All honor to Jefferson—to the man who, in the concrete pressure of a struggle for national independence by a single people, had the coolness, forecast, and capacity to introduce into a merely revolutionary document, an abstract truth, applicable to all men and all times, and so to embalm it there, that to-day, and in all coming days, it shall be a rebuke and a stumbling-block to the very harbingers of re-appearing tyrany [*sic*] and oppression." Abraham Lincoln, Letter to Henry L. Pierce and others, April 6, 1859, *The Collected Works of Abraham Lincoln*, ed. Roy P. Basler, vol. III, 376, http://name.umdl.umich. edu/lincoln3, retrieved 23 April 2010. If Obama was right in 2006, Lincoln was wrong in the argument he used so effectively against Douglas and slavery in 1859. As Peter J. Colosi perceptively noted, when paraphrasing the preamble to the Declaration of Independence as "the God-given promise that all are equal, all are free, and all deserve a chance to pursue their full measure of happiness" in his own inaugural address, "President Obama gave up 'created', 'Creator', and 'Life.'" Peter J. Colosi, Unpublished manuscript, July 2, 2010. Rather than Lincoln, Obama followed liberal constitutional scholars who express the Epicurean world view by routinely omitting Lincoln's words "under God" from the Gettysburg Address, as Robert George has documented. Robert George, "God and Gettysburg: 'Under God' were Lincoln's immortal words," *First Things*, August/September 2010, retrieved 9 August 2010 from http://www.firstthings. com/article/2010/07/god-and-gettysburg.

Acknowledgments

I owe a great debt to several editors and publishers at or engaged by ISI Books, (especially) Jeremy Beer, Jeffrey Nelson, Jed Donahue, Jennifer Fox, David Mills, and Adam Kissel, and to ISI's president, T. Kenneth Cribb Jr.

Many friends, acquaintances, and friendly critics have been extraordinarily generous with their scarce time in making suggestions about the manuscript of *Redeeming Economics* or articles related to it: Andrew V. Abela, Maria Sophia Aguirre, Dale Ahlquist, Kevin Andrews, Margaret Andrews, Hadley P. Arkes, Dean Baker, Stephen Balch, Doug Bandow, Fred Barnes, Francis J. Beckwith, Richard Behn, Jeffrey Bell, Herman Belz, Ralph Benko, Matthew Berke, Kenneth W. Bickford, Joseph Bottum, Rev. J. Ian Boyd, CSB, Gerard V. Bradley, Richard Brake, J. Budziszewski, Josiah Bunting III, Francis P. Cannon, James C. Capretta, Merrick Carey, Allan C. Carlson, James W. Ceaser, José Joaquín Chaverri, Stephen Clements, Peter Colosi, Matthew Cowper, Michael Cromartie, Thomas D'Andrea, John DeIulio, Patrick J. Deneen, Brian Domitrovic, Daniel Doron, Patrick Fagan, Don Feder, Edwin Feulner, Sean Fieler, Joseph Fornieri, John M. Finnis, David F. Forte, Gregory Fossedal, Logan Gage, Robert P. George, Kenneth B. Gray, Samuel Gregg, Earl Grinols, Khalil Habib, Stephen J. Haessler, Phillip Hamilton, Kelly Hanlon, Carson Holloway, John C. Hardin, Martin Holmer, Larry Jacobs, Adam Keiper, John Kelly, James P. Kemp, Jeff Kemp, Ken I. Kersch, Charles R. Kesler, Rev. Kestutis Kevalas, David Kidd, John B. Kienker, William Kristol, Lawrence Kudlow, James M. Kushiner, John L'Arrivee, Peter Augustine Lawler, Lewis E. Lehrman, Thomas D. Lehrman, John Lenczowski, François Lepoutre, Yuval Levin, Rev. Charles Lohr, SJ, G.A. "Sandy" Mackenzie, Gabriel Martinez, Tom Masters, Ken Masugi, Richard B. McPherson, Lawrence Mead, John Médaille, Carrie A. Miles, Marc Miles, Robert I. Mochrie, Gerson Moreno-Riano, Jennifer Roback Morse, Mark Mueller, Richard Mueller, Justin Mundy, Saulius Naujokaitis, Michael J. New, Jarl Nischan, Edd S. Noell, David Novak, Michael Novak, Joseph O'Brien, Mark O'Brien, Matthew O'Brien, Robert W. Patterson, John L. Pisciotta, Gary Quinlivan, Dermot A. Quinn, Richard W. Rahn, Jacques Raiman, Ann Robertson, Brian Robertson, Daniel N. Robinson, Maureen Rodger, Mark Rodgers, Mark Ryland, William Saunders, Rev. James V. Schall, SJ, Kevin Schmiesing, Gary Scott, Roger Scruton, Colleen Sheehan, Peter Singer, David M. Smick, Russell J. Snell, Matthew Spalding, Richard Starr, Robert Stein, James R. Stoner Jr., Michael Sugrue, Seana Sugrue, Luis Tellez, Dennis E. Teti, Lee Trepanier, Frank Trotta, Pete Wehner, George Weigel, M. Edward Whelan III, W. Bradford Wilcox, Bradford P. Wilson, Christopher Wolfe, Andrew Yuengert, and John Zmirak.

My sincere thanks to Georgetown University Press and David F. Forte for their kind permission to incorporate brief passages and footnotes from my essay "Taxation", in *Natural Law and Contemporary Public Policy*, and to Elliott Banfield and the *Claremont Review of Books* for their kind permission to use the graphic in Figure 8–3, which appeared with my review of *Freakonomics*.

My other half, Linda D. Mallon, provided what Chesterton calls "general sanity" along with valuable editorial advice. Christian T. Mueller designed the book jacket and guided me through the thickets of software to make it possible to publish the many graphs and tables. Lucy F. and Peter J. Mueller, besides making cameo appearances in chapter 7 to instruct me about the marginal utility of soup, provided the intelligent good cheer that kept us all on an even keel through what turned out to be a long decade.

Finally, my thanks to the Lehrman Institute, the Lincoln Institute, and Princeton University's James Madison Program in American Ideals and Institutions for allowing me take leaves of absence from business to pursue my hypothesis, and to my colleagues at the Ethics and Public Policy Center for permitting me to expound it. I am deeply grateful to their magnanimous, farsighted leaders and staff for making *Redeeming Economics* possible.

Index

Note: Page numbers ending in "f" refer to figures. Page numbers ending in "t" refer to tables.

Abela, Andrew V., 451
"Abortion and Crime," 516n8
abortion rates, 176–81, 181f, 224–26, 225f,
    278, 298f, 319–26, 322f, 324t, 434n6
"Abortion statistics and other data," 434n6
Accounting for Tastes, 100, 404n57, 404n62,
    404n66, 411n28, 413n17
Ackrill, John Lloyd, 446n5
Acton, Lord John Dalberg-, 370n3
"Adam Smith and the Invisible Hand,"
    387n3
adult labor status, 304f, 305f
Against the Gods, 412n3
Age of Inflation, The, 406n15, 441n6
Age of Reason, The, 388n7, 446n4, 447n7
Aguirre, Maria Sophia, 368n9, 369n9, 451
Ahlquist, Dale, 451
Akerlof, George A., 225, 226, 415n8,
    427n49, 428n49
Albert the Great, 26–28, 32, 377n31,
    378n35, 420n1
"Albert the Great and Medieval Culture,"
    378n35
Alexander Hamilton, 380n62
Alfarabi, 356
altruism, 103–4, 109, 144, 165–69, 198,
    206, 235
Ambrose, 373n27, 378n46
"America the Fertile," 434n4

American Chesterton Society, 448n19
American Founders, 34, 44–45, 90, 283,
    350, 385n115, 387n3, 434n2, 449n26
American Marriage and Divorce, 427n45,
    427n46
American National Election Studies (ANES),
    6, 284, 285f, 286f, 287, 288, 288f, 289f,
    291f, 435n6, 435n7, 435n10
American public choice, 283–302
"Analysis of Out-of-Wedlock Childbear-
    ing in the United States, An," 427n48,
    428n49
Ancient Law, 384n101
Anderson, John, 444n26
Andrews, Kevin, 451
Andrews, Margaret, 451
Annual Statistical Digest, 442n19
Anselm, 448n12
Applied Theory of Price, The, 412n3
Aquinas, 379n50
Aquinas, Thomas
    and benevolence and beneficence,
    381n72; and classical economics, 51, 59,
    73–74, 396n74; and division of moral
    philosophy, 47t, 106t, 368n7, 373n1;
    and division of sciences, 47t, 106t,
    373n1; and elements of economics, 1–6,
    367n7; and money, 385n96; and Moth-
    er's Problem, 142; and neoclassical eco-

nomics, 78, 87, 106t; and neo-Scholastic economics, 117–25, 368n6; and proofs of God's existence, 447n8; and property, 383n86, 383n87; and scarcity, 142, 190, 193–97; and Scholastic economics, 13–32, 35–39, 41–42, 46, 47t, 370n2, 372n16, 373n1, 378n36, 378n40, 378n41, 381n72, 382n77, 383n86, 384n96, 384n102, 384n104, 384n105, 385n106; and scientific method, 371n14; and social bonds, 205–6, 421n10; and worldviews, 356, 359, 363, 378n45, 379n50, 388n7, 447n8. *See also* organic unity vs. unity of order

"Archeology and St. Paul's Journey in Greek Lands," 445n1

Aristotelian Analysis of Usury, The, 380n55

Aristotle
and classical economics, 58–59, 64, 72, 392n34; and definition of love, 139, 409n14; and division of moral philosophy, 28, 47t, 368n7, 373n1; and elements of economics, 1–6, 22, 370n2, 371n12, 374n7, 376n18, 377n29, 392n34, 411n31; and language, 368n6; and mathematical economics, 375n13; and metaphysics, 446n5; and money, 384n94; and monopoly, 377n32; and Mother's Problem, 137–39; and neoclassical economics, 78, 83–84, 87, 96–97, 371n12; and neo-Scholastic economics, 112, 117–25, 130t, 175, 275, 368n6; and organic unity vs. unity of order, 38, 123–4, 382n85; and property, 382n77, 383n86, 383n87; and rhetoric, 52, 390n13; and scarcity, 191–92; and Scholastic economics, 13–31, 34–38, 46, 47t, 371n10, 371n12, 374n7, 376n16, 376n17, 376n18, 376n25, 377n29, 377n30, 377n31, 377n34, 382n77, 383n86, 383n87, 383n88, 383n89, 383n90, 385n95, 420n4; and social bonds, 112, 203–9, 405n1, 420n4, 420n5, 420n6, 420n7, 420n8, 420n9, 420n12; and utility, 27, 372n16; and worldviews, 28–9, 356, 359, 362–63, 371n14, 378n45, 379n50, 381n68, 382n77, 447n8

Arkes, Hadley P., 74, 451

Armey, Dick, 293, 295, 435n12

arrestees, 176–77, 177f, 181f

Arrow, Kenneth, 91, 165–66, 401n34

Ashley, Sir William J., 41–42, 124, 384n102, 384n103

Atlas of World Cultures, 426n39

Audacity of Hope, The, 449n26

"August Comte," 398n3

Auguste Comte, An Intellectual Biography, 398n2, 398n4

Auguste Comte and Positivism, 398n2, 398n5

Augustine
and classical economics, 56–59, 72; and commensurability of goods, 137–150, 368n7, 377n27; and elements of economics, 1–6, 367n4, 368n6, 377n27; and personal love, 368n6; and love and hate, 142t; and mathematical economics, 46, 409n8; and Mother's Problem, 133–53; and neoclassical economics, 77, 81–82, 87–92, 96, 155, 162, 170–73; and neo-Scholastic economics, 108, 118–19, 123–28, 130t, 175, 246, 368n8, 377n27; and personal distribution, 144t; and public vs. private goods, 25, 377n28; and scarcity, 37, 183, 186–99; and Scholastic economics, 15, 17, 18, 22, 23–30, 33, 34, 35, 36, 38, 46, 372n16, 375n26, 376n20, 376n21, 376n22, 376n23, 376n26, 377n27, 379n49, 379n50; and Schumpeter, 373n27; and social bonds, 206–9, 421n16; and worldviews, 52, 356, 359, 363

Augustine: Earlier Writings, 367n4, 376n22, 376n23, 378n46, 408n7

Avicenna, 356

Backhouse, Roger, 372n25

Baker, Dean, 451

balance of payments, 334–35

Balance of Payments, 445n31

Balch, Stephen, 451

Bandow, Doug, 451

Banfield, Elliott, 417n25, 451

Banking and Monetary Statistics, 442n19

banking standard, 335–36

Barnes, Fred, 451

Barnett, A. H., 405n3

Bartley, Robert L., 408n28

"basic commodities," 98, 101–2, 168

Beccaria, Cesare, 14

Becker, Gary S., 84, 95–106, 128, 166–69, 175, 198–99, 246, 358, 400n20, 403n49, 403n50, 403n51, 403n54, 403n55, 403n56, 404n57, 404n58,

404n62, 404n66, 404n68, 404n70, 404n72, 411n28, 413n15, 413n17, 414n20, 414n22, 414n23, 414n24, 414n25, 414n26, 414n29, 414n31, 415n3, 431n6
Becker–Barro assumption, 234–35
Becker-Stigler-Bentham assumptions, 101–2, 167–68, 176, 182–83
Beckwith, Francis J., 451
Beer, Jeremy, 451
Behn, Richard, 451
Being and Some Philosophers, 379n50
Bell, Jeffrey, 436n12, 451
Belloc, Hilaire, 121, 124, 406n14, 407n23
Belz, Herman, 451
Benedict XVI, 445n3
beneficence, 36, 56–58, 142, 142t, 190–91
benevolence, 36, 55–57, 98, 142, 142t, 190–91
Benko, Ralph, 451
Bentham, Jeremy, 81, 82, 89, 96–102, 198, 199, 399n15, 401n28, 404n58, 411n28. *See also* Becker-Stigler-Bentham assumptions
Berke, Matthew, 451
Bernanke, Ben, 341–42, 347, 441n21, 445n29
Bernholz, Peter, 404n63
Bernoulli, Daniel, 395n71, 412n3
Bernstein, Peter L., 412n3
Berry, Wendell, 116, 405n5, 405n6
Bettenson, H., 376n26, 409n7
betting, 160–61, 161f
Bible and Science, 448n17
biblically orthodox natural law, 3–4, 51–52, 355–56, 361, 363–64, 365t, 445n22. *See also* natural law
Bickford, Kenneth W., 451
birth rates, 176, 225–27, 225f, 277–78
Black, Duncan, 91, 402n37
Blanchard, Calvin, 446n4
Blaug, Marc, 372n25
Bloendal, S., et al., 431n5
Boland, Lawrence, 413n19
Boldrin, Michele, 235, 237, 429n8, 429n11, 429n13
Boldrin–Jones assumption, 235
bonds of human society, 203–29
"Born in the USA," 434n4
Bottum, Joseph, 451
Boudrieu, Pierre, 411n28
Bourgeois Virtues, The, 392n33

Bourke, Vernon J., 379n50
Bowling Alone, 411n28
Boyd, Rev. J. Ian, CSB, 451
Bradley, Senator Bill, 407n25
Bradley–Gephardt tax reform bill, 435n12
Bradley, Gerard V., 451
Bradley, Phillips, 387n5
Brake, Richard, 451
Breaking the Spell, 446n6
Bridget, J. H., 398n2
Buchanan, James M., 91–92, 402n37, 402n38, 402n39, 402n40
Buchholz, Todd G., 384n98
Budziszewski, J., 451
builder, 31–32
"Building Automatic Solvency into Social Security," 434n10
Bunting, Josiah III, 451
Buridan, Jean, 31
Burleigh, John H. S., 367n4, 376n22, 376n23, 377n28, 378n46, 408n7, 409n8
Bush, George W., 289–91, 296, 300, 347–48
Butterfield, Herbert, 370n2
"buying and selling," 18

Calculus of Consent, The, 402n36
Call, Vaughn R. A., 428n53
Cannan, Edwin, 61, 389n12, 390n20, 393n42
Cannon, Francis P., 436n12, 451
"Canon in the History of the Adam Smith Problem, The," 390n15
Cantillon, Richard, 70, 395n62
capital, kinds described, 20, 25, 84–85, 107, 215, 431n7
Capital, 80, 397n89, 399n7
Capitalism and Freedom, 432n14
Capretta, James C., 434n10, 451
cardinal utility, 81–82, 90, 235
Carey, Merrick, 451
Caritas in Veritate, 125, 355–56, 407n24, 445n3
Carlson, Allan, 121, 406n12, 451
Carmichael, Gerschom, 50, 386n3
Carter, Jimmy, 348
Catechetical Instructions of St. Thomas Aquinas, The, 381n72, 420n13
Catechism of Positive Religion, The, 106t, 398n4
Ceaser, James W., 398n5, 399n5, 451
Chafuen, Alejandro, 368n9
Chambre, Henri, 397n88

"Changing times," 427n43
Chaverri, José Joaquín, 451
Chesterton, G. K., 121, 124, 131, 201, 213, 231, 256, 273, 283, 353, 361, 363, 406n14, 422n20, 426n41, 432n8, 448n16, 452
"Chicago Counter-Revolution, The," 369n1
children, rearing, 231–43
choice of goods, 145–47, 146f
choice of means, 139–40
choice of persons, 143–44
choice of scarce, 145–47
Christendom in Dublin, 273
Christian Philosophy of St. Thomas Aquinas, The, 409n10
Christianity, 29, 356, 361, 363–64, 387n5, 406n20, 408n7, 413n18, 421n11, 445n3, 446n4, 447n6
Christians for Freedom, 368n9
"Christmas and the Aesthetes," 353
Chrysostom, 373n27
church–state relations, 43–44
City of God, The, 24, 27, 29, 30, 119, 139, 373n27, 376n26, 409n7, 409n12, 409n17, 419n1, 421n13, 421n14, 445n2
Claremont Review of Books, 417n25
Claridge, Tristan, 411n29
classical economics, 2, 46, 49–76, 355–65, 365t, 367n6, 371n12, 372n19, 375n13, 394n61, 395n71, 396n71
Clements, Stephen, 451
Clinton, Bill, 289–91, 348
Clippinger, Lancie, 116, 121
Coase, Ronald H., 93, 115–16, 402n44, 402n45, 402n46, 403n46, 403n47
Coase Theorem, 93–96, 114–15, 403n47
Coleman, James S., 411n28
Collected Works of Abraham Lincoln, 434n12
Collected Works of Philip Henry Wicksteed, 400n25
collectivism, 120, 127
Collings, Jesse, 406n14
Colosi, Peter J., 449n26, 451
Commentary on Aristotle's Nicomachean Ethics, 123, 373n1, 378n36, 378n41, 384n96, 420n1
Commentary on Aristotle's Politics, 27, 378n36, 382n40, 383n86
commodity money, 334, 345–47
Common Sense of Political Economy, 87, 133, 376n24, 399n6, 400n24, 401n26, 408n1, 408n2, 408n29, 432n10

commutative justice, 26, 40, 41, 42, 47t, 57, 58, 106t, 125, 373n1, 377n33, 392n34, 392n35. See also justice in exchange
compensation and income, 270f
compensation of factors, 32, 71–73, 308, 310, 380n63
compensation, labor vs. property, 271f, 374n9
Complete Writings of Thomas Paine, 446n4
Comte, Auguste, 78, 79, 106t, 398n2, 398n3, 398n4, 398n5, 399n5
"Concept of the Just Price, The," 384n93
Condillac, Étienne Bonnot, Abbé de, 71, 395n67
Confessions, 373n27
consumer price index, 328–32, 329f, 330t, 345–46
consumer price inflation, 346f
consumer prices and deposits, 341f
consumption, and income, 246f
consumption, and taxes, 295f
consumption theory, 1, 18, 20, 374n6, 377n28, 380n64, 431n3, 432n13
Copleston, F. C., 379n50
Cotton, John, 32
Cournot, Antoine Augustin, 395n71
Cowper, Matthew, 451
"Crash Course for Central Bankers, A," 442n21
Crell, Johannes, 32
Cribb, T. Kenneth Jr., 451
crime, 2, 176–81, 418n32; and abortion, 176–81; and arrests, 176–77, 177f, 181f
"Crime and Punishment," 414n26, 415n3
Crisis of Civilization, The, 407n23
"Critical Notes on the Wealth of Nations," 395n69
Critique of Political Economy, 396n73, 397n88
Critique of the Gotha Program, 397n87
Cromartie, Michael, 451
Cronin, Julie-Ann, 433n19
Crusoe, Robinson, 20, 79–80, 87–88, 133, 136, 408n6
Current Contents, 402n40
current predicament, 86–105

D'Andrea, Thomas, 451
Davanzati, Bernardo, 31
Dawkins, Richard, 446n6
Deane, Herbert A., 448n20
Declaration of Independence, 357, 364

"Défense et illustration de l'étalon-or,"
442n18
"Definitions of Social Capital," 411n29
Defoe, Daniel, 133, 408n6
Degrees of Knowledge, The, 373n1
"De Gustibus Non Est Disputandum,"
404n62
DeIulio, John, 451
De l'Aube au Crépuscule, 437n5
demand, 31–32, 39, 41–42, 86, 210. *See also*
utility theory
Democracy in America, 387n5
demographic exceptionalism, 276–77
demographic suicide, 276–77, 281
demographic transition, 232f
Dempsey, Bernard W., 372n15, 384n93,
384n105, 385n105
DeNavas-Walt, Carmen, et. al., 420n16
Deneen, Patrick J., 451
Dennett, Daniel, 446n6
Denuc, Jean, 437n6
deposits
and consumer prices, 341f; and stock
market, 337–41, 340f
Descartes, René, 448n12
"Determinants of Children's Attainments,
The," 404n62
Deus Caritas Est, 125, 407n24
"Development of Adam Smith's Ideas on the
Division of Labour, The," 391n27
"Development of Utility Theory, The,"
399n13
Dickens, Charles, 75, 77, 375n13
"Did Legalized Abortion Lower Crime?"
415n8
Discourses Concerning Government, 448n24
disequilibrium, 40–41, 303–6, 304f, 327–32
Dismal Science, The, 398n5
Distributive Justice, 384n99
distributive justice theory
and classical economics, 56–59, 72, 76,
371n12, 375n13, 392n34, 400n23; and
"distribution," 374n7; and elements
of economics, 5; and infant industry,
275; and marriage, 204, 214–16; and
Mother's Problem, 411n32; and neoclassical economics, 173, 371n12, 375n13,
411n31; and neo-Scholastic economics, 107, 112, 117–28, 405n2, 411n32,
429n14; and public choice, 283; and
Scholastic economics, 20–22, 28, 41–45,
373n1, 376n17, 376n19, 379n50; and

unemployment, 326; and worldviews,
358
divine economy, 7, 51, 121, 284, 353–65
division and methods of the sciences, The,
373n1
division of labor, 13, 57, 68, 71, 100–4,
110, 255, 327, 403n49
divorce
and abortion rates, 224–25, 225f; and
income, 262–63; statistics of, 223–24,
224f, 228t
"Does Economics Have a Useful Past?"
370n2
domestic economy, 6, 25, 37, 110–12, 129,
201–71
domestic monetarism, 341, 343
domestic trade, 37, 39–40
Domitrovic, Brian, 407n26, 451
Donahue, Jed, 451
Donohue, John J., 175–87, 415n1, 415n2,
415n4, 415n5, 415n6, 415n7, 415n8,
416n8, 416n9, 416n12
Donohue–Levitt paper, 175–87, 416n8
Doron, Daniel, 451
Douglas, Stephen, 449n26
Downs, Anthony, 91, 283, 402n37, 435n5
Dubner, Stephen, 198, 415n1
Dupuit, Arsène Jules Etienne, 395n71
Dye, Jane Lawler, 427n44

earnings
by age, 245–48, 247f, 254f; by education,
248–53, 248f, 249f, 268f; life earnings,
245–71, 246f; by marital status, 261–63
by sex, 253–61; and spending, 245–71;
year-round earnings, 249f, 255f
Eberstadt, Nicholas, 434n4
Eclipse of Keynesianism, The, 369n1
Econoclasts, 407n26
economic analysis, 12–15, 33–35, 371n10,
371n12, 371n14
"Economic Analysis of Fertility, An"
413n15, 414n22
Economic Approach to Human Behavior, The,
99, 403n50, 403n51, 403n54, 403n56,
404n58, 413n15, 414n20, 414n21,
414n22, 414n23, 414n25, 414n29,
415n3
economic behavior, 359
"Economic Consequences of Jacques Rueff,
The," 442n22
economic equations, 21

"economic fatherhood," 162, 175–87, 184f, 417n26, 418n30, 418n32, 419n32
Economic Imperialism, 404n63
"Economic Imperialism," 404n67
economic policies, 281t
Economic Recovery Tax Act of 1981, The, 407n25
Economic Sentiments, 387n3
economic theory
    "filing cabinet" of, 361f; history of, 11–13; Scholastic development of, 30–35; scholastic outline of, 17–35; structure of, 130t; worldviews of, 355–65, 365t
Economic Theory in Retrospect, 372n25
Economic Theory of Democracy, An, 402n37
"Economic Theory of Political Action in a Democracy, An," 402n37, 435n5
"Economic Way of Looking at Life, The," 404n66, 413n17
economics
    birth of, 9–130; death of, 9–130; definition of, 127–29; education on, 11–12; elements of, 1–8, 19–20, 30–35, 46, 49; "founder" of, 1, 12–15; oversimplification of, 15; redeeming, 8; resurrection of, 9–130; stepping stones of, 2–3; structure of, 45–46, 130t; theories of, 1–8
Economics in the Medieval Schools, 380n55
Economics of Heinrich Pesch, The, 118, 405n8
"Economics of Information, The," 403n47
Economics of the Family, 414n20, 414n25, 414n29
Economics of the Free Society, 407n22
Economics of Welfare, The, 401n29, 401n30
economies, growth in, 35
"Economist as Preacher, The," 4, 359
Economist as Preacher and Other Essays, The, 369n2, 370n2, 393n42
economists, predicament of, 86–105
Edgeworth, Francis Ysidro, 399n15
education and earnings, 248–53, 248f, 249f, 268f
egoism, 24, 109, 144
Einstein, Albert, 3
Eisenhower era, 288
Elam-Evans, Laurie D., 416n15
elements of economics, 1–8, 19–20, 30–35, 46, 49
Elements of Pure Economics, 399n12
empirical test, 175–87
employment and population, 269f

Encyclopedia of Law and Economics, 403n48
End of Faith, The, 446n6
"End of the Externality Revolution. The," 405n3
"Energetic America," 440n25
Epicurean materialism, 55, 75–76, 78, 283–84, 355–61, 365t, 445n22, 446n3, 449n26
equilibrium
    and classical economics, 49, 64–66; and elements of economics, 1, 5; and marriage, 215–16; and Mother's Problem, 411n31; and neoclassical economics, 85–86, 401n31, 411n31; and neo-Scholastic economics, 260, 425n36, 426n36; and Scholastic economics, 20, 26, 41–43, 46, 376n15, 378n36, 380n61
"Equilibrium Theory of the Distribution of Income, An," 403n49
Escape from Hunger and Premature Death, 1700–2100, The, 426n42
Essai sur la Nature du Commerce en Général, 395n62
Essay on the Nature and Significance of Economic Science, An, 399n14, 409n18
Essays in Positive Economics, 381n68, 448n14
Essays in the History of Economics, 369n2, 370n2
Essays on Philosophical Subjects, 389n8
Essential Augustine, The, 379n50
Ethics. See Nicomachean Ethics
Everlasting Man, The, 131
evolution, 361
"Evolution, development and timing of puberty," 427n43
"Exposition of a New Theory on the Measurement of Risk," 395n71

factor compensation, 32, 71–73, 308, 310, 371n12
Fagan, Patrick, 447n6, 451
Faith and Liberty, 368n9
"Fallacies of Lord Keynes General Theory, The," 437n7
"Family and Economic Development, The," 368n9
family income, 267f, 285f, 288f
"Famine, Affluence and Morality," 419n6
Farmer Refuted, The, 74, 380n62
"Father absence, parental care and female reproductive development," 427n43
fatherhood, 175–87, 184f, 185f

fatherhood vs. homicide, 184f, 185f
Feder, Don, 451
Federal Reserve, 327–32, 334, 336–44,
347–48, 351, 441n11, 442n19, 443n32
federal spending projections, 321f, 434n7
Federalist, The, 34, 44, 385n112, 385n113,
385n117, 385n224, 386n117, 434n1,
435n3, 435n8, 435n9
Feldstein, Martin, 299, 301
Ferrara-Ryan-Sununu, 301
"Fertility and Mortality in the United
States," 426n42, 428n5
"Fertility and Social Security," 429n8
"Fertility of American Women," 427n44
fertility rates, 232–43, 232f, 233f, 236f,
237f, 239f, 240t–41t, 319–24, 323t,
324t, 428n3, 428n4
fertility status, 221–22, 222f
"Fertility Tables for Birth Cohorts by Color,"
427n44
fertility vs. national saving, 237f
fertility vs. social spending, 236f
fertility vs. weekly worship, 239f
Festy, Patrick, 427n44
Feulner, Edwin, 451
Fieler, Sean, 451
"filing cabinet" of economic theory, 361f
final distribution theory
and classical economics, 49, 56–58,
72–73; and elements of economics, 1;
and marriage, 213–16; and neoclassical economics, 86, 103; and Scholastic
economics, 20, 22–24, 46, 374n7; and
worldviews, 363
Finnis, John M., 451
Firm, the Market and the Law, The, 403n46
fiscal policy, 40, 74, 212, 243, 277, 302,
309, 319–21
Flat Tax, The, 435n12
flat taxes, 195, 293–98, 294f, 295f
"Fluctuations Comparées du Chômage et
des Salaires, Les," 437n6
Fogel, Robert William, 426n42
Foner, Philip S., 446n4
Foote, Christopher L., 415n8
Forbes, Steve, 293, 295, 435n12, 436n12
Ford, Gerald, 348
foreign dollar deposits, 337–41, 340f, 341f
foreign trade, 37, 39–40
Formation and Stocks of Total Capital, The,
400n21, 406n21
Fornieri, Joseph, 451

Forte, David F., 369n9, 451, 452
Fossedal, Gregory, 451
Foundations of Technique, The, 369n9
"founder" of economics, 1, 12–15, 371n10
Fox, Jennifer Connolly, 451
Fratscher, Oliver, 444n24
Freakonomics, 5, 175, 198, 415n1, 452
"free to choose," 101, 127, 357, 364
Free to Choose, 357, 447n10
Friedman, David, 385n108
Friedman, Milton, 265–66, 341–43, 347,
357, 359, 364, 381n68, 432n14, 442n20,
444n26, 445n29, 447n10, 448n14
Gage, Logan, 447n6, 451
Galiani, Ferdinando, 31, 33
gasoline prices, 347–48
gasoline prices vs. voter approval, 348f
General Theory, 307, 437n7
General View of Positivism, A, 398n2
George, Robert P., 196, 373n5, 449n26, 451
Gephardt, Rep. Dick, 407n25
"Gifts and Exchanges," 413n14
Gilson, Étienne, 362, 379n50, 409n10,
447n9
globalization, 39–40
global monetarism, 443n22
"Glory of Grey, The," 426n41
Gluckman, Peter D., 427n43
"Go Forward to Gold," 440n1
"God and Gettysburg," 449n26
God Delusion, The, 446n6
God Is Not Great, 446n6
Goetz, Christopher F., 415n8
Gold Commission Report, 445n32
gold standard, 306, 330–31, 334–40,
349–51, 442n17, 443n22, 445n32
Gold Standard, The, 442n17
Gold Standard Act of 1984, The, 445n34
Golden Franc, The, 441n14
Golden Rule, 192, 194
Goldstein, Joshua, 427n44
"Good Farmer of the Old School, A,"
405n5
Good Samaritan, 37, 189–99
goodwill, 30, 36, 142, 142t, 190
Goodwin, Robert P., 409n10
Goss, Stephen C., 300
Gossen, Hermann Heinrich, 395n71
government, purpose of, 38–39, 73–75
government subsidies, 303, 310–11
Granger, C. W. J., 416n10, 416n11, 417n27

Gray, Kenneth B. Jr., 451
Great Depression, 7, 162–63, 314, 328, 340–43, 347
"Great Gap," 13, 28–30, 362
Great Recession, 7, 328
Gregg, Samuel, 451
Grinols, Earl, 451
Grotius, Hugo, 33, 49
Growth of Economic Thought, The, 369n10, 372n25
Grundsätze der Volkswirtschaftslehre, 399n12

Habib, Khalil, 451
Haessler, Stephen J., 451
Haines, Michael, 426n42
Hall, Robert E., 435n12
Hall–Rabushka tax reform plan, 435n12, 436n12
Hamilton, Alexander, 34, 45, 74–75, 350, 380n62, 385n117, 386n117, 396n81, 396n82, 397n82, 439n17, 440n25
Hamilton, Phillip, 451
Hanlon, Kelly, 451
Hansel and Gretel, 166
Hanson, Mark A., 427n44
Hardin, John C., 451
Harris, Sam, 446n6
Hasson, Seamus, 44, 385n111
Hasting, Donald W., 427n44
hate explanation, 169–73. *See also* love and hate
Haveman, Robert, 404n67
Hawtrey, Ralph George, 442n17
Hayek, Friedrich, 121, 124, 406n17
Hayward, J. E. S., 406n20
Heap, Shaun Hargreaves, 405n74
Heaton, Tim B., 428n52
Hegel, Georg Wilhelm Friedrich, 75–76
Heinrich Pesch on Solidarist Economics, 405n10
Henry of Friemar, 31, 32
Heretics, 353
Herford, Charles Harold, 399n11, 400n25
Hetherington, Norriss S., 387n3
Heuser, Robert, 427n44
Himmel in Stein, 385n107
Historical Statistics of the United States, 417n23, 441n3
History of Christian Philosophy in the Middle Ages, 447n9
History of Economic Analysis, 4, 12–13,

118, 369n2, 370n4, 370n5, 371n6, 371n7, 371n8, 371n9, 371n10, 371n11, 371n12, 371n13, 371n14, 372n15, 372n16, 372n17, 372n18, 372n19, 372n20, 372n22, 372n23, 372n24, 373n4, 373n27, 381n67, 381n69, 386n1, 390n21, 397n91, 402n43
"History of Law and Economics," 403n48
History of Monetary and Credit Theory, 441n9
Hitchens, Christopher, 446n6
Hobbes, Thomas, 58, 113, 364, 392n35
Holloway, Carson, 451
Holmer, Martin, 451
homicide, 175–87, 184f, 185f
Hoover, Herbert, 339
Human Action, 405n11, 413n13
"human approach," 175–87
human behavior, 175–87
"human capital"
  and classical economics, 70–71, 394n61, 395n61; and marriage, 210–16; and Mother's Problem, 151; and neoclassical economics, 82–85, 97–100; and neo-Scholastic economics, 123–24, 245–53, 264–68, 431n7; and public choice, 292–99; and Scholastic economics, 20, 25–26, 34–35, 374n8, 374n10, 374n11
Human Capital, 400n20
human nature, view of, 47t, 79, 97, 106t, 164–65, 365t
human society, bonding, 203–29
Humane Economy, A, 122, 406n18
humans and animals, 137–39
Hume, David, 55, 75–76, 78–79, 81, 164, 357, 365t, 388n6, 391n24, 391n25, 398n1, 398n5, 412n7, 447n12, 448n12
Hutcheson, Francis, 50, 55, 386n3, 390n23, 397n91
Huxley, Thomas H., 398n4

ideology, 291f
"Impossibility of a Paretian Liberal, The" 402n36
"Incidence of Divorce, The," 427n47
"In defense of Thomas Aquinas and the just price," 385n108
income
  by age, 245–48, 247f, 254f; and consumption, 215f, 246f; increase in, 51; and taxes, 278–79, 294f, 296f; indifference curves, 173, 399n15, 410n26, 414n30, 414n31; individualism, 91,

120–21, 126–29, 136; infant industry,
saving, 275–81, 408n26, 433n1
infant mortality, 232–33, 428n4, 429n6,
429n13, 430n16, 430n19
inflation, 304f, 327–32
injustice in exchange theory
causes of, 40–41; and classical economics, 64–65; and elements of economics, 5;
and inflation, 327–51; and production,
66–68; and unemployment, 7, 303–26.
See also commutative justice
*Inquiry into the Nature and Causes of the
Wealth of Nations, An,* 390n20. *See also
Wealth of Nations*
*Inquiry into the Original of Our Ideas of
Beauty and Virtue, An,* 390n23
"Institution Structure of Production, The,"
402n45
Interest and Usury, 372n15
interest on loans, 35
international balance of payments, 334–35,
445n31
International Economics, 442n22
intrafamily gifts, 6, 216, 247, 263–66
*Introduction to English Economic History and
Theory, An,* 384n102, 384n103
Introduction to Moral Theology, An, 368n8
Introductory Lectures on Political Economy,
395n68
"Investment in Human Capital," 399n17,
406n21, 411n30
"Investment in Human Capital Through
Post-Compulsory Education and Train-
ing," 431n5
investments vs. monetary reserves, 349f
"invisible hand," 4, 53–54, 72, 361, 364,
367n4, 387n6, 388n6, 446n3
"Invisible Hand and Economic Man, The,"
388n6
"Iron Law of Wages," 70, 77
"Isaac Newton's Influence on Adam Smith's
Natural Laws in Economics," 387n3
Italian Merchant in the Middle Ages, The,
382n75

Jacobs, Larry, 451
Jacobson, Paul H., 224–25, 427n45,
427n46, 427n47
Jaki, Stanley, 362, 448n17
James Madison Program, 373n5, 420n18,
452
J.-B. Say, 395n69

Jefferson, Thomas, 357, 364, 449n26
"Jesse Collings," 406n14
Jesus, 3, 18, 385n109
Jevons, William Stanley, 81, 399n12,
399n15
John Paul II, 199, 420n20, 445n3
Johnson era, 288
Johnston, William Robert, 434n6
Joyce, Ted, 415n8
"Just Price in a Functional Economy,"
372n15
Justice as Fairness, 402n36
justice in exchange theory
and classical economics, 49, 64–66; and
elements of economics, 1, 5; and marriage, 215–16; and neo-Scholastic economics, 85–86; and neoclassical economics, 260; and Scholastic economics, 20,
26, 41–43, 46, 377n33; and worldviews,
363
"Justum Pretium," 384n93

Kasten, Senator Bob, 407n25
Katz, Michael L., 415n8, 428n49
Keiper, Adam, 451
Kelly, John, 451
"Kemp-Bradley Monetary Conference, The,"
443n22
Kemp, Jack, 6, 125–26, 295, 407n25,
407n26, 435n12, 436n12, 443n22,
445n32
Kemp, James P., 451
Kemp, Jeff, 451
Kemp–Kasten tax reform bill, 407n25,
436n12
Kendrick, John W., 84–85, 124, 359,
400n21, 406n21, 407n22
Kennedy, John F., 288, 289
Kennedy era, 288–89
Kennen, Patricia Ann, 382n75
Kenney, Catherine T., 427n44
Kersch, Ken I., 451
Kesler, Charles R., 451
Ketteler, Wilhelm Emmanuel Freiherr von,
124, 407n23
Kevalas, Rev. Kestutis, 451
Keynes, John Maynard, 126, 307, 342–43,
437n7, 442n22
Keynesians, 11, 126, 307, 359–60, 369n1,
408n28
Kidd, David, 451
Kienker, John B., 451

Kinnaman, David, 447n6
Kissel, Adam, 451
Knight, Frank H., 369n2
Kohler, Thomas C., 387n3, 406n20
Korotayev, Andrey, 426n38
Kristol, William, 451
Kudlow, Lawrence, 451
Kunze, Konrad, 385n107
Kushiner, James M., 451

labor compensation, 20, 67–68, 84, 114,
    215, 246–56, 266–71, 270f, 287–98,
    306–17, 375n12
labor costs, 307–26, 313f, 314f, 315f, 317f,
    319f, 325f, 326t
labor, division of, 13, 57, 68, 71, 100–4,
    110, 255, 327, 403n49
labor income, 316–18, 317f
labor market, 315f, 319–21, 320f, 324f
labor status, 304–5, 304f, 305f
"labor theory of value," 4, 14, 55, 61–64,
    69, 71–81, 126
labor vs. compensation, 271f
Lactantius. 373n27
Laffer, Arthur, 126, 438n10
Langholm, Odd, 31, 32, 377n31, 380n51,
    380n54, 380n55, 380n57, 380n59,
    380n60, 394n55, 395n66
L'Arrivee, John, 452
Lawler, Peter Augustine, 452
Lazear, Edward P., 102, 404n67
Lectures on Jurisprudence, 390n12
Lectures on Justice, 389n12, 391n27
Lectures on Rhetoric and Belles Lettres, 386n5,
    390n12, 390n14
Leeson, Robert, 369n1
Lehrbuch der Nationalökonomie, 117, 118,
    119, 405n10
Lehre von der Wirtschaft, Die, 407n22
Lehrman, Lewis E., 327, 386n118, 436n1,
    436n12, 440n1, 440n25, 443n22,
    445n32, 452
Lehrman, Thomas D., 452
Lemaître, Georges, 3, 367n1
lemonade stand, 209–16, 269, 309–13,
    333–34, 422n19
Lenin, Vladimir Ilyich [né Ulyanov], 75–76,
    397n86, 397n90
Lenczowski, John, 452
Lenzer, Gertrud, 398n2, 398n5
Lepoutre, François, 452
Lethem, Yvonne, 400n21

Letter to Fortunatianus, 367n4
Leviathan, 392n35, 448n23
Levin, Yuval, 452
Levitt, Steven D., 5, 175–87, 198–99, 358,
    415n1, 415n2, 415n4, 415n5, 415n6,
    415n7, 415n8, 416n8, 416n9, 416n11,
    416n12, 427n47
Liberalism, Socialism and Christian Social
    Order, 117
life earnings, 245–71
life expectancy, 219f
life expectancy and fertility rates, 232f
life expectancy increase, 34, 51, 218–20,
    219f, 231–32. See also mortality decline
Life of Adam Smith, The, 386n2, 388n6,
    392n34, 394n55
lifetime income and consumption, 246–47,
    246f
Lincoln, Abraham, 45, 90, 275, 281, 288,
    301, 386n118, 386n119, 434n12,
    440n25, 449n26
Lincoln at Peoria, 386n118
List, Friedrich, 75, 397n84
Litzinger, C.I., 373n1, 378n36, 378n41,
    378n42, 420n1, 420n3, 421n4, 421n5
Living Wage, A, 384n99
Lodge, Henry Cabot, 380n62, 396n81
loans, interest on, 35
Locke, John, 364, 449n25
Logic of Collective Action, The, 402n37
Lohr, Rev. Charles SJ, 452
London Times, 306, 437n5
"Long-Term Budget Outlook, The," 434n7
Lott, John R. Jr., 415n8
love, 23–24, 36–37, 171f, 172f
Love and Economics, 368n9
love and hate, 103, 142t, 143–44, 169–73
love and morality, 189–90
love of self, 23, 44, 56–59, 109, 144, 148,
    172, 181
Luke, 355
Lyons, Gabe, 446n6

Macaulay, Thomas Babington, 370n3
Mackaay, Ejan, 95. 403n48
Mackenzie, George Alexander, 452
MacCrimmon, Kenneth R., 412n4
Madison, James, 44–45, 283, 287, 385n112,
    385n113, 385n114, 385n115
Maimonides, 356
Maine, Sir Henry, 41, 124, 384n101
Mair, Johannes, 32, 65, 394n55

Mallon, Linda D., 452
Malthus, Thomas, 70, 440n25
Manual of Political Economy, 401n31
"Map" of the Human Person, 47t, 106t
marginal utility, 60, 81–82, 88, 126–28,
    142, 155–62, 158f, 167, 170, 193, 259
"marginal value," 156, 156f
Marglin, Stephen A., 398n5
Maritain, Jacques, 373n1
marital and fertility status, 221–22, 222f
marital dissolution, 224f
marital status, 220, 221f, 222f, 261–63
market, order in, 363–64
marriage
    and abortion rates, 225–26, 225f; being
        given in, 18; and bonding, 203–29;
        disappearance of, 216–29, 218f; and
        divorce, 224f, 228–29; and family, 218f
"Marriage and Divorce," 427n47
"Marriage and Divorce in Twentieth Cen-
    tury American Cohorts," 427n44
"Marriage and the Family in Economic
    Theory and Policy," 368n9
"Marriage Delayed or Marriage Foregone?"
    427n44
Marshall, Alfred, 21, 85–86, 89, 375n13,
    400n22
Martineau, Harriet, 398n2
Martinez, Gabriel, 452
Marx, Karl, 4, 49, 69–70, 73–82, 120,
    126–27, 364, 396n73, 397n86, 399n6,
    399n7, 445n2, 446n3
"Marxian Theory of Value, The," 399n6
"Marxism," 397n88
Maslow, Abraham, 162, 412n6
Masters, Thomas, 452
Masugi, Ken, 452
Mathematical Psychics, 399n15
"Mathematics in Economics," 448n15
"matrimonial" nature, 5, 83, 127, 203–4,
    206, 209, 216, 220, 266, 357, 373n1,
    422n18
Maurer, Armand, 373n1
Mauss, Marcel, 392n33
May, William E., 368n8
McCloskey, Deirdre (Donald) N., 391n33,
    392n33, 412n3
McDonald, William A., 445n1
McPherson, Richard B., 452
Médaille, John C., 369n9, 452
Meek, Ronald L., 390n12, 391n27
Melanchthon, Philip, 32

McDonald, John, 427n47
McInerny, Ralph, 373n1, 378n36, 378n41,
    420n1
Mead, Lawrence, 452
"Measurement of Utility and the Economics
    of Risk, The," 412n3
Melitz, Jacques, 370n2
Mellon, Andrew, 339
Memoirs of an Unregulated Economist, 370n2,
    403n47
Memorials of Alfred Marshall, 375n13
Menger, Carl, 81, 85, 399n12
Merchant in the Confessional, The, 380n55
Metaphysics, 446n5
"Methodology of Positive Economics, The,"
    381n68, 448n14
Michael, R.T., 403n51, 403n52, 403n53,
    404n70
Miles, Carrie A., 452
Miles, Marc A., 438n10, 452
Mill, John Stuart, 12, 14, 71–72, 74, 78,
    372n21
Millar, John, 389n12
Mills, David, 451
Mises, Ludwig von, 118, 120–25, 164–65,
    405n9, 405n11, 406n17, 412n8,
    413n11, 413n12, 413n13
missing element, 1–8
Mitchell, Broadus, 380n62
Mochrie, Robert I., 452
"Monetarism Revisited," 444n24
Monetary History of the United States, A, 341,
    442n20
monetary policy, 278, 326–34, 339, 341–43
monetary reform, 280–81
monetary reserves vs. investments, 349f
Monetary Sin of the West, The, 441n13,
    442n18
monetary standards, 328–32, 329f
monetary theory, 31, 442n22
Monetary Theory, 442n22
money, uses of, 327–32
monopoly regulation, 40, 42–43, 121,
    372n15, 377n32, 377n33
"Monopoly Theory Prior to Adam Smith,"
    372n15
Montanari, Geminiano, 31
Monthly Treasury Bulletin, 442n19
moral choice, 189–99
Moral Foundations of Civil Society, The,
    406n16
moral Newtonianism, 4, 51–55, 61, 446n4

Moreau, Émile, 441n14
Moreno-Riano, Gerson, 452
Morse, Jennifer Roback, 368n9, 369n9, 452
mortality decline, 34–35, 218, 222–24, 231–33, 245, 264–65, 381n66. *See also* life expectancy increase
"Mother's Problem," 5, 87–89, 96, 103, 108, 133–53, 148f, 149f, 162–70, 199
Moure, Kenneth, 441n15
"Mouse Assumption," 70
movable type invention, 33
Mueller, Christian T., 452
Mueller, John D., 367n3, 369n9, 373n5, 398n5, 399n16, 406n17, 407n24, 412n2, 417n25, 420n18, 420n19, 427n48, 428n1, 430n20, 431n2, 432n12, 433n1, 434n8, 434n9, 437n2, 437n9, 438n10, 439n22, 440n1, 440n23, 440n24, 442n22, 443n22, 444n24, 444n28, 446n3
Mueller, Lucy F., 452
Mueller, Mark, 452
Mueller, Peter J., 452
Mueller, Richard, 452
Mulcahy, Richard E., SJ, 405n8
Mundell, Robert A., 126, 342–43, 442n22
Mundy, Justin, 452
Murdock, George P., 426n39
Myers, Robert, 280, 301

Nagel, Thomas, 413n14
national income, 265–71, 315–16, 315f, 317f, 438n11, 438n12
"National Income Gap," 269, 303, 315–16, 315f, 325f
national saving vs. fertility, 237f
National System of Political Economy, The, 397n84
"Nature and Role of Originality in Scientific Progress, The" 370n2
"Nature of the Firm, The," 402n46
natural law
    and classical economics, 50–52; and elements of economics, 3, 7; and neoclassical economics, 78; and neo-Scholastic economics, 117; and public choice, 284 and scarcity, 199; and Scholastic economics, 14, 33–36, 43–44, 380n61, 386n3; and worldviews, 355–57, 363–64, 365t, 379n50, 445n3
Natural Law, 369n9

Natural Law and Contemporary Public Policy, 369n9
natural lawyers, 7, 368n8
Naujokaitis, Saulius, 452
neighborhood yard sale, 332–34
Nelson, Jeffrey, 451
neoclassical economics, 5–6, 46, 77–106, 155–73, 355–65, 365t
neo-Scholastic economics, 5–7, 107–30, 245–71, 355–65, 365t, 367n6
neo-Thomism, 118, 124, 367n6
New, Michael J., 452
New Aristotle Reader, A, 446n5
New Ideas From Dead Economists, 384n98
"New Welfare Economics," 90–95, 401n31, 402n42
New York Times Magazine, 198, 419n12
"New Yorker's Eye View" of economics, 12, 369n2
Newbold, P., 416n10
Newton, Isaac, 51, 387n5, 446n4
Newtonianism, 4, 51–55, 61, 377n5, 446n4
Nicomachean Ethics, 22, 24, 26–28, 31, 119, 203–4, 205, 206, 209, 376n16, 376n25, 377n30, 378n44, 380n53, 381n72, 384n95, 392n34, 400n25, 405n7, 420n3, 420n4, 421n5, 423n25, 448n18
Nischan, Jarl, 452
Nixon, Richard, 348
Noell, Edd S., 452
nominalism, philosophical, 365t, 371n14, 372n14
nondurables vs. oil supply, 347f
"nonhuman capital"
    and classical economics, 70–71; and marriage, 210–16; and neoclassical economics, 82–85, 97–100; and neo-Scholastic economics, 123–24, 245–53, 264–68, 431n7; and public choice, 292–99; and Scholastic economics, 20, 25–26, 34–35, 374n11
normative economics, 17, 31, 34–45, 73–76, 88–89, 124, 175, 238, 369n9, 381n68, 381n69, 402n40
Norton, D.F., 387n3
"Notion of Solidarity, The," 387n3, 406n20
Novak, David, 452
Novak, Michael, 452

Oakeshott, Michael, 392n35
Obama, Barack, 399n25, 449n26
O'Brien, Joseph, 452
O'Brien, Mark, 452

O'Brien, Matthew, 452
"Observations on the History of Cohort Fertility in the United States," 428n3
Odishelidze, Alexander, 438n10
Odonis, Gerald, 32
"Of the Good of Marriage," 422n18
oil supply vs. nondurables, 347f
"Ökonomisches Kapital, kulturelles Kapital, soziales Kapital," 411n28
Olson, Mancur, 91, 402n37
O'Meara, J., 376n26, 409n7
On Being and Essence, 409n10
On Christian Doctrine, 130t, 376n20, 376n21, 377n28, 381n71, 381n73, 408n7, 409n7, 409n15, 410n19, 419n2
On Free Will, 139, 376n23, 377n28, 408n7, 409n8, 409n9, 409n16
On the Moral Behavior of the Catholic Church, 379n50
"On the New Theory of Consumer Behavior," 403n51, 404n70
On Kingship, 38, 123, 382n79, 382n80, 382n81, 382n82, 382n83, 382n84, 382n85, 383n91, 385n109
On the Duty of Man and Citizen According to Natural Law, 33, 50, 380n61, 380n62, 385n110, 386n3
"On the Futility of Criticizing the Neo-classical Maximization Hypothesis," 413n19
"On the rationale of group decision making," 402n37
On the Wealth of Nations, 395n69
order in market, 363–64
ordinal utility, 81–82, 90, 107
Ordinary Business of Life, The, 372n25
Oresme, Nicole, 31, 32, 40
organic unity vs.unity of order, 38, 128, 205–6, 382n85, 406n20, 421n10, 421n11
Orthodoxy, 283, 448n16
oversimplification, 15
ownership rights, 38–39, 382n77, 383n86, 383n87

Paine, Thomas, 52, 356, 388n7, 446n4, 447n7
Palmer, R.R., 395n69
Papers of James Madison, The, 434n2
"paradox of value," 59
parenting, 231–43
Pareto, Vilfredo, 401n31, 402n42
Parkinson, C. Northcote, 343–44, 444n25
"Parkinson's Debt Corollary," 345f

Parkinson's Law, 343–44, 345f, 444n25, 444n26
"Parkinson's Law," 444n25
Patterson, Robert W., 452
Paul, 29, 208, 355, 406n20, 445n1
Pay to the Order of Puerto Rico, 438n10
pay-as-you-go system, 114, 235, 242, 265–66, 279, 298–301, 311–12, 351
personal distribution function, 5, 143–45, 144f, 238, 358
personal distribution theory
and classical economics, 56–57; and elements of economics, 5; and marriage, 209; and Mother's Problem, 133, 151–53; and neoclassical economics, 155; and scarcity, 186, 191; and Scholastic economics, 22–28; and worldviews, 357–58, 363
personal economy, 5, 36, 108–10, 127–29, 131–99
personal gifts, 214–16, 368n6
personal income, 267f
personalism, 127–29, 136
Pesch, Heinrich, 117–25, 130t, 405n8, 405n10
Peters, Richard S., 392n35
Peters-Fransen, Ingrid, 390n15
Philip Henry Wicksteed, 399n11, 400n25
Pickering, Mary, 398n2
Piedra, Alberto M., 369n9
Pigou, Arthur C., 89–90, 93, 114, 375n13, 401n29, 401n30
Pisciotta, John L., 452
"planting and building," 18
Plato, 205, 356, 364, 379n50, 383n87, 384n94, 392n33
"Poet's Knowledge," 360, 361f
"Policeman as a Mother, The," 199, 422n20
Political and Social Ideas of St. Augustine, The, 448n20
political distribution theory, 5, 22–24, 44, 58, 363
political distributive justice, 45, 58, 214, 275, 283, 326, 363, 376n19, 446n3
political economy, 5–7, 12, 37–38, 87–96, 112–29, 273–351, 376n19, 408n5, 411n32, 424n30, 432n10
Political Economy, 401n27
Politics, 25, 112, 119, 205–6, 209, 377n29, 377n32, 377n34, 378n36, 382n77, 382n78, 383n86, 383n87, 405n1, 419n5, 421n6, 421n7, 421n8, 421n9, 421n12

"Polygamy and Monogamy," 404n61
Pope Benedict XVI, 125, 355, 407n24,
445n3
Pope John Paul II, 199, 420n20, 445n3
Pope Leo XIII, 117, 118
Pope Pius XI, 118
population, and employment, 269f
population, and relative size, 276–77, 276t,
336–37
Population Economics, 413n16
population increase, 34, 51
Populism and Elitism, 436n12
positive economics, 17, 35–36, 381n68,
381n69, 448n14
Positive Philosophy of Auguste Comte, The,
398n2
Positivism, 78–79
Posner, Richard, 95
poverty levels, 178, 195, 262–63, 278,
291–97
"Pre-Adamite" economics, 372n25
Précis of *The calculus of consent*, 402n40
preference, scale of, 140–41
prescriptive economics, 17, 34–45, 124, 238
Preston, Samuel H., 427n47
*Price and Value in the Aristotelian Tradi-
tion*, 377n31, 380n49, 380n51, 380n54,
380n55, 380n57, 380n60, 394n55,
395n66
price deflation, 330–32, 339, 342, 347
price regulation, 309–10
Principles of Economics, 400n22
Principles of Legislation, 98
Principles of Political Economy, 12, 372n21,
395n63, 395n70, 396n72, 397n83,
397n85
Pringsheim, F., 385n116
private goods, 25, 377n28, 401n32, 405n73
"Problem of Social Cost, The," 402n44
"Problems of Majority Voting," 402n37
"Process and Progress of Economics, The,"
370n2
producer price index, 328–32, 329f
product market, 316f
product subsidies, 303, 310–11
production assumptions, 70
production theory
and classical economics, 49, 61–64; and
elements of economics, 1; and marriage,
215–16; and neoclassical economics,
82–85; and Scholastic economics, 18–20,
25–26, 46, 374n11; and worldviews, 363

Production and Distribution Theories, 369n2
"Property," 385n115, 434n2
"property" definition, 44–45
property ownership, 38–39, 382n77,
383n86, 383n87
providence, theory of, 3–4, 18–19, 29, 30,
50–54, 129, 361, 364, 367n4, 370n2,
377n27, 379n50, 383n89, 388n6,
389n10, 389n11
Psychology of Science, The, 412n6
"Public Choice," 402n38
public choice theory, 91–93, 113, 126–27,
282, 283–302, 343, 402n38, 402n39,
402n40
public goods, 25, 34, 44–45, 90, 275, 281,
284–86, 383n88, 385n117, 386n117,
401n32, 405n73, 433n3
Pufendorf, Samuel, 4, 33, 43, 49, 50,
380n61, 380n62, 385n110, 386n3
"Pure Theory of Public Expenditure, A,"
401n32
Putnam, Robert D., 411n28

quasi-public goods, 45, 281, 284–86,
385n117
Quinlan, Robert J., 427n43
Quinlivan, Gary, 452
Quinn, Dermot A., 452

Rabushka, Alvin, 435n12
Raditzky, Gerard, 404n63
Rahn, Richard W., 452
Raiman, Jacques, 452
Rationale of Reward, The, 401n28
"Rational Fools," 402n41
Rawls, John, 402n36, 405n2
Razin, Assaf, 413n16
Reagan, Ronald, 6, 126, 275, 281t, 288,
301, 343, 407n26, 436n12, 444n26,
444n27
realism, philosophical, 365t, 371n14
rearing children, 231–43
"redeeming economics" definition, 8
"Re-Examination of Hernes' Model on the
Process of Entry Into First Marriage, A,"
427n44
*Reflections on the Classical Canon in Econom-
ics*, 390n15
Reid, Thomas, 387n3
relative size, 276–77, 276t, 336–37
Religious Thought and Economic Society,
370n2

Report on Manufactures, 74
reproduction rates, 204, 232–43, 243f
Rerum Novarum, 117
reserve currencies, 7, 327–32, 337–41, 349–50
"reserve currency curse," 7, 327–32, 349–50, 440n1
"Rethinking polygyny," 426n39
"retirement problem," 263f, 264–65
rhetoric, 4, 51–52, 59, 61, 76, 389n12, 390n13, 409n14
Ricardo, David, 68–71, 76–77, 394n60, 394n61
Right to Be Wrong, The, 385n111
risk aversion, 159–61
Rist, Charles, 339, 441n9
Robbins, Lionel, 82, 90, 104, 129, 141, 376n24, 400n24, 408n1
Robertson, Ann, 452
Robertson, Brian, 452
Robinson Crusoe, 408n6
Robinson, Daniel N., 452
Robinson, J. Gregory, 427n44
Rodger, Maureen, 452
Rodgers, Mark, 452
Roe v. Wade, 178, 220, 226, 440n24
Role of Providence in the Social Order, The, 370n2, 377n27.
Ronald Reagan, 444n27
Roosevelt, Franklin Delano, 275, 281t, 301
"Roots of Obama Worship, The," 399n5
Roover, Raymond de, 372n15, 384n93
Röpke, Wilhelm, 121–24, 406n16, 406n17, 406n18, 407n22
Ross, Ian Simpson, 57, 386n2, 388n6, 392n34, 394n55, 395n69
Ross, Sir David, 376n13, 420n4, 446n5
Rowley, Jennifer, 400n21
Rueff, Jacques, 121–24, 303, 337–43, 406n15, 407n26, 436n1, 437n4, 437n5, 437n7, 441n6, 441n13, 442n18, 442n22, 443n22, 445n31
Rueff's Law, 305–16, 307f, 315f, 316f
Ryan, John A., 384n99
Ryder, Norman B., 428n3
Ryland, Mark, 452

Sadka, Efraim, 413n16
St. Antonino of Florence, 32
St. Bernardino of Siena, 32
Saint-Simon, 398n3

Samuelson, Paul, 90, 401n32, 401n33, 414n30, 414n31
Sapori, Armando, 382n75
Saunders, William, 452
Say, Jean-Baptiste, 71–72, 395n69, 395n71
"scale of preference," 140–41
"scale of values," 141, 377n27
scarce goods
  and benevolence, 190–92; and children, 238; and classical economics, 60, 395n71; and marriage, 215; and Mother's Problem, 141–43; and neoclassical economics, 81, 96, 100, 167–68; and neo-Scholastic economics, 108, 123; and poverty levels, 195; and Scholastic economics, 36–39; and worldviews, 363
scarcity implications, 189–99
scarcity of means, 141–43
Scarry, Richard, 373n2
Schall, Rev. James V. SJ, 452
Schmiesing, Kevin, 452
Schoen, Robert, 428n3
Schoen, Robert et al., 427n44
Scholastic development, 30–35
Scholastic economics, 1–2, 13–47, 75, 372n25, 373n27
"Scholastic Economics," 372n15
Scholastic "Map," 47t, 106t
Scholastic outline, 17–35, 45–46, 54–73, 133
Scholasticism and Welfare Economics, 368n9, 382n76, 384n100
Schultz, Theodore W., 83–85, 95, 97, 124, 151, 292, 359, 399n17, 399n18, 399n19, 406n21, 407n22, 411n30, 414n20, 414n25, 414n29, 435n11
Schumpeter, Elizabeth Boody, 370n4
Schumpeter, Joseph, 4, 12–14, 29, 31–32, 35, 49, 93, 118, 362, 369n2, 370n2, 370n4, 370n5, 371n6, 371n7, 371n8, 371n9, 371n10, 371n11, 371n12, 371n13, 371n14, 372n15, 372n16, 372n17, 372n18, 372n19, 372n20, 372n22, 372n23, 372n24, 372n25, 372n26, 373n3, 373n4, 373n27
"Schumpeter's *History of Economic Analysis*," 370n2
Schwartz, Anna, 341, 347, 442n20
"Scope and Method of Political Economy, The," 432n10
Scott, Gary, 452
Scruton, Roger, 452

Seabury, Samuel, 74
Second Treatise on Government, 449n25
Selected Writings of St. Thomas Aquinas,
   409n10
self-love, 23, 44, 56–59, 109, 144, 148, 172,
   181, 385n113
Sen, Amartya, 91, 402n35, 402n36,
   402n41
Senior, Nassau, 71, 395n71, 401n27
Shaw, George Bernard, 80
Sheehan, Colleen, 452
Sidney, Algernon, 364, 448n24
Singer, Peter, 5, 167, 192–99, 358, 373n5,
   419n6, 419n8, 419n12, 452
"Singer Solution to World Poverty, The,"
   419n12
Skinner, Andrew S., 391n27
slavery, 25–26, 37–38, 45, 145, 151, 205–9,
   251–53, 265–66, 382n77, 382n78,
   386n118, 386n119
Smick, David M., 436n12, 452
Smith, Adam
   and classical economics, 54–73, 372n19,
      389n12, 391n33, 392n34; and elements
      of economics, 1–4, 371n12, 374n7; and
      neoclassical economics, 79–86, 164; and
      neo-Scholastic economics, 126–27, 255;
      reevaluation of, 49–77, 370n3; revision
      of, 79–86; and Scholastic economics,
      12–15, 46, 386n2, 386n3; and world-
      views, 356–61, 364, 387n3, 387n4,
      387n6, 396n74
Smithology, 11–15
Snell, Russell J., 452
social benefits reform, 279–80
"Social Capital in the Creation of Human
   Capital," 411n28
social capital theory, 102, 151, 410n28,
   411n28, 411n29
Social Choice and Individual Values,
   401n34
Social Choice and Justice, 401n34
"Social Choice and Justice: A Review
   Article," 402n35
Social Conservatism, 436n12
social distribution theory, 24
social graces theory, 151–53, 411n32,
   411n33
"social income," 103–4, 168–69
"Social Indifference Curves," 401n33,
   414n30
social order, 37, 38, 205, 208–9

social relationships, 2
Social Security
   and abortion rates, 298f, 322f; imbal-
      ances in, 229; options for, 300f; reform
      for, 265–66, 278–90, 297–98; and repro-
      duction rates, 243f; retirement pensions,
      114, 242, 243f, 265–66
social spending vs. fertility, 236f
Socialism, 405n9, 412n8, 413n11, 413n12
Sollicitudo rei socialis, 445n3
"Some Properties of Time Series Data,"
   417n27
Sophistical views, 4, 51–52
Sourcebook of Criminal Justice Statistics,
   417n23
Spalding, Matthew, 452
spending/earnings, 245–71. *See also* earn-
   ings
Spiegel, Henry William, 7, 32, 369n10,
   372n25, 380n58
"Spurious Regressions in Econometrics,"
   416n10, 416n11
Stamp, Sir Josiah, 437n5
Star Wars, 363
Starr, Richard, 452
Statistical Abstract of the United States,
   417n23
"Staying Power," 447n6
Steedman, Ian, 400n25
Steen, Ron, 432n15
Stein, Herbert, 126
Stein, Robert, 452
Steinberg, Saul, 12
stepping-stones, 2–3
Stevenson, Betsey, 427n47
Stewart-Robertson, J. C., 387n3
Stigler, George J., 4, 11, 61, 94–96, 101–2,
   115, 167–69, 175, 359–60, 369n1,
   369n2, 370n2, 372n14, 378n37,
   393n42, 399n13, 403n47, 404n62,
   404n63, 404n68, 405n4, 448n13,
   448n15. *See also* Becker-Stigler-Bentham
   assumptions
stock market and dollar deposits, 337–41,
   340f, 345
Stoic pantheism, 4–5, 51–54, 78, 283–84,
   355, 361–64, 365t, 388n8, 445n22
Stoner, James R. Jr., 452
structure of economics, 45–46, 130t
"Successes and Failures of Professor Smith,
   The," 393n42
successful economic policy, 281t

Sugrue, Michael, 452
Sugrue, Seana, 452
Summa Contra Gentiles, 117, 379n50
Summa Economica, 118
Summa theologiae, 27, 117, 368n7, 378n37,
  378n40, 378n45, 379n50, 383n87,
  383n89, 383n92, 384n92, 384n102,
  384n104, 384n105, 385n106, 388n7,
  410n22, 419n3, 419n10, 419n11, 447n8
supply and demand, 31–32, 39, 41–42, 86,
  210. *See also* production theory; utility
  theory
supply-side economics, 125–26, 364
supply-side fiscalism, 126
"Sur un point d'histoire," 441n14

Taking Risks, 412n4
Talleyrand, 307, 437n8
Tax Reform Act of 1986, 407n25
"Taxation," 369n9
taxes
  and consumption, 295f, 435n12; and
  income, 294f, 296f; reform for, 278–79,
  290–302; and transfer payments, 313f
Tellez, Luis, 452
terrorist attacks, 43, 152
"Testing Economic Hypotheses with State-
  Level Data," 415n8
Teti, Dennis E., 452
Theological Works of Thomas Paine, 446n4
Theory of Choice: A Critical Guide, The, 104,
  405n74
Theory of Justice, A, 402n36
"A Theory of Marriage," 414n20
Theory of Moral Sentiments, 53–58, 387n6,
  388n6, 389n9, 389n10, 389n11,
  389n12, 390n15, 390n16, 390n17,
  390n18, 390n22, 391n24, 391n26,
  391n30, 392n33, 392n34, 397n91
Theory of Political Economy, The, 399n12
Theory of Price, The, 448n13
"Theory of Social Interactions, A," 414n23
"Theory of the Allocation of Time, A," 98,
  403n50, 404n69
"Thomas Reid on Adam Smith's Theory of
  Morals," 387n3
"three acres and a cow," 406n14
"Three Sources and Three Component Parts
  of Marxism, The," 397n86
time, allocating, 149–50, 150f
"Timing Effects and the Interpretation of
  Period Fertility," 428n3

Tomes, Nigel, 403n49
"To Simplician—On Various Questions,"
  30, 367n4, 376n22, 378n46, 379n47,
  379n48, 379n49, 448n20
"Total Capital and Economic Growth,"
  400n21, 406n21
Traité d' économie politique, 395n69
transfer payments, 214–16, 311–14, 313f,
  318–21, 320f, 324f, 326t, 374n9,
  376n17, 429n7
Treatise of Human Nature, A, 391n24,
  391n25, 398n1, 398n5, 412n7, 448n12
Treatise on Political Economy, A, 395n69
Treatise on the Family, The, 99, 403n49, 403n55,
  404n61
Trepanier, Lee, 452
Triffin, Robert, 342
Trotta, Frank, 452
Tullock, Gordon, 91, 402n36
Turgot, Anne-Robert-Jacques, Baron de
  Laune, 14
Two Great Commandments, 3, 34, 36, 139,
  238, 277, 380n61, 409n13, 419n13,
  430n17

unChristian, 446n6
"Underinvestment in College Education?"
  431n6
"Undervaluing the Franc Poincaré," 441n15
unemployment
  and inflation, 304f; and injustice in
  exchange, 7, 303–26; and labor costs,
  307–26, 314f, 325f, 326t
"Unique Character of Classical Roman Law,
  The," 385n116
Unity of Philosophical Experience, The,
  379n50
university requirements, 11–12, 369n1,
  369n2
"U.S. Treasury Distributional Analysis Methodology," 432n19
utility, absence of, 69–70
utility theory
  and classical economics, 49, 58–61,
  69–70, 395n71; and elements of economics, 1; and marriage, 214–15; and neoclassical economics, 79–82, 103, 155–62; and
  Scholastic economics, 18, 20, 24–25, 46,
  374n10; and worldviews, 363

"value" definition, 59–61. *See also* "labor
  theory of value"

value paradox, 59
values scale, 141
"Variations du Chômage en Angleterre, Les,"
    437n4
Varro, Marcus Terentius, 355
Viner, Jacob, 369n2, 370n2, 377n27,
    387n6, 388n6
Vocation of Business, The, 369n9
von Thuenen, Johann Heinrich, 395n71
voter approval vs. gasoline prices, 348f
voter family income, 285f, 288f
voter party ID, 286f, 288f, 289f
voters, 284–90, 347–48

wages and prices, 306f
Wall Street Journal, 357
Walras, Leon, 81, 85, 90, 93, 126, 130t,
    371n12, 399n12
Wanniski, Jude, 125, 364, 443n19
Washington, George, 34, 74, 275, 280, 301,
    350
Way the World Works, The, 125, 408n27
Wealth and Money in the Aristotelian Tradi-
    tion, 380n55
Wealth of Nations, 2, 12–15, 49, 51, 54–58,
    60–61, 65–66, 68, 74, 388n6, 390n12,
    390n15, 390n19, 390n20, 391n28,
    391n32, 393n36, 393n37, 393n41,
    393n43, 393n44, 393n45, 394n48,
    394n50, 394n51, 394n52, 394n56,
    394n57, 394n58, 394n59, 395n69,
    396n74, 396n75, 396n76, 396n77,
    396n78, 396n79, 396n80
Weber, Max, 79, 371n14
Wehner, Pete, 452
Wehrung, Donald A., 412n4
Weigel, George, 420n20, 452
Weisheipl, James A., 378n35
"Welfare Costs of Tariffs, Monopolies, and
    Theft, The," 402n37
What Do People Do All Day?, 18, 373n2
Whately, Richard, 71, 77, 395n68
What's Wrong With the World, 432n8
Whelan, M. Edward III, 452
Whig history, 11, 370n3
Whig Interpretation of History, The, 370n3
White, Douglas R., 426n39
Whitley, John, 415n8
"Why Religion Matters Even More,"
    447n6
Wicksteed, Philip, 5, 24, 79–82, 87–88,
    127–29, 133–36, 260, 376n20, 399n6,

399n8, 399n9, 399n10, 399n11,
    400n24, 400n25, 432n10
Wilcox, W. Bradford, 452
Wilcox, Walter, 224
Wilson, Bradford P., 452
Winch, Donald, 370n2
Witness to Hope, 420n20
Wolfe, Barbara, 404n71
Wolfe, Christopher, 452
Wolfers, Justin, 427n47
"Work and Wages," 437n4
Works of Alexander Hamilton, The, 380n62,
    396n81, 397n82
Worland, Stephen, 41, 368n9, 382n76,
    384n93, 384n100
World Congress of Families, 437n2
world dollar base, 342–47, 342f, 344f, 346f,
    347f, 436n1, 444n24
"World Dollar Base and Causality, The,"
    444n24
World Economy: A Millennial Perspective,
    The, 426n42
World Is Curved, The, 436n12
World Religions and Social Evolution of
    the Old World Oikumene Civilizations,
    426n38
worldviews, 29–30, 38, 45, 52, 73, 88, 99,
    138–41, 153, 189–90, 206, 208, 229,
    238, 242, 277, 355–65, 365t, 378n45,
    378n46, 379n50, 381n72, 388n6,
    388n7, 445n3, 446n3, 446n4, 446n5,
    446n6, 447n6, 447n7, 447n8, 448n12,
    449n26
Writings of Gershom Carmichael, The, 386n3
Writings on an Ethical Life, 419n20
Wyatt, Terrance, 432n15

Xu, Zeyu, 234–35, 429n8, 429n9

Yandle, Bruce, 405n3
yard sale, 332–34
year-round earnings, 249f, 255f
Yellen, Janet L., 225, 226, 415n8, 427n49,
    428n49
Yuengert, Andrew M., 369n9, 452

Zeno of Citium, 364
Zmirak, John, 452

"125-Year Picture of the Federal Govern-
    ment's Share of the Economy, A," 434n7